THE BLACKWELL ENCYCLOPEDIA OF WRITING SYSTEMS

THE BLACKWELL ENCYCLOPEDIA OF WRITING SYSTEMS

Florian Coulmas

First published 1996
First published in paperback 1999

Blackwell Publishers Ltd
108 Cowley Road
Oxford OX4 1JF, UK

Blackwell Publishers Inc
350 Main Street
Malden, Massachusetts 02148, USA

British Library Cataloguing in Publication Data
A CIP catalogue record for this book is available from the British Library

Library of Congress Cataloging in Publication Data
Coulmas, Florian.
The Blackwell encyclopedia of writing systems / Florian Coulmas.
p. cm.
Includes bibliographical references (p.).
ISBN 0–631–19446–0 (hbk) — ISBN 0–631–21481–X (pbk)
1. Writing—Encyclopedias. I. Title. II. Title: Encyclopedia of writing systems.
Z40.C67 1995 94–47460
411—dc20 CIP
REV.

Typeset in 10 on 12pt Palatino
by Graphicraft Typesetters Limited, Hong Kong
Printed and bound in Great Britain
by MPG Books Ltd, Bodmin, Cornwall

This book is printed on acid-free paper

CONTENTS

LIST OF FIGURES

A

B

C

D

O

P

V

W

X

Y

Z

LIST OF TABLES

A

B

C

D

E

F

R

S

T

Z

PREFACE

The principal purpose of this encyclopedia is to provide basic concise information on the writing systems, scripts and orthographies of the world's major languages, and about theoretically important issues concerning the relationship between speech and writing. The variety of writing systems, past and present, is stupendous, and several profound books have been written about them. No student of writing can dispense with the seminal works of Marcel Cohen, David Diringer, Ignace Gelb and Hans Jensen which have laid the groundwork for the scientific study of writing. More than 40 years ago Gelb proposed the term 'grammatology' for this field of inquiry. New findings have come to light since then, and a great deal of research in various fields has advanced our understanding of how writing systems evolved, how they work, and how they differ from each other. Among the many scientific fields that have an interest in writing, four stand out: history and palaeography are concerned with the origin, spread and development of writing; psychology studies the perceptual and cognitive conditions of producing and processing written texts; linguistics investigates the mapping relations between speech and writing underlying the visual representation of language; and sociology has an interest in the social conditions and consequences of literacy. It would be preposterous to try to do justice to all of these aspects of writing in a single volume, and this encyclopedia makes no such attempt. Its emphasis is on concision. Yet, it takes into account that the study of writing cannot be confined to a narrowly circumscribed field, but rather has to draw on different scientific disciplines. The fact that writing is a common concern of many domains of scholarship testifies to its great importance for humanity.

Each of the writing systems dealt with in this volume warrants full monograph treatment. The same is true of entries dealing with technical aspects of writing, such as handwriting, printing and word processing; practical problems, such as decipherment, alphabet making and spelling reform; and theoretical issues, such as distinguishing writing from pre-writing and other notation systems, typology of writing systems, functions of writing etc. Major writing systems and writing systems not described in generally accessible works are described and illustrated in detail, and major theoretical problems are discussed in a manner that familiarizes the reader with the relevant issues. Bibliographic references given at the end of these entries enable the reader to look for more comprehensive accounts where such exist. These references are compiled in a selected bibliography of some 600 titles at the end of the book. For more in-depth research the reader may want to consult the comprehensive bibliography on writing and its use by Ehlich Coulmas and Graefen (1995) which comprises in excess of 25,000 titles.

While making available essential information is the paramount objective of this encyclopedia, it does not deny that it is based on certain theoretical assumptions. Most importantly, writing systems are considered as incorporating a linguistic analysis. They are based on and hence contain meta-linguistic knowledge. This theoretical outlook makes it desirable to include entries about how writing systems and their units relate to language. Since the development of writing is characterized by mutual influences between outer graphical form and inner structural form, entries pertaining to the physical appearance of writing systems have also been included.

The entries are arranged in alphabetical order. They vary in length between short explanations of terms and concepts, and accounts of individual writing systems or theoretical issues several pages long. Cross-references at the end of an entry guide the reader to thematically related entries. Cross-references in the main body of the text are intended to inform the reader that the subject in question is also an entry of this encyclopedia.

No work such as this is ever complete. If, however, this volume proves useful as a reference work to students who have an active interest in writing, it will have fulfilled its purpose.

In imperfectu valor.

F. C.
Berlin
April 1995

ACKNOWLEDGEMENTS

In writing this book I have benefited from assistance of various kinds from many people. Without their generosity I could not have brought it to a conclusion, however imperfect.

It gives me great pleasure to acknowledge my gratitude to the members of the study group on writing and written language at the Reimers Foundation, Bad Homburg, FGR, of which I had the privilege to be a member for more than ten years: Jürgen Baurmann, Konrad Ehlich, Peter Eisenberg, Heinz Giese, Helmut Glück, Hartmut Günther, Klaus Günther, Ulrich Knoop, Otto Ludwig, Bernd Popino-Marschall, Eckart Scheerer. Many fruitful discussions with these friends regarding virtually every aspect of written language have done more than anything else to sharpen my understanding of the diversity of writing as a human achievement.

At a very early stage of this project Henry Rogers reviewed a general outline of the encyclopedia and some draft chapters. His constructive comments have served me as a valuable guide for the work that followed.

I have also consulted numerous colleagues who are specialists in areas where my own expertise is limited. Many more than I remember have provided valuable information in informal discussions, and with others I had correspondence about various technical aspects of individual writing systems and languages: Matthias Brenzinger, William Bright, Chander J. Daswani, Konrad Ehlich, Paulin G. Djité, Yehuda Elkana, Joshua A. Fishman, Hartmut Haberland, David P. B. Massamba, Sun Hongkai, Matsumoto Kazuo, Raja Ram Mehrotra, Miyamoto Masaru, Nonna Nielsen-Stokkebye, Hans J. Nissen, J. Noorduyn, Antoon Postma, Taniq Rahman, Harold F. Schiffman, Judith Stalpers, Danny D. Steinberg, Wendy Du Steinberg, Umemura Haruo, Wu Tie-ping, Peter Zieme. I may not always have wisely used the information they kindly offered, and the responsibility for any mistakes and incomplete descriptions is, of course, solely my own. I hope, however, that I have done justice to their invaluable help.

I owe a special debt of gratitude to Iriya Reiko, the reference librarian of Chuo University Library, who helped me with unfailing patience to locate bibliographical references in a most diverse field.

During the final stage of writing this book I had the good fortune to be a fellow at the Institute for Advanced Study, Wissenschaftskolleg zu Berlin. The stimulating intellectual atmosphere and privileged working conditions characteristic of this five-star academic institution have enabled me to finish this work sooner than I could have hoped under normal circumstances. I am deeply grateful for being given this unique opportunity.

ABBREVIATIONS AND NOTATIONAL CONVENTIONS

CE	Common Era
BCE	Before Common Era
C	consonant
V	vowel
CV	consonant-vowel syllable
CA	Classical Arabic
Gk	Greek
Lat.	Latin
IPA	international phonetic alphabet
c.	about
d.	died
lit.	literally
*	prefixed to a word indicates a reconstructed form
< >	enclose graphemes
[ ]	narrow phonetic transcription
/ /	broad phonemic transcription

Where sound values of graphic signs are known they are typically given in the conventional Roman transliteration system most widely used for the language in question, unless indicated otherwise. In many cases, however, especially regarding very ancient writings, transliteration conventions are only very vaguely associated with actual sound values. Where no square brackets or slashes are used, italicized alphabetic letters represent conventional transliterations rather than transcriptions, i.e. sound values.

The art of writing is one of the ancient arts and crafts in which the science of language has its origin.

W. Haas, *Alphabets for English*

A, a /ɛi/ The first letter of the English alphabet goes back to Phoenician ≮'*āleph*, whence Greek *alpha* (Α, α). The small letter derives from Latin cursive *a*.

accent A prominence given to a syllable in a word. Latin *accentum* is the literal translation of Greek προσῳδία (prosody), lit. 'song added to'. The most general distinction is between pitch accent and stress accent. In the study of writing, the graphical marks placed over letters by which the nature and position of phonetic accent are indicated are also called accents. Classical Greek had three distinctive pitch accents which were marked in writing in Hellenistic times by <´> (known as acute) for rising pitch, <`> (grave) falling pitch, and <˜> (circumflex) for contour pitch. English orthography does not include accent marks, except in certain loan words or where they serve the purpose of graphic disambiguation, e.g. *résumé, resume*. Other languages, French for example, use the said accent marks (circumflex as <ˆ>) both to indicate pronunciation and to differentiate meaning as in *je, espérer, espèce, rêver* and *ou* 'or' vs *où* 'where'. Accents are commonly placed on vowel letters, especially where they indicate stress and pitch. However, accent marks are also used for other functions, and are then occasionally found on consonant letters. In Croat, for example, <ć> and <č> indicate different phonemes. In some languages, for example Dutch, the acute is used for marking emphasis in a sentence and is independent of word orthography. In a loose sense a variety of auxiliary signs such as aspiration marks or the tone marks of Chinese PINYIN are sometimes also called accents.
See also ACUTE ACCENT; ASPIRATION MARKS; CIRCUMFLEX; DIACRITIC; DIAERESIS; GRAVE ACCENT; TONE.

acronym A word composed as an abbreviation of the initial letters of other words, often used as a label for new organizations (IMF, NATO), inventions (TV, radar) and discoveries (HIV, AIDS). The term is sometimes limited to abbreviations which are pronounced as whole words such as *scuba* (from *s*elf-*c*ontained *u*nderwater *b*reathing *a*pparatus). The first items of the three sets of examples would thus be excluded.
See also ALPHABETISM.

acrophonic principle [Gk ἄκρο– 'tip' + φωνία 'voice', 'the initial sound'] As in telephone spelling, 'A for apple, B for book, etc.', acrophony uses the initial sound of a word. In the history of writing this principle refers to the use of a written sign which originally took the form of a pictorial or logographic symbol of an object to represent the initial syllable or phoneme of the name of that object. For example, in Egyptian the hieroglyph *ft* depicting a 'horned viper' is used for *f*. Acrophony has played an important role in theories about the origin of the alphabet because, of the 22 Phoenician consonant letters, 16 are named after common objects. It was hypothesized that forerunners of the Phoenician

letters may have represented these objects in a prior pictographic stage of writing. This principle has also been invoked to interpret proto-Sinaitic inscriptions and establish an Egyptian origin of Semitic writing (Gardiner 1916). This hypothesis, however, could not be confirmed. Further, the Greek alphabet is said to derive from the initial sounds of the Phoenician letter names. There is no agreement about the significance of acrophony in the evolution of writing. Some stress its importance for the coming into existence of Semitic scripts, portraying the Phoenician consonant script as a natural result of the fact that Old Phoenician has consonant initial words only (Voegelin and Voegelin 1961). Others reject the idea that acrophony played a general role in the evolution of writing, emphasizing that there is no evidence for it in other early writings, especially Sumerian, Hittite hieroglyphic, Chinese and Mayan (Gelb 1963).
See also EGYPTIAN WRITING SYSTEM; GREEK ALPHABET; LETTER NAMES; SEMITIC WRITING.

acute accent [Lat. *acūtus* 'sharp'] The accent <´> which in Classical Greek is used as a marker of pitch accent. In modern languages such as French it is used to mark the high vowels [e,o] as opposed to the lower [ɛ,ɔ]. Spanish uses the acute to indicate stress (the grave is not used). The accent <´> is usually placed on vowel letters, e.g. <é, á>, but also occurs on consonants, e.g. <ć> in Polish for palatalization. It is occasionally used to mark length, as in Slovak where the letters for the liquids [l:] and [r:] are <ĺ> and <ŕ>, contrasting with <l> [l] and <r> [r].
See also ACCENT.

Africa alphabet A script for African languages based on the Latin alphabet. It was first proposed in 1928 by Diedrich Westermann in collaboration with a group of Africanists and phoneticians working at the International Institute of African Languages and Cultures in London as an attempt to provide a suitable script for African languages that would be both scientifically satisfactory and practical. The revised version presented in table 1 was published in 1930 by the institute under the title *Practical Orthography of African Languages*. Developed under the influence of the IPA, it is based, by and large, on the principle of a simple one-letter/one-sound correspondence, although a number of exceptions are admitted. Since many African languages have relatively complex phonemic systems, the 26 letters of the Latin alphabet were supplemented by ten additional letters such as <Đ> and <ŋ>. The absence of these letters from the keyboards of standard typewriters is seen as a major reason why the Africa alphabet, in spite of being welcomed by many, failed to gain universal acceptance. Another problem was that, where a Latin-based orthography had been introduced for African languages, it was generally employed in accordance with the conventions of the various European colonial languages which continued to play an important role in post-colonial Africa. In order to facilitate the transition from one to the other, the users of African orthographies have a practical interest in their being similar to the orthographies of European languages. This precept, however, interferes with the analytic principles that would yield scientifically motivated orthographies.
See also ALPHABET MAKING.
Reading Tucker 1971; Westermann 1930.

Roman.	*Italic.*	*Written Forms.*	*Roman.*	*Italic.*	*Written Forms.*
a A	*a A*	*a A*	l L	*l L*	*l L*
b B	*b B*	*b B*	m M	*m M*	*m M*
ɓ Ɓ	*ɓ Ɓ*	*ɓ Ɓ*	n N	*n N*	*n N*
c C	*c C*	*c C*	ŋ Ŋ	*ŋ Ŋ*	*ŋ Ŋ*
d D	*d D*	*d D*	o O	*o O*	*o O*
ɖ Ɖ	*ɖ Ɖ*	*ɖ* or *d Ɖ*	ɔ Ɔ	*ɔ Ɔ*	*ɔ Ɔ*
e E	*e E*	*e E*	p P	*p P*	*p P*
ɛ Ɛ	*ɛ Ɛ*	*ɛ Ɛ*	r R	*r R*	*r* or *r R*
ə Ə	*ə Ə*	*ə Ə*	s S	*s S*	*s* or *s S*
f F	*f F*	*f F*	ʃ Σ	*ʃ Σ*	*ʃ Σ*
ƒ Ƒ	*ƒ Ƒ*	*ƒ Ƒ*	t T	*t T*	*t T*
g G	*g G*	*g G*	u U	*u U*	*u U*
ɣ Ɣ	*ɣ Ɣ*	*ɣ Ɣ*	v V	*v V*	*v V* or *v V*
h H	*h H*	*h H*	ʋ Ʋ	*ʋ Ʋ*	*ɣ Ɣ* or *ʋ Ʋ*
x X	*x X*	*x X*	w W	*w W*	*w W*
i I	*i I*	*i I*	y Y	*y Y*	*y Y*
j J	*j J*	*j J*	z Z	*z Z*	*z Z*
k K	*k K*	*k K*	ʒ Ʒ	*ʒ Ʒ*	*ʒ Ʒ*

Order of the letters:

a b ɓ c d ɖ e ɛ ə f ƒ g ɣ h x i j k l m n ŋ o ɔ p r s ʃ t u v ʋ w y z ʒ '

Names of consonant letters:

b	ɓ	c	d	ɖ	f	ƒ	g	ɣ	h	x	j	k	l	m	n
be	ɓa	ce (tʃe)	de	ɖa	ef	iƒ	ga	ɣe	ha	ex	je (dʒe)	ke	el	em	en

ŋ	p	r	s	ʃ	t	v	ʋ	w	y	z	ʒ	'
iŋ	pe	ra	es	iʃ	te	ve	ʋi	wa	ya	ze	ʒi	a'a

Table 1 The Africa alphabet
Source: *International Institute of African Languages and Cultures 1930*

African writing systems Africa, meaning sub-Saharan Africa, is often described as the continent of oral tradition and unwritten languages which came into contact with literacy from the outside, in the form of Arabic and Roman letters. Even Ethiopic writing came from the Arabian peninsula to Africa. Likewise, Old Nubian writing is not of African origin but rooted in Greek letters. Evidence for pre-Portuguese writing in southern Nigeria is not conclusive, although a spectacular claim has been made that the script of the West African Obɛri Ɔkaimɛ is derived from Minoan LINEAR A (Hau 1967). Yet, if Egypt is included, Africa is home of the sudden invention of hieroglyphic writing as well as a multiplicity of ancient systems of writing of which the Tifinagh alphabet of the Tuareg is a modern descendant. Africa is rich in systems of graphic as well as plastic symbols which have been regarded as precursors of writing. Africa has also played a significant part in the spread of the LATIN ALPHABET and the ARABIC ALPHABET for centuries. These scripts were largely distributed among African languages following religious divisions between Christian and Islamic communities. But several language communities, such as the Hausa and the Fula, have considerable corpora of written texts in both Arabic and Latin scripts. Swahili, too, was first written in Arabic letters in pre-colonial times and only adopted a Roman orthography around 1900.

In modern times, from the early nineteenth century, Africa witnessed the appearance of many indigenous vernacular writing systems, syllabic and alphabetic. These include scripts for Vai, Mende, Loma, Kpelle and Bassa, covering adjacent areas of Liberia and Sierra Leone. Further to the north along the Atlantic coast other languages including Manding, Wolof, Fula, Bamum and Bagam developed scripts of their own. Many of these scripts were associated at their inception with revelations and supernatural inspirations of one kind or another. Their creation and employment was in many cases governed by a spirit of secretiveness, which may be one of the reasons why relatively little is known about them. As they have to compete with the widespread Roman and Arabic alphabets, most of these systems are limited in use with respect to both literary functions and communities of users, but they are remarkable for their originality and precision in the transcription of sounds.

See also AFRIKUANDIKA; BAMBARA WRITING; BAMUM WRITING; BASSA ALPHABET; BETE WRITING; DIGRAPHIA; DJUKA SYLLABIC WRITING; INTERNATIONAL NIAMEY KEYBOARD; KISWAHILI WRITING; KPELLE SYLLABARY; LOMA SYLLABARY; MENDE SYLLABARY; NUBIAN ALPHABET; TIFINAGH; VAI WRITING.

Reading Battestini 1994; Dalby 1967; 1968; 1969; Gregersen 1977a; Hau 1967; Zima 1969; Gérard 1984; *L'Afrique et la lettre* 1986.

Afrikuandika A modern script invention by Paul A. Barton, an African West Indian from St Lucia. Proposing it as a pan-African writing system, its creator has aimed at a transcription system capable of representing all African languages in such a way that each sign represents one and only one sound. The system is meant to be iconic in that the signs, called 'hieroglyphs' by Barton, are designed to depict place and manner of articulation by indicating tongue positions and opening or constriction of the air stream (figure 1). The individual signs are thus stylized diagrams of articulation configurations. Superscript numerals are used to distinguish homonyms graphically. The system is not based on a comprehensive

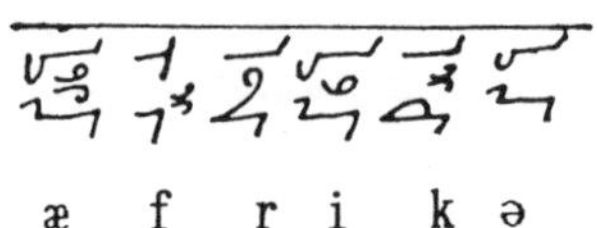

æ f r i k ə

Figure 1 A sample of Afrikuandika with transcription

analysis of African sound systems but seems to take English as a reference point. It is not used by any speech community.
Reading Barton 1991.

agraphia A pathological disturbance of written language abilities. It is usually part of a complex aphasic syndrome in which writing is the most damaged component. However, research in neurolinguistics and in the psychology of reading has found evidence that impairment of writing also occurs in isolation from other speech disturbances. Research on agraphia is of great interest for the study of writing because it sheds light on the relationship between language, speech and writing, and the question of whether or to what extent different language faculties are independent of each other. It also offers one of the most promising pathways for investigation of the conditions that different writing systems pose for the processing of written language by the human brain. Some case histories involving native speakers of Japanese and Chinese have revealed certain differences between phonetic writing and logographic writing which would suggest differences in neural storage and processing. For example, some Japanese patients had better retention of Chinese characters (CHINESE SCRIPTS) than of HIRAGANA signs. The former are assumed to provide access to items of the mental lexicon without phonetic mediation, whereas the latter necessarily involve phonetic coding. Written language is considered the most complex and fragile of language skills. Not all of its disturbances are related to neurological syndromes.
See also DYSLEXIA.
Reading Hu et al. 1990; Morton and Sasanuma 1984; Henderson 1984; Ulatowska et al. 1979.

***ajami* script** [Arabic *aȁjàmí* 'foreign'] The ARABIC ALPHABET adjusted to non-Arabic languages, for example Hausa and Fula in Africa, which have been written in the Arabic script for many centuries. The term *ajami* also refers to literature written in this way. Today its use is restricted to Islamic texts.
See also HAUSA WRITING.

Akkadian One of the major languages of cuneiform writing, Akkadian is an east Semitic language that was spoken between the early third and the late first millenniums BCE in what corresponds to modern Iraq and Syria.

As of about 2800 BCE, Akkadian was widely spoken in Mesopotamia, but Sumerian was the written language. Early attempts at writing Akkadian in cuneiform are attested from around the middle of the third millennium, but a significant body of written documents appeared only under King Sargon I (about 2350). Akkadian was used in writing until the first century CE, serving speakers of many different languages in south-western Asia as the primary medium of graphic communication rather divorced from speech. Babylonian and Assyrian are the two main dialects which are further classified in terms of Old (2000–1500 BCE), Middle (1500–1000) and Neo periods (1000–500).

Akkadian is unrelated to, and typologically different from, the isolating Sumerian language. Writing Akkadian with the largely logographic Sumerian script, therefore, caused difficulties and brought about important changes in the system. The need to write grammatical morphemes was one of the developmental forces that strengthened the phonetic element of cuneiform writing. Many logographic signs of the Sumerian script were revalued to serve as syllabic signs. This is clearly evidenced by the shift in the ratio of the different kinds of signs of which cuneiform writing makes use, LOGOGRAMS, SYLLABOGRAMS and DETERMINATIVES, shown in table 2.

SIGNS	SUMERIAN %	AKKADIAN %
Logograms	60 – 43	7 – 4
Syllabograms	36 – 54	86 – 96
Determinatives	3	8 –1

Table 2 Ratio of logograms, syllabograms and determinatives in Sumerian and Akkadian cuneiform

Another reason for the relative increase of phonetic signs in Akkadian is that the syllable structure of Akkadian is quite different from that of Sumerian, so the set of Sumerian syllabograms was insufficient for writing Akkadian. Hence, many Sumerian logograms came to be used for their syllabic value in Akkadian. Since the Sumerian values were also retained, this adaptation brought about POLYVALENCE for many signs, adding to the complexity of Akkadian writing. The three kinds of Sumerian signs were adapted to Akkadian as follows.

Logograms The adaptation of logograms was a kind of translation: the Sumerian word signs were associated with the Akkadian equivalents of the respective Sumerian words. Thus, the logogram 𒀭, *dingir* 'god' in Sumerian, was used to write the Akkadian word *ilu* – a simple strategy which, however, made for a complex system. Together with the script the bilingual Akkadian scribes adopted many Sumerian loan words. In this way numerous signs came to be associated with two readings, one Sumerian and one Akkadian. Many Sumerian signs were polyvalent to begin with. The logogram 𒀭, for example, was not only *dingir* 'god' but also *an* 'sky'. Since it was recruited to write the Akkadian words for both 'god' and 'sky', it eventually had four different values in Akkadian writing: *dingir/ilu* 'god' and *an/šamû* 'sky'.

Determinatives This class of mute signs which indicate the semantic range of a polyvalent sign is an important reading aid. The Sumerian system was quite simple, making use of noun determinatives only. In addition to the semantic noun determinatives of Sumerian, a system of phonetic determinatives developed in Akkadian. These were essential for disambiguating polyvalent logograms, because semantic determinatives could not indicate whether a Sumerian or an Akkadian reading was intended. Thus for *šamû* 'sky' the Akkadians wrote *šamû-u*, where the final *u* is not pronounced but only indicates Akkadian rather than Sumerian reading, which would be *an*. Phonetic complements were also used to indicate inflectional endings.

Syllabic signs Syllabic signs were taken from Sumerian as they were. Thus Sumerian *mu, ti, šu* etc. were also *mu, ti, šu* etc. in Akkadian writing. However, the Akkadians also pressed other logograms into service as additional syllabic signs which were needed for representing all Akkadian syllables. CVC syllables were often broken up in writing into two parts, CV + VC. Thus *lum* would be written *lu-um* and *gir* as *gi-ir*.

Although Akkadian cuneiform is more phonetic and less logographic than Sumerian, it is a very involved system consisting of polyvalent signs often serving two or three functions in the same text which are not graphically distinguished. To illustrate, was used as a logogram for both *šadû* 'mountain' and *mâtu* 'country', as a determinative for names of mountains and countries, and also as a syllabic sign with as many as five different values, *kur, kin, šat, nat* and *gin*.

The operative sign inventory of Akkadian cuneiform writing ranges between 200 and 400 signs depending on the text genre. Literary texts may have a variety exceeding these numbers.

See also ASSYRIAN; BABYLONIAN; CUNEIFORM WRITING; DECIPHERMENT; SUMERIAN WRITING.

Reading Civil 1973; Gelb 1963; Labat and Malbran-Labat 1988; Reiner 1966; Soden and Röllig 1969.

akṣara [Sanskrit] A CV syllable represented by a symbol consisting of a consonant with a short inherent /a/ vowel. Phonetically this is variously realized as [a], [å] or [ə], although the exact phonetic value cannot always be determined uniformly, especially in archaic inscriptions. For this reason, the inherent vowel of the *akṣara* is generally transcribed as *a* in this encyclopedia. The *akṣara* is the characteristic unit of Indic writing.

See also INDIAN WRITING SYSTEMS; INHERENT VOWEL.

Alaska script *See* YUPIK WRITING

Albanian writing The Albanian language was first documented in the fifteenth century. It consists of two dialect groups, the southern Tosk and the northern Gheg. Both were written, the former in Greek letters and the latter in the Latin alphabet. An official written standard was codified in 1916 on the basis of Gheg, but in 1945 Tosk was taken as the norm of a reformed standard (table 3).

In addition, Albanian has been written locally in seemingly autochthonous scripts. One is called 'Elbasan script' after the city of Elbasan in central Albania where it was used and is thought to have been created in the mid-eighteenth century (table 4). Another which was created around 1840 is know as 'Beitha Kukju script' after its inventor (table 5).

Alcuin of York (*c.*730–804) Anglo-Saxon scholar who in 781 was called to France by Charlemagne to restore the educational system of antiquity. His ideas concerning language reform had a significant effect on the coming into existence of the Romance vernaculars as written languages.

See also CAROLINGIAN REFORM.

Aldine A book printed by ALDUS MANUTIUS, a celebrated Venetian printer of the sixteenth century, especially his editions of the Greek classics.

a [a]	g [g]	n [n]	t [t]
b [b]	gj [ǵ]	nj [ṇ]	th [θ]
c [ts]	h [h]	o [o]	u [u]
ç [tš]	i [i]	p [p]	v [v]
d [d]	j [j]	q [ḳ]	x [dz]
dh [ð]	k [k]	r [r]	xh [dž]
e [e]	l [l]	rr [r:]	y [y]
ë [ə]	ll [ł]	s [s]	z [z]
f [f]	m [m]	sh [š]	zh [ž]

Table 3 The Albanian alphabet of 1945

Symbol	Value	Symbol	Value	Symbol	Value	Symbol	Value	Symbol	Value	Symbol	Value
[illegible]	a	[illegible]	ts	[illegible]	r	[illegible]	ṅ'	[illegible]	θ	[illegible]	š
[illegible]	e	[illegible]	ds	[illegible]	r̄	[illegible]	γ	[illegible]	b	[illegible]	ž
[illegible]	i	[illegible]	nds	[illegible]	f	[illegible]	ps	[illegible]	mb	[illegible]	št
[illegible]	o	[illegible]	w	[illegible]	δ	[illegible]	h	[illegible]	p	[illegible]	te
[illegible]	u	[illegible]	l	[illegible]	m	[illegible]	χ	[illegible]	n	[illegible]	ń
[illegible]	ü	[illegible]	l'	[illegible]	y	[illegible]	χ'	[illegible]	tš	[illegible]	as
[illegible]	e̥	[illegible]	k'	[illegible]	χ́	[illegible]	t	[illegible]	dž	[illegible]	o̲
[illegible]	s	[illegible]	k	[illegible]	ṅ	[illegible]	d	[illegible]	ndž	[illegible]	jü
[illegible]	dz	[illegible]	ks	[illegible]	χ́'	[illegible]	nd	[illegible]	st		

Table 4 The Elbasan script of Albanian

Aldus Manutius Born 1449 in Bassiano, Aldus opened his own printing office in 1495 in Venice, concentrating on Greek classics and textbooks of Classical Greek. Many of his editions became the recognized versions of the classical texts (figures 2, 3).

alexia Disturbances in reading due to cerebral lesions in the occipitoparietal areas and characterized by the inability to recognize written words, numerals or individual letters.
See also DYSLEXIA.

alloglottography The practice of using one language in writing and another in reading, known from situations of restricted literacy. For example, the Achaemenid multilingual empire under Darius the Great (522–486 BCE) was

Symbol	Value	Symbol	Value	Symbol	Value	Symbol	Value
	a		b		kj		s
	e		g		l		t
	e		'j		m		f
	i		đ		n		ḫ
	o		d		ng		ks
	y		þ		p		ts
	ü		dz		r		tsj
	v		k		z		ts

Table 5 The Beitha Kukju script of Albanian

administered largely in Aramaic, then the dominant medium of written communication (ARAMAIC WRITING). Bilingual Aramaic scribes would translate the sender's message phrased in a Persian language for recording into Aramaic which the recipient's scribe would in turn read out in Persian or another language. The Japanese method of reading Chinese in translation (*kundoku kanbun*) is a similar if more involved practice, because the written text itself blends features of Chinese and Japanese.
See also ALLOGRAM; XENOGRAPHY.
Reading Gershevitch 1979.

allogram A term used to characterize the practice of integrating logograms or spellings of one writing into another by changing their values. For example, the Sumerian syllabic spelling *in-lá-e*, 'he will weigh out', was adopted for the corresponding Akkadian phrase *išaqqal*.
See also XENOGRAPHY.

allograph **1** Graphical variants which have developed in the history of writing, for instance, the interchangeable use of <i> and <j> or of <u> and <v>, or the writing of <ÿ> for Dutch <ij>. **2** Realized variants of a GRAPHEME understood as the smallest functional unit of a language-specific writing system. For example, in Greek the same /s/ sound is represented in writing by two allographs, <σ> and <ς>. Other examples include the systematic differentiation of initial, medial and final letter forms in Arabic which can be understood as contextually determined allographs.

alphabet [αλφα βῆτα, the first two Greek letters] **1** A writing system characterized by a systematic mapping relation between its signs (graphemes) and the minimal units of speech (phonemes). **2** The total number of elementary signs

17.

ΑΡΙΣΤΟΦΑΝΟΥΣ ΠΛΟΥΤΟΣ.

Καρίων οἰκέτης.

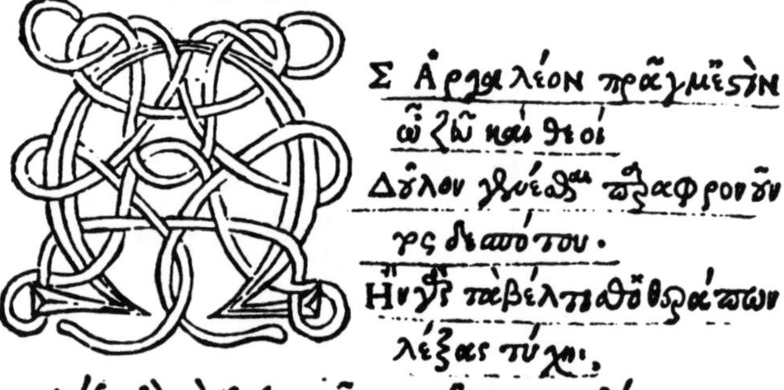

Σ Ἀργαλέον πρᾶγμ' ἐστὶν
ὦ Ζεῦ καὶ θεοί
Δοῦλον γενέσθαι παραφρονοῦν-
τος δεσπότου.
Ἢν γὰρ τὰ βέλτισθ' ὁ θεράπων
λέξας τύχῃ,
Δόξῃ δὲ μὴ δρᾶν ταῦτα τῷ κεκτημένῳ,
Μετέχειν ἀνάγκη τὸν θεράποντα τῶν κακῶν.
Τοῦ σώματος γὰρ οὐκ ἐᾷ τὸν κύριον
Κρατεῖν ὁ δαίμων, ἀλλὰ τὸν ἐωνημένον.
Καὶ ταῦτα μὲν δή, ταῦτα. Τῷ δὲ Λοξίᾳ

Σ ἀργαλέον. [illegible] δύσφορον δεσπότου ἑπομένου τυφλῷ ἀνδρί. [illegible] πλέκεται ἡ διάνοια [illegible] ἀργαλέον, χαλεπόν. δύσκολον. δυσχερές. [illegible] παλαιοῖς, τὸ δυσχερές. ἐκ τούτου παράγωγον ἀργαλέον. [illegible]

Ὦ Ζεῦ. τὸν Δία παρέλαβε κατ' ἐξοχὴν τῶν ἄλλων θεῶν, ὥσπερ [illegible] καὶ Ἕκτορα ὀνομάζουσι, κατ' ἐξοχὴν τῶν ἄλλων. Δοῦλον γενέσθαι. χαλεπὸν ὄντως φύσει τὸ δουλεύειν, χαλεπώτερον δὲ [illegible], ἐὰν ἀνοήτῳ τις δεσπότῃ ὑπηρετῇ. Μὴ δρᾶν ταῦτα. οἱ γράφοντες ταυτά, οὐ καλῶς γράφουσιν. εὕρηται γὰρ ἐν πολλοῖς τῶν παλαιῶν ἀντιγράφων τὸ ταῦτα. καὶ ἔστι κρεῖττον ἐκείνου. Μετέχειν ἀνάγκη. πρὸς τὸ ποιητικόν. Ἥμισυ γάρ τ' ἀρετῆς ἀποαίνυται εὐρύοπα Ζεὺς ἀνέρος, εὖτ' ἄν μιν κατὰ δούλιον ἦμαρ ἕλῃσι. τί γὰρ κακώτερον τοῦ τὰ ἐναντία ἑαυτῷ διαπράττεσθαι [illegible] βούλεται [illegible] ἀφροσύνης ἀνέχεσθαι. Τῶν κακῶν. τῆς ἀφροσύνης ὧν ὁ δεσπότης ἔχει [illegible] τοῖς ἀπειθοῦσι τοῖς δεσπόταις ὀφείλονται. εἰώθασι δὲ οἱ Ἀττικοὶ τὰ ἄρθρα πλεονάζειν. ὥσπερ οὖν ἐνταῦθα, τὰ βέλτιστα, περισσὸν κατ' Ἀττικῶς τὸ ἄρθρον, οὕτω κἀνταῦθα τὸ τῶν. [illegible] τὸ δὲ ταῦτα τὸ δεύτερον [illegible] ἀντὶ τοῦ ταύτῃ [illegible] ἀλλ' ἀντὶ τοῦ ταῦτα πάλιν Ἀττικῶς. Τοῦ σώματος γάρ. οἷον αὐτὸν ἑαυτοῦ τὸν δοῦλον οὐκ ἐᾷ κρατεῖν. μάλιστα γὰρ κύριος τοῦ σώματος ἕκαστος αὐτὸς ἑαυτοῦ. Τὸν ἐωνημένον. ἀντὶ τοῦ τὸν ὠνησάμενον [illegible] Καὶ ταῦτα μὲν δὴ ταῦτα. [illegible] Τῷ δὲ Λοξίᾳ. τῷ Ἀπόλλωνι [illegible] λοξὰ γὰρ μαντεύεται ὁ θεός. ἢ τὴν λοξὴν πορείαν ποιούμενος [illegible]

Figure 2 A page from the Aristophanes-Aldina

Figure 3 Aldus's emblem

in an alphabetic writing system, bar punctuation marks. **3** The fixed order of the written signs of a language, ABC.

The set of letters used in writing the Greek language was called *alphabet(a)* by combining the first two letter names which in turn derive from west Semitic *ʾāleph* and *bēth*. The term itself is of Latin origin whence it came into general use for any set of the elementary signs of a phonetic script. Alphabetic writing can be defined as a system of recording language which makes use of this inventory of letters or any historically related variant thereof. The alphabet most widely used nowadays is the English alphabet consisting of 26 letters. They are arranged in a fixed order each having its own name. Each letter has two different forms, one called 'capital' letter and the other 'small' letter, or 'upper case' and 'lower case', respectively.

In a wider sense the term 'alphabet' applies both to consonant scripts such as Hebrew and Arabic, and to segmental scripts comprising letters for consonants and vowels, for example Greek. While generally representing the most important sounds of the language for which they are employed, alphabetic writing systems vary greatly in complexity and in the kind and regularity of grapheme–phoneme (letter–sound) correspondence. Alphabets with a one-to-one correspondence based on the principle of only one symbol for each sound are called 'phonemic alphabets'. Such alphabets or systems approximating this ideal have been and are being used for several languages including Spanish, Finnish and Serbo-Croatian as well as many languages recently provided with an alphabet. However, one-to-one consistency on the phonemic level is by no means the predominant characteristic of alphabetic writing systems. Many are highly irregular or exhibit regularities on the morpho-phonological or lexical rather than the phonological level. Alphabetic writings that are not periodically adjusted have a tendency to preserve etymological spellings rather than strict grapheme–phoneme correspondence.

See also Alphabetical order; Alphabetic hypothesis; Alphabet making; Arabic alphabet; English spelling; Greek alphabet; Hebrew writing; International phonetic alphabet; Letter; Orthography; Phoenician alphabet; Roman alphabet; Transcription; Writing system.

Reading Diringer 1943; Driver 1976; Gelb 1963; Gordon 1970; Jensen 1969; Naveh 1982.

alphabet making Selecting a script and constructing an orthography for a language that never had one. It is a form of encoding the language visually so that it can be used efficiently in written communication. In modern times a great number of languages spoken in Africa, in Latin America, on the Indian subcontinent and in other parts of Asia and in the Pacific have been given a written form for the first time. The erstwhile Soviet government was quite active in this regard and so were Christian missionaries in many countries. Linguistic techniques such as phonemics (PHONEME) were developed in close connection with the problems of creating suitable scripts for unwritten languages. From a linguistic point of view a broad phonemic transcription which is systematically transparent, precise and economical is the ideal orthography, but these criteria are known to determine the success of a newly proposed orthography only to a limited extent – for scripts and orthographic conventions are never socioculturally neutral for those concerned. Rather than being mere instruments of a practical nature, they are symbolic systems of great social significance. Both scripts and orthographies often carry cultural and political overtones.

There may be non-linguistic reasons for speech communities to want their writing to be similar to, or different from, that of another language. For example, in India the task of reducing an unwritten language to writing must be considered within the context of India's literary heritage and the government's literacy programmes. Literacy in vernacular languages is promoted as a bridge to literacy in one of the regional literary languages. This notion implies that a new writing for a vernacular language should be designed on the model of that of the regional language that is dominant in the state where the vernacular language is spoken. Similarly, many languages were given a Cyrillic alphabet in the Soviet Union both in order to facilitate transfer and for political reasons.

Such considerations notwithstanding, the script most widely employed for creating new writings in this century is the Roman alphabet, if only because this is the script that Western linguists are most familiar with. New orthographies often reflect conventions of existing ones, especially in multilingual settings where a colonial language plays the role of the dominant written language. For example, in Bolivia the Aymara allophones of /u/ and /i/, [o] and [e] respectively, are represented in writing because the Spanish orthography includes the letters <o> and <e>. Since in Aymara [o] and [e] are contextually determined, there is no linguistic need for assigning them separate letters; but, from a sociolinguistic viewpoint, to some Aymaras the Aymara alphabet would look defective if it had fewer letters than the Spanish.

Linguistic adequacy and economy have no cultural prestige, but existing orthographies, irregular and flawed as they may be, often do. Therefore, the acceptability of a new alphabet to the speech community concerned is not wholly determined by its linguistic fit and efficiency.

Another problem to be reckoned with in designing new orthographies is dialect differences. Where different dialects present a variety of different forms, choices have to be made if there is to be a uniform written language. Again, these cannot be determined on the basis of linguistic criteria alone. For such choices may influence the development of a standard variety and, therefore, need careful consideration. Often speakers have strong feelings about which dialect should or should not be used as the basis on which to build a written form of their language. Ideally, the variety that is to be written should be a common reference point for speakers of all dialects.

In alphabet making, a balance must be struck between linguistic and extra-linguistic requirements. A new writing should be based on a variety of the language acceptable to the majority of the speech community; it should be phonemic to the extent that this requirement does not impede its acceptability and, where useful, should also incorporate morphophonemic and lexical information; it should be easy to learn and write both by hand and with the available printing (word-processing) equipment; it should be easy to read; and it should transcend as little as possible the limitations of the sign inventory of the orthography of the major contact language.

See also Africa alphabet; Orthography reform.

Reading Westermann 1930; Pike 1947; Berry 1958; 1977; *Orthography Studies* 1963; Pattanayak 1979; Winter 1983.

alphabet, origin of *See* Greek alphabet

alphabetic hypothesis The idea that the development of writing was brought to completion by the Greeks who first devised a phonetic writing with letters for both consonants and vowels. Rather than stressing the continuity in the history of writing and the fact that the Greeks adopted an extant system from the Phoenicians which they adjusted to their own language, adherents of the alphabetic hypothesis highlight the new quality of the Greek alphabet which they view as the necessary conclusion of a development that leads from logograms through syllabic signs to the decomposition of syllables into signs for segments. They regard the Greek alphabet as qualitatively new and altogether different from other writing systems, seeing in it a decisive force of Western civilization. The gist of the argument is that only the simplicity of the Greek alphabet made widespread literacy possible. The Greek alphabet is consequently credited with bringing about such fundamental achievements as democracy, logical thinking and philosophy.

Opponents of this view emphasize the commonalities of the archaic writings of the fertile crescent and the eastern Mediterranean. They hold that the alphabetic hypothesis is itself a product of alphabetic culture. It was produced by scholars who, owing to their upbringing, were most familiar with alphabetic writing and thus tended to overemphasize differences and advantages distinguishing it from other writing systems, especially the various Semitic systems but also late forms of Cuneiform writing. They also contend that the alphabetic hypothesis is based on a simplistic and misguided notion of how alphabetic writing works, one that assumes (1) there is a simple mapping relation between letters and sounds and (2) meaning is only provided through the representation of sounds. In the 1970s and 1980s the relative simplicity of writing systems has become an object of renewed interest, and the notion that, because of its small inventory of letters, the alphabet by and of itself makes for simple writing systems has given way to the more differentiated view that alphabetic writings can vary on a large scale in complexity.

See also GREEK ALPHABET; WRITING, DEVELOPMENT OF.
Reading (*pro*) Gelb 1963; McLuhan 1962; Havelock 1982; Illich and Sanders 1988; (*contra*) Coulmas 1989; Powell 1981; Scholes and Willis 1991.

alphabetical order In one definition, alphabets are ordered sets of letters. Various ordering principles exist. The ARABIC ALPHABET is ordered by letter forms; Indian alphabets are ordered by sound values. The order of the Greek and Latin alphabets follows no transparent principle, but stems from that of the ancient Semitic scripts. The fixed order is of great importance, because the alphabet fulfils a pervasive function as an index system. Chess boards, geographical maps, seat rows in aircraft and theatres, grades on school reports are commonly coded alphabetically. Lexicographers use the fixed order of the alphabet as a macro-system for arranging headwords. This macro-system is an *n*-position system, where *n* is the number of the letters of the alphabet and where each letter has the numerical value corresponding to the position at which it occurs in the sequence: $a = 1$, $b = 2$, $h = 8$, $s = 19$ etc. Each item to be recorded in the system thus gets a numerical code: for example, 19–3–18–9–16–20 would be *script*, according to the conventional order of the English alphabet. If the longest item is taken as a measure and the numerical value of all others is filled up with zeros at the end, then the code assigned to each item read as a number will determine its position in the system. The lower the value, the earlier its place in the sequence. Filling up empty positions with zeros is necessary in order to prevent the length of words affecting the sequencing in such a way that, for example, *but*, with its low value, preceded *antivivisectionist* with its much higher value. The alphabetical order as it is understood nowadays is thus equivalent to an enumeration. However, full alphabetic order of reference works and indices appeared only in the fourteenth century, although alphabetic arrangement by first letter was common in medieval times.

In many archaic cultures, counting was associated with primitive forms of recording. It has been hypothesized, therefore, that writing was connected with numeracy from early times and perhaps originally derived from tally systems. The alphabet has been a numerical code since antiquity. Letters were associated with numerical values as shown in table 6.
See also ORIGIN OF WRITING.
Reading Daly and Daly 1964; Brincken 1972; Schwarz 1915; Gerschel 1960; Harris 1986; O'Connor 1991.

alphabetism An acronym of separately pronounced initial letters of other words, such as IQ, PLO and VIP.
See also ACRONYM.

American spelling This differs from British spelling in a number of respects. The most important differences are the following: British *-our* becomes *-or* as in *labour* → *labor*; *-re* becomes *-er* as in *centre* → *center*; *-ce* becomes *-se* as in *defence* → *defense*; most derivatives of verbs ending in *-l* or *-p* do not double the final consonant as in *traveled, worshiped* vs British *travelled, worshipped*; British *ae* and *oe* are often reduced to *e* as in *anaemia* → *anemia*; a silent *e* is sometimes omitted as in *judgement* → *judgment*; silent endings of French origin words are often omitted,

The Hebrew alphabet and its numerical values

א	1	י	10	ק	100
ב	2	כ	20	ר	200
ג	3	ל	30	ש	300
ד	4	מ	40	ת	400
ה	5	נ	50		
ו	6	ס	60		
ז	7	ע	70		
ח	8	פ	80		
ט	9	צ	90		

The Greek alphabet and its numerical values

Α	1	Ι	10	Ρ	100
Β	2	Κ	20	Σ	200
Γ	3	Λ	30	Τ	300
Δ	4	Μ	40	Υ	400
Ε	5	Ν	50	Φ	500
Ϝ*	6	Ξ	60	Χ	600
Ζ	7	Ο	70	Ψ	700
Η	8	Π	80	Ω	800
Θ	9	Ϙ	90	Ϡ	900

*Ancient Greek digamma.

Table 6 The Hebrew and Greek alphabets and the numerical values of their letters

e.g. *catalogue* → *catalog*; the prefix *en-* is sometimes spelt with an *i* as in *enclose* → *inclose*. Other alternative American spellings such as *nite* for *night*, *thru* for *through* are not generally recognized. The American departure from British spelling conventions goes back to the time of independence whence it originated as an expression of linguistic nationalism.

See also Franklin; Spelling reform; Webster.

Reading Baron 1982; Clemens 1967.

Amharic writing The national language of Ethiopia, Amharic is a Semitic language but is written in the Ethiopic script, which conspicuously differs from all other Semitic scripts. It is a syllabic alphabet with consonant letters modified for seven 'orders' of vowels (table 7). The vowel diacritic may appear on either the left or the right of the consonant symbol. The unit of writing is a (C)V syllable, but the individual graphs clearly encode segmental information. This type of

	a	u:	i:	a:	e:	(ə)	o:
h	ሀ	ሁ	ሂ	ሃ	ሄ	ህ	ሆ
l	ለ	ሉ	ሊ	ላ	ሌ	ል	ሎ
ḥ	ሐ	ሑ	ሒ	ሓ	ሔ	ሕ	ሖ
m	መ	ሙ	ሚ	ማ	ሜ	ም	ሞ
s	ሠ	ሡ	ሢ	ሣ	ሤ	ሥ	ሦ
r	ረ	ሩ	ሪ	ራ	ሬ	ር	ሮ
š	ሸ	ሹ	ሺ	ሻ	ሼ	ሽ	ሾ
q	ቀ	ቁ	ቂ	ቃ	ቄ	ቅ	ቆ
b	በ	ቡ	ቢ	ባ	ቤ	ብ	ቦ
t	ተ	ቱ	ቲ	ታ	ቴ	ት	ቶ
ẖ	ኀ	ኁ	ኂ	ኃ	ኄ	ኅ	ኆ
n	ነ	ኑ	ኒ	ና	ኔ	ን	ኖ
’	አ	ኡ	ኢ	ኣ	ኤ	እ	ኦ
k	ከ	ኩ	ኪ	ካ	ኬ	ክ	ኮ
w	ወ	ዉ	ዊ	ዋ	ዌ	ው	ዎ
‘	ዐ	ዑ	ዒ	ዓ	ዔ	ዕ	ዖ
z	ዘ	ዙ	ዚ	ዛ	ዜ	ዝ	ዞ
j	የ	ዩ	ዪ	ያ	ዬ	ይ	ዮ
d	ደ	ዱ	ዲ	ዳ	ዴ	ድ	ዶ
g	ገ	ጉ	ጊ	ጋ	ጌ	ግ	ጎ
ṭ	ጠ	ጡ	ጢ	ጣ	ጤ	ጥ	ጦ
p̣	ጰ	ጱ	ጲ	ጳ	ጴ	ጵ	ጶ
ṣ	ጸ	ጹ	ጺ	ጻ	ጼ	ጽ	ጾ
ḍ	ፀ	ፁ	ፂ	ፃ	ፄ	ፅ	ፆ
f	ፈ	ፉ	ፊ	ፋ	ፌ	ፍ	ፎ
p	ፐ	ፑ	ፒ	ፓ	ፔ	ፕ	ፖ

Table 7 The Ethiopic syllabic alphabet for Amharic

'alpha-syllabic' writing suggests a connection with Indian writings, perhaps a result of stimulus diffusion. The Ethiopic script runs from left to right, another feature distinguishing it from other Semitic scripts. It is the system of the classical language Ge'ez which for many centuries served as the language of the Ethiopic church and other literary functions. The standardization of Amharic was achieved in modern times. Although the Ethiopic script is highly systematic in its structural make-up, its adaptation to Amharic has introduced a number of complications. Some of the graphic distinctions are today only etymological. There are two consonant symbols for the vowel *a*, formerly representing *'ayin* and the glottal stop, and three symbols for *h*, formerly *h*, *ḫ*, *ḫ*. The Ethiopic script has been adapted to Amharic as well as Oromo, Tigr, Tigrinya and other languages of Ethiopia.
Reading Bender et al. 1976; Leslau 1987; Mulugeta 1988.

anagram [modern Lat. *ana* 'back' + *gramma* 'letter'] A transposition of the letters of a word or phrase to create new words; often used to form pen-names, e.g. AROVET L[e] J[eune] → Voltaire.

Anglo-Saxon alphabet The Anglo-Saxons were introduced to the Roman alphabet by Irish missionaries. For Old English it consisted of 25 letters, the same letters as the present English alphabet except <j>, <q>, <v> and <w>. In addition, the Anglo-Saxon alphabet included the following letters which are no longer in use: <æ>, representing the vowel of modern English *ash*; and <ð>, called *eth*, and the runic letter <þ>, called *thorn*, both represented in modern English spelling by <th> (table 8).

A a	a	F ꝼ	f	L l	l	R ꞃ	r	X x	ks
B b	b	Ᵹ ᵹ	g	₥ m	m	S ꞅ ſ	s	Y y Ẏ ẏ	ü
C c	q	Ƅ h	h	N n	n	T ꞇ	t	Z	dz
D ꝺ	d	I ı	i	O o	o	U u	u	Ð ꝺ	ð
Ɛ e	e	K k	k	P p	p	V ƿ	w	Þ þ	θ

Table 8 The Anglo-Saxon alphabet

Letter <y> represented a sound much like the IPA symbol corresponding to the French vowel [y] in *lune*. But in late Middle English it came to be used for [θ] because Caxton, who in 1476 brought the art of printing from the continent, had no letter <þ>: instead he used <y>. In books up to the eighteenth century <y^{e}> and <y^{t}> are common contractions of *the* and *that*, as in *He y^{t} hath ears to heer let him heer* (Matthew in Sir John Cheke's rendition, *c.*1550). That <ye> came to be pronounced [jə] rather than [ðə] in pseudo-archaic phrases such as *Ye Olde Bull's Head* is a peculiar case of SPELLING PRONUNCIATION induced by the printing technology.

Anglo-Saxon spelling was haphazard and irregular in many other respects, partly as a result of the fact that it was a makeshift system that had to build a relationship between spelling and pronunciation with fewer letters than phonemes. The discrepancy between sounds and letters was further confounded by spellings on Latin models which inserted letters in words with no corresponding sounds, such as <b> in *debt* or *doubt* after Latin *debitum, dubitare.* Proposals for rectifying the spelling system appeared as of the sixteenth century. In 1568 Thomas Smith published a *Dialogue Concerning the Correct and Emended Writing of the English Language*, and William Bullokar's *Booke at Large, for the Amendment of Orthographie for English Speech* of 1580 was an attempt at phonetic reform. About the contemporary orthography Bullokar complained thus:

> Of which default, complaine we may, in the old A.B.C.
> Wherein be letters twentie fower, whereof but six agree,
> In perfect use, of name and sound, besides misplacing some,
> other are written unsounded, wherein concord is none.
> But he that will in Inglish knowe, divisions in voice,
> shall find therein fortie and fower, without any more choice.

This complaint has been echoed many times since, reflecting the fact that English spelling is highly involved not only because, over the past three or four centuries, speech underwent considerable changes while writing remained largely what it was in the sixteenth century, but also because the Anglo-Saxon alphabet was poorly fitted to the English language to begin with.
See also ENGLISH SPELLING; SPELLING; SPELLING REFORM.
Reading Baugh 1951, appendix; Vallins 1973.

Annamese writing *See* CHŨ'NÔM; VIETNAMESE ALPHABET

antique A style of display type developed in the nineteenth century which is characterized by almost uniform thickness of all lines (figure 4). It belongs to a family of display types known as 'egyptian', reminiscent of the monumental Egyptian architecture after which it is named.
Reading Druet and Grégoire 1976.

anusvāra [Sanskrit 'after-sound'] A diacritic device of Indian writing systems for expressing nasal quality, usually a dot placed above a letter which is thus modified, for example DEVANĀGARĪ तं /tam/ vs त /ta/.

Arabic alphabet One of the major Semitic scripts descended from the Aramaic and the Nabataean alphabets. It originated in the fourth century CE, but the oldest document – a trilingual inscription in Greek, Syriac and Arabic – dates from 512 CE. Like other Semitic scripts, the Arabic alphabet is a consonant alphabet typically applied to the writing of consonant roots. It comprises 28 basic letters (table 9), six more than the classical Aramaic alphabet from which it derived, reflecting the richer inventory of consonants in the Arabic language. Some of the additional letters were created by adding diacritical marks to others. For instance, a dot was added to the letter *hā* to distinguish the tense voiceless velar

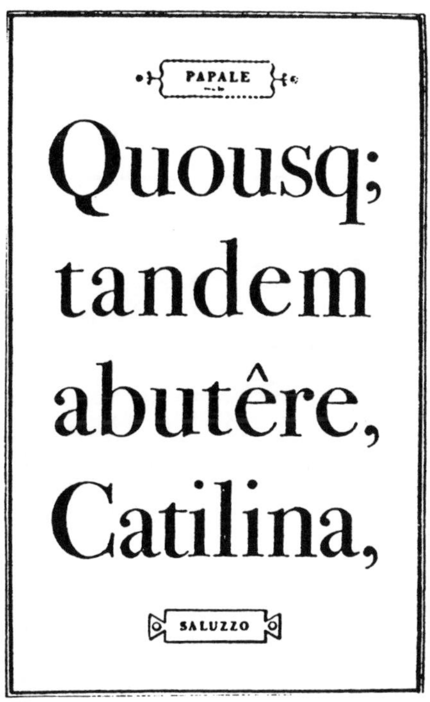

Figure 4 Antique style of Giovanni Battista Bodoni's Manuale Tipografico, *1818*

/ḫ/. New letters were also created by adding diacritics for voiced and voiceless fricatives, emphatic /d/ and /z/, as well as for /s/. In addition, a ligature formed of *lām* and *'elif* is often counted as the 29th letter. In Arabic there are three pairs of vowels, /a/ /a:/, /i/ /i:/ and /u/ /u:/. The long vowels are generally represented by the consonant letters *'elif*, *jā* and *wāw*, while diacritics are used for the short ones: a horizontal bar over the consonant letter (*fat'hā*) for /a/; a horizontal bar under the consonant letter (*kasrā*) for /i/; and a little hook over the consonant letter (*damnā*) for /u/. Further, a little circle above a consonant letter (*sukūn*) is sometimes used to show doubling of a consonant, that is, the absence of a vowel.

It is a characteristic feature of the Arabic alphabet that all letters except *'elif*, *dāl*, *rā*, *zā* and *wāw* occur in four different forms: independent, initial, medial and final (table 10). Some of the letters cannot be joined to others, which makes for the articulated appearance of Arabic writing. Like other Semitic scripts, the Arabic alphabet is written from right to left.

In the wake of the Islamic religion, the Arabic alphabet has spread throughout much of the world. In current use it stands second only to the Roman alphabet. Of the many languages to which it was applied – including Turkish, Farsi, Pashto, Urdu, Kashmiri, Malay, Uighur, Kazakh, Somali, Hausa, Fula, Swahili, Sudanese, Hebrew, Berber, Portuguese, Spanish and Serbo-Croatian – some have a richer inventory of phonemes than Arabic which led to the introduction of new or derived letter signs. For writing Persian, for example, four additional letters for /p/, /č/, /ž/ and /g/ were added, and its extension to Urdu produced another

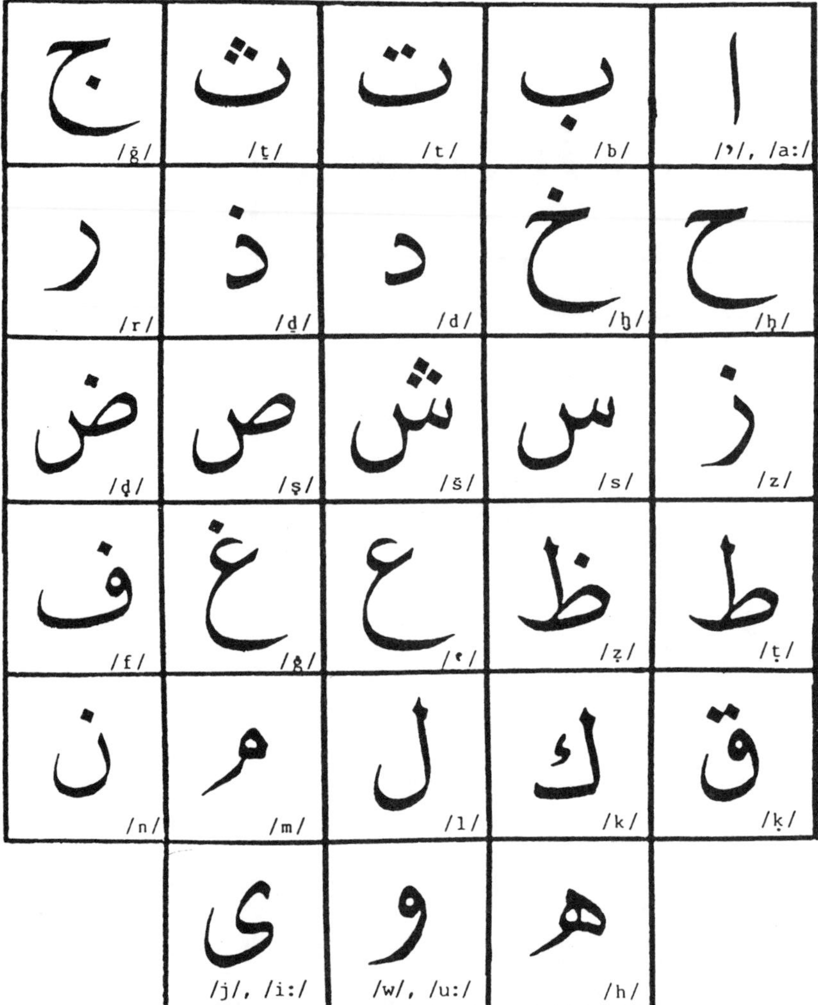

Table 9 The Arabic alphabet: independent letter forms and sound values

four letters for /t/, /d/, /r/ and /ğ/. For Malay the *nūn* was modified with a diacritic to represent the palatalized nasal /ŋ/.
See also ARABIC SCRIPTS; ARABIC WRITTEN LANGUAGE; ARAMAIC WRITING; CALLIGRAPHY; NABATAEAN SCRIPT; SEMITIC WRITING.
Reading Barr 1976; Beeston 1970; Naveh 1982.

Arabic scripts Evolved from the Nabataean script during the fourth and fifth centuries CE, the Arabic script spread with the Arabic language as the Arabs conquered territories stretching from North Africa at the Atlantic coast in the west to Sind in the east. The many scripts that developed over the centuries can be broadly classed into two types, the *kūfīc* book style and the *naskhī* cursive style. *Kūfīc* means the script of Kufah, a city founded in 638 CE in Mesopotamia which

Name	Initial	Medial	Final	In isolation	Sound value	Name	Initial	Medial	Final	In isolation	Sound value
'elif			ـا	ا	'	ṭā	طـ	ـطـ	ـط	ط	ṭ
bā	بـ	ـبـ	ـب	ب	b	ẓā	ظـ	ـظـ	ـظ	ظ	ẓ
tā	تـ	ـتـ	ـت	ت	t	'ain	عـ	ـعـ	ـع	ع	'
ṯā	ثـ	ـثـ	ـث	ث	ṯ	ġain	غـ	ـغـ	ـغ	غ	ġ
ǧīm	جـ	ـجـ	ـج	ج	ǧ	fā	فـ	ـفـ	ـف	ف	f
ḥā	حـ	ـحـ	ـح	ح	ḥ	ḳāf	قـ	ـقـ	ـق	ق	ḳ(q)
ḫā	خـ	ـخـ	ـخ	خ	ḫ	kāf	كـ	ـكـ	ـك	ك	k
dāl			ـد	د	d	lām	لـ	ـلـ	ـل	ل	l
ḏāl			ـذ	ذ	ḏ	mīm	مـ	ـمـ	ـم	م	m
rā			ـر	ر	r	nūn	نـ	ـنـ	ـن	ن	n
zā			ـز	ز	z	hā	هـ	ـهـ	ـه	ه	h
sīn	سـ	ـسـ	ـس	س	s	wāw			ـو	و	w
šīn	شـ	ـشـ	ـش	ش	š	jā	يـ	ـيـ	ـي	ي	j
ṣād	صـ	ـصـ	ـص	ص	ṣ	lām-elif			ـلا	لا	lā
ḍād	ضـ	ـضـ	ـض	ض	ḍ						

Table 10 The Arabic alphabet: letter names and variant forms

was a major centre of early Islamic learning. The *kūfīc* script has many angular forms, probably because it was initially used in inscriptions in stone. It is the script of the earliest copies of the Qur'ān. The stretched-out horizontal letters and the omission of diacritical marks are characteristic features of this script, as illustrated in figure 5. The *kūfīc* script went out of general use in the eleventh

Figure 5 Part of an inscription on a tomb, in Arabic: Egypt, tenth century, kūfīc *style (Museum für Islamische Kunst, Berlin)*

century except for decorative purposes. It was replaced by a new script called *naskhī* which then became the major medium for copying the Qur'ān. It is a cursive script governed by principles regulating the proportions between the letters. The notion of regulating letter proportions gave rise to a number of variant scripts including the *tūmār* script of fourteenth-century Egypt and the *maghribī* or 'western' script of North Africa (figure 6). The normal variety used for handwriting is *rīgāl*.
See also CALLIGRAPHY.
Reading Ettinghausen 1974.

Figure 6 A page from the Qur'ān in the maghribī *script, from north-west Africa, early fourteenth century (Bayerische Staatsbibliothek, Munich)*

Arabic written language The language that developed into Classical Arabic (CA) is first attested in inscriptions from the second century CE. It received its refined form during the seventh century in pre-Islamic poetry, and then in the Qur'ān. The period of the Arab conquests (seventh and eighth centuries CE) brought CA as the language of Islam to various non-Arabic-speaking countries. The ensuing process of language contact and the expansion of the language area are thought to have led to a surge of linguistic normativism manifested in the production of a large number of grammars, dictionaries and anthologies. As of that time, writing was closely linked with the Islamic faith. Since the sacred text of the Qur'ān was thought to be inspired, copying the Qur'ān was a literary activity of great importance. The Qur'ān language of the time provided the model of what subsequently became a highly artificial and eventually atrophied written language far removed from any spoken variety. This religiously inspired establishment of a written standard for Arabic reinforced the normative attitude towards the written language and a growing cleavage between spoken and written Arabic. Eventually a situation of DIGLOSSIA developed with CA as the universally recognized written variety. Vernacular varieties of Arabic were first used in writing in the present century, the Egyptian variety of Cairo or a koine based on

it being the strongest contender to replace CA as the primary means of written communication, formal instruction and education in the Arabic-speaking world.
Reading Mahmoud 1979; Fischer 1982; Ibrahim 1989.

Aramaic writing The Aramaic language is an offshoot of Phoenician. It is first attested in writing in the ninth century BCE on documents found in the nineteenth century CE in northern Syria. A north Semitic consonant script was adapted to Aramaic, perhaps in the late tenth or early ninth centuries, but numerous inscriptions appear only in the sixth century, reflecting the spread of the Aramaic alphabet throughout the Near East. This writing had an enormous influence, gradually replacing Assyrian cuneiform as the Assyrian empire adopted Aramaic as the principal administrative language. The Aramaic script must be considered the ancestral writing of the scripts of several Semitic languages as well as the KHAROṢṬHĪ SCRIPT of India which like it was written from right to left. In the late Assyrian period (1000 to 600 BCE) the Aramaic language became the international language of contact throughout the Near East and Asia Minor, serving as an administrative language of the Persian empire as far afield as Egypt in the west and India in the east. Owing to its political importance the Aramaic script was quite uniform for many generations, but at the end of the third century BCE it split up into several new scripts such as the Syriac, Nabataean, Palmyran and Hebrew square.

ʾ	𐡀	l	𐡋
b	𐡁	m	𐡌
g	𐡂	n	𐡍
d	𐡃	s	𐡎
h	𐡄	ʿ	𐡏
w	𐡅	p	𐡐
z	𐡆	ṣ	𐡑
ḥ	𐡇	q	𐡒
ṭ	𐡈	r	𐡓
y	𐡉	š	𐡔
k	𐡊	t	𐡕

Table 11 The Aramaic alphabet

The early Aramaic alphabet consists of 22 consonant letters as shown in table 11. Formal modifications which were fully developed by the fifth century made the script appear more fluid with rounded forms and letters such as *bēth, dāleth, rēš* and *'ayin* open at the top.
See also ALLOGLOTTOGRAPHY; PHOENICIAN ALPHABET; SEMITIC WRITING.
Reading Naveh 1982; Segert 1975; Gershevitch 1979.

Armenian writing Created in the early fifth century CE by Mesrọp, a clerk at the Armenian royal court, the Armenian alphabet accurately maps the Old Armenian phonology. Its earliest form, used until the eleventh century, is known as *erkat 'agir* 'iron script'. Armenian texts were always written from left to right. Moreover, the order of the vowel letters corresponds to that of the Greek alphabet. These features suggest Greek influence, while some letter shapes betray Semitic models. However, the inventory of its 38 letters and their close phonological fit point to an otherwise original creation (table 12). Old Armenian was used as a classical language until the nineteenth century when it was replaced by the modern language as the major vehicle of written communication. The latter exhibits two main varieties, the western and eastern dialects. The western or Constantinople dialect is more widely spoken, but the variety taught at school is closer to the eastern dialect which deviates little from the written norm, although its orthography has some historical (etymological) features. The letters for [o] and [f] are additions to the original alphabet introduced during the late Middle Ages for writing the many loan words which came into the language, mainly from Middle French.
Reading Thomson 1975.

ash The name of the letter *æ* used by the Anglo-Saxons.
See also ANGLO-SAXON ALPHABET.

Aśoka edicts Emperor Aśoka Maurya, who ruled from 272 to 231 BCE, propagated Buddhist doctrines throughout the Indian subcontinent. The inscriptions with his famous edicts, dating from around 253 to 250, are found over a large part of South Asia. While Greek and Aramaic versions were discovered in the north-western frontier region, most of the inscriptions were redacted in the Prakrit of Māgadha using two different writing systems, Kharoṣṭhī and Brāhmī, which are said to have been invented by order of the Emperor. The appearance of these scripts marks the commencement of writing proper on the Indian subcontinent.
See also BRĀHMĪ WRITING; INDIAN WRITING SYSTEMS; KHAROṢṬHĪ SCRIPT.
Reading Gopal 1977; Verma 1971.

aspiration marks Diacritical marks used in ancient Greek to indicate breathing quality: δασεία <'>, called *spiritus asper* in Latin, indicates the presence of /h/; and Ψιλή <'>, *spiritus lenis,* stood for the glottal stop. In modern Greek, aspiration marks are redundant because all initial vowels are articulated without glottal stop. Diacritic <'> in Greek words that have entered other languages as loans is usually represented by <h>, e.g. ἅδης ['a ðīs] whence *Hades* ['heidi:z] 'hell'.

1.	2.	3.	4.	5.	1.	2.	3.	4.	5.
Ա	ա	a		aĭb	Մ	մ	m		men
Բ	բ	b	p‘	ben	Յ	յ	h-, j		hi
Գ	գ	g	k‘	gim	Ն	ն	n		nu
Դ	դ	d	t‘	da	Շ	շ	ʃ		ʃa
Ե	ե	e, je-		jetʃ‘	Ո	ո	o, vo-		vo
Զ	զ	z		za	Չ	չ	tʃ‘		tʃ‘a
Է	է	e		e	Պ	պ	p’	b	p’e
Ը	ը	ə		ət‘	Ջ	ջ	dʒ	tʃ‘	dʒe
Թ	թ	t‘		t‘o	Ռ	ռ	rr		rra
Ժ	ժ	ʒ		ʒe	Ս	ս	s		se
Ի	ի	i		ini	Վ	վ	v		vev
Լ	լ	l		ljʉn	Տ	տ	t’	d	t’jʉn
Խ	խ	x		xe	Ր	ր	r		re
Ծ	ծ	ts’	dz	ts’a	Ց	ց	ts‘		ts‘o
Կ	կ	k’	g	k’en	Ւ	ւ	v, u		hjʉn
Հ	հ	h		ho	Փ	փ	p‘		p‘jʉr
Ձ	ձ	dz	ts	dza	Ք	ք	k‘		k‘e
Ղ	ղ	ɣ		ɣad	Օ	օ	o		o
Ճ	ճ	tʃ’	dʒ	tʃ’e	Ֆ	ֆ	f		fe

Table 12 The Armenian alphabet. Column headings: (1) capital letters (2) small letters (3) sound values in eastern Armenian (4) sound values in western Armenian where different (5) letter names in eastern Armenian

Assamese writing One of India's constitutionally recognized languages, Assamese is written in the Bengālī syllabic alphabet with slightly altered characters for /r/ and /w/.
See also BENGĀLĪ WRITING.

Assyrian One of the major languages of CUNEIFORM WRITING. It is an offshoot of Old Akkadian originating in the north of Mesopotamia. Assyrian cuneiform writing is commonly divided into Old, Middle and New or Late Assyrian periods. Old Assyrian is attested in the records of traders in Asia Minor, the so-called Cappadocian tablets (*c.*1950 BCE), while Middle Assyrian (*c.*1200) is preserved in numerous legal documents. The New Assyrian period was the era of Assyrian dominance from which extensive records have come down to us, especially from the library at Nineveh of the seventh century BCE. The cuneiform of the Cappadocian tablets is characterized by a relatively small inventory of only about 100 syllabograms and a small number of logograms. In the texts each cuneiform sign is separated from its neighbours by a dividing line. In the later periods the sign

Figure 7 A specimen of Assyrian cuneiform: the annals of the Assyrian king Tiglath-Pileser I inscribed on a clay cylinder, eleventh century BCE *(by permission of Staatliche Museen Berlin: Vorderasiatisches Museum zu Berlin)*

inventory expands. Especially in the New Assyrian period, Assyrian cuneiform is characterized by a high degree of symmetry and regularity, as illustrated in figure 7, a clay cylinder bearing an inscription of Tiglath-Pileser I, King of Assyria (1115–1077). This regularity distinguishes Assyrian cuneiform from the older Babylonian variety. Table 13 illustrates the difference in appearance of early Babylonian and Assyrian cuneiform signs.
See also AKKADIAN; BABYLONIAN; CUNEIFORM WRITING.
Reading Edzard 1980.

autograph [Gk αὐτό 'by oneself' + γραφος 'writing', 'written with one's own hand'] **1** The author's own manuscript written in his/her own hand-writing.

Early Babylonian	Assyrian	Meaning
[illegible]	[illegible]	bird
[illegible]	[illegible]	fish
[illegible]	[illegible]	donkey
[illegible]	[illegible]	ox
[illegible]	[illegible]	sun day
[illegible]	[illegible]	grain
[illegible]	[illegible]	orchard
[illegible]	[illegible]	to plough to till
[illegible]	[illegible]	boomerang to throw to throw down
[illegible]	[illegible]	to stand to go

Table 13 Some early Babylonian and Assyrian cuneiform signs and their meanings

2 A person's own signature. The individual signature, thought to be unique and therefore authentic, is a modern Western practice. In East Asia, the personal seal is still more common than the autograph, the rationale being that anybody can write anybody else's name, while the authentic seal impression can only be produced with one's own seal. Figure 8 shows Charlemagne's autograph *Karolus* of which he, however, only inscribed the hook in the centre, since he was not able to write.

autonomy of writing The idea that writing is, at least partly, independent of speech. Mainstream linguistics in the first half of the twentieth century has assumed that writing is a secondary system of symbols derived from speech and designed solely as a means of making a visible recording of speech, of which, however, it is never more than an imperfect and corrupt reflection. Under this

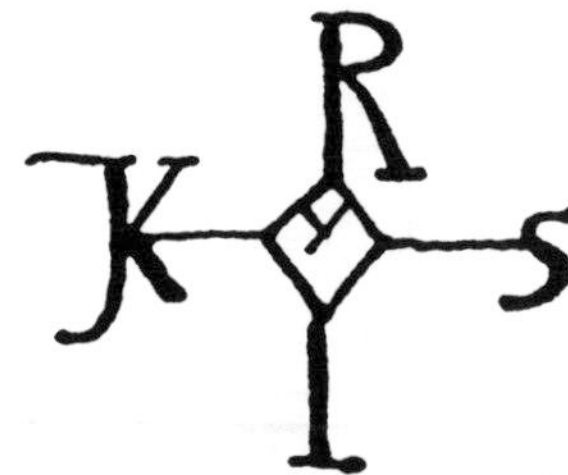

Figure 8 Charlemagne's autograph

assumption, language was equated with speech for the purposes of linguistic study. As a result, the relation between speech and writing as well as that between spoken and WRITTEN LANGUAGE has received little attention. Only the Prague school of linguistics was ahead of its time in according writing equal significance with speech. It was in this context that the notion of partial autonomy of writing was first discussed. Writing and speaking, the Prague scholars taught, serve different functions. And although there is no clear-cut collection of features that differentiate written from spoken language, writing can be expected to exhibit properties and patterns which have no equivalent in speech and vice versa. Writing is thus to be investigated as a means of linguistic expression in its own right.

During the second half of the twentieth century, the notion that writing is just a way of setting down speech has been repeatedly challenged and the Prague idea of partial autonomy of writing has gained ground. The relation between writing and speech, their commonalities and differences, and the role that writing systems play in this relation have been addressed in a growing body of literature. But the degree of independence of writing from speech, the extent to which it is divorced from sound, remains a highly contentious issue. Among the relevant questions to be further explored in this connection are the following relating respectively to the ORIGIN OF WRITING, its communicative functions, its place in the language system, its styles and its constituent units:

Origin Were written messages originally substitutes for spoken messages?
Communication How do (spoken) utterances differ from (written) texts in terms of conveying messages?
Style How do writing styles differ from speaking styles?
Language system Where is the place of the writing system within the overall system of language, and how does it relate to other systemic levels?
Constituent units What are the operative units of a writing, and how do they relate to the relevant units of speech?

Reading (*pro* autonomy) Ginneken 1939; Bolinger 1946; Vachek 1973; Feldbusch 1985; Harris 1986; (*contra*) Saussure 1916; Bloomfield 1933; DeFrancis 1989.

Avesta alphabet A writing created in the third century CE for recording the Avestan hymns composed by Zarathustra (also Zoroaster) in the Persian language or Gathic, as it was known at the time (sixth century BCE). Since the old texts had become incomprehensible, a Middle Persian commentary (*zend*) was

added: hence Zend Avestan. The Avesta alphabet (table 14) consists of 48 letters many of which are derived from the older Pahlevi writing of Persian which in turn can be traced to ARAMAIC WRITING. Some letters were created by uniting Pahlevi letters in cursive writing. Avestan is written in Semitic fashion from right to left. However, the complete representation of vowels testifies to Greek influence. In the wake of the Islamization of Persia, the Avestan alphabet was replaced by the Arabic script.
Reading Reichelt 1909; Mills 1913.

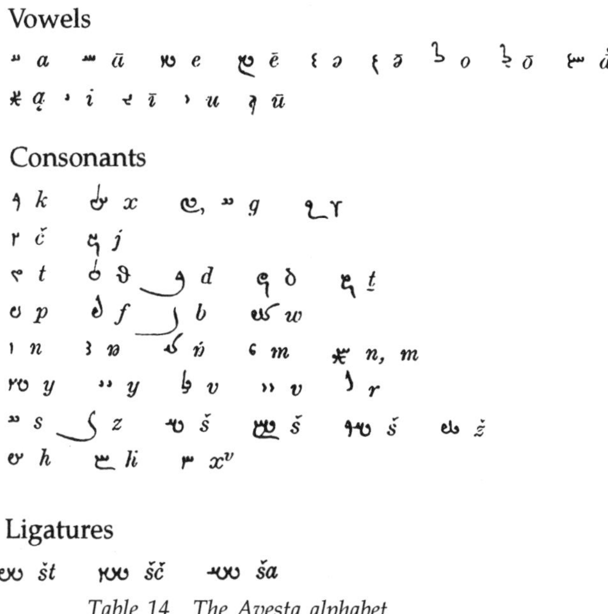

Table 14 The Avesta alphabet

Azerbaijani (*also* Azeri) A Turkic language spoken in the Republic of Azerbaijan, in Nagorno-Karabakh and in Iran. Azerbaijani was written traditionally from the fifteenth century CE in the Arabic alphabet, but in 1924 the Soviet government introduced a new orthography in Roman letters. Another reform brought a change to the Cyrillic alphabet in 1940, but in 1991 the new republic once again reverted to the Roman alphabet. The Cyrillic alphabet contains eight special letters not used in Russian: ғ, ә, ј, K, ө, ү, һ and ҹ (table 15).

Azeri *See* AZERBAIJANI

Aztec writing One of the autochthonous writings of Central America which is often classified as a borderline case of writing proper. In pre-colonial times the Aztecs, who were at the pinnacle of their power when the Spaniards arrived, had produced a great body of historical and administrative literature. Much of it was destroyed as satanic stuff by the *conquistadores* and the clergymen in their entourage. The Aztecs themselves, moreover, had a habit of burning each other's records when they demolished the temples of the cities they subdued. Yet a number of documents have been preserved, some of which were recorded at the

Roman 1922–33	Roman 1933–39	Cyrillic 1940–58	Cyrillic 1958	Arabic	Value
A a	A a	А а	А а	ا، آ	a
B b	B b	Б б	Б б	ب	b
V v	V v	В в	В в	و	v
K k	Q q	Г г	Г г	ق	g[1)]
G g	Ƣ ƣ	Ғ ғ	Ғ ғ	غ	ɣ
D d	D d	Д д	Д д	د	d
E e	E e	Э, Е э, е	Е е	—، ء، اء	e
Ə ə	Ə ə	Ә ә	Ә ә	—، ا	ä
Ƶ ƶ	Ƶ ƶ	Ж ж	Ж ж	ژ	ž
Z z	Z z	З з	З з	ز	z
I i	I i	И и	И и	ای، ی	i
Ꞁ ꞁ	Ь ь	Ы ы	Ы ы	ی	ï
J j	J j	Й й	Ј ј	ی	y
Q q	K k	К к	К к	ك	k
Ƣ ƣ	G g	Ӄ ӄ	Ҝ ҝ	گ	g[2)]
L l	L l	Л л	Л л	ل	l
M m	M m	М м	М м	م	m
N n	N n	Н н	Н н	ن	n
O o	O o	О о	О о	او، و	o
Ɵ ɵ	Ɵ ɵ	Ө ө	Ө ө	اؤ، و	ö
P p	P p	П п	П п	پ	p
R r	R r	Р р	Р р	ر	r
S s	S s	С с	С с	ص، ث، س	s
T t	T t	Т т	Т т	ت	t
Y y	U u	У у	У у	او، و	u
U u	Y y	Ү ү	Ү ү	اؤ، و	ü
F f	F f	Ф ф	Ф ф	ف	f
X x	X x	Х х	Х х	خ	x
H h	H h	Һ һ	Һ һ	ح، ه	h
Ç ç	C c	Ч ч	Ч ч	چ	č
C c	Ç ç	Ҷ ҷ	Ҹ ҹ	ج	ǰ
Ʒ ʒ	Ş ş	Ш ш	Ш ш	ش	š
Ņ ņ	Ņ ņ	—	—	(ڭ)	ŋ
—	—	Е е	—	—	ye
—	—	Ю ю	—	—	yu
—	—	Я я	—	—	ya

1) before back vowels; 2) before front vowels.

Table 15 The Azerbaijani alphabets

request of the European intruders, the most famous example being the Codex Mendoza, so called after Antonio de Mendoza, first viceroy of New Spain (from 1535 to 1550). This document, which is kept at the Bodleian Library in Oxford, has an extensive Spanish commentary written at the time by a priest who had some knowledge of Classical Nahuatl, the language of Aztec writing. Classical Nahuatl, also called Classical Aztec, is now extinct, but several descendant languages survive in Hidalgo, Puebla and Veracruz, Mexico.

Aztec glyphs are conspicuous for their vivid graphic outer form. Many of the signs are pictorial and, within a given cultural context, more or less self-explanatory. They are clearly of iconic origin, although they exhibit a considerable degree of standardization. Notice, for example, in figure 9 the complex glyph that designates the conquest of a city. It depicts a burning temple which falls off its elevated terrace. On this page of the Mendoza it appears eight times (on the top, at the right side and on the bottom), indicating that Uitzilihuitl, the Aztec ruler from 1396 until 1417, vanquished eight cities. The chronology is indicated in the glyphs of the L-shaped column at the left side of the page which contain calendrical information. Thus these and similar historical events were unambiguously recorded, but the Aztec system of writing did not allow the registering of messages verbatim in such a way that the exact wording of connected sentences could be retrieved from the written text. Rather, to some extent the Aztecs had to rely on pictorial representation, the wording being supplied by the reader. That Aztec writing was only feebly related to language is also evidenced by the fact that only nouns appear to be written, some of them deverbal.

The inner form of Aztec writing was thus not highly developed. It had no clearly delimited corpus of signs, and a fixed direction of writing was not established. Rebus phonetic writing was used, but never played an important role, perhaps because homonyms are exceedingly rare in Classical Nahuatl. Among the glyphs with definite semantic denotations many show polyvalence, being associated with more than one lexeme. Polyvalence is also evident where glyphs are used both as logograms and as phonetic indicators.

Phonetic indicators are of two kinds, suppletive and constitutive. Suppletive phonetic indicators are added to word signs in order to identify the target word unequivocally by eliminating possible synonyms. A set of logograms was routinely used as initial phonetic indicators. The word properly indicated by such a sign would have the same initial segment, syllable or any other submorphemic unit as the target word to whose glyph it was added. Constitutive phonetic glyphs, on the other hand, provide information not otherwise indicated in the pictographic mode. This is particularly common in toponyms. The eight conquered cities referred to on the page of the Codex Mendoza in figure 9 are identified by constitutive phonetic indicators, each of which is connected with one of the burning temple glyphs. For instance, the city in the top right corner of the page is Chalco. (In the Mendoza the place names of the cities followed by *pu.* as an abbreviation for *pueblo* 'people' are written in alphabetic letters above the pictogram plus toponym combinations.) The toponym is indicated by a glyph that depicts a ring of jade stones, *chalchihuitl*. Only part of the word sign that is being pressed into phonetic service here is functional. The difficulty with this procedure is that there is no definite convention telling the reader exactly which part of a word sign is

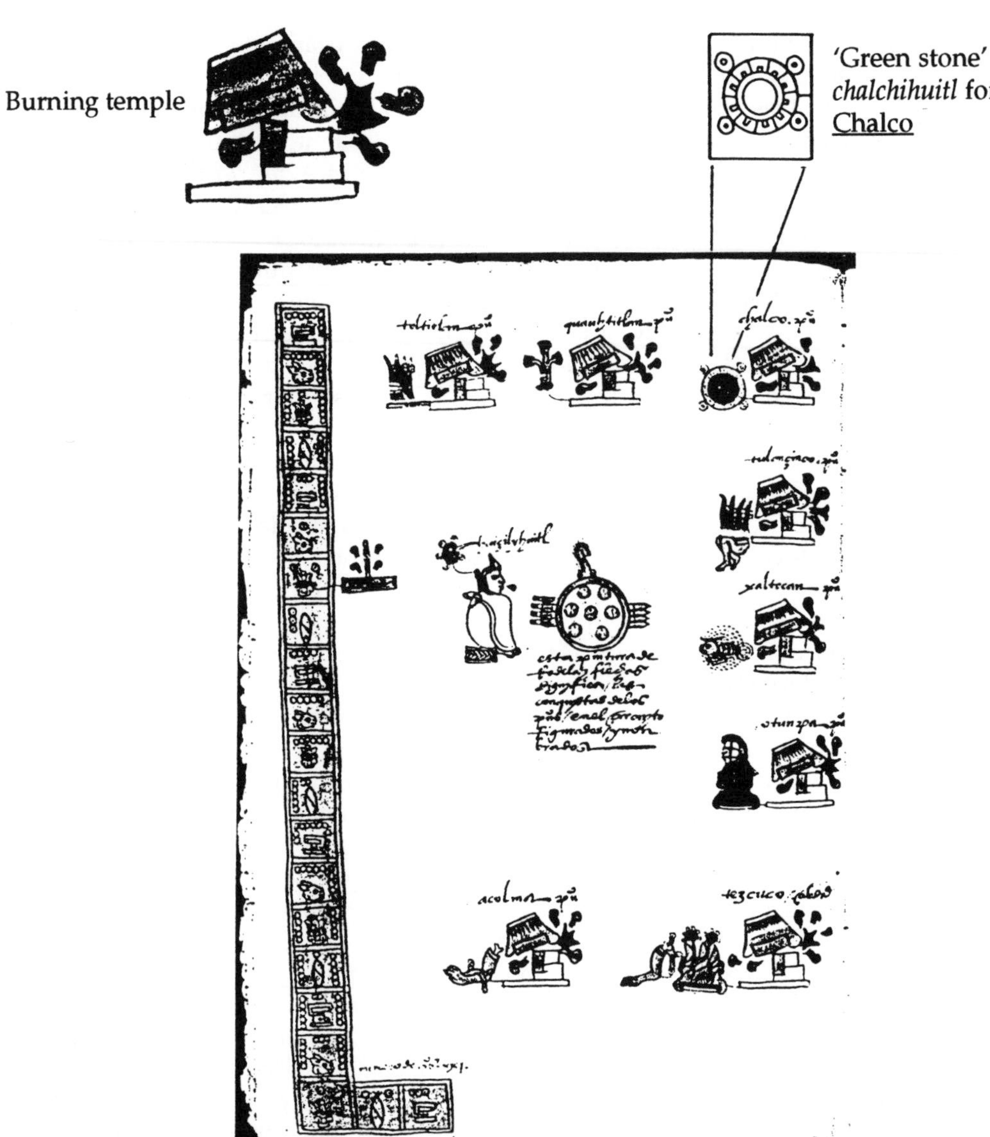

Figure 9 A page from the Codex Mendoza. *The 'burning temple' glyph is enlarged at upper left. The jade stone glyph, which serves as the toponym of the city of Chalco, is enlarged at upper right: as a logogram the same glyph has the reading* chalchihuitl *'green stone'*

to be interpreted as a phonetic indicator. In restricted contexts such as place names the informed reader can readily arrive at the intended reading, but as a general mode of writing this kind of polyvalence is impractical.

Another feature of Aztec hieroglyphic writing is that, much like compounding in word formation, individual glyphs were joined to designate new concepts. However, no conventional patterns for constructing or deriving new complex glyphs could be determined as yet.

The Aztec scribes understood the principle of phonetic writing and applied it where pictorial symbols and logograms failed, especially for personal and place names, but they never developed phonetic writing into a fully fledged system.
Reading Cooper-Clark 1938; Prem and Riese 1983; Berdan and Rieff Anwalt 1992.

B

B, b /bi:/ The second letter of the English alphabet derives from Semitic *bēth* through Greek *beta* (Β, β). The small letter is a derivative of the cursive *B* of which the upper loop was eliminated.

Babylonian One of the major languages of cuneiform writing. It is an offshoot of Old Akkadian originating in the south of Mesopotamia. Babylonian and Assyrian are considered dialects of Akkadian by some and separate languages by others. Regional and chronological divisions overlap, since the southern Babylonian and northern Assyrian were predominant as written varieties during different epochs. Babylonian cuneiform writing is commonly divided into Old, Middle, New and Late Babylonian periods. In the eighteenth century BCE, King Hammurapi (reign *c*.1792–1750) established Babylon as the principal centre of southern Mesopotamia. The Code of Hammurapi is written in Old Babylonian, which then became the dominant style of cuneiform writing. Babylonian cuneiform spread far beyond Babylon itself to become a medium of contact throughout the entire Near East for almost a millennium (figure 1). It was one of the languages of the famous trilingual rock inscription at Behistun, along with Elamite and Old Persian, which was produced in the late fifth century BCE by the Achaemenid Persians at a time when Babylon's glory was long past. It is not clear when Babylonian ceased to be a spoken language of everyday use, but the language of the Late Babylonian period (fifth to first century) is likely to have been a learned one. The New Babylonian (New Assyrian) period once again witnessed Assyrian dominance in Mesopotamia, and the Assyrians adopted Aramaic with its much simpler writing as their administrative language.

Babylonian cuneiform was a rather involved writing system making use of three kinds of signs: logograms, syllabograms and determinatives.

See also AKKADIAN; ARAMAIC WRITING; ASSYRIAN; CUNEIFORM WRITING; ELAMITE WRITING; OLD PERSIAN WRITING.

Reading Borger 1981; Bottéro 1982; Hawkins 1979; Jensen 1969.

Babylonian pointing One of the systems of vowel indication in ancient Hebrew writing. The spelling system of ancient Hebrew was highly homographic. Vocalization by means of the consonant letters ה *h*, ו *w* and י *y* (MATRES LECTIONIS) was insufficient and not consistent in all positions. This problem was alleviated through the insertion of 'points' into the consonantal text. The Babylonian system reflects the Babylonian tradition of reading the Bible. It distinguishes six contrasting vowel qualities.

See also HEBREW WRITING; TIBERIAN POINTING.

Reading Bauer and Leander 1922.

*Figure 1 Babylonian inscription on the so-called border stone (*kudurru*) from the era of Shamash-shum-ukins of Babylon, seventh century* BCE *(by permission of Staatliche Museen Berlin: Vorderasiatisches Museum zu Berlin)*

Balinese writing The oldest inscriptions from the island of Bali, Indonesia, were found on copper plates dating from the beginning of the eleventh century CE. It is thought that the texts were originally written on palm leaves which were reproduced in size and shape by the copper plates. Typologically the Balinese writing is a syllabic alphabet of the Indic kind. It is derived from the Old Kawi script which in turn belongs to the northern Indian group of Brāhmī-derived scripts. This writing is traditionally associated with religious texts. After the Hindu–Javanese culture of east Java was replaced by Islam, Hinduism re-established itself in Bali during the sixteenth century (figure 2). The literary language of that time has continued up to the twentieth century, but is substantially different from modern spoken Balinese. Its use is diminishing as the number of those who can handle the script declines. The Balinese language is nowadays written both in its traditional script and in Roman letters.
See also KAWI SCRIPT.
Reading Stutterheim 1930; Casparis 1975.

Figure 2 A section of the Ramayana in Balinese script incised on thin wooden plates held together by a cord

Bambara writing The Bambara reportedly used graphic symbols associated with blacksmiths and other craftsmen for many centuries before their language was reduced to writing in the colonial age. One of the Mande languages which constitute a branch of the Niger–Congo family of languages, Bambara is spoken primarily in Mali where it enjoys official status jointly with French and is systematically cultivated as a means of modern communication and literacy. It has an alphabetic orthography making use of Roman letters. Much like French, it used accents for open vowels <è> and <ò> which, however, were replaced in 1989 by special letters, following a proposal by Mali's Direction Nationale de l'Alphabétisation Fonctionelle et de la Linguistique Appliquée. Since the reform, the writing system includes the four letters given in table 1 in addition to the French alphabet (figure 3).

UNTIL 1989	AS OF 1990	EXAMPLES
è	ɛ	tègè : tɛgɛ
ny	ɲ	nyè : ɲɛ
ò	ɔ	mògò : mɔgɔ
ng	ŋ	ngana : ŋana

Table 1 Four special letters of Bambara

a bè bò kalo o kalo "AMAP" ka yamaruya kònò

A bɛ bɔ kalo o kalo "AMAP" ka yamaruya kɔnɔ

Figure 3 Specimens of Bambara writing before and after the 1989 reform

Bamum writing The Bamum (also Bamun) script is the result of one of several modern West African script inventions. Spoken in western Cameroon, the Bamum language belongs to the south Bantoid branch of the Niger–Congo languages. Around the end of the nineteenth century King Njoya of the Bamum was inspired by a dream to provide his language with a writing of its own. He ordered his subjects to draw simple images and symbols from which he then chose the signs for his script. The initial version had an inventory of more than 500 pictographic signs, not yet suitable for a complete and flexible representation of the language. The symbols functioned as memory aids rather than elementary signs for representing consecutive text. But as the number was reduced and the forms of the individual signs were stylized in subsequent versions which quickly followed one another, the system evolved into a full-blown script which by 1910 had a signary of just 80 symbols. In its intermediary stages, Njoya exploited the homophony of many words, making use of the REBUS PRINCIPLE, but eventually he arrived at a syllabic system. The syllabary came to be known as *a-ka-u-ku* from the values of the first four signs. Its basic unit is the CV syllable, but it also has signs for independent, i.e. syllabic vowels. A structurally interesting feature of the Bamum script is the pleonastic representation of syllables such that a vowel sign is added to an open syllable, as in the word *lam* written *la-a-m* 'marriage' in the first line of the text in figure 4.

pua a la a m fe ŋʒuə ə mɔ ɔ pa mɔ m
i puaʔ le wa ŋga lam mfe yɯə mə
this is the book thing wedding new which I Paməm

m fu ɔ n n ʃɯ ɔ i ya yɯ e r na ɔ n ʃi i
mfɔn (the sign nʒɯəya ka ɣet nə pa nʒi tɯ
king nʒəmli) Njoya have made for the notables in

fu ɔ mbɛn puə a pɯ ɔ n m fu ɔ n ŋkwən e n na
fumbɛn pua pɯən mfɔn tɯ ŋgwən'a
Fumban and people king in country side

Figure 4 A text written in the sixth version of the Bamum script

The script is written from left to right, allegedly because Njoya did not want it to bear any resemblance to Arabic. By compiling a history of his kingdom in the Bamum script he laid the foundation of a literature. On his orders copper dies of the sixth and last version of the script were created by French printers. The script was taught to many of his subjects and gained some popularity, but after Njoya was exiled in 1931, it quickly fell into disuse. The Bamum script has attracted considerable attention among scholars of writing, because it developed from a crude pictographic system of largely mnemonic function into a sophisticated syllabic writing system with alphabetic tendencies within a couple of decades.
Reading Schmitt 1963; Dalby 1968.

Bassa alphabet A modern West African script devised by or with the help of American missionaries in the 1920s. It is used to write Bassa, a Kru language spoken mostly in Liberia. No reliable reports on the usage of the script are available, but dies were created for printing, and an association for the promotion of the script was established in Liberia in 1959.

The script is an alphabet with a tone marking system consisting of 23 consonant letters, seven vowel letters and five tone diacritics. In table 2 the consonant letters are arranged in *lenis/fortis* pairs. The numbering refers to the conventional order of the alphabet which is also known as *ni-ka-se-fe* using the first four consonant letter names. Vowels are taken as a separate set not included in the sequence. In the table they are arranged roughly in phonological order from unrounded to rounded and front to back vowels. As illustrated for the letter *i* in

CONSONANTS			
LENIS		FORTIS	
p	22	**b**	19
kp	9	**gb/gm**	14
m/ɓ	5		
f	4	**v**	20
t	18	**ḍ**	8
n	1		
dy/ny	6		
ɖ (l)	15		
r	23		
s	3	**z**	13
c	16	**j**	10
k	2	**g**	7
w	12	**h**	21
xw	11	**hw**	17

VOWELS AND TONES					
	HIGH	MID	LOW	MID-LOW	HIGH-LOW
i					
a			etc.		
u			etc.		
e			etc.		
ɛ			etc.		
ɔ			etc.		
o			etc.		

Table 2 The Bassa alphabet: numbering refers to conventional order (see text)
Source: *Dalby 1967*

the table, tone marks are placed as diacritics within vowel letters. The sign + is used as a punctuation mark corresponding to a full stop.
See also AFRICAN WRITING SYSTEMS.
Reading Pichl 1966; Dalby 1967.

Batak script (*also* Battak script) One of several indigenous scripts of the Indonesian archipelago, the Batak script originates from central Sumatra. It is derived from the Old Kawi script, but its outer appearance is substantially different. The script was reportedly written from bottom to top in vertical columns arranged from left to right, a peculiarity that has been attributed to the writing surface. It consists of long strips of bamboo placed next to one another and held together by a string. However, if the resulting bundle of plates is turned 90 degrees clockwise, an arrangement of right-running horizontal lines results which may well have been the conventional order of reading. Typologically the Batak script is a syllabic alphabet of the Indian type. Its 18 basic consonant letters have an inherent *a* vowel which is modified by diacritical marks for other vowels (table 3). They are always written separately without connection. A short transliterated text is given in figure 5. The slash-like mark (VIRĀMA) indicates a syllable-final consonant, i.e. the absence of a vowel.
See also KAWI SCRIPT.
Reading Terrien de Lacouperie 1894; Jensen 1969.

Battak script *See* BATAK SCRIPT

Consonant letters

ka	*ga*	*na*	*ċa*	*ġa*	*ṅa*	*ta*	*da*	*na*
pa	*ba*	*ma*	*ya*	*ra*	*la*	*va*	*sa*	*ha*
a	*i*	*u*	*e*	*o*				

Vowel indication

pa	*pi*	*pu*	*po*	*pe*	*pang*

Table 3 The consonant letters of the Batak script and the vowel diacritics

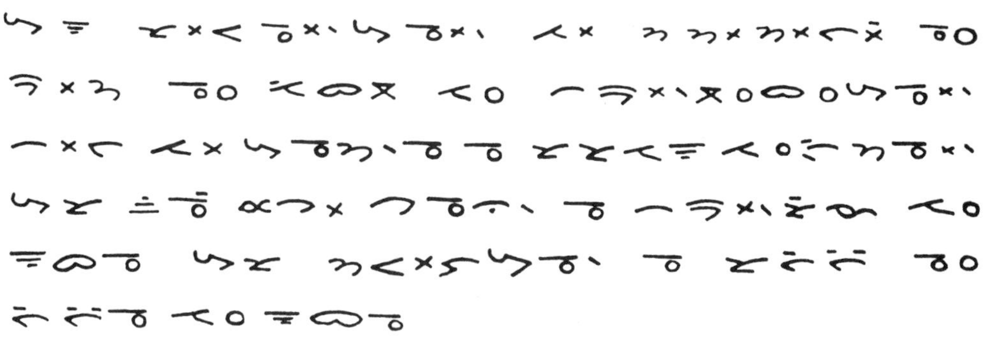

Transcription

Ai songon on do hahoholong ni roha ni debata di portibi on, pola do anakna, na sasada i dilehon, asa unang mago ganup na porsea di ibana, asa hangoluan na saleleng ni lelengna di ibana.

Translation

For God so loved the world, that he gave his only begotten Son, that whosoever believeth in him should not perish, but have everlasting life.

Figure 5 A text in Batak script with transcription: St John 3:16
Source: *Jensen 1969*

Bengālī writing Like all other modern Indian scripts, that of Bengālī derives from the Brāhmī script. In its appearance it resembles DEVANĀGARĪ from which it began to diverge in the eleventh century CE. Like Devanāgarī it makes use of the characteristic horizontal top line to connect letters forming a word. The script of the Bengālī language, which is closely related to Sanskrit, is a syllabic alphabet written from left to right (table 4). The consonant letters have an inherent *a* vowel which can be muted by an oblique stroke at the foot of the character, called *hasanta*: thus ক *ka*, but ক্ *k*. In word-final position the inherent vowel is not pronounced unless indicated by a diacritic. Other vowels are indicated by means of diacritic satellites added to the consonant signs. Geminate consonants are expressed by doubling the consonant letter, for example ড্ড *ḍḍa*, ন্ন *nna*, ব্ব *bba*, ম্ম *mma*. Many other ligatures for consonant clusters are formed by modifying consonant letters. In addition to Bengālī, the national language of Bangladesh as well as the official language of West Bengal in India, the modern script is also used with slight modifications for other languages spoken in West Bengal or neighbouring states of the Indian Union such as Assamese, Manipurī and some Munda languages.
See also BRAHMI WRITING.
Reading Dimock 1976.

Berber writing *See* TIFINAGH.

Consonant letters (initial forms)

ক	খ	গ	ঘ	ঙ	চ	ছ	জ
ka	*kha*	*ga*	*gha*	*nga*	*cha*	*chha*	*ja*
ঝ	ঞ	ট	ঠ	ড	ঢ	ণ	ত
jha	*nya*	*ṭa*	*ṭha*	*ḍa*	*ḍha*	*ṇa*	*ta*
থ	দ	ধ	ন	প	ফ	ব	ভ
tha	*da*	*dha*	*na*	*pa*	*pha*	*ba*	*bha*
ম	য়	র	ল	ব	শ	ষ	স
ma	*ya*	*ra*	*la*	*va*	*sa*	*sha*	*sa*
হ							
ha							

Vowel letters (initial forms)

অ	আ	ই	ঈ	উ	ঊ	ঋ
a	*ā*	*i*	*ī*	*u*	*ū*	*ri*
এ	ঐ	ও	ঔ	অং	অঃ	
ē	*ai*	*ō*	*au*	*aṅ*	*a'*	

Vowel letters (satellite forms)

◌া *–ā*	ি◌ *–i*	◌ী *–ī*	◌ু *–u*	◌ূ *–ū*
◌ৃ *–ri*	ে◌ *–ē*	ৈ◌ *–ai*	ে◌া *–ō*	◌ৌ *–au*

Table 4 The Bengālī syllabic alphabet

Bernard Shaw alphabet A proposal for altering the mode of writing English. As a professional writer, Bernard Shaw was greatly annoyed by what he considered a waste of time, energy, paper and ink involved in mastering and using the English orthography. He therefore provided in his will that a competition be held for the creation of a new alphabet for English. A prize of £500 was offered for the best design by the public trustee who executed the will. The Bernard Shaw alphabet is the result of this competition, for which 467 entries were made in 1958. It was designed by Kingsley Read. As stipulated in his will, Shaw's play *Androcles and the Lion* was printed in the new writing, but the Shaw alphabet was never seriously considered as an alternative writing for English. This demonstrates among other things that the systematic virtues of a spelling or writing reform proposal are only marginally relevant for its acceptance.

The Shaw Alphabet for Writers

Double lines = between pairs show the relative height of Talls, Deeps, and Shorts. Wherever possible, finish letters rightwards; those starred * will be written upwards.

Tall	Deep
peep	bib
tot	dead
kick	gag
fee	vow
thigh	they
so	zoo
sure	meaSure
church	judge
yea	*woe
hung	ha-ha
Short	**Short**
loll	roar
mime*	nun

Short	Short
if	eat
egg	age
ash*	ice
ado*	up
on	oak
wool	ooze
out	oil
ah*	awe
are	or
air	err
array	ear
	Tall
Ian	yew

Table 5 The Bernard Shaw alphabet. Double lines = between pairs show the relative height of talls, deeps and shorts. Wherever possible, letters are finished rightwards; those starred are written upwards

The Shaw alphabet is an ingenious system consisting of 48 letters, elegantly shaped and simple to write (table 5). The number of letters is almost double that of the English alphabet, substantially reducing the incidence of POLYVALENCE and complex grapheme–phoneme correspondences. No distinction is made between capital and small letters, or between initial and other forms. The sign inventory includes a raised 'namer' dot to mark proper names. Although only a few texts in the Shaw alphabet are available, it is evident that the relationship of letters to sounds is coherent and carefully thought through. The letter forms moreover have an iconic quality in that they map certain relations of the English phonology. For example, the symmetry of voiced and voiceless consonants is reflected by pairs of inverted letters for /k/ and /g/, /t/ and /d/, /ø/ and /ð/ etc.

See also SPELLING REFORM.

Reading MacCarthy 1969.

Bete writing A script for the Bete language invented in 1956 by Frédéric Bruly-Bouarbé, a well-educated Bete from Ivory Coast who was literate in French, the official language of that country. A syllabic system consisting of 401 signs, this script has never been used to any significant extent.

See also AFRICAN WRITING SYSTEMS.

Reading Monod 1958; Dalby 1968.

bilinguis Document written or inscribed in parallel versions of two different languages and often different scripts. Inscriptions of this sort have proved invaluable for the decipherment of unknown writings. Perhaps the most famous bilinguis is the Rosetta Stone which bears a decree passed by a council of Egyptian priests on the occasion of the first anniversary of the coronation of Ptolemy V Epiphanes, King of Egypt, in 196 BCE (figure 6). The text is provided in Egyptian and Greek because the rulers and high-ranking officers were Greeks rather than Egyptians. The Egyptian version of the text is given in two scripts, the formal hieroglyphic and the cursive demotic. The discovery of the Rosetta Stone by Napoleon's soldiers in 1799 greatly facilitated the decipherment of Egyptian hieroglyphs. Just as treaties and other agreements are often bilingual nowadays when the parties concerned speak different languages, it was quite common in antiquity to redact international documents in two or more languages. Babylonian was often used side by side with other languages such as Aramaic, Elamite and Old Persian. In South and South East Asia many bilingual inscriptions combine Sanskrit with various local languages such as Vietnamese and Javanese; in China and Central Asia, Chinese, Mongolian, Manchurian, Uighur and several other languages appear on bilingual or multilingual inscriptions. Such documents are important objects of palaeographic research not only where decipherment is at issue, but also for the dating of styles of languages and scripts.

See also DECIPHERMENT; PALAEOGRAPHY.

biliteracy A speech situation where an individual or society is literate in two languages and possibly two scripts. Social bilingualism is often function specific,

Figure 6 The Rosetta Stone (British Museum)

each language being used for complementary functions. A common pattern is using only one of the languages in writing while restricting the other to the oral mode of communication: bilingualism is then not coextensive with biliteracy. In other situations, however, the distribution of the languages is less clearly based on a functional division of labour: rather, both are used in speech and in writing. For example, most of Israel's Arabs are bilingual and biliterate using both Arabic and Hebrew with their respective scripts.
See also DIGLOSSIA; LITERACY.
Reading Ferguson 1978.

black letter An early Latin Gothic script (table 6), not related to the Gothic script created by Bishop Ulfilas for his Bible translation. It came into use about 1600 and was developed mainly in German-speaking areas, known there as *Fraktur*.
See also GOTHIC TYPE.

Table 6 The Latin alphabet in black-letter type

Bokmål [lit. 'book language'] The literary variety of Norwegian which is an offshoot of the written form of Danish evolved during the more than 400 years of Norway's union with Denmark (1380–1814). Also known as 'Riksmål', it is co-official with Nynorsk, 'new Norwegian', a form of Norwegian which was codified by Ivar Aasen in the mid-nineteenth century based on western rural dialects, originally intended to replace Bokmål to stress independence from Danish. However, the two varieties continue to coexist in a situation of diglossia with Bokmål as the prestige variety used for most literary purposes (figure 7).
See also DIGLOSSIA.
Reading Haugen 1961; Gundersen 1977; Vikør 1989.

book A document comprising several sheets or pages bound together in a cover, intended as a material record for the preservation and transmission of immaterial, spiritual goods. In the European context, palaeographers typically distinguish between books and manuscripts, thus reserving the notion of a book for printed material. On the basis of this definition, the first books appear about the middle of the fifteenth century. Their production presupposed the technique of making movable type and paper. A wider definition includes other kinds of written records, in particular scrolls made of papyrus, vellum or parchment, as were used throughout the ancient Near East as well as in Greece and Rome; the palm leaves bound together with fine twine which the Hindus used for their sacred writings; and the Maya codices written on tree bark.

The most ancient written documents recognizable to modern readers as books were indubitably in existence in China. Among the oldest attested Chinese

Bokmål	**Nynorsk**
Det rette heimlinge mål i landet er det som landets folk har arvet ifra forfedrene, fra den ene ætt til den andre, og som nå om stunder, trass i all fortrengsle og vanvørnad, ennå har grunnlag og emne til et bokmål, like så godt som noe av nabomålene.	Det rette heimlinge mål i landet er det som landets folk har arva ifrå forfedrene, frå den eine ætta til den andre, og som no om stunder, trass i all fortrengsle og vanvørnad, enno har grunnlag og emne til eit bokmål, like så godt som noko av grannfolk-måla.

Translation

The right native tongue in this country is the one that the people of the country have inherited from their ancestors, from one generation to the next, and which nowadays, in spite of all displacement and contempt, still has the basis and material for a written language just as good as any of the neighbours' languages.

Figure 7 Comparison of Bokmål and Nynorsk

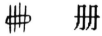

Figure 8 The most ancient form of the Chinese character for book *and its modern equivalent*

characters found in Oracle-bone script dating from the second millennium BCE is one which to this day signifies a volume or book (figure 8). The four vertical lines represent wooden or bamboo tablets inscribed vertically with a pointed stylus and later with a brush. The set of tablets was held together by leather thongs or silk cords as shown in figure 9: such were the most ancient books. In later times the Chinese continued to spearhead the development of the art of the book. They developed the technique of Xylography and block printing, and around the beginning of our era they invented Paper to replace the more costly silk as the most common writing surface. As of the eleventh century CE they experimented with movable Type, the technique which in the fifteenth century

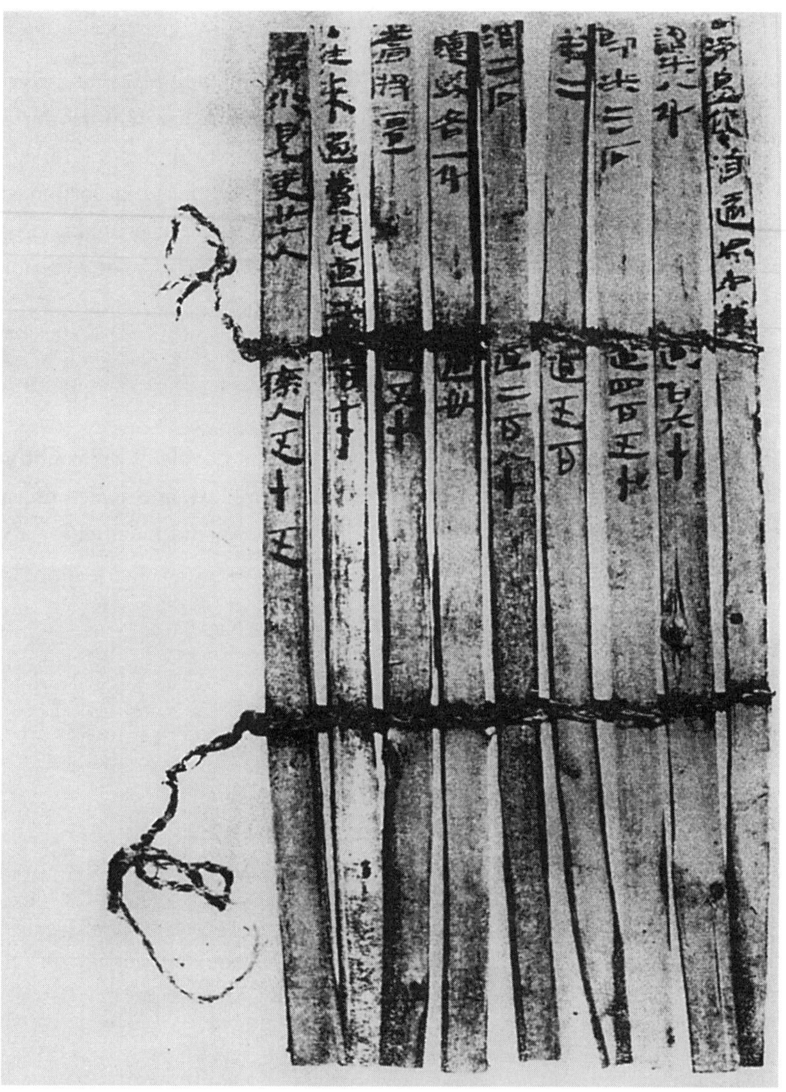

Figure 9 A Chinese book made out of wooden tablets inscribed vertically with a brush, dating from 22 CE

eventually led to the beginning of mass production of books in Europe. Since that time the printing technology has been variously improved and refined, but not fundamentally altered. The advent of electronic techniques for information processing and storage has induced some to declare the end of the age of the book, but there is little evidence to suggest that the book will be dispensable in the foreseeable future. It continues to be the most important vehicle of written language, serving as the primary medium of scholarship and literature.

See also PRINTING.

Reading Febvre and Martin 1958; Gray 1979.

bookkeeping One of the earliest attested functions of writing and, perhaps, the most important force behind its development. Property marks are found in all ancient civilizations at the threshold of writing, and in what is considered the earliest literate culture, that of Mesopotamia, a system of accountancy led to the creation of a full-blown writing system. Counters or tokens made of clay, and cylinder seals used for securing the covers of containers holding such tokens, eventually gave way to signs impressed and later incised on a wet clay surface which gradually assumed the function of the tokens. In Mesopotamia, early writing was employed for economic and administrative purposes rather than for divination or the veneration of rulers and gods. That some 85 per cent of the most ancient texts excavated in Uruk are economic records is clear testimony that the Mesopotamians needed writing as a device for controlling the economy. It was necessary for organizing complex irrigation systems and for administering agricultural surplus. In Egypt, too, accounting is seen as having played a principal role in the origin of writing. Bookkeeping, rather than being a humble by-product of the invention of writing, may thus more properly be regarded as its true parent.
See also ORIGIN OF WRITING.
Reading Gelb 1965; Schmandt-Besserat 1977; Nissen 1985; Baines 1983.

boustrophedon [Gk βου-στρόφος 'ox-turning'] Writing alternately in lines running from left to right and right to left:

——————————→
←——————————
——————————→
←——————————

Following the Phoenician practice, the earliest Greek inscriptions were from right to left. Then followed a period of writing in both directions like the course of the plough in successive furrows. The direction of Greek writing stabilized only in the fifth century BCE whence all inscriptions are from left to right. Two varieties of boustrophedon writing can be distinguished: in one, only the direction of reading changes with every line; in the other, the orientation of asymmetric letters is also inverted, as illustrated in figure 10.
See also DIRECTION OF SCRIPT.

brackets A pair of punctuation marks typically used for enclosing a word or phrase as a parenthetic unit. Both parentheses or round brackets ( ) and square brackets [ ], formerly 'crotchets', are common in ordinary prose, whereas braces or curly brackets { } and angles or pointed brackets < > are typically reserved to technical writing.
See also PARENTHESIS; PUNCTUATION.

Brāhmī writing The parent script of all modern Indian scripts. It is thought to be derived from Semitic and to have been established on the Indian subcontinent

Figure 10 Archaic Greek inscription in boustrophedon writing with inversion of letters, clearly recognizable in letters such as E, K and S. The text is a legal code of the city of Gortyn drafted in the Dorian dialect around 475 BCE

before 500 BCE. It is first attested in left-running inscriptions in the Semitic fashion, but as of the AŚOKA EDICTS of the third century BCE its direction is from left to right (figure 11).

Typologically the Brāhmī script is a syllabic alphabet which treats CV sequences as its basic units of writing. Yet consonant and vowel components are clearly distinguishable, as illustrated in table 7. The unit of writing, the syllable, is hence not the same as the unit of the underlying analysis, the segment. The principles of vowel indication in the Brāhmī script can be summarized as follows:

1 The Brāhmī script has graphemes for syllabic – that is, word-initial – vowels: 𑀅 /a/, 𑀇 /i/, 𑀉 /u/ and 𑀏 /e/.
2 Every basic grapheme has a consonant and the inherent vowel /a/ as its value.
3 Other vowels are represented by modifying the respective C + *a* grapheme in a like manner for all basic consonant graphemes.
4 Consonant clusters are represented by ligatures, of which all but the last consonant graphemes lose their inherent vowel.
5 The inherent /a/ vowel can be muted by a special diacritic, typically used at the end of a line.

These structural principles enable the representation of syllables of various different kinds: V, CV, CCV, CCCV, CVC, VC etc. However, since vowels are indicated by diacritical marks attached as satellites to the consonant graphemes,

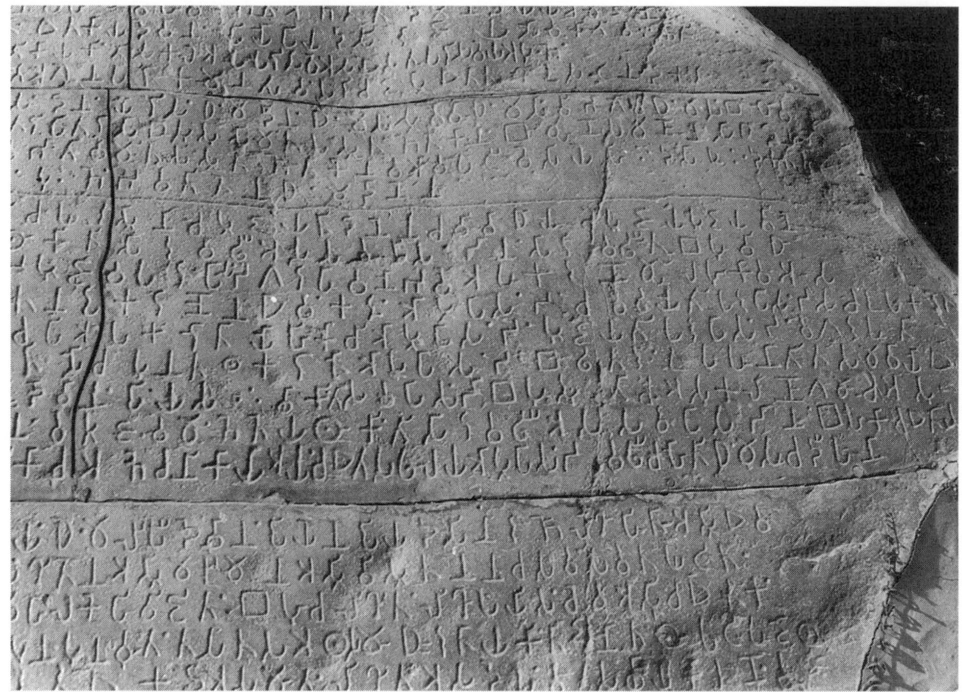

Figure 11 *Stele with inscription of Aśoka edict in Brāhmī script (National Museum, New Delhi)*

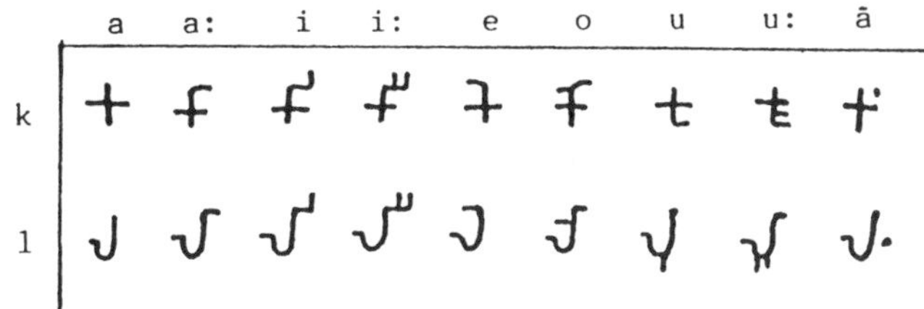

Table 7 *Vowel indication in the Brāhmī script*

the writing cannot justly be called 'syllabic'. Writings of the Brāhmī type have, therefore, been described as 'alpha-syllabic' or 'augmented consonantal' systems (table 8).

Brāhmī-derived scripts are commonly divided into a northern Indian group and a southern Indian group. The most important members of both groups are given in figure 12. Many of these scripts are used for several different languages to which they have been adapted, giving rise to some variation and subtypes.

See also INDIAN WRITING SYSTEMS.

Reading Dani 1963; Gupta and Ramachandran 1979.

braille A system of raised symbols to enable blind people to read, designed by Louis Braille (1809–52), a French teacher of the blind. The symbols consist of

Consonant letters

ka	ṭa	pa	ha
kha	ṭha	pha	
ga	ḍa	ba	
gha	ḍha	bha	
ṅa	ṇa	ma	
ča	ta	ya	
čha	tha	ra	
ja	da	la	
jha	dha	va	
ña	na	sa	

Vowel letters

a i u e ā

Table 8 The Brāhmī syllabic alphabet

3 × 2 configurations of embossed dots arranged in sequences of cells (table 9). Each cell represents a letter, numeral or punctuation mark. For example, one embossed dot in the upper left corner of the cell represents *A*, three dots in the left column of the cell *L* etc. Some frequently used words are provided with a one-cell code of dots. Hence, conversion of alphabetically written text into braille is straightforward and mechanical. The system can also be used to take notes on a writing pad equipped with a plastic grid of lines divided into cells of 3 × 2 points each of which can be embossed with a stylus. Braille is an ingenious invention which has helped many blind people to use written language. However, because material written in the tactile medium takes up much more space than printed text, books are relatively expensive to produce and store.

Bugis script One of several indigenous scripts of the Indonesian archipelago. It is used to write the Buginese language which belongs to the south Sulawesi languages spoken on the island of Celebes. The Bugis script came into existence not later than the seventeenth century, and probably earlier. A relationship with the KAWI SCRIPT seems likely, but the details of the derivation are unknown. That

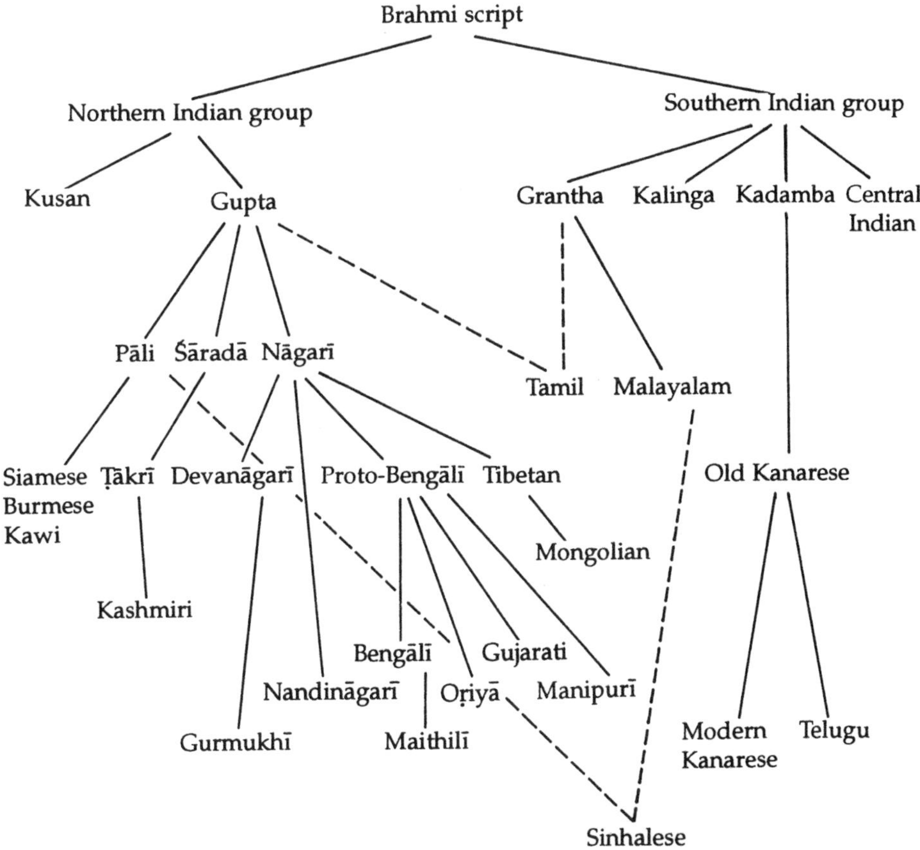

Figure 12 The most important Brāhmī-derived scripts

A B C D E F G H I J K L M N O P Q R

S T U V W X Y Z and for of the with

Table 9 Braille symbols and their corresponding alphabetic letters

the Bugis script descended from the MAKASARESE SCRIPT, with which it shares a number of characteristics, has been posited but not established. Rather than one being derived from the other, it seems more likely that both go back to a common but unknown proto-script which was closer to the Kawi script.

Bugis writing is a syllabic alphabet of the Indic type, each of the 23 letters denoting a C with inherent *a*. Other vowel values are indicated by dots and hooks placed as diacritics above, before or after the consonant letters. The conventional order of Bugis letters is systematic, relating to the places of articulation of the depicted sounds, a feature which is also reminiscent of the Indian tradition:

first the velars, then the labials, dentals and palatals, followed by /re/, /la/, /wa/, /sa/, /a/ and /ha/ (table 10).

The script is written from left to right (figure 13). Bugis documents have a very regular and well-proportioned appearance, especially in the printed characters which were produced in Rotterdam in the mid-nineteenth century. However, the script is not easy to read as most letters consist of arcs and dots and resemble each other. Moreover, a number of distinctions of the language are not represented in writing. There is no letter for the phonemic glottal stop, and geminated consonants remain likewise unexpressed in the script.

The Bugis script has been adapted to write a number of neighbouring languages including Bimanese and Ende, but only scanty records have been preserved.
Reading Hilgers-Hesse 1967; Noorduyn 1992.

Table 10 The basic letters of the Bugis script in their conventional order

Figure 13 A specimen of Bugis writing

Bulgarian A south Slavic language of some 8 million speakers which is written in the Cyrillic alphabet in a form close to that of Russian (table 11). Written Bulgarian is based on the north-eastern variety of the language. Prior to the spelling reform of 1945 two additional letters were in use: <ѫ> for the neutral vowel, which has been replaced by <ъ>; and <Ѣ> [ɛ'dvojno] for which, depending on the environment, <Е> or <Я> have come to be used. Former бѢх 'I was' is бях in the new spelling.

Аа [a], Бб [bɛ], Вв [vɛ], Гг [gɛ], Дд [dɛ], Ее [ɛ],
Жж [ž ɛ], Зз [zɛ], Ии [i], Йй [i kratko], Кк [kɛ],
Лл [lɛ], Мм [mɛ], Нн [nɛ], Оо [o], Пп [pɛ], Рр [rɛ],
Сс [sɛ], Тт [tɛ], Уу [u], Фф [fɛ], Хх [xɛ], Цц [tsɛ],
Чч [tšɛ], Шш [šɛ], Щщ [štɛ], Ъъ [ɛr goljam],
Ьь [ɛr malek], Юю [ju], Яя [ja]

Table 11 The Bulgarian alphabet

Bulgarian has a literary tradition that goes back to the tenth century CE whence Old Bulgarian or Old Church Slavonic became the first Slavic language to be written.
See also CYRILLIC; OLD BULGARIAN.
Reading Scatton 1984.

Burmese writing A member of a group of northern Indian Brāhmī-derived scripts which are known as 'Pāli scripts'. Between 700 and 1200 CE the Old Pāli script spread in the wake of Buddhism to southern India, Sri Lanka, Indo-China and Indonesia. In Burma (Myanmar) it assumed the form of the *kyok-cha* script which is documented in a large body of inscriptions dating from the eleventh to the fifteenth century. The Burmese script is a descendant thereof. The distinguishing feature of its outer form is the curvilinear appearance, the letters consisting almost entirely of circles or portions of circles in various configurations. It is hence known as *ca-lonh* or 'round script'. This characteristic is attributed to the writing surface in general use during the script's formative period, namely palm leaves on which the letters were drawn with a sharp stylus. Straight lines and angular forms were more likely to break the leaf.

The inner form of the Burmese script is that of an Indian-type syllabic alphabet with each consonant letter containing an inherent *a* vowel (table 12). Diacritic satellites are used to mark other V values. A member of the Tibeto-Burman family of languages, Burmese is a tone language. Each syllable is pronounced in one of four tones, high short falling, low long falling, high long falling, and high flat. Tonality is expressed in Burmese writing. Some vowel letters have an inherent tone; the low tone remains unmarked; and the other two are indicated by additional diacritics, a following double dot <:> for the high long falling tone and an underdot <◦> for the flat tone. Geminate Cs and other C clusters are represented by ligatures. In ligatures the letters for *ya*, *ra*, *wa* and *ha* change their forms to ျ, ြ, Δ and ှ, respectively. An overdot is used to mark nasalization, and vowel muting is indicated by a superscript half-circle.

The orthography of Burmese (figure 14) is etymological rather than phonemic, containing many historical spellings that preserve Pāli values of the letters. The script is written from left to right, each letter or ligature separately. Pause groups

Consonant letters

Symbol	Value	Symbol	Value	Symbol	Value	Symbol	Value
က	ka	ည	ńa	ဓ	dha	လ	la
ခ	kha	ဋ	ṭa	န	na	ဠ	ḷa
ဂ	ga	ဌ	ṭha	ပ	pa	ဝ	wa
ဃ	gha	ဍ	ḍa	ဖ	pha	သ	sa
င	ṅa	ဎ	ḍha	ဗ	ba	ဟ	ha
စ	ca	ဏ	ṇa	ဘ	bha		
ဆ	cha	တ	ta	မ	ṃa		
ဇ	ja	ထ	tha	ယ	ya		
ဈ	jha	ဒ	da	ရ	ra		

Vowel letters

Symbol	Value	Symbol	Value
အ	a	ဧ	e
အာ	ā	အဲ	ai
ဣ	i	ဩ	o
ဤ	ī	ဪ	au
ဥ	u	အံ	ã
ဦ	ū	အား	aḥ

Table 12 The Burmese syllabic alphabet

မြန်မာပြည်မကိုတိုင်း၊ ခရိုင်၊ မြို့နယ်နဲ့ ကျေး
ရွာတွေအဖြစ်ခွဲချမ်းထားတယ်။

Transliteration

myanmapyimakau 'tain khayain myounene

'caiywatweiaphyi ' 'khwe'chan'thate

Translation

Burma proper is divided in provinces,

districts, townships and villages.

Figure 14 A specimen of Burmese writing with transliteration and translation

rather than words are separated by spacing. A double vertical bar ‖ marks the end of a sentence.
See also PĀLI WRITING.
Reading Roop 1972.

Byblos script An ancient Semitic script discovered in 1929 at the northern Phoenician coast in Byblos, Syria. Documentation is scant as only about a dozen relatively short inscriptions on stone and bronze plates have been brought to light (figure 15). On the basis of archaeological evidence the script is dated to the middle of the second millennium, but this assignment remains uncertain. Virtually nothing is known about the development of the Byblos script or its

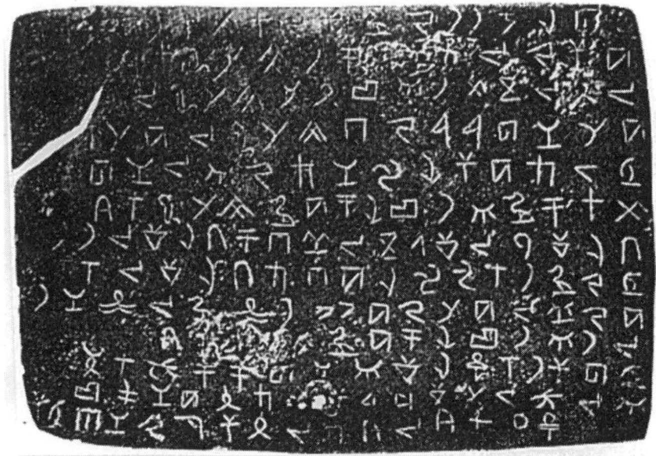

Figure 15 Enigmatic stone inscription from Byblos in Syria

relation to other scripts of the ancient Near East, although similarities of individual signs with, on the one hand, Egyptian hieroglyphs and, on the other, Old Phoenician letters have been pointed out. The inventory of more than 100 different signs suggests a syllabic system. According to the most credible decipherment by Edouard Dhorme, the script has both syllabic and alphabetic properties and includes CV signs. The language of the inscriptions is thought to be Phoenician.

See also SEMITIC WRITING.

Reading Dunand 1945; Dhorme 1948; Martin 1962.

C, c /si:/ The third letter of the English alphabet developed from Semitic *gīmel* and Greek *gamma* (Γ, ᒋ). It was adapted from Greek by the Etruscans who used it for both voiceless and voiced velar plosives (*k* and *g*). The letter assumed its present form in Latin. In Semitic scripts and in Greek the shape was angular and facing to the left (ᒣ).

Cadmus [Gk Κάδμος] The mythological son of Phoenician king Agenor and founder of Thebes in Boeotia who is said to have introduced the alphabet into Greece. Greek letters have been referred to as 'Cadmean letters'.

calligraphy [Gk καλλος 'beauty' + γράφειν 'to write'] The art of beautiful writing. Most literate cultures have invested writing with aesthetic significance. In Europe calligraphy was cultivated as an art together with manuscript illumination, especially prior to the invention of printing with movable type. These exercises often served the purpose of normalizing and standardizing the Roman letters that had come down from antiquity. The introduction of the Caroline minuscule under Charlemagne was an attempt to unify the writing of his empire by creating a common style for the chanceries (CAROLINGIAN REFORM). However, new designs of letters continued to be made from the Middle Ages until the present, and a great variety of styles developed as documented in numerous copy-books of penmanship that were published in every European country. The principal implement of penmanship was the quill, later replaced by metal pens (figure 1). Balance, legibility and ornament were aspired to by 'command of hand'. The writing masters enjoyed considerable prestige, yet in the European context penmanship always remained a craft (figure 2). Its cultivation as an artistic achievement was much more pronounced in the Far East and in the Arabic-speaking world of Islam.

Chinese calligraphy

In China and under her influence in East Asia generally, a distinguished hand has for many centuries been considered the mark of every cultured man and woman. The art of the brush is still taught regularly at school and held in high esteem in all countries that use Chinese characters. The appreciation of ornate writing is very much in evidence in public places everywhere between Singapore in the west and Tokyo in the east. In the Chinese tradition calligraphy is more than a craft. Its aim is to develop the practitioner's character and moral stature. Among the traditional arts, calligraphy is the most highly regarded.

Although Chinese characters were first incised in bone and cast in bronze, Chinese calligraphy is the art of the brush. Its basic implements are the inkstick, the inkstone for liquefying the ink by rubbing it in a few drops of water, and a number of brushes varying in thickness and length (figures 3, 4). Inscriptions in stone abound, but they are usually chiselled after a brush-drawn model.

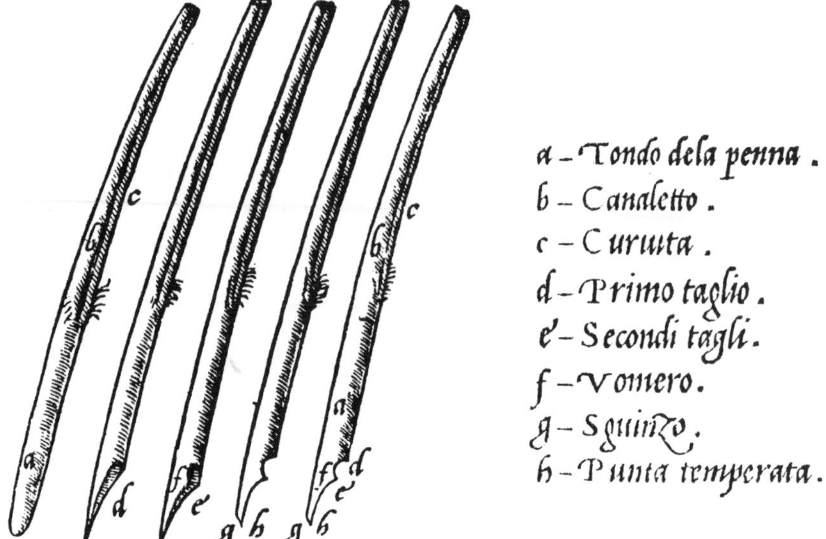

Figure 1 Tools of penmanship: quills cut in various shapes as explained by Ludovico degli Arrighe of Rome, sixteenth century

Figure 2 Strokes of the Pen *by Francesco Pisani of Genoa, 1640*

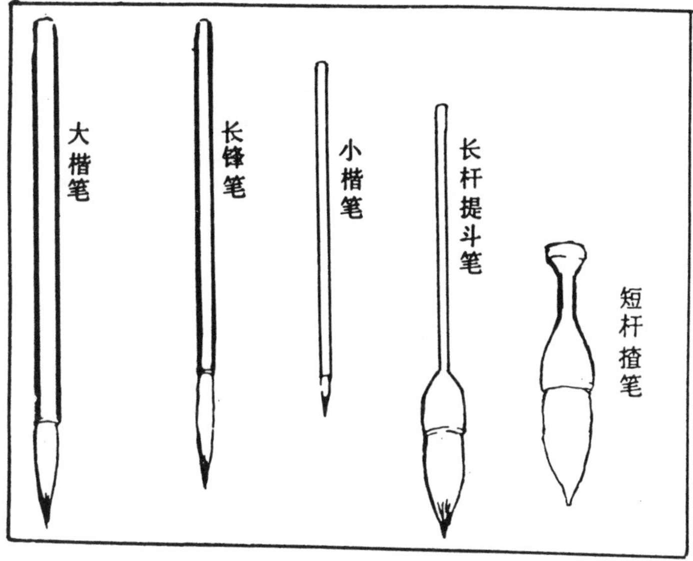

Figure 3 Five different kinds of brush for Chinese calligraphy

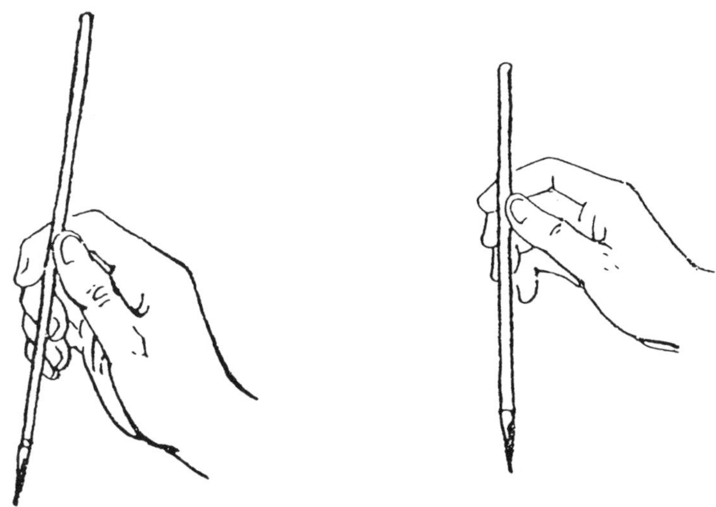

Figure 4 Instruction for holding a brush

The tradition of Chinese calligraphy spans more than 3,000 years, going back to the archaic bronze script of the Shang dynasty and the oracle-bone script (*jiagu wenzi*). Several other script types followed, eventually leading to the most influential clerical script (*lishu*) of the second century CE. It is this script from which all modern scripts are derived. Three types are generally distinguished: standard script (KAISHU), running script (XINGSHU) and cursive script (CAOSHU). The ancient script forms of the bone and bronze inscriptions are characterized by unwavering strokes of even breadth. It is only with the clerical script which introduced more curving forms that the brush's potential for expressive form is fully

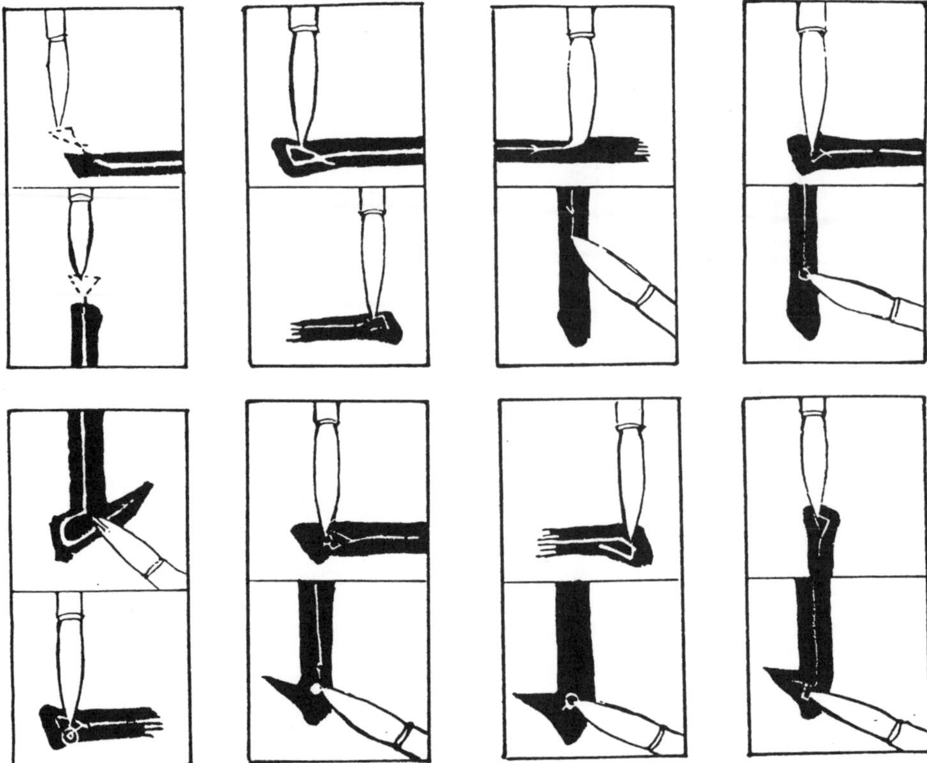

Figure 5 Instruction for producing basic strokes

exploited. The running and cursive scripts in particular presented calligraphers with a high degree of formal flexibility allowing for individual expressiveness (figures 5, 6, 7).

A great many variations of the *kaishu*, *xingshu* and *caoshu* scripts were introduced in the course of the centuries. However, owing to the Chinese reverence for past achievements, older types were not necessarily discarded but often survived to become an integral part of the stylistic repertoire. To this day the bronze and seal scripts are used for decorative purposes. Also, archaic forms have frequently been re-employed in slightly modified form to add yet another nuance to the many script styles of China's cultural heritage.

Korea and Japan adopted writing from China, and they both followed the Chinese example of cultivating brushwork as a sublime art and a means of moral education. They developed their own styles and schools, especially after writing systems for the Japanese (ninth century) and Korean (fifteenth century) languages had evolved. However, notwithstanding their many innovations and idiosyncrasies, they are essentially extensions of the Chinese tradition.

Arabic calligraphy

This developed in close connection with the spread of Islam. The Prophet Muhammad stated God's message in his native tongue which hence became the

Figure 6 *Instruction for writing three and four separate dots as one stroke in cursive script*

Figure 7 *Chinese calligraphy. The sentence* Jīn shēng lí shuǐ *'Gold can be found in Lishui' is often used for practising calligraphy, because it contains both simple and complex characters. The five columns illustrate five different script styles in order of increasing cursivity from left to right: small seal, clerical, standard, running and cursive*

language in which the Qur'ān was written. Arabic has, therefore, been revered as God's language, and every letter of the Arabic alphabet is regarded as a manifestation of God. Thus for many Muslims the Qur'ān should not be rendered in any other language. As the written version of the revelation it must always be copied in Arabic. Since in the wake of the Islamic conquest Islam was carried to regions of many different tongues, written Arabic acquired an important function as a unifying bond of the various Islamic peoples. Writing itself came to be regarded as an expression of faith. In this spirit it developed into a religiously inspired art with a special status that no other form of aesthetic expression was able to attain (figure 8).

Figure 8 Seventeenth-century calligraphic inscription from a tomb in Agra, India, in Arabic: 'He who was cherished created things that made him cherished, he has gone to a faraway place'

A great variety of materials was used to receive calligraphic writing: stone, glass, ceramics, metalwork, woodwork, carpets and other textiles, as well as parchment, paper and other surfaces of manuscript writing. The adaptability of Arabic scripts and their ability to be modified is attributed to the early use of such a variety of surfaces. In addition, the formal simplicity of the 28 letters of the Arabic alphabet allows for great flexibility. They are composed of three basic strokes: horizontal, vertical and diagonal.

The development of Islamic calligraphy can be traced back to the ninth century CE. Numerous inscriptions in *mail* المائِل and *kūfīc* الكوفِي scripts remain of that time,

Figure 9 A page from a Qur'ān in thuluth *script, Egypt, mid fourteenth century (by permission of the Freer Gallery of Art)*

two monumental angular scripts first associated with the copying of the Qur'ān, the latter being the more important one. Originating in the city of Kufah in present-day Iraq, *kūfīc* evolved into a number of monumental and manuscript scripts. *Kūfīc* writing is often highly stylized, omitting all diacritical marks used to indicate vowels. This practice both emphasized simplicity for aesthetic reasons and demonstrated the scribe's familiarity with the scriptures, exemplifying the essential quality of Islamic calligraphy, to glorify God's word by cloaking it in visual beauty.

During the early centuries of Islamic calligraphy, copies of the Qur'ān produced in Iraq were very similar to those made in Iran and North Africa. But since with Islam the Arabic alphabet spread across such a vast area stretching from the Atlantic coast in the west to Indonesia and Central Asia in the east, many script forms evolved in addition to *kūfīc*. In the tenth century, Abū 'Ali Muḥammad Ibn Muqlah, a vizier in Baghdad, invented the *sitta*, a canon of six cursive scripts. They are known as *thuluth, naskhī, rīhānī, muḥaqqaq, tauqī'* and *rīqā'*. This canon was later augmented to include four more scripts, *ghubar, tūmār, ta'līq* and *nasta'līq,* which came to be used throughout the Islamic world. While these cursive scripts became popular with calligraphers and illuminators (figures 9, 10), they never replaced *kūfīc* altogether. In many religious writings *kūfīc* headings are combined with the main body of the text written in a cursive script.

Because of its religious significance, great importance is attached to the literal contents of Islamic calligraphy. Yet, sometimes the verbal message is pushed into the background by the decorative function. As many students of Islamic calligraphy have pointed out, there are a great number of inscriptions which defy easy reading. Orthographic mistakes and peculiarities as well as typographic idiosyncrasies render inscriptions on such sanctuaries as the Dome of the Rock in Jerusalem (seventh century), the Qutab Minar in Delhi (eleventh century), and the Masjid-i Shah Mosque in Isfahan (seventeenth century) virtually impossible to decipher. This suggests that the viewer of these works of art was not always expected to read the text. In many instances of decorative writing the symbolic message was conveyed by other means. For instance, an inscription on a tomb or the wall of a mosque would be recognized as a holy phrase, no matter whether it could actually be read or not.

In the Chinese tradition, too, many calligraphies are hard to read without special training. This is to show that *reading* a calligraphic inscription is not always of the first importance. By its very nature calligraphy combines two functions, the recording of verbal contents and the expression of visual beauty. Whether both are held in equilibrium or one is emphasized at the expense of the other depends on the purpose of the work and on the inclination of the artist.

See also ARABIC SCRIPTS; CHARACTER; CHINESE SCRIPTS; HANDWRITING; WRITING SURFACE; WRITING TOOLS.

Reading Fu et al. 1986; Gaur 1994; Lucas 1984; *Ku-kung fa-shu*, 1962–8; Ledderose 1979; Nakata 1973; Schimmel 1984; Druet and Grégoire 1976.

Canaanite alphabet *See* PHOENICIAN ALPHABET

Cantonese writing *See* YUE WRITING

Figure 10 Silverwork penbox signed by Shadhi, Iran, dated 1210: human-headed naskhī *script (by permission of the Freer Gallery of Art)*

caoshu [Chinese 草書] (*ts'ao-shu*) A cursive Chinese script type used since the fourth century CE. Its English name 'grass script' is a literal translation of the Chinese term. In *caoshu*, parts of Chinese characters are connected with each other and sometimes abbreviated, resulting in supple and curvilinear writing (figure 11). The Japanese reading of the Chinese term is *sōsho*.
See also CHINESE SCRIPTS; KAISHU; XINGSHU.

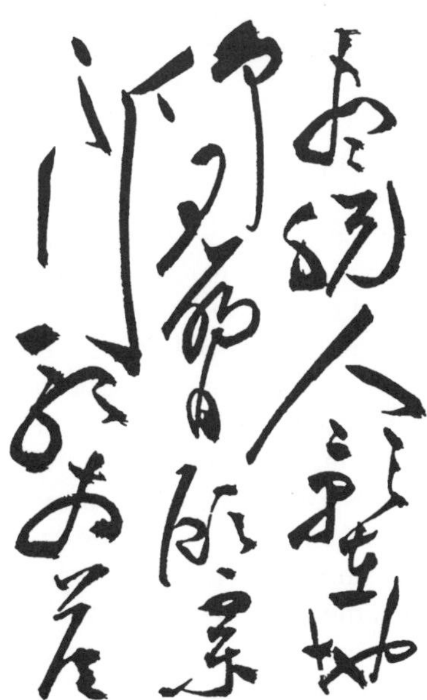

Figure 11 A specimen of the Chinese caoshu, *cursive or grass script, Ming dynasty (1368–1644)*

Figure 12 Caroline minuscule

Caroline minuscule *See* CAROLINGIAN REFORM.

Carolingian reform The period of Charlemagne was an epoch of reform in education. With the revival of learning came a revision of church books which brought about great activity in the writing schools of the monastic centres of France. The changes initiated at that time had consequences for the development of writing in Europe. As a visible manifestation of the reforms the Caroline minuscule came into existence, developed under the direction of Alcuin of York, abbot of St Martin's in Tours from 796 to 804 (figure 12). What has become known as the 'dual alphabet', the combination of capital letters and small letters in a single system, is a development which followed the introduction of the Caroline minuscule.

At a deeper level, the relationship between spoken and written language was affected. In Charlemagne's name Alcuin demanded that the corruption of the language of the church should be checked, by which he meant that Latin should be pronounced in a unified way throughout the empire: it should be pronounced *ad litteras*, as it were. Each word was to be pronounced such that each letter could be 'heard' in a way that was thought to have been its pronunciation in classical times. In modern descriptive terms this was an attempt at standardizing and simplifying sound–letter correspondences. This pronunciation reform came to be known as *reparatio*. It was successful in that it led to a more standardized pronunciation of Latin, but it had unforeseen consequences. Henceforward, the written representation of Latin came to be regarded as the model of the language, a model however which could provide guidance only to the literati who constituted but a small part of the speech community. As a consequence, the gulf between spoken and written Latin, which the reform was intended to eliminate, widened and Latin was gradually reduced to a written language only. The reform thus marked the beginning of diglossia in Romania, with Latin remaining for some time the only written language and Romance evolving, more or less unaffected by the interventionist language policy, into the vernaculars which were eventually established as written languages in their own right.

The *ad litteras* movement is interesting as an early instance of language planning. It offers important aspects of research into the complicated relationships between spoken and written language, demonstrating as it does that a written norm cannot arrest linguistic change, and that its influence can be only limited in a speech community with highly restricted literacy.

See also DIGLOSSIA; SPELLING REFORM.

Reading Fleckstein 1953; Bullogh 1991; Wright 1991.

cartouche **1** Oval or oblong figures in Egyptian hieroglyphic writing, enclosing royal or divine names or titles. The conspicuity thus given to proper names was instrumental in the decipherment of Egyptian hieroglyphics. Figure 13 shows a cartouche with the name of King Ptolemy. **2** A tablet for inscriptions in the form of a sheet of paper or parchment with the ends rolled up; a drawn enclosure of a printed or engraved text.

See also DECIPHERMENT; EGYPTIAN WRITING SYSTEM.

P T O L M Y S

Figure 13 A cartouche with Egyptian hieroglyphs representing the name of King Ptolemy

Caxton, William The first English printer (*d.*1492) who brought the printing technology to England from the continent and set up his press at Westminster about 1476 (figure 14). His first dated book (18 November 1477) was *The Dictes and Sayengs of the Philosophers*. He and other printers who soon followed his lead had a far-reaching influence on the development of written English. He did

Figure 14 William Caxton's printer's mark

much to establish a common standard and to make the improvements in the English language of which he thought it had great need. He was very conscious and critical of the great variation in the speech of his time:

> That comyn Englysshe that is spoken in one shyre varyeth from a-nother in so moche, that in my dayes happened that certayn marchauntes were in a shippe in Tamyse; and for lacke of wynde thei taryed atte forlond, and wente to lande for to refreshe them. And one of theym, named Sheffelde, a mercer, came into an hows, and axed for mete; and specyally he axed after eggys. And the goode wyf answerde, that she coude speke no Frenshe. (from Caxton's preface to his *Eneydos*, 1490)

Like many of his contemporaries Caxton aspired for English to become as uniform and as suitable for all communication functions as Latin. The new technology allowed him to contribute substantially to this purpose. However, much as he looked ahead, his views were anchored in the past. By and large he adopted the late Middle English word patterns for his spelling conventions, disregarding the great vowel shift which was already much in evidence at his time. His spelling was conservative from the very beginning. Sound–letter correspondences in English vowels still bear witness to Caxton's usage. For example, as a result of the great vowel shift a long /a:/ became diphthongized in modern English. Yet, the sound /ei/ is spelt <a> as in *mate* and *sake*. Similarly, /i:/ became the diphthong /ai/ which, however, is spelt <i> as in *time, ride* etc. Caxton also introduced some entirely haphazard features into English spelling. For example, for want of a thorn <þ> in his letter case he used <y>, whence the pseudo-archaic article *ye*. This is perhaps the most conspicuous instance of how the new technology affected the written language. Thanks to it, Caxton's total effect on the language was considerable. The numerous books that issued from his press gave currency to London speech and promoted its adoption as the general standard of English.
See also ENGLISH SPELLING; PRINTING.
Reading Hellinga 1982; Vallins 1973.

cedilla [Italian *zēticula* 'little zed'] The cedilla is a diacritic mark <¸> derived from the letter <z> which in French and Portuguese was placed under a letter, often <c>, to indicate a pronunciation that deviates from its normal pronunciation in a certain environment. Thus, French <c> is usually pronounced [k] before [a] and [o] as in *franco* [frãko], but it is [s] with the cedilla as in *français* [frãsɛ]. Similarly, Portuguese *jaca* [žaka], a fruit, vs *jaça* [žasa] 'flaw'.
See also DIACRITIC.

Celtic writing The family of Celtic languages comprises continental Celtic and Cornish, both extinct, as well as Gaelic Irish, Gaelic Scottish, Manx, Pictish, Welsh and Breton. Their earliest attestations in writing are mainly in glosses of Latin manuscripts dating from the eighth and ninth centuries CE. There are, however, a number of stone inscriptions found only in the British Isles which allow the tracing of Celtic language history to an earlier age. Known as 'Ogham inscriptions', the majority of the approximately 500 known inscribed stones are found in southern Ireland, some in Wales and Scotland. They have been dated to the fourth century CE.
See also OGHAM SCRIPT.

cenemic writing A term used by students of writing to distinguish writing systems whose basic units denote meaningless sounds from those whose units operate on a level of meaningful linguistic entities. *Cenemic* (Gk κενός 'empty') indicates that the unit of a writing system, for example, an alphabetic letter or a Japanese *kana*, is devoid of any inherent meaning. By contrast, a Chinese character is associated with both a sound and a meaning: systems of this kind are called *pleremic*. Thus, in the analysis of writing systems, two basic types are distinguished: those operating on the level of sense-discriminative elements (phonemes, syllables), i.e. cenemic; and those operating on the level of sense-determinative elements (lexemes, morphemes), i.e. pleremic.
See also PLEREMIC WRITING; WRITING SYSTEM.
Reading French 1976; Coulmas 1989.

ceriph *See* SERIF

Champollion, Jean-François (1790–1832) The decipherer of Egyptian hieroglyphics. Champollion had an interest in Egyptian palaeography since his early youth (figure 15). He studied oriental languages and became an expert in Coptic,

Figure 15 Jean-François Champollion

which turned out to be the key for the decipherment of Egyptian since Coptic is the final developmental stage of the Egyptian language written in Greek letters. He received in 1808 a copy of the bilingual inscription on the Rosetta Stone (for illustration see BILINGUIS), but it was not before 1821 that it occurred to him to count and compare the number of signs in the Greek and hieroglyphic texts. Since there were 1,419 signs for 486 words, and since the 1,419 were made up by only 66 different signs, he was led to conclude that the Egyptian script was partly at least a phonetic one. His first success was the identification of King Ptolemy's name in a CARTOUCHE to which he was soon able to add the names of other royalty such as Cleopatra, Alexander and Ramses from other inscriptions (figure 16). It took him some time, however, to realize that the phonetic use of hieroglyphs was not a special ancillary code restricted to proper names, but the central element of Egyptian writing. In 1824 Champollion published his *Précis du système hiéroglyphique* of over 400 pages including 46 plates. It is acclaimed as one of the greatest and most original works of modern scholarship.
See also COPTIC ALPHABET; DECIPHERMENT.
Reading Hartleben 1906; Lacouture 1988.

Figure 16 A page from Champollion's manuscript explaining the cartouche with the name of Cleopatra

character **1** One of the elementary signs of a written language, e.g. a letter, a cuneiform sign or a hieroglyph. **2** The series of elementary signs peculiar to any writing; a set of letters. **3** A single sign of the Chinese writing system. Chinese characters are internally structured configurations of basic strokes to be written in a fixed sequence. Character dictionaries in China, Korea and Japan are organized on the basis of the compositional principles of Chinese characters.
See also CHINESE WRITING SYSTEM; RADICAL; STROKE.

Cherokee syllabary A writing devised around 1820 by SEQUOYAH, who is said to have been a monolingual speaker of Cherokee, an Iroquoian language indigenous to Tennessee, but now only spoken in Oklahoma. Sequoyah was reportedly illiterate when he created his syllabary, but it is clear that he had contact with literacy and literate people. He must have been familiar with the sight of alphabetic writing, for many of the symbols he used resemble Roman letters. But he assigned these letters sound values completely unrelated to English or any other written language he might ever have seen. Thus, the signs <A>, <B>, <C>,

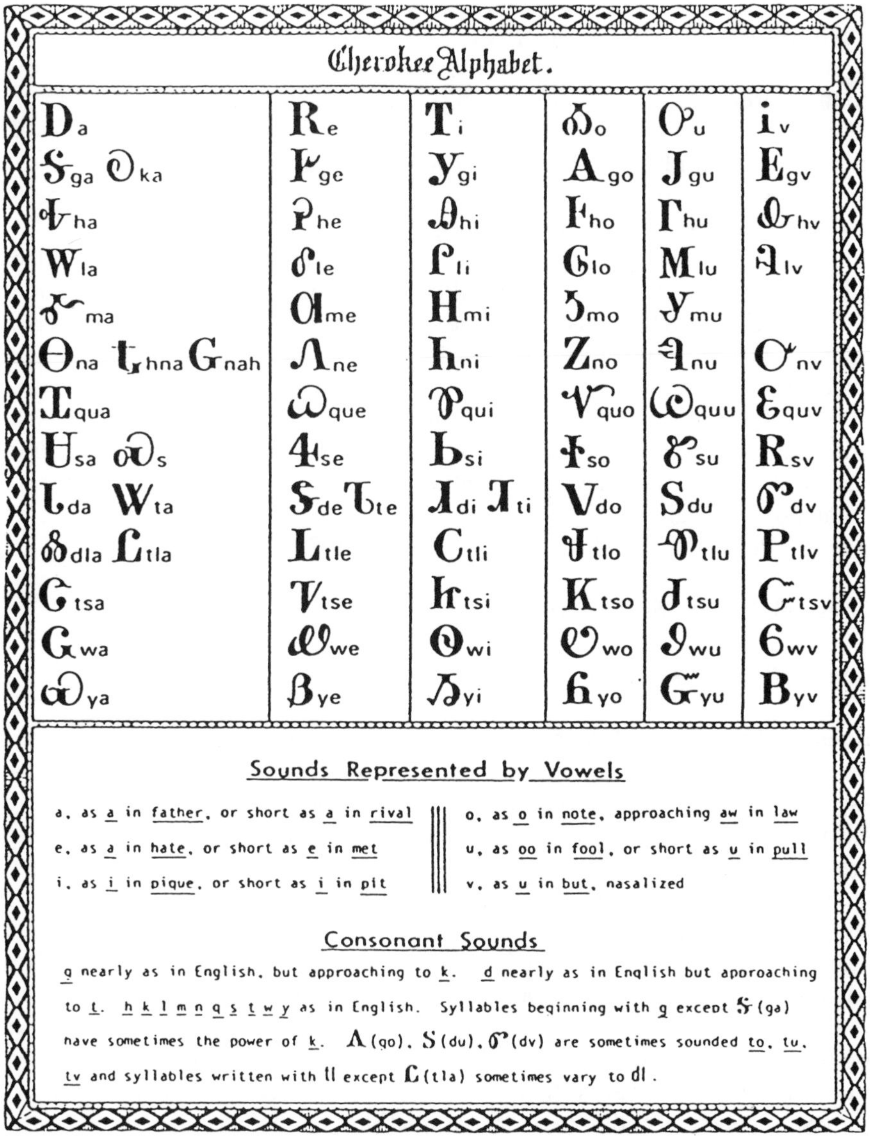

Cherokee Alphabet.

Ꭰ a	Ꭱ e	Ꭲ i	Ꭳ o	Ꭴ u	Ꭵ v
Ꭶ ga Ꭷ ka	Ꭸ ge	Ꭹ gi	Ꭺ go	Ꭻ gu	Ꭼ gv
Ꭽ ha	Ꭾ he	Ꭿ hi	Ꮀ ho	Ꮁ hu	Ꮂ hv
Ꮃ la	Ꮄ le	Ꮅ li	Ꮆ lo	Ꮇ lu	Ꮈ lv
Ꮉ ma	Ꮊ me	Ꮋ mi	Ꮌ mo	Ꮍ mu	
Ꮎ na Ꮏ hna Ꮐ nah	Ꮑ ne	Ꮒ ni	Ꮓ no	Ꮔ nu	Ꮕ nv
Ꮖ qua	Ꮗ que	Ꮘ qui	Ꮙ quo	Ꮚ quu	Ꮛ quv
Ꮜ sa Ꮝ s	Ꮞ se	Ꮟ si	Ꮠ so	Ꮡ su	Ꮢ sv
Ꮣ da Ꮤ ta	Ꮥ de Ꮦ te	Ꮧ di Ꮨ ti	Ꮩ do	Ꮪ du	Ꮫ dv
Ꮬ dla Ꮭ tla	Ꮮ tle	Ꮯ tli	Ꮰ tlo	Ꮱ tlu	Ꮲ tlv
Ꮳ tsa	Ꮴ tse	Ꮵ tsi	Ꮶ tso	Ꮷ tsu	Ꮸ tsv
Ꮹ wa	Ꮺ we	Ꮻ wi	Ꮼ wo	Ꮽ wu	Ꮾ wv
Ꮿ ya	Ᏸ ye	Ᏹ yi	Ᏺ yo	Ᏻ yu	Ᏼ yv

Sounds Represented by Vowels

a, as a in father, or short as a in rival
e, as a in hate, or short as e in met
i, as i in pique, or short as i in pit
o, as o in note, approaching aw in law
u, as oo in fool, or short as u in pull
v, as u in but, nasalized

Consonant Sounds

g nearly as in English, but approaching to k. d nearly as in English but approaching to t. h k l m n q s t w y as in English. Syllables beginning with g except Ꭶ (ga) have sometimes the power of k. Ꭺ (go), Ꮪ (du), Ꮫ (dv) are sometimes sounded to, tu, tv and syllables written with tl except Ꮭ (tla) sometimes vary to dl.

Table 1 The Cherokee syllabary
Source: *Holmes and Smith 1976 (by permission of University of Oklahoma Press)*

<D> are pronounced /go/, /yī/, /tli/, /a/ respectively. Other signs resemble Greek letters Sequoyah found in a book, and yet others are of his own devising.

The Cherokee syllabary consists of 85 signs of which one represents the consonant /s/ and six others represent independent vowels; the remaining 78 are CV syllabic signs (table 1). In Sequoyah's original design there was an 86th letter which was deleted when the script was slightly modified for printing in 1827. The system is generally well fitted to the Cherokee language which has a phonotactic structure allowing almost only VCV or CV syllables. The only closed syllables end in /s/, hence the one sign that represents an independent consonant.

There are a number of both over- and underdifferentiations in the writing relative to the phonological structure. The graphic distinction between /t/ and /d/ is unnecessary. Conversely, the distinction between long and short vowels remains unrepresented in the writing, although vowel length is distinctive. Likewise pitch, which is distinctive in some words, is not marked in syllabic writing. For example, the spelling for *á:ma* 'salt' and *àma* 'water' is the same. However, on the whole over- and underdifferentiation of the system are slight and do not hamper its functionality.

The facts that thousands of Cherokee speakers accepted Sequoyah's syllabary and became literate in it very shortly after he introduced it to the public, and that fonts were cut and type was cast for the publication of Cherokee newspapers and magazines, testify to its systematic clarity and practical usefulness. The spelling conventions are certainly easier to learn for a fluent speaker of Cherokee than are the English conventions for a fluent speaker of that language. Sequoyah's syllabary is still used by some Cherokee in the religious domain and in that of Indian medicine. It is also preserved on street signs and other public writings in the city of Tahlequah, Oklahoma.

Reading Pulte 1976; Walker 1981; Scancarelli 1992.

Chinese alphabet *See* PINYIN

Chinese phonetic symbols *See* ZHÙYĪN ZÌMǓ

Chinese scripts In the long history of Chinese writing a great many script types have evolved (table 2). The most archaic characters recognizably related to the present system of writing were incised on ox and sheep scapulas and tortoise shells for purposes of divination. This angular script, known as oracle-bone script (*jiagu wenzi*), dates from early in the second millennium BCE. Inscriptions on bronze vessels of the Shang dynasty (1523–1028 BCE) followed. Some 2,000 different characters with modern counterparts have been identified. As of the eighth century BCE the large-seal script (*dazhuan*) is attested in its mature form. It was predominant until the second century BCE, when the small-seal script (*xiaozhuan*) made its appearance. The next step in the development brings the Chinese script close to its typographically mature form. The clerical script (*lishu*) of the eastern Han (25–220 CE) gave rise to three basic types which continue to be used today. They are, respectively, the standard script (*kaishu*), the running script (*xingshu*) and the cursive script (*caoshu*), all in use since about the fourth century CE. In modern times the Chinese script has undergone some modification as a result of

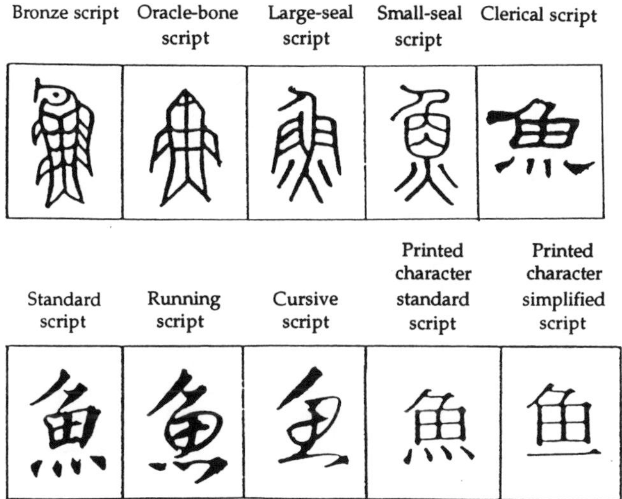

Table 2 The Chinese character 魚 yú *'fish' in different scripts*

the character simplification carried out in the People's Republic of China. Many abbreviated varieties of characters have become the standard forms.
See also CALLIGRAPHY; CAOSHU; CHARACTER; CHINESE WRITING REFORM; CHINESE WRITING SYSTEM; KAISHU; LISHU; XINGSHU.
Reading Liang 1959; Tsien 1962.

Chinese telegraphic code A numerically ordered list of almost 10,000 characters each of which is assigned a four-digit code. These codes are used for data transmission such as telegraphy. For example, the three characters 明天到 *míngtiān dào* 'arriving tomorrow' would be coded as 2494 1131 0451. At the receiving end the four-digit code is converted back into characters.

Chinese transliteration In Chinese writing, non-Chinese proper names have to be transliterated using Chinese characters. Since every Chinese syllable can be represented by a multiplicity of Chinese characters, a selection must be made for the use of certain characters rather than others for certain syllables. Transliterating non-Chinese proper names into Chinese hence involves two steps: (1) choosing a string of Chinese syllables that approximate the sound of the original name; and (2) assigning those syllables Chinese characters. Since both steps allow for many different options, a convention must be established. The Chinese standard list of transliteration characters which is used in mainland China is given in table 3. No comparable list exists in Taiwan or Hong Kong, but transliterations there differ significantly from those practised on the mainland, as illustrated with some examples in table 4.
Reading Lou 1992.

Chinese writing reform Attempts at reforming the Chinese script have been made periodically and since the 1890s there have been repeated calls for both Romanization and simplification, but in modern times effective reforms were first implemented in the People's Republic of China. The reform programme of

IPA (transliteration / IPA)		b	p	d	t	g	k	v	f	z dz	s	ʃ	dʒ
IPA		布	普	德	特	格	克	符(夫)	弗(夫)	兹	斯	希	季
ɑ:, æ, ʌ	阿	巴	帕	达	塔(大)	加	卡	伐	法	扎	萨	夏	贾
ai	艾	拜	派	代	太	盖	凯	魏	法	宰	赛	夏	贾
ei, e, ɛ	埃	贝	佩	德	特	格	克	佛	费	泽	塞	谢	杰
ɔ:, ə	厄	伯	珀	德	特	格	克	佛	弗	泽	塞	歇	哲
i:, i	伊	比	皮	迪	提	吉	基	维	菲	济	西(锡	希	季
u:, u	乌	布	普	杜	土	古	库	武	富	祖	苏	休	朱
ɔ:, ɔ, o	沃	博	波	多	托	果	科	伏	福	佐	索	肖	焦
ou	欧	博	颇	窦	透	苟	寇	浮	福	奏	叟	首	周
au	奥	包	泡	道	陶	高	考	窝	福	澡	骚	晓	焦
ju:	尤	布	普	杜	土	纠	丘	武	富	久	修	休	朱
æm, ɑ:m æm ɑ:m	安	班	潘	丹	坦	甘	坎	范	凡	赞	散	香	江(姜)
ain	艾恩	拜恩	派恩	代恩	太恩	盖恩	恩	伐因	法因	宰恩	赛恩	夏因	贾恩
en, n em, m	恩	本	彭	登	顿	根	肯	文	芬	曾	森	兴	靳
in, im	因(英)	宾	平	丁	廷	京	金	文	芬	津	辛	欣	今
ɔ:n, ɔn, ʌn ɔ:m, ɔm, ʌm	昂	邦(榜)	庞	当	汤	冈	康	房	方	臧		尚	璋
u:n, un, oun u:m, um, oum	翁	崩	蓬	东(栋)	通	贡	孔	冯	丰	宗	宋	雄	琼

Table 3 Transliteration chart for writing foreign proper names in Chinese characters. Top row represents syllable onsets and left column vocalic rhyme. Resulting matrix contains characters for basic Chinese syllables without tones. Alternative characters are given in parentheses

the 1950s and 1960s defined three main tasks: (1) the standardization and simplification of Chinese characters, (2) the creation of a Romanized orthography, and (3) the promotion of the standard language.

Under the direction of the officially appointed Committee for Reforming the Chinese Written Language, 2,238 Chinese characters have been simplified and 1,055 variants ruled out since 1956. Character simplification has been achieved on the basis of several principles. Some many-stroked characters were replaced by simpler ones. In other cases, complex characters were reduced to one of their compound parts. A very prolific principle has been the adoption of cursively

tʃ	θ	h	m	n	l	r	w	hw	kw	j	ts	transliteration	IPA
奇	思	赫	姆	恩	耳	尔	伍			伊	次		
恰	撒	哈	马	纳	拉	腊	瓦	华	夸	亚	察	阿	ɑː, æ, ʌ
柴	赛	海	迈	奈	来	赖	怀	怀	快		蔡	艾	ai
切	塞	黑	梅	内	累	雷	韦	惠	奎	耶	策	埃	ei, e, ε
彻	瑟	赫	默	纳	勒	勒	沃			耶	策	厄	ɔː, ə
契	锡	希	米	尼	利	里	威	惠	魁	伊	戚	伊	iː, i
丘	素	胡	穆	努	路	鲁	伍		库	尤	促	乌	uː, u
乔	梭	霍	莫	诺	洛	罗	沃	霍	廓	约	措	沃	ɔː, ɔ, o
裘	叟	侯	谋	诺	娄	娄	沃		寇	尤	凑	欧	ou
乔	扫	豪	毛	瑙	劳	劳	渥		考	耀	曹	奥	au
丘	修	休	缪	纽	刘	留			丘		秋	尤	juː
强	散	汉	曼	南 (楠)	兰	兰	万	环	宽	延	粲	安	æm, ɑːm æm ɑːm
柴恩	赛恩	海恩	迈恩	奈恩	来恩	赖恩	怀恩	怀恩	快恩		蔡恩	艾恩	ain
琴	森	亨	门	嫩	冷	伦	温	珲	昆	要	吟	恩	en, n em, m
钦	信	欣	明	宁	林	临	温	珲	昆	英	青	因 (英)	in, im
昌	桑	杭	芒	囊	郎	朗	旺	黄	匡	杨	仓	昂	ɔːn, ɔn, ʌn ɔːm, ɔm, ʌm
群	松	洪	蒙	农	隆	龙	翁		孔	荣	聪	翁	uːn, un, oun uːm, um, oum

handwritten characters as the standard form. Character simplification is a reform that caters more to the writer than to the reader. While characters become easier to write if the number of strokes is reduced, their distinctness for the reader is reduced by the same measure (table 5). The advantage of simplified characters is thus hard to assess. The fact that in recent years old forms have reappeared in public life suggests that character simplification met with mixed public approval, perhaps because some simplifications were better and easier to grasp than others.

The second measure was implemented in 1958 when the People's Congress adopted the Chinese phonetic alphabet, *hànyǔ pīnyīn*, as the standard system of writing Chinese with Roman letters. Since the seventeenth century numerous Romanization systems have been developed and used, resulting in a rather chaotic situation of rivalling conventions. Pinyin is a phonemic orthography which is

	PR China	Pronunciation	Taiwan, Hong Kong	Pronunciation
Italy	意大利	Yìdàlì	義大利	Yìdàlì
Nigeria	尼日利亞	Nírìlìyà	奈及利亞	Nàijílìyà
Tunisia	突尼斯	Túnísi	突尼西亞	Tuníxīyà
Sydney	悉尼	Xīní	雪梨	Xuělí

Table 4 Transliteration of foreign proper names in the People's Republic of China, Taiwan and Hong Kong

迠 〔建〕	旦 〔蛋〕
江 〔豇〕	弫 〔弹〕
夺 〔酱〕	𧿒 〔蹈〕
交 〔跤〕	𥝌 〔稻〕
茭 〔椒〕	辺 〔道〕
亍 〔街〕	佟 〔懂〕
井 〔阱〕	斗拱 〔枓栱〕
垪 〔境〕	𥎆 〔短〕
𨱔 〔镜〕	𧿳 〔蹲〕
艽 〔韭〕	炖 〔燉〕

Table 5 Some simplified Chinese characters with their earlier forms in square brackets

superior to the older systems in terms of analytic consistency. It has been adopted by the United Nations as the standard system of transcribing Chinese names, which is why *Peking*, *Nanking*, *Taipei* and *Sinkiang* are now generally spelled *Beijing*, *Nanjing*, *Taibei* and *Xinjiang*. Although Pinyin has been created also with the idea in mind that Chinese characters may one day be abolished and replaced by an alphabetic orthography, nothing points towards such a drastic reform in the near future.

The third measure of the Chinese writing reform is a necessary corollary of the second. As a phonemic script Pinyin depends to a greater extent than do characters on the phonology of the standard language, *pǔtōnghuà*, and is hence of little use to those who do not understand this language. Knowledge of the standard language is thus a precondition for employing Pinyin as an effective means of written communication in China. To date the standard language is not used in everyday life throughout the country, and as long as this is so, Pinyin cannot be expected to gain ground in public communication. Owing to the extensive differences between the various Chinese regional dialects this is a considerable challenge yet to be faced.

See also CHINESE WRITING SYSTEM; PINYIN.

Reading DeFrancis 1984b; Seybolt and Chiang 1979; Coulmas 1983; 1991; Rohsenow 1986.

Chinese writing system Chinese writing appeared no later than the Shang dynasty, said to have begun in 1766 BCE. The earliest inscriptions found on bronze vessels and oracle bones dating from early in the second millennium are already highly stylized, although many characters were clearly derived from naturalistic representations of objects (ORACLE-BONE SCRIPT). It is assumed, therefore, that in China writing was present considerably earlier. China can consequently claim the longest literary tradition that still continues today. Many of the characters of the earliest inscriptions closely resemble their modern equivalents. Out of more than 2,500, some 1,400 could be identified as the original forms of present standard Chinese characters and hence interpreted unequivocally. Table 6 lists some such pairs of equivalents.

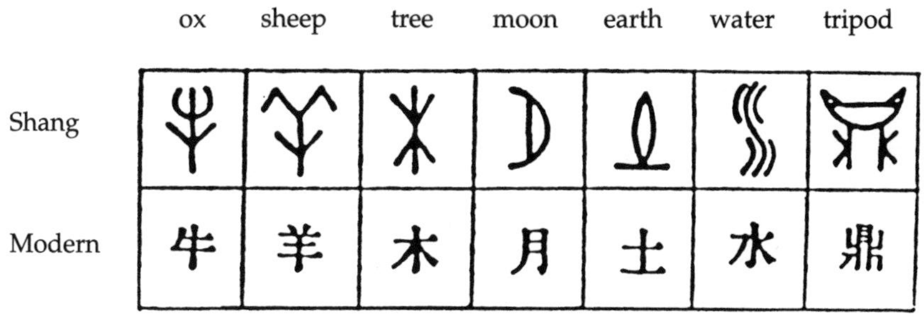

	ox	sheep	tree	moon	earth	water	tripod
Shang							
Modern	牛	羊	木	月	土	水	鼎

Table 6 Ancient Chinese characters of the Shang period and their modern equivalents

Outer form

Pictures of concrete objects stood at the beginning of Chinese writing. Linearization, reduction and conventionalization set in early. Hard surfaces like bone and shell favoured an angular rather than rounded appearance of early characters, a design feature that was preserved in brush writing. Since early characters were pictographic, their numbers proliferated with little conformity in their creation. Prior to the writing reform of the Qin dynasty (221–206 BCE), there was a great deal of unsystematic variation. About 200 BCE the small-seal script (XIAOZHUAN) made its appearance, leading to some measure of standardization. In the Han dynasty (206 BCE to 220 CE), from which Chinese characters derived their name *hànzì*, the small-seal script gave way first to the clerical script (LISHU) and then to the standard script (KAISHU), which is still used today in many publications.

Each Chinese character consists of between one and 25 strokes (table 7, figure 17). In order to determine the number of strokes of a given character, it is essential to know what counts as one stroke (table 8). Chinese characters are also analysed as consisting of configurations of strokes, many of which recur as building blocks of more complex characters. For example, the character 語 'word' is composed of three parts, 言, 五 and 口, all of which also occur independently as characters (figure 18). These recurring configurations are variously called 'keys', 'classifiers', 'determinatives' or 'radicals'. Ordered for number of composant strokes, they provide the ordering principle of dictionaries: there are 540 in the *Shuowen jiezi* of 120 CE, and 214 since the *Kang xi* of 1716, the number still used in modern dictionaries.

Stroke	Name		
	点	diǎn	dot
	横	héng	horizontal
	竖	shù	vertical
	撇	piě	left-falling
	捺	nà	right-falling
	提	tí	rising
	钩	gōu	hook
	折	zhé	turning

Table 7 The eight basic strokes of which all Chinese characters are composed

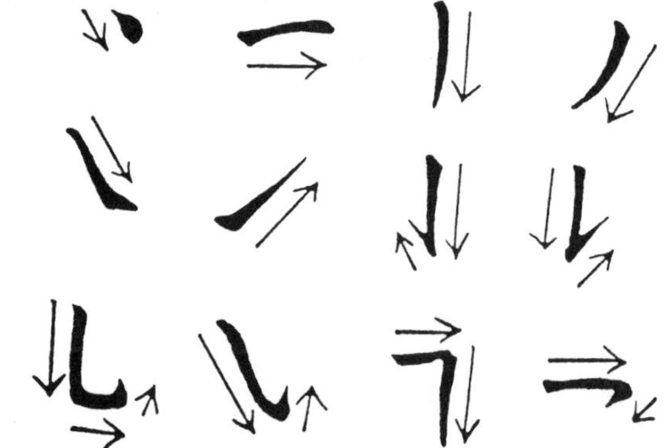

Figure 17 The direction of basic strokes for Chinese characters

Inner form

As a means of representing the Chinese language, the Chinese writing system combines the representation of sound and meaning. Each character denotes a morpheme and a syllable. Since Chinese is an isolating language with no inflectional morphology, morphemes (and words) appear in the same form in all contexts. In this regard Chinese characters are quite suitable for the Chinese language. Yet, the graphic representation of Chinese is rather involved. In principle, there is a one-to-one mapping relation between characters and morphemes, while that between characters and syllables is a set of many-to-one relations, there being more characters than syllables. Referring to both sound and meaning, Chinese characters are built following a number of different structural principles.

Traditionally, six classes of characters called 六書 *liù shū* 'the six writings' are distinguished:

Example	Stroke order	Rule
十	一 十	First horizontal, then vertical
人	丿 人	First left-falling, then right-falling
三	一 二 三	From top to bottom
州	丶 丶丿 丶丿丶 丶丿丶丨 丶丿丶丨丶 州	From left to right
月	丿 冂 月 月	First outside, then inside
四	丨 冂 叮 叩 四	Finish inside, then close
小	亅 亅丿 小	Middle, then the two sides

Table 8 The order of strokes of some simple Chinese characters

Figure 18 Composition of the Chinese character for 'word'

1 *Pictographic* characters in their ancient form were pictures of natural objects, e.g. ᐞᐞ → 山 'mountain'.
2 *Simple ideographic* characters denote abstract concepts such as numbers or the notions of above and below: 一 '1', 二 '2', 三 '3', 上 'above', 下 'below'.
3 *Compound ideographic* characters have a meaning which is a function of that of the composing parts, as in 信 *xin* 'honest' consisting of 人 *ren* 'man' and 言 *yúan* 'word'.
4 *Phonetic loans* or rebus characters resulted from borrowing a character for writing a homophonous or phonetically similar word. Thus the pictograph 來 of *leg* 'wheat' came to be used for *leg* 'to come', a word more difficult to represent pictographically.
5 *Semantic-phonetic compound* characters consist of a classifier and a phonetic, an element indicating meaning and another indicating sound, as in 糖 *táng* 'sugar',

Phonetic	Meaning		Classifier*	
	糖	'sugar'	米	(cereal)
唐	塘	'embankment'	土	(earth)
táng	搪	'to block'	手	(hand)
	溏	'pond'	水 = 氵	(water)

Table 9 The phonetic táng *(* The shape of characters varies slightly depending on whether they occur independently or as a part of another character)*

consisting of the classifier 米 'cereal' and the phonetic 唐 *táng*, which as an independent character stands for a proper name (table 9).

6 *Mutually interpretative* characters are unclear as a category, but they comprise characters which by semantic extension were used to write words of the same or similar meaning, but different pronunciation. For instance, 樂 *yuè* 'music' was also used for *lè* 'pleasure'.

Of all Chinese characters, 90 per cent or more belong to the fifth class, being composed of a phonetic and a classifier. This is one reason why Chinese characters are very inadequately described as ideographs, if this notion means that the written symbol refers to an idea rather than to a linguistic unit. In modern treatments of Chinese writing the notion of ideography is therefore often avoided, although it is still frequently found in popular accounts.

The formation of Chinese characters of the fifth category clearly relies on the representation of sounds, that is on syllables. However, Chinese writing never developed into a purely phonetic system. Although many characters were employed in rebus fashion for the representation of sounds, they were never completely stripped of their meaning. Whenever a character was used to represent a homophonous word, it was felt necessary to also indicate the meaning of that word. In other writing systems, for example, CUNEIFORM WRITING, similar processes occurred in the early phase of development, but with very different consequences. Cuneiform also developed determiners to add semantic information where the representation of sounds was felt to be inadequate or ambiguous, but these determiners stood by themselves, allowing the number of signs gradually to decrease. In Chinese by contrast they became integral components of characters, leading to an enormous expansion of the sign inventory. Some 2,500 different characters were used on Shang inscriptions. This number quadrupled in the Han dynasty and by the twelfth century had soared to about 23,000. The most comprehensive dictionaries list almost 50,000 characters. This is a cumulative figure comprising current and obsolete characters. It must also be noted that only a fraction of this inventory has been used at any one time, never more than about 6,000. Yet, it is obvious that such an order of magnitude in the sign inventory had to affect the system not just in quantitative terms. On the level of individual

Table 10 The position of phonetics (solid) and classifiers (outline) in compound Chinese characters. Source: *Alleton 1970*

characters it meant higher graphic complexity, an increase in the number of composant strokes being a corollary of the need to graphically distinguish ever more characters.

As for the mapping relation of characters, syllables and morphemes, classifiers and phonetics can be described as disambiguating each other: the classifier marks a semantic domain rather than a precise concept. Similarly, many phonetics are associated with more than one syllabic value, and for many syllables there are several phonetics. For example, there are more than ten different phonetics each indicating the syllables /ji/, /xi/ and /ši/; and it would be difficult to find a syllable that is represented by one phonetic only. Mandarin Chinese has some 1,270 tonal syllables. Swedish sinologist Bernhard Karlgren has identified 1,260 phonetics under which he has classified some 6,000 of the most common characters. These two figures suggest an average one-to-one syllable/graph ratio; but a simple comparison is misleading, because there is a great deal of POLYVALENCE. Another difficulty is the absence of any convention determining the positions of phonetics and classifiers within a character. Both can appear in any position. Moreover, phonetics and classifiers are not graphically distinct, both making use of the same set of formal elements. The resulting difficulty of determining classifier and phonetic in a compound character is illustrated in table 10, where classifiers appear as (1) left, (2) right, (3) bottom, (4) top, (5) enclosure and (6) centre parts of characters.

How are Chinese characters read? This question touches on the function of classifiers and phonetics. Since there are only 214 classifiers, they clearly play only a limited role in semantic decoding. Although classifiers and phonetics are composed of the same graphic elements, the latter outnumber the former by at least six to one, as many phonetics are composed of several classifiers. From this it follows that the overall contribution of phonetics to the decoding of characters in reading must be greater than that of the classifiers. This does not make Chinese a phonetic writing system, but it shows that its phonetic component is stronger than is generally recognized.

The Chinese writing system has often been criticized as cumbersome and uneconomical, yet it has survived from antiquity to the present. Systemically it is a peculiar mixture of marking sound and meaning. Although it is hard to learn, its proficient users emphasize its efficiency and speed as well as the fact that it adds a dimension to the visual manifestation of language which has no counterpart in purely phonetic writing.

Literacy made China the dominant culture in East Asia. Chinese characters were borrowed to write other languages, notably Vietnamese, Korean and Japanese. As in the case of cuneiform, the transfer to other languages resulted in major modifications and the eventual emergence of other writing systems.
See also CALLIGRAPHY; CHARACTER; CHINESE SCRIPTS; CHINESE WRITING REFORM; CHỮ'NÔM; JAPANESE WRITING; KOREAN WRITING; VIETNAMESE ALPHABET.
Reading Karlgren 1923; Alleton 1970; Leon 1981; DeFrancis 1984b; Coulmas 1991.

Chinese written language For many centuries China's classical literary language *wényán* was the medium of literature not only in China but also in adjacent countries – Vietnam, the Korean peninsula and, in particular, Japan. During its formative epoch from the warring states period (445–221 BCE) to the early Han period (206 BCE to 25 CE) it was not very different from spoken Chinese. However, as of the late Han period the relationship between the spoken and written language was characterized by increasing divergence. This was partly a result of the canonization of the five classics of Confucianism, *The Book of Changes* (*Yi jing*), *The Book of Documents* (*Shu jing*), *The Book of Odes* (*Shi jing*), *The Book of Rites* (*Li ji*) and *The Spring and Autumn Annals* (*Chun qiu*). It became customary to put the study of these texts at the centre of one's education. They also came to form the basis of the civil service examinations in China, the backbone of selecting the bureaucratic elite. These examinations, which were held until the end of the nineteenth century, did much to perpetuate the use of *wényán* and uphold its status. As a result, the classical language which was far removed from vernacular speech was the primary medium of literary prose throughout the centuries. Vernacular varieties of Chinese were also written, especially beginning in the Tang dynasty (608–906), many of them Buddhist scriptures. However, until modern times Classical Chinese was unrivalled as the prestigious language of writing. It was nobody's mother tongue, but a learned language acquired through formal education. It differed from vernacular Chinese in vocabulary and grammar. For example, unlike the vernacular it had no aspect marker, no copula, no verbal classifiers, and no plural suffixes for nouns or pronouns. For many centuries, then, the linguistic situation in China was what is commonly characterized as diglossia, namely a pronounced dichotomy between Classical Chinese and vernacular Chinese. As of Han times, these two were differentiated as separate systems. Attempts at overcoming this gap were beginning to be made early in the twentieth century. The literary renaissance that began in 1917 led to the *báihuà* or 'plain language' movement, promoting the idea that the classical written style should be replaced by a vernacular style. This process can be compared with the gradual replacement of Latin as the primary written language that marked the transition from medieval to modern times in Europe. An important difference is, however, that Latin gave way to several written Romance vernaculars, whereas Classical Chinese was replaced by a single vernacular based largely on the Beijing dialect, called *pǔtōnghuà* 'common language'.
See also DIGLOSSIA; WRITTEN LANGUAGE.
Reading DeFrancis 1984b; Peyraube 1991.

chirography [Gk χειρό 'hand' + γραφος 'writing'] A formal written document. The term 'chirographic' is occasionally used in the study of orality and LITERACY, especially where it is important to mark the distinction between handwriting and print. Learned or classical languages such as Latin, Classical Arabic and Classical Chinese have been called 'chirographically controlled languages' as they depend on the written medium rather than speech for their development.
See also HANDWRITING; WRITTEN LANGUAGE.
Reading Ong 1982.

chữ'nôm [Vietnamese *chữ'* 'writing' + *nôm* 'south', 'southern writing'] *Chữ'nôm* is a vernacular writing system devised probably in the thirteenth century CE in Vietnam. The earliest known document is a stele discovered in Ho Thanh Son, Ninh Binh Province, Vietnam. The inscription dating from 1343 lists the names of 20 villages. *Chữ'nôm* consists of modified Chinese characters (figure 19). The adaptation of Chinese characters for writing Vietnamese followed three strategies (table 11):

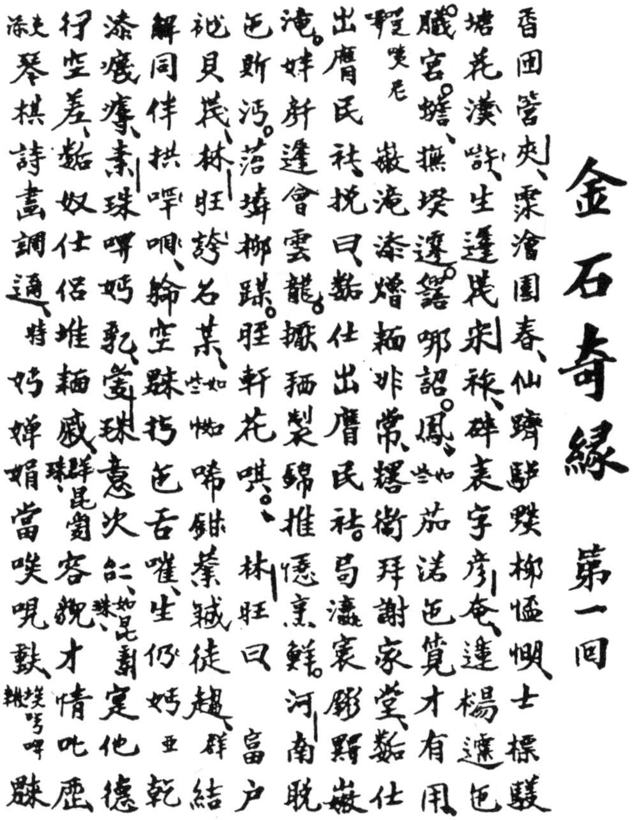

Figure 19 A specimen of chữ'nôm *writing from the drama* The Marvellous Union of Gold and Jade

		Chinese		Vietnamese
1	sound	hàng	行	hàng
	meaning	to go		line order
2	meaning	to hit	打	to hit
	sound	ta		dánh
3	new character:		口安	
	meaning			to eat
	sound	an	安	an

classifier 口 `mouth' + phonetic 安 an

Table 11 The three adaptation strategies of chữ'nôm *for writing Vietnamese with Chinese characters*

1. A character was used for the syllable it represented in Chinese, irrespective of its meaning, for a homophonous or phonetically similar Vietnamese word. For example, 行 'to go', pronounced *hàng* in southern Chinese, was adopted for Vietnamese *hàng* 'line, order'.
2. A character was used for the meaning of the Chinese word it represented, but given a Vietnamese pronunciation. For example, 打 stands for Chinese *tǎ* 'to hit'. The Vietnamese word for 'to hit' is *dánh,* which thus became the new reading of this character.
3. Using elements of Chinese characters, new characters were formed that did not exist in Chinese. For example, to write the word *an* 'to eat' the character 口安 was formed, consisting of 安, pronounced *an* in southern Chinese, and 口, the character for 'mouth'. The new character does not occur in Chinese.

See also CHINESE WRITING SYSTEM; VIETNAMESE ALPHABET.
Reading Nguyên 1959.

chu yin *See* ZHÙYĪN ZÌMǓ

cipher (*also* cypher) **1** An arithmetic symbol such as Arabic number signs. **2** A secret or concealed way of writing by using transposed, substitute or re-valued letters or other written symbols. For example, a cipher alphabet may be created by assigning each letter of the alphabet the value of the letter which corresponds to its position when recounting the alphabet backwards: *a* = *z*, *b* = *y*, *c* = *x* etc. Provided the enciphered text is long enough, such simple transpositions are easily deciphered, because a frequency distribution analysis can uncover the true value of the letters (figure 20). More complex ciphers therefore use several transpositions as well as multiple equivalents of letters which are

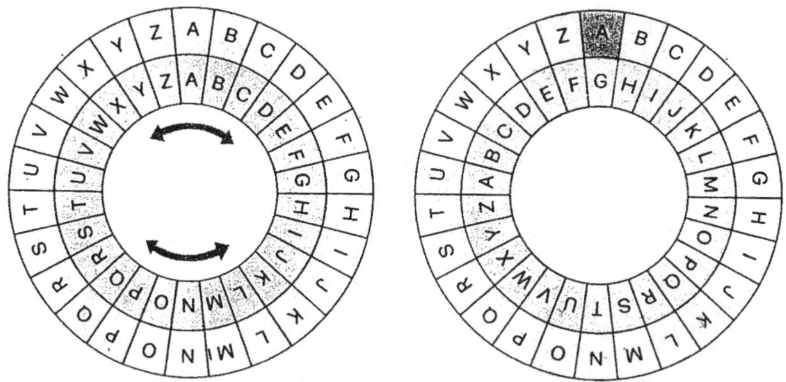

Figure 20 The ciphering disk developed by Italian philosopher Leon Battista Alberti (1404–72) as a key for transposing letters, from his book Modus scribendi in ziferas

selected at random. Computer programs can produce highly opaque cipher systems which are virtually impossible to decode without the help of a machine.
See also CRYPTOGRAPHY.
Reading Beckett 1988.

circumflex [Lat. *circumflexus* 'bent about'] A diacritic sign of the form <˜> or <ˆ>, originally used in Greek to mark long vowels with a rising-falling pitch. In Latin the circumflex was sometimes used to indicate contraction. In Germanic languages such as Old High German it marked long vowels. It was introduced into French as a mark of the long open vowel [ɛ] resulting from contraction, as in *bête* from *beste,* but also the closed vowel [o], as in *rôle.*
See also ACCENT; DIACRITIC.

Classical Chinese *See* CHINESE WRITTEN LANGUAGE; WÉNYÁN

clay tablets The surface on which the cuneiform writing system evolved. Clay is a very durable material. When baked it is virtually indestructible, but even unbaked clay will keep longer than most other writing materials. It is thanks to this property of clay that tens of thousands of documents have come down to us from the earliest period of writing in Mesopotamia. Tablets were inscribed with a pointed stylus when the clay was still moist and hence plastic. When completely dry or baked the inscription can be preserved indefinitely (figure 21). Babylonian clay tablets came in various sizes, but most commonly they were the size of the human palm. Typically inscribed on both sides, this format made them easy to handle for the scribe. Clay was also used for writing in other parts of the ancient world. Many tablets were unearthed in Crete bearing seal impressions and inscriptions. The richest heritage of ancient writing is, however, found on the clay tablets of Mesopotamia.
See also CUNEIFORM WRITING; WRITING SURFACE.
Reading Chiera 1938.

clicks A kind of consonant which is pervasive in southern Africa's Khoisan languages. Clicks have also been incorporated into the phonological systems of

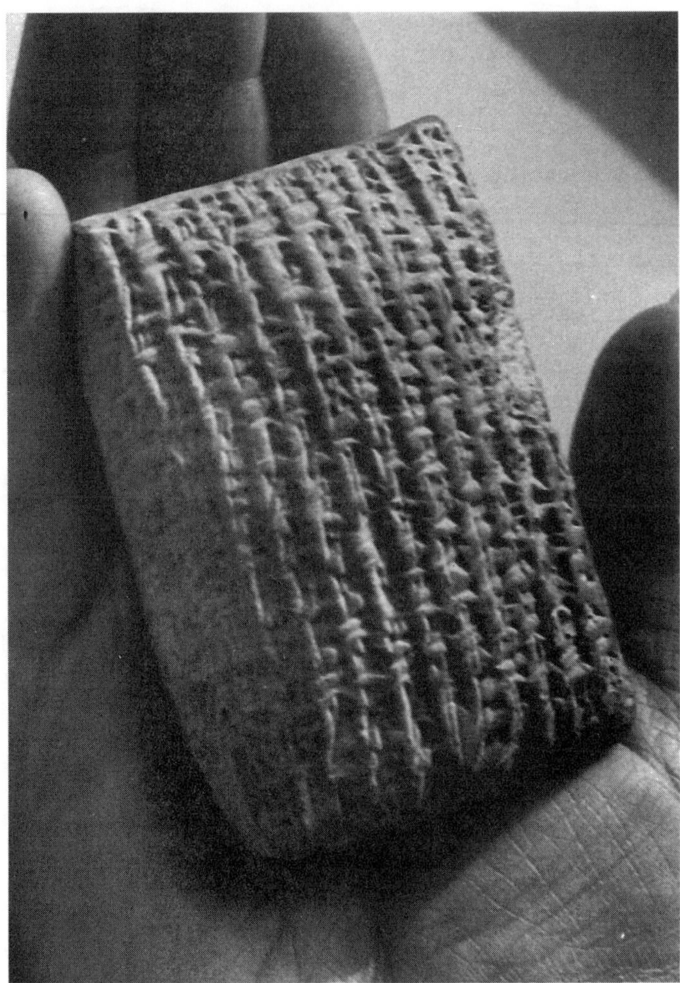

Figure 21   Neo-Babylonian clay tablet with cuneiform inscription (by permission of Staatliche Museen Berlin: Vorderasiatisches Museum zu Berlin)

some Bantu languages. They vary with respect to place of articulation (bilabial, lateral, dental, palatal) and manner of articulation (plain, breathy, aspirated, nasalized). Since they have no equivalent in Semitic or Indo-European languages, for which alphabetic writing was first developed, clicks present a particular problem for the creation of Latin-based orthographies. Various solutions have been proposed. For practical reasons it was deemed advisable to use symbols that are present on the keyboard of conventional typewriters. Alphabetic letters have therefore been used, in particular <g>, <gb>, <k>, <c>, <q> and <x>, because their various pronunciations come closest to the places of articulation of clicks. In Zulu and Xhosa, dental, palatal and lateral clicks are thus written <c>, <q> and <x>, respectively. However, Roman letters do not suggest anything about the peculiar manner of click articulation. To mark their special quality, an alternative notation makes use of non-alphabetic symbols: <⊙> for bilabial clicks,

</> for dental clicks, <!> for palatal clicks and <//> for cerebral clicks (table 12). Turned letters, for example a turned <t> for a voiceless velar ingressive dental stop, i.e. a dental click, have also been used, the disadvantage once again being their absence from ordinary keyboards. As word-processing technology becomes more widely available, this will be ever less of a problem.
Reading Bleek 1926; Herbert 1990; Ladefoged and Traill 1984.

Median clicks	ʘ	Bilabial
	ǀ	Dental or alveolar
	!	Postalveolar
Lateral click	ǂ	(Post)alveolar

Table 12 The IPA symbols for click consonants

code **1** Any system of symbols used for communicating messages. In information theory the term is used for systems that assign the elements of one sign system to those of another which can thus represent the same information contents. For example, the so-called binary code makes use of only two elements, 0 and 1, which in various combinations can represent the elements of another system, for instance decimal numbers. The combinations 00, 01, 10, 11 can be assigned the numbers 1, 2, 3, 4. The two inventories of signs are then 'semantically equivalent'. Writing systems are codes which convert audible into visible units of speech. **2** Derived codes are systems of signals used to secure secrecy in conveying a message. The Morse code is a derived code which, however, is generally known. It converts alphabetic letters into sequences of dots and dashes. Other derived codes arbitrarily assign code words, code numbers, or other code signs to words, syllables, letters etc. In order to decode the message, the receiver must know the secret code.
See also Cipher; Writing system.

codex In ancient Greece and Rome Wax tablets were used to receive writing. Such a tablet, held together by rings much like a modern notebook, was called a *caudex* or *codex*. In palaeography, important ancient manuscripts are called codices, for instance the *Codex* Mendoza of Aztec writing or the Dresden and Madrid codices of Maya writing. Collections of statutes or recipes for the preparation of drugs are also referred to as codices, for example, the Codex Hammurapi which is at the same time one of the most significant Babylonian inscriptions.

codification The regulation of a language by prescriptive rules based on an analytic description of its structure. Such a description typically takes the variety of a cultural and/or political elite as its object. For example, when Samuel Johnson attempted to codify the English language in his famous dictionary, he selected middle- and upper-class usage, clearly favouring the written forms of groups with social prestige over the spoken language of the lower classes. Through codification, rules are accorded normative status, that is they are designated models

for guiding correct usage. Languages are codified in varying degrees and at different linguistic levels: lexical, phonological, orthographical and grammatical. Codification typically presupposes writing, if only because a comprehensive description of all levels of a language system is hard to memorize without written record. There is a long and significant research tradition which assumes that the Sanskrit grammar of Pāṇini may have been elaborated without the use of writing. However, there is mention of writing in Classical Sanskrit texts, and the question of the beginning of writing in the Sanskrit tradition is yet to be resolved conclusively. In any event, codification in the modern sense relies on writing, even with respect to pronunciation. Dictionaries and grammars are the main tools of codification. The task of codification is often entrusted to language academies, such as the Académie Française, which publish the results of their deliberations, providing the language in question with a normative scaffold laid down in writing.
Reading Haas 1982; Milroy and Milroy 1985.

colon [Gk κῶλον 'portion of strophe, member of sentence'] **1** In Greek rhetoric a member of a sentence or rhythmical period. **2** A punctuation mark consisting of two dots placed one above the other <:> used to separate a clause that introduces a list, a conclusion or a quotation. Where the item introduced by that clause is set off in a new paragraph, the colon is sometimes combined with a dash <:->, but this usage is antiquated and declining.
See also PUNCTUATION.
Reading Carey 1958.

Columbian alphabet An attempt made in 1798 by American businessman James Ewing at reforming the spelling system of English. He advocated the abolition of silent letters, a one-to-one correspondence of sounds and letters, and a pronunciation of letters according to their 'real' values.
See also SPELLING REFORM.
Reading Ewing 1801.

comma [Gk κόμμα 'cut off, short clause'] **1** In Greek rhetoric a dependent clause or group of words less than a sentence period. **2** The punctuation mark <,> used to separate clauses, appositions and other subordinate members of a sentence. There is considerable variation across languages in the conventions guiding the use of commas.
See also PUNCTUATION.
Reading Carey 1958.

consonant roots In Semitic languages the invariant or root part of morphemes consists of consonants. The triconsonantal root is a distinctive characteristic of these languages, many of which share a common lexical stock of such roots. For example, the root *qbr* 'to carry' is the nucleus of a word common to Hebrew, Syriac, Ugaritic, Arabic and Ethiopic (table 13). Combining consonant roots with variable vowels is a major word formation mechanism of Semitic languages. In Arabic, *ktb* is the consonant root of a variety of words having to do with writing:

		Hebrew	*Syriac*	*Ugaritic*	*Arabic*	*Ethiopic*
Singular	2 m.	qəbur	qəbor	qbr	'uqbur	qəbər
	f.	qibri	qəbor	qbr	'uqburi	qəb(ə)rī
Plural	2 m.	qibru	qəbor	qbr	'uqburu	qəb(ə)rū
	f.	qəborna	qəbor	qbr	'uqburna	qəb(ə)rā

Table 13 The Semitic root qbr *'to carry', imperative forms*

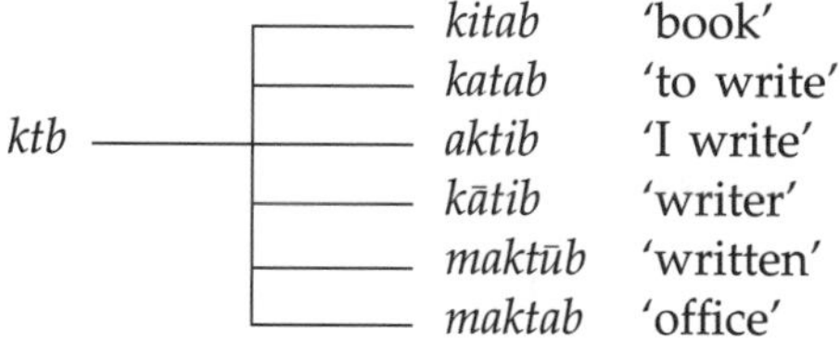

The fact that consonant roots contain the most important semantic information of Semitic words is seen as the underlying reason for the development of writings which leave vowels unmarked.
See also ARABIC WRITTEN LANGUAGE; CONSONANT SCRIPT; HEBREW WRITING.

consonant script Also called 'defective alphabets', consonant scripts operate on the level of segments but do not indicate vowels. They came into existence in the context of Semitic languages, reflecting one of their most conspicuous structural characteristics, the CONSONANT ROOTS. In the languages of this family, vowels serve mainly to indicate grammatical or derivational changes – parts of speech, voice, mood, tense – while lexical content is carried by consonant roots. This feature clearly favoured the creation of consonant scripts. The Canaanite, Aramaic, Phoenician and Hebrew alphabets came into existence during the second half of the second millennium BCE and all belong to this type, as do many other writings derived from any of them at a later time, such as Punic, Syriac, Nabataean and Arabic.

The origin of consonant scripts is a matter of considerable controversy, as the known developmental stages of west Semitic writing in Syria and Palestine leave the exact circumstances of the invention of alphabetic writing in the dark. The other Semitic tradition of writing, that of CUNEIFORM WRITING in Mesopotamia, never led to a consonant script, with the sole exception of the UGARITIC ALPHABET, which is thought to be an adaptation of the extant west Semitic alphabet to writing on clay, whence the cuneiform letter shapes. The origin of the Semitic consonant scripts has also been sought in the west, in Egypt. However, if in fact there was a link between the EGYPTIAN WRITING SYSTEM and Old Semitic writing it could not be established beyond doubt. An additional problem is that there is a great deal of disagreement about the classification of Egyptian hieroglyphic writing. In particular, Ignace Gelb, one of the most influential students of writing, considers Egyptian to be syllabic rather than consonantal, assuming that Egyptian phonetic signs indicate syllables each consisting of a C plus neutral or unspecified V. Egyptologists tend to disagree with Gelb, but no matter how this dispute is resolved, the Egyptian influence on Old Semitic writing remains an open question. Likewise, a Mediterranean origin has also been suggested, but could not be established.

The origin of the Semitic consonant scripts may be elusive, but there is no doubt that even the earliest scripts used letters solely for phonetic representation of Cs. This is a point of great significance for the theory of writing and its evolution, as it shows that alphabets evolved not as mimetic representations of speech, but rather as graphic systems of linguistic expression linked to speech in a more complex way than faithful representation of sounds. Given the systematic nature of consonant writing, it is clearly mistaken to look at it as something incomplete, an imperfection of the technology which was to be fully developed only by the Greeks. Mrvr, cnsnnt scrpts r nt s dffclt t rd s n mght thnk. Even non-Semitic languages with no consonantal roots can be written and, with minimal practice, quite easily read in consonant scripts. It should also be noted that vowels are underdetermined in virtually all alphabetic writings derived from the Phoenician model, most alphabetically written languages having two to three times as many Vs as V letters. The poverty of vowel letters in Greek- and Latin-derived alphabets still testifies to their Semitic source.

See also GREEK ALPHABET; MATRES LECTIONIS; SEMITIC WRITING; TIBERIAN POINTING.

Reading Jensen 1969; Gelb 1963; Diringer 1968; Naveh 1982.

Coptic alphabet Coptic is the final developmental stage of the Egyptian language and was strongly subject to the influence of Hellenization. The Coptic script derives from the Greek uncial alphabet. Coptic writing is one of many examples of the diffusion of a script by virtue of the expansion of a religion. Egypt was receptive to the influence of Greek culture for many centuries, even prior to the Hellenistic age which began with the foundation of the city of Alexandria in 332 BCE. The Greek language was used extensively in Egypt, as attested in many bilingual inscriptions. The Egyptians were hence quite familiar with Greek letters. At the same time they had a venerable literary tradition of their own. The desire to write the Egyptian language with Greek letters emerged only in the wake of the spread of Christianity in the second century CE. Two factors favoured the adoption of Greek letters: one is that written demotic Egyptian had become quite removed from the spoken language, and the other is that the Egyptian Christians were eager to have their own letters as a visible symbol of their faith. Hence Coptic, which through Arabic mediation (*qopt/qipt*) is the Greek name of Egyptian (γύπτιος short for αἰγύπτιος 'Egyptian'), came to be written in Greek letters. The Copts adopted the entire Greek alphabet, including the letters Γ, Δ, Χ, Θ and Φ for their numerical values, although the corresponding sounds were absent from their language. On the other hand, the Greek alphabet was supplemented by six additional letters apparently derived from the demotic script (tables 14, 15). There are still some uncertainties as to the time when these additions were made, but the full 32 letters of the Coptic alphabet are already attested on inscriptions dating from the second century (figure 22).

Adopting the Greek alphabet for the Egyptian language was not just a visible break with the past and a testimony to Hellenization; it also meant that, for the

Demotic	Coptic	Value
	ϣ	š
	ϥ	f
	ϧ	χ
	ϩ	h
	ϫ	dž
	ϭ	tš

Table 14 Six Coptic letters derived from demotic letters

Name	Symbol	Value	Name	Symbol	Value
Alpha	Ⲁ ⲁ	a	*Thita*	Ⲑ ⲑ	th
Bida	Ⲃ ⲃ	b v	*Jauta*	Ⲓ ⲓ	i
Gamma	Ⲅ ⲅ	g	*Kapa*	Ⲕ ⲕ	k
Dalda	Ⲇ ⲇ	d	*Laula*	Ⲗ ⲗ	l
Ei	Ⲉ ⲉ	e	*Mi*	Ⲙ ⲙ	m
So	Ⲋ ⲋ	6	*Ni*	Ⲛ ⲛ	n
Zita	Ⲍ ⲍ	dz	*Ksi*	Ⲝ ⲝ	ks
Ita	Ⲏ ⲏ	e ī	*O*	Ⲟ ⲟ	o
Pi	Ⲡ ⲡ	p	*Au*	Ⲱ ⲱ	ū ō
Ro	Ⲣ ⲣ	r	*Šei*	Ϣ ϣ	š
Sima	Ⲥ ⲥ	s	*Fei*	Ϥ ϥ	f
Tau	Ⲧ ⲧ	t	*Khei*	Ϧ ϧ	χ
He	Ⲩ ⲩ	ū	*Hori*	Ϩ ϩ	h
Phi	Ⲫ ⲫ	ph	*Džan-džia*	Ϫ ϫ	dž
Khi	Ⲭ ⲭ	kh	*Tšima*	Ϭ ϭ	tš
Psi	Ⲯ ⲯ	ps	*Ti*	Ϯ ϯ	ti

Ⲙ̇ ⲙ̇ ẹm, Ⲛ̇ ⲛ̇ ẹn, Ⲣ̇ ⲣ̇ ẹr, Ⲁ̇ ⲁ̇ a, Ⲉ̇ ⲉ̇ e, Ⲏ̇ ⲏ̇ i, Ⲓ̇ ⲓ̇ i, Ⲟ̇ ⲟ̇ o, Ⲩ̇ ⲩ̇ u, Ⲱ̇ ⲱ̇ o.

ⲁⲓ ai, ⲉⲓ ei, ⲟⲓ oi, ⲁⲩ au, ⲉⲩ eu, ⲟⲩ u, ⲟⲟⲩ ou.

Table 15 The Coptic alphabet

Figure 22 Pistis Sophia, *a Coptic treatise expounding the doctrines of the Gnostic teacher Valentius, late fourth century (By permission of the British Library)*

first time, the language could be transcribed without regard to etymological and historical writing. As a consequence, and in contradistinction to demotic Egyptian with its very variable and often opaque conventions, Coptic developed a rather stringent normative orthography, a novelty for Egyptian scribes. Coptic died out in the fourteenth century.

Reading Morenz 1973.

Cree syllabary A script invented around 1840 by missionary James Evans for the Cree-speaking peoples of northern Canada. The system makes use of an extremely small set of basic signs (table 16). Most Cree dialects can be written in this script using 12 signs or fewer. Each sign indicates a CV syllable or an independent V. The great economy of signs is made possible by exploiting the orientation of each sign's position as a distinctive feature. For example,

	E	I	O	A	Finals	
	ᐁ	ᐃ	ᐅ	ᐊ		
T	ᑌ	ᑎ	ᑐ	ᑕ	ᐟ	ᑦ
K	ᑫ	ᑭ	ᑯ	ᑲ	ᐠ	ᒃ
N	ᓀ	ᓂ	ᓄ	ᓇ	ᐣ	ᓐ
M	ᒣ	ᒥ	ᒧ	ᒪ	‹	ᒻ
Ch	ᒉ	ᒋ	ᒍ	ᒐ	-	ᒡ
S	ᓭ	ᓯ	ᓱ	ᓴ	^	ᔅ
Sh	ᔐ	ᔑ	ᔓ	ᔕ	˘	ᔥ
P	ᐯ	ᐱ	ᐳ	ᐸ	•	ᑊ
Y	ᔦ	ᔨ	ᔪ	ᔭ		
L	ᓓ	ᓕ	ᓗ	ᓚ	ᐪ	ᓪ
R	ᕃ	ᕆ	ᕈ	ᕋ	ᐠ	ᕐ
W	·ᐁ	·ᐃ	·ᐅ	·ᐊ	•	•

Table 16 The Cree syllabary

independent vowel quality is indicated by a triangle. Depending on whether it faces south, north, east or west, the vowel is /e/, /i/, /o/ or /a/, respectively. In the same manner, each CV sign changes its vowel quality with its orientation. Since Cree has seven vowels rather than only four, a few diacritical marks are needed to indicate the three additional vowels. For example, a large dot placed over the CV sign modifies the vowel quality by marking length. A set of 'finals' is employed to indicate syllable-final consonants.

Although not an indigenous creation, the syllabic script was adopted enthusiastically by the Cree people. Within a short time virtually the entire community became literate in this script. The ingenious simplicity of the system clearly played a part in this achievement. However, it is also thought that the four orientations contributed to the system's acceptability, because the number four has religious significance among native northern American peoples. Its popularity among the Cree encouraged adaptation of the script to other languages of the region. It was accordingly modified to fit some phonologically more complex languages of the

ᑲᑲᓂᑲᑕ:ᐚᔮᒋ ᒥᐢᒋᓇ ᑭᔮ ᒥᑕᓱᒪ ᑭᔮ ᐊᒥᐢ ᒍᔮᓐ
Kakanikatawayach missin kea miskwhyan kea mitasuch

Long legged boots in beaver with socks

Figure 23 Specimen of Naskapi writing in the Cree script with transliteration and translation

Athabaskan family, especially Carrier, Chipewyan and Slavey, as well as the Algonkian language Naskapi, necessitating an expansion of the sign inventory (figure 23). It was also adapted for Inuktitut (Eskimo). Among the Cree, the writing is still widely used, although competence seems to be declining in the younger generations.
Reading Murdoch 1982; Bennett and Berry 1991.

Cretan writing The Mediterranean island of Crete is home to several ancient writings which are only partially deciphered. The oldest epigraphic documents were found on small seal stones, called 'Cretan hieroglyph' by Arthur EVANS who first studied them (figure 24). The excavation of Knossos, the centre of

Figure 24 Cretan hieroglyph seals

Minoan culture in Crete, and other sites in central and eastern Crete brought to light a number of inscriptions which illustrate the development of Cretan writing. Dating from the end of the third millennium BCE, the hieroglyphs are thought to form a logographic script much like HITTITE HIEROGLYPHIC. Many of the signs depict natural objects such as animals. What seems to be a variety of the plastic seal inscriptions is a more linear script found on baked clay tablets. Some 45 of these so-called 'proto-linear' signs could be identified with hieroglyphs. Both scripts consist of about 90 signs. Their exact relationship is yet to be determined.

During the Middle Minoan period (about 1700–1550 BCE) the proto-linear signs developed into two scripts known as LINEAR A and LINEAR B (figure 25). The former was used up to about 1450 BCE and the latter up to about 1200 BCE. Although Linear A inscriptions were found throughout central and eastern Crete while Linear B is only attested in Knossos, the latter is deemed more important because the documents are more numerous and because it could be deciphered. Yet another writing of Cretan origin is found on a single document, the famous PHAISTOS DISK, which has defied all attempts at decipherment.

In sum, the Minoan culture of Crete has produced at least five different writings, most of which, however, are sparsely documented and therefore poorly understood. All Minoan inscriptions pre-date Greek alphabetic writing. However fragmentary and partially undeciphered, they are of great significance for the history of writing since they constitute the first instances of writing in the Aegean Sea and in the Greek language.
Reading Evans 1909; Dow 1954; Ekschmitt 1969.

Figure 25 Cretan hieroglyphs and Linear A on clay documents
Source: *Ekschmitt 1969*

cryptography [Gk κρυπτός 'hidden' + γραφος 'writing'] The various methods for concealing the meaning of what is written by using arbitrarily designed letters or a system of ciphers for substituting and interchanging letters or other units of writing. Texts produced in such a manner are called 'cryptograms' (figure 26). They can be read by means of a key or, in the absence of such, can be made readable by 'cryptanalysis', a procedure which relies mainly on statistical methods of distribution and frequency analysis.
See also CIPHER; CODE; DECIPHERMENT.
Reading Devos and Seligman 1967.

Figure 26 Cryptograms designed by the earliest Christians who were forced to keep their meetings secret. Many used the chi-rho *sign, made from the first two letters of Gk* χρηστος Christos, *χ and ρ*

cuneiform writing The oldest and most widespread writing system in the ancient Middle East which was in active use for a variety of languages for three millenniums BCE. The name is a modern coinage first introduced as *litterae cuneatae*, from Lat. *cuneus* 'wedge', by Thomas Hyde, a professor of Hebrew and Arabic at the University of Oxford, in his book on Persia, published 1700. It refers to the wedge-shaped strokes of which cuneiform signs consist. Cuneiform writing owes this characteristic feature of its outer form to the physical medium on which it evolved, namely clay. The writing tool was a pointed stylus cut from reed which left wedges of various orientations when impressed upon wet clay (figure 27).

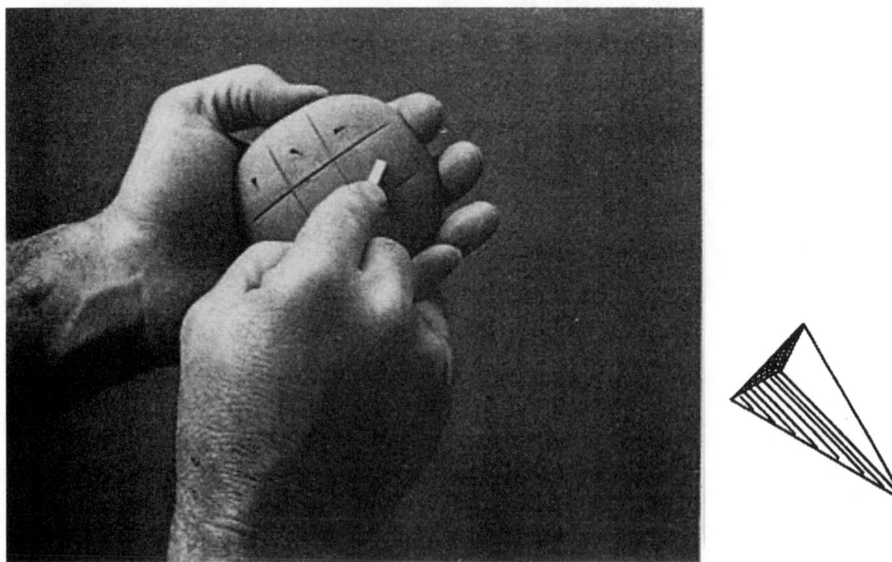

Figure 27 Standard writing position of stylus and tablet. Right: the wedge made, oriented in standard reading position
Source: *Powell 1981*

Figure 28 Early Sumerian inscription dating from around 3000 BCE

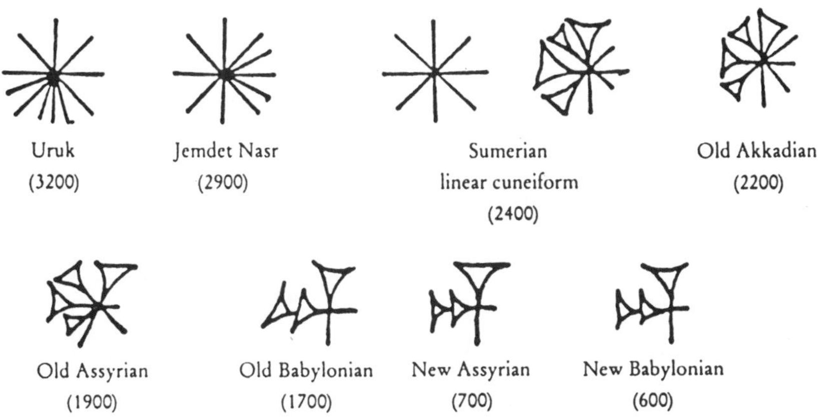

Figure 29 Gradual stylization and simplification of the cuneiform sign for both an *'sky' and* dingir *'god' (numbers refer to years BCE)*

Origin and development of outer form

Near the end of the fourth millennium BCE the Sumerians who inhabited southern Mesopotamia had developed a civilization with food production above subsistence level. In addition to major inventions such as the wheel and the plough they also developed a system of recording. Starting out as representations of natural objects, the earliest signs were pictures, then pictograms (figure 28). Stylization set in early, leading to a complete loss of the pictorial appearance of cuneiform signs (figure 29). This was an immediate result of the practice of writing on CLAY TABLETS. The earliest tablets were rather small and square, and writing was from top to bottom. Later, bigger rectangular tablets were used, which forced the scribes to change the position of their left hand in which the tablets were held for writing. As a result, the signs were rotated 90 degrees counterclockwise and lost their iconic quality (table 17). From around the middle

Original pictograph	Pictograph in position of later cuneiform	Early Babylonian	Assyrian	Original or derived meaning
				bird
				fish
				donkey
				ox
				sun day
				grain
				orchard
				to plough to till
				boomerang to throw to throw down
				to stand to go

Table 17 Rotation and loss of iconicity of some Sumerian signs

of the second millennium, tablets were written and read from left to right in horizontal lines.

Stylization and conventionalization of the script made the wedge the elementary building block of all signs. Once the script was fully developed, the orientations of wedges were restricted. Only five different types were permissible for the composition of more complex signs: four pointed south, east, south-east and north-east, and the fifth formed a 90-degree angle by superimposing the latter two (figure 30). Since every sign is a configuration of permissible wedges, simple signs may form parts of more complex ones, a composition principle also found in the Chinese writing system. However, complex signs are not to be interpreted as compounds of constituent configurations, because the graphic structure is independent of the phonetic structure of the referent. For example, the graphs

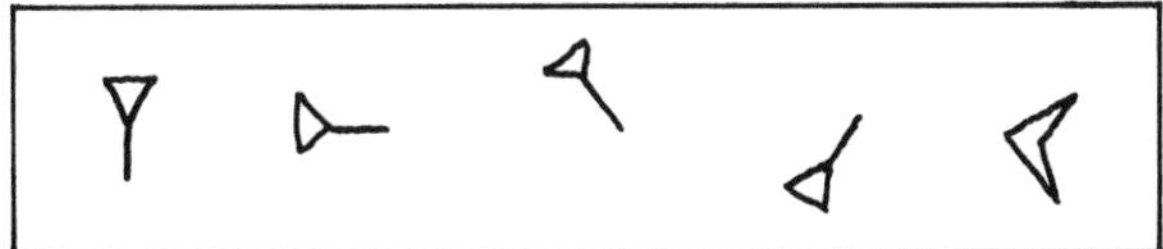

Figure 30 The permissible wedges of cuneiform

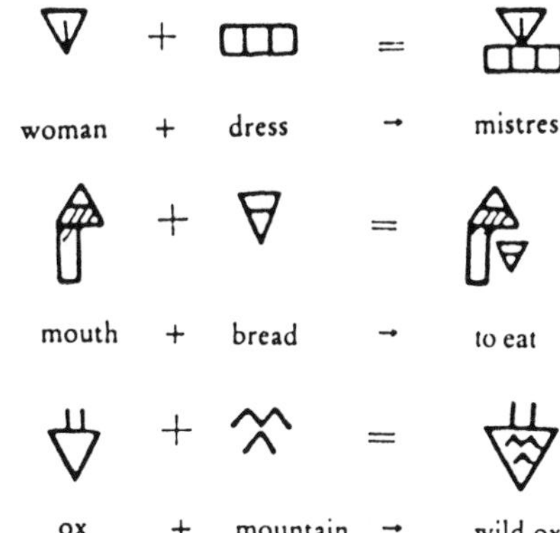

Table 18 Graphical composition of new signs in Sumerian writing

which (in Akkadian) are read *pa* and *ib* in combination yield not the graph *pa* + *ib* but the graph for *sab*.

Development of the inner form

Early Sumerian writing was word writing, mostly depicting concrete nouns which could be represented easily with pictograms. The expressive power of this system was very limited, and it took a long time before it was expanded when new signs were formed by combining others by virtue of their meaning. For example, the sign for 'mistress' was formed by connecting the signs for 'woman' and 'dress' (table 18).

Another strategy for increasing the expressive power of the system consisted in expanding the meaning of existing word signs. The sign *APIN* 'plough' came to be used for *uru* 'to plough', even though the two words were unrelated in Sumerian. Ultimately, it was even used for 'ploughman'. But eventually the exploitation of phonetic similarities in accordance with the REBUS PRINCIPLE, that is the transfer of word signs motivated by their sound values rather than by their meanings, proved to be more effective. Thus the sign for *ti* 'arrow' could be used for writing the word *ti(l)* 'life', which is much more difficult to depict. This was the first step towards the development of syllabic writing.

Gradually the sound value of signs became increasingly important and their meanings receded into the background. The transfer was always first from one content word to another and then to a function word. Thus a syllabary of sorts came into existence whose elements, like Egyptian hieroglyph with phonetic values, are formally indistinguishable from logograms. The relationship between syllables and signs was far from being simple. Rebus and syllabic writing greatly increased the range of words that could be expressed, but they also introduced considerable ambiguity into the system since many signs became polyvalent, having several different meanings as well as phonetic values. In order to remedy this weakness, a third type of sign was introduced in addition to word signs and syllable signs: determinatives. These signs were mute. Logograms for generic terms such as 'man', 'god', 'land', 'city', 'wood', 'stone', 'copper', 'plant' and 'fish' were placed in front of – or, less frequently, behind – a word sign in order to specify its meaning. The sign for 'wood' put in front of that of 'plough', transcribed as ^{giš}*apin*, where the superscript is not pronounced, made it clear that the tool *apin* was meant rather than the activity. And 'man' instead of 'wood' in the same position could only be interpreted as *engar* 'ploughman'.

Another strategy to cope with polyvalence, which however further increased the multifunctionality of signs, was employing syllabic signs as phonetic complements. Where one sign was used to represent several related meanings, a phonetic complement was added to single out the intended one. For example, whenever the sign *DU* 𒁺 'leg' was used for *gin* 'to go' a phonetic complement *na* was added to indicate the ending *-n*. This method of determining the reading *gin* amounts to an instruction to find a word in the semantic range of 'leg' with the ending *-n*.

With three kinds of signs – word signs indicating meaning and sound, syllable signs and phonetic complements indicating sound only, and determinatives indicating meaning only – the cuneiform system was fully developed. Graphically all three were indistinguishable, being composed of the same standard wedges. This made for considerable complexity. Further modifications of the cuneiform system were brought about when it was applied to other languages, first to Babylonian and Assyrian and then to several other languages of the region belonging to different language families.

Languages written in cuneiform

Sumerian, a language of unknown affiliation, is the language for which the cuneiform system was developed, and was presumably the first to be written in it. Sumerian was superseded by Old Akkadian, the Semitic parent language of Babylonian and Assyrian. It is these two languages, sometimes identified as dialects, in which the bulk of cuneiform literature is written. Cuneiform was, however, also adapted to languages of other stock. Elamite, typologically an ergative language of uncertain extraction, was in contact with the languages of Babylon as early as the third millennium. It was written with cuneiform syllabic signs from *c.*2200 to 400 BCE. Hurrian, which is related to the poorly attested language of the Urartian kingdom of eastern Anatolia, became extinct around the end of the second millennium. It was written in a variety of cuneiform derived from Old Akkadian which, however, was almost free of logograms. Another language of Anatolia, Hittite, belongs to the Indo-European family. During the second millennium BCE when the Hittite empire was at the crest of its power (*c.*1600–1200), the language was written in a variety of cuneiform containing several new syllable signs because the phonological structure of Hittite did not match that of Akkadian well. Hittite cuneiform also made extensive use of logograms. This language is well attested on numerous clay tablets excavated in the Hittite capital Boğazköy in central Turkey. Old Persian, too, is Indo-European. It came to be written with the simplest and the latest of all cuneiform scripts, consisting of just

36 syllable signs (often used with segmental rather than syllabic values) plus a few logograms and auxiliary signs. Most written records date from between the sixth and the fourth centuries BCE. Old Persian is one of the languages of the famous trilingual rock inscription of Behistun (Achaemenid Elamite and Late Babylonian being the others). While Old Persian is structurally at the threshold of alphabetic writing, Ugaritic cuneiform is alphabetic: it consists of 30 signs, of which 27 are consonants and three are (long) vowels. The system was apparently used in Ugarit at the northern Syrian coast in the fourteenth and thirteenth centuries BCE, when it was supplanted by a west Semitic script. Other Semitic languages, especially Akkadian, were also written in Ugarit using the Ugaritic alphabet, although documentation is sparse. The sign inventory of cuneiform is shown in table 19.

Sumerian	Old Akkadian	Babylonian-Assyrian	Elamite	Old Persian	Ugaritic
2000	800	700	113	41	30

Table 19 Sign inventory of cuneiform

The spread of cuneiform from its Mesopotamian heartland to Elam in the east, Persia in the south, Anatolia in the north and Ugarit in the west concurs with its development from a logographic to a phonetic writing system. In this sense, the development of cuneiform is a story of one script (outer form) and several writing systems (inner form): word writing, word-syllable writing, word-syllable writing with determinatives and phonetic complements, purely syllabic writing, and, if Ugaritic is included, consonant-alphabetic writing (figure 31). The outer form was remarkably stable with the wedge as its characteristic element for more than 25 centuries, although the graphic complexity of individual signs was gradually reduced as the number of different signs decreased. The inner form, however, changed drastically, the most significant innovations being made whenever cuneiform was adapted to a new language. Akkadian cuneiform, consisting of an extensive inventory of three functionally different kinds of sign, remained stable for two millenniums, but attempts at using the script for other

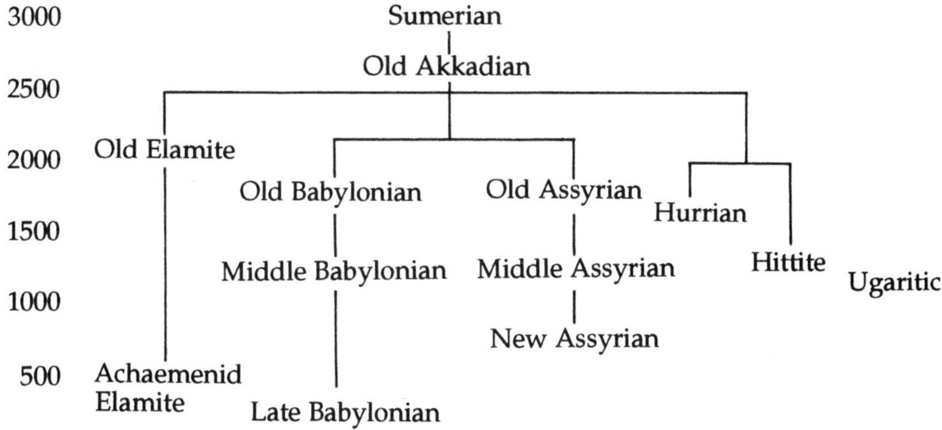

Figure 31 The lineage of cuneiform scripts (numbers refer to years BCE)

languages resulted in drastic changes and simplifications. Where a writing is transferred from the language for which it first evolved to another, the bonds of established usage are much easier to cast off in the interests of efficiency than within the traditional system itself.

Documentation

Cuneiform writing was in use for 3,000 years. The latest known text dates from 74 CE. It is thanks to the writing surface on which cuneiform developed – clay, a most durable material – that the oldest inscriptions could survive in perfect shape for thousands of years. Hundreds of thousands of clay tablets with inscriptions of various kinds have been preserved in addition to many monumental inscriptions in stone. These documents hold more information about the history, culture and everyday life of the early civilizations of Mesopotamia and Asia Minor than any archaeological evidence. To decipher, edit and interpret them is hence a task of great significance. Today, modern technology is applied to this

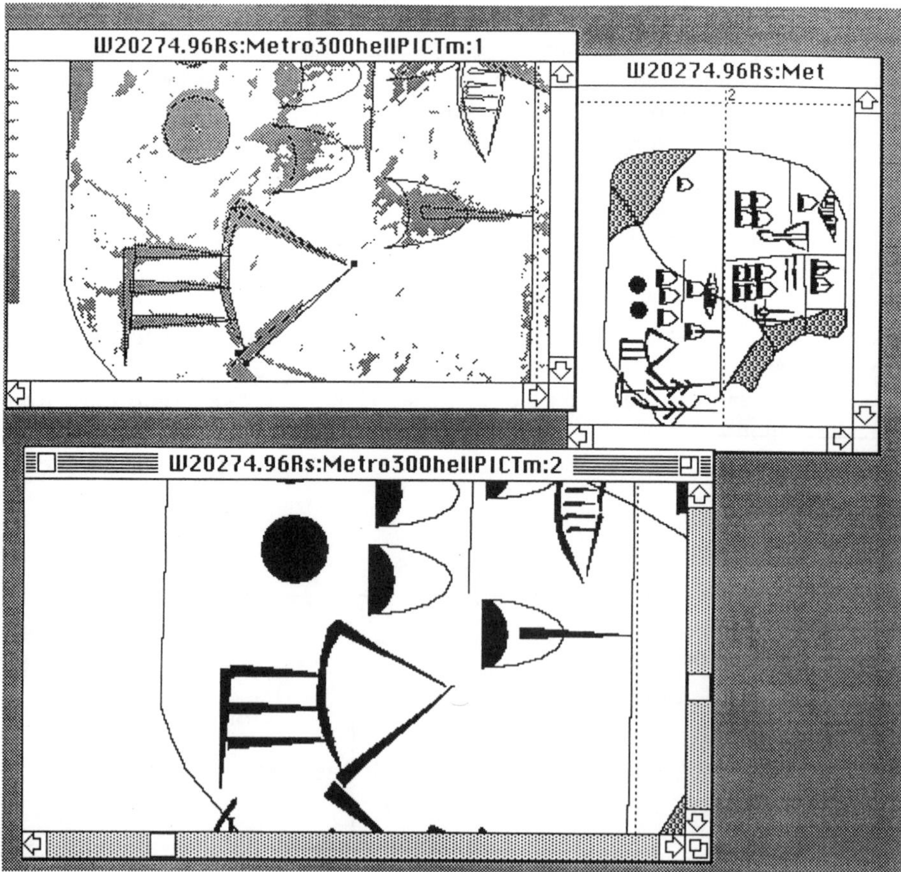

Figure 32 A computer graphics program redraws archaic cuneiform records from photographs of clay tablets for filing and analysing purposes: above, drawing screen; below, window showing the result (Institute of Classical Archaeology, Free University, Berlin)

research. Computer-assisted processing of cuneiform inscriptions makes them more accessible, as texts are edited, translated and filed in data banks. Copying cuneiform texts by hand is laborious and very time-consuming, but until recently was common practice among Assyrologists. It was only in the late 1980s that computer graphics programs were designed to handle inscriptions from photographs of clay tablets, an innovation which facilitates filing and reproduction of the many cuneiform texts still waiting to be read (figure 32).

See also AKKADIAN; ASSYRIAN; BABYLONIAN; EGYPTIAN WRITING SYSTEM; ELAMITE WRITING; HITTITE CUNEIFORM; OLD PERSIAN WRITING; SUMERIAN WRITING; UGARITIC ALPHABET.

Reading Gelb 1963; Jensen 1969; Edzard 1980; Bottéro 1982; Reiner 1973; Green 1981; Powell 1981; Walker 1987; Nissen, et al., 1990.

cursive [Lat. *currere* 'to run'] A style of writing with a running hand, so that individual letters are connected, have their angles rounded, and become slanted (figure 33). Cursive writing styles are attested from antiquity, for example on OSTRACA and GRAFFITI wall inscriptions. In palaeography the cursive style is distinguished from the more formal uncial writing. In print cursive scripts are characterized by slightly slanted forms.

Figure 33 Specimen of cursive script by Rudolf Koch, 1916

cypher *See* CIPHER

Cypriote writing Three different ancient writings are known from Cyprus. The oldest one is documented on a single clay tablet bearing a short inscription of three lines with 20 different signs dating from approximately 1500 BCE. Although some of the signs are reminiscent of Minoan LINEAR A, this script cannot be derived from Cretan writing. It also has no apparent relationship with the next Cypriote writing, which is documented on a small number of clay tablets excavated in Enkomi. Because of its non-figurative appearance and because, much as in Babylonian cuneiform, the individual signs are broken down into wedge-like parts reflecting the plastic nature of the surface on which they were written, it is called 'Cypriote cuneiform' (table 20). This writing dates from around 1200

Table 20 Sign inventory of Cypriote cuneiform writing (undeciphered)

BCE. Its origin remains obscure, although a connection with the cuneiform alphabet from Ugarit at the Syrian coast opposite the most easterly cape of Cyprus has been suggested (UGARITIC ALPHABET).

Finally, there is the Cypriote syllabic writing, also known as 'Cypro-Minoan' writing because it is thought to be derived from the Linear A script of Crete. However, its exact genealogy is still uncertain, if only because it is separated from the Minoan script by about half a millennium. Cypriote syllabic writing appeared around 700 BCE, at a time, that is, when Greek was already written in the Phoenician-derived alphabet. Normally written from right to left, it was used for several centuries until the Hellenistic period, mostly for writing Greek and to a lesser extent for local languages which cannot yet be read. The syllabary consists of 45 signs, of which five mark the vowels /a/, /e/, /i/, /o/ and /i̯/ or /u/, and the remainder indicate open syllables, i.e. CV groups (table 21). Hence geminate consonants, other consonant clusters and final consonants pose difficulties. The last are indicated by C + /e/ syllabic signs, while clusters are written as CV–CV sequences. Double consonants are not marked at all, and nasals are left out in front of consonants. With respect to the Greek language the syllabary is underdifferentiated in yet another respect, failing as it does to mark voicing and aspiration of consonants. Hence /b,p,p^h/, /g,k,k^h/ and /d,t,t^h/ are marked by only one sign each. For example, Gk ἄνδριάς is written as *a-ti-ri-a-se*. These features make the script difficult to read (figure 34). In view of the much simpler contemporary alphabetic writing for Greek it is a matter of some surprise that Cypriote syllabic writing continued to be used for several centuries.

Reading Masson 1961; Ekschmitt 1969.

Cyrillic An alphabet derived from the Greek uncial script first used by Greek Orthodox Slavs, also known as *asbuka* after the Slavic names of its first two

Symbol	Value	Symbol	Value	Symbol	Value
	a		e		i
	ta		te		ti
	ga				
	ka		ke		ki
	pa		pe		pi
	la		le		li
	ma		me		mi
	na		ne		ni
	ra		re		ri
	sa		se		si
	va		ve		

Symbol	Value	Symbol	Value
	o		i̯
	to		ti̯
	ko		ki̯
	po		pi̯
	lo		
	mo		
	no		
	ro		
	so		si̯
	vo		

Table 21 The Cypriote syllabary

letters. Its creation is attributed to the ninth-century apostle of the Slavs, Saint Cyrillus. Most of its letters are of Greek origin; five, ж /ž/, ч /č/, ш /š/, щ /št/ and Ѧ /ę/, were taken from the GLAGOLITIC ALPHABET. The Cyrillic alphabet contains a number of combined letters such as ю /yu/, composed of F + O. Under Peter the Great the Cyrillic alphabet was simplified and made graphically similar to Latin antique. In its modern form it is used for Byelorussian, Bulgarian, Russian, Serbian, Ukrainian and other non-Slavic languages spoken in the erstwhile

'Ανδρο	*a-to-ro*
ιν τυχαι	*i-tu-ka-i*
ης λογαρια	*e-se-lo-ka-ri-ja*
λαμπαδων Ζωϝαρ	*la-pa-to-ne zo-va-ra*
Μεγαλαθεω Φιλοδαμω	*mi-ka-la-te-o pi-lo-ta*
'αζαρϝων Ζωϝορω	*a-za-ra-vo-ne zo-vo-ro*

Translation: When Andro was in good luck. The calculation of torches was Zovar's, Megalotheos' and Philodamos' chore, that of what has been raised by collection Zovoras' chore.

Figure 34 Left-running Cypriote syllabic inscription with transliteration (right), Greek transcription (left) and translation of the first six lines

Аа	Бб	Вв	Гг	Дд	ЕЕ	Ёё	Жж	Зз	Ии	Йй
a	b	v	g	d	e	e,ë	ž	z	i	j
Кк	Лл	Мм	Нн	Оо	Пп	Рр	Сс	Тт	Уу	Фф
k	l	m	n	o	p	r	s	t	u	f
Хх	Цц	Чч	Шш	Щщ	Ъъ	Ыы	Ьь	Ээ	Юю	Яя
h	c	č	š	šč	i	y	’	ė	yu	ya

Table 22 The Cyrillic alphabet with Latin transliterations

Soviet Union, such as Chuvash. Romanian, too, was written in it until the mid-nineteenth century, and for its variety Moldavian it continued to be used until 1991 when Moldavia became independent and replaced it with the Latin alphabet. As the script of the Russian language the Cyrillic alphabet consists of 33 letters (table 22).

D, d /di:/ The fourth letter of the English alphabet derives from Semitic *dāleth* through Greek *delta* (Δ, δ), taking its present form in the Latin alphabet.

Danish alphabet Three letters are added in Danish to the Latin alphabet: <Æ æ>, <Ø ø> and <Å å>. Prior to the latest spelling reform of 1948, <Aa> and <aa> were used instead of <Å> and <å>, respectively. This reform also abolished the practice of writing nouns with capital initials. The orthography is based on a number of different principles which taken together make the system deviate in many instances from a one-to-one grapheme–phoneme correspondence. It is an orthography with a strong morphological element. For instance, the principle of morpheme constancy requires the spelling of a morpheme to be retained in different contexts even where its phonetic shape differs considerably. Another morphological principle is to make different morphemes look dissimilar. Thus many homophones are not homographs, for instance *løg* 'onion' vs *løj* 'lied', both [lçi']. In some cases where graphemic distinctions do not correspond to phonemic distinctions they are introduced to compensate for lacking graphemic distinctions in another part of the word. For instance, the only phonological distinction between *mor* 'mother' and *mord* 'murder' is in the vowel which, however, is spelt the same in both cases, while <r> vs <rd> distinguish the two words.

Figure 1 Specimen of the Chinese dazhuan *or large-seal script by Chen shi-ri, Qing dynasty (seventeenth century* CE*)*

dazhuan (*ta-chuan*) An archaic Chinese script known as the large-seal script. It originated in the Shang dynasty (1523–1028 BCE) and was used in several varieties during the Chou dynasty (1027–221 BCE) before the Chinese script was fully standardized in the small-seal script (XIAOZHUAN). The large-seal script is mostly documented in bronze inscriptions (figure 1). It is still occasionally used for carving official seals or stamps.
See also CALLIGRAPHY; CHINESE SCRIPTS.

***dbu-med* script** A cursive type of the Tibetan script written without the characteristic horizontal bar on top of each letter, whence the name which literally means 'headless' (figure 2).
See also TIBETAN WRITING.

Figure 2 Specimen of Tibetan dbu-med *script: the title of the Chinese newspaper Red Flag,* tar-ma *in Tibetan*

Dead Sea scrolls A loose collective designation of several manuscripts on parchment bearing biblical texts discovered in 1947 in Qumran on the north-west shore of the Dead Sea (figure 3). On the basis of palaeographic evidence and the application of the radiocarbon test to some of the linen in which these manuscripts were wrapped before being sealed in jars, the scrolls could be dated to between the first century BCE and the first century CE. They were written by the Essenes in Hebrew and Aramaic, using the Old Hebrew script and the Jewish script, which is one of the offshoots of the Aramaic cursive script.
Reading Pearlman 1980; Yadin 1984; Eisenman and Robinson 1991.

decipherment The recovery of the key to an extinct writing system. Decipherment is a relatively modern undertaking which has been successfully attempted only in the last two or three centuries. Because of the difficulties it involves and the reward it often yields in the form of unlocking entire histories, it is rightly regarded as one of the most glamorous achievements of scholarship.

All writing is meant to be read, yet there are many texts which cannot be read at all, because nobody knows how to relate the visual symbols of which they are composed to linguistic units. Before such texts can be read, the code that links writing to meaning or sound or both must be recovered.

Three kinds of decipherment can be distinguished, as summarized in table 1. Where the language is known but not the script, as in (1), no message can be extracted from the text. For example, the text in figure 4 is in a language well known to the reader of these lines, English. But only those familiar with the BERNARD SHAW ALPHABET will be able to identify it as the beginning of Lincoln's Gettysburg address. A historical decipherment of this kind is that of LINEAR B, an unknown Mycenean syllabic script which Michael Ventris found to be used for writing Greek. In (2) a familiar script is used to write a text in a language unknown to the reader. Again the encoded meaning remains obscure, and as in

1. כי לוא רמה תודה לכה ולוא תספר חסדכה תולעה
2. חי חי   יודה לכה יודו לכה כול מוטטי רגל בהודיעכה
3. חסדכה להמה וצדקתכה תשכילם כי בידכה נפש כול
4. חי נשמת כול   בשר אתה נתתה עשה עמנו 𐤉𐤄𐤅𐤄
5. כטובכה כרוב רחמיכה וכרוב צדקותיכה שמע
6. 𐤉𐤄𐤅𐤄 בקול אוהבי שמו ולוא עזב חסדו מהמה
7. ברוך 𐤉𐤄𐤅𐤄 עושה צדקות מעטר חסידיו

   את
8. חסד ורחמים שאגה נפשי להלל שמכה להודות ברנה
9. חסדיכה להגיד אמונתכה לתהלתכה אין חקר למות

Figure 3 Fragment of one of the Dead Sea scrolls with a commentary on the biblical verses of Hosea 2:8–14. The Tetragrammaton, the four-letter divine name, appears in the Old Hebrew script in lines 4, 6 and 7. The rest of the text is in the Jewish script (transcription and translation by M. Horgan)

	Language known	Script known	
1	+	–	
2	–	+	
3	–	–	
4	+	+	Reading

Table 1 Three kinds of decipherment

(1) the text cannot be read. The ETRUSCAN ALPHABET is very similar to that of early Greek. It is possible, therefore, to reconstruct the pronunciation of many words. However, very little is known about the Etruscan language which appears to be unrelated to any other, and therefore many inscriptions are quite unintelligible. Etruscan inscriptions can be pronounced, but only insufficiently read. Reading in the proper sense of the word presupposes knowledge of both the script and the language, as in (4). Conversely, a situation where script and language are unknown as in (3) presents the most difficult case of decipherment. Nothing was known about the Egyptian language when CHAMPOLLION and some of his contemporaries set out to reveal the secret of the hieroglyphs and make the message they preserved from Ptolemaic times once again accessible.

All decipherments belong to one of these three types, although it is not always immediately clear whether a given case falls under (1), (2) or (3), because decipherers may not be aware of the fact that they are ignorant only of the script but not of the language. For example, certain inscriptions in Greek letters from Crete could be identified as Semitic only decades after their discovery. This is so because all writing systems are full of imperfections and irregularities, and to discover the functional units of a writing system and the regulations by virtue of which they relate to a particular language can be quite difficult even where the language is known. Historically evolved writing systems have, therefore, proved more difficult to decipher than artificially construed CIPHER codes.

The fundamental assumption of any decipherment is that a set of graphic marks harbours a message which can be understood. Certain features such

Figure 4 Language known, script unknown: the beginning of Lincoln's Gettysburg address written in the Bernard Shaw alphabet

Figure 5 Early Mycenaean inscription from Orchomenos
Source: *Jensen 1925*

as regularities, repetition, a limited set of units, as well as statistically variable distributions of individual signs, reveal to the keen observer that the marks are actually writing rather than ornament, meaningless strokes or accidental cracks as on the surface of pottery. This first step of establishing that a sign configuration constitutes writing is especially difficult where inscriptions are fragmentary and short such as the Mycenaean inscription in figure 5, or where the data base is limited to a single inscription, as in the case of the unique and as yet undeciphered PHAISTOS DISK. But even where a great many inscriptions exist such recognition may not be a foregone conclusion. For example, in spite of a large corpus of Mesoamerican monumental inscriptions, the glyphs of MAYA WRITING were not regarded as writing proper until the 1950s. The fundamental assumption that there is a message that can be understood implies, equally importantly, that the message is expressed in a particular language and that therefore the writing depicts that language, however involved and deviating from systematic principles is the mapping relation. No successful decipherment is achieved unless, as a result, it can be shown how a particular language is represented visually. The decipherment of the Maya script was greatly retarded, because until three decades ago a thorough grounding in the Mayan language was not considered important. From whatever clues are available the decipherer must determine the systematic properties of the script as they relate to a given language. A distribution analysis of recognizable units can reveal certain features of a script such as its direction, its systematic type, its elements and the concurrence restrictions governing those elements. Under condition (3) all of this is, however, not sufficient for successful decipherment. Two things have generally been instrumental in completing the task: a BILINGUIS, one part of which is in a known language and script, and proper names occurring therein. They provide a reference point for testing hypotheses about the working of a forgotten system.

The primary function of a proper name is to identify a person or place rather than to express a meaning. Therefore foreign proper names are not usually translated but represented phonetically. Many important decipherments took advantage of this fact. Herodotus's historical account of Achaemenid kings and their names provided the crucial data for the decipherment of the cuneiform inscriptions of Persia and Mesopotamia. The names of Ptolemy, Cleopatra and Alexander the Great were the opening wedge needed for deciphering the Egyptian hieroglyphs; and solving the riddle of Linear B was greatly aided by the occurrence of the

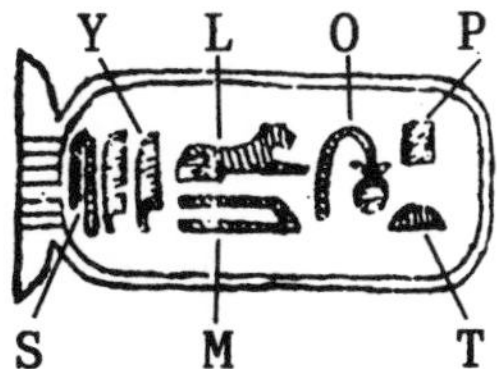

Figure 6 Cartouche with King Ptolemy's name as it appears on the Rosetta Stone with alphabetic values

place names *Knossos* and *Pylos* in inscriptions from Knossos and Pylos, respectively. If an inscription can be put into a historical and linguistic context, proper names are the most promising words to look for. They are moreover the most likely words to supply the data needed for establishing the first phonetic values of elements of the system.

The crucial steps of the decipherment of Egyptian hieroglyphs exemplify the general principles of scientifically sound decipherment referred to so far. In 1808 Étienne Quatremère, a French orientalist, suggested that Coptic was descended from the language of ancient Egypt (Coptic alphabet). His compatriot Jean-François Champollion was persuaded by this argument and used Coptic as a reference language for the reconstruction of Egyptian words. His determination to break the hieroglyphic code received a spectacular boost by the accidental discovery of a bilinguis: Napoleon's troops stumbled over the Rosetta Stone, an inscription dating from 197 BCE redacted in Greek and Egyptian, the Egyptian text being written in two scripts, hieroglyphic and demotic (for illustration see Bilinguis). As the Greek text contains several proper names, it was a reasonable assumption that the same names should also be present in the Egyptian text. Champollion believed that these names were written phonetically, an assumption that flew in the face of the general perception of the hieroglyphs at his time. He had arrived at this hypothesis by a very simple but pivotal observation: the Greek text had *fewer* than 500 words, while the hieroglyphic text consisted of 1,419 sign instances made up of only 66 types. This ruled out the possibility of an ideographic system which hieroglyphs were believed to be. Working, therefore, under the hypothesis that hieroglyphic writing was basically phonetic, Champollion tried to find the name of Ptolemy which occurs several times in the Greek version. Assuming that the royal name was graphically distinct, he identified a word enclosed in a Cartouche as the equivalent of the Greek *PTOLEMAIS*. He then gave the signs in the cartouche hypothetical alphabetic values as indicated in figure 6. The sound assignments could be validated by applying them to other cartouches as illustrated in figure 7. Repeating this procedure with as many as 80 cartouches known from other inscriptions, Champollion ascertained the basic phonetic signs of the Egyptian hieroglyphs. This was the breakthrough, although many details remained to be clarified. By relying on his knowledge of Greek and Coptic, and by reckoning with inaccuracies, polyvalence, systematic inconsistencies and the occurrence of unpronounced determinatives as in Cleopatra's name cartouche (figure 8), he eventually arrived at a complete system for the decipherment of the Egyptian hieroglyphs. The decipherments of other forgotten scripts were no less remarkable, and some were perhaps even more difficult,

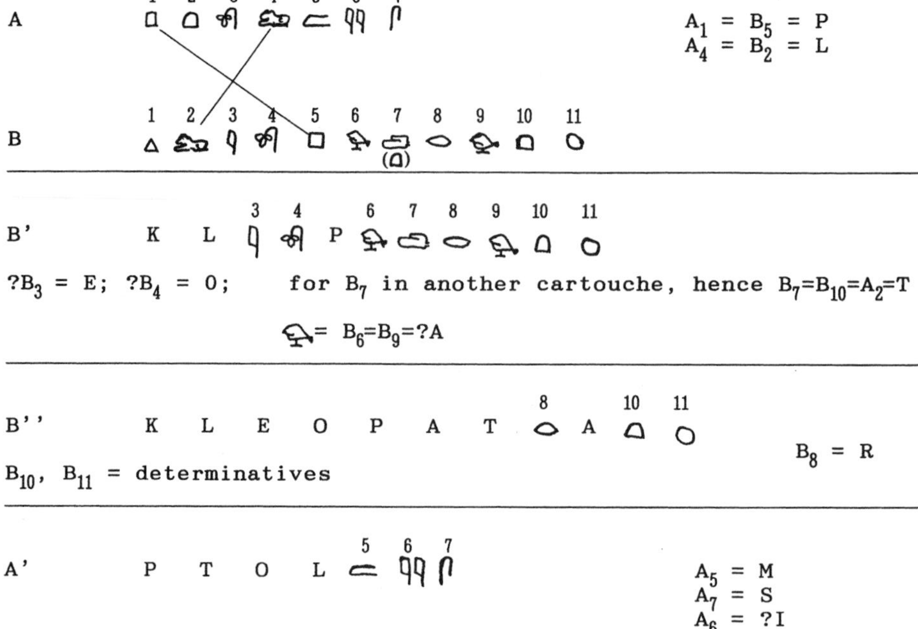

Figure 7 Champollion's successive steps in forming hypotheses about the phonetic values of signs in cartouches on the Rosetta Stone

but none was so universally acclaimed and celebrated as Champollion's accomplishment, perhaps because of the exceptional beauty of hieroglyphic inscriptions and because they were the key to what was clearly one of the grandest civilizations that ever existed.

The decipherment in the first half of the nineteenth century of cuneiform, associated with the names of Georg Friedrich Grotefend, Cornelius de Bruin (also known as Le Brun), Rasmus Rask, Henry Creswicke Rawlinson and Fox Talbot, among others, began with the simplest cuneiform script, that of OLD PERSIAN WRITING. From there it proceeded with the help of the great triscripts of Persepolis

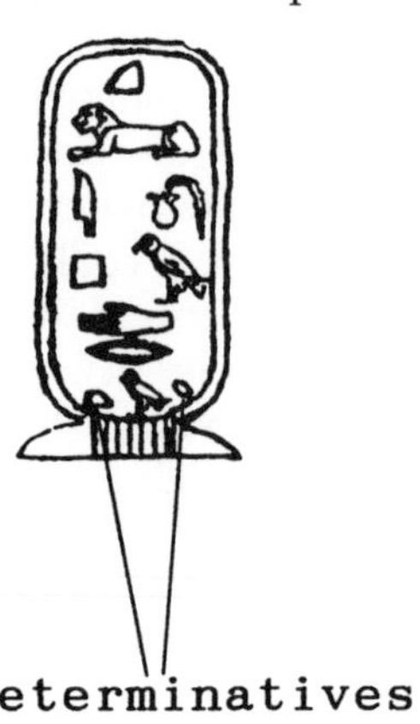

Figure 8 Determinatives in the cartouche with Cleopatra's name

and Behistun (in Old Persian, Babylonian and Elamite) to the more involved systems of ASSYRIAN, BABYLONIAN, AKKADIAN, SUMERIAN WRITING, ELAMITE WRITING and HITTITE CUNEIFORM. It opened up the world of cuneiform writing which in its cultural diversity and linguistic variety proved an even richer source of historical knowledge than the Egyptian literature.

The decipherment of Cretan Linear B by Michael Ventris in the 1950s is considered a brilliant intellectual feat chiefly for the method that led to success rather than for the contents of the documents it made accessible. Two obstacles had to be overcome: no bilingual inscription was available, and the language was unknown. Collateral evidence suggested that the language might be Greek. The number of different signs, 87, indicated a syllabic system. Working on these two hypotheses, Ventris developed an abstract 'syllabic grid', and by studying co-occurrence patterns of sign groups he was able to fill in the grid by matching the signs to the syllabic values. His method was purely experimental and systematic (figure 9).

a, a_2	e	i	o	u
ai				
ja	je		jo	
wa	we	wi	wo	
da	de	di	do	da_2
ka	ke	ki	ko	ku
ma	me	mi	mo	
na	ne	ni	no	nu, nu_2?
pa, pa_2?	pe	pi	po	pu
	qe	qi	qo, qo_2?	
ra, ra_2	re	ri	ro, ro_2	ru
sa	se	si	so	
ta, ta_2?	te, pte	ti	to	tu
	z?e		z?o, z?o_2	

Figure 9 Experimental syllabic grid for the decipherment of Linear B
Source: *Ventris and Chadwick 1953*

The decipherment of HITTITE HIEROGLYPHIC was perhaps the least dramatic of all, because it progressed slowly over some 70 years after the first inscriptions were published in the 1870s. There was no breakthrough, and no one scholar was solely or chiefly responsible. Ignace J. Gelb and Emil Forrer deserve major credit during the final phase, but many other scholars contributed to the decipherment. Part of the difficulty lay in the great number of signs, 497, of which some 60 syllabic signs had to be filtered out by scrupulous DISTRIBUTION ANALYSIS. The secret of Hittite hieroglyphic was solved by persistence and a multiplicity of avenues of approach rather than one imaginative technique or an ingenious mind.

Similarly, and even more so, the epigraphic history of Maya hieroglyphics was protracted and cumbersome. For a long time Maya inscriptions were considered incomplete writing which no one would ever be able to read again. Even after Yuri Valentinovich Knorosov made a credible case in the early 1950s for the phonetic element in the Maya script, it took another two decades before this insight bore fruit and the decipherment really took off, using Yucatec Maya as the reference language.

In the history of decipherment, individual genius has played an important role. As a field of inquiry, however, it progressed to the extent that the language dependency of all writing and its systematic character, however contaminated, became better understood, and linguistic insight was taken into account. The conceptual tools and techniques of decipherment have been refined and systematized. But there are still several early scripts, such as the Indus script, which have withstood their onslaught, for one or a combination of the following reasons: the text corpus is too small; the language is unknown; and no bilingual documents have shown up.

The fundamental principles on which successful decipherment rests can thus be summarized as follows:

1 The language should be known, at the very least its typological and genetic affiliation.
2 The text corpus should include texts of sufficient length rather than just emblematic inscriptions.
3 A bilinguis should be available.
4 The analysis of the data should be based on a linguistic approach, taking into account the segmentation of linguistic units, their distribution and their possible systematic links with units of writing.
5 Due attention should be paid to the defective and unsystematic nature of writing systems.
6 Collateral evidence, especially from historical and archaeological sources, should be made use of.

See also Polyvalence; Writing system.
Reading Champollion 1833; Chadwick 1958; Friedrich 1954; Laroche 1960; Vaillant 1972; Bibliothèque nationale 1990; Pope 1975; Coe 1992; Parpola 1993.

defective alphabet A term sometimes used to refer to consonant scripts where vowels are indicated by diacritics or not at all. The standard against which segmental writing systems are judged as 'defective' or 'full' is usually the Greek alphabet which because of its vowel letters has often been portrayed as a revolutionary innovation rather than a gradual improvement of the Semitic system on which it is based. This view has lost currency since the history of Semitic vowel indication, especially the Matres lectionis of Aramaic, has become better understood, and the Greek alphabet has come to be viewed as a continuation of rather than a radical break with the earlier tradition.
See also Consonant script; Greek alphabet.
Reading Millard 1976; Daniels 1992.

Dehong writing A vernacular writing used since the eleventh century CE by the Jingpo people in China's Yunnan province close to the border with Myanmar

ᥐ	ᥑ	ᥒ	ᥓ	ᥔ	ᥕ
ka	xa	ŋa	ŧsa	şa	ja
ᥖ	ᥗ	ᥘ	ᥙ	ᥚ	ᥛ
ta	tha	la	pa	pha	ma
ᥜ	ᥝ	ᥞ	ᥟ	ᥠ	ᥡ
fa	va	ha	ʔa	kha	ŧsha
ᥢ	ᥣ	ᥤ	ᥥ	ᥦ	ᥧ
na	a	i	e	ia	u
ᥨ	ᥩ	ᥪ	ᥫ	ᥬ	ᥭ
o	ua	ɯ	ə	aɯ	ai

Table 2 The basic consonant signs of Dehong writing with inherent a

(Burma). The name of the writing and the people using it is Chinese, the autonym being *laitai* 'Thai writing'. The system is clearly derived from PĀLI WRITING although its exact genealogy is unclear. Its vowel indication displays the typical Indian pattern, that is, consonant letters have an inherent *a*, other Vs being expressed by diacritics added thereto (tables 2, 3). The Dehong dialect of the Jingpo language has six tones which between 1956 and 1963 were experimentally indicated by Roman letters <r>, <e>, <a>, <v> and <c> inserted between the standard letters, the first tone being left unmarked. As of 1964, tones have been marked by the following diacritics: <¨>, <ˇ>, <`>, <·> and <´>. Two versions of the same sample text illustrate these modes of tone indication (figure 10).
Reading Kao 1992.

deities of writing All civilizations that possessed writing regarded it as extremely valuable, but its evolution was never recorded and hence invited mythological explanations. It is not surprising, therefore, that we find many legends which describe writing as a divine gift. In the Sumerian–Babylonian pantheon, the 'clear-eyed' lord of the sea Ea (Gk *Oannês*) was revered as the philanthropic originator of writing (figure 11). The Egyptians believed that Tehuti, commonly known by his Greek name Thoth, the god of wisdom, learning and magic, was also the inventor of numbers and letters as well as the scribe of all gods. The master of papyrus who was in charge of keeping the score of time, he is usually represented as a man with the head of an ibis or of a baboon (figure 12). In the

a	i	e	u	o	ɔ	ɯ,ə,ɯɯ,əu
aɯ						
ai,a:i			ui, oi		ɔi	ɯi, əi
au,a:u	iu.eu,ɛu					
am,a:m	im,em,ɛm		um,om		ɔm	ɯm,əm
an,a:n	in,en	ɛn	un,on		ɔn	ɯn,ən
aŋ,a:ŋ	iŋ,eŋ,ɛŋ		uŋ,oŋ		ɔŋ	ɯŋ,əŋ
ap,a:p	ip,ep,ɛp		up, op		ɔp	ɯp, əp
at,a:t	it,et,ɛt		ut, ot		ɔt	ɯt, ət
ak,a:k	ik,ek,ɛk		uk, ok		ɔk	ɯk, ək

Table 3 Vowels, diphthongs and consonant-final syllables in Dehong writing

Greek mythology he plays an important role as Hermes Trismegistus, a multifarious character blending features of Thoth and the ancient Greek messenger of the gods, Hermes, the golden-voiced interpreter who was also the god of commerce and cunning and the patron of thieves (figure 13). The Chinese knew of a heaven-sent turtle which emerged from a river, a set of characters incised on his back as a gift to a legendary emperor. In India, too, the invention of writing was considered a feat quite beyond human capacities. Ganesha, the elephant-faced god of wisdom and remover of obstacles, is credited with this achievement (figure 14). He is said to have broken off one of his tusks to use as a stylus. And Devanāgarī, the principal script of the Hindus, is the 'heavenly script'. In the Islamic tradition God himself was the creator of writing, which is why every

Tone indication with roman letters

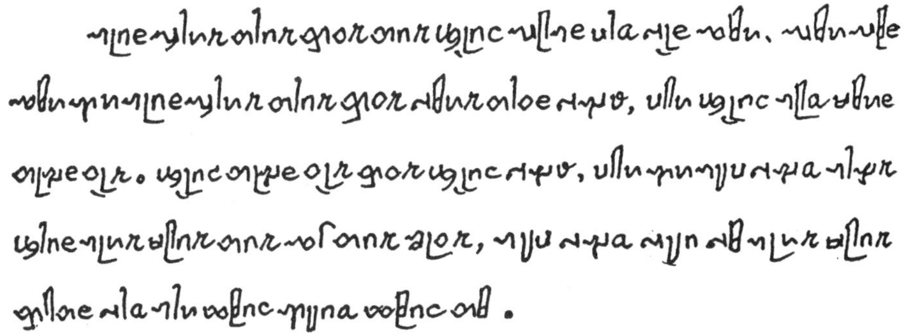

Tone indication with diacritics

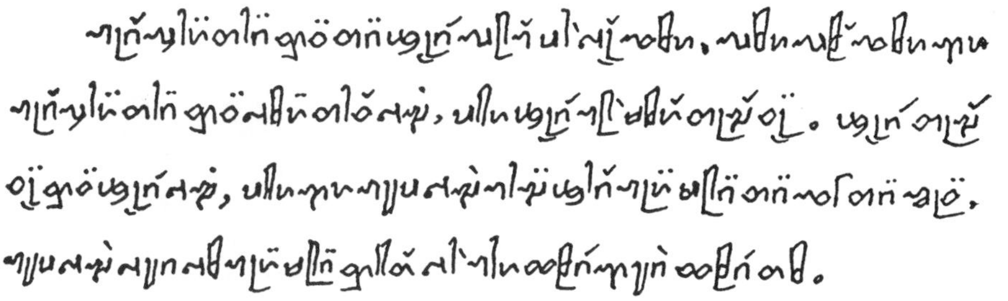

Translation

Our Communist Party and the 8th army and the new 4th army under the leadership of the Communist Party are the revolutionary army.

Figure 10 Specimen of Dehong writing in two versions of the script, making use of different modes of tone indication

Figure 11 Ea

Figure 12 Thoth

Figure 13 Hermes Trismegistus

letter is exalted. Odin of the *Northern Saga* is another god of writing, the inventor of the runes, just like his Mesoamerican colleague Itzamná, the supreme creator divinity of the Mayas (figure 15).

These and many similar legends reflect an important aspect of the early history of writing. Once fully developed, ancient scripts were rather complex. They were quite beyond the reach of the vast majority of the population. Scribes were a small and privileged class, often priests. For the masses engaged in productive

Figure 14 Ganesha

Figure 15 Maya rabbit god of the scribes

labour, writing was a mystery, a secret code understood only by those nearest to the gods whence it originated.

demotic script The most cursive of the three Egyptian scripts was called 'demotic', that is a popular script by Herodotus. Its origin and derivation from the hieratic book script is not fully understood, but all available evidence suggests that it first evolved as an administrative script used in the chanceries of upper Egypt. The first known text in demotic dates from 660 BCE, the last from 470 CE. During the 1,100 years of its use it changed relatively little. As a running script demotic was mostly used on papyrus, mummy wrappings and other soft surfaces, but it is also attested in monumental inscriptions, for instance in the middle section of the Rosetta Stone (for illustration see BILINGUIS). Although demotic is isomorphic with the other Egyptian scripts in that it reproduces in more cursive shapes the signs of hieratic and hieroglyphic, it also developed orthographic conventions of its own. In particular, new words not present in earlier stages of the Egyptian language were written phonetically as no word signs were available. However, in demotic the majority of Egyptian words continued to be written in the traditional fashion.
See also EGYPTIAN WRITING SYSTEM; HIERATIC SCRIPT.
Reading Brunner 1973.

determinatives Unpronounced key signs employed in many early logographic writing systems to specify meaning by indicating the class of words of related meaning to which the referent word belongs. The need for determinatives generally arose when word signs were used in rebus fashion for their sound values and hence became associated with several meanings. Determinatives were thus initially a means of coping with POLYVALENCE. The Sumerians used noun determinatives only, a relatively simple system which was adapted to Akkadian. However, the increased complexity of Akkadian writing required a greater number and more intensive use of determinatives for disambiguation. The Egyptian system of determinatives was similar in function but was more elaborate, comprising both general and specific determinatives as in the case of signs for *dog* and for *animal*. Moreover, Egyptian had determinatives for both nouns and verbs. Use of this sign class in Egyptian was often redundant, with at times several determinatives being used for a single referent word. Determinatives are also a common feature of HITTITE HIEROGLYPHIC and MAYA WRITING. The signs used as determinatives were usually existing logograms which were assigned a new function. Thus in Egyptian as well as in some of the cuneiform systems one and the same sign can be a logogram in one context and a determinative in another. In Chinese alone among the ancient scripts, determinatives – often called 'radicals' – were incorporated into logograms whenever disambiguation was felt necessary. This led to a proliferation of logograms as ever more compound characters were formed by adding determinatives to existing ones.
See also AKKADIAN; CHINESE WRITING SYSTEM; EGYPTIAN WRITING SYSTEM.
Reading (cuneiform) Reiner 1973; (Egyptian) Meltzer 1980; (Chinese) DeFrancis 1989, ch. 7; (Maya) Coe 1992.

Devanāgarī [Sanskrit *deva* 'heavenly' + *nāgarī* 'script of the city'] As the script of Sanskrit literature and other major Indo-Aryan languages such as Hindi, Marāṭhī, Sindhī and Nepali as well as many languages of other affiliations such as Mundari-Ho and Gondi, Devanāgarī is today the foremost script of India. It is a Brāhmī derivative of the northern Indian group which has been known under its present name since the eleventh century CE.

The Devanāgarī alphabet consists of 48 letters, 13 vowels and 35 consonants (with inherent /a/ V), which supposedly represent every sound of the Sanskrit language (table 4). The order of the alphabet in table 4 is that devised by the ancient Indian grammarians. The vowel letters at the beginning of the list appear

Vowels

*	+	
अ / अ	–	a
आ / आ	ा	ā
इ	ि	i
ई	ी	ī
उ	ु	u
ऊ	ू	ū
ऋ	ृ	ṛ (or ṛi)
ॠ	ॄ	ṝ (or ṝi)
ऌ	ॢ	ḷ (or ḷi)
ए	े	e
ऐ	ै	ai
ओ	ो	o
औ	ौ	au

Consonants

क	k	gutturals	प	p	labials
ख	k-h		फ	p-h	
ग	g		ब	b	
घ	g-h		भ	b-h	
ङ	ṅ		म	m	
च	c	palatals	य	y	semivowels
छ	c-h		र	r	
ज	j		ल	l	
झ / झ (or झ)	j-h		व	v	
ञ	n̄				
ट	ṭ	cerebrals	श	ś (or ç)	spirants
ठ	ṭ-h		ष	ṣ	
ड	ḍ		स	s	
ढ	ḍ-h		ह	h	
ण	ṇ				
त	t	dentals	:	ḥ (visarga)	
थ	t-h		·	ṃ or ṁ (anusvāra)	
द	d				
ध	d-h				
न	n				

* initial form of letters + medial form of letters

Table 4 The Devanāgarī script for Sanskrit

in two forms, initial and medial. There is no medial form for the short /a/ because this V does not occur in post-vocalic position and, at the same time, is the inherent V of the unmodified C letters. Medial V letters neutralize the inherent *a* of the C letter to which they are attached. The inherent V can also be muted, in word-final position, by a *virāma*, an oblique stroke added to the C letter, as in प /pa/, but प् /p/. Weak aspiration is represented by the *visarga*, a colon after the letter, as in सः /sah/. C clusters are represented by conjoining two or more C letters to form ligatures (table 5). As all of the basic letters have a vertical stroke

क्क /kka/	क्ख /kkha/	क्त /kta/	क्त्य /ktya/
क्त्र /ktra/	क्त्व /ktva/	क्थ /ktha/	क्न /kna/
क्म /kma/	क्य /kya/	क्र /kra/	क्ल /kla/
क्व /kva/			

Table 5 Some common Devanāgarī ligatures

व्यवहारान्नृपः पश्येद्विद्वद्भिर्ब्राह्मणैः सह ।
धर्मशास्त्रानुसारेण क्रोधलोभविवर्जितः ॥१॥

vyavahārān nṛpaḥ paśyed Vidvadbhir brāhmanaiḥ
saha dharmaśāstrānusāreṇa Krodhalobhavîvarjitaḥ

The ruler shall examine the trials together with learned Brahmins in accordance with the law, free of ire and passion.

Figure 16 Specimen of Sanskrit text in Devanāgarī script with transliteration and translation

and the characteristic horizontal bar on top, ligatures are often formed by adding a distinctive stroke only to the letter which keeps its inherent vowel. For example, the C cluster /nt/ is represented by conjoining the letters for /n+a/ न and /t+a/ त to form the ligature न्त /nta/. The non-linear marking of Vs has resulted in certain inconsistencies. For example, both /i/ and /i:/ were originally written as curves above the consonant sign, the former to the left and the latter to the right. For the sake of clear distinction the curves were later prolonged with a vertical downward stroke on the respective side. As a result, medial or final /i/ is now written before the consonant after which it is pronounced.

Like all Indian scripts, Devanāgarī is written from left to right. Word boundaries are not marked, as the horizontal top bars are usually linked to form an unbroken line. The line is only broken between words with final V, diphthong, nasal (*anusvāra*) or weak spirant (*visarga*) and words with initial C. Rather than writing successions of isolated words, Sanskrit orthography is sensitive to breath groups representing connected discourse. Sentences are marked by a perpendicular stroke at the end, as shown in the text specimen in figure 16. Two such strokes are used at the end of a text.

See also Brāhmī writing; Indian writing systems.

Reading Agrawala 1966; Daswani 1976; McGregor 1977.

diacritic [Gk διακριτικύς 'that distinguishes'] A mark added to a basic letter to alter its pronunciation, for example <a, á, à, â, ä, å, ă, ā, ą, ǎ, ã>. Diacritics are widely used to augment the Latin alphabet. Among the more common diacritics are accent marks <´, `, ˆ> as used in French, the Cedilla <¸> as in French and Portuguese, the Spanish Tilde <˜>, the Diaeresis or umlaut sign <¨> as in German, and the háček or wedge <ˇ> and under-hook <¸>, both used in several Slavic orthographies. Some diacritics are superimposed upon letters, such as the Polish slashed L<Ł ł>. Barred letters with a hyphen or short dash through the body of the letter as in <Đ Ħ Ŧ> are also occasionally used. Certain diacritics, especially those found on a standard typewriter, serve a variety of different functions. For example, the accent marks mentioned above are used both for pitch accent (French) and as tone marks (Chinese). The macron <¯> is used as a marker of vowel length (Classical Latin) or to indicate a high flat tone (Chinese). By contrast, the breve sign <˘> is used as a pedagogical aid to mark short Vs in Classical Latin.

In other alphabets and writing systems, diacritics are also common. In addition to accents, Classical Greek had two breathing marks known by their Latin names *spiritus asper* <‘> for rough breathing and *spiritus lenis* <’> for soft breathing (at first representing the left and the right half of the letter <H>). Hebrew, Syriac, Arabic and other CONSONANT SCRIPTS rely on diacritics for vowel indication. These systems of 'pointing' consist of dots, strokes or circles placed above, below or inside the consonant letter. The INDIAN WRITING SYSTEMS, too, can be understood as consisting of sets of consonant letters with inherent /a/ vowel, with other Vs being indicated by diacritic satellites attached to the basic letters. Japanese *kana* use diacritics systematically to mark a number of phonological distinctions. For instance, two small strokes (*nigoriten*) placed on the right shoulder of the letter differentiate voiced from unvoiced consonants. This device exploits a regularity of the Japanese phonology, thereby reducing the number of necessary basic signs. As a general rule, the need for diacritics tends to increase as the inventory of a writing system's basic signs becomes smaller.
See also ACCENT; TRANSCRIPTION.

diaeresis [Gk διαίρεσις] A diacritic mark of two dots placed over a vowel letter, also referred to as 'umlaut', depending on the function it serves. The diaeresis used over the second of two consecutive vowel letters indicates that the Vs are to be pronounced as two syllables rather than a diphthong or long V, e.g. English *coördinate*, French *naïf*. Marks of diaeresis for this function occur already in early Greek papyri, being a single or a double dot or, occasionally, an accent mark. In later manuscripts the form is usually a double dot <¨>. As an umlaut, on the other hand, <¨> indicates a change in the vowel quality: for example, in German it is used to mark the Vs [ɛ], [ø] and [y] which originally resulted from a vowel fronting sound change called *umlaut* (e.g. *älter* 'older', *schön* 'beautiful', *über* 'above').
See also DIACRITIC.

dictionary A reference book which lists the words of one, two or more languages providing information about their meaning, usage, pronunciation, spelling, parts of speech and history. The monolingual dictionary, which uses one language as a closed system where every definition refers back to itself, is a modern invention, but embryonic dictionaries and bilingual word lists were already compiled 5,000 years ago on Sumerian clay tablets. Word lists, the core of all dictionaries, are the prototypical example of decontextualized speech. Their objects are words rather than communicative units of language. In a list, words are isolated from their communicative context. They can be ordered on purely formal grounds and inspected with regard to formal properties. Dictionaries are the pre-eminent example of text genres which came into existence as a consequence of writing.

The internal organization of every dictionary depends on the structure of the writing system used for recording the language(s) in question. The alphabet is a powerful conceptual ordering system which determines the place of a word in a dictionary. In English, for example, words are arranged by their graphemes. As a result homophonous words often show up in very different places in the dictionary (e.g. *filter* and *philtre*). Other writing systems impose different ordering

principles on the organization of dictionaries and hence, to a large extent, on their users' perception of the language. In Chinese dictionaries words are arranged for semantic determinatives or radicals and the number of constituent strokes, the 214 radicals also being ordered for number of strokes. In Hebrew dictionaries and those of other Semitic languages the triconsonant root is the key for the arrangement of entries, again a principle which relies on graphemic form rather than pronunciation. A major by-product of the development of WRITTEN LANGUAGE, dictionaries also serve as an indispensable tool of language cultivation and standardization by using written lexemes as their elements and by setting up literary rather than vernacular usage as the reference standard of the language.
See also ALPHABETICAL ORDER; CONSONANT ROOT; RADICAL.
Reading Goody 1977; Harris 1980; Zgusta 1992.

digamma <F> [Gk δι 'twice' + γάμμα 'the letter Γ'] The sixth letter of the archaic Greek alphabet corresponding to Semitic ו *wāw*. It was called *digamma* by Roman grammarians of the first century CE because of its shape F resembling two superposed gammas <Γ>. It fell into disuse in Attic and Ionic Greek at an early time, apparently because there was no need to represent its sound value. It was retained, however, in some other varieties, especially in western Greek alphabets whence it entered the Latin alphabet as the letter <F>.
See also GREEK ALPHABET.

diglossia A language situation characterized by a conspicuous divergence between a literary or 'high' variety (H) and the colloquial or 'low' variety (L). In many cases such divergence is a consequence of the attempt to conserve a written variety in a form recognized as classic or associated with religious significance. This variety then came to be recognized as the proper incarnation of that language, although only a minority of speakers had access to it, those who were literate. Hence, diglossia is typically an outgrowth of restricted literacy.

For instance, Sanskrit became a language whose spoken realization depended on the rules that were committed to writing, while the substandard Prakrits were corrupted by perpetual change. Many of the modern literary languages of India conform to this pattern, as does Arabic, Javanese and a number of other languages. If the phenomenon of diglossia cannot without undue simplification be reduced to a dichotomy of spoken and written language, there can be no doubt that a literary language harnessed by the superimposed structure of a deliberately created graphical form is a key ingredient of diglossia, and that diglossia without writing is extremely rare, if it exists at all. The specific circumstances of socially and functionally differentiated H and L varieties differ greatly, as does the meaning of the term 'diglossia' as used by different investigators. In Arabic H is the classical language of the Qur'ān, a book language, as it were, and L is a set of unwritten dialects; in Greek both the archaizing Katharevousa (H) and the modern Demotiki (L) were used in writing. The Swiss–German diglossic situation is basically one characterized by a strong hiatus between very pronounced dialects and the written standard of German, usually referred to as *Schriftdeutsch* or 'literary German' in Switzerland. In some instances H and L represent different

historical stages of a language. There is also a difference in mode of acquisition, L being naturally acquired as a first language, while H is learned on the basis of grammatical rules laid down in writing. In a wider sense 'diglossia' also refers to the social coexistence of two genetically unrelated languages, such as Spanish (H) and Guarani (L) in Paraguay. What all these different cases have in common is that the functions of written communication are preferably if not exclusively carried out in H, while L is typically not used in writing at all.
Reading Britto 1986; De Silva 1976; Hudson 1991.

digraph **1** A combination of two letters to represent one sound, as initial and final in *thrash* for /θ/ and /š/, respectively. Using digraphs is one of the more common strategies in alphabetic writing to compensate for the disparity between letters and phonemes, alphabetically written languages typically having fewer letters than phonemes. When listing the complete inventory of graphemes of a given language, digraphs (and TRIGRAPHS) are included and recognized as units of the system. For English, such a list includes <ch, ck, gh, ph, sh, th, wh, ng, pn, ps, pt, ea, ee, ie, oo>, among others. Some letters, for example <q> in many European languages, occur exclusively in digraphs. **2** In a narrower sense the term refers to two letters graphically combined to form a new unit such as <Æ>, <Œ> and Dutch <ij>.
See also ORTHOGRAPHY.

digraphia The use of two or more different writing systems or scripts for the same language. Historically this is a very common phenomenon, since many languages have been reduced to writing more than once or used in writing by different communities with different preferences for a writing system or script. Often such preferences are indicative of other alignments, for instance religious or political.

Perhaps the earliest instance of digraphia is found in Egypt where a cursive script, called 'hieratic' by the Greeks, has been used for almost as long as the hieroglyphs. Here both scripts represent the same writing system: the signs of the HIERATIC SCRIPT (and later the DEMOTIC SCRIPT) differ from the hieroglyphs in their outer form, but not structurally in the way they relate to units of the language. From this case must be distinguished a digraphic situation involving different writing systems, as for instance that of Chinese written in Chinese characters and PINYIN, a script based on the Latin alphabet. This distinction can be summarized in the matrix shown in table 6. Modern examples of case (1) include Albanian, which used to be written in both the Greek and the Latin alphabets; Finnish, which until 1940 was known as Karelian in Cyrillic letters;

Digraphia	Different script	Different writing system
1 Egyptian	+	–
2 Chinese	+	+

Table 6 Two forms of digraphia

Romanian and Moldavian in Latin and Cyrillic, respectively; and Serbo-Croatian divided along the same lines, the Orthodox Serbs using the Cyrillic and the Roman Catholic Croats the Latin alphabet. Javanese may be cited as another instance of case (2), being written in Javanese and Latin scripts, the former a syllabic alphabet of the Indian type and the latter a segmental alphabet. Similarly, Sindhī is written in Perso-Arabic and Devanāgarī; Azerbaijani and Tadjik in Arabic and Cyrillic; and Mongolian in Mongolian and Cyrillic. Both Hausa and Swahili have been written in Arabic and Latin letters at different times but also overlapping. Some languages are, or were, written in three different scripts or writing systems, for example Kurdish which uses Latin letters in western Europe and in Turkey, Arabic in Syria, Iraq and Iran, and Cyrillic in the Commonwealth of Independent States. Uighur has been recorded in the same three scripts in China, Mongolia and the CIS, respectively. Digraphia is thus frequently encountered in regions of cultural contact and is often a result thereof. Religious schism is often expressed typographically: antique is Catholic, black letter Protestant. On the level of orthography, digraphic differentiations can also be observed. British and American spelling conventions are an example, as is the Swiss variety of German which does not include the grapheme <ß>.

Perhaps the most consequential aspect of digraphia is that it fosters linguistic divergence where such is desired. Claims of linguistic autonomy gain credibility in cases such as Hindi/Urdu or Serbian/Croatian where the two members belong to a continuum of varieties on linguistic grounds, but are strictly differentiated on the level of written representation. Since these graphic distinctions symbolize pronounced religious, cultural and political differences, and since there is a general tendency to regard the written form of a language as its proper embodiment, digraphia favours the development of two different language identities.
Reading Dale 1980; DeFrancis 1984a; Hodgson and Sarkonak 1987.

digraphic literacy The simultaneous use of two writing systems or scripts for one language by the same community. For several centuries Korean literati continued to use the Chinese script after their king had promulgated HAN'GŬL in the fifteenth century, because they considered it more dignified than the new vulgar script. When Turkey replaced the Arabic by the Latin alphabet in the 1920s both were used side by side during a transition period. In China, proponents of a writing reform advocate a policy of digraphia in which the Latin orthography PINYIN serves not as a replacement for the traditional system but as an addition, such that there will be a functional division of labour between the two systems: characters for literary and historical scholarship, and Pinyin for computers and other modern media of communication.
See also DIGRAPHIA; SCRIPT REFORM.
Reading DeFrancis 1984a.

direction of script The conventional course in which a script is written and (usually) read. Herodotus observed that 'the Greeks write their letters and reckon with counters from left to right, but the Egyptians go from right to left'. At that time, Greek writing had been fixed in the left-to-right direction in which it is used today, but it was also known that other orientations were customary elsewhere.

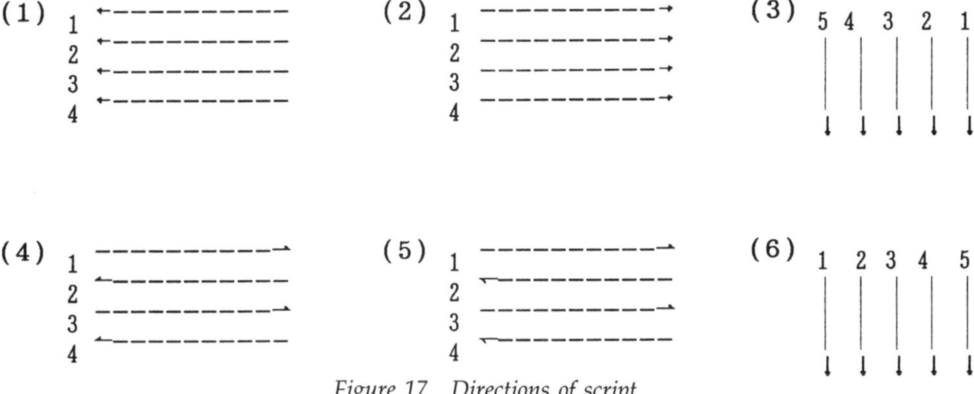

Figure 17 Directions of script

In earlier times, Greek was written from right to left, like Semitic scripts, and then BOUSTROPHEDON, changing direction on alternate lines. In the writing systems of the world a great variety of directions are attested, but the direction of writing is usually the same as that of reading. A system such as the MANGYAN SCRIPT, which is written in vertical columns from bottom to top but read horizontally from left to right, is exceptional.

The most common directions of script are shown as (1), (2) and (3) in figure 17. Direction (1), right to left in horizontal lines shifting downwards, is the direction of ancient and modern Semitic scripts including Phoenician, Aramaic, Hebrew and Arabic, as well as the numerous derivatives of Arabic such as Ottoman Turkish and Urdu. Direction (2), left to right in horizontal lines shifting downwards, is the direction of all descendants of Brāhmī and Greek. These include Kawi, Burmese, Tibetan, Thai, Devanāgarī, Gurmukhī, Latin, Cyrillic, Armenian and many others. Direction (3), top to bottom in vertical columns shifting from right to left, is the direction used since ancient times in Chinese writing and, under its influence, in several other scripts including Korean, Japanese, Hsi-hsia and *Chũ'nôm* (Vietnamese). Directions (4), (5) and (6) in figure 19 are also attested, although less commonly. Directions (4) and (5) are two varieties of BOUSTROPHEDON. In (4) the direction in which the signs are read changes with every line, while in (5) the orientation of the letters is also inverted or mirror image, as in some archaic Greek texts and in Hittite hieroglyphic. Direction (6) is again a vertical arrangement, but with columns shifting from left to right. The 'PHAGS-PA SCRIPT of Central Asia is written in this way, as well as the Mongolian script which evolved from it. Other arrangements have also been found. Inscriptions of the Celtic OGHAM SCRIPT are usually cut into the edge of a stone from bottom to top, whence longer inscriptions turn downward on another edge. Even more extraordinary is the arrangement of the Easter Island script where lines alternate in boustrophedon fashion as in (4), but the characters on the alternate lines are upside down. This suggests that the reader, moving from line to line, had to turn the wooden tablets on which the texts were inscribed.

Some scripts have changed their direction. In the formative period of cuneiform scribes turned their tablets 90 degrees when they increased in size. As a result, pictorial signs lost their iconic quality, becoming entirely conventional symbols.

Another case of change of direction is that of the Uighur script, a derivative of Aramaic which was originally written in (1), but changed to (3) under the influence of Chinese. Some scripts are habitually written in more than one direction. Modern Chinese and Japanese books are printed both in (3) and in (2), and in handwriting (2) is becoming ever more common. Newspapers and other popular print media moreover use both directions simultaneously, often on the same page.

Another aspect of the direction of scripts is the orientation of signs. The Latin alphabet has symmetrical letters such as *H, M, T, U* and *W*, and asymmetrical ones such as *C, E, F, P* and *R*. The latter are facing to the right and give the script a right-running orientation. In a similar manner every script has an orientation which reflects the mechanical aspects of how the graphic shapes were physically produced. It is here that the DECIPHERMENT of unknown scripts begins, because the orientation of elementary signs is often the key to determining the direction of a script. For instance, alternating orientations of signs indicate boustrophedon writing. Unless the direction of a script has been identified, decipherment cannot proceed.

See also ARABIC SCRIPTS; BRĀHMĪ WRITING; GRAPHETICS; GREEK-DERIVED SCRIPTS; INDIAN WRITING SYSTEMS; SEMITIC WRITING.

Reading Powell 1981; Sirat 1987; Van Sommers 1989.

distribution analysis A structuralist method of linguistic analysis which excludes any non-observable evidence and, in order to determine the systematic relations and structural properties of language elements, relies on the formal description of their distribution alone. The identification and classification of elements is accomplished by formal *discovery procedures* of segmentation and substitution. This method was designed in the 1940s and early 1950s chiefly for recording and analysing languages unknown to the linguist. In theoretical linguistics it has been largely superseded by the paradigm of generative grammar which relies on introspection and sophisticated informants. But in one field where such are not available it still offers a fruitful avenue of approach: decipherment. It can help to determine the DIRECTION OF SCRIPT and to recognize and classify the signs.

See also DECIPHERMENT.

Reading Harris 1954.

Divehi hakura (*also Dives akuru*) A southern Indian script formerly used in the Maldive Islands, probably derived from the SINHALESE SCRIPT in the twelfth century CE (table 7). Little is known about the exact genealogy of this writing which is sparsely documented on a few tombstones. It was replaced by the Maldivian alphabet, an unrelated script adopted after the Islamic conquest of the Maldives.

See also MALDIVIAN SCRIPT.

Dives akuru *See* DIVEHI HAKURA

Djuka syllabic writing A script invented in 1910 by Afaka Atumisi, a Bush Negro from eastern Surinam (at the time a Dutch colony), for the Djuka language,

h	ś	n	r	b	ḷ	k	ɔ	w	m	f	d

t	l	g	ñ	s	ḍ	z	ṭ	y	j	c

Table 7 The Old Maldivian script Divehi hakura

an English-based creole also known as Aukaans. Like Chief Njoya, the inventor of the West African BAMUM WRITING, Afaka claims to have been inspired by a visitation indicating that a script would be revealed to him. He subsequently devised a number of characters, drawing on a variety of shapes including some Roman letters and Arabic numerals as well as traditional African graphic symbols, some of which are used as pictographs. The presence of the last class of signs in the script is a matter of some interest, because it suggests an African cultural inheritance in the field of graphic symbolism in spite of the Bush Negroes' separation from West Africa for over 150 years at the time the script was devised. The syllabary consists of 58 signs, five with the vocalic values [a], [e], [i], [o] and [u], and the remainder syllabic CV signs (table 8).
Reading Dalby 1968.

Drāvidī writing (*also* Dāmilī) A variety of the Brāhmī script documented in a few inscriptions of central India dating from the second century BCE. Although most letters are those of Brāhmī, there are some differences, especially in the vowel indication. Unlike Brāhmī, consonant letters have no inherent *a* V which instead is expressed by a horizontal bar (which in Brāhmī marks vowel length).
See also BRĀHMĪ WRITING; INDIAN WRITING SYSTEMS.
Reading Chatterji 1966.

dual alphabet The combination of capital and small letters in a single system. MINUSCULE or small letters are derived from MAJUSCULES; but notwithstanding early cursive specimens of what became minuscules, a full minuscule alphabet was only slowly developed. The dual alphabet making use of capital and small letters followed the introduction of the Caroline minuscule.
See also CAROLINGIAN REFORM.
Reading Thompson 1906.

duality of patterning A universal structural characteristic which distinguishes human languages from less complex sign systems. Also known as 'double articulation', it means that language is structured on two different levels: the units of the 'lower' level of phonology are arranged to form units of the 'higher' level of grammar. Hence many thousands of morphemes can be represented economically by different combinations of a small set of phonemes. In alphabetic writing

	a	e	i	o	oe
	1 [a:]	2 [e]	3 [i:]	4 [ɔ]	5 [u]
b	6 [ba:]	7 [be]	8 [bi:]	9 [bɔ]	=9 [bu]
d	10 [da:]	11 [de]	12 [di:]	13 [dɔ]	=13 [du]
dj				14 [djɔ]	=14 [dju]
f	15 [fa:]	16 [fe]	17 [fi:]	18 [fɔ]	=18 [fu]
g	19 [ga:]	20 [ge]	21 [gi:]	22 [gɔ]	=22 [gu]
j	23 [ja:]	24 [je]			25 [ju]
k	26 [ka:]	27 [ke]	28 [ki:]	29 [kɔ]	=5 [ku]
kw	30 [kwa:]				
l=r	31 [la:]	32 [le]	=32 [li:]	33 [lɔ]	=33 [lu]
m	34 [ma:]	35 [me]	=35 [mi:]	36 [mɔ]	=36 [mu]
n	37 [na:]	38 [ne]	39 [ni:]	40 [nɔ]	=40 [nu]
nj	41 [nja:]				
p	=6 [pa:]	42 [pe]	43 [pi:]	44 [pɔ]	45 [pu]
s	46 [sa:]	47 [se]	=47 [si:]	48 [sɔ]	=48 [su]
t	49 [ta:]	50 [te]	51 [ti:]	52 [tɔ]	53 [tu]
tj	54 [tja:]				
w	55 [wa:]	56 [we]	=56 [wi:]		

Table 8 Afaka's syllabary for the Djuka language with sound values indicated in the Dutch alphabet. Source: *L'Afrique et la lettre 1986*

this duality is reproduced as letters are combined to form (visual) morphemes. Logographic writing systems are often thought to lack this feature, which is why their sign inventories are much more numerous than alphabets. However, closer inspection reveals that duality of patterning also underlies these systems, although it is structurally independent of the relationship between the phonological and morphological strata of language. Rather, the graphic system itself exhibits double articulation. For example, Chinese characters have an internal structure, being composed of smaller elements known as radicals. These radicals also occur independently, thus fulfilling a double function as building blocks and as self-sufficient characters. This is a structural analogue of phonemes, e.g. /eɪ/, which can function as morphemes or parts thereof, e.g. *a* and *able*, by exploiting the duality of sense-determinative and sense-discriminative units of language. Thus,

in their graphical make-up Chinese characters are based on a universal principle of human language.
Reading Martinet 1965; Coulmas 1984.

Dutch alphabet The 26-letter Latin alphabet is used for Dutch with an additional digraph <IJ ij> for the diphthong [ɛi] which is considered a separate letter. The present spelling conventions are laid down in the *Woordenlijst* of 1954, a document jointly commissioned by the Dutch and Belgian governments. It is the result of several schemes for standardizing and simplifying the spelling during the past 150 years, most recently the orthography reform of 1934 and the *Spellingwet* 'Spelling Act' of 1947. The spelling system is quite regular, largely following phonological principles with some aspects of the morphology also reflected in the spelling. The difference between open and closed syllables is clearly shown in writing, the former being spelt with a single vowel letter whereas the vowel letter is geminated in the latter, unless the vocalic nucleus of the syllable is short and unstressed.

Dutch uses the acute <´> and grave <`> accents. The numerous French loan words usually retain their accent except in initial position: thus *etage* rather than *étage*. Likewise, words ending in *-ée* drop the accent, as in *orchidee*. Accents are also used for emphasis. The grave is usually placed on the letter <e> as in *tè behoudend* '*too* conservative'. The acute is used on all other letters for emphasis, to mark difference in meaning and to avoid ambiguity, for instance: *een* 'a' vs *één* 'one'; *voor* 'for' vs *vóór* 'in front of'; *verstrekkend* 'supplying' vs *vèrstrekkend* 'far-reaching'. Although the Dutch orthography is a highly standardized system, it allows for some variation. The 1954 *Woordenlijst* makes provisions for alternative spellings, listing preferred and permissible varieties, especially regarding the many loans. Thus there are *cultuur/kultuur* 'culture', *cadeau/kado* 'present', *historisch/histories* 'historical' etc., the first members of these pairs being the traditional, the second members the Dutchified spellings. There is also some divergence between Dutch and Belgian (Flemish) usage, as the Flemings tend to give preference to the Dutchified version to counteract the influence of French.
Reading *Woordenlijst* 1954; de Rooij and Verhoeven 1988.

dyslexia A general cover term for disturbances in the ability to read. A broad distinction is made between *developmental* and *acquired* dyslexia. The former is observed in children with otherwise normal intelligence who are up to two years behind expected grade level in reading and exhibit serious difficulties in the acquisition and use of written language. The incidence of developmental dyslexia is estimated at between 5 per cent and 10 per cent of the population, depending on the definition that is applied. It is higher by a factor of three to five in males than in females. Acquired dyslexia often results from brain injury and is usually associated with pathological conditions such as AGRAPHIA and other aphasic syndromes. Etiologies vary on a wide scale from a disconnection between the visual and language areas of the cerebral cortex, through a disorder of perceptual recognition, to a disruption of the internal lexicon. Although disturbances of written language skills were late to be taken up in neurological and neurolinguistic research, both acquired and developmental dyslexia are now fields of very active research.

See also READING DISABILITY.

Reading Ellis 1984b; Vellutino 1979.

E, e /iː/ The fifth letter of the English alphabet developed from Semitic *hē*, in the Phoenician script. In Semitic scripts it indicated the consonant /h/ which, at the time the Greeks adopted the Phoenician script, had no equivalent in Greek. The letter ∍, called *epsilon*, was thus revalued to represent a vowel. The small letter <e> was derived from the uncial form of the capital.

Easter Island script (*also* Rongo-rongo script) This script is an indigenous development of the Easter Islands, probably used to write the eastern Polynesian language Rapanui. The script is documented on a few wooden tablets and some other artefacts (figure 1). It is based on some 120 elementary signs of which between 1,500 and 2,000 logograms have been composed. In as far as the script has been deciphered, it would seem that Rongo-rongo inscriptions consist of key words which in reciting the texts were syntactically augmented and perhaps transformed to produce comprehensible discourse. The individual signs are strung together in unbroken sequence without any apparent structure.

A noteworthy feature of the Easter Island script concerns its outer form. In addition to the boustrophedon alternation of the direction of the lines, the signs in every other line are upside-down. This suggests that the reader turned the tablet when moving from one line to the next.

Reading Barthel 1969.

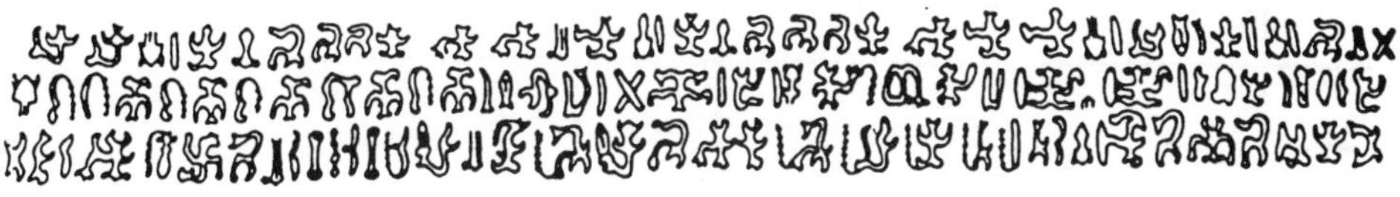

Figure 1 Three lines of Easter Island script from a wooden tablet (Musée de Braine-le-Comte, Belgium)

economy of writing A principle proposed by Ignace Gelb (1963, p. 72) governing the development of writing systems which aims 'at the effective expression of the language by means of the smallest possible number of signs'. Hence the gradual reduction of the number of basic signs as writing systems develop from the representation of words to syllables to phonemes. Certain conclusions can be drawn about unknown writings simply by looking at the number of different signs. An inventory of several hundred signs points to a logographic system, while a system consisting of between 50 and 100 signs should be syllabic. In this regard the internal economy of writing systems is clearly informative. However, the thesis that the principle of economy generally determines the development of writing is hard to defend. Many systems across the ages exhibit features which hardly support a general principle of economy. The redundant use of determinatives in the Egyptian writing system is one; modern English spelling is another. Gelb's principle has also been criticized for focusing too narrowly on the writing system's inventory of signs. In determining the facility of using a system and hence presumably its development this feature interacts with others, especially simplicity, unequivocalness and faithfulness. Most existing writing systems could be more efficient and economical than they are, had they been constructed solely for maximizing efficiency. As the most conspicuous linguistic subsystem, a language's writing system lends itself more easily than any other to linguistic conservatism resisting change. This inevitably corrupts the economy of the system.

See also Writing, development of; Writing system.

Reading Gelb 1963; 1974; Coulmas 1992.

Egyptian scripts Three scripts were developed in Egyptian writing, known as hieroglyphic, hieratic and demotic. They represent successive stages of cursivization while being structurally identical. Although the pictorial appearance of the individual hieroglyphic signs of monumental inscriptions was highly stylized in the hieratic book script (mid second millennium BCE) and completely lost in the popular demotic script (seventh century BCE), these changes in the outer form of Egyptian writing (table 1) did not result in any functional changes concerning

Hieroglyphic					Hieroglyphic book script	Hieratic			Demotic
2900–2800 BCE	2700–2600 BCE	2000–1800 BCE	c.1500 BCE	500–100 BCE	c.1500 BCE	c. 1900 BCE	c. 1300 BCE	c.200 BCE	500–100 BCE

Table 1 Three Egyptian scripts: hieroglyphic, hieratic and demotic (with years BCE)

the inner form of the writing system. The older hieroglyphic script continued to be used side by side with the two younger scripts until the end of Egypt's literary tradition. For example, two of the three text blocks on the famous Rosetta Stone dating from 196 BCE are in Egyptian, one hieroglyphic and one demotic.
See also BILINGUIS; DEMOTIC SCRIPT; EGYPTIAN WRITING SYSTEM; HIERATIC SCRIPT; HIEROGLYPH.
Reading Helck 1973.

Egyptian writing system Egyptian writing is logosyllabic with beginnings of phoneme representation. It represents both words and meaningless sounds. In the earliest inscriptions dating from about 3000 BCE, hieroglyphic signs are already used for their sound values rather than for the semantic contents indicated by their pictorial form. In the fully developed system the individual signs serve three different functions which are not graphically distinguished: as logograms, phonograms and determinatives. Hence, the same sign can be used as a phonogram or as a determinative, depending on the context. Logograms or word signs are mostly used for concrete nouns or verbs signifying perceptible actions or movements, such as *to hit, to fly, to walk, to eat*. Phonograms are of various kinds. In accordance with the REBUS PRINCIPLE, one logogram may stand for a homophonous word. Homophony is perceived as identity of the sequence of consonants, which is another way of saying that, as phonograms, Egyptian signs represent Cs only, while Vs must be supplied by the reader. Phonograms are not limited to rebus words, but are also used to represent parts of words. There are phonograms standing for three and two Cs as well as a small set representing single Cs. This set of 27 letters is sometimes referred to as the hieroglyphic alphabet (table 2). Monoconsonant signs are also used as phonetic complements to reinforce the pronunciation of a C already given in another sign. They often augment bi- or triconsonant signs, repeating their final C as a reading aid. This practice results in spellings such as $C_1C_2C_3 + C_3$: for instance, the word *netjeret* 'goddess' is spelt *nrt* + *t* + *r* + *t* + determinative (figure 2).

The true sound value of the phonograms has been a controversial issue. The view that monoconsonant signs stand for individual Cs has been challenged by Gelb, who argued on theoretical grounds that these must be considered to have syllabic values, that is, C* where * is an unspecified vowel. However, the prominence of Cs in Egyptian writing agrees well with the fact that, like Semitic languages, Egyptian has a word structure based on CONSONANT ROOTS.

In popular transcriptions the letter <e> is conventionally inserted between consonants except after the glottal stop which is transcribed as <a>. In scholarly works only the Cs are written: thus *nfrt* rather than *neferet*. The actual pronunciation of many Egyptian words remains unknown, although comparison with Coptic, the last developmental stage of the Egyptian language, has clarified some uncertainties (COPTIC ALPHABET). Whatever their real sound value, with monoconsonant signs Egyptian writing comes to the threshold of phonetic writing, but throughout its long history it never parts with logograms or determinatives.

While exploiting homophony strengthens the phonographic side of the system, it also creates confusion, as more words are represented by the same signs. As a remedy such words are supplemented with determinatives. For example, the

Sign	Transcription
𓄿	(vulture) *3*
𓇋	(flowering reed) *i͗*
𓇌	(two flowering reeds) *y*
𓏭	(oblique strokes) *y*
𓂝	(forearm and hand) *ʿ*
𓅱	(quail chick) *w*
𓏲	(cursive development of 𓅱) *w*
𓃀	(foot) *b*
𓊪	(stool) *p*
𓆑	(horned viper) *f*
𓅓	(owl) *m*
𓈖	(water) *n*
𓂋	(mouth) *r*
𓉔	(reed shelter) *h*
𓎛	(wick of twisted flax) *ḥ*
𓐍	(placenta?) *ḫ*
𓄡	(animal's belly) *ẖ*
𓊃	(door bolt) *s*
𓋴	(folded cloth) *s*
𓈙	(pool) *š*
𓈎	(hill) *ḳ*
𓎡	(basket with handle) *k*
𓎼	(jar-stand) *g*
𓏏	(loaf) *t*
𓍿	(tethering rope) *ṯ*
𓂧	(hand) *d*
𓆓	(snake) *ḏ*

Table 2 The hieroglyphic alphabet

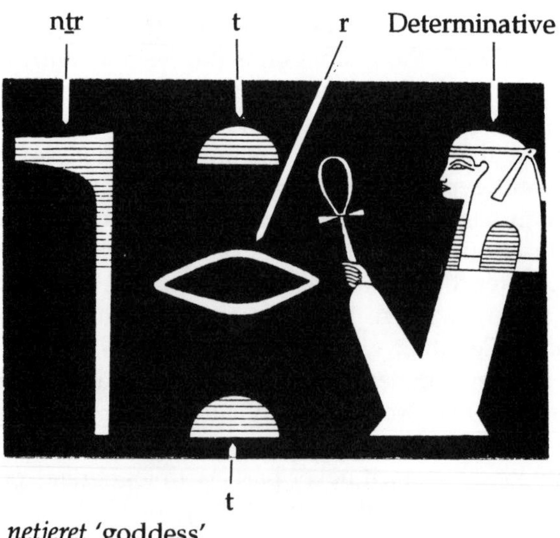

Figure 2 Phonetic complements in the word netjeret *'goddess'*

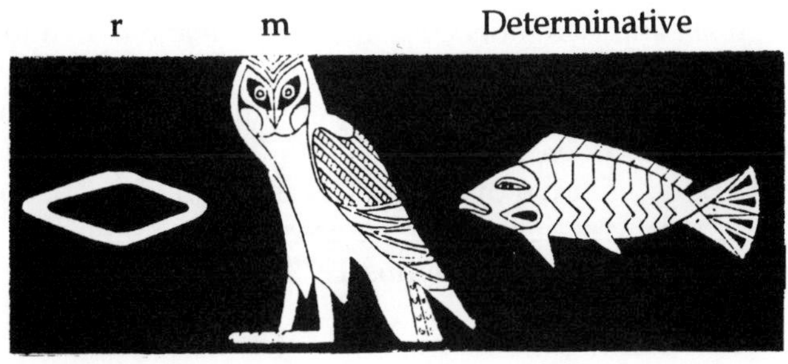

rem 'fish'

rem 'to cry'

Figure 3 Phonograms supplemented by determinatives

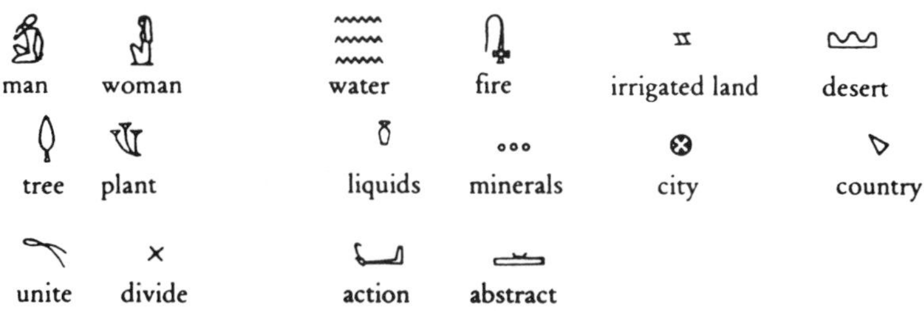

Table 3 Some common determinatives

words for 'fish' and 'to cry' are both spelt with the phonograms for *r* and *m*. To distinguish them, the first is supplemented with a determinative depicting a fish, and the second with a determinative showing a tear-shedding eye (figure 3). Determinatives are extensively used: only the most common words are written without any, and more than one are commonly used in one word (table 3). Hence they are often redundant, as when a fully spelt-out word with no obvious homophone counterpart is still supplemented with a determinative. Where such writing is moreover augmented with phonetic complements it becomes rather pleonastic. For instance, the word *menhedj* 'writing palette' is phonetically spelt with a biconsonant sign *mn* and two monoconsonant signs *h* and *d*. In addition, there is a phonetic complement *n* and a determinative depicting the object (figure 4).

Egyptian writing spans one of the longest continuous literary traditions, having been in use for some 3,000 years.

See also BILINGUIS; CHAMPOLLION; DECIPHERMENT; DEMOTIC SCRIPT; DETERMINATIVES; HIERATIC SCRIPT; HIEROGLYPH.

Reading Gelb 1963; Schott 1973; Vernus 1977; Meltzer 1980; Ray 1986.

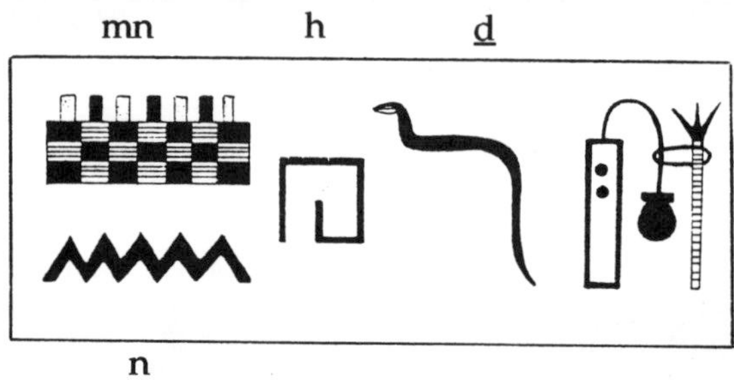

Figure 4 Pleonastic writing for the word menhedj *'writing palette': the second consonant of the biconsonant sign* mn *is repeated and the phonetically written sequence is supplemented with a determinative*

Elamite writing Elam, a region in western Iran, knew two different kinds of writing. A still undeciphered pictorial script which is generally known as proto-Elamite is documented on several hundred clay tablets dating from the twenty-eighth century BCE. In the first half of the second millennium the Elamites began to write their language with Sumerian-Akkadian cuneiform imported from neighbouring Mesopotamia. Since Elamite, a language of unknown affiliation, was unrelated to either of these languages, the adaptation of cuneiform led to drastic changes of the system. A major shift towards sound writing brought about an almost completely syllabic system by the thirteenth century. The inventory of cuneiform signs was reduced to 113. The general principle of adaptation was to use the Sumerian-Akkadian signs for their sound value, although in Elamite some signs assumed different values. Only 25 signs were also used as logograms for highly frequent words. The number of DETERMINATIVES was reduced to seven. One of them, a single perpendicular wedge originally used as a determinative for place names and other nouns, came to be used so frequently that in late inscriptions it virtually assumed the function of a WORD BOUNDARY marker.

See also CUNEIFORM WRITING.

Reading Friedrich 1966; Vallat 1986.

English phonotypic alphabet A phonetic script for English designed in 1847 by Isaac Pitman and Henry Ellis. It was never widely used, although a few issues of the *Phonotypic Journal* were printed in it (figure 5). However, it became important as the basis of the INTERNATIONAL PHONETIC ALPHABET.

Reading Kelly 1981.

FONOTIPIC JURNAL:

PUBLIST AT ƷE

FONETIC INSTITUSUN, 5, NELSUN PLAS, BAT.

[Nr. 62. FEBRUERI, 1847. Vol. 6.]

ƷE INTRODUCSUN OV PRINTIŊ, AND ƷE SPELIŊ REFORM.

Befor ƌe invenʃun ov ƌe inestimabl art ov Printiŋ, mancind war suŋc in ƌe grosest ignorans, and oprest undur ƌe most abject despotizm ov tirani. Ʒe clurji, hu befor ƌis era held ƌe ce ov ol ƌe lurniŋ in Urup, war ƌemselvz ignorant, ƌo proud, prezumtuus, arogant, and artful. Ʒar devisiz war sun detected tru ƌe invenʃun ov Tipografi. Az it ma naturali be imajind, meni ov ƌem, az wel az ƌe bref men, or riturz, hu livd bi ƌar manuscripts for ƌe laiti, war veri avurs tu ƌe progres ov ƌis invenʃun. Ʒa went so far az tu atribut it tu ƌe instigaʃun ov ƌe devl; and sum ov ƌem wornd ƌar herurz agenst uziŋ suc diabolical buks az war ritn wiƌ ƌe blud ov ƌe victimz hu devoted ƌemselvz tu hel for ƌe profit or fam ov instructiŋ auƌurz.

Figure 5 The phonotypic alphabet in use

English spelling Among alphabetic orthographies the English spelling system is one of the most complex. Criticism launched against it has a long tradition. Usually, English orthography is condemned because it is far removed from a simple phonemic script which is often thought to be the hallmark of alphabetic notation. Some linguists though have taken a different view. In a widely quoted assessment Chomsky and Halle (1968) have praised English spelling as coming 'remarkably close to being an optimal orthographic system for English'. Venezky's (1970) extensive study also emphasizes the underlying regularities of the system rather than the superficially irregular spellings. However, because such underlying rules are highly abstract, they may not be easily discovered. Such scholars who defend English orthography on the grounds that it is based on some kind of relationship between spelling and phonological and/or morphological patterns, however complex, have usually ignored the practical needs of ordinary readers and writers. While English spelling is an acceptable system for proficient readers, it clearly presents considerable difficulties to the writer as well as to young or foreign learners.

On the level of grapheme–phoneme correspondence, which most people are likely to perceive as relevant for a good spelling system, English exhibits a great deal of irregularity and polyvalence. Irregularity means that the spelling of a sound or a sequence of sounds in a word is unique and hence cannot be accounted for by a rule (table 4).

among	eye	quay
answer	friend	shoe
build	hour	sugar
clerk	monk	two
comb	once	who
do	people	you

Table 4 Irregular English spellings

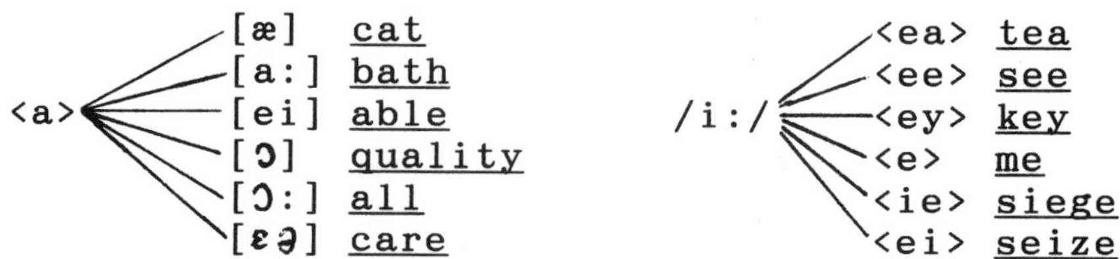

Figure 6 Polyvalence in English spelling

Polyvalence means that the same letter represents several different sounds and vice versa (figure 6). Conversely, the same sound is represented by several letters. For instance, the phoneme /s/ can be spelt <c> as in *mice*, <s> as in *send*, <sc> as in *scent*, or <ss> as in *miss*. Polyvalence of a much more serious proportion has been discovered for the spelling of vowels by Nyikos (1988). In a survey of common words he found 80 different GRAPHEMES for the back V phoneme /u/ as in *truancy*, and, more generally, 1,120 different graphemes for the 40 phonemes of English. Not all of these spellings are arbitrary. Many can be explained by historical processes or morphological rules. Nevertheless, many of these relationships are so complex and opaque that they are of little help to the learner. English spelling is more abstract in its principles than a grapheme–phoneme correspondence system. Consequently it takes little advantage of the fact that English speech makes do with some 40 phonemes. Clearly, many of the conventions of the written language are not paralleled in speech. How did such a situation evolve?

Three major developments account for the complexities of the English spelling system. When the Latin alphabet was first used to write English, there were just 23 letters for some 40 phonemes. No distinction was made between <i> and <j> or <v> and <u>, and there was no <w>. Some additional letters were then taken from the runic alphabet, such as the thorn <þ> for /θ/. Since, however, these were not sufficient, some letters were used for more than one sound, and some sounds were represented by DIGRAPHS and other letter combinations.

Additional complications arose when, after the Norman conquest, English spelling was influenced by French. As a result, the gap between sound and symbol continued to widen. For instance, <u> was replaced by <ou> in several words such as *house*. The Latin suffix <-or> became <-our> in Norman French whence it was adopted into Middle English, although not all existing loan words were affected. General lack of consistency accounts for rival spellings such as *honour, humour* vs *governor, actor*. The Normans also helped to establish <sh> and <wh> spellings, and instead of <cw> as in *cween* they introduced <qu>. In some words they inserted <g> in front of <h>, for example *night*. During the same period <u> was replaced by <o> before <m>, <n> or <v> for graphical reasons, a succession of arcs being difficult to read: hence *come, love* and *son*. Many French and Latin loan words which entered the language between the twelfth and the fifteenth centuries retained their original spelling. In Old English <c> was used to represent /k/, but with the adoption of French and Latin derivatives such as *ceiling, precede, receive* it came to represent /s/ as well. Similarly, <th> and <ph> spellings came into the language with Greek and Latin origin words, some as reformations based on false etymologies, e.g. *author* vs Lat. *auctor*. In the sixteenth and seventeenth centuries many words were re-Latinized to show their etymologies: examples are *debt, doubt* and *salmon,* which were formerly written as *dette, doute* and *samon* in Middle English.

The third formative event in the development of English spelling was the introduction of printing towards the end of the fifteenth century. William CAXTON and other printers who followed his lead did much to reduce the extensive variation in spelling common at the time. But they also introduced some peculiar spelling rules from Holland where Caxton was raised. By using the speech of London as their point of reference, they greatly contributed to the creation of a written norm and the notion of a 'correct' spelling. The printing press thus became a powerful agent of language standardization and stabilization. By the mid-seventeenth century printers had agreed on a fixed spelling system, one which has remained relatively stable ever since. However, because the spoken language underwent substantial changes, over time this led to a serious discrepancy between spelling and pronunciation.

The present spelling system reflects its complex history and the various influences it absorbed. Correspondences between written and spoken English can be ascertained on different levels. Orthographic words indicate pronunciation, often in a regular phonemic manner, but pronunciation is not always predictable from spelling, and the representation of individual phonemes is often complicated and perplexing. At the same time correspondences are functional between spelling and the morphemic and word levels. In word paradigms, preserving the visual identity of morphemes is generally given preference over the representation of phonetic differences. A massive intake of loan words has furthermore introduced many exceptional spellings which cannot be subsumed under any rule, e.g. *bizarre, czar, gazette, moustache.* The complexities of the English spelling system, then, can be accounted for by the fact that it rests on a number of structurally different and often competing principles.

Despite all these problems, the system has withstood more than three centuries of reform proposals with only slight changes. Even the most serious and successful revision, Noah Webster's formulation of an AMERICAN SPELLING, produced only minor simplifications. Its stability over time and throughout a vast speech community is remarkable. As an orthography where uniformity and consistency are regarded as more important than transparency and simplicity of rules, it is a prime example for showing that the developmental forces at work in the spoken and the written language are not the same. It furthermore illustrates the fact that alphabetic writing systems are not always or exclusively employed to graphically represent phonologic structures.

See also ETYMOLOGICAL SPELLING.

Reading Vallins 1965; Chomsky and Halle 1968; Venezky 1970; Albrow 1972; Vachek 1973; Stubbs 1980; Skousen 1982; Nyikos 1988.

epigraph [Gk ἐπι 'upon' + γράφειν 'to write'] **1** An inscription, especially on a monument. **2** The imprint on a title page. **3** A moral or summarizing sentence or quote placed at the beginning of a work.

epigraphy The science concerned with the study, classification and interpretation of inscriptions. Also used in the narrow sense of PALAEOGRAPHY.

Esperanto alphabet The script of the Esperanto language consisting of 22 Roman letters with the following names: *A* /a:/, *B* /bo:/, *C* /tso:/, *D* /do:/, *E* /e:/, *F* /fo:/, *G* /go:/, *H* /ho:/, *I* /i:/, *J* /jo:/, *K* /ko:/, *L* /lo:/, *M* /mo:/, *N* /no:/, *O* /o:/, *P* /po:/, *R* /ro:/, *S* /so:/, *T* /to:/, *U* /u:/, *V* /vo:/, *Z* /zo:/. In addition, the following letters are used with a circumflex: *Ĝ* /džo:/, *Ĥ* /xo:/, *Ĵ* /žo:/, *Ŝ* /šo:/. The velar back vowel is indicated by *Ŭ*/wo:/. Both upper and lower case letters are used, but only proper names and sentence-initial words are capitalized.
Reading Szerdahelyi 1984.

***Esṭrangelā* script** *See* SYRIAC SCRIPTS

eth /eð/ The name of the letter <ð>, also called 'crossed *d*'. In Old English and Icelandic it was used to write the voiced interdental fricative which in modern English spelling is spelt <th>, as in *the*, like its voiceless counterpart /θ/, as in *think*.

Ethiopian writing Old Ethiopic, a Semitic language, was first written in the Semitic manner without vowel signs, but as of the fourth century CE a script with vowel indication evolved, probably under Indian influence. This script which runs from left to right is alpha-syllabic, vowels being indicated as diacritic satellites to a consonant base. It is the script of Ge'ez, the liturgical language of the Ethiopian church. With minor modifications it was adjusted to Amharic in the fifteenth century.
See also AMHARIC WRITING.

Etruscan alphabet An offshoot of the Greek alphabet of Euboea. The origin of the Etruscan alphabet is not completely clear, but it is certain that varieties of the Greek alphabet became known on the Italian peninsula at the beginning of the Greek colonization. The ivory tablet of Marsiliana d'Albegna shown in figure 7 is the earliest known inscription dating from the middle of the sixth century BCE. In addition to the alphabet of Marsiliana d'Albegna, table 5 lists an archaic variety from the seventh to the fifth century (second column) and a late variety dating from the fourth to the first century (third column). Most of the more than 10,000 known inscriptions were found on tombstones (see also figure 8). They usually run from right to left; some are BOUSTROPHEDON. No literary or historical documents are known.

Some of the 26 letters of the tablet of Marsiliana d'Albegna do not appear in any of the inscriptions, as they do not seem to correspond to any units of the Etruscan phonology. The letter <8> for /f/ was added later. Its origin is not known. The letter <V>, which first signified /u/, is also an Etruscan invention which was later adopted into the Roman alphabet. Thanks to its Greek origin, Etruscan writing can be read easily. There are also a few bilingual inscriptions with Phoenician and Etruscan texts dating from the early fifth century BCE. Nevertheless, the Etruscan language is poorly understood because the available text corpus is severely limited in scope and variety. Many of the documents are still awaiting interpretation and translation.
See also GREEK-DERIVED SCRIPTS.
Reading Bonfante and Bonfante 1983; Bundgard 1965.

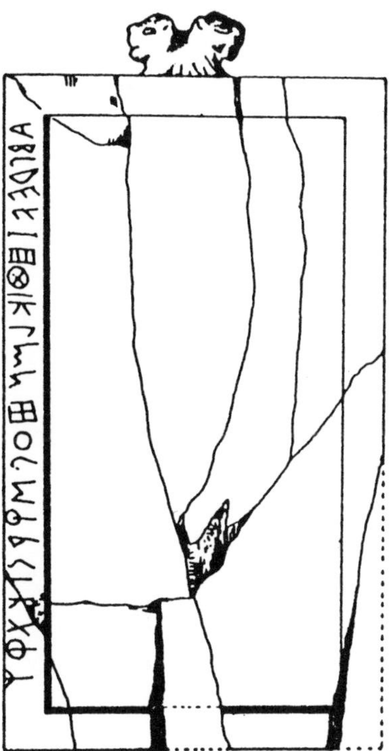

Figure 7 The ivory writing tablet of Marsiliana d'Albegna with a model of the Etruscan alphabet engraved at the side, seventh century BCE *(Museo Archeologico, Florence)*

etymological spelling Etymology is a rival principle of phonemic representation in many alphabetic orthographies. It is evidence of the speech community's linguistic awareness and its readiness to acknowledge the independent existence of the written norm of its language. In English etymological spelling is rampant, because the spelling system has not been adjusted for several centuries. For example, <w> in *acknowledge* indicates the etymological relation with *to know*. 'Silent' letters such as <l> in *folk*, <k> in *knife* and <w> in *wrestle* are etymological remnants. Etymological spellings are often preserved to indicate morphological derivation, as in many learned words of Latin origin. Thus *sign-* in *signal* and *paradigm-* in *paradigmatic* are spelt phonemically, but as isolated words they contain a letter, <g>, which has no counterpart in the phonemic representation. In this way etymological spellings relate to other words belonging to the same paradigm, or to historically earlier word forms.
See also SPELLING.
Reading Smith 1980.

Evans, Arthur, Sir (1851–1941) British archaeologist who excavated Knossos in Crete and thus became the founder of Minoan archaeology and the study of Minoan writing.
See also LINEAR A; LINEAR B; MINOAN WRITING.
Reading Evans 1921.

Marsiliana d'Albegna	Archaic period	late period	Roman transliteration
			a
			(b)
			c (= k)
			(d)
			e
			v
			z
			h
			ϑ (= th)
			i
			k
			l
			m
			n
			(s)
			(o)
			p
			ś
			q
			r
			s
			t
			u
			ṡ
			φ (= ph)
			χ (= kh)
	(8 8)	8	f

Table 5 Varieties of the Etruscan alphabet

Evans, James English missionary who around 1840 invented a syllabary for the use of the Cree and other Algonkins.
See also CREE SYLLABARY.
Reading McLean 1890.

eye dialect A deviation from standard orthography to represent spoken language, standard or non-standard, without resorting to a phonetic notation. Eye dialect is a common means of literary prose for identifying and characterizing

Figure 8 Toy jug in the shape of a cock, incised with the Etruscan alphabet, seventh century BCE, *found at Viterbo (by permission of the Metropolitan Museum of Art, Fletcher Fund, 1924)*

speakers by hinting at their regional or social pronunciations (*dem* for *them*, *wiv* for *with*, *cyar* for *car*). It is a deliberate violation of orthographic norms, but it rarely violates the underlying spelling principles, because the reader must be able to associate the unfamiliar spelling with the intended word. Eye dialect is a graphic means of expression. Although it manipulates an orthography which supposedly maps pronunciation, the alterations of which it consists often involve irregular spellings and do not affect pronunciation. For example, *women* may be replaced by *wimin* or *business* by *bizness*. Here the effect is on the graphic level alone. Similarly, the apostrophe is used to indicate the absence of a sound, but in eye dialect it is often placed in positions where the sound in question would not usually be pronounced anyway, as in *I jus' don't know* or *good fo' nothing*. Thus the non-standard spellings of eye dialect go beyond representing particular aspects of pronunciation, portraying levels of formality and other aspects of ambience and style.

Reading Bowdre 1982.

F, f /ef/ The sixth letter of the English alphabet is derived from Phoenician *wāw*, a letter resembling *Y*. A variant of that letter became the Greek *digamma* <F> which was used to represent a bilabial semivowel /w/. However, the *digamma* fell out of use in Classical Greek. It was restored to the alphabet in Latin. The small letter is derived from the capital.

facsimile [Lat. *facere* 'to do' + *similis* 'like'] An exact reproduction of a manuscript, printed document or drawing. Rubber or metal stamps are used for facsimile signatures, while phototechnical printing devices are used for larger reproductions.

Faliscan script One of several Old Italic scripts, Faliscan is most closely related to the Latin script. Consisting of 18 letters, it also exhibits some commonalities with the ETRUSCAN ALPHABET, notably the letters for /t/ and /u/. In the third century BCE the Faliscan script was driven out by the Latin script, the major alphabet of Rome.
See also OLD ITALIC SCRIPTS.

fǎnqiè [Chinese: 反 *fǎn* 'opposite' + 切 *qiè* 'cut']. (*fan-ts'ie*) A method of indicating the pronunciation of Chinese characters traditionally attributed to Sun Yen, a scholar of the third century CE. It consists in using two characters whose syllabic values are commonly known for their initial and final sounds, respectively. Chinese syllables are conventionally analysed by dividing them into an initial, or the beginning sound, and a final, or the rest of the syllable. In *fǎnqiè* about 40 characters are used for initials and some 200 for finals. The syllable of the unknown character is thus represented by combining the initial of one character with the final of another. For example, the pronunciation *nài* of the character 耐 is given by combining 奴 *nú* and 代 *tài*: [*n*(*ú*) + (*t*)*ài* = *nài*]. The representation of syllables by this method is sometimes imperfect. For instance, *fěi* might be given as *f*(*ú*) + (*g*)*uěi* or *fàn* as *f*(*āng*) + (*o*)*uàn*. Although *fǎnqiè* was never standardized as a system, there was general agreement about which characters were used in this manner for indicating pronunciation. As an auxiliary device it was largely confined to lexicographic applications. It is no longer in use.
Reading Yin 1979.

Filipino alphabet *See* PILIPINO ALPHABET

finger alphabet A mapping of the alphabet on fingers and parts of the hand. Finger spelling is a method of visual communication in the absence of writing devised for the deaf. One of the earliest systematic layouts was proposed in 1680 by George Dalgaro in his treatise *Didascalocophus or the Deaf and Dumb Man's Tutor* (figure 1). Modern one-handed and two-handed finger alphabets are used

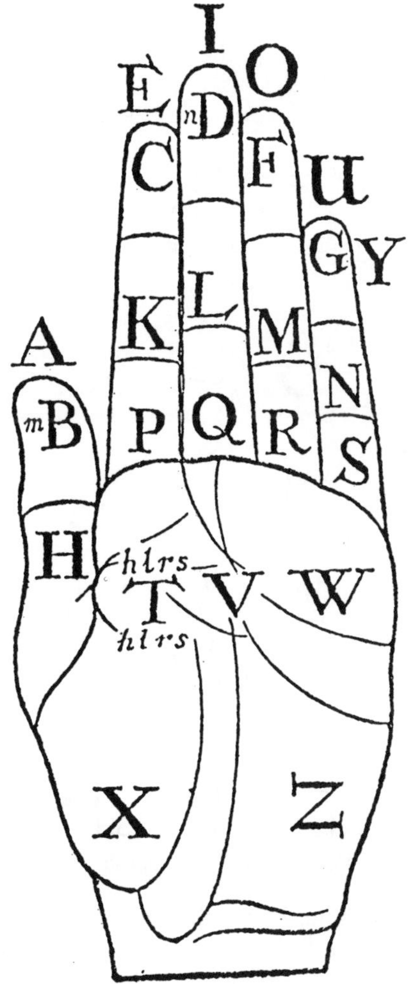

Figure 1 George Dalgaro's finger alphabet

to supplement sign language whenever words need to be represented that have no conventional signs (table 1).
Reading Kyle and Woll 1985.

Finnish spelling A member of the Baltic-Finnic branch of the Finno-Ugric family of languages, Finnish has been used in writing since the sixteenth century, but standardization of the written language was only achieved in the mid-nineteenth century. Finnish is written in the Roman alphabet of which the following 21 letters are used: vowels <a, e, i, o, u, y, ä, ö>; consonants <d, g, h, j, k, l, m, n, p, r, s, t, v>. Since not much time has elapsed since the Finnish orthography was stabilized, the relationship between phonological and graphemic structure is highly systematic. In standard pronunciation the orthography approximates a phonemic representation with a one-to-one correspondence of phonemes and graphemes, although the glottal stop is not indicated in writing. Its occurrence is, however,

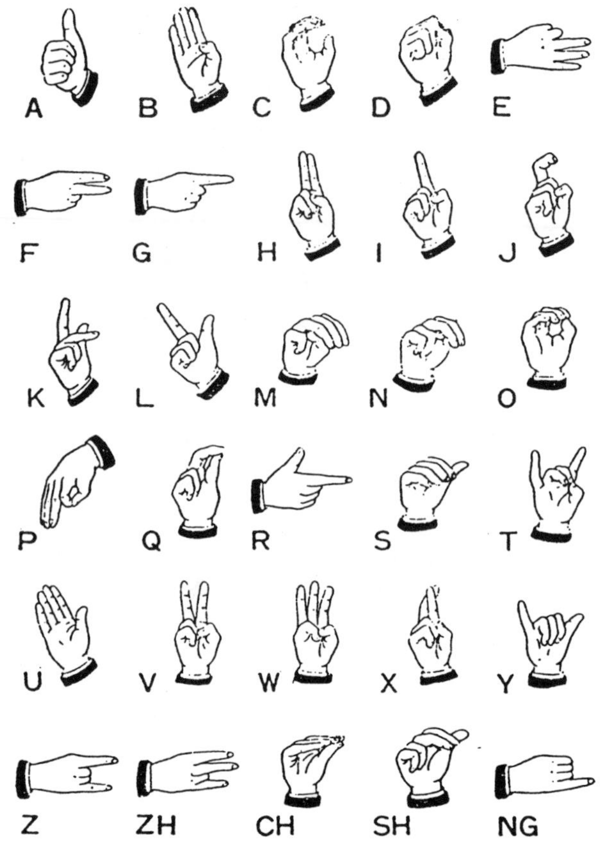

Table 1 One-handed finger alphabet for Chinese

contextually highly predictable, being limited to word-final position. Another minor deviation from the one-to-one correspondence is the spellings <ng> and <nk> for /ŋŋ/ and /ŋk/, respectively. Although vowel reductions in casual speech interfere with the simple mapping relation, Finnish orthography deserves its reputation of being basically phonemic.
Reading Hakulinen 1961.

font The total assortment of type of one style and size. What constitutes the style of a letter, and how the letters of one font share the same style, are difficult questions. Graphical properties of letter shapes such as SERIFS, slants, proportions, angularity and roundness can be defined, but it is hard if not impossible to specify sufficiently many parameters for all letters to eliminate all potential deviation (table 2). The question then is how much deviation can be tolerated for a given letter shape to still be recognized as belonging to a particular font (figure 2). Designers of typefaces and letter forms have an intuitive grasp of the problem, but it has proved extremely difficult to formalize a mathematics of shapes in such a way that computer programs can be employed for parametric letter design. In the field of artificial intelligence the concept of a 'meta-font' has been proposed by Donald Knuth to achieve just that. It is still unclear, however, whether

Century Oldstyle Roman	ABCDEFGHIJKLMNOPQRSTUVWXYZ 1234567890 abcdefghijklmnopqrstuvwxyz
Century Oldstyle Italic	*ABCDEFGHIJKLMNOPQRSTUVWXYZ 1234567890* *abcdefghijklmnopqrstuvwxyz*
Century Oldstyle Bold	**ABCDEFGHIJKLMNOPQRSTUVWXYZ 1234567890** **abcdefghijklmnopqrstuvwxyz**
Gothic 720 Roman	ABCDEFGHIJKLMNOPQRSTUVWXYZ 1234567890 abcdefghijklmnopqrstuvwxyz
Gothic 720 Italic	*ABCDEFGHIJKLMNOPQRSTUVWXYZ 1234567890* *abcdefghijklmnopqrstuvwxyz*
Gothic 720 Bold	**ABCDEFGHIJKLMNOPQRSTUVWXYZ 1234567890** **abcdefghijklmnopqrstuvwxyz**

Table 2 A variety of modern fonts of the Roman alphabet for English

abstract letter forms can be captured by finite sets of parameters that would tell us not only whether or not a letter belongs to a given font, but also how one font differs from all others.

See also LETTER; TYPOGRAPHY.

Reading Zapf 1960; Jaspert 1970; Knuth 1982.

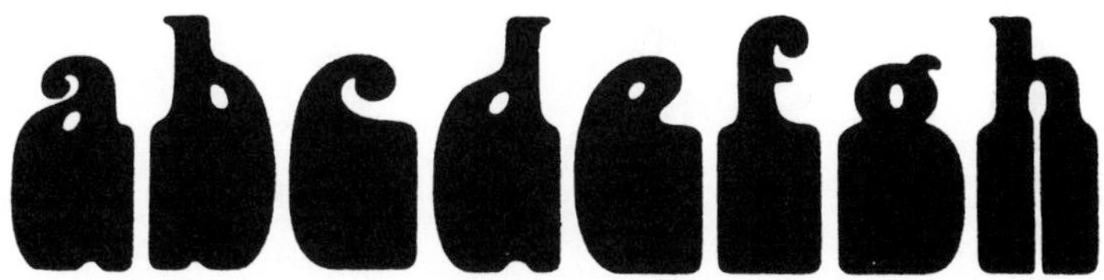

Figure 2 How much variation is tolerable (Tulo typeface)?

Fox syllabary A writing devised in the 1870s for the Mesquakie, Sauk and Kickapoo dialects of Fox, a central Algonkian language formerly spoken in Michigan, but today only used by a small group of speakers in Oklahoma. Several varieties of the Fox writing have been reported. What they share is the basic design of a syllabary which indicates Vs, by means of diacritics placed around a C base. The 'dot notation' variant uses letters of the Latin alphabet plus two other symbols as the base characters which without any diacritics stand for C + *a* sequences (table 3). One dot placed at the centre on the right side of the base letter indicates /e/; one dot at the right shoulder /i/; and two dots /o/. The Roman letters are assigned arbitrary sound values. The '*x* and scored-line notation' is structurally identical, but it uses *x*s and scored lines for the Vs and a different set of base symbols for the Cs (table 4). The Fox syllabary was adapted

	/a/	/e/	/i/	/o/
/p/	l	l.	l˙	l..
/t/	t	t.	t˙	t..
/s/	s	s.	s˙	s..
/š/	&	&.	&˙	&..
/č/	tt	tt.	tt˙	tt..
/y/	9	9.	9˙	9..
/w/	w	w.	w˙	w..
/m/	m	m.	m˙	m..
/n/	n	n.	n˙	n..
/k/	K	K.	K˙	K..
/kw/	8	8.	8˙	8..

Table 3 *The Fox syllabary for the Mesquakie dialect: dot notation. Phonetic values are indicated by the vowels and consonants added in phonemic notation*
Source: *Walker 1981*

	/a/	/e/	/i/	/o/
/p/	x	H	HI	HH
/t/	+x	+H	+HI	+HH
/s/	Cx	CH	CHI	CHH
/š/	Qx	QH	QHI	QHH
/č/	λx	λH	λHI	λHH
/v/	ñx	ñH	ñHI	ñHH
/y/	=x	=H	=HI	=HH
/w/	ƨƨx	ƨƨH	ƨƨHI	ƨƨHH
/m/	⊞x	⊞H	⊞HI	⊞HH
/n/	#x	#H	#HI	#HH
/k/	C′x	C′H	C′HI	C′HH
/kw/	ƨCx	ƨCH	ƨCHI	ƨCHH

Table 4 *The Fox syllabary for the Mesquakie dialect: x and scored-line notation. Phonetic values are indicated by the vowels and consonants added in phonemic notation*
Source: *Walker 1981*

to Siouan Winnebago in the 1880s. Since the Fox orthography distinguishes just ten Cs and four Vs, it was not very suitable for Siouan Winnebago which has 20 Cs and eight Vs. As a consequence, a number of phonemic distinctions of Siouan Winnebago are not represented. Length and stress of Vs are disregarded, and no distinction is made between /o/ and /u/. For Cs, additional lower case letters of the Roman alphabet were added.

Reading Walker 1981.

Franklin, Benjamin (1706–1790) The American statesman and inventor also tried his hand at improving ENGLISH SPELLING. In 1768 he proposed a 'reformed alphabet for English' (table 5). He introduced some diacritics and some new

Characters	Sounded as now in	Names of the letters expressed in the reformed sounds and characters
o	old	o
a [ɑ]	John, Folly	a
a	man, can	a
e	mane, lane	e
i	een, seen	i
u	tool, fool	u
ɥ [ɥ; Ɏ]	um, un, as in umbrage, unto, etc	ɥ
h	hunter, happy, high	huh
g	give, gather	gi
k	keep, kick	ki
s [ʃ]	sh, ship, wish	ish
ŋ [ŋ]	ng, ing, reaping, among	ing
n	end	en
r	art	ar
t	teeth	ti
d	deed	di
l	ell, tell	el
h [h]	th, think	eh
dh [dh; Ð]	dh, thy	edh
s	essence	es
z	ez, wages	ez
f	effect	ef
v	ever	ev
b	bees	bi
p	peep	pi
m	ember	em

Table 5 Benjamin Franklin's reformed alphabet
Source: *Wilcox, 1972, facing p. 175*

letters. For example, to replace the digraph <sh> and its voiced counterpart <j>, he invented the letter *ish*. For <ng> he also introduced a single letter called *ing*. Franklin's purpose was to design a spelling system which was easier to learn than the standard system. He was concerned, moreover, that over time English spelling would lose all connection with pronunciation.
See also SPELLING REFORM.
Reading Wilcox 1972.

French spelling With the CAROLINGIAN REFORM of the ninth century CE, French emerged as a written language independent of Latin. Since the scribes continued to use the letters of the Latin alphabet largely with their traditional sound values, French spelling was not a phonetically faithful system to begin with, although it was much more phonetic than it is today. Etymologizing and pseudo-etymological spellings from early times have further removed the orthography from a phonemic representation. In its present form French spelling is largely historical reflecting, however imperfectly, the speech of the eleventh to the thirteenth centuries. Grapheme–phoneme correspondences are, accordingly, complex and obscure for historically uninformed readers (figure 3). Many spellings are those of Latin etymons, e.g. [tã], spelled *temps* after Lat. *tempus*. Such a spelling is not predictable, as the same sound sequence [tã] could also be spelled *tant*, *tans* or *ten*, among others. Conversely, however, pronunciation is quite predictable from spelling, since most grapheme–phoneme discrepancies reflect regular historical changes which can be captured in orthographic and orthoepic rules. For example, from the following spellings it can be concluded that <oi> is pronounced [wa] and that final <s> and <e> are not pronounced. A more comprehensive set of examples will reveal that <e> is indeed always mute in final position and that <s> and other consonant letters in final position are only pronounced in clearly specifiable contexts.

bois [bwa] 'wood' *lois* [lwa] 'law' *fois* [fwa] 'time' *foie* [fwa] 'liver'

The 26 letters of the French alphabet are identical with those of English. In addition, the following orthographic diacritics are employed: ACCENTS, DIAERESIS, CEDILLA, apostrophe and HYPHEN.

Oreille, exaspéré, ordonna à sa femme de lui
[ɔRɛ:j egzaspeRe ɔRdɔna a sa fam: də lɥi

choisir un nouveau riflard, en soie fine, de
ʃwazi:R œ̃ nuvo Rifla:R ã swa fin də

vingt francs, et d'apporter une fracture justificative.
vɛ̃fRã e dapɔRte yn fakty:R ʒystifikati:v]

Exasperated, Oreille ordered his wife to pick a new umbrella for him of fine silk for twenty francs, and to bring a receipt.

Figure 3 Sample of French grapheme–phoneme correspondence: from Guy de Maupassant, Le Parapluie

Grapheme	Phoneme	Example
<a>	[a]	patte [pat]
<â>	[ɑ:]	âme [ɑ:m]
<e>	[ə], [Ø]	bretelle [brətɛl], cupide [kypid]
<é>	[e]	été [ete]
<è>	[ɛ]	flèche [flɛʃ]
<i>	[i]	vite [vit]
<î>	[i:]	pire [pi:r]
<y>	[i]	mythe [mit]
<o>	[o], [ɔ], [ɔ:]	auto [oto], flotte [flɔt], mort [mɔ:r]
<ô>	[o:]	rôle [ro:l]
<u>	[y], [y:]	tu [ty], cure [ky:r]
<û>	[y:]	mûre [my:r]
DI- AND POLYGRAPHS		
<au>	[o], [o:]	auto [oto], haute [o:t]
<eau>	[o]	eau [o]
<eu>	[ø]	peu [pø]
<œu>	[œ]	bœuf [bœf]
<ou>	[u], [u:]	sous [su], jour [ʒu:r]
<oi>	[wa]	coi [kwa]
<ille>	[i:j]	fille [fi:j]
<ail>	[a:j]	travail [trava:j]
<œil>	[œ:j]	œil [œ:j]

Table 6 Canonical pronunciation of French vowel graphemes

Three different accent marks are placed on vowel letters to specify their pronunciation and, in some cases, to differentiate words. The acute is generally placed on the <e> to indicate the pronunciation [e] as opposed to [ɛ] and [ə], as in *fermé*. The grave is placed on <e> and <a> in stressed syllables (*procès, voilà*) as well as on <a> and <u> in some words as a means of homonym distinction, as in *là* 'there' vs *la* article and pronoun feminine, and *où* 'where' vs *ou* 'or'. The circumflex occurs on all vowel letters to indicate vowel length (*diplôme* [diplo:m]). It is also placed on vowels after which an <s> has dropped out, as in *tête*, formerly *teste*.

The diaeresis (*tréma*) is placed on <e,i,u> to indicate separate pronunciation in the context of an adjacent vowel letter that is not marked by an accent, e.g. *naïf, bisaïeul*. The cedilla is placed under <c> before <a,o,u> where it is to be pronounced /s/ rather than /k/, which would be the regular pronunciation: thus *licorn* [likɔrn] but *leçon* [ləsɔ̃]. The apostrophe indicates the omission of a vowel letter and its elision in pronunciation, e.g. *d'abord*. The hyphen (*trait d'union*) is used to connect the elements of compound words such as *vis-à-vis, contre-attaque*.

The canonical pronunciation of the vowel graphemes of the French writing system is given in table 6. Canonical spellings for French vowel phonemes are more difficult to specify, since there is more polyvalence. For example, there are more than 50 different spellings for each of the three vowels [o], [ɛ̃] and [ɛ]. The canonical sound values of the consonant graphemes are closer to their Latin values. Some peculiarities are as follows: <h> is mute, but sometimes serves as boundary marker (*le hasard*: the article cannot be elided with the initial V of [aza:r]); final Cs are also mute; and in post-vocalic positions, <n> and <m> are interpreted as giving the preceding vowel a nasal quality.

Under the guidance of lexicographers, printers and the Académie Française – created in 1635 by Cardinal Richelieu – French spelling was relatively early to be standardized and turned into a proper orthography. The first edition of the Academy's dictionary of 1694 adopted an archaizing stand, and although it recognized a number of alterations until its eighth edition (1935), it never changed its conservative outlook. Ever since it first appeared, the notion took root that an elaborate written language has an existence quite distinct from the spoken language. Reform proposals intended to simplify spelling and to narrow the gap between speech and writing have been advanced periodically, but resistance by the literati and printers prevented any substantial changes (figure 4). Like the English, French spelling has thus proved very conservative, with the result that a great number of words have to be learned individually before regularities become apparent.

Reading Clédat 1930; Dournon 1974; Guion 1974; Catach 1978; Grevisse 1980.

functions of writing Speech and writing are communication practices which are subject to the physical conditions of, respectively, the visual and auditory senses. As to the interpretation of the resulting differences, there are two schools of thought: those who emphasize the qualitative disparity of spoken and written language and the communicative functions that writing alone allows; and those who conceive of writing as a gradual expansion of speech and highlight the diversity of written language uses in different sociocultural settings. Among those who represent the former, Jack Goody in his earlier works may be mentioned as well as David Olson and Walter Ong. Two prominent advocates of the latter are Brian Street and Harvey Graff.

Writing evolved as a visual medium of communication which circumvents or transcends certain limitations of speech. Five functions in particular stand out as distinguishing writing from speech: the mnemonic function, the distancing function, the reification function, the social control function, and the aesthetic function.

Memory

Although members of oral societies are often said to command a memory that far surpasses that of literate people, the amount of information that can be stored by means of writing and retrieved from written records clearly transcends the capacity of individual remembrance. Accumulation of knowledge on a large scale and historical reflection – as opposed to myth and legend – developed thanks to the memory supportive potential of writing.

Distance

Communicating in speech requires the co-presence of speaker and listener. Writing, by contrast, enables communication over any spatial or temporal distance. Hence, the three essential components of linguistic communication – speaker,

Projet
D'une
Nouvelle forme D'orthographe
à l'usage
Des Sans culottes

Au moment où les français cherchent à remonter à tous les principes pour perfectionner chaque point de leur existence phisique et morale; au moment où la Convention s'occupe à nous former une constitution et un code fondés sur les bases éternelles de la justice; au moment où une troupe de savants vient d'extraire des éléments mêmes de la nature, une mesure commune de la pesanteur et des distances, pour servir aux besoins de notre commerce journalier; au moment où un nouveau calendrier va diviser, d'une manière plus égale, les différentes parties du tems qui règle nos destinées: au moment enfin, où toutes les institutions humaines sont brisées et rejetées au moule, pour être reconstruites sur les principes immuables de la raison: la plus belle des inventions, la plus utile des sciences, celle dont toutes les autres tirent leur perfection, restera-t-elle imparfaite elle meme? et la verrons-nous couverte de la rouille et de la poussière des siècles dont elle aura aidé les autres à se secouer? je veux ici parler de l'écritture: cette ingénieuse image de la parole; cet art précieux au quel notre révolution doit presque tous ses succès, et qui peut seul les propager dans les générations futures et les régions éloignées.

Dans toute autre circonstance que celle où nous nous trouvons, la réforme que je vais proposer paroitroit peut être impossible; mais l'expérience a fait voir qu'il n'est rien dont ne puisse venir à bout, un Peuple courageux, quand il est guidé par des hommes fermes et persévérants, qui pour le conduire aux grandes choses savent lui faire braver

Figure 4 Reform proposal for a new orthography by the French Revolutionaries

listener and utterance – can be separated from each other. The same message can be received by many in different places and at different times. If messengers carrying bad news were sometimes punished by the recipients of their oral reports, it was because no distinction was made between author and voice. In writing the distancing function brings about such conceptual differentiations, as the written word is typically detached from the 'here', 'now' and 'I' of its production.

Reification

The essence of oral communication is to determine what the *speaker* means by the utterance. In writing the utterance is detached from its sender and given a stable physical presence on clay tablets, paper or some other surface. The focal question about its interpretation then becomes what the *words* mean. There is hence a gradual shift from the intentional to the conventional aspects of linguistic meaning. Reification means that in writing a linguistic message becomes an interpretable object which must be self-sufficient because the author may not be at hand for clarification. Accordingly, written messages rely much less on context and situation than spoken ones. Reification further fosters an attitude towards language as an object which has an existence in its own right that can be studied and manipulated. Normalization and standardization of form, prescriptions about proper usage, rely largely on reducing language to writing. In the form of dictionaries and grammar books language is given a stable form which is harder to detect and to arrest in the flux of ephemeral speech.

Social control

As in language, codified standards of correctness laid down in writing bring about changes in social organization. The permanence of writing gives written documents the character of seemingly objective guidelines of human conduct independent of personal interests. Writing also creates a larger speech community, tying together people in communication many of whom never meet each other. New and larger networks come into existence, making social relations, obligations and rights impersonal. In modern societies one's entire social existence depends on written records, and it is written records that allow the execution of social control in such matters as registering the members of a community for compulsory education, taxation, military draft and voting. On the linguistic side, elevating one variety to the status of *the* written language is likewise an act of social control, as elites invariably accord their own speech this privilege. Often this reflects and reinforces power structures, as the respected standard language affords advantages in gaining access to socially desirable positions.

Aesthetic

Language is used for aesthetic purposes both orally and visually, but the form and appeal of verbal and written language arts clearly differ. The written medium has added to the range of artistic expression by means of language. Certain genres, such as novel and drama, as well as some kinds of poetry, require the aid of writing for composition and the visual impression for proper reception. The aesthetics of writing is less immediate, for the consumption of literature is potentially a solitary experience which again is a result of the physical properties of writing as visible language. In a wider sense the stylistic traits associated with written texts and spoken discourse are also to be subsumed under the aesthetic function.

Clearly, writing has other functions, many of which it shares with speech. And those identified here are not realized in all writing. However, in order to

understand the differences between speech and writing, the most promising approach is an investigation of the functions these communication practices fulfil.
See also LITERACY; ORIGIN OF WRITING.
Reading Goody and Watt 1968; Olson 1977; Ong 1982; Street 1993; Graff 1987.

furigana [Japanese 振る *furu* 'to attach' + 假名 *kana* 'the Japanese syllabary'] *Kana* attached in small print as a reading aid at the side of Chinese characters of which readers are not expected to know the pronunciation. This may be because the readers are still learning the written language, as in children's books (figure 5), because they lack sufficient literacy education, because the text is archaic, or because the writer chooses to give a character an unconventional reading.
See also JAPANESE WRITING.

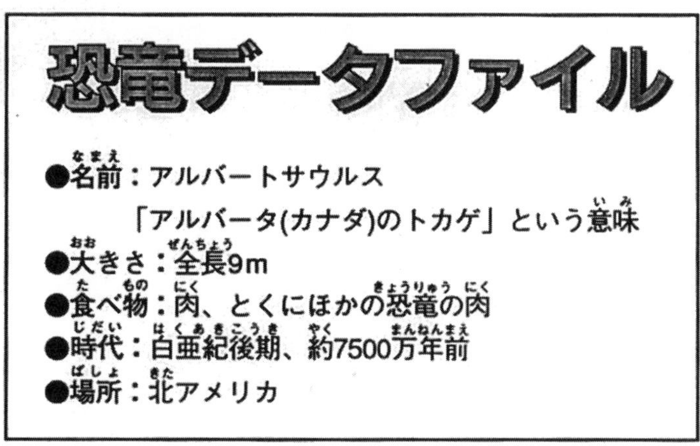

Figure 5 Caption from a Japanese children's book fully annotated with furigana

futhark (*also futhork*) The runic alphabet used for writing various Germanic languages including proto-Nordic, the Scandinavian parent language, and Old English. The name *fuþark* (*futhark*) consists of the first six letters of the early alphabet of 24 letters dating from the second century CE (table 7). In the wake of Christianization the Latin alphabet spread through Scandinavia and the British

Table 7 The older futhark

Isles, superseding the runes. However, for folk literacy the *futhark* continued to be used until the seventeenth century, though in reduced form with just 16 letters. The origin of the *futhark* is not well documented, but the symbols are clearly related to the ETRUSCAN ALPHABET and the LATIN ALPHABET. The individual runic letters have names chosen in accordance with the ACROPHONIC PRINCIPLE. The initial sounds of the Old Nordic names were the sound values of the runes they denoted: *fehu* 'wealth', *ūruz* 'aurochs', *þurisaz* 'giant', *ansuz* '(?)month', *raidō* 'ride', *kaunan* 'torch' etc. A conspicuous graphic feature of the *futhark* symbols is that they consist almost exclusively of straight lines, which made them easy to scratch and carve in stone, wood, bone and metal.
See also RUNE.
Reading Elliott 1971.

G, g /dʒiː/ The seventh letter of the English alphabet developed from Semitic *gīmel* and Greek *gamma* (Γ, γ). In the Etruscan adaptation of the Greek alphabet it was used for both voiceless and voiced velar plosives (/k/ and /g/). In Latin the two had to be distinguished, and hence a stroke was added to the lower curve of the *C*.

Gelb, Ignace J. (1907–) One of the foremost orientalists of his generation, Gelb played a major role in the decipherment of HITTITE HIEROGLYPHIC. With his seminal book *A Study of Writing* he presented a systematic account of the history and evolution of writing. Not everyone accepts his view of the history of writing as a quasi-necessary progression from the representation of meaning to that of sound, with the alphabet as the crown of the development. However, by formulating a clear hypothesis, he provided a common focus for what had previously been largely isolated afterthoughts of various disciplines and thereby made a major contribution to establishing the study of writing as a scientific field in its own right. Until his retirement Gelb was affiliated with the Oriental Institute and the Department of Near Eastern Languages and Civilizations and Linguistics at the University of Chicago.
See also GRAMMATOLOGY.
Reading Gelb 1963.

Georgian alphabet The creation of the Georgian alphabet in the fifth century CE is attributed to MESRỌP, an Armenian court secretary and missionary. The Chutsuri or Xutsuri script of 38 letters was primarily employed in ecclesiastical writing and is no longer in use. It was replaced by the Mkhedruli (secular) script which is still used today. The origin of the latter is uncertain. Some scholars describe it as having evolved from a cursive form of the Chutsuri script, but according to others it pre-dates the church script. The order of the letters betrays Greek influence, but like the Armenian script some letters of the Mkhedruli alphabet also point to a connection with northern Iranian scripts of the Arsakidian period, i.e. early forms of the PAHLAVI SCRIPT. In its modern form the Mkhedruli alphabet has 33 letters. In Old Georgian another five symbols were in use (table 1). The modern orthography is largely phonetic, approximating a one-to-one mapping relation between phonemes and graphemes.
Reading Aronson 1982.

German spelling German emerged as a written language in the wake of the CAROLINGIAN REFORM, although Latin continued to be the Germans' proper language of education and culture for many centuries thereafter. While initially several varieties of German were written with a pronounced contrast between Upper and Lower German, the advent of printing technology and the Reformation movement led to gradual convergence as of the sixteenth century. In the process,

Letter	Name	Value	Letter	Name	Value
ა	ani	a	ს	sani	s
ბ	bani	b	ტ	t’ani	t’
გ	gani	g	უ	uni	u
დ	doni	d	ფ	p‘ari	p‘
ე	eni	ɛ	ქ	k‘ani	k‘
ვ	vini	v	ღ	γani	γ
ზ	zeni	z	ყ	qari	q
თ	t‘ani	t	შ	ʃini	ʃ
ი	ini	i	ჩ	tʃ‘ini	tʃ‘
კ	k’ani	k’	ც	ts‘ani	ts‘
ლ	lazi	l	ძ	dzili	dz
მ	mani	m	წ	ts’ili	ts’
ნ	nari	n	ჭ	tʃ’ari	tʃ’
ო	oni	ɔ	ხ	xani	x
პ	p’ari	p’	ჯ	dʒani	dʒ
ჟ	ʒani	ʒ	ჰ	haɛ	h
რ	raɛ	r			

Table 1 The Mkhedruli alphabet of Georgian

spelling conventions were altered and regularized with a tendency to accept etymological rather than phonetic representations of words. As a consequence, modern German orthography is governed more by morphological than by phonological principles. Full standardization was achieved only in the nineteenth century. An official orthographic norm which is still in effect was adopted in 1901.

German uses the Latin alphabet with one additional lower case letter, <ß>, originally a ligature of Gothic type <s> and <z> and hence called *Eszett*, a combination of the German names of these two letters. The diaeresis or umlaut <¨> is placed on <a>, <o> and <u> in derivative forms to indicate the front vowels /ɛ/, /ø/ and /y/. A conspicuous feature of German texts is the use of initial capitals to distinguish nouns.

The underlying order of German spelling is largely a result of spontaneous developments, although conscious interventions have produced a number of regularities. Some of these clearly deviate from a one-to-one correspondence of sounds and letters or groups of letters. There is considerable polyvalence resulting from the fact that different principles are at work in the system (table 2). For example, the vowel [o:] is variously represented as <o>, <oh>, <oo>, <au> and <ot>, among others:

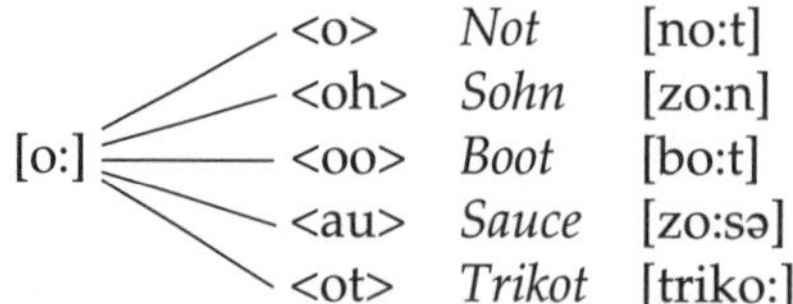

Similarly, many consonants have various written representations. The distinctive feature of voicing in consonant pairs such as /b,p/, /d,t/, /g,k/ is ignored in some cases, but graphically represented in others. Thus final /k/ appears as <g>

Grapheme	Phoneme	Example
<a>	[a]	hat [hat]
<aa>	[a:]	Aal [a:l]
<ah>	[a:]	kahl [ka:l]
<ä>	[ɛ], [ɛ:]	Getränk [gətrɛŋk], Käse [kɛzə]
<e>	[ɛ], [e],[e:]	Ente [ɛntə], lebendig [lebɛndiç], ehe [e:ə]
<ee>	[e:]	See [ze:]
<i>	[i], [i:]	mit [mit], wir [vi:r]
<ie>	[i:]	wie [vi:]
<ih>	[i:]	ihr [i:r]
<o>	[ɔ], [o:]	Ort [ɔrt], Ozean [o:tsea:n]
<oo>	[o:]	Boot [bo:t]
<oh>	[o:]	Sohn [zo:n]
<ö>	[œ], [ø:]	öfter [œftər], schön [ʃø:n]
<u>	[u], [u:]	Hunger [hunər], zu [tsu:]
<uh>	[u:]	Kuh [ku:]
<ü>	[y], [y:]	Küche [kyçə], Lüge [ly:gə]
<y>	[y], [y:]	Typ [typ], Elysium [ely:zium]
DIGRAPHS		
<ai>	[ai]	Kai [kai]
<ei>	[ai]	Keil [kail]
<au>	[au]	Frau [frau]
<eu>	[ɔy]	teuer [tɔyər]
<äu>	[ɔ:y]	Mäuse [mɔ:yzə]

Table 2 Canonical pronunciation of German vowel graphemes

in *Tag* and as <k> in *Gequak*. Underlying these differences are different principles of the spelling system which, therefore, cannot be described adequately by just listing the observable GRAPHEME–PHONEME CORRESPONDENCES.

A key principle in the German spelling system is that of preserving paradigm similarity. Consonant alternations which can be predicted from general morphophonological rules are neglected in writing in order to keep the variation of the graphic form of a word or morpheme minimal. For example, the morpheme *KÖNIG* has three different pronunciations – [køniç] in *König* (i.e. in isolation), [kønik] in *königlich*, and [kønig] in *Könige* – but its graphic representation is always the same, <könig>.

No attempts were made at maintaining paradigmatic similarity in spelling in earlier forms of written German. Middle High German spelled *tac, tage; gap, gaben; leit, leiden* etc. (modern *Tag, Tage; gab, gaben; Leid, leiden*). However, in modern German the principle of minimal variation in the written form of morphemes occupies a position of central importance. Usually, the stem form and the derivatives of a given morpheme are spelled alike. Sometimes this results in redundant spellings, as in *sieht* 'sees', where both *e* and *h* serve the function of indicating vowel length. The *h* is there because the stem form of the verb *seh-en* has an *h* where it is regularly employed to mark the length of the first vowel [zé:ən]. The *e*, on the other hand, is employed because [i:] is usually spelled <ie>:

<ie> ⇔ /iː/ is a regular grapheme–phoneme correspondence in German. At the same time, the principle of minimal graphical morpheme variation requires the copying of the *h* from the stem form.

Another important principle is homonym differentiation. Different spellings in homonym pairs such as the following reflect different meanings: *Lied* 'song', *Lid* 'eyelid'; *Leere* 'emptiness', *Lehre* 'teaching'; *malen* 'to paint', *mahlen* 'to mill'. Sometimes this principle interacts with that of minimal morpheme variation. Thus [wɛndə] is spelled *Wände* as the plural of *Wand* 'wall', but *wende* as an inflected form of *wenden* 'to turn'. Hence, such multiple phoneme representation is not arbitrary, but the underlying rationale is not necessarily apparent without an intimate knowledge of the regularities of the language. Moreover, what appears to benefit the reader – homonym differentiation on semantic grounds – is an additional burden for the writer since many sound patterns allow for more than one spelling. The spelling of a large number of words has to be memorized before the underlying regularities become apparent.

The German spelling system rests on different structural principles, not all of which are related to the phonological structure of German speech. The spelling of sound patterns is, therefore, much less predictable than pronunciation is predictable from spelling (figure 1). Various proposals at simplifying the system by eliminating irregularities and overly involved rules have been discussed, but, however moderate, they have invariably met with conservative resistance on the part of intellectuals and the media.

Reading Duden 1991, 1994; Eisenberg 1993; Kohrt 1987.

Freude, schöner Götterfunken
[frɔydə ʃøːnər gœtərfuŋkən

Tochter aus Elysium
tɔxtər aus elyːzium

Wir betreten feuertrunken
viːr bətreːtən fɔyərtruŋkən

Himmlische, dein Heiligtum!
himliʃə dain hailiçtuːm]

Joy, bright spark of divinity,
Daughter of Elysium,
Fire-inspired we tread
Thy sanctuary.

Figure 1 Sample of German grapheme–phoneme correspondence: from Friedrich Schiller, Ode 'An die Freude'

Glagolitic alphabet The first alphabet of any Slavic language, the Glagolitic script was created in the ninth century CE for the translation of the Bible into Old Bulgarian, which hence became known as Old Church Slavonic. Also called *asbuka* after the names of the first two letters, *as* and *buka*, the name 'Glagolitic' derives from that of its third letter, *glagol* 'word'. The origin of Glagolitic has long been obscure, but modern research sees the Slav apostle Konstantin, later St Cyrillus (*d.* 869), who is traditionally credited with inventing the CYRILLIC alphabet, as the likely inventor of this script. The shapes of Glagolitic letters seem to be freely designed, although derivations from the Greek and Hebrew alphabets have been suggested for some of them. The order of Glagolitic is basically that of the Greek alphabet, with additional letters for sounds non-existent in Greek (e.g. /š/, /ž/, /št/, /č/, /dž/) appended at the end of the sequence (table 3). Glagolitic was

Ⰰ Ⰰ	a	Ⱆ Ⱆ	u
Ⰱ Ⰱ	b	Φ Φ / Ⱇ Ⱇ	f
Ⰲ Ⰲ	v		
Ⰳ Ⰳ	g	Ⱈ Ⱈ	χ
Ⰴ Ⰴ	d	Ⱉ Ⱉ	ō
Ⰵ Ⰵ	e	Ⱋ Ⱋ	št
Ⰶ Ⰶ	ž	Ⱌ Ⱌ	ts
Ⰷ Ⰷ	dz	Ⱍ Ⱍ	tš
Ⰸ Ⰸ	z	Ⱎ Ⱎ	š
Ⰹ Ⰹ	ī	Ⱏ Ⱏ	o, e
Ⰻ Ⰻ	i		
Ⰼ Ⰼ	d', y	ⰟⰊ ⰟⰊ	ü
Ⰽ Ⰽ	k	Ⱐ Ⱐ	i̯
Ⰾ Ⰾ	l	Ⱑ Ⱑ	ye, ya
Ⰿ Ⰿ / M M	m	Ⱓ Ⱓ	yu
		Ⱘ Ⱘ	õ
Ⱀ Ⱀ	n	Ⱔ Ⱔ	ẽ
Ⱁ Ⱁ	o	Ⱗ Ⱗ	yõ
Ⱂ Ⱂ	p	Ⱙ Ⱙ	yẽ
Ⱃ Ⱃ	r	Ⱚ Ⱚ	θ
Ⱄ Ⱄ	s	Ⱛ Ⱛ	ü
Ⱅ Ⱅ	t		

Table 3 The Glagolitic alphabet

used for a relatively short period, mainly by south-western Slavs in Croatia and Dalmatia. In the twelfth century it was replaced by Cyrillic, the script of the Orthodox Church.
Reading Schenker and Stankiewicz 1980.

glyph A term derived by contraction from HIEROGLYPH. It has sometimes been used in the description of writing systems whose units were not well understood. For example, in Maya epigraphy, where the phonetic component of the writing system has long been in doubt, it is used as a collective designation to indicate a logogram, a phonetic sign or a compound sign.

Gothic alphabet Gothic is the oldest known Germanic language. First documented in 'pagan' runic letters, it was given a Christian script in the fourth century CE in what is now Bulgaria. The alphabet created for this purpose was designed by Bishop Ulfilas or Wulfila (311–83), a Greek missionary who

Symbol	Value	Symbol	Value
𐌰	a	𐌽	n
𐌱	b	𐌾	3
𐌲	g	𐌿	u
𐌳	d	𐍀	p
𐌴	e	𐍁	
𐌵	q	𐍂	r
𐌶	z	𐍃	s
𐌷	h	𐍄	t
𐌸	θ	𐍅	v
𐌹	i	𐍆	f
𐌺	k	𐍇	ks
𐌻	l	𐍈	w
𐌼	m	𐍉	o
		𐍊	

Table 4 Ulfilas's Gothic alphabet

Christianized the west Goths. Largely derived from the Greek alphabet, it contains six Latin letters (those for /q, h, j, r, s, f/) and two of runic origin (those for /u/ and /o:/). In addition to the 25 letters, two characters were used only as numerals: ч for 90 and ↑ for 900 (table 4). Almost all preserved Gothic documents are parts of Ulfilas's translation of the Gospels and other sections of the New Testament.
See also GOTHIC RUNES.
Reading Schulz 1939.

Gothic runes The first letters used for recording the Gothic language (table 5). This particular variety of the runic alphabet is documented only in very few inscriptions. According to one theory, the Goths were the first to write runes, but scarcity of data has not allowed this to be established as fact.
See also RUNE.
Reading Elliott 1971.

ᚠ	f	ᛇ	kw
ᚢ	u	ᛈ	p
ᚦ	ð	ᛉ	uu
ᚨ	a	ᛊ	s
ᚱ	r	ᛏ	t
ᚲ	k	ᛒ	b
ᚷ	g	ᛖ	e
ᚹ	w	ᛚ	l
ᚺ	h	ᛗ	m
ᚾ	n	ᛜ	ñ
ᛁ	i	ᛞ	θ
ᛃ	ʒ	ᛟ	o

Table 5 Gothic runes

Gothic type Also known as 'black letter', Gothic type is the script associated with the German scribal tradition. It was derived in the thirteenth century CE from the Caroline minuscule. While England and other western European countries adopted Roman very early, Germany retained Gothic type. It was the script that GUTENBERG used in his famous Bible which later became known as *Fraktur*, i.e. a script with 'broken' vertical strokes. It remained the most common German type until the present century (figure 2). However, since 1945 all major newspapers have adopted roman type and Gothic type has been largely relegated to decorative purposes.

Vollständigere und Neuerläuterte
Deutsche
Sprachkunst,

Nach den
Mustern der besten Schriftsteller
des vorigen und itzigen Jahrhunderts
abgefasset,
und bey dieser fünften Auflage merklich verbessert,
von
Johann Christoph Gottscheden,
P. P. der Univ. Leipzig Decemv. des großen Fürstencoll. u. der
phil. Facult. Sen. der churf. Stipend. Aufs. u. verschie-
dener Akad. der Wiss. Mitgliede.

Mit Röm. Kaiserl. wie auch Königl. Pohln. und Churf. Sächs.
allergnädigster Freyheit.

Leipzig,
Verlegts Bernh. Christ. Breitkopf und Sohn, 1762.

Figure 2 Gothic type: sample from Johann Christoph Gottsched's Deutsche Sprachkunst *(1748)*

graffito Writing or drawing scratched on a wall or other surface (figure 3), such as the wall inscriptions of Pompeii which contain quotations from poets, salutations, idle words, obscenities, love addresses and satirical remarks (figure 4). *See also* PALAEOGRAPHY.

grammar The word *grammar* derives from Gk γράμμα 'letter, written mark'. Until recently there was never any doubt that grammar had to do with written

Figure 3 Modern graffiti

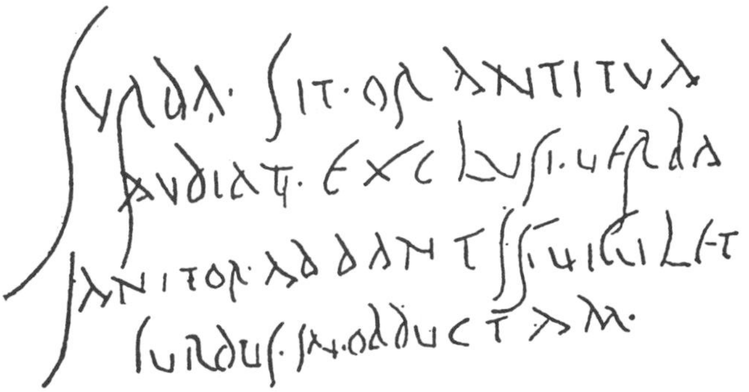

Surda sit oranti tua
audiat exclusi verba
ianitor ad dantis vigilet
surdus in obductam

Figure 4 Ancient graffiti in Latin from a wall in Pompeii, first century CE. *The four lines are fragmented verses from Ovid* (Amores *1, 8, 77f.) and Properz* (Elegies *IV, 5, 47f.) which command a watchman to keep the door closed to him who begs but to open it to him who gives – a reference to a Roman brothel* language. The data of grammatical description were drawn from written texts, and for the most part this is still the case. But in this century many linguists have concerned themselves with unwritten languages and, because of the primacy and universality of speech as opposed to the recency and restrictedness of writing, they declare speech the proper object of linguistic investigation regardless of whether the language under study has a written form. Yet, although most practitioners in the field have consequently turned their back on spelling and written language and profess to be interested in speech alone, they continue to use analytic concepts which were developed on the basis of written language. The essential difficulties involved in making unwritten languages susceptible to grammatical analysis are only rarely acknowledged, as in Kenneth Pike's 1947 book *Phonemics: A Technique for Reducing Languages to Writing*. Instead, the potentially serious differences between written and spoken language have been largely ignored in grammar theory, which has tacitly assumed a written language framework using theoretical concepts and applying methods designed for the description of language as it manifests itself in writing.

For example, in grammatical analysis prosody – stress, tone, intonation, melody, rhythm – is often treated as an independent phenomenon. It is abstracted from the discrete units distinguished in writing: sentences, words and letters. These units are treated as if they corresponded to autonomous units of speech to which intonation is added. However, the intonationless sentence never occurs in speech, but only in writing. Imperfect as it was, the Greek alphabet was not adjusted to express 'suprasegmental' phenomena. It is this alphabet on which the supposedly universal phonetic transcription system, the linguist's most basic tool, is based.

There is strong evidence that laypeople's perception and conceptualization of language is shaped, partly at least, by literacy. They perceive distinctions that are coded in writing more readily than those that are not. Linguists assume that their training enables them to escape these preconceptions, but this assumption may not be true. The syntactically complete sentence is not the only writing-induced concept which plays a major role in linguistic theorizing. Words are linguistic units that one finds in dictionaries, and the similarity between the notion of a morphological word and that of an orthographic word is hardly coincidental. A stable form with an invariant literal meaning is precisely what is suggested by the disconnected unit recorded in a dictionary. In keeping with this notion, morphological and phonological analysis is primarily concerned with word-internal relationships. More generally, the study of grammar has been restricted, by and large, to the kind of decontextualized autonomous language appropriate for written texts. The linguistic units are, moreover, often given by the analysis that is inherent in the writing (recording) system in question.

No writing system is only a means of recording language. Writing always both represents and imposes structure. But the interrelations between the structures of languages and those of writing systems have not received much attention in linguistics. Therefore linguists have failed to sufficiently recognize the intimate relationship between written language and grammar and its implications for the very foundations of the scientific study of language.

See also Phoneme; Word; Written language.

Reading Lüdtke 1969; Linell 1982; Derwing 1992.

grammatology A modern formation from Gk γραμματο-, the combining form of γράμμα 'letter', and -λογία 'teaching', this term was suggested by Ignace GELB as a name for the science of writing. Rather than dealing with writing only as far as is necessary to retrieve the information it is employed to record, the study of writing as a scientific discipline in the intended sense describes and analyses the structural properties of writing systems, much like the science of phonology deals with the structural properties of linguistic sound systems. Gelb's term has not gained wide currency, but the scientific field that he envisaged has begun to take shape.

In a somewhat different though also related sense, the French philosopher Jacques Derrida has used the term *grammatologie* to designate a theory of writing which he understands as a critique of the logocentrism of the Western intellectual tradition since Aristotle, which considers the sign (writing) as a mere supplement rather than an epistemic force in its own right.
See also GRAPHEMICS; GRAPHETICS.
Reading Gelb 1963; Derrida 1967.

Grantha script Epigraphically identifiable as of the sixth century CE, the Grantha script is a member of the southern Indian branch of Brāhmī-derived scripts. Like all Indian scripts it is a syllabic alphabet consisting of independent V letters and C letters with an inherent *a* (table 6). It is the parent script of the MALAYALAM SCRIPT which took on a distinct form in the twelfth century. Apart from the Malayalam language, this script was also used as the southern Indian script for Sanskrit. Through this usage it influenced the development of the TAMIL WRITING. Grantha is written from left to right. Today it survives in its Malayalam derivative.
See also INDIAN WRITING SYSTEMS.
Reading Dani 1963.

graph The smallest formal unit of written language on the level of handwriting or print. This comprises all signs occurring in writing including capital and small letters, spaces, punctuation marks, numerals, abbreviations such as *Ltd, n.d.* and *etc.*, special symbols such as %, £ and ©, as well as typographic distinctions such as *italics* and superscripts and subscripts ^{123}, $_{456}$. From the set of all graphs of a writing its graphemes must be sorted out by distributional or representational analysis. Several graphs may form allographs of one grapheme. For example, the two Greek graphs σ and ς are allographs of the grapheme <σ>, their occurrence being contextually determined, since ς occurs exclusively in word-final position. Capital and small letters are also sometimes described as allographs of a common abstract grapheme. Such an analysis is language dependent and can only be justified if the distribution of capital and small letters can be shown to be contextually determined rather than indicating differences in meaning. In German, for example, capital letters signify a special word class, nouns. The semantic difference between the members of pairs such as *wand* 'wound' and *Wand* 'wall', *grab* 'dig!' and *Grab* 'grave', is indicated by the choice of a capital or small letter alone, which would suggest that both should be treated as graphemes rather than allographs of a common abstract grapheme. However, the factors underlying

a	ǧha	pha
i	ña	ba
u	ṭa	bha
e	ṭha	ma
ā	ḍa	ya
ka	ḍha	ra
kha	ṇa	la
ga	ta	va
gha	tha	sa
na	da	ṡa
ča	dha	ṣa
čha	na	ha
ǧa	pa	la

Table 6 The Grantha syllabic alphabet

the distribution of capital and small letters in various orthographies are little understood, and no general theoretical model for categorizing graphs as allographs of a grapheme in a given writing system has yet been established.
See also GRAPHEME.

grapheme Coined on analogy with 'phoneme', this term designates the unit of analysis in the study of written language understood as an abstract entity. In linguistics the graphemes of a language are commonly enclosed in angle brackets < >. Every analysis of a writing system starts out with compiling a complete list of the graphemes of that system on the basis of a set of data that comprise all of its GRAPHS, that is, all visually distinct formal elements. However, just as there are different understandings of the notion 'phoneme', the analogy is understood differently by different researchers.

There are basically two views of how the notion of a grapheme should be defined. Some students of writing (e.g. Pulgram 1976) have defined it as the smallest functional unit of writing on whatever structural level of language the writing system operates. In word writing systems, individual logograms are hence regarded as graphemes; in syllabic systems it is syllable signs; and the graphemes of segmental systems are letters, digraphs etc. In this sense the notion of a grapheme clearly departs from its model analogue in that it transcends the level of sound patterning. Other theoreticians prefer to avoid this conceptual inconsistency and reserve the notion of grapheme to segmental writing systems alone. The notion of grapheme then depends on that of phoneme.

Difficulties are associated with both uses of the term 'grapheme'. Where it is restricted to segmental systems, the problem arises of finding appropriate terms for graphic units referring to units of speech on levels other than phonology, in particular syllables, morphemes and words. As a solution Catach (1978) has proposed the term 'archigrapheme' to which are related 'primary graphemes' (i.e. transcriptions of phonemes) and 'secondary graphemes' (i.e. positional or morphological graphemes) which may be mute. On the other hand, where 'grapheme' is understood as the smallest functional unit of any writing system, the problem is that the term suggests the comparability of the units of different writing systems, although it is unclear in what sense they are comparable.

Another question about the definition of 'grapheme' has to do with the theoretical conception of how written and spoken language are related. *Representationalistic* theories, as advocated for instance by DeFrancis (1989), regard writing as a representation of speech and, accordingly, a grapheme as the smallest segment of speech represented in writing, a visual unit which in a given script corresponds to a unit of speech – a phoneme in the narrow sense of 'grapheme' mentioned above. By contrast, *distributionalistic* theories, as advocated among others by Eisenberg (1985), define the grapheme autonomously without reference to speech, taking into account the structural characteristics of written language alone. A grapheme is thus understood as the smallest identifiable unit of the writing system of a given language which differentiates meaning. Every writing system is to be analysed in terms of the distribution and visual distinctness of these units, the question of their relation to speech being left until a full structural description of the writing system on the basis of independently defined graphemes is available. This approach does not rule out the existence of systematic relationships between the structural levels where the minimal units of spoken and written language are specified; but it starts out from the assumption that these minimal units are affected by their respective contextual environments, and therefore cannot be expected to relate to each other in straightforward bidirectional correspondences. Conceiving the grapheme in this manner as conceptually autonomous is the most promising theoretical approach for coming to grips with the complex relationships between units of writing and units of speech.

See also GRAPHEMICS; GRAPHETICS; ORTHOGRAPHY; PHONEME.

Reading Catach 1978; Pulgram 1976; Eisenberg 1985; Kohrt 1986; Henderson 1986; DeFrancis 1989.

grapheme–phoneme correspondence Representationalistic theories of written language take as their point of departure that a linear order of graphic elements usually corresponds to a temporal succession of phonological elements. Determining these correspondences – grapheme–phoneme correspondences in the case of alphabetic scripts – is seen as the crucial component of a linguistic analysis of writing, and their complexity as one criterion for measuring the relative difficulty of orthographies. In phonemic transcription this correspondence is ideally one-to-one. However, most alphabetic orthographies such as English spelling, French spelling, and German spelling deviate to a greater or lesser extent from such a simple relationship in as much as they exhibit Polyvalence in both directions between alphabetic symbols and phonemes. It is very common that the correspondence between graphemes and phonemes is either 'one-to-many', for instance <c> corresponding to /s/ and /k/ in *cipher* and *come*, respectively; or 'many-to-one', for instance both <c> as in *cat* and <k> as in *king* corresponding to /k/; or both. Moreover, the sequential order of elements on the graphic level may not be the same as that of the phonological level. In *cat* this is the case, and the relationship between the elements of the spoken and written word is accordingly simple:

```
<c a t>
 | | |
/k æ t/
```

But many words exhibit much more complex relationships. For example, the final <e> in English words such as *tone* is not pronounced at the end of the word, but that is not to say that its presence in the orthographic word corresponds to nothing on the phonological level. Rather, it corresponds to certain features of the preceding vowel, which is readily apparent when we compare the pronunciation of the same vowel grapheme <o> in *ton*:

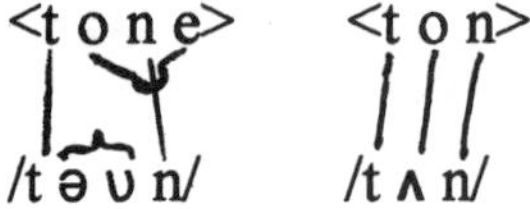

It is because of such complexities that some scholars reject the idea that establishing grapheme–phoneme correspondences is suitable as a method for analysing alphabetic writing systems, emphasizing instead the importance of higher-level correspondences between spoken and written language.

See also Grapheme; Graphemics; Orthography.

Reading Haas 1970; Luelsdorff 1987.

graphemics The linguistic study of writing systems based on a description of their elements and the graphotactic rules specifying the systematically permissible combinations thereof. Research in this field has concentrated on alphabetic writing systems since the term Grapheme was coined on analogy with Phoneme, and it has been the relationship between phonology and graphemics which has dominated the theoretical discussion. The case for an autonomous graphemics has been made most forcefully and consistently since the 1930s by members of the linguistic school of Prague. There are two aspects to the question of the autonomy of graphemics: do the regularities of written language constitute an independent level of linguistic structure, and should the study of these regularities be construed as an independent subdiscipline of linguistics? Although mainstream linguistics has long relegated writing to a backstage position as supposedly a mere substitute of speech, both of these questions are now generally answered

affirmatively. The relative recency of writing, as well as the fact that not all languages have a written form, are no longer considered valid reasons to disregard the specific properties of written language or to reduce them to surrogates of properties of speech. An autonomous graphemics treats WRITTEN LANGUAGE as a linguistic system in its own right. The relationship to spoken language is not eliminated from the research agenda, but written language is no longer reduced to, and described as, a secondary system of representation. Instead, an autonomous graphemics recognizes that written language has properties not found in spoken language, and vice versa, and that therefore a structural description of both must precede an analysis of how sound system and writing system relate to each other.
See also GRAMMATOLOGY.
Reading Haas 1970; Vachek 1973; Augst 1986.

graphetics The study of the physical properties of written signs. This term is a conceptual analogue of phonetics and accordingly two divisions can be distinguished: *visual graphetics* and *mechanical graphetics*, corresponding to auditory and articulatory phonetics, respectively.

Visual graphetics investigates the graphic design features of written signs, including the geometric shapes of which they are composed; frequency distributions of certain features such as descenders and ascenders of alphabetic letters; similarities and minimal distinctions of the signs belonging to one system; their orientation, if any; and features critical for recognition. What is it that all tokens of capital *A* have in common? To what extent is it defined contrastively by the features it must *not* share with all other letters? How far can geometric features be distorted before recognition becomes impossible? And so on.

Mechanical graphetics, on the other hand, is concerned with how written signs are mechanically generated, trying to answer questions such as the following. What are the possible and the preferred movements of the human hand? How are strokes produced on a surface, and how do writers connect strokes with one another? What does it take to maintain contact with the writing surface in drawing curved and angular lines of various directions? What kinds of cursivization and abbreviation tendencies can be attributed to the mechanics of the hand? Are there any movements and strokes that are rare across many different scripts? More generally, how do the mechanical conditions of manually producing successions of signs on a surface influence the shapes of the individual signs?

Clearly, there are analogies between the mechanics of the hand and those of the articulation apparatus, but in other respects the production of signs in the two media – the modulation of an air stream and the tracing of visual marks on a surface – are subject to specific physical conditions that have no parallel. For example, there is nothing in the temporal linearity of speech sounds that corresponds to the direction of a script. Hence, a BOUSTROPHEDON piece of writing has no analogue in vocal utterances; there is nothing in speech that can be likened to left-running or right-running scripts. Further, speech is realized as a continuous sound stream which can be analysed as a succession of segments, whereas written signs are segments to begin with. Other articulation characteristics of writing such as lines and columns also have no counterpart in spoken

language. Thus the function of graphetics in the analysis of writing can be compared to, but not derived from, that of phonetics in the analysis of speech. The task of graphetics can be defined as describing the graphic design features of writing systems (visual graphetics) and the physical conditions of the writing process (mechanical graphetics). How the latter influence the former is the general question to be tackled cooperatively by both divisions of graphetics. Research in this area is in its infancy.
Reading Sirat 1987.

graphology [Gk γραΦο- 'writing' + λογία 'discourse'] **1** The study of handwriting from the point of view of diagnostic psychology. The basic assumption is that features of handwriting such as size, slant, direction, the construction of letter forms with strokes, loops, circles and angles, angularity, roundedness, protrusion of descenders and ascenders, writing speed and pressure, junctions of letters, and spacing of letters and words are indicative of character and personality traits. Ascertaining the authorship of handwritten documents is one of the areas where graphology has been put to practical use in the context of both historical and criminal investigations. More controversial is its employment since the beginning of the twentieth century in the screening of job applications. Clinical personality studies usually combine graphological tests with other psychodiagnostic methods rather than relying on the analysis of handwriting alone. **2** Sometimes the term 'graphology' is also used in analogy with 'phonology', that is, in the sense of Graphemics.
Reading **1** Ansell 1979; Hertz 1970; Hargreaves 1992.

grashdanskaja asbuka [Russian 'civil script'] The Cyrillic alphabet in the form that in 1708 Peter the Great had designed for it by typecasters in Amsterdam. *See also* Cyrillic.

grave accent The accent mark <`> is used in the orthographies of several alphabetically written languages as a diacritic to mark pitch accent, stress or tone, to distinguish sound values and, occasionally, to differentiate words. In ancient Greek, presumably the origin of this and other accent marks, the grave indicated low pitch. In modern languages it is more frequently used to distinguish manner of articulation. For example, in French spelling it indicates an open articulation of <e>, as in *père* [pɛ:r]. Italian spelling (Italian alphabet) uses the grave accent whenever a word of more than one syllable stresses the final vowel, as in *città*. Semantic discrimination is also sometimes achieved, as for example *e* 'and' vs *è* 'is'. In the alphabetic orthography of Chinese, Pinyin, the grave serves as a tone marker for the fourth, falling tone. This latter usage coincides with the recommendations of the IPA to use the grave as a transcription for a high falling tone. *See also* Accent.

Greek alphabet The first fully phonetic system of writing which represents both C and V segments by individual letters arranged in a linear fashion, the Greek alphabet is a successful adaptation of an earlier north Semitic script, generally thought to be Phoenician or Canaanite. The Greek alphabet is a prime example of the developmental tendency of writing systems to undergo a change of type when transferred to languages unrelated to that for which they first

Phoenician			Greek		
name	sign	value	name	sign	value
'aleph	𐤀	/'/	alpha	A	/a/
he	𐤄	/h/	epsilon	϶	/e/
waw	Y	/w/	upsilon	Y	/u/
yod	𐤉	/y/	iota	I	/i/
ʻayin	o	/ʻ/	omicron	O	/o/

Table 7 Greek vowel values assigned to Phoenician consonant letters

evolved. What distinguishes the Greek alphabet from all earlier systems of the eastern Mediterranean is that it represents Cs and Vs by means of independent letters of the same kind rather than relying on diacritics or C letters for V indication. It is not known exactly when the Greeks first used the Semitic script for their own language, but an increasing corpus of early Greek inscriptions suggests that the borrowing took place around the turn of the second millennium BCE.

Although there are ways of indicating Vs in Semitic scripts, the 22 letters of the Phoenician alphabet include no V signs. In the Greek adaptation five Phoenician C letters were reinterpreted and assigned vocalic values (table 7). Whether this happened by accident or ingenious design is not clear, but it seems that these changes were made in a single move for, apart from *omega*, the classic vowels are present in the earliest Greek documents; no developmental state of Greek writing with defective V representation is known. It has been suggested that the assignment of Greek Vs to Phoenician C signs was the result of a misinterpretation of the Phoenician system. The letter names *alpha, beta, gamma* etc. are meaningless in Greek, but in Phoenician they are meaningful words designating the letters in accordance with the ACROPHONIC PRINCIPLE by virtue of the initial sounds of these words, *'āleph* 'ox' for /'/, *bēth* 'house' for /b/, *gīmel* 'camel' for /g/ etc. However, certain phonological differences between Phoenician and Greek made it difficult to apply the acrophonic principle in exactly the same way as it was applied in Phoenician. All Phoenician words have initial Cs, but many Greek words begin with a V. Moreover, the glottal stop /'/ represented by the letter *'āleph*, and the emphatic sound /ʻ/ represented by the letter *ʻayin*, are not phonemic in Greek and therefore not readily perceived by native speakers of Greek. Thus the Greeks were likely to pronounce the names of the first letter of the Phoenician alphabet not with an initial glottal stop, but with an initial /a/. The result was that *alpha* came to represent a V, whereas *'āleph* represents a C. In this way the Greeks augmented the Phoenician consonant script with vowel letters. It must also be noted, however, that the letters which acquired V values in Greek had been used in Semitic scripts to indicate Vs in the form of MATRES LECTIONIS in word-final position.

The system of V letters at which the Greeks had thus arrived underwent considerable changes from the earliest attested documents to the classical period. In the archaic period V length was not marked, but in the classical system only *alpha* and *iota* continued to be used for both long and short Vs. Short /e/ was differentiated from /e:/ when the consonant /h/ expressed by Phoenician *hēth* was lost and its letter acquired the value /e:/ of *eta*, distinguishing it from /e/ of *epsilon*. The 'big o' <Ω ω> *omega* was introduced to distinguish /o:/ from 'little o' /o/ *omicron*, written as <o>. The representation of /u/, which was first expressed by Phoenician *wāw*, also changed as this sound came to be realized as /y/ in many contexts. A digraph combining *omicron* and *upsilon* was consequently used to represent /u/. Originally another sign F, called DIGAMMA in Greek, had been derived from Phoenician *wāw* for the representation of a labiodental /w/, which soon fell out of use together with the letter, which, however, was later re-employed in Latin as the letter *F*.

Further modifications of the archaic alphabet followed later as the letters Φ *phi* and X *chi* were introduced for the aspirated stops /p^h/ and /k^h/ respectively, and the letters Ψ *psi* and Ξ *xi* for the C clusters /ps/ and /ks/. These letters were added at the end of the list which the Greeks left in the conventional Semitic order (*xi* was originally listed before *phi*). With these supplementary letters the Greek alphabet was complete, but the writing system and the script underwent further changes. A number of local forms of the alphabet developed to fit the various dialects spoken in different parts of Greece. They are usually divided into eastern and western scripts (table 8). In 403 BCE Athens made an attempt at script unification, officially adopting the eastern Greek variety. It is basically in this form that the 24-letter Greek alphabet has come down to us.

In the early documents the Greeks followed Phoenician practice by writing from right to left, the letter forms having a left-facing orientation. For some time both horizontal directions of writing were possible as documented in numerous BOUSTROPHEDON (refer to illustration) inscriptions. By the fifth century BCE, the left-to-right direction had become standard practice. When the direction of writing was firmly established, the orientation of letter forms also became fixed. In some boustrophedon inscriptions non-symmetric letters such as B, Γ, E, K, P changed orientation with the alternating directions of the lines; but once the left-to-right direction of writing was fixed, all of these letters were given a uniform right-facing orientation (table 9). Further, in early inscriptions the Greeks did not mark WORD BOUNDARIES which apparently were not essential for the type of reading they engaged in. Neither was there a distinction between capital and small letters. The latter evolved from later uncial letter forms which came to be employed in combination with capitals only in Byzantine times. Modern Greek orthography uses capital letters as initials of proper names, place names, titles and government offices, and for emphasis.

The archaic alphabet had no ACCENT or breathing marks. Diacritics for high, low and contour pitch were added by Alexandrian grammarians in the middle of the third century BCE. Conventionally referred to by its Latin name, the *spiritus asper* (rough breathing) was originally expressed by the letter which later became *eta*, but the *spiritus lenis* (smooth breathing) was not represented (table 10). In modern Greek the three pitch accents have been superseded by a single stress accent, rendering the orthographic distinction unnecessary. The orthography reform of 1982 introduced 'monotone' writing, recognizing only the acute for

	Eastern	Western
alpha	A A	A A
beta	B B	B B
gamma	𐌂 Γ Λ	Γ Γ
delta	Δ D	Δ ▷ D
epsilon	𐌄 E	𐌄 E
digamma	[𐌅]	𐌅 F
zeta	𐌆	𐌆
eta	𐌇 H	𐌇 H
theta	⊗ ⊙	⊗ ⊙
iota	I	I
kappa	K	K
lambda	𐌋 Λ	𐌋 Λ
mu	M M	M M
nu	N N	N N
xi	Ξ	X +
omikron	O	O
pi	𐌐 Π	𐌐 Π
koppa	[Ϙ]	Ϙ
rho	P R R	P R R
sigma	Σ Ϛ	Σ Ϛ
tau	T	T
upsilon	V Y	V Y
phi	Φ Φ	Φ Φ
chi	X +	↓ Ψ
psi	↓ Ψ	✱
omega	Ω	

Table 8 Eastern and western varieties of the Greek alphabet

Right to left	Left to right

Table 9 Reversal of non-symmetric letter forms after left-to-right direction of writing became established

Accent marks	Breathing marks
<ά> acute (ἡ ὀξεία)	<ἁ> rough breathing (δασεία)
<ὰ> grave (ἡ βαρεία)	<ἀ> smooth breathing (ψιλή)
<ᾶ> circumflex (ἡ περισπωμένη)	

Table 10 Greek accent and breathing marks

marking stress accent (figure 5). The reform has also done away with the subscript iota <ᾳ> placed below α, η and ω in Classical Greek and the archaizing Katharevousa style. The DIAERESIS <¨> is placed on ι and υ to indicate separate pronunciation of two consecutive Vs: και [kɛ:] vs καϊ [kai]. Modern Greek uses the following punctuation marks: full stop <.>, semicolon <·>, comma <,>, colon <:>, question mark <;>, exclamation mark <!>, quotation marks <« »>, dash <–> and brackets <( )>. Although not completely phonemic, with two letters for C clusters, the alphabet of Classical Greek closely mapped the phonological structure of the language. The modern orthography is more complicated (table 11). A number of sound changes are reflected in the use of digraphs (table 12).

See also ALPHABET; ALPHABETIC HYPOTHESIS; ALPHABETICAL ORDER; PHOENICIAN ALPHABET.

Reading Millard 1976; Diringer 1968, 1977; McCarter 1975; Jeffery 1982; Isserlin 1983; Gaur 1992.

Δϖσε μου δυόσμο να μυρίσω
[ðɔsɛ mu ðiɔzmɔ na mirisɔ

λουîζα κι βασιλικω
luiza kɛ vasilikɔ

Μαζι μ' αυτα να σε φιλησω
mazi mafta na sɛ filisɔ

και τι να πρωτοϑυμηϑϖ
kɛ ti na prɔtɔθimiθɔ]

Let me smell the bush of mint
basil and balm
I want to kiss you with this scent
Waiting for remembrance

Figure 5 Sample of modern Greek writing: from Odysseas Elytis, Marina

Letter	Name	Ancient pronunciation	Modern pronunciation	Translit-eration
Α α	alpha	[a]	[a]	a
Β β	beta	[b]	[v]	b/v
Γ γ	gamma	[g]	[j],[y]	g/y,j
Δ δ	delta	[d]	[ð]	d(h)
Ε ϵ	epsilon	[ɛ]	[ɛ]	e
Ζ ζ	zeta	[zd]	[z]	z
Η η	eta	[ɛ:]	[i]	e,ē/i
Θ θ	thēta	[tʰ]	[θ]	θ/th
Ι ι	iota	[i]	[i]	i
Κ κ	kappa	[k]	[k]	k,c/k
Λ λ	lambda	[l]	[l]	l
Μ μ	mu	[m]	[m]	m
Ν ν	nu	[n]	[n]	n
Ξ ξ	xi	[ks]	[ks]	ks/x
Ο ο	omicron	[o]	[o]	o
Π π	pi	[p]	[p]	p
Ρ ρ	rho	[r]	[r]	r
Σ σ ς	sigma	[s]	[s]	s
Τ τ	tau	[t]	[t]	t
Υ υ	upsilon	[u],[y]	[i]	u,y/i
Φ φ	phi	[pʰ]	[f]	ph/f
Χ χ	chi	[kʰ]	[x]	kh,ch/h,x
Ψ ψ	psi	[ps]	[ps]	ps
Ω ω	omega	[ɔ:]	[o]	ō/o

Table 11 The Greek alphabet with ancient and modern pronunciation and Roman transliteration

αι	[a:]	ηυ	[iv]	γκ	[g]
αυ	[av]	οι	[i:]	γγ	[ŋg]
αϋ	[ai]	οϊ	[ɔi]	γχ	[ŋx]
ει	[i:]	ου	[u:]	μβ	[b]
εϊ	[εi]	υι	[i:]	τζ	[dz]
ευ	[εv]			χι	[ç]

Table 12 Digraphs in modern Greek

Greek-derived scripts The Greek idea of writing spread through the Mediterranean world of antiquity (figure 6). In Asia Minor several non-Hellenic peoples such as the Carians, Lycians, Lydians, Pamphylians and Phrygians developed their own alphabets on the Greek model. In Egypt it eventually supplanted the EGYPTIAN WRITING SYSTEM in the form of the COPTIC ALPHABET. From the Hellenic colonies in Sicily it swept across the Italian peninsula, inspiring the creation of the ETRUSCAN ALPHABET and the Messapian alphabet and indirectly other OLD ITALIC SCRIPTS, from which in turn the LATIN ALPHABET is a direct descendant. And on the mainland it was carried north in the wake of Christian missionary work to become the rootstock of the GOTHIC ALPHABET, CYRILLIC and the GLAGOLITIC ALPHABET. Although the Greek alphabet is today used only for the Greek language, it is, through Latin, the parent script of the most widely disseminated family of scripts now in existence.

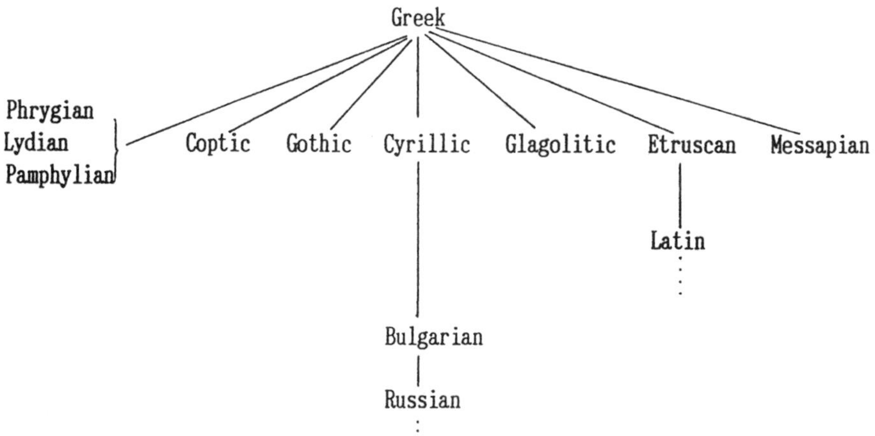

Figure 6 Descendants of the Greek alphabet

Grotefend, Georg Friedrich (1775–1853) In his treatise *Praevia de cuneatis quas vocant inscriptionibus Persepolitanis legendis et explicandis relatio* (*Preliminary Report on Reading and Explaining the Cuneiform Inscriptions of Persepolis*), published in 1802, Grotefend, a German philologist, explained the names of the Persian kings Darius and Xerxes in Old Persian inscriptions. His idea was that the introductory lines of a Persepolis inscription probably contained the name, title and genealogy of the ruler who had caused the inscription to be carved. He assumed that a certain group of cuneiform characters repeated several times represented 'king' and set up a hypothetical formula: 'so-and-so, great king, king of kings, son of so-and-

so, the king'. On this assumption the first of the two inscriptions he worked on read 'king Y, son of X', while the second was 'king Z, son of king Y'. This fitted perfectly with the genealogy of King Xerxes known from Herodotus: Xerxes, son King Darius, son of Hystaspes (who was not a king). On the basis of this discovery Grotefend was able to read several proper names and thus opened the path for the decipherment of cuneiform writing.
See also CUNEIFORM WRITING.

grotesque A family of square-cut printing type without SERIFS or hair-lines first created in England early in the nineteenth century (figure 7). Because it was inspired by inscriptions of Roman brick stamps, it was formerly called 'stone letter'.
See also TYPOGRAPHY.

Gujarati script Derived from an early version of the Bengālī script, the Gujarati script is the syllabic alphabet of the Gujarati language which, with its approximately 45 million speakers, is one of the major languages of India. It belongs to the northern Indian group of Brāhmī-derived scripts. The system of the Gujarati script resembles that of Devanāgarī, but its outer form is conspicuously different since it has no horizontal top bar. It is written from left to right with word spacing and a perpendicular stroke marking the end of a sentence. The consonant letters are shown in table 13. Independent vowel letters are available for *a*, *i*, *u* and syllabic *r*, while those for *ā*, *ī*, *ū*, *ō* and *au* are derived thereof by means of diacritics (tables 14, 15). Except for *-a* which is the inherent V of all unmodified C letters, Vs are also indicated by diacritics placed around the C letters. The inherent V is thus replaced by another V. A small under-hook is used for V muting, and a dot placed on top of a letter (ANUSVARA) shows nasalization. The Gujarati orthography is quite systematic on the phonemic level, but the ligatures that have to be learned to read the script are numerous.

Gupta script One of the major northern Indian scripts, the Gupta script is a direct descendant of BRĀHMĪ WRITING. It was created under the Gupta dynasty in the fourth century CE. Vowel indication follows the usual Indian pattern with diacritic satellites placed around a consonant base letter which in isolation has an inherent *a* V. In addition, it has four independent V letters for *a*, *i*, *u* and *e* (table 16). The Gupta script is the parent script of both the Nāgarī and Pāli scripts, and a cursive variety was carried to Central Asia where it was further developed into the Tocharian script, also known as 'Central Asian slanting'.
See also INDIAN WRITING SYSTEMS.
Reading Bühler 1980; Jensen 1969.

Gurmukhī script One of the Brāhmī-derived scripts, *Guru-mukhī*, 'the script that issued from the mouth of the guru', is a direct descendant of Nāgarī to which it bears close formal resemblance because of the characteristic horizontal top bar. Associated with the Sikh religion, it was devised in the sixteenth century CE by the second Sikh guru to replace the Laṇḍā script for writing the Punjabi language. Like the other Brāhmī derivatives, Gurmukhī is a syllabic alphabet written from

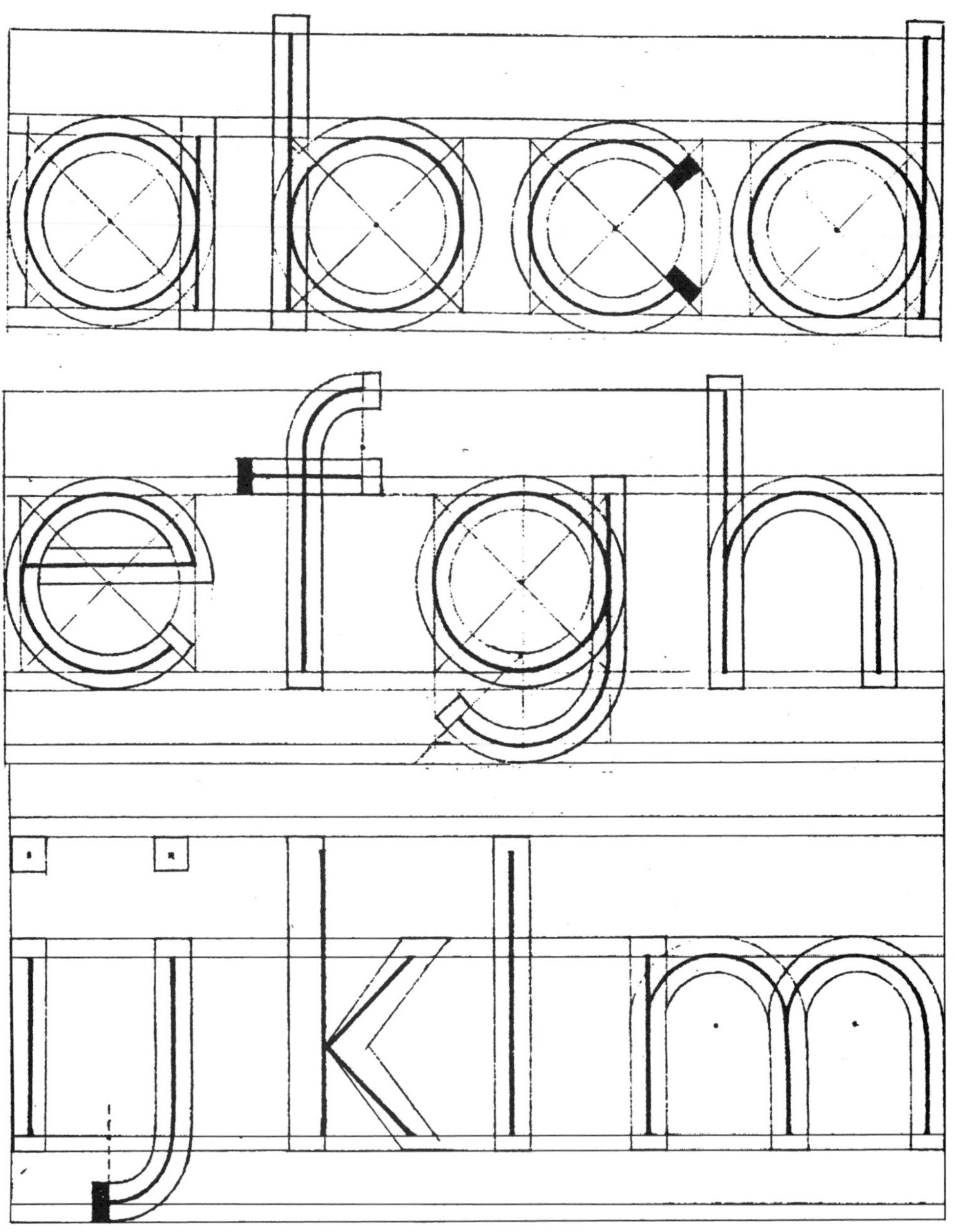

Figure 7 The architecture of lower case grotesque letters

ક	ka	ખ	kha	ગ	ga	ઘ	gha	ઙ	na
ચ	ca	છ	cha	જ	ja	ઝ	jha	ઞ	ña
ટ	ṭa	ઠ	ṭha	ડ	ḍa	ઢ	ḍha	ણ	ṇa
ત	ta	થ	tha	દ	da	ધ	dha	મ	ma
પ	pa	ફ	pha	બ	ba	ભ	bha		
ય	ya	ર	ra	લ	la	વ	va	ળ	ḷa
શ	śa	ષ	ṣa	સ	sa	હ	ha		

Table 13 Gujarati consonant letters

અ	a	આ	ā
ઇ	i	ઈ	ī
ઉ	u	ઊ	ū
ઋ	ṛ		
એ	e	ઐ	ai
ઓ	ō	ઔ	au

Table 14 Gujarati vowel letters

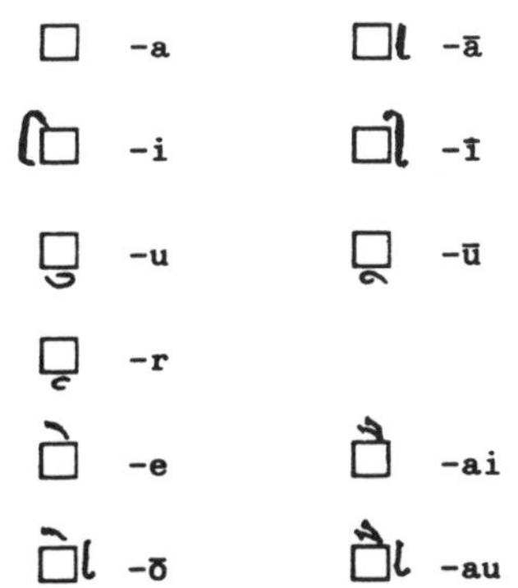

Table 15 Gujarati vowel diacritics

Consonant letters				Vowel letters
ka	ña	pa	va	a
kha	ṭa	pha	śa	i
ga	ḍa	ba	ša	u
gha	ta	bha	sa	e
ṅa	tha	ma	ha	
ca	da	ya		
cha	dha	ra		
ja	na	la		

Table 16 The Gupta syllabic alphabet

left to right. A vertical stroke indicates a period. Punjabi has three tonal accents which, however, are not systematically marked in writing, although the letter *ha*, sometimes reduced to a subscript hook, is used to indicate a high tone on the preceding V. The ten independent V letters given in table 17 are organized on three base forms for *a*, *i* and *u*, from which the others are derived by diacritic modification. A dot (*bindi*) or a small semicircle (*tippi*) placed on the right shoulder of the letter indicate nazalization of the V. The inherent *a* V of the consonant letters is muted whenever a V letter follows, but its pronunciation is not mandatory in the context of a subsequent C letter. Gurmukhī has no special character for vowel muting: hence C clusters are typically spelled as C-*a* + C-*a* with the first -*a* being left unpronounced.
See also INDIAN WRITING SYSTEMS.
Reading Gill and Gleason 1963.

Gutenberg, Johannes Gensfleich zum (1397–1468) A citizen of Mainz, Gutenberg was trained as a goldsmith and was hence well versed in the art of forging metal. He applied his technical expertise to perfecting the process of mechanical text reproduction by inventing movable type around 1445. His famous 42-line Latin Bible, traditionally regarded as the first printed book, dates from 1455 (table 18). In addition to the letters of the Latin alphabet he used a variety of LIGATURES and abbreviations as were common in medieval MANUSCRIPT writing (table 19). These characters were a typical by-product of the slow technology of handwritten reproduction. As the advantages of the new technology became fully understood and exploited, ligatures and abbreviations gradually disappeared from the printer's letter case. Gutenberg was a pioneer who is often credited with

Consonant letters								**Vowel letters**	
ਕ	ka	ਟ	ṭa	ਪ	pa	ਸ	sa	ਅ	a
ਖ	kha	ਠ	ṭha	ਫ	pha	ਹ	ha	ਆ	ā
ਗ	ga	ਡ	ḍa	ਬ	ba	ਗ੍ਯ	gya	ਇ	i
ਘ	gha	ਢ	ḍha	ਭ	bha	ਨ੍ਹ	nha	ਈ	ī
ਙ	ṅa	ਣ	ṇa	ਮ	ma	ਮ੍ਹ	mha	ਉ	u
ਚ	ca	ਤ	ta	ਯ	ya	ਰ੍ਹ	rha	ਊ	ū
ਛ	cha	ਥ	tha	ਰ	ra	ਲ੍ਹ	lha	ਏ	e
ਜ	ja	ਦ	da	ਲ	la	ੜ੍ਹ	rha	ਐ	ai
ਝ	jha	ਧ	dha	ਵ	va	ਸ਼	š	ਓ	o
ਞ	ña	ਨ	na	ੜ	ṛa	ਜ਼	z	ਔ	au
						ਲ਼	ḷa		
						ਤ੍ਰ	tr		

Table 17 The Gurmukhī syllabic alphabet

A A a	a	H h	h	O o	o	V u	v
B b	b	I î ı	i	P p	p	W w	w
C c	c	J j	j	Q q	q	x x	x
D d	d	K k	k	R r ꝛ	r	y	y
E e	e	L l l	l	S ſ ſ s	s	Z z	z
F f	f	M m	m	T t	t		
G g	g	N n	n	U u	u		

Table 18 Alphabet of the Gutenberg Bible

ā	am, an	do	do	pa	pa	ꝛ	r
ä	ar	ḋ	nd	pe	pe	r̄ r̄	re
ba	ba	ē	em, en, est	p̄	per	ꝝ	rum
be	be	ė	er, re	p̄	præ	ſ	s
bet	bet	fi	fi	po	po	ſ̄	ser
bo	bo	fl	fl	pp	pp, pop	ſſ	ss
ch	ch	ffl	ffl	ppe	ppe	ſt ſt	st
cha	cha	ġ	gi	ṗ	pre, pri	t̄	ta
che	che	g̈	gra	pⁱ	pri	ṫ	ter, tur
cho	cho	ha	ha	ꝓ	pro	th	th
co	co	he	he	ꝓp	prop	the	the
ꝯ	com	î	im, in, min, mni, ni	q̈	qua, qui	ü	ua
c̄	cra, cri	ĵ	j	q̈ꝫ	quam, quan	û	uer, ver
ċ	cri	ł	el, il, les, ul	qꝫ	que	ū	um, un
ct	ct	m̄	mm, mn	q̄	que, quod	ꝰ ꝫ	us
da	da	ä	an	q̂	qui	va	va
de	de	n̄ ā	nn, omin	q̊	quo	ve	ve
ḋe	dem	ö	ao	ꝗ	quod	⁊	et
dē	den	ō	io, on	q̊ꝫ	quoque		

Table 19 Some of Gutenberg's ligatures and abbreviations

Figure 8 Anonymous portrait of Johannes Gutenberg from the seventeenth century (by permission of the Gutenberg Museum, Mainz: photograph Ludwig Ridefer)

revolutionizing intellectual life in Europe (figure 8). Although printing with movable type in Korea pre-dates Gutenberg by several centuries, the historical context of humanism and then the Reformation movement guaranteed his invention immediate impact, providing as it did a means for the popularization of literacy.
See also Printing; Type.
Reading Febvre and Martin 1958; Raabe 1990.

Gwoyeu Romatzyh [國語羅馬字] Gwoyeu Romatzyh (GR) or National Language Romanization is a system of phonetic writing for Chinese created in 1926 by a team of Chinese linguists headed by Yuen Ren Chao. Designed for the national language, it represents Mandarin, that is, an educated variety of the Beijing dialect. Although it gained official recognition and was promulgated in 1928 by the Ministry of Education in Nanjing, its use as a practical system of writing remained restricted to a few dictionaries and textbooks. A distinguishing formal characteristic of GR is its mode of indicating the four Tones of Mandarin. Instead of diacritics it uses a system of 'tone spelling' that indicates tones with

alphabetic letters. Thus, the four tonal syllables [fen] are spelled *fen, fern, feen, fenn*. In this manner GR forms a different graphic image for each tonal syllable in Mandarin.
See also ROMANIZATION; PINYIN.
Reading Newnham 1987.

Gypsy alphabet *See* ROMANI ALPHABET

H, h /ɛitʃ/ The eighth letter of the English alphabet goes back to Semitic *hēth*, a letter which had a consonant value similar to /x/. In the Greek alphabet it was first used to express rough breathing (*spiritus asper*) and later became the letter *eta* (Η, η) which was sometimes used to represent the long vowel /ɛː/. In English this letter represents an aspirated sound or a glottal stop.

háček [Czech 'little hook'] The háček or 'wedge' <ˇ> is a diacritic commonly used in Slavic orthographies. Placed on letters for alveolar or palatal Cs it serves to represent palato-alveolar fricatives or affricates, for example <š> for [ʃ], <ž> for [ʒ], <č> for [tʃ], <ǰ> for [dʒ]. It is also placed on some other letters, for instance <ř>, to indicate flapped articulation. As a tone mark the wedge is used iconically for a falling-rising tone as in Chinese PINYIN.
See also DIACRITIC.

handwriting At the beginning of the second millennium CE, Abū Ḥayyān at-Tawḥīdī, a leading Arab philologist of Persian origin, characterized handwriting thus: 'Handwriting is the tongue of the hand. Style is the tongue of the intellect. The intellect is the tongue of good actions and qualities. And good actions and qualities are the perfection of man' (Rosenthal 1948). This description captures well the multifaceted nature of handwriting. In modern parlance handwriting is a highly specialized human skill involving coordinated precision motions of the arm, the wrist, the hand and the fingers, neurally controlled and with immediate visual feedback. 'The tongue of the hand' is a fitting metaphor, since the articulated movements of thumb and fingers necessary for producing legible handwriting are just as complex as those of the articulatory tract necessary for producing intelligible speech. Moreover, as in speech, motor control is exercised in response to instructions by the language and orthographic systems (figure 1). Letter forms must be produced and they must be placed in the correct order to form words and higher-level units suitable for conveying linguistic meaning. There is hence a double feedback link to the motor command system and to the language system, one controlling letter shapes and the other higher-level language patterns such as spelling configurations. In addition, there is also sensory feedback from the hand's contact with the writing surface which controls the writing point pressure – a mechanism that can be likened to volume control through auditory feedback in speech.

Another systematic characteristic that handwriting has in common with speech is that it involves the physical production of variable tokens representing invariant types (the ideal letter shapes). Two dimensions of variation which are generally recognized are individual and national. National hands have a distinctive appearance partly for linguistic reasons: letter frequencies and other characteristic spelling patterns reflect structural properties of the languages in question. But there may even be national differences where the same script and the same

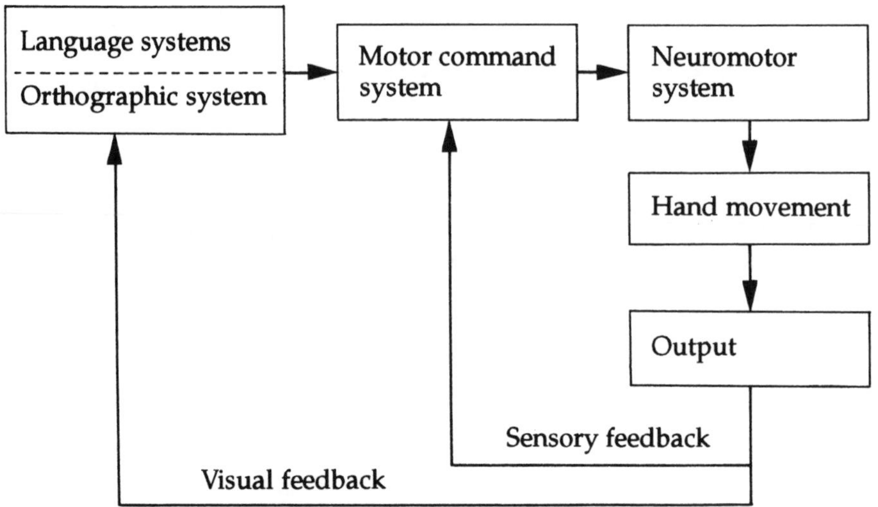

Figure 1 Simplified block diagram of systems involved in handwriting

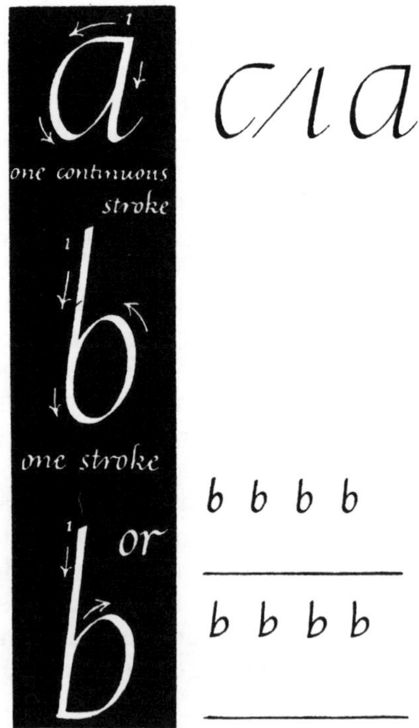

Figure 2 Sample of letter models with directions of strokes indicated for elementary instruction in British schools

language are involved, e.g. a British and an American hand. Such differences reflect different traditions of teaching handwriting and different underlying concepts of letter shapes (figures 2, 3). For instance, a small *b* may be taught as a single perpendicular stroke beginning at the top and turning right at the bottom into a loop that bends back to reconnect with the initial stroke; or as a forward-turning loop added to the perpendicular stroke. An *x* may be taught as consisting of two crossed oblique bars or as two curves that touch in the middle. Instructions of this sort result in routinized movements and rhythms which are at the basis of the common features of national hands.

Individual variability in handwriting reflects educational and cultural influences as well as age, practice and personal choice (figure 4). Individual style in handwriting is commonly interpreted as an expression of personality, a perception which graphology has tried to put on a scientific footing as a psychodiagnostic technique.

Because of the many subskills (linguistic, neural, motor, visual) that must be coordinated in handwriting if legible output is to result, it is a common object of interest for experimental and diagnostic psychologists, neurologists and neurolinguists.

See also CALLIGRAPHY; GRAPHETICS; GRAPHOLOGY; MANUSCRIPT; WRITING TOOLS

Reading Fairbank 1970; Wing 1979; Kao, et al. 1986.

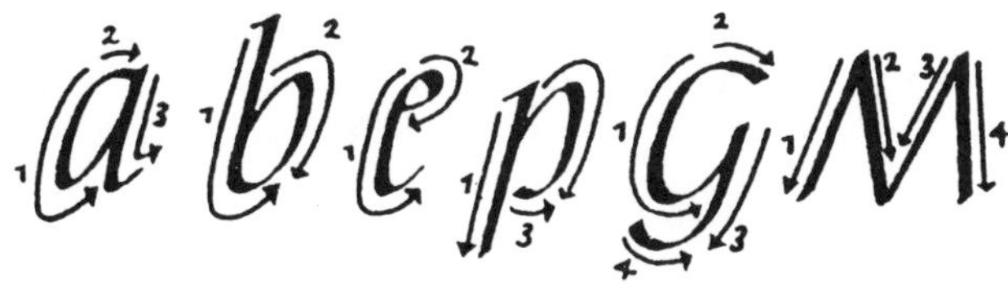

Figure 3 Sample of letter models with directions of strokes indicated for elementary instruction in German schools

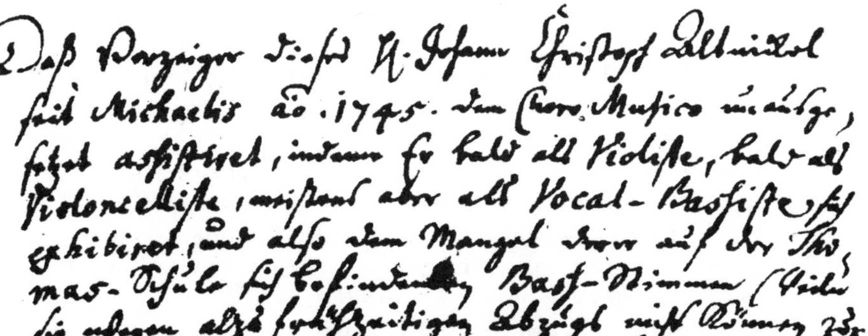

Figure 4 Johann Sebastian Bach's autographed letter of recommendation for his son-in-law, J. Christoph Altniko

han'gŭl [Korean 한글] (*han-geul*) The name of Korea's phonetic system of writing, promulgated in 1446 by King Sejong.

See also KOREAN WRITING.

hanja [Korean 漢字 'Chinese character'] Chinese characters as they are used in Korean.
See also KOREAN WRITING.

hànyŭ pīnyīn [lit. 'Chinese language spell sounds'] The name of the Latin-based phonetic script for Chinese adopted in 1958 by the People's Republic of China.
See also PINYIN.

hànzì [Chinese 漢字 'Chinese character'] *See* CHINESE WRITING SYSTEM

Harappan seals Steatite seals used in the neolithic culture of Pakistan and India. The small stone instruments, most of which measure no more than a few square centimetres, bear elaborate figurative and geometric designs of plants and animals as well as inscriptions of a still undeciphered writing system. Harappa in the Punjab is one of the most important archaeological sites of the early Indus valley civilization which dates back to the seventh millennium BCE. Some Harappan seals were excavated in Iraq, indicating contacts between the Indus civilization and Mesopotamia at the time of Sargon the Great (twenty-fourth century BCE).
See also INDUS SCRIPT.
Reading Allchin and Allchin 1982; Parapola 1993

Hatrene script A Semitic consonant script derived near the end of the first millennium BCE from the ARAMAIC WRITING.

Hausa writing A member of the west branch of the Chadic languages, Hausa (also Hawsaa) is the most important regional language and lingua franca of West Africa, with more than 25 million speakers in Nigeria and Niger. Hausa has been written at least since the eighteenth century in a variety of the Arabic script known as the AJAMI SCRIPT. To deal with phonological complexities of Hausa (and other West African languages) this script includes a more complex system of pointing than is necessary for writing Arabic. It was taught in Koranic schools and is still used for writing Islamic literature (figure 5).

At the beginning of this century the colonial administrators introduced a modified Roman alphabet called *boko* or *bóokòo* from *book*, which gradually replaced *ajami* in other than Islamic religious domains. The orthographic rules for writing Hausa in Roman letters are not uniform, since anglophone Nigeria spells in an English-like manner, while francophone Niger uses essentially French-based sound values. Hence there are differences such as *farko* (Nigeria) vs *hwarkoo* (Niger) 'beginning', which are especially bothersome for lexicographic purposes. In both orthographies tone and vowel length are ignored, although English–Hausa dictionaries use a macron to mark a long V and accent marks over V letters to indicate tone: a grave indicates a low tone and a circumflex a falling tone. The high tone remains unmarked. In Nigeria, Hausa is now written in pan-Nigerian, a font designed in 1985 by Hermann Zapf, a German typographer, and

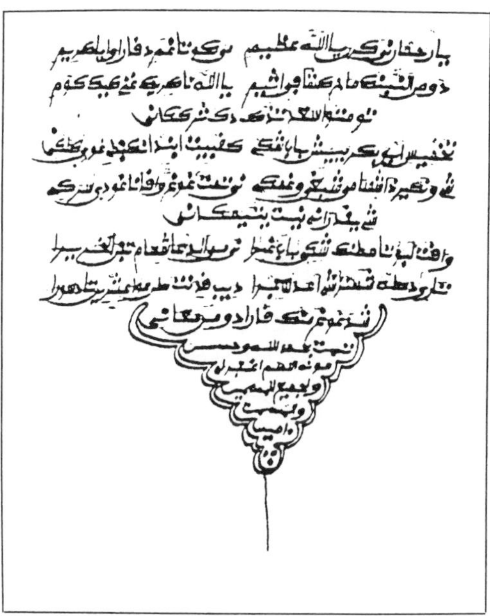

Figure 5 Hausa in Arabic letters: a page from a manual introducing the ajami *script to speakers of Hausa*

à b ɓ c d ɗ e ə ẹ́ f g

À B Ɓ C D Ɗ E Ǝ Ẹ́ F G

h i î ị́ j k ƙ l m n ò ọ

H I Î Ị J K Ƙ L M N Ò Ọ

p r s ṣ t û ụ̄ v w y z

P R S Ṣ T Û Ụ̄ V W Y Z

1 2 3 4 5 6 7 8 9 0 ₦

[. , : ; (& ’ ” * ‘ “ %) — - ! ?]

Table 1 The pan-Nigerian alphabet

adjusted to write the many languages of the country (table 1). This alphabet includes three 'hooked' letters, <ɓ, ɗ, ƙ>, to represent glottalized Cs which are distinct from /b/, /d/, /k/. The digraph <ts> represents a glottalized /s/. **Reading** Gregersen 1977b.

Hebrew writing The literary tradition of Hebrew spans some 3,000 years. The oldest known inscription in Hebrew is the Gezer Calendar dating from the late eleventh or early tenth centuries BCE (figure 6). The script of this period is generally known as Old Hebrew to distinguish it from the later Hebrew square script. Old Hebrew is a consonant script derived from the Phoenician script, now

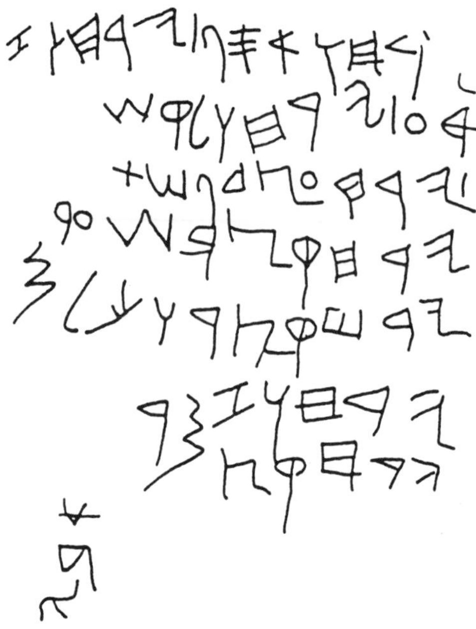

Figure 6 *The Gezer Calendar, an ancient Hebrew record of the annual agricultural cycle, tenth century* BCE *(Israel Museum, Jerusalem)*

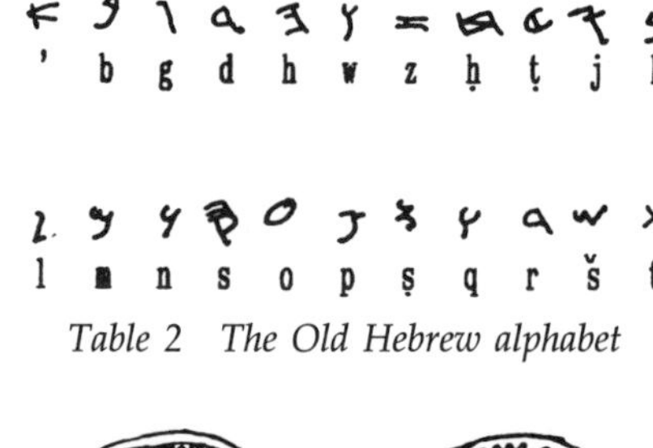

Table 2 *The Old Hebrew alphabet*

Figure 7 *Coins dating from the early second century* CE *with Old Hebrew legend*

often called Old north Semitic. It is essentially a graphic variation of the 22-letter Old north Semitic alphabet (table 2). The Hebrews used this script until the sixth century BCE when it was supplanted by the Aramaic script and then its offshoot, the Hebrew square script or *kĕtāb mĕrubbā'*. In later times a stylized variety of Old Hebrew was used on Jewish coins from 135 BCE to 132 CE (figure 7).

Initially the square script did not differ structurally from the Old Hebrew script (table 3). Both systems represented all Hebrew Cs and none of the Vs. The absence of V letters did not at first impede the comprehensibility of written texts,

Name	Symbol	Value
ʼāleph	א	ʼ
bēth	ב	b
gīmel	ג	g
dāleth	ד	d
hē	ה	h
wāw	ו	w
zayin	ז	z
ḥēth	ח	ḥ
ṭēth	ט	ṭ
yodh	י	j
kaph	כ ך*	k
lāmedh	ל	l
mēm	מ ם*	m
nūn	נ ן*	n
sāmekh	ס	s
ayin	ע	ʻ
pē	פ ף*	p
ṣādhē	צ ץ*	ṣ
qōph	ק	q
rēš	ר	r
šin	ש	š
tāw	ת	t

***Final forms**

Table 3 The alphabet of the Hebrew square script

/i/	/e/	/ä/	/a/	/ɔ/	/o/	/u/	/ə/

Table 4 Vowel diacritics of Hebrew: the Tiberian pointing system

since the core of the Hebrew lexicon is formed by CONSONANT ROOTS, while Vs mainly indicate inflections which can be supplied by readers on the basis of their knowledge of the language. But Hebrew was replaced as the vernacular language of the Jews by Aramaic, and consequently knowledge of the spoken language dwindled. It became desirable, therefore, to indicate Vs in order to unambiguously represent pronunciation, especially of biblical texts.

Two solutions were found to compensate for the absence of V letters in the Hebrew alphabet. One of them is known as MATRES LECTIONIS or 'mothers of reading'. Four of the 22 C letters were given an additional function, to signify long Vs: *'āleph* for /a:/, *hē* for /o:, a:/, *wāw* for /o:, u:/, and *yōdh* for /e:, i:/. Since these letters retained their original consonant values, this solution was not always satisfactory. For disambiguation *wāw* and *yōdh* were sometimes reduplicated where they had consonantic values. Also, short Vs were not represented in this system. Writing with *matres lectionis* is known as *scriptio plena 'plene* writing' or 'full writing'.

The second solution was the introduction of diacritics for all vowel distinctions. These are dots and dashes grouped in various ways around C letters. Historically there was more than one system of diacritic marks, 'pointing' or PUNCTUATION, for the vocalization of Hebrew writing. The system still in use was first developed at the beginning of the ninth century CE by the masoretes. It is known as the 'Tiberian' system after the city of Tiberias in Palestine. The representation of the Vs of biblical Hebrew by means of the Tiberian system is as in table 4. Together with the *matres lectionis,* which remained part of Hebrew writing, the diacritical marks represent the five basic Vs, /ä/, /i/, /o/, /u/ and /e/, both long and short. As a result there is some redundancy in the V indication of modern Hebrew because vowel length is still marked in writing, although it has been neutralized in speech. Some Vs thus have multiple representations. For example, /i/ may be represented either by the letter ' *yōdh* as a *mater lectionis,* or by a dot under the preceding C letter, or both.

The two devices of V indication have not led to the abandonment of C writing; rather, V punctuation is used for certain purposes only. Thus two orthographies of modern Hebrew coexist: the pointed system which specifies Vs; and the unpointed system which omits every indication of Vs, relying on context for their correct identification. Modern Hebrew is usually written without V indication. The vowelized orthography is only used for the Bible and other religious texts, children's books, and poetry (figure 8).

Since antiquity Hebrew has been written from right to left. Over the centuries several varieties of the square script evolved, the most important ones being the *Sephardic,* that is of oriental Spanish type characterized by rounded lines, and the *Ashkenasic,* which is angular. In addition to Hebrew some other languages have

בְּרֵאשִׁית בָּרָא אֱלֹהִים אֵת הַשָּׁמַיִם וְאֵת הָאָרֶץ׃ 2 וְהָאָרֶץ
הָיְתָה תֹהוּ וָבֹהוּ וְחֹשֶׁךְ עַל־פְּנֵי תְהוֹם וְרוּחַ אֱלֹהִים מְרַחֶפֶת עַל־פְּנֵי
הַמָּיִם׃

bə-rē'šīþ bārā' älōhīm' eþ ha-ššāmajim wə' eþ hā-'āräṣ. wə hā-'āräṣ hājəþā þōhū wā-βōhū wə ḥošäχ 'al-pənē þəhōm, wə rūăḥ 'älōhīm məraḥäſäþ 'al-pənē ha-mmājim.

In the beginning God created the heavens and the earth. Now the earth was unformed and void, and darkness was upon the face of the deep; and the spirit of God hovered over the face of the waters.

Figure 8 Specimen of Hebrew writing: Genesis 1:1–2

been written in the square script, notably Arabic, Turkish, Spanish (Ladino) and German (Yiddish).
See also BABYLONIAN POINTING; SEMITIC WRITING; TIBERIAN POINTING.
Reading Birnbaum 1971; Driver 1976; Renz and Röllig 1995; Weinberg 1985.

hentai-kanbun [Japanese 變體漢文 'variant Chinese'] A now defunct literary style often used in official Japanese documents, *hentai-kanbun* combines the Chinese written language *kanbun*, as it is called in Japanese, with native Japanese elements. In the form of the *sōrōbun* epistolary style it was still used in the 1920s.
See also KANBUN.

Hepburn system The most widely used Romanization system for Japanese, so called after its first popularizer, James Curtis Hepburn (1815–1911). In 1885 a group of Japanese and foreign scholars developed a system of writing Japanese with the Roman alphabet (table 5). Hepburn, an American missionary, contributed to its promotion by adopting this system in his Japanese–English dictionary which became very popular. The sound values of consonant letters are based on English, those of vowel letters on Latin/Italian. The Hepburn system puts pronounceability by the linguistically naïve reader (whose first language is English) above systematic consistency; hence *shi, chi, tsu, fu* rather than *si, ti, tu, hu*. The latter spelling is used in the *kunrei* system which is more phonemically systematic, the actual pronunciation of these syllables being /ʃ i/, /tʃ i/, /tsu/, /ɸu/.
See also HIRAGANA; JAPANESE WRITING; RŌMAJI; TRANSLITERATION.
Reading Saeki and Yamada 1977.

a	ka	sa	ta	na	ha	ma	ya	ra	wa	
i	ki	shi	chi	ni	hi	mi		ri	(i)	
u	ku	su	tsu	nu	fu	mu	yu	ru		
e	ke	se	te	ne	he	me		re	(e)	
o	ko	so	to	no	ho	mo	yo	ro	wo	n

Table 5 The basic chart of the Hepburn system arranged in the traditional order of the 50-sounds table of five lines and ten columns

heterograph A differentiation in spelling which distinguishes different meanings of homophonous words or phrases, e.g. *read, reed, Reed, Reid; right, rite, write, wright; frays, phrase;* or French *elle se lève à sept heures* 'she gets up at seven o'clock' vs *elles ses lèvent à cette heure* 'they get up at this hour'. While heterography inevitably adds to the complexity of a spelling system, it also fulfils a function of disambiguation on the graphic level and thus contributes to the autonomy of written language. From the perspective of spoken language heterographs are also called 'homophones', i.e. cases of two or more spellings with one pronunciation.
See also HOMOGRAPH; ORTHOGRAPHY.

hieratic script [Gk ἱερατικός 'priestly'] A cursive style of Egyptian writing normally written in ink on papyrus, hieratic was in evidence from the middle of the second millennium BCE. It was originally a secular book script used for literary texts and business documents, but in these domains it was replaced from about the seventh century BCE by the even more cursive DEMOTIC SCRIPT and hence became a specialized medium of religious writing. When the Greek name of this script was coined in the second century CE, it was the script of the cult in other

Hieroglyph	Hieratic	Value	Hieroglyph	Hieratic	Value
		god			*a, am* to eat, to speak
		goddess			*aft* to rest
		ra sun god			*r* mouth
		ma, šu truth			*t* tongue
		npt			*th* to spoil
		ntr divine			*šm* to walk
		a man			*pt, rt* foot, thigh
		bk woman			*kb, bk*

Table 6 Some hieratic signs and the hieroglyphs from which they are derived

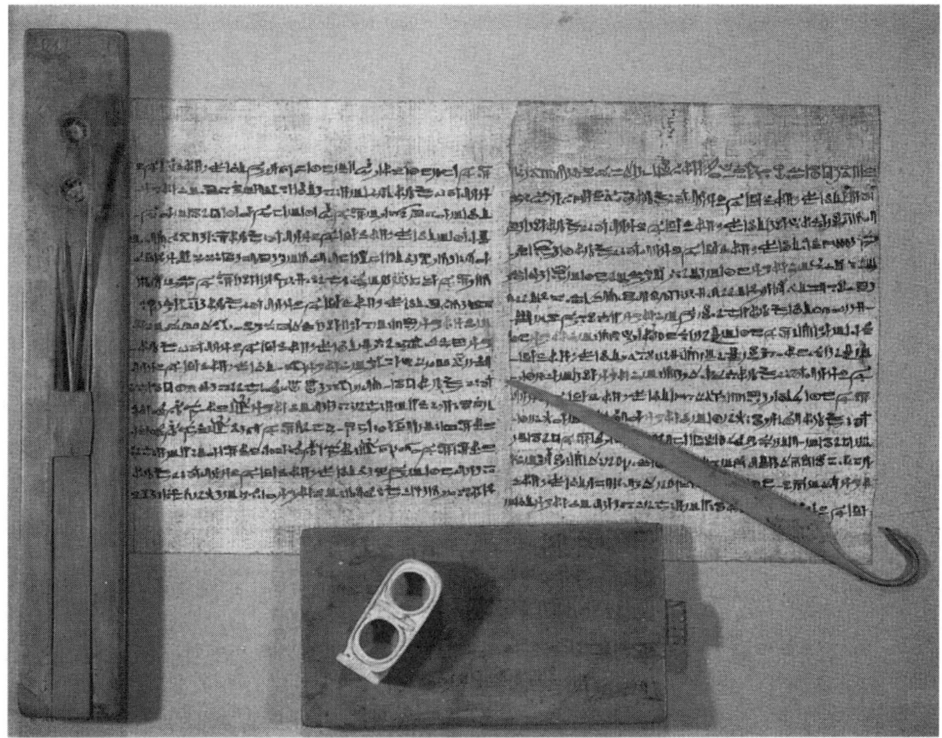

Figure 9 Fragment of a papyrus of a book of the dead in hieratic script, 27th to 30th dynasties (by permission of Staatliche Museen zu Berlin: reference 186/64, Ägyptisches Museum)

than monumental inscriptions, which were always in hieroglyphics. On papyrus hieratic is written in horizontal lines from right to left. Structurally hieratic differs little from the hieroglyphic script, making use of three kinds of signs: logograms, syllabograms and determinatives (table 6).

During its long coexistence with the hieroglyphic script, hieratic underwent further cursivization and stylistic changes. By the 12th dynasty (*c.*2000–1790) it had developed into a distinctive script with well-defined signs and ligatures, generally referred to as middle hieratic. The high point of hieratic papyrus literacy was during the new kingdom (*c.*1550–1330) (figure 9). It was only in later periods that hieratic was occasionally carved in stone.

See also Egyptian scripts; Egyptian writing system.

Reading Brunner 1973a; 1973b; Schlott 1989.

hieroglyph [back formation from Gk ἱερός 'sacred' + γλυφή 'carving'] A term first coined when the make-up of the Egyptian writing system was not well understood, to describe its supposedly sacred nature. The pictorial signs of the Egyptian monumental script which were incised in stone had already been referred to as holy or divine in classical antiquity, for instance by Herodotus who visited Egypt in the fifth century BCE and by Diodorus Siculus who described hieroglyphic writing in the first century BCE. The term has been maintained for convenience to denote a single unit of the monumental script. Some 4,500 Egyptian hieroglyphs are known from the inscriptions that have been preserved. In addition there are some 5,000 graphic variants. Rather than for their readings, hieroglyphs are conventionally ordered in lexical lists for the objects they depict, e.g. gods, plants, animals, parts of the human body and tools.

The term 'hieroglyph' is occasionally used in analogy with the Egyptian monumental script to refer to writings consisting of signs which are (assumed to be) non-phonetic, such as MAYA WRITING, HITTITE HIEROGLYPHIC and CRETAN WRITING.
See also EGYPTIAN WRITING SYSTEM.

hieroglyphic alphabet The Egyptian syllabary consists of three series of syllabograms, namely mono-, bi- and triconsonantal signs. Each C is understood to be associated with any or no V. The monoconsonantal series, a set of between 24 and 27 hieroglyphic signs, is often referred to as the 'hieroglyphic alphabet'. To what extent this terminology is appropriate is a matter of controversy, but most scholars regard Egyptian as a logosyllabic script. However, with the monoconsonantal series, Egyptian writing came to the threshold of alphabetic representation of language.
See also (for illustration) EGYPTIAN WRITING SYSTEM.

Hindi writing A member of the Indo-Aryan family, Hindi is one of India's foremost languages in terms of the size of its speech community of more than 200 million. It is also the national language of the Republic of India. The development of Hindi into a modern standard language was promoted by the British administrators who, from the beginning of the nineteenth century, cultivated it as a standard among government officials. The literary tradition of Hindi goes back to the twefth century CE. The identity of Hindi as a language is closely associated with the DEVANĀGARĪ script in which it is written. Based on the *Khaṛī bolī* variety of Delhi and the surrounding region, the language has also been called 'Hindavi' and 'Hindustani', among others. Linguists often refer to 'Hindi-Urdu', because from a structural point of view Urdu and Hindi are not different languages, not even different dialects, but rather different literary styles based on the same dialect. These different styles are given visual expression by two different writing systems, a modified Perso-Arabic for Urdu and Devanāgarī for Hindi. The Devanāgarī script links Hindi with its parent language Sanskrit on which it relies as a source for its higher lexicon (figure 10).

The order of the Devanāgarī alphabet for Hindi follows the conventional pattern of Indic scripts which is based on the phonological analysis of the ancient Indian grammarians (table 7). First come the Vs, syllabic liquids and V-like nasals. Then come series of Cs ordered for place of articulation from back to front: gutturals, palatals, cerebrals, dentals and bilabials. Finally, there are semivowels and sibilants. Every written sign represents a syllable since the C letters have an inherent neutral V which is usually transliterated as *a*. For the representation of non-initial Vs there is a second set of V signs which do not occur independently but only appear as diacritics to C letters (table 8). Whenever any of these signs is attached to a C letter the inherent *a* is cancelled out. The correspondence between letters and sounds is quite regular in Hindi, although the inherent *a* of

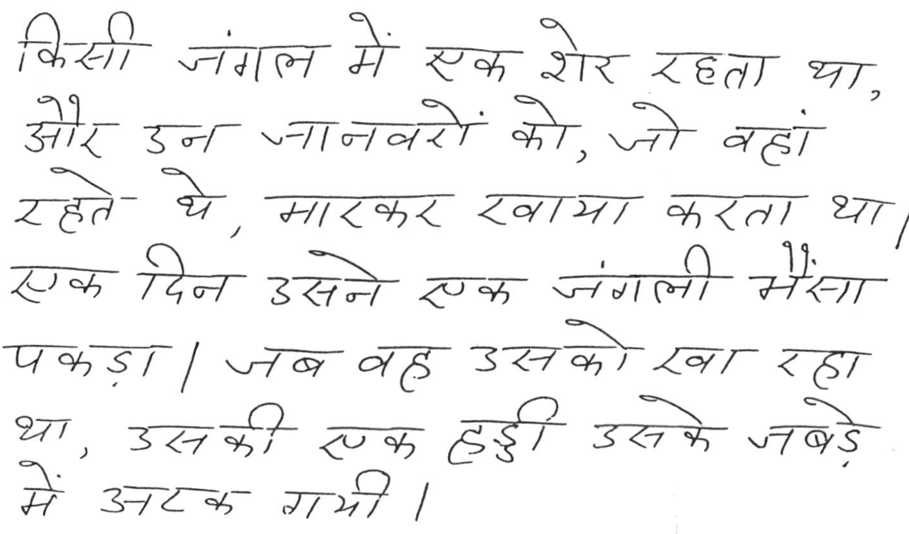

किसी जंगल में एक शेर रहता था,
और उन जानवरों को, जो वहां
रहते थे, मारकर खाया करता था।
एक दिन उसने एक जंगली भैंसा
पकड़ा। जब वह उसको खा रहा
था, उसकी एक हड्डी उसके जबड़े
में अटक गयी।

Transliteration

Kisī jangal mẽ ek sher rahtā thā, aur un jānvarõ ko, jo wahā̃ rahte the, mārkar khāyā kartā thā. Ek din us ne ek jangalī bhaisā pakṛā. Jab wah us ko khā rahā thā, us kī ek haḍḍi us ke jabṛe mẽ aṭak gaī.

Translation

In a certain forest, there used to dwell a tiger who was in the habit of killing and devouring all the beasts that lived there. One day he caught a wild buffalo bull. While he was eating it, one of its bones stuck in his jaw.

Figure 10 Specimen of Hindi writing with transliteration and translation (courtesy R. R. Mehrotra)

the C letters is not always pronounced. The *Virāma* V muting device, an oblique stroke under the C letter called *halant* in Hindi, can be used to represent vowel-less Cs, but this sign is mainly used for final Cs. In Hindi some C clusters are written without indicating the absence of the inherent V. However, it has been shown that such pronunciations follow simple phonological rules, making a simpler orthography possible. Certain sounds that have entered Hindi with loan words mainly from Persian are represented by means of a diacritic, a dot placed under a Devanāgarī letter of a related sound (table 9).
See also INDIAN WRITING SYSTEMS; URDU WRITING.
Reading Masica 1991; Ohala 1983.

hiragana [Japanese ひらがな] One of the two Japanese syllabaries. In its modern form the *hiragana* syllabary consists of 48 syllable signs used primarily for writing indigenous Japanese words (as opposed to Sino-Japanese words and Western loans). Five signs represent syllabic Vs, one the syllabic nasal /n/, and

अ, अ	ʌ	क	kʌ	ट	ʈʌ	प	pʌ	श	ʃʌ
आ, आ	a	ख	khʌ	ठ	ʈhʌ	फ	phʌ	ष	ʂʌ, ʃʌ
इ	ɪ	ग	gʌ	ड	ɖʌ	ब	bʌ	स	sʌ
ई	i	घ	ghʌ	ढ	ɖhʌ	भ	bhʌ	ह	hʌ
उ	ʊ	ङ	ŋʌ	ण, ण	ɳʌ	म	mʌ		
ऊ	u							र्‍	r before consonant
ऋ	rɪ	च	cʌ	त	tʌ	य	jʌ		
ए	e	छ	chʌ	थ	thʌ	र	rʌ		
ऐ	æe	ज	ɟʌ	द	dʌ	ल, ल	lʌ		
ओ	o	झ, झ	ɟhʌ	ध	dhʌ	व	vʌ, ʋʌ		
औ	ɔo	ञ	ɲʌ	न	nʌ				

Table 7 The Devanāgarī syllabic alphabet for Hindi listed in the conventional order of Hindi dictionaries with sound values given in IPA

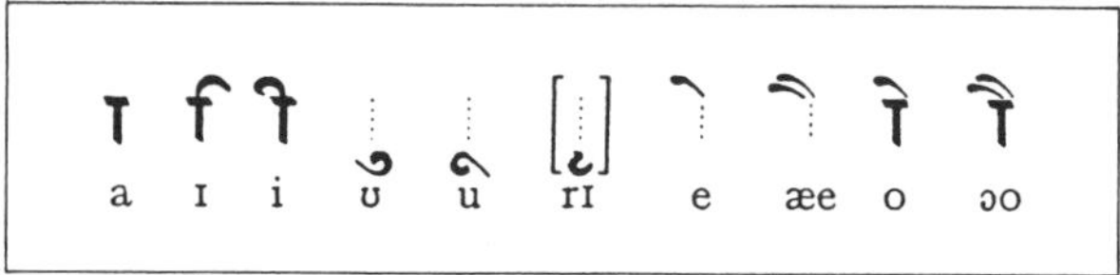

Table 8 Devanāgarī vowel signs used in combination with consonant letters

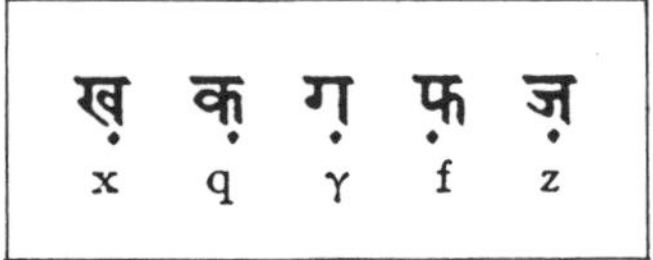

Table 9 Devanāgarī letters with underdot for sounds occurring in loan words only

the rest syllables of the CV type. The *hiragana* signs were derived from Chinese characters as of the eighth century CE. *Hira* means 'commonly used', 'rounded', referring to the curvilinear shapes of the signs which are simpler and more rounded than the original Chinese characters (table 10).

Hiragana is based on *manyōgana*, that is, Chinese characters used as phonograms irrespective of their meaning in Chinese as they appear in the eighth-century poetic anthology *Manyōshū*. In the *Manyōshū* this method of writing Japanese was still in its incipient stage which exhibits a great deal of POLYVALENCE: many different characters were used to represent the same syllable. Gradually these were reduced in number, and simplified and stylized in form. Known as *sōgana*, these characters were eventually developed into a fully fledged syllabary with a one-to-one relationship between symbols and Japanese syllables. Owing to sound changes and variation in writing conventions, this neat correspondence gave

a	安	あ	i	以	い	u	宇	う	e	衣	え	o	於	お
ka	加	か	ki	幾	き	ku	久	く	ke	計	け	ko	己	こ
sa	左	さ	si	之	し	su	寸	す	se	世	せ	so	曽	そ
ta	太	た	ti	知	ち	tu	川	つ	te	天	て	to	止	と
na	奈	な	ni	仁	に	nu	奴	ぬ	ne	祢	ね	no	乃	の
ha	波	は	hi	比	ひ	hu	不	ふ	he	部	へ	ho	保	ほ
ma	末	ま	mi	美	み	mu	武	む	me	女	め	mo	毛	も
ya	也	や				yu	由	ゆ				yo	与	よ
ra	良	ら	ri	利	り	ru	留	る	re	礼	れ	ro	呂	ろ
wa	和	わ	wi	為	ゐ*				we	恵	ゑ*	wo	遠	を
												n	无	ん

* No longer in use

Table 10 Hiragana *signs and the Chinese characters from which they are derived, arranged in the traditional order of the 50-sounds table. The Roman transliteration follows the official* kunrei *system*

way to more polyvalent usage, and the principle of one *kana* for one syllable was not restored until the beginning of this century.

Hiragana was originally known as *onnade* 'women's hand', since it was first used primarily by women while men used Chinese characters. But by the early tenth century this gender-based distinction in use had broken down and *hiragana* had become a generally accepted writing system for literature (figure 11). The high point of literary works written in *hiragana* script is the *Genji monogatari* (*The Tale of Genji*) by Murasaki Shikibu, a female novelist of the early eleventh century.

The present orthography (*gendai kanazukai*) was officially codified in a cabinet order of 1946. It is intended to map the phonology of present-day standard Japanese. However, in some cases it reflects historical usage, especially in representing the grammatical particles for topic [wa], direct object [ɔ] and direction [ɛ] which are written with the *hiragana* は *ha*, を *wo* and へ *he*, respectively. Although the system is highly systematic and simple, a few conventions have to be observed. In addition to the basic symbols the system uses two diacritics. Two small strokes (*nigoriten*) are placed on the right shoulder of the sign to distinguish voiced from unvoiced C onset, e.g. か /ka/ vs が /ga/, さ /sa/ vs ざ /za/. A small circle (*maru*) on the right shoulder of the *h kana* transforms these symbols to represent a voiceless bilabial plosive onset /p/ plus the V in question: は /ha/ vs ぱ /pa/. Since no separate *kana* exist for palatalized syllables, the signs for *ki, si, ni, hi, mi* and *ri* are used in conjunction with those of the *y* series.

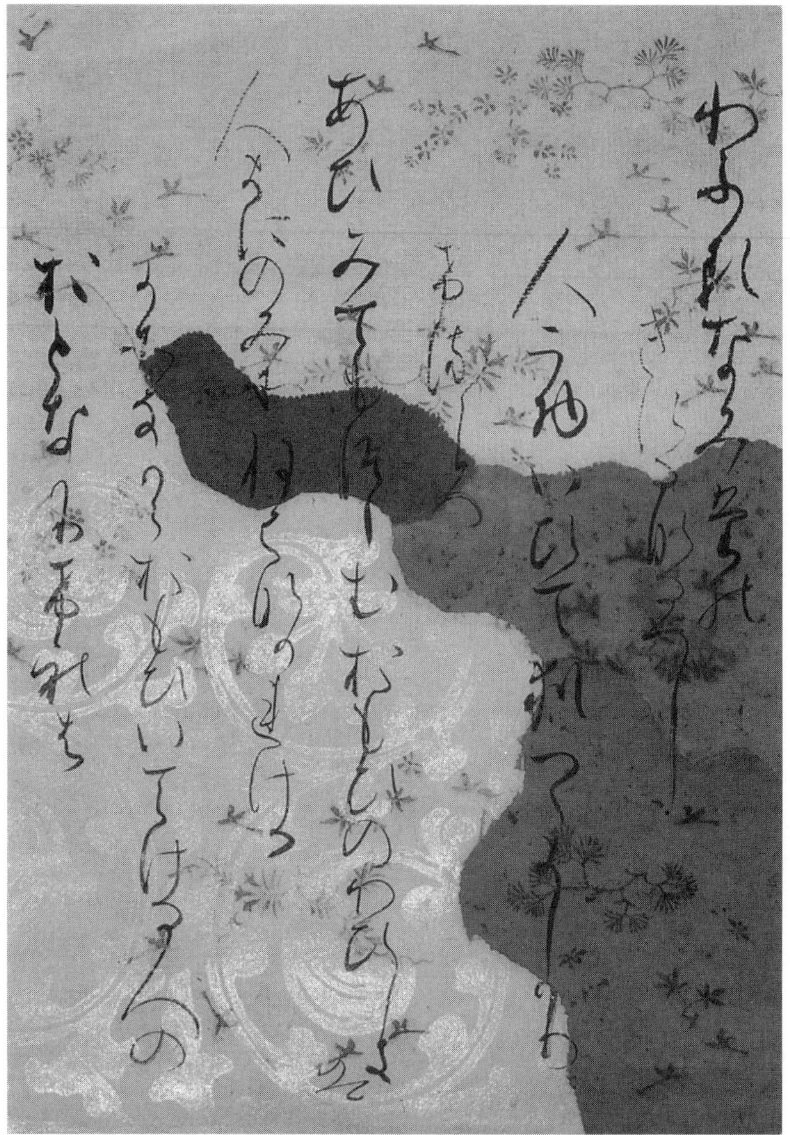

Figure 11 Poem written entirely in hiragana *from the anthology* Ise-shū *on a hanging scroll of the twelfth century* CE *(by permission of Idemitsu Museum of Arts, Tokyo)*

In modern orthography the latter are put in smaller size: きゃ *kī* + ^{ya} [kya]. Further, a small subscript *tu* is used for indicating tense Cs which are pronounced with a glottal stop or as two Cs. It precedes the *kana* whose onset C is geminated: かた /kata/ vs かった /katta/.

As a mnemonic, all 47 signs of the old *hiragana* syllabary are used without repetition in a poem composed in the tenth century. The poem is called *I-ro-ha uta* '*I-ro-ha* song' after its first three syllables (figure 12). The *i-ro-ha* arrangement is still occasionally used in indexes and for short enumerations, but dictionaries generally use the *a-i-u-e-o* order of the '50-sounds table'.

i ro ha ni ho he to ti ri nu ru [w]o

wa ka yo ta re so tu ne ra mu

u [w]i no o ku ya ma ke fu ko e te

a sa ki yu me mi si [w]e hi mo se su

Colours are fragrant, but they fade away.

In this world of ours none lasts forever.

Today cross the high mountain of life's illusions,

and there will be no more shallow dreaming,

no more drunkenness.

Figure 12 Poem I-ro-ha uta (translation by A. N. Nelson 1962)

Japanese can easily be written in *hiragana* alone, but except in children's books the syllabary is generally used in combination with Chinese characters.

See also JAPANESE WRITING; KATAKANA.

Reading Sato Habein 1984; Seeley 1991.

Hittite cuneiform In their first written documents around the beginning of the second millennium BCE, the Hittites of central Anatolia used Akkadian cuneiform, the literary and diplomatic language of the time. Hittite scribes subsequently borrowed the CUNEIFORM WRITING for writing their own language, closely following the writing practice of Babylonian scribal schools. Being of Indo-European stock, Hittite was typologically quite different from the Semitic languages of Mesopotamia. This made adjustments of the script inevitable, the biggest problem being the representation of C clusters. The Akkadian syllabary was simplified, but the representation of the Hittite language remained imperfect. Redundant 'plene' spellings of Vs were widespread. For example, **trijanalli-* 'third' was spelled *tar-ri-ja-na-al-li*, and *li-in-ik-ta* represented what in speech must have been something like **linkt* 'he vowed'. Because of such cumbersome spellings the phoneme inventory of Hittite remains uncertain, as does the exact form of many words.

Unlike other adaptations of the cuneiform script, such as those of ELAMITE WRITING and HURRIAN, WRITING, Hittite cuneiform continued to employ a large number of Sumerograms, i.e. Sumerian loan words written with logograms, as well as Sumero-Akkadian allograms, i.e. Akkadian phonetic spellings to be read in Hittite. The latter practice was used instead of spelling out the respective Hittite words with syllabograms which were used only to indicate Hittite morphological endings. Thus, to write the Hittite word *haššu-* 'king' the scribes supplemented the logogram for 'king' (*lugal* in Sumerian, *šarru* in Akkadian)

Figure 13 Bilingual and biscriptual Hittite seal of King Suppiluliuma I (1380–1346 BCE*). The Luwian text in the centre under the winged sun is written in Hittite hieroglyphic, stating the king's name and that of his wife Tawananna with the titles 'Great King' and 'Great Queen'. The Hittite cuneiform text of the concentric circles reads: 'Seal of Suppiluliuma, Great King, King of Hatti, favourite of the Thunder God, seal of Tawananna, Great Queen, daughter of the King of Babylon'*

with the singular nominative ending *-uš* to write *haššuš*, or with the singular accusative ending *-un* for *haššun*, and so on.

The bulk of Hittite cuneiform documents were excavated in a clay tablet archive at Boğazköy, the capital of the Hittite empire (figure 13). The literary tradition of cuneiform Hittite lasted until about 1200 BCE when the Hittite empire collapsed.
Reading Friedrich 1960 (for signary); Gramkrelidze 1961.

Hittite hieroglyphic A writing of the Bronze Age used for writing Luwian, an Indo-European language closely related to Hittite. Because of its largely pictorial appearance, the logosyllabic script which was used by the Hittites in addition to the imported cuneiform script is conventionally termed 'Hittite hieroglyphic'. It is attested mainly on monumental stone inscriptions and on seals dating from two distinct periods: the Hittite empire period (*c*.1400–1200 BCE) overlapping with HITTITE CUNEIFORM writing; and the neo-Hittite period (*c*.1000–700 BCE) of the Hittite empire successor states. The inscriptions of the second period were discovered in south-east Anatolia and north-west Syria at the periphery of the former Hittite empire. As of the middle of the eighth century the Assyrian empire expanded into this area, bringing the Hittite hieroglyphic tradition to an end.

The inhabitants of the sites of Hittite hieroglyphic inscriptions were called *Hatti* 'Hittites' by their neighbours, but the decipherment of this script has shown that the language written in it is actually Luwian, not Hittite (figure 14). Hittite hieroglyphic has been deciphered only in this century as a result of collaborative effort by several scholars including Ignace GELB. This work was aided by the discovery between the two world wars of some cuneiform/hieroglyphic bilingual seals.

The script of the second period is clearly a continuation of early Hittite hieroglyphic but more polished and developed. Structurally it resembles Egyptian and Babylonian writing, comprising three kinds of signs which are used in combination: logograms, syllabograms and determinatives (tables 11, 12, 13). The syllabary is quite regular with CV syllabograms for C*a*, C*i*, C*u* as well as signs

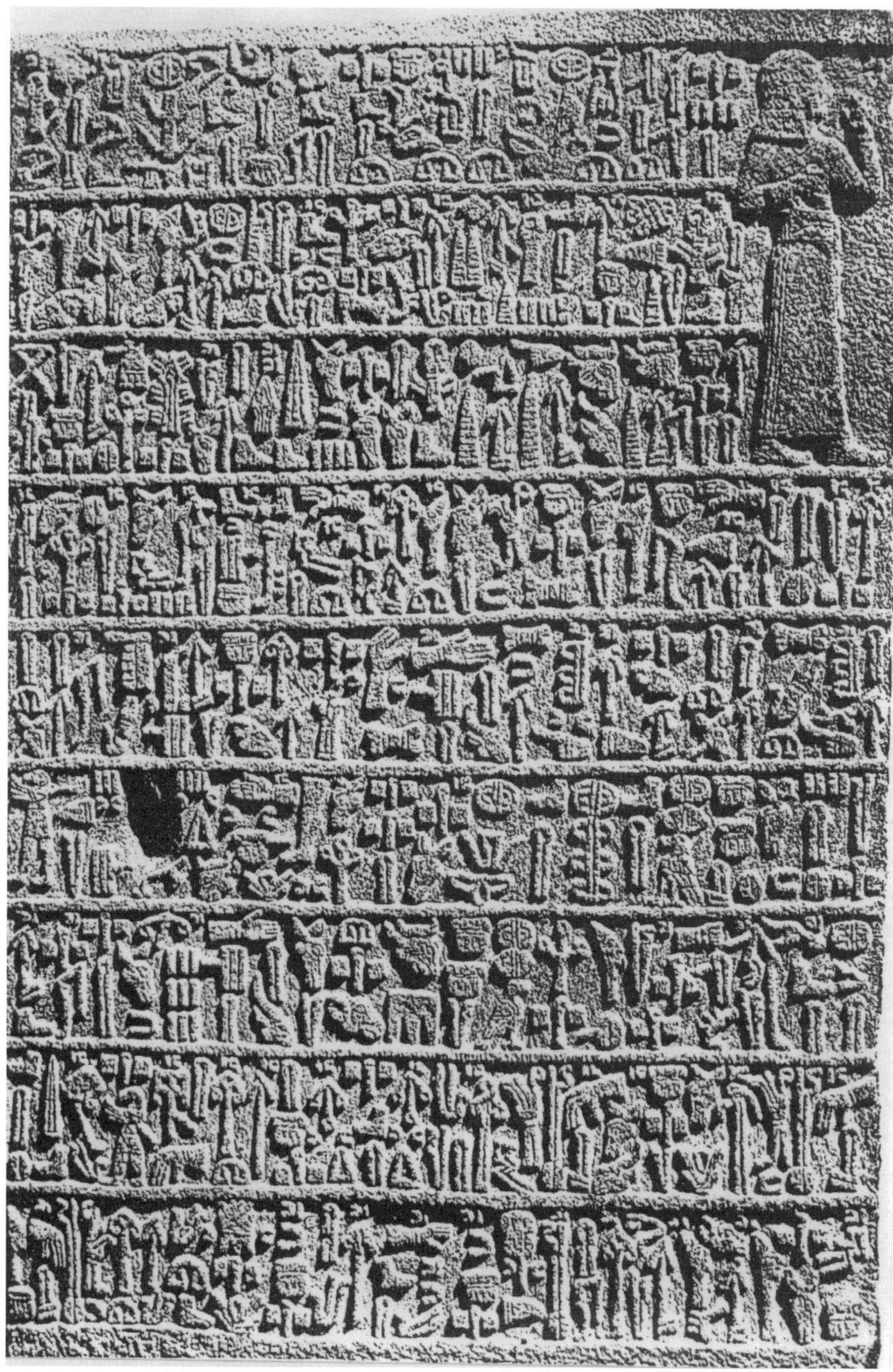

Figure 14 *Stone inscription of King Araras in Hittite hieroglyphic: the language of the inscription is Luwian*

ANNUS		DOMINUS		LUNA		REGIO	
ARHA		DOMUS		MAGNUS		REX	
AUDIRE AURIS.tu+mi		EGO		MALLEUS		SARMA	
AVIS		EQUUS		MALUS		SCALPRUM	
AVUS		EXERCITUS		MANUS		SCRIBA	
BONUS		FEMINA		MONS		SOL	
BOS		FINES		NEG(ative)		SOLIUM	
CAELUM		FRATER	see INFANS	NEG ; NEG		STELE	
CAPUT		FRONS		NEPOS		SUB	see INFRA
CASTRUM		HALPA		OCCIDENS		SUPER	
CERVUS		HEROS		OMNIS		TERRA	
CERVUS,		INFANS		ORIENS		THRONUS	
CORNU		INFRA		OVIS		TONITRUS	
CRUS		IRA		PANIS		URBS	
CRUX		LEPUS		PES		VAS	
CULTER		LIBARE		PES		VERSUS	
CUM		LINGUA		PONERE		VIA	
CURRUS		LITUUS		POST		VINUM	
DARE		LOCUS	see TERRA	PRAE		VIR	
DEUS		LOQUI		PUGNUS		VIS	

Table 11 Some logograms of Hittite hieroglyphic with conventional Latin transcriptions
Source: *Hawkins 1986*

for independent Vs /a/, /i/, /u/. It consists of some 60 commonly used signs and a number of lesser used alternatives. (The numbers in table 12 follow Laroche 1960.) More than 200 logograms were identified in the inscriptions, of which a body of some 150 were in regular use. In the literature these are usually given Latin rather than Luwian names as the exact forms of many Luwian words are still in doubt.

See also DECIPHERMENT.

Reading Laroche 1960; Hawkins 1986.

a	i	u
á 19	i 209	u 105
à, 450	í 299	
ha 215	hi 413	hu 307
há 196		
ka 434	ki 446	ku 423
la 175	li 278	
lá/í 445	→	→ (lu)
	lì[6] 125	
ma 110	mi 391	mu 107
	mí 387	
	mì 419	
na 35	ni 411	nu 153
ná 332	ní 214	nú 395
pa 334	pi 66	pu 328
pá 462		
ra/i 383	→	ru 412
		rú 103
sa 415	si 174	su 370
sà 433	sí?[7] 456	sú 108
sà 104		sù 448
sa 402		
sa 327		

a	i	u
sa 223		
sa 316		
ta 100	ti 90	tu 89
tá 29	tí 488	tú 325
tà 41		tù 326
ta_4[8] 319	→ (tì?)	
ta_5[6] 172	→ (ti?)	
wa/i 439	→	
wá/í 105	→	
wà/ì 166	→	
la 210		
lá 299		
là 379		
za 371	zi 376	zu? 432
zá 335	zí 313	
zà 336	zì 336	
za 112	zi 128	
ara/l 134		
tara/l 389		
kar 315		

Table 12 The syllabary of Hittite hieroglyphic (numbers follow Laroche 1960)

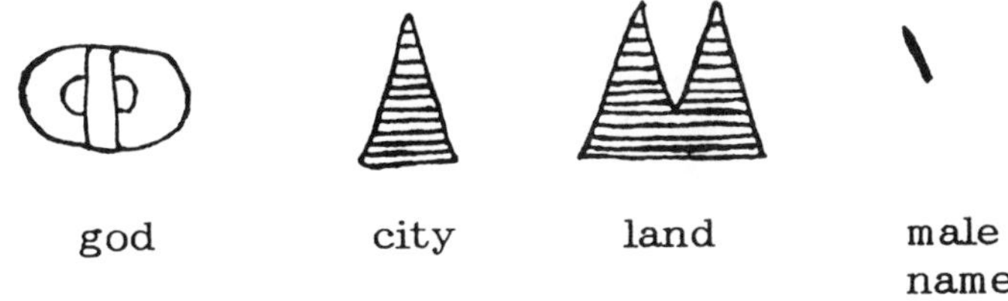

Table 13 Some determinatives of Hittite hieroglyphic

Hmong writing The Hmong language, also known by its Chinese name *Miao*, is spoken in several dialects in southern China, Vietnam, Laos and Thailand. The literary traditions of neighbouring languages have inspired the creation of a number of writing systems for the Hmong language. In Sichuan province it has been written in Chinese characters, and in Thailand the Thai syllabic alphabet has been adjusted for writing it. In addition, there are a number of Roman-based scripts created by foreign missionaries. Among these the 'Pollard Miao script'

𖬀	𖬁	keeb	keev
𖬂	𖬃	kib	kiv
𖬄	𖬅	kaub	kauv
𖬆	𖬇	kub	kuv
𖬈	𖬉	keb	kev
𖬊	𖬋	kaib	kaiv
𖬌	𖬍	koob	koov
𖬎	𖬏	kawb	kawv
𖬐	𖬑	kuab	kuav
𖬒	𖬓	kob	kov
𖬔	𖬕	kiab [kab]	kiav [kav]
𖬖	𖬗	kab [kaab]	kav [kaav]
𖬘	𖬙	kwb	kwv

Table 14 Two sets of Pahawh Hmong vowel symbols with inherent tones (by permission of William A. Smalley et al. 1990)

(also Old Miao writing) of the Chinese Hmong which uses Roman capital and inverted letters, and the 'Romanized popular alphabet' of the Laotian Hmong, gained the widest currency. According to Huang (1992) the Pollard system is still in use in southern China.

Yet another writing system for Hmong known as 'Pahawh Hmong' was designed in Laos and Vietnam between 1959 and 1971 by Shong Lue Yang, who came to be regarded by many Hmong as a prophet who was given an alphabet for their language by divine revelation. In South East Asia there is a widespread feeling that a respectable language should have a distinctive writing system. This view, reinforced by a strong sense of ethnic identity, led to the rapid spread of the new writing system among the Hmong in Laos and Vietnam. Refugees of the Vietnam War subsequently carried it to the United States where in the 1970s and 1980s first a typewriter and then word-processing equipment were developed for writing Pahawh Hmong texts.

Hmong has a simple CV syllable structure but a rich inventory of as many as 80 phonemes, 13 Vs, 59 Cs and eight tones. To cope with this variety the writing system makes use of two sets of 13 V symbols with inherent tones. In isolation the symbols in table 14 each represent a V with a tone and an associated initial /k/. In combination they stand for Vs with a tone. The conventions of the Roman transliteration in table 14 are as follows. Romanized *keeb* in the first line indicates both the name of the symbol and its sound value in isolation. The first *e* represents the V /e/, the second *e* indicates nasalization, and the final *b* gives the tone. (C letters of the Roman script can conveniently be so employed for transliteration, since the language has no syllable-final Cs.) The other tones are represented by means of diacritics on the V symbols in such a way that the same diacritic placed on different V symbols indicates the same tone value.

The C symbols are usually combined with V symbols to form syllables, but in certain contexts a C symbol can represent the syllable that is its name without any additional V symbol. As is apparent in table 15, C symbols are also composed with the help of diacritics which, however, have no linguistic significance. They only reduce the number of necessary basic signs.

In order to represent the syllables of the Hmong language the C and V symbols are combined with each other on horizontal lines running from left to right. The

C	Ċ	Ĉ	vau	nrau	fau
n	ṅ	n̂	nkau	ntxau	rhau
A	Ȧ	Â	xau	[?]au	nyau
V	V̇	V̂	cau	ntshau	txau
m	ṁ	m̂	lau	dau [dlau]	dhau [dlhau]
K	K̇	K̂	ntsau	tsau	phau
Ч	Ч̇	Ч̂	hlau	zau	ntxhau
ʉ	ʉ̇	ʉ̂	rau	nphau	nphlau
Ж	Ж̇	Ж̂	hnau	khau	ntau
m	ṁ	m̂	plhau	tshau	pau
M	Ṁ	M̂	nthau	nplau	nkhau
Ӿ	Ӿ̇	Ӿ̂	chau	xyau	tau
ɾ	ɾ̇	ɾ̂	nau	nqau	nqhau
F	Ḟ	F̂	nlau	hnlau	gau
E	Ė	Ê	qhau	nyhau	hmau
r	ṙ	r̂	hau	thau	plau
a	ȧ	â	nchau	nrhau	npau
R	Ṙ	R̂	mau	txhau	qau
w	ẇ	ŵ	yau	ncau	sau
G	Ġ	Ĝ	'au	ndlau	ndlhau

Table 15 Pahawh Hmong consonant symbols (by permission of William A. Smalley et al. 1990)

peculiar feature of the writing system is that the V symbol with its inherent tone or tone diacritic is treated as the nucleus of the syllable to which the C symbol is attached. The order of writing, V^t(C), is thus the reverse of the order of the spoken syllable, (C)V^t. Thus Pahawh Hmong writes syllables rather than segments, but the structural analysis underlying the system recognizes the relevant segmental and suprasegmental features of the language. In addition to punctuation marks adapted from languages written with the Roman alphabet, the system has signs for reduplication and for indicating intonation rhythms.

See also MIAO WRITING SYSTEM.

Reading Smalley et al. 1990.

homograph Orthographic words which have the same spelling but different pronunciations, such as *read* as present [ri:d] and past tense [rɛd] forms of the verb, or *lead* as a verb [li:d] and a noun [led]. In English homographs are much rarer than homophones (words which sound alike but are differentiated in spelling).

See also HETEROGRAPH.

Hsi-hsia writing The Hsi-hsia (Xīxìà in Pinyin) was used in the eleventh century CE for writing Tangut, a Tibeto-Burman language then spoken in northwestern China which is now extinct. *Hsia* is the Chinese dynastic name adopted by the Tangut rulers, called in history 'Hsi-hsia', or 'western Hsia'. In 1038 Li Yuan-hao, the ruler of the Tanguts, declared his independence from China of the Sung dynasty. On his orders a new writing system was invented as an act of asserting linguistic independence. In 1226 Djingis Khan conquered and destroyed the Hsi-hsia empire, but the literary tradition lived on for another century. The youngest known Hsi-hsia inscription dates from the fourteenth century CE.

Meaning	Character	Construction	Pronunciation
same	[illegible]	□□	ləw
head	[illegible]	▭ over □□	ndɛ̣
solitude	[illegible]	□□□	?
strength	[illegible]	□□□	ɣkɪě

Table 16 Graphical composition of some Hsi-hsia characters
Source: *Nishida 1982*

Hsi-hsia writing is clearly inspired by CHINESE SCRIPTS with which it bears superficial resemblance, as characters are composed of individual strokes and recurring elementary configurations of strokes resembling Chinese radicals and phonetics. The graphical composition principles, too, resemble those of Chinese characters, and like Chinese the Hsi-hsia script is written in vertical columns. However, rather than using existing Chinese characters, the creators of the Hsi-hsia script designed new characters of their own (table 16). More than 6,000 different characters have been identified so far.

In a few inscriptions the Hsi-hsia script was used for transliterating Buddhist texts in Sanskrit. On this basis the sound values of many characters could be reconstructed, but others remain obscure (table 17). While the large number of characters points to a logographic script, the writing system also includes a syllabographic element.

The Hsi-hsia literature includes numerous Buddhist sūtras as well as a Chinese–Tangut dictionary and a five-volume encyclopedia (figure 15). Nevertheless, some of the literature is still unintelligible, since the meaning and reading of many characters are uncertain.

Reading Piehl 1940; Nishida 1982.

Hungarian alphabet A member of the Ugric branch of the Finno-Ugric languages, Hungarian (autonym Magyar) is written in the Roman alphabet. The earliest written document is a funeral oration dating from the beginning of the thirteenth century CE. A stable orthography had been established by the sixteenth century. The spelling system is largely phonetic. In addition to the letters listed in table 18 in the order of modern Hungarian dictionaries, the letters <q>, <w> and <x> occur in loan words. Hungarian has a complicated V system with pairs of long and short Vs. The acute accent is used as a diacritic to mark long Vs except on the letters <ö> and <ü>. The long counterparts of these two letters are marked with the characteristic double acute accent; hence <ö> [ø], <ü> [y] vs <ő> [ø:], <ű> [y:]. An example of modern Hungarian is shown in figure 16.

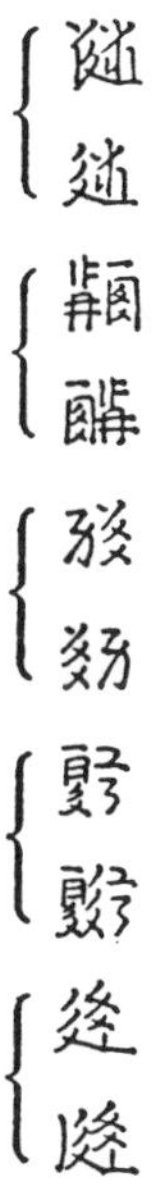

Meaning	Character	Pronunciation
rabbit	[illegible]	ɣɔɦ
	[illegible]	łị
whirlwind	[illegible]	sʷĭ
	[illegible]	ŋgeɦ
incomplete	[illegible]	kew
	[illegible]	tšha
harmony	[illegible]	phow
	[illegible]	šɪɦ
rest	[illegible]	ndĭeɴ
	[illegible]	tạ

Table 17 Some Hsi-hsia characters used for their sound values to represent bisyllabic words
Source: *Nishida 1982*

Figure 15 Specimen of Hsi-hsia writing: a passage from the Avataṃsaka-sūtra (The Great Extensive Buddha Garland Sūtra)

a [ɔ]	e [ɛ, æ]	j [j]	ö [ø]	u [u]
á [aː]	é [eː]	k [k]	ő [øː]	ú [uː]
b [b]	f [f]	l [l]	p [p]	ü [y]
c [ts]	g [g]	ly [j]	r [r]	ű [yː]
cs [tʃ]	gy [ɟ]	m [m]	s [ʃ]	v [v]
d [d]	h [h]	n [n]	sz [s]	z [z]
dz [dz]	i [i]	o [o]	t [t]	zs [ʒ]
dzs [dʒ]	í [iː]	ó [oː]	ty [c]	

Table 18 The Hungarian alphabet with canonical pronunciation of letters in IPA in brackets

Öt vagy hat éves voltam. Kis városunkban valami társas
[øt vɔɟ hɔt eːvɛʃ voltɔm. kiʃ vaːroʃ uŋgbɔn vɔlɔmi taːrʃɔʃ

mulatságot adtak, hol több család szerzi össze a
mulɔtʃ aːgot ɔtːɔk hol tøb tʃɔ laːd sɛrzi øsːɛ ɔ

készleteket. Valami barbár néven ugy híják hogy piknik.
keːslɛtɛkɛt. vɔlɔmi bɔrbaːr neːvɛn uɟ hiːjaːk hoɟ piknik]

Translation

I was five or six years old. In our little town they held one of those parties where several families pool their supplies. With some barbaric name they called it a picnic.

Figure 16 Specimen of modern Hungarian writing: from Jókai Mór, Húsz év múlva (Twenty Years Later)

Hun min jong um [Korean 訓民正音 'The correct sounds for instructing the people'] The title of a royal rescript issued in 1446 by King Sejong to promote the newly designed Korean alphabet called HAN'GŬL.
See also KOREAN WRITING.

Hurrian writing Hurrian, a language of unknown descent, is documented in north-eastern Mesopotamia as of the middle of the second millennium BCE. It was written in a variety of CUNEIFORM WRITING which was almost completely syllabic. The longest and most important Hurrian text is the so-called Mitanni letter from King Tushratta of Mitanni to Pharaoh Amenhotep IV of Egypt. Dating from about 1400 BCE, this letter of more than 400 lines was discovered in a clay tablet archive of diplomatic correspondence in Tell-el-Amarna in Egypt (figure 17). The Hurrian syllabary goes back to the Old Akkadian syllabary, but it also testifies to later Babylonian influence. Vs were more important in Hurrian than in Akkadian: the Hurrian writing system distinguishes five Vs, /a/, /e/, /i/, /o/, /u/, while Akkadian wrote only three, /a/, /i/, /u/. Highly redundant indication of Vs is a conspicuous characteristic of Hurrian writing. For example, the names of the gods Šimigi and Teššupa are written *Ši-mi-i-gi* and *Te-e-eš-šu-pa*, respectively, and *ennašuš* 'the gods' is rendered *e-e-en-na-šu-uš*. The literary tradition of Hurrian breaks off at the end of the second millennium.
Reading Speiser 1941; Wilhelm 1982

Figure 17 The Mitanni letter by King Tushratta of Mitanni to Pharaoh Amenhotep IV of Egypt, c.1400 BCE: cuneiform script, Hurrian language (by permission of Staatliche Museen Berlin)

hyphen The punctuation mark <-> used for graphic compound formation and word division. Greek grammarians of the Hellenistic period used a subscript semicircle (ἡ ὑφέν 'together') <‿> placed under a compound to indicate that it was to be pronounced as one word. Today's hyphen, which consists of a small dash, serves a similar function in English and other alphabetically written languages. While there is considerable variation in using the hyphen, a sense of growing attachment between the component words of an incipient compound is generally given expression by connecting them with a hyphen, as in *high-rise, in-laws, day-care,* until the two words become one and the hyphen drops out, as in *highway, inmate, daylight*. Other uses of the hyphen include indication of the scope of a modification, *lost-property office,* and attributive compounds, *a never-to-be-forgotten scene.*

I

I, i /aɪ/ The ninth letter of the English alphabet derives from the Semitic consonant letter *yōdh*. The absence of an equivalent consonant in Greek led to its revaluation to the vowel letter *iota* (Ι, ι). The dot on the small letter came into use in Greek because other letters were also written with simple vertical strokes, in particular *n* || and *m* |||.

Iberian writing Documented in numerous inscriptions and legends on coins that were excavated on the Iberian peninsula and the Balearic Islands, the Iberian literary tradition can be traced back to the fourth century BCE. The script is regarded as a derivative of the PUNIC SCRIPT, but the language of the inscriptions, which cannot be related to either Semitic or Indo-European, is still unknown (figure 1). The identification of Iberian proper names in Greek and Latin documents with Iberian coin legends has made it possible to assign sound values to the graphemes of the script (table 1), but, since nothing is known about the language, the inscriptions cannot be understood. On the basis of the readings of coin legends it appears that several of the signs have syllabic rather than segmental values. The script is attested in two slightly different varieties, the left-running older southern form, also called *Bastulo-Turdetanian*, and the right-running younger northern form.
Reading Gomez-Moreno 1962.

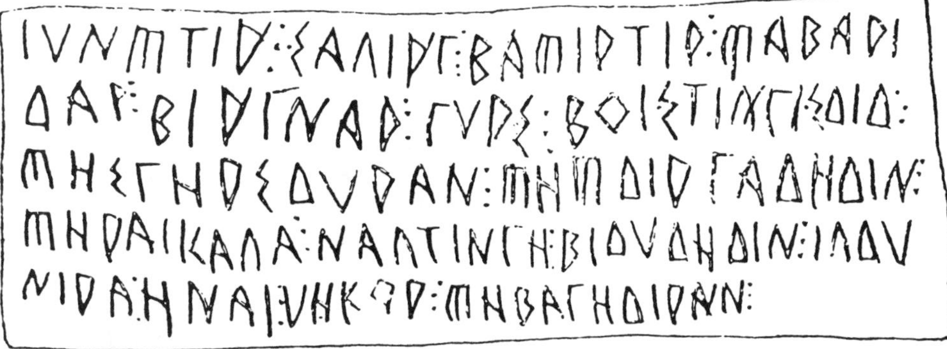

Figure 1 Lead plate from Alcoy, Spain, with Iberian inscription, fourth century BCE

icon [Gk εἰκών 'image'] A sign which bears physical resemblance with the object to which it refers. Since all known original creations of writing took pictorial representations of objects as their point of departure, iconic signs played an important role in the early history of writing (figure 2). In archaic SUMERIAN WRITING, for example, the sign meaning 'heaven' took the form of a star; the Egyptian hieroglyph for 'sun' is a circle with a dot in the centre; and in CHINESE SCRIPTS the earliest character, meaning 'moon', is still recognizable as the crescent

Sign	Sound value	Sign	Sound value
	a		ba
	e		be
	i		bi
	o		bo/po
	u		bu
	l		da/ta
	r		te/de
	m		ti/di/ili
	n		to
	s		tu/du/llu
	ṣ		ca/ga
			ce
			ci/gi
			co/go
			cu/gu

Table 1 Signary of the Iberian script

Sumerian **Egyptian** **Chinese**

Figure 2 Early written characters for the word 'fish' which developed from iconic signs shape familiar from national flags of Islamic countries. Modern creations such as the BAMUM WRITING also started out with iconic (pictorial) signs. In the course of time the original iconic devices typically became stylized and simplified out of all recognition, since the function of the signs changed from depicting objects to representing words. The hieroglyphic EGYPTIAN SCRIPT is exceptional in this regard, as the pictorial quality of its signs was preserved throughout its history, although it lost its original function of referring to objects.

In modern times, iconic signs are used in many public places, especially where linguistic communication by writing is unreliable (figure 3). At airports and in hotels, on fairgrounds and in tourist spots one finds little figures with trousers or skirts, pictures of a drinking fountain, running figures or pointing hands for indicating escape routes. Instruction manuals also make use of icons to facilitate orientation.

Figure 3 Modern icons: air transportation, car rental, restaurant, coffee shop

Iconicity in a different sense has been sought in the development of phonetic writing systems, in that the shapes of letters have been related to the physiological conditions of the production of the sounds they represent. For example, in a treatise of 1667, *Alphabeti vere naturalis hebraici brevissima delineatio, quae simul methodum suppliciat, juxta quam, qui surdi nati sunt, sic informari possunt* (*A Briefest Outline of the Natural Hebrew Alphabet, Demonstrating How Sounds are Engendered and can be Formed*), Mercurius ab Helmont argued, rather fantastically, that Hebrew letters represented positions of articulation organs (figure 4). However, in the nineteenth century the same basic idea was developed into a physiological alphabet. Melville Bell's 'visible speech' is a graphic system that schematically depicts the actions of the speech organs.

Usually the relationship between the individual signs of writing systems and the linguistic units they represent is arbitrary rather than iconic. The only writing system in actual use which has been created with this kind of iconicity in mind is *han'gŭl*, the KOREAN WRITING. The explanation that was published when it was first introduced to the public stated that the letter for *k* ㄱ 'depicts the outline of the base of the tongue blocking the throat', while that for *n* ㄴ 'depicts the tongue touching the upper palate' and that for *m* ㅁ 'depicts the outline of the mouth'. Other consonant letters were formed along similar lines, and vowel letters too are related to place and manner of articulation. An iconic relationship between points and manner of articulation and character shapes thus underlies the *han'gŭl* script.

See also ORIGIN OF WRITING; PICTOGRAM; VISIBLE SPEECH.

Reading Morris 1938.

Figure 4 Hebrew letter as an iconic depiction of the tongue position involved in the production of the sound it represents, according to Mercurius ab Helmont (1667)

ideogram *See* IDEOGRAPHY

ideography [Gk εἶδος 'idea, concept' + γράφειν 'to write'] An outmoded term widely used to refer to non-alphabetic writing of various kinds. Its literal meaning suggests a mode of writing consisting in symbolizing an idea directly, as distinguished from the linguistic form by which it is expressed. 'Ideography' in this sense was long thought to be a transitional stage in the development of writing between pictography and logography. It is distinguished from the former by the criterion that it lacks iconic pictorial qualities, and from the latter by the alleged lack of unequivocal linguistic reference. Mathematical and typographic symbols such as ≡ , ∞ , †, ♂ and ♀, meaning 'identical with', 'infinity', 'died', 'male' and 'female', respectively, can be cited as examples of ideographic writing. Since their association with meaning is not mediated by the representation of sounds, they can be pronounced in any language. Most modern scholars agree that no writing ever worked in this way, but in former times writing systems such as Egyptian hieroglyphic and Chinese were thought to be ideographic or to contain ideographic elements.

The misconception about Egyptian writing was introduced into Western scholarship by the Greeks. In the first century BCE Diodorus Siculus wrote of the Egyptians that 'their script works not by putting syllables together to render an underlying sense, but by drawing objects whose metaphorical meaning is impressed on the memory'. The notion that hieroglyphic writing was based on the association of symbols with ideas survived basically unchanged until

Champollion's spectacular decipherment which revealed the true nature of the EGYPTIAN WRITING SYSTEM as logosyllabic with a strong phonetic component. In Egyptian writing only DETERMINATIVES – key signs which specify a semantic domain and are not pronounced – can be said to be ideographic.

Characters in CHINESE SCRIPTS were also regarded by Western scholars as forming a system that speaks almost directly to the mind by means of visual images without mediation by the representation of sound shapes of linguistic units. Early reports by Christian missionaries who travelled to China from Europe did much to establish the common view that Chinese characters are ideographs or ideograms, each of which represents an idea. Modern scholarship has abandoned this view, although it is still a matter of controversy to what extent Chinese writing relies on the representations of sound and of meaning.

The term 'ideographic' is often used in a loose sense to refer to both semasiograms (e.g. numerals) and logograms (i.e. word signs) as they occur in conjunction with signs of other categories in several writing systems such as Egyptian, Akkadian and Maya. No writing system is purely ideographic in the strict sense of the term, but many writing systems contain ideographic elements.

See also LOGOGRAM; PICTOGRAM; SEMASIOGRAPHY.

Reading Sampson 1985; Coulmas 1989; DeFrancis 1989.

ido [Korean 吏道 'clerical writing'] A system of using Chinese characters for writing Korean. In the second century CE the Koreans adopted both the Chinese script and the Chinese written language, called *hanmun* 'Chinese writing'. Korean proper names posed a problem for *hanmun* writing which was solved by using some Chinese characters (*hanja* in Korean) for their phonetic value. The next step in using the Chinese script for writing Korean was to write *hanja* in Korean word order. Gradually this usage of Chinese characters developed into a written language of its own, known as *ido* or *imun* 吏文, which became the official writing of the chanceries of Silla, a Korean kingdom of the three-kingdom period (first to seventh centuries CE). *Ido* was systematized at the end of the seventh century CE by Solch'ong, a scholar in the service of King Sin-mun. It was a mixed system with both logographic and syllabographic elements. A special set of Chinese characters was selected for their phonetic values and used for writing grammatical morphemes. Lexical morphemes, many of which were Chinese words, were written in the usual (i.e. Chinese) manner. Since the characters used for writing grammatical morphemes were not graphically distinct from those for lexical morphemes, a rather cumbersome system resulted, later to be replaced by *han'gŭl*, an entirely new writing system promulgated in the fifteenth century CE by King Sejong.

See also KOREAN WRITING; KUGYOL.

Reading Yi 1975.

illiteracy Lack of formal education, specifically the inability to read and write. Illiteracy is one of the strongest indicators of underdevelopment, closely correlated with poverty and social inequality. The United Nations Educational, Scientific and Cultural Organization (UNESCO) estimated the number of illiterate people world-wide to be 948 million in 1990, or 27 per cent of the world's population.

Since the absolute number has remained more or less stable since the early 1980s, this represents a slight drop in the illiteracy rate of a growing world population. This is a result of the many campaigns to eradicate illiteracy which have been sponsored by UNESCO as well as national and regional governments. The disparities in literacy rates between rural and urban areas and between females and males, strongly disfavouring the former in both cases, reflect the historical association of literacy with empowerment. These disparities are still very pronounced in the developing countries of Africa, Asia and Latin America.

Historically, the meaning of 'illiteracy' has undergone considerable changes. In the Middle Ages, when literacy in Europe was largely restricted to the social elites, 'illiterate' was almost synonymous with 'layman', while the *literatus* was the *clericus*, the educated clergyman. 'Literate', then, meant 'knowledgeable of letters' in the sense of 'literature'. In modern times, 'literate' and 'illiterate' have come to refer more to the basic technical skills of reading and writing, although these have not remained unchanged either. While attempts to assess social literacy rates in the eighteenth and nineteenth centuries have often taken the ability to write one's name as a criterion, much more sophisticated written language skills are at issue when measuring literacy rates at the end of the twentieth century. Reflecting such changes in contents, the notion of 'functional (il)literacy' has gained currency, which is defined as the (in)ability to execute common daily tasks involving written language in a given society, such as reading a bus schedule, finding a telephone number in a directory, or filling in a health-care application form in Western industrialized societies.

The universal spread of literacy across all social strata is a modern phenomenon approximated only in the most highly industrialized countries in which, as a consequence, illiteracy has become a critical social stigma and an obstacle to social and economic advancement. In these countries the negative evaluation of illiteracy hinders an easy assessment of the extent of the problem, which is further frustrated by the varied nature of the criteria adopted in defining it. For example, depending on how 'illiteracy' is defined, between 10 per cent and 20 per cent of the US population are estimated to be functionally illiterate. For this reason and because literacy practices vary widely from one sociocultural setting to another, it is hard to draw meaningful comparisons of illiteracy rates across countries.
See also LITERACY.
Reading Wagner 1987; Winterowd 1989; Clanchy 1993; *Literacy Mission.*

Illyrian script The younger script form of the GLAGOLITIC ALPHABET with angular letter shapes, mostly used in Croatia, as opposed to the older Bulgarian variety with rounded letter shapes.

incunabula [Lat. *cunæ* 'cradle'] Books printed in Europe before 1500 CE, i.e. in the infancy of printing with movable type. The earliest incunabula looked much like MANUSCRIPTS with ornate initials and many ligatures. It took some time to accept the idea that the new technology altered the way not only of distributing and using books, but also of producing them. Initially, printing was primarily seen as a means of duplicating books, that is, of manufacturing copies which were as good as manuscripts. Therefore, not all advantages of printing with

movable type were immediately recognized and exploited, which is evidenced by the physical appearance of the incunabula.
See also PRINTING.
Reading Febvre and Martin 1958.

Indian writing systems The systems of writing used on the Indian subcontinent form a large family of dozens of scripts evolved from a single source, the Brāhmī script, first documented extensively in the AŚOKA EDICTS of the third century BCE. The members of this family, which extends to the TIBETAN WRITING in the north, the SINHALESE SCRIPT in the south, and the BURMESE WRITING and KAWI SCRIPT with their various derivatives in the east, are quite diverse in graphic appearance (table 2). The formal variety of the numerous scripts is much more pronounced than, for example, that of the many descendants of Roman capital. But in spite of this divergence in appearance they all share basic features of structural make-up.

Development and classification
In the earliest epigraphic documents (in Prakrit) Brāhmī is left-running, pointing to a Semitic connection. In the case of Kharoṣṭhī, the other script of the Aśoka edicts, which remained without descendants, derivation from the Aramaic script is generally regarded as an established fact. Other evidence too, such as the graphic similarity of some Brāhmī letters with letters of north Semitic scripts, also suggests a relationship between Brāhmī and the sphere of Semitic writing, although some scholars, especially Indian epigraphers, prefer to look at it as an autochthonous invention. This question may eventually be resolved on the basis

	a	ā	i	ī	u	ū	e	o
Brāhmī	𑀅	𑀆	𑀇		𑀉		𑀏	𑀑
Devanāgarī	अ	आ	इ	ई	उ	ऊ	ए	ओ
Gurmukhī	ਅ	ਆ	ਇ	ਈ	ਉ	ਊ	ਏ	ਓ
Bengālī	অ	আ	ই	ঈ	উ	ঊ	এ	ও
Gujarati	અ	આ	ઇ	ઈ	ઉ	ઊ	એ	ઓ
Telugu	అ	ఆ	ఇ	ఈ	ఉ	ఊ	ఎ	ఒ
Oṛiyā	ଅ	ଆ	ଇ	ଈ	ଉ	ଊ	ଏ	ଓ
Sinhalese	අ	ආ	ඉ	ඊ	උ	ඌ	එ	ඔ

Table 2 Graphic diversity of Indian scripts: vowel letters of Brāhmī, Devanāgarī, Gurmukhi, Bengālī, Gujarati, Telugu, Oṛiyā, Sinhalese

Table 3 Vowel indication by means of diacritic satellites attached to consonant letters: k *in Brāhmī and Devanāgarī*

of more epigraphic evidence. Nevertheless, Brāhmī differs from Semitic systems significantly in its vowel indication which is the most characteristic structural feature of all Indian scripts: Vs are represented by means of diacritic satellites attached to C graphemes (table 3). Although it has been suggested that this method may have originated from the Semitic practice of optional vowel indication by means of MATRES LECTIONIS, there is no positive evidence to verify this hypothesis. On the other hand, the fully developed Indian vowel indication device was taken to south Arabia by Indian traders where it was adopted to form the Ethiopic script.

The descendants of Brāhmī are conventionally divided into two groups which emerged around the beginning of the present era, the northern group and the southern group. The northern group includes the Gupta script which spread across north India during the Gupta empire in the fourth and fifth centuries CE, which in turn gave rise to the Nāgarī script in the east and the Śāradā script in the west, the forerunner of Tākrī and Kashmiri as well as Gurmukhī which latter, however, was also under the influence of Nāgarī. Nāgarī is the richest source of modern Indian scripts. It is at the origin of the proto-Bengālī script and Devanāgarī, both of which were adapted to several languages to yield new scripts including Nandināgarī, the southern counterpart of northern Devanāgarī, Assamese-Bengālī, Oṛiyā, Gujarati (Kaithi) and Maithilī, among others. Another branch of the northern group extends to the (Buddhist) Pāli script and its Mon-Burmese, Cambodian-Siamese, and Kawi offspring in Indo-China and Indonesia. The Tibetan script, too, and its derivative the Lepcha script of Sikkim, can also be traced to Nāgarī.

The southern group of Indian scripts comprises mostly those of the Dravidian languages of south India: the archaic Grantha, Kalinga and Kadamba scripts which further developed between the sixth and eighth centuries CE to yield the Telugu-Kannada script as a descendant of Kadamba which lives on in modern Kanarese and Telugu. Grantha is the source of Malayalam and Tamil which also integrated elements of the northern Gupta. The Vaṭṭeḻuttu and Pallava-Cola scripts are local varieties of Tamil. Another script which draws on both northern and southern sources is Sinhalese, which is derived from Malayalam but also reflects features of Pāli.

The scripts of the southern group share with those of the northern group most features of their structural make-up: both are written from left to right. Certain differences between the various systems are related to structural differences between the languages for which they evolved, but the most salient distinctions are superficial in a systematic sense, pertaining as they do to the outer forms of the various scripts.

With the exception of Devanāgarī which is employed for several different languages including Sanskrit, Hindi and Sindhī, most Indian scripts are primarily associated with the language for which they first evolved. Many script appellations are identical with those of their languages, although some scripts have been given names referring to places (e.g. *Nandināgarī*), empires (e.g. *Gupta*), religious practices (e.g. *Grantha* meaning 'book', a script for writing religious texts in Sanskrit), religious affiliations (e.g. *Gurmukhī*, the Sikhs' 'script of the guru') or particular inscriptions (e.g. *Siddhamāṛkā*, a cursive variety of Gupta).

Formative principles

The mode of vowel indication defines Indian writing systems as syllabic alphabets. They are syllabic in that the unit of coding is a syllable, and they are alphabetic in that the unit of the underlying analysis is a segment. Each syllable, no matter whether it consists of a single V or a CV, CCV, CVC or VC group, is written as a graphic unit. Yet these units, except for those of syllabic Vs, display internal structure reflecting a segmental analysis. C graphemes are coded with an inherent neutral vowel, usually transliterated as *a*. Independent V graphemes are used in initial position; otherwise Vs are marked by diacritics known as *mātrās* grouped around the C graphemes. There is no need to mark an [a] or [ə] following a consonant, since this vowel inheres the C letters and hence has no *mātrā*. This assumption has the following structural consequences for the combination of letters. *Mātrās* supersede the inherent *a*. Consonant clusters are generally represented by compound ligatures, conjunct C letters which, excepting the last of the sequence, lose the inherent *a*. Another device for suppressing the inherent *a* is a subscript diacritic known as *virāma* in Sanskrit. The *virāma* indicates the absence of a vowel. Its use is generally restricted to mark final consonants, although more extensive use could substantially reduce the number of necessary ligatures. Ligatures are often formed by combining elements of two C letters, but these graphic compositions are rarely transparent and thus have to be learned separately.

The economic advantage of the *virāma* device is exploited only in the Tamil script which has comparatively few ligatures. Many other graphemic and orthographic peculiarities distinguish Indian scripts from one another. For example, Sinhalese has different letters for short and long *e* : *ē* and *o* : *ō*, a distinction not made in other scripts. Gurmukhī has a special sign (*addak*) for geminates. And in many scripts etymology plays a role in determining grapheme–phoneme correspondences, as in Bengālī which preserves graphemes for *i* : *ī* and *u* : *ū*, although the corresponding phonological distinctions have been lost. Notwithstanding such differences, all Indian scripts are structurally very similar, having preserved most of the formative principles of the Brāhmī script which can be summarized as follows:

1 graphemes for independent, i.e. initial, Vs
2 C graphemes with inherent *a*

3 V indication in non-initial position by means of *mātrās* (V diacritics)
4 ligatures for C clusters
5 muting of inherent V by means of *virāma*.

The order in which Indian scripts are arranged is systematically motivated, being based on phonological principles which were determined by the ancient Indian grammarians. First come the graphemes of Vs in pairs, short and long, and syllabic liquids followed by diphthongs. Then come the C + *a* graphemes: stop consonants, semivowels and spirants. The stops are arranged in four sets, gutturals, palatals, cerebrals and dentals, each consisting of five elements: graphemes for voiced and voiceless unaspirated and aspirated sounds, and nasals. In Devanāgarī, the most widely used Brāhmī-derived script, these groups add up to a total of 47 graphemes. The number increases slightly when variant letter forms, i.e. initial and medial forms of V graphemes, and the *anusvāra* (nasalization) and *visarga* (weak aspiration) devices are included. Give or take a few graphemes, all Indian syllabic alphabets have a sign inventory of roughly the same size, testifying to the essential uniformity of these systems in spite of the diversity of their outer form.
See also BRĀHMĪ WRITING; (for illustrations of signaries) BENGĀLĪ WRITING; DEVANĀGARĪ; GUJARATI SCRIPT; GURMUKHĪ SCRIPT; KANNADA SCRIPT; KASHMIRI SCRIPT; KHAROṢṬHĪ SCRIPT; MOḌI SCRIPT; OṚIYĀ SCRIPT; TAMIL WRITING; TELUGU WRITING.
Reading Dani 1963; Chatterji 1966; Masica 1991.

Indonesian alphabet The Indonesian variety of Malay is called *Bahasa Indonésia* 'Indonesian language'. Its orthography in Roman letters was standardized and unified with that of Malay in Malaysia in 1972. It is very regular and largely phonemic. Prior to the 1972 reform the spelling system was based on the Dutch values of the letters of the alphabet, having evolved during the colonial period (table 4). The conspicuous Dutch <oe> spelling for [u] was replaced by <u> in 1947, whence *Soerabaja* became *Surabaya*.

grapheme old	new	phoneme
ch	kh	x
dj	j	j
é	e	e
j	y	y (initially)
'	k	'
nj	ny	ñ
sj	sy	š
tj	c	c

Table 4 Indonesian spellings until and since 1972

Indus script The earliest writing on the Indian subcontinent, found at archaeological sites in north Sind and south Punjab, and also known as 'Mohen-jo-Daro' and 'Harappa seal script'. It belongs to the highly developed pre-Aryan Indus civilization, which between the fourth and first millenniums BCE covered a large area stretching from Sind and Gujarat to the Punjab, northern Rajasthan and even into Maharashtra. Although links between the Indus valley civilization and Mesopotamia and north-eastern Iran are attested by archaeological findings dating from the mid third millennium, the origin of the Indus script remains enigmatic, as does the language written in it. In spite of various claims to the contrary which have tried to relate it to both the Dravidian and the Austric (Munda) families of languages, the Indus script remains undeciphered. The case for a Dravidian connection is much stronger than an Austric interpretation, since statistical evidence derived from co-occurrence frequencies of signs suggests a left-branching language which points towards Dravidian. However, so far no Harappan text can be read with any degree of confidence in whatever language. Neither is there any hard evidence to suggest that the Indus script relates to INDIAN WRITING SYSTEMS proper.

The Indus script is documented in more than 2,200 inscriptions from some 60 excavation sites. These inscriptions are, however, short and limited in nature (figures 5, 6). Most of them are found on small seals with an average length of just five signs and on small tablets made of steatite and copper. The longest text consists of 26 signs on three sides of an inscribed stone. No bilingual inscription has been discovered. In view of these limitations, the Indus script may well be undecipherable unless further archaeological evidence opens up a new avenue of approach.

Some scholars have estimated the number of basic signs as high as 400, while others who recognize a wider range of variant forms would distinguish only some 50 signs. The most informed estimate based on careful corpus analysis (Parpola 1986) puts the number of distinct graphemes at no less than 200. This rules out the possibility of an alphabetic script. The fact that many inscriptions consist of a single sign strongly suggests a restricted system which represents words, leaving grammatical information largely unexpressed (as did the early form of Sumerian writing).

See also DECIPHERMENT.

Reading Dani 1963; Parpola 1993.

Figure 5 Steatite seals with bull and inscription, from Mohen-jo-Daro, Pakistan, c.2000 BCE *(New Delhi, National Museum)*

Figure 6 Specimens of seal inscriptions in Indus script

inherent vowel A V which is assumed to be associated with a C grapheme without being marked as such. The writing system underlying Indian scripts makes the assumption of an inherent V necessary because, although Vs are indicated by means of diacritic marks (*mātrās*) attached to basic C graphemes, the value of the latter is a syllable C + [*a*] or C + [ə]. In order to denote a C alone, the inherent V thus needs to be muted by means of another diacritic (*virāma*). Indian writings are therefore called 'alpha-syllabic' or SYLLABIC ALPHABETS.
See also AKṢARA; INDIAN WRITING SYSTEMS.

initial **1** An initial letter; especially the first letters of a person's surname and given name(s), often used instead of a full signature to authenticate a document or indicate consent with a provision, as in a contract. **2** In typography the first letter of a paragraph or page. In MANUSCRIPTS initials are often put in larger size, coloured and ornamented (figure 7). This practice dates from the fourth century CE and continued for a long time after the introduction of printing.

initial teaching alphabet (ITA) An alternative, largely phonemic orthography for English designed in 1959 by James Pitman (1901–85). First called the 'augmented Roman alphabet', the ITA was intended not as a spelling reform proposal but as a transition alphabet designed to facilitate the acquisition of literacy in traditional orthography. The ITA consists of 44 graphemes with simple and mostly monovalent phoneme correspondences (table 5). The traditional letters of the English alphabet except <q> and <x> are retained, and 20 new symbols are added for phonemes represented by polyvalent graphemes or combinations of phonemes in traditional orthography. In the 1960s and 1970s the ITA was being widely used in English classrooms, but although the results of many studies

Figure 7 Page with ornamented initial from Mira Calligraphiae Monumenta, *written by Georgii Bochkaj and illuminated by Joris Hoefnagel, 1562–96 (Every effort has been made by the publishers to trace the copyright-holder.)*

Table 5 James Pitman's initial teaching alphabet

indicate that it is quite successful in teaching to read more quickly, and although children who were exposed to this experimental reading instruction achieved the changeover to traditional spelling without difficulties (table 6), the use of ITA in British schools has declined.
See also SPELLING REFORM.
Reading Pitman and St John 1969.

ITA		"Traditional"
æ	pæn	pain
ϵϵ	hϵϵ	he
ie	wield	wild
œ	œver	over
ue	dispuet	dispute
au	pauzd	paused
ou	hou	how
oi	emploiment	emploiment
ω	intω	into
ꝏ	rꝏmerd	rumoured
ɑ	mɑrz	Mars
ʃh	ʃhϵϵ	she
ţh	ţhin	thin
ɟh	ɟhe	the
ʒ	aʒuer	azure
ŋ	fϵϵliŋ	feeling
ȼh	muȼh	much

Table 6 Some ITA spellings

inner form of writing systems A term which refers to the structural constitution of writing systems in their relation to language, as opposed to the outer form which has to do with graphic characteristics. For example, the Egyptian and Babylonian writings are very different in outer form, but share important characteristics in inner form, both being logosyllabic. Similarly, Ugaritic is a cuneiform script which, however, is identical in its inner form with Semitic consonant scripts. Conversely, writing systems can make use of the same script and hence be very similar in outer form, but differ substantially in inner form, that is, in how they represent linguistic units. For instance, both English and Spanish use the Roman alphabet, but GRAPHEME–PHONEME CORRESPONDENCES and with them the inner forms of these systems are very dissimilar, since the Spanish spelling system works almost exclusively on the phonemic level, while the English operates on the morphophonemic and often lexical levels.
Reading Haas 1983; Coulmas 1989.

international Niamey keyboard In 1984 at a meeting of coordinators of linguistic projects in Niamey, Niger, the Agence Francophone de Coopération

Culturelle et Technique advocated a new typewriter keyboard with an expanded Roman alphabet suitable for writing African languages (figure 8). The keyboard excludes all upper case letters, using their space for a series of new letters.
See also AFRICA ALPHABET.

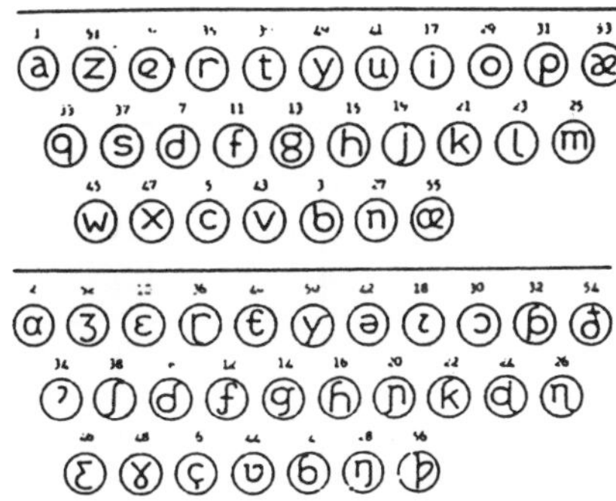

Figure 8 The international Niamey keyboard

international phonetic alphabet (IPA) Today the most common system for transcribing the sounds of a language, the IPA was first published in 1888 by the Association Phonétique Internationale, an organization of foreign language teachers founded by French phonetician Paul Passy. The practical purpose of this association was to create a standardized system of transcribing speech sounds independent of any language, but applicable to all languages. Rather than on the exact representation of the articulation of individual sounds, the emphasis was on furnishing pronounceable texts. A phonetic script for English designed in 1847 by Isaac Pitman and Henry Ellis served the creators of IPA as a model. IPA was last revised in 1989 (table 7). It has been employed in many instances for first reducing a language to writing. However, functional orthographies usually do not adhere to IPA principles strictly, if only because orthographies can rely on the users' knowledge of the language in question and hence incorporate other than phonetic (e.g. morphophonemic) information, ignoring contextually predictable phonetic variation.
See also ENGLISH PHONOTYPIC ALPHABET; ORTHOGRAPHY; TRANSCRIPTION.
Reading Albright 1958.

Italian alphabet The literary standard of Italian evolved in the fourteenth century, mostly based on the dialect of Tuscany under the influence of Dante's *Divina Commedia* and works by Petrarch and Boccaccio. Like all daughter languages of Latin, Italian uses the Roman alphabet in a highly regular and largely phonemic orthography (table 8), although some phonemic distinctions, such as [dz/tz], both spelt <z>, remain graphemically undistinguished. Also, the seven

Consonants

	Bilabial	Labiodental	Dental	Alveolar	Postalveolar	Retroflex	Palatal	Velar	Uvular	Pharyngeal	Glottal
Plosive	p b			t d		ʈ ɖ	c ɟ	k ɡ	q ɢ		ʔ
Nasal	m	ɱ		n		ɳ	ɲ	ŋ	ɴ		
Trill	ʙ			r					ʀ		
Tap or Flap				ɾ		ɽ					
Fricative	ɸ β	f v	θ ð	s z	ʃ ʒ	ʂ ʐ	ç ʝ	x ɣ	χ ʁ	ħ ʕ	h ɦ
Lateral fricative				ɬ ɮ							
Approximant		ʋ		ɹ		ɻ	j	ɰ			
Lateral approximant				l		ɭ	ʎ	ʟ			
Ejective stop	pʼ			tʼ		ʈʼ	cʼ	kʼ	qʼ		
Implosive	ƥ ɓ			ƭ ɗ			ƈ ʄ	ƙ ɠ	ʠ ʛ		

Where symbols appear in pairs, the one to the right represents a voiced consonant.
Shaded areas denote articulations judged impossible.

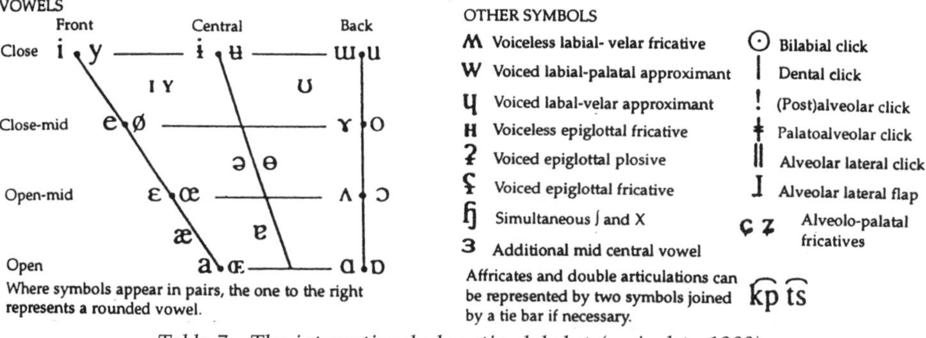

Table 7 The international phonetic alphabet (revised to 1989)

V phonemes [i, e, ɛ, a, ɔ, o, u] are represented by the conventional five V graphemes <i, e, a, o, u> (figure 9). Moreover, <è> is used for accented [ɛ], <é> for accented [e], and <ò> for accented [ɔ]. The grave and acute accents are also used to mark final stress, e.g. *città* 'city', *perciocché* 'because', and to distinguish monosyllabic words such as *si* 'oneself', *sì* 'so, thus'. The oppositions [e/ɛ] and [o/ɔ] are often ignored in spelling, e.g. *venti* [e] 'twenty', *venti*, [ɛ] 'winds'; *ho* [ɔ] 'I have', *o* [o] 'or'. Italian uses capital letters at the beginning of a sentence, for proper names, for designations of historical eras (*il Duecento* 'the thirteenth century'), and personal and possessive pronouns referring to the addressee.
Reading Lepschy and Lepschy 1988.

DIACRITICS

̥ Voiceless n̥ d̥	̹ More rounded ɔ̹	ʷ Labialized tʷ dʷ	˜ Nasalized ẽ
̬ Voiced s̬ t̬	̜ Less rounded ɔ̜	ʲ Palatalized tʲ dʲ	ⁿ Nasal release dⁿ
ʰ Aspirated tʰ dʰ	̟ Advanced u̟	ˠ Velarized tˠ dˠ	ˡ Lateral release dˡ
̤ Breathy voiced b̤ a̤	̠ Retracted i̠	ˤ Pharyngealized tˤ dˤ	̚ No audible release d̚
̰ Creaky voiced b̰ a̰	̈ Centralized ë	̴ Velarized or pharyngealized ɫ	
̼ Linguolabial t̼ d̼	̽ Mid centralized e̽	̝ Raised e̝ ɹ̝ (ɹ̝ = voiced alveolar fricative)	
̪ Dental t̪ d̪	̘ Advanced tongue root e̘	̞ Lowered e̞ β̞ (β̞ = voiced bilabial approximant)	
̺ Apical t̺ d̺	̙ Retracted tongue root e̙		
̻ Laminal t̻ d̻	˞ Rhoticity ə˞	̩ Syllabic ɹ̩	̯ Non-syllabic e̯

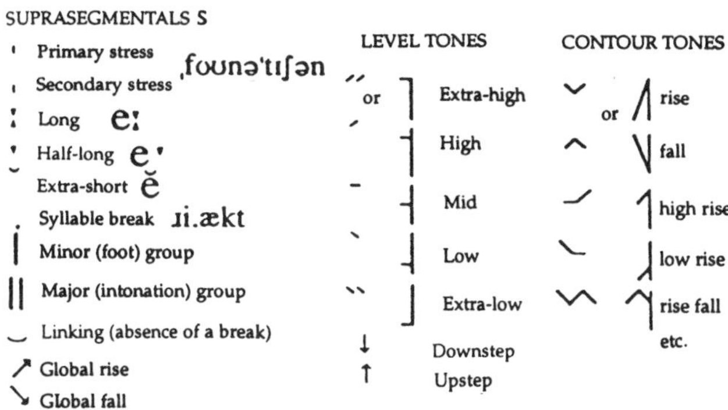

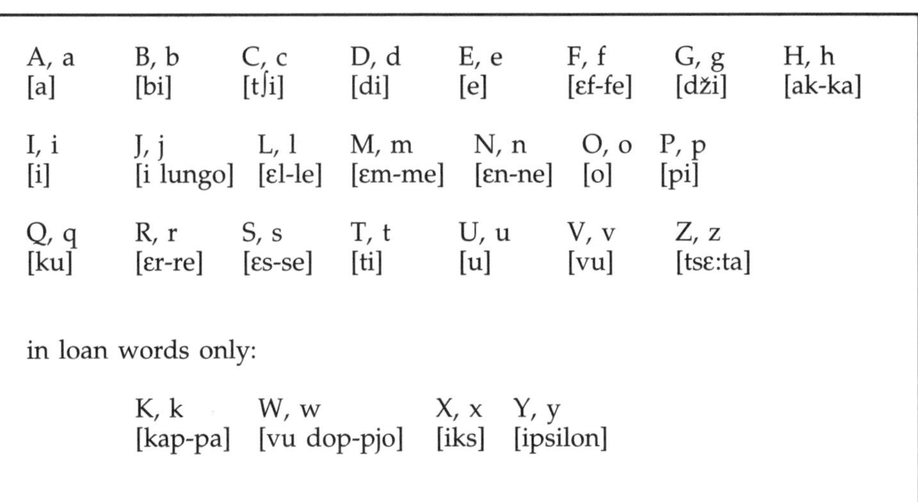

A, a [a]	B, b [bi]	C, c [tʃi]	D, d [di]	E, e [e]	F, f [ɛf-fe]	G, g [dži]	H, h [ak-ka]
I, i [i]	J, j [i lungo]	L, l [ɛl-le]	M, m [ɛm-me]	N, n [ɛn-ne]	O, o [o]	P, p [pi]	
Q, q [ku]	R, r [ɛr-re]	S, s [ɛs-se]	T, t [ti]	U, u [u]	V, v [vu]	Z, z [tsɛ:ta]	

in loan words only:

K, k [kap-pa]	W, w [vu dop-pjo]	X, x [iks]	Y, y [ipsilon]

Table 8 The letters of the Italian alphabet and their names

E Don Fabrizio si commosse di nuovo, ricordando
[e don fabritsio si kom-mɔse di nuɔ:vo rikɔrdando

la sua cara Giulia, la cui vita spregianta era
la sua ka:ra dʒulia la kui vi:ta sprɛ:dʒanta ɛ:ra

stata un perpètuo sacrificio dinanzi alle
sta:ta un perpɛ:tuo sakrifi:tʃo dinantsi al-le

stravaganze frenètiche del padre di Tancredi.
stravagantse frenetike del pa:dre di Tankre:di]

Figure 9 Sample of Italian grapheme–phoneme correspondence: from Giuseppe Tomasi di Lampedusa, Il Gattopardo

italic A printing type which was introduced by Aldus Manutius of Venice (figure 10). Instead of being perpendicular in orientation as in ROMAN TYPE, the letters slope towards the right. The italic is derived from a cursive form of Caroline minuscules. It has become the most common supplementary type used by printers in combination with roman and other types for purposes of contrast and emphasis.

P.V.M. GEORGICORVM,
LIBER QVARTVS.

P Rotinus aerii mellis, cœlestia dona
Exequar, hanc etiam Mœcenas aspice
partem.
Admiranda tibi leuiũ spectacula rerũ,
M agnanimosq; duces, totiusq; ex ordine gentis
M ores, et studia, et populos, et prælia dicam.
I n tenui labor, at tenuis non gloria, si quem
N umina leua sinunt, auditq; uocatus Apollo.
P rincipio, sedes apibus, statioq; petenda,
Q uo neq; sit uentis aditus (nam pabula uenti
F erre domum prohibent) neq; oues, hœdiq; petulæ

Figure 10 Specimen of italic from Aldus Manutius's Virgil, *Venice, 1501*

Italic scripts *See* OLD ITALIC SCRIPTS

Itzamná The supreme Maya god, inventor of writing.
See also DEITIES OF WRITING.

J

J, j /dʒeɪ/ The tenth letter of the English alphabet derives from Semitic *yōdh* and developed as a variant of *I* in medieval Latin. Both *I* and *J* were used to represent the vowel [i] and the semivowel [j]. Its present phonetic value in English developed under French influence.

Japanese writing Japanese uses a mixed writing system consisting of Chinese characters, *kanji* in Japanese, and the two KANA syllabaries HIRAGANA and KATAKANA. For certain purposes, such as decoration, abbreviation and quotation, Roman letters are also used in Japanese writing. Arabic numerals are predominant, but Chinese numerals are still in evidence in lettering, addresses, dates etc. Like Chinese, Japanese is traditionally written in vertical lines proceeding from right to left, but horizontally printed material with right-running lines is also common. Horizontal inscriptions are found in both directions, from left to right and from right to left. The mixed nature of the system and the multiformity of its calligraphy and typography lend Japanese writing an ornate and distinct appearance (figure 1).

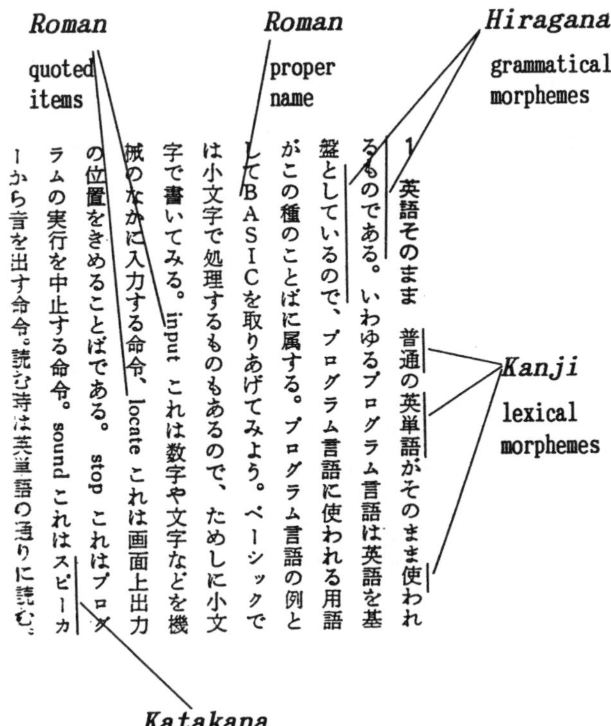

Figure 1 A paragraph of contemporary Japanese writing, combining kanji, hiragana, katakana *and Roman letters*

Historical development

The literary history of Japan begins with Chinese inscriptions dating from the fifth century CE. Having no writing of their own, the Japanese imported both the Chinese script and the Chinese written language, known as KANBUN 'Chinese writing' in Japanese. A distinction is made between *jun-kanbun* 'genuine Chinese' and *hentai-kanbun* 'abnormal *kanbun*', which deviates in grammar and character usage considerably from Chinese. *Hentai-kanbun* became the normal way of reading and writing Classical Chinese in Japan.

In addition to using Chinese for the purposes of written communication, the Japanese adapted Chinese characters for writing their own language. Two adaptation strategies were employed, one based on meaning, the other based on sound. Following the meaning-based strategy, a *kanji* was used to write a Japanese word which was synonymous with the Chinese word written with it. Thus, the Japanese word *fitö* 'man' (*hito* in modern Japanese) came to be written with the Chinese character 人 for *ren* 'man'. The Japanese reading of Chinese characters resulting from this adaptation strategy is called *kun* 'meaning' in Japanese philology. The other, sound-based strategy emerged in response to the need to write grammatical morphemes. *Kanji* were used for their sound values irrespective of meaning. For example, the topicalization particle *fa* came to be written with the character 波 'wave' which was pronounced *pua* in Middle Chinese. The Sino-Japanese reading of *kanji* resulting from this adaptation strategy is called *on* 'pronunciation' in Japanese philology. During the formative period of the Japanese writing system, Japanese was, moreover, enriched by a massive intake of Chinese loan words which entered the language through the written medium and were hence naturally written as they were in Chinese. Three different functions of *kanji* resulted: (1) representing native Japanese words as logograms; (2) representing Japanese syllables that resembled Chinese words; (3) representing Chinese loan words.

Many Chinese characters were adapted in accordance with both strategies and as loan words. As a consequence, there are now many words in the Japanese lexicon which are semantically closely related in the sense that, for instance, *water* and *hydro-* share the same semantic core. These words are written with the same *kanji*, although their phonetic form is unrelated. 人 of the above example is thus used to write both *hito* (Japanese reading) and *jin* (Sino-Japanese reading), much as if *man* and *anthropo-* were written with the same character.

The adaptation was even more confounded, because it took place over an extended period of almost 1,000 years, many characters being introduced into Japanese writing more than once with different Chinese dialect pronunciations. Accordingly, various Sino-Japanese readings of *kanji* coexist: *go-on* is the oldest pronunciation of *kanji* in Japanese dating from the sixth century CE, while *kan-on* reflects seventh- and eighth-century pronunciations. *Tō-on* (also *Tōsō-on*) is based on the fourteenth-century speech of the Hangchow region. The result is a high degree of POLYVALENCE in the Japanese use of Chinese characters. In order to determine which reading is intended in a given case, the reader has to rely on contextual information and certain general principles (figure 2, table 1).

The great complexity of writing Japanese with *kanji* only led to the development of a simpler, phonetic script. Graphic stylization and systematization brought

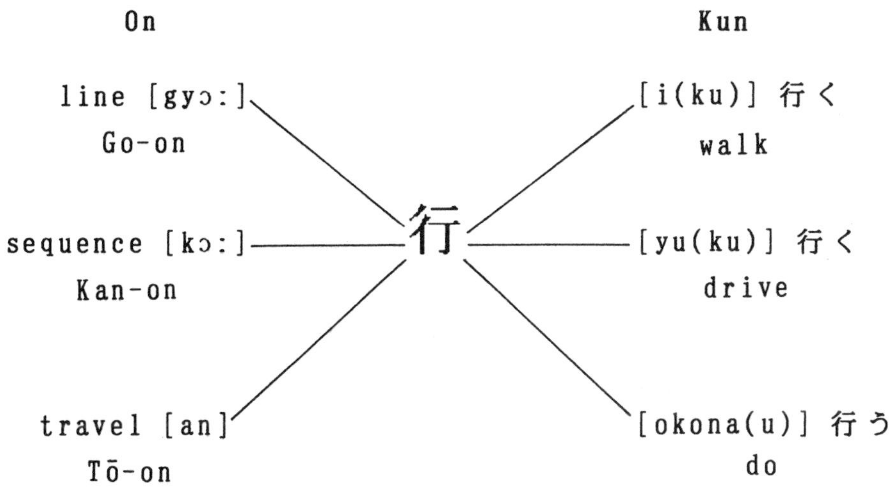

Figure 2 Multiple readings of the Chinese character 行 *in Japanese*

	go-on	kan-on	tō-on	kun
京	kyô	kei	kin	miyako
外	gyô	gai	ui	soto
行	gyô	kô	an	kudari
明	myô	mei	min	akashi
和	wa	ka	o	nagi

Table 1 On *and* kun *readings of* kanji

two syllabaries into existence, *katakana* and *hiragana*. The former evolved in the ninth century CE from parts of Chinese characters used as reading aids written alongside Chinese characters. *Hiragana* were drawn from simplified and stylized Chinese characters known as *sōgana*. Whereas *katakana* were always used in conjunction with, and as auxiliary signs for, *kanji*, *hiragana* came to be used without *kanji* to write Japanese in a completely phonetic fashion, and were thus instrumental in establishing the Japanese written style *wabun* (tenth century). Until the end of the nineteenth century the Japanese wrote in various styles, ranging from Classical Chinese, in *kanji* only, to Classical Japanese, mostly in *kana*, and a variety of mixed styles combining *kanji* and *kana* in differing proportions. The Chinese style was always the prestige variety, and to the present time a style that makes use of many *kanji* is regarded as a sign of erudition. Although a reform movement at the end of the nineteenth century known as *genbun itchi* 'unification of speech and writing' has brought spoken and written styles much closer together, the gap between spoken and written varieties of Japanese is still very noticeable.

俤	omokage	one's look	柾	masaki	spindle tree
俥	kuruma	jinrikisha	栃	tochi	horse chestnut
俣	mata	thigh	栂	tsuga	hemlock spruce
働	hatara-ku	to work	凧	tako	kite
凪	nagi	lull	辻	tsuji	crossroad
辷	sube-ru	to slip	込	ko-mu	congested
匂	nio-i	smell	迚	totemo	very
腺	sen	gland	膵	sui	pancreas
峠	touge	pass	噸	ton	ton
鋲	byou	tack	鑓	yari	spear
畑	hatake	field	笹	sasa	bamboo grass
杢	moku	woodworker	枠	waku	frame
鱈	tara	codfish	鴫	shigi	snipe
蓙	goza	mat	籾	momi	unhulled rice
麿	maro	you	杣	soma	timber

Table 2 Kokuji*: kanji designed in Japan in accordance with the formative principles of Chinese characters*

Current usage

In modern times, the Japanese have limited the number of *kanji* and of their readings. The *Jōyō kanjihyō* (*List of Chinese Characters for General Use*), which was promulgated by cabinet decision in 1981 to replace the *Jōyō kanjihyō* (*List of Chinese Characters for Current Use*) of 1946, contains 1,945 characters and an appendix giving irregular *kun* readings as well as one listing 166 name characters. A total of 4,087 readings are associated with the 1,945 *kanji* in the list. Of these characters, 1,168 have one *on* and one *kun* reading each, while 737 have only an *on* reading and 40 only a *kun* reading. The last group comprises mainly *kokuji* or Japanese-made characters not used in Chinese (table 2). In addition, some *kanji* are also used to write non-Chinese loan words such as 珈琲 [kɔːçiː] 'coffee'. While writers are free to use any historically attested *kanji*, government documents, newspapers, textbooks and similar publications directed at a general readership are expected to use only *kanji* included in the list.

Although these regulations have made *kanji* easier to handle, the system is still very demanding. It can be difficult, for example, to determine the correct reading of a character. In compounds *kanji* tend to have Sino-Japanese (i.e. *on*) readings, but compounds with Japanese (i.e. *kun*) readings are also common. Furthermore, there are some 170 mixed *on-kun* or *kun-on* compounds as well as bi-*kanji* compounds with two or more possible readings usually associated with different meanings.

As regards the spelling conventions for using *kanji* and *kana* in combination, the general principle is that lexical morphemes are written in *kanji* and grammatical

(1) 山にも海にもやっと夏が来た。

(2) やまにも、うみにも、やっとなつがきた。

(3) yamanimo uminimo yatto natsuga kita.

Figure 3 Three ways of writing Japanese: (1) regular style combining kanji *and* kana, *(2)* hiragana *only, (3)* rōmaji *or Roman letters*

morphemes in *hiragana* (figure 3). This implies that words which take agglutinative suffixes such as adjectives and verbs are written as *kanji* plus *kana* combinations. *Katakana* are used for emphasis, for non-Chinese loan words, and for onomatopoeic words. Japanese is normally written without word spacing, each character, *kanji* or *kana*, occupying the same space. However, the functional allocation of the different scripts to different form classes conveys much of the information that word spacing would make available.

Where a *kanji* is unknown, the word in question can be written in *kana*. Repeated proposals have been made to write Japanese in *kana* only, but simplicity arguments have never been embraced by wide sections of the population, let alone by the literary elites. Similarly, suggestions for a Romanized orthography have never attracted more than curiosity, although the RŌMAJI system for writing Japanese in Roman letters has been standardized and approved by the Japanese government. While proposals directed at replacing the Japanese mixed system of writing by a simpler phonetic orthography have thus come to nothing, there is statistical evidence that the number of different *kanji* as well as the proportion of *kanji* in running text has been declining steadily in the course of the twentieth century, which means that the number of content words written in *kana* has increased. At the same time it must be noted that word-processing technology may help to arrest if not reverse this trend, as there are virtually no limitations on the number of characters stored in computer software. The two 1990 Japanese Industrial Standard lists of *kanji* (JIS X20H-1990) coded for computers and word processors include as many as 6,353 characters, of which 2,965 belong to the first level and are considered essential.

Reading Seeley 1991; Coulmas 1991; Unger 1984.

Javanese writing A member of the Hesperonesian branch of the Malayo-Polynesian family, Javanese is Indonesia's oldest literary language, spoken by some 70 million of its inhabitants.

Literary history

Throughout its varied literary history, which goes back to the fourth century CE, Javanese was written in several different scripts, beginning with the Pallava script, a variety of Indian Devanāgarī. In the east Javanese *kakāwin* literature of the tenth to the fourteenth centuries, the Old Javanese or Kawi script had already assumed a distinct Javanese form (figure 4). While Old Javanese orthography generally followed Sanskrit conventions, the ancient orthography was eventually discarded and even the numerous Sanskrit loan words were given an approximate phonetic spelling. After the rise of Islam in Java in the fifteenth century, Javanese was also

Transcription

1. Oṃ sri sarasoti krĕta wukir - hadi umalung uri-
2. p - ing buwana añakra murusa patirtan - palĕmaran hapan - yang
3. widi hani deni yang raditya yang wulan hanĕlĕ i halahayu
4. ni dewamanusa yang hanut - yang hagawe bajaran - tapak - tangtu kabaḥha
5. deni dewamanusa muwaḥ sang tumon sang ṅamanah - arĕṅĕ luputa
6. ring ila-ila paḍa kadĕlana tutur - jati yen - ana ṅabah ta-
7. npa bĕkĕl - apatik - wĕnang tanpa baktaha histri pitung hajama tan - wawa
8. dona wastu . sri syati sakawarsa * 1371.

* Representation of a *liṅga*.

Figure 4 Stone inscription from Ngadoman, dated 1449 CE: the script is a variety of the Old Javanese script (transcription Cohen 1875, no. XXVII: by permission of E. J. Brill, Leiden)

written in an adaptation of the Arabic script, called *pégon* or *gundil* script (figure 5), but the Javanese script tradition continued. In subsequent stages of Javanese literature the script underwent further changes, arriving at its present form in the literature of the Mataram period of the seventeenth and eighteenth centuries (figure 6). The nineteenth century saw the introduction by the Dutch of the Roman script for writing Javanese, which has since gradually supplanted the Javanese

Figure 5 Sample page of Javanese pégon *(adapted Arabic) script*

script. Today, few Javanese are literate in the traditional script, most of them scholars, although it continues to be taught at school and those who can read and write it are highly esteemed.

Modern Roman orthography

By the mid-twentieth century, the Roman script had become the predominant written medium of Javanese. In 1972, a spelling reform fixed a new standard. The resulting orthography has five V graphemes to represent nine phonemes using a grave and acute accent on <e> for distinction (table 3). The 29 C phonemes are represented by the following 19 letters, from which 29 graphemes are formed by

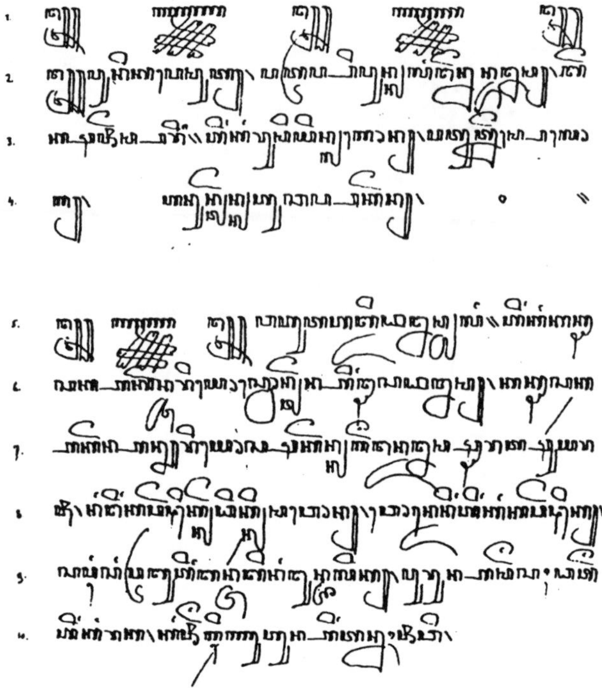

Transliteration

1
2 punika pémut / patrappipun kalaŋṅĕnnan dalm / bĕ
3 kṣa jĕmpariŋ//hiŋkaŋ rumiyin lagon / patut nĕm pélo
4 g / hanuntĕn kahucappakĕn /
5 // // wahu ta habdi dalm ḍalaŋ // hiŋkaŋ kakṛ
6 sakakĕn cariyos wontĕn hiŋ ṅṛsa dalm / kakṛsak
7 hakĕn hanñariyossakĕn kagĕŋṅan dalm ṣrat ṣurya ra
8 ja / naŋniŋ kapĕṭik kĕḍik kimawon / wondéniŋ hiŋkaŋ kap ĕṭik /
9 saṛŋ saŋ prabu hiŋ bañjar binaŋṅun balik / purun hamĕŋsaḥ datĕŋ
10 hiŋkaŋ raka / kaŋjĕŋ śṇuhun hiŋ tanaḥ jawi /

Translation

1
2 Note! The arrangement of the King's Play,
3 "The Arrow Dance". First: *lagon patut nĕm pélog*
4 Then is recited:
5 Here is the King's servant the *dalang* who
6 has been requested to narrate in the King's presence. He was requested
7 to narrate the tale of the King's book Surya Raja,
8 but only a chosen passage. What was chosen is the tale of the episode
9 when the Prince of Bañjar Binangun rebelled, daring to wage war against
10 his elder brother His Majesty the Emperor of Java.

Figure 6 Passage of Javanese manuscript written about 1800 CE *in the ornate* Kraton *script: beginning of a libretto of a theatrical ballet at the Yogyakarta Court*
Source: *Pigeaud 1975, plate 21 (by permission of Franz Steiner Verlag, Wiesbaden)*

Grapheme	Phoneme
a	a, å
e	e
é	é
è	è
i	i
o	o, ɔ
u	u

Table 3 Javanese vowel graphemes and phonemes

means of including ten DIGRAPHS and TRIGRAPHS: <p, t, c, k, q, b, d, j, g, m, n, f, v, s, h, l, r, w, y>. Digraphs are <th, dh, ny, ng> for alveolar, palatal and velar occlusives, <mb, nd, nj,> for nasals, and <lh> for a dental lateral. The two trigraphs <ndh, ngg> are for 'heavy' alveolar and velar nasals. The glottal stop is spelt <k>. Largely morphophonemic in structure, the orthography disregards many predictable phonetic alternations.

Javanese script

The Javanese script (native term *tjarakan* or *carakan*) is a syllabic alphabet of the Indian type consisting of 20 C graphemes with an inherent V *a* (table 4). These are called *akṣara*, using the Sanskrit term. Two *akṣara* placed next to each other thus stand for two syllables, C-a + C-a. Vowels other than the neutral inherent V are expressed by diacritic satellites attached to the *akṣara*. (The base lines in table 4 show where the V diacritics are placed in relation to the *akṣara*.) These V diacritics are called *sandangan* in Javanese. In combination with any *akṣara* they neutralize the inherent V. The latter can also be muted in other contexts, as when Cs occur in syllable-final position or as clusters. For V muting in final position a special diacritic called *patèn* is used, its vertical part being put under the *akṣara* whose inherent V is to be cancelled. The *patèn* corresponds to the VIRĀMA device of Devanāgarī.

An extra set of letters exactly paralleling the *akṣara* is available for representing C clusters. These conjunct letters are called *pasangan*. Many of them closely resemble their *akṣara* counterparts. In running text, *pasangan* letters are placed under or, less frequently, next to *akṣara* letters in horizontal lines running from left to right. No *pasangan* can follow *hå, rå* and *nyå* because special diacritics (*sandangan panyigeging wanda*) are available for representing *h, r* and *ny*. Another limitation on the use of *pasangan* letters is that each *akṣara* can be combined with only one *pasangan*. Therefore, the *patèn* V muting device must be employed for writing clusters consisting of more than two Cs.

Word-initial Vs are usually spelt with initial *hå*. In addition, there are special graphemes indicating initial Vs called *akṣara swara* which, however, are optional. Likewise, there is another set of optional graphemes known as *akṣara murda* or *akṣara gedhé* 'great or important letters' (table 5). These are derived from the Indian letters for *ṇå, khå, thå, šå, śå, phå, dhå* and *bhå* which were not needed in Javanese, the difference in pronunciation between these letters and *nå, kå, tå, så,*

Consonant letters: akṣara and pasangan

Akṣara	Pasangan	Value	Akṣara	Pasangan	Value
ꦲ	꧀ꦲ	hå	ꦝ	꧀ꦝ	dha
ꦤ	꧀ꦤ	nå	ꦗ	꧀ꦗ	jå
ꦕ	꧀ꦕ	cå	ꦪ	꧀ꦪ	yå
ꦫ	꧀ꦫ	rå	ꦚ	꧀ꦚ	ńå
ꦏ	꧀ꦏ	kå	ꦩ	꧀ꦩ	må
ꦢ	꧀ꦢ	då	ꦒ	꧀ꦒ	gå
ꦠ	꧀ꦠ	tå	ꦧ	꧀ꦧ	bå
ꦱ	꧀ꦱ	så	ꦛ	꧀ꦛ	thå
ꦮ	꧀ꦮ	wå	ꦔ	꧀ꦔ	nyå
ꦭ	꧀ꦭ	lå			
ꦥ	꧀ꦥ	på			

Vowel letters: sandangan

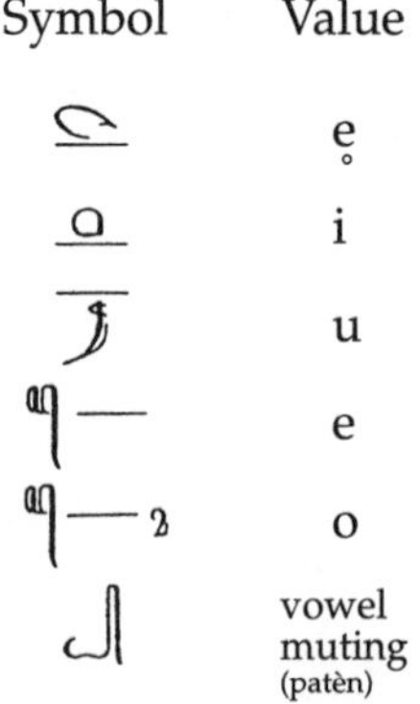

Table 4 The Javanese script

Devanāgarī	ण	ख	थ	ष	श	फ	घ	भ
Akṣara murda	ꦟ	ꦑ	ꦡ	ꦰ	ꦯ	ꦦ	ꦓ	ꦨ
Value	nå	kå	tå	så	så	på	gå	bå

Table 5 Aksara murda *and the Devanāgarī letters from which they are derived*

Beginning of a poem

End of a poem

Figure 7 Poetic signs of the Javanese script

så, på, gå and *bå* having been neutralized. Javanese spelling makes no regular distinction between capital and small letters, but *akṣara murda* are used for honorific purposes, especially to distinguish names and titles of respected persons. Whenever such designations are graphically marked in this way, *akṣara murda* are used throughout the word rather than as initials only.

Another peculiarity of the Javanese script is special graphemes for poetic purposes marking the beginning and the end of a poem (figure 7).

Typography

The Javanese script was first used in print in the 1830s when the Dutch produced a type font of erect letters. A cursive font was developed shortly thereafter and widely used during the second half of the nineteenth century. Two other cursive varieties came into existence early in the twentieth century, marking the end of the typographic development of the Javanese script. From 1942 to 1945 the Japanese occupation prohibited the use of the Javanese script. Already weakened by the irreversible inroads of the Roman script, the traditional Indo-Javanese script never recovered from this blow. Outside scholarly contexts its use is reduced to decorative functions.

See also Indian writing systems; Kawi script.

Reading Dumont 1923; Van der Molen 1993; Pigeaud 1975.

Jingpo writing A member of the Tibeto-Burman branch of the Sino-Tibetan language family, Jingpo (also called Jingpho, Jinghpaw, Chingpo and, in Myanmar, Kachin) is spoken by some 560,000 people in China and Myanmar (Burma). A writing system based on the Latin alphabet was created for it at the end of the nineteenth century by the British missionary O. Hansen. It consisted of 46 graphemes including accented V letters for tones as well as 19 Digraphs and Trigraphs.

b	[p]	p	[p-]	hp	[ph]	m	[m]	w	[w]	f	[f]
d	[t]	t	[t-]	ht	[th]	n	[n]	l	[l]		
z	[ts]	ts	[ts-]	zh	[tsh]	s	[s]				
j	[tʃ]	chy	[tʃ-]	ch	[tʃh]	sh	[ʃ]	r	[ʒ]	y	[j]
g	[k]	k	[k-]	hk	[kh]	ng	[ŋ]	h	[x]		
br	[pʒ]	pr	[pʒ-]	hpr	[phʒ]						
gr	[kʒ]	kr	[kʒ-]	hkr	[khʒ]						
by	[pj]	py	[pj-]	hpy	[phj]	my	[mj]				
gy	[kj]	ky	[kj-]	hky	[khj]	ny	[ŋj]				

Table 6 Jingpo consonant grapheme–phoneme correspondences

Hpa–ji n htum ai masha she arong nada sha–ok, n hpring ai ntsin nhtung go gaprok.

Translation

A half-full bucket of water is easily splashed out; a half-informed person is prone to show off.

Figure 8 Sample sentence of Jingpo

In 1957 a reformed spelling system was adopted in China where Jingpo is one of the officially recognized minority languages. Its 48 graphemes, 39 for Cs and nine for Vs and diphthongs, allow for a largely phonemic notation, although the four tones of Jingpo are not marked in writing. The V letters <a, e, i, o, u> represent four different tonal segments each, and the digraphs <ai, au, ui, oi> two tonal diphthongs each. Phoneme values of C graphemes are indicated in table 6. A sample sentence is given in figure 8.
Reading Kao 1992.

Jurchen script *See* NÜZHEN SCRIPT

K, k /keɪ/ The eleventh letter of the English alphabet is derived from Semitic *kaph* through Greek *kappa* (Κ, κ). Having been used interchangeably with *C* in Etruscan, it fell into disuse in Latin. In English it was introduced under Norman French influence, its principal function being to distinguish native from Romance origin words. Hence *cyng* became *king*, *cnif* became *knife* etc. Its present use is no longer so restricted.

Kadamba script A southern Indian offshoot of the Brāhmī script first attested in the fifth century CE. By the tenth century the Kadamba script (table 1) had developed into the Old Kanarese script which was widely used across south India and became the parent script of the modern Kanarese (Kannada) and Telugu scripts.
See also BRĀHMĪ WRITING; INDIAN WRITING SYSTEMS.

Consonant letters

ka	kha	ga	gha	ṅa	ča	čha	ǧa	ña
ṭa	ḍha	ta	tha	ḍa	dha	na	pa	pha
ba	ma	ra	la	śa	ṣa	sa	ha	

Vowel letters

a	i	u	e	ā

Table 1 The Kadamba script

kaishu [Chinese 楷書] (*k'ai-shu*) An angular, straight-lined form of the Chinese script, *kaishu* (*kaisho* in Japanese) developed during the later Han dynasty (25–220 CE) from the earlier clerical script (figure 1). The *kaishu* is the non-cursive standard style of Chinese characters which continues to be used today.
See also CALLIGRAPHY; CHINESE SCRIPTS.

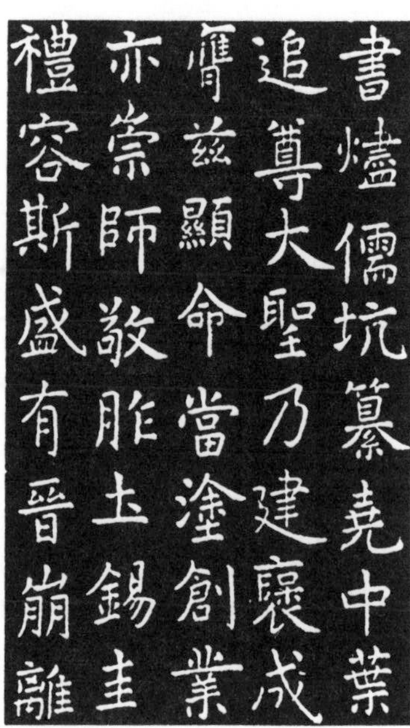

Figure 1 A specimen of the Chinese kaishu, *standard script, Tang dynasty (618–906)*

Kalmyk writing A variety of western Mongolian, the Kalmyk language, which is also known as Kalmyk-Oirat or Qalmaq, has a literary tradition going back to the mid-seventeenth century CE when an alphabet for the language was derived from the Uighur-Mongolian script by Ĵaya Pandita (1599–1662), Chief Lama of Dzungaria (table 2). Like the Mongolian script it runs from top to bottom in vertical columns shifting from left to right. Each letter appears in three forms: initial, medial and final. This script was used until 1927. Under Soviet rule a Cyrillic orthography was introduced in 1923 which was replaced in 1931 by the Latin alphabet. However, as of 1938 Kalmyk was once again written in Cyrillic.
See also MONGOLIAN WRITING.
Reading Aalto 1964.

kana A general term for a number of syllabic writing systems developed in Japan on the basis of Chinese characters for writing Japanese. Etymologically the word *kana* derives from *kari* 'temporary, non-regular' plus *na* 'name' or 'writing'. In the early literary history of Japan 'regular' writing was Chinese writing, whereas *kana* evolved as an alternative system suitable to write the Japanese language. The *kana* signs were derived from Chinese characters used as reading aids in annotating Buddhist texts. Considering the important role that the study of these texts played in the evolution of the *kana* syllabaries, it is not surprising to find traces of Indian influence. The sequence of *kana* Vs (*a, i, u, e, o*) and *kana* Cs (*k, s, t, n, h, m, y, r, w*) largely corresponds to the usual arrangement of Indian writing systems.

Manyōgana, the *kana* used in the eighth-century CE *Manyōshū* anthology of Japanese poetry, still look like standard Chinese characters, although they function as phonograms used irrespective of their Chinese meaning. There were 87

initial	mid	final		initial	mid	final		initial	mid	final	
[illegible]	[illegible]	[illegible]	a	[illegible]	[illegible]	[illegible]	n	[illegible]	[illegible]	[illegible]	m
[illegible]	[illegible]	[illegible]	o	-	[illegible]	[illegible]	ŋ	[illegible]	[illegible]	-	č
[illegible]	[illegible]	[illegible]	u	[illegible]	[illegible]	-	x	[illegible]	[illegible]	-	ǰ
[illegible]	[illegible]	[illegible]	e	[illegible]	[illegible]	-	γ	[illegible]	[illegible]	-	y
[illegible]	[illegible]	[illegible]	ö	-	[illegible]	[illegible]	k*	[illegible]	[illegible]	-	k
[illegible]	[illegible]	[illegible]	ü	[illegible]	[illegible]	-	g	[illegible]	[illegible]	-	g
[illegible]	[illegible]	[illegible]	i	[illegible]	[illegible]	-	k	[illegible]	[illegible]	[illegible]	r
[illegible]	[illegible]	[illegible]	ā	[illegible]	[illegible]	[illegible]	b	[illegible]	[illegible]	-	w
[illegible]	[illegible]	[illegible]	ō	[illegible]	[illegible]	-	p	[illegible]	[illegible]	-	dž
[illegible]	[illegible]	[illegible]	ū	[illegible]	[illegible]	[illegible]	s	[illegible]	[illegible]	-	h
[illegible]	[illegible]	[illegible]	ē	[illegible]	[illegible]	[illegible]	š	-	[illegible]	-	v
[illegible]	[illegible]	[illegible]	ȫ	[illegible]	[illegible]	[illegible]	t	[illegible]	[illegible]	-	ñ
[illegible]	[illegible]	[illegible]	ǖ	[illegible]	[illegible]	-	d	-	[illegible]	-	ṇ
[illegible]	[illegible]	[illegible]	ī	[illegible]	[illegible]	[illegible]	l		[illegible]		ṣ

[illegible] bo ~ bü, [illegible] bö, [illegible] bu, [illegible] bō, [illegible] bȫ, [illegible] bū, [illegible] bǖ.

* before consonants and in final position.

Table 2 The Kalmyk alphabet

different syllables in eighth-century Japanese which were represented by some 970 *manyōgana*. The system was still highly complex and redundant. Gradually the number of characters was reduced and their form stylized, by and large losing their graphic resemblance to the Chinese characters of which they were derived.

The two KANA systems used in contemporary Japanese, HIRAGANA and KATAKANA, are isomorphic consisting of 48 characters each, five of which represent independent Vs and the rest syllables of the CV type plus one syllabic nasal (table 3). The unit represented by each of the basic 48 *kana* characters is a *mora*, that is a short syllable. Syllables with long Vs count as two *mora* and are represented by two *kana*. Two diacritics are employed to mark systematic phonological contrasts: two little strokes (*dakuten* or *nigoriten*) are added to a character to mark voicing where a contrast between voiced and unvoiced Cs exists; and a small circle (*handakuten*) is added to those of the *h* column to mark initial *p*-. Further, the *kana* for *tsu* is put in smaller type next to full-sized characters to indicate geminate Cs. No separate *kana* exist for palatalized syllables. The characters for *ki, si, ni, hi, mi* and *ri* are therefore used in conjunction with those of the *y* column, the latter in smaller type. What would have to be transliterated

Katakana

nasal	w	r	y	m	h	n	t	s	k		
n ン	ワ	ラ	ヤ	マ	ハ	ナ	タ	サ	カ	ア	a
	(ヰ)	リ		ミ	ヒ	ニ	チ	シ	キ	イ	i
		ル	ユ	ム	フ	ヌ	ツ	ス	ク	ウ	u
	(ヱ)	レ		メ	ヘ	ネ	テ	セ	ケ	エ	e
	ヲ	ロ	ヨ	モ	ホ	ノ	ト	ソ	コ	オ	o

パ	バ	ダ	ザ	ガ
ピ	ビ	ヂ	ジ	ギ
プ	ブ	ヅ	ズ	グ
ペ	ベ	デ	ゼ	ゲ
ポ	ボ	ド	ゾ	ゴ

リャ	ミャ	ヒャ	ニャ	チャ	シャ	キャ
リュ	ミュ	ヒュ	ニュ	チュ	シュ	キュ
リョ	ミョ	ヒョ	ニョ	チョ	ショ	キョ

ピャ	ビャ	ヂャ	ジャ	ギャ
ピュ	ビュ	ヂュ	ジュ	ギュ
ピョ	ビョ	ヂョ	ジョ	ギョ

Table 3 The two Japanese syllabaries, katakana *and* hiragana

Hiragana

ıasal	w	r	y	m	h	n	t	s	k		
n ん	わ	ら	や	ま	は	な	た	さ	か	あ	a
	(ゐ)	り		み	ひ	に	ち	し	き	い	i
		る	ゆ	む	ふ	ぬ	つ	す	く	う	u
	(ゑ)	れ		め	へ	ね	て	せ	け	え	e
	を	ろ	よ	も	ほ	の	と	そ	こ	お	o

ぱ	ば	だ	ざ	が
ぴ	び	ぢ	じ	ぎ
ぷ	ぶ	づ	ず	ぐ
ぺ	べ	で	ぜ	げ
ぽ	ぼ	ど	ぞ	ご

りゃ	みゃ	ひゃ	にゃ	ちゃ	しゃ	きゃ
りゅ	みゅ	ひゅ	にゅ	ちゅ	しゅ	きゅ
りょ	みょ	ひょ	にょ	ちょ	しょ	きょ

ぴゃ	びゃ	ぢゃ	じゃ	ぎゃ
ぴゅ	びゅ	ぢゅ	じゅ	ぎゅ
ぴょ	びょ	ぢょ	じょ	ぎょ

bisyllabically as <ni-ya>, for example, according to the usual values of the *kana* characters thus stands for the single syllable [nja] or [ña]. Together with these auxiliary devices the basic *kana* characters suffice to express all 102 syllables of Japanese in a straightforward and economic way. *Kana* orthography has changed considerably over the centuries. Contemporary usage is regulated in a report by the Deliberative Council on the National Language (*Kokugo shingikai*) of 1986.
See also JAPANESE WRITING.
Reading Komatsu 1968; Seeley 1991.

***kanamajiri* writing** A style of written Japanese which first came into use in the early ninth century CE. It combines KANJI or Chinese characters and KANA syllabic signs.
See also JAPANESE WRITING; KANBUN.

kanbun A Japanese term which literally means 'Chinese writing'. It refers to classical Chinese as used in Japan, a language variety which exists in writing alone. A distinction is made between *jun-kanbun* 'genuine Chinese' and *hentai-kanbun* 'abnormal *kanbun*', a hybridized form of Chinese which displays many features of Japanese grammar.

Hentai-kanbun texts make difficult reading because, rather than following a fixed pattern, the hybrid features are highly variable, leaning more in the direction of Chinese or Japanese as the case may be (figure 2). It is even difficult in many instances to say whether a *hentai-kanbun* text represents the Chinese or the Japanese language, that is whether it is basically Chinese with occasional Japanese word order or heavily Sinicized Japanese. In fact, there was a gradual transition from one to the other. Since most Japanese literati learned Chinese as a written language only, and since Chinese characters expressed morphemes rather than meaningless syllables, the Japanese developed the practice of reading Classical Chinese sentences in Japanese, in much the same way as speakers of English usually read *e.g.* as 'for example', rather than *exempli gratia*. This 'translating while reading' procedure was gradually formalized and marked in the text by *okurigana*, i.e. KANA which indicate Japanese particles and suffixes, and *kaeriten* or 'return markers' which transform Chinese into Japanese word order. These reading aids are called *kunten* and this style *kundoku* style. *Kanbun* texts without reading aids are called *hakubun* 'white or blank writing'.
Reading Komai and Rohlich 1988; Seeley 1991.

kanji The Japanese term for 'Chinese character', also widely used in Western writings about Japanese. *Kanji* differ from Chinese characters *sensu stricto* in important respects. While Chinese characters each represent a Chinese morpheme syllable, this simple correspondence has been destroyed in the process of adapting them to writing Japanese. Most *kanji* are associated with multiple pronunciations and many with multiple meanings. The so-called *ateji* 'substitute characters' are characters that are assigned irregular, unpredictable readings.

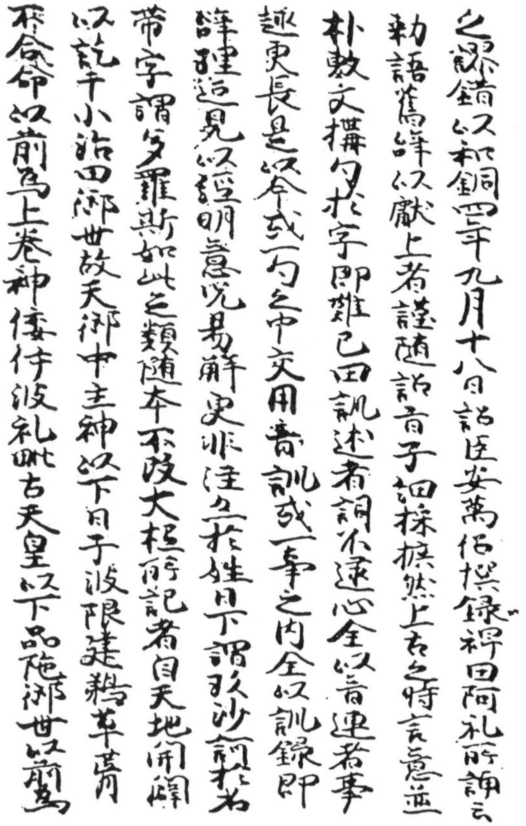

Figure 2 A page in hentai-kanbun *from the* Kojiki (Record of Ancient Matters), *one of Japan's oldest written documents, conventionally dated to 712* CE. *The oldest surviving manuscript is a scroll copied in 1371*

Furthermore, more than 150 *kanji* known as *kokuji* or 'domestic characters' were created in Japan and are not used in China.
See also JAPANESE WRITING.
Reading Nelson 1962; Yoshino 1988.

Kannada script One of the major scripts of south India, Kannada is a descendant of the KADAMBA SCRIPT and Old Kanarese script. The latter was used from about the thirteenth century CE for both Kannada and Telugu, but the introduction of printing in the early decades of the nineteenth century has accentuated some minor distinctions, giving rise to two systems. Yet the two remain very similar, the differences being limited to some variant letter forms such as the letter for *ka* which is ಕ in Kannada and క in Telugu.

The script is a syllabic alphabet consisting of independent V graphemes and C graphemes with inherent *a* (table 4). In post-consonant position other Vs are expressed by diacritics added to the basic C graphs. C clusters are expressed by conjunct letters mainly formed by subscripts. The first C graph in a cluster which

Symbol	Value	Symbol	Value	Symbol	Value	Symbol	Value	Symbol	Value
ಅ	a	ಎ	e	ಙ	ṅa	ಣ ಣ	ṇa	ಮ ಮ	ma
ಆ	ā	ಏ ಏ	ē	ಚ	tša	ತ	ta	ಯ ಯ	ya
ಇ	i	ಐ	ai	ಛ	tšha	ಥ ಥ	tha	ವ ವ	va
ಈ ಈ	ī	ಒ ಒ	o	ಜ	dža	ದ ದ	da	ರ ರ	ra
ಉ	u	ಓ ಓ	ō	ಝ	džha	ಧ ಧ	dha	ಲ ಲ	la
ಊ	ū	ಔ	au	ಞ	ńa	ನ	na	ಸ ಸ	sa
ಋ	ṛ	ಕ ಕ	ka	ಟ	ṭa	ಪ ಪ	pa	ಶ ಶ	śa
ೠ	ṝ	ಖ	kha	ಠ	ṭha	ಫ ಫ	pha	ಷ ಷ	ša
ಌ	ḷ	ಗ ಗ	ga	ಡ	ḍa	ಬ ಬ	ba	ಹ ಹ	ha
ೡ	ḹ	ಘ	gha	ಢ	ḍha	ಭ ಭ	bha	ೞ ೞ	t'a

Vowel indication

ಕಾ kā ಕಿ ki ಕೀ kī ಕು ku ಕೂ kū

Table 4 The Kannada syllabic alphabet

thus loses its inherent V is written on the ordinal line and the succeeding ones are subscribed in truncated form or transformed in some other way. The absence of the inherent V is also indicated by the V muting sign (*virāma*) ್ placed above the C graph. The Kannada *anusvāra* or *bidu*, used instead of a nasal letter, has the characteristic form of a circle placed on the ordinal line between the C letters rather than a dot attached to the preceding letter. Kannada letters are characterized by rounded forms typical of all southern Indian scripts.
See also INDIAN WRITING SYSTEMS.
Reading Rao 1966.

Kashmiri script A variant of Nāgarī, the Kashmiri script is a member of the northern Indian group of Brāhmī-derived scripts which can be traced back to the Śāradā script of the early ninth century CE. It is still in use in Jammu and Kashmir and adjacent states in India and Pakistan, although Kashmiri is also written in the Urdu variety of Perso-Arabic. Usage of the two scripts is largely distributed along religious lines, the former generally being used by Hindus, the latter by Moslems. Like all Brāhmī descendants the Kashmiri script is a syllabic alphabet

with independent V letters and diacritic satellites grouped around the C letters to indicate Vs other than the inherent *a* (table 5).
See also BRĀHMĪ WRITING; INDIAN WRITING SYSTEMS.

Symbol	Value	Symbol	Value	Symbol	Value
अ	a	ग	ga	ध	dha
आ	ā	घ	gha	न	na
इ	i	ङ	ṅa	प	pa
ई	ī	च	tša	फ	pha,fa
उ	u	छ	tšha	ब	ba
ऊ	ū	ज	dža,za	भ	bha
ऋ	r̥	झ	džha	म	ma
ॠ	r̥̄	ञ	ña	य	ya
ऌ	l̥	ट	ṭa	र	ra
ॡ	l̥̄	ठ	ṭha	ल	la
ए	e	ड	ḍa	व	va
ऐ	ai	ढ	ḍha	स	sa
ओ	o	ण	ṇa	श	śa
औ	au	त	ta	ष	ša
क	ka	थ	tha	ह	ha
ख	kha	द	da		

Vowel indication

का kā, कि kī, कु ku, के ke, कं kã, क् k

Table 5 The Kashmiri syllabic alphabet

katakana [Japanese カタカナ] One of the two Japanese syllabaries. Etymologically *kata* means 'partial, fragmentary' and *kana* means 'non-regular writing'. This designation refers to the form of *kana* graphemes which were drawn from parts of Chinese characters, mostly of block letters and sometimes of semi-cursive letter forms. *Katakana* came into being in the ninth century CE as a supplementary writing system, with forerunners appearing in texts from the middle of the eighth century (figure 3, table 6). The *katakana* symbols derive from abbreviated Chinese characters used as phonograms by Buddhist monks studying Chinese texts (table 7). They were used for annotations indicating the correct pronunciation of Chinese characters.

In the initial period of writing the Japanese language, unabbreviated Chinese characters were also used as phonograms, but since they were not graphically

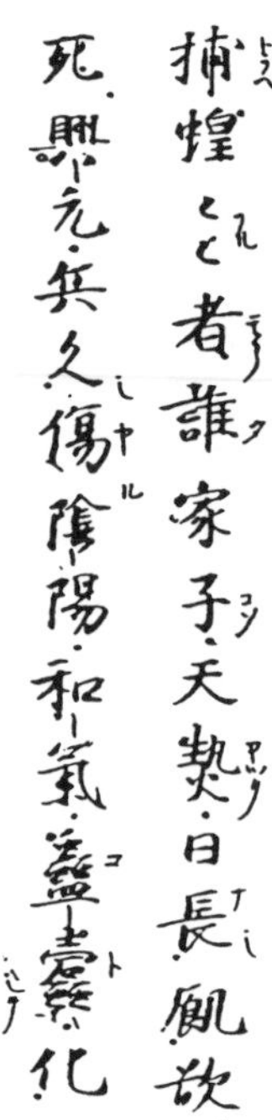

Figure 3 Chinese characters annotated with reading aids of which katakana *evolved: from the* Hakushichō *anthology of poems (824 CE)*

ア	カ				ハ		ヤ	ラ
イ					ヒ	ミ		リ
	ク			ヌ	フ	ム		ル
エ						メ		レ
オ		ソ	ト	ノ			ヨ	ロ

Table 6 Katakana *already used before 1000 CE*

distinct from standard Chinese characters, this kind of writing was extremely cumbersome. Owing to their truncated form, *katakana* were immediately recognizable as phonograms. The system developed gradually. In the beginning many different *katakana* were in use for any one syllable, but by the tenth century the system had been greatly streamlined, and by the fourteenth century a near one-to-one correspondence between *katakana* and Japanese syllables had been achieved.

From Buddhist texts the use of *katakana* spread to Japanese texts in which lexical morphemes were represented by Chinese characters and grammatical morphemes by *kana*, a style which came to be known as *kanamajiri* writing. In this function *katakana* were used until the beginning of the twentieth century (figure 5).

Nowadays HIRAGANA, the other syllabary, is used in combination with Chinese

a	阿	ア	i	伊	イ	u	宇	ウ	e	江	エ	o	於	オ
ka	加	カ	ki	幾	キ	ku	久	ク	ke	介	ケ	ko	己	コ
sa	散	サ	si	之	シ	su	須	ス	se	世	セ	so	曽	ソ
ta	多	タ	ti	千	チ	tu	川	ツ	te	天	テ	to	止	ト
na	奈	ナ	ni	二	ニ	nu	奴	ヌ	ne	祢	ネ	no	乃	ノ
ha	八	ハ	hi	比	ヒ	hu	不	フ	he	部	ヘ	ho	保	ホ
ma	万	マ	mi	三	ミ	mu	牟	ム	me	女	メ	mo	毛	モ
ya	也	ヤ				yu	由	ユ				yo	輿	ヨ
ra	良	ラ	ri	利	リ	ru	流	ル	re	礼	レ	ro	呂	ロ
wa	和	ワ	wi	井	ヰ*				we	恵	ヱ*	wo	乎	ヲ
												n	无	ン

Table 7 Katakana *and the Chinese characters of which they are derived, arranged in the traditional order of the 50-sounds table: the Roman transliteration follows the official* kunrei *system (*no longer in use)*

アリストテレス a-ri-su-to-te-re-su Aristotle	シェクスピア si-e-ku-su-pi-a Shakespeare
ウェストミンスター u-e-su-to-mi-n-su-ta-a Westminster	ヨーロッパ yo-o-ro-p-pa Europe

コンピュータ ko-n-pi-yu-u-ta computer	メロドラム me-ro-do-ra-mu melodrama	ロンドン ro-n-do-n London

Figure 4 Foreign names and loan words in katakana *spelling and back transliteration*

characters, while *katakana* is chiefly limited to writing non-Chinese loan words, onomatopoeic words and foreign place names, and for emphasis. Usage has always been characterized by considerable variation, with many alternative spellings. In 1954, guidelines were published for the use of *katakana* to represent Western loan words and non-Chinese foreign place names (figure 4), and in 1959 the Japanese Ministry of Education published a guide entitled *Chimei no yobikata to kakikata* (*The Pronunciation and Spelling of Place Names*) which has helped to reduce orthographic variation.
See also JAPANESE WRITING; KANA.
Reading Seeley 1991; Kabashima 1979.

十三日暁天ノ高潮ニ乗ジテ郵船ハ滞ルコトナク横濱港ヘ着セリ抑モ此港ハ北米洲ヨリ太平洋ヲ踰エテ支那日本呂宋ノ地方ヘ往來スル船舶ノ寄港スル処ナレバ実ニ要衝ノ地ナリ其位置ハ日本帝国第二ノ首府ナル江戸ヲ距ルコト遠カラズ其海湾ニ臨ンデ新タニ設ケタル開市場ナリ江戸府ハ昔時曾テ将軍ノ居城ニシテ万機ノ首府ナレバ神孫帝子ノ居地京都ト繁盛ヲ頡頏スル廣大ノ一都府ナリ。

Figure 5 A paragraph from a Japanese translation of Jules Verne's Around the World in Eighty Days, *published in 1870. The writing style combines* kanji *for lexical morphemes with* katakana *for grammatical morphemes*

Kawi script The word *kawi* means 'poet' in Sanskrit. It is the name of the literary language of pre-Islamic Java. The Kawi script, a syllabic alphabet of the

Value	Nāgarī	Kawi forms
k	क	
g	ग	
ng	ङ	
ch	च	
j	ज	
ng	ञ	
ṭ	ट	
ḍ	ड	
t	त	
d	द	
n	न	
p	प	
b	ब	
m	म	
y	य	
r	र	
l	ल	
v	व	
ṣ	श	
h	ह	

Table 8 Variant Kawi letter forms and the corresponding Nāgarī letters

Indian type, is a descendant of the Pallava script, a member of the southern Indian group of Brāhmī-derived scripts, although its exact genealogy is unknown (table 8). The oldest inscription, on a stele near Salatiga, central Java, dates from 750 CE, marking the beginning of what is conventionally classified as the period of the early Kawi script (*c*.750–925 CE) as opposed to the later Kawi script (*c*.925–1250).

Most Kawi inscriptions are from eastern Java, but the script is also attested in Bali and southern Sumatra. After 1250 its several varieties are usually referred to as Javanese script. The development from Old Kawi to Javanese concerns graphic style more than structural make-up. The development of Kawi is well documented in a substantial corpus of inscriptions which, however, are all engraved in stone or metal, the only writing materials that do not perish quickly in the humid climate of Indonesia (figure 6).

See also JAVANESE WRITING.

Reading Casparis 1975; Cohen Stuart.

Kazakh writing A member of the western branch of Turkic languages, Kazakh, (also Kazak, Kaisak, Qazaq) is spoken in the Republic of Kazakhstan, in China

Transcription

1. cca // jagatāṃ śivam ·astu sadā godvijarājñāṃ tathā śivaratānāṃ
2. śrutibhaktidānadharmmā bhavantu nārātirogerṣyāḥ // o //
3. // tuṅgang dawĕt - laṅka sĕrĕḥ wulakan - niwalā walaing lo-
4. dwāng wanwanira - ng dhīmān kumbhayoni ṅarannira // o //

Figure 6 Sanskrit and Old Javanese stone inscription from Pereng, dated 863 CE*: the script is an early form of the Kawi script (transcription De Casparis 1975: by permission of E. J. Brill, Leiden)*

and in Mongolia. It has been used in writing since the mid-nineteenth century in Arabic letters. In the USSR a shift to a Latin-based orthography was made in 1929 (table 9), which, however, was replaced by Cyrillic in 1940 (table 10). In China, the Arabic alphabet continues to be used (table 11, figure 7), although an attempt was made in the 1970s to introduce the Latin alphabet.

A	a	*A*	*a*	R	r	*R*	*r*
B	b	*B*	*b*	S	s	*S*	*s*
C	c	*C*	*c*	T	t	*T*	*t*
D	d	*D*	*d*	U	u	*U*	*u*
E	e	*E*	*e*	V	v	*V*	*v*
F	f	*F*	*f*	W	w	*W*	*w*
G	g	*G*	*g*	X	x	*X*	*x*
H	h	*H*	*h*	Y	y	*Y*	*y*
I	i	*I*	*i*	Z	z	*Z*	*z*
J	j	*J*	*j*	Ol	ol	*Ol*	*ol*
K	k	*K*	*k*	Ḩ	ḩ	*Ḩ*	*ḩ*
L	l	*L*	*l*	Ķ	ķ	*Ķ*	*ķ*
M	m	*M*	*m*	Ə	ə	*Ə*	*ə*
N	n	*N*	*n*	Ɵ	ɵ	*Ɵ*	*ɵ*
O	o	*O*	*o*	Ü	ü	*Ü*	*ü*
P	p	*P*	*p*	Ê	ê	*Ê*	*ê*
Q	q	*Q*	*q*				

Table 9 The Roman alphabet for Kazakh

А	а	Аа	Р	р	Рр
Б	б	Бб	С	с	Сс
В	в	Вв	Т	т	Тт
Г	г	Гг	У	у	Уу
Д	д	Дд	Ф	ф	Фф
Е	е	Ее	Х	х	Хх
Ё	ё	Ёё	Ц	ц	Цц
Ж	ж	Жж	Ч	ч	Чч
З	з	Зз	Ш	ш	Шш
И	и	Ии	Щ	щ	Щщ
Й	й	Йй		ъ	ъ
К	к	Кк	Ы	ы	ы
Л	л	Лл		ь	ь
М	м	Мм	Э	э	Ээ
Н	н	Нн	Ю	ю	Юю
О	о	Оо	Я	я	Яя
П	п	Пп			

Table 10 The Cyrillic alphabet for Kazakh

ketav meruba' (*kĕtāb mĕrubbā'*) The Hebrew name of the Hebrew square script which developed from the late Aramaic script to become the principal medium of Jewish religious and secular literature.
See also HEBREW WRITING.

Kharoṣṭhī script The beginning of Indian writing proper is usually associated with the AŚOKA EDICTS issued in the mid third century BCE. These were redacted in two scripts, Brāhmī, the parent script of all modern Indian scripts, and Kharoṣṭhī, which remained without descendants. The Kharoṣṭhī script, which is also known as 'Indo-Bactric', was widely used in north-west India and Central Asia from the time of Aśoka until the fourth century CE (figure 8). Although nothing is known about its origin, it is generally thought to be derived from the Aramaic script. Its direction from right to left as well as similarities with Aramaic letter forms support this assumption, and since at the time Aramaic was the most important ad-ministrative language from Syria to Afghanistan, it seems likely that the northern Indian empire borrowed the Aramaic script (table 12).

If the assumption of Aramaic origin is correct, the typological differences between the two systems are yet to be explained. Aramaic, like all Semitic scripts, is a consonant script, while Kharoṣṭhī is a syllabic alphabet. The basic C letters have an inherent V *a* and are modified with diacritic satellites for other Vs (table

Independent	Initial	Medial	Final	Value	Independent	Initial	Medial	Final	Value
ا	ا	–	ـا	a	و	و	–	ـو	o
اٴ	اٴ	–	–	æ	ٴو	ٴو	–	–	ø
ب	بـ	ـبـ	ـب	b	پ	پـ	ـپـ	ـپ	p‘
ۋ	ۋ	–	ـۋ	v	ر	ر	–	ـر	r
گ	گـ	ـگـ	ـگ	g	س	سـ	ـسـ	ـس	s
ع	عـ	ـعـ	ـع	ʁ	ت	تـ	ـتـ	ـت	t‘
د	د	–	ـد	d	ۋ	ۋ	–	ـۋ	w, uw yw
ە	ە	–	ـە	e	ۇ	ۇ	–	ـۇ	u
ج	جـ	ـجـ	ـج	ʤ	ٴۇ	ٴۇ	–	–	y
ز	ز	–	ـز	z	ف	فـ	ـفـ	ـف	f
ي	يـ	ـيـ	ـي	j.əj.ɨj	ح	حـ	ـحـ	ـح	χ
ك	كـ	ـكـ	ـك	k‘	ھ	ھـ	ـھـ	–	h
ق	قـ	ـقـ	ـق	q‘	چ	چـ	ـچـ	ـچ	tʃ
ل	لـ	ـلـ	ـل	l	ش	شـ	ـشـ	ـش	ʃ
م	مـ	ـمـ	ـم	m	ى	ىـ	ـىـ	ـى	ə
ن	نـ	ـنـ	ـن	n	ٴى	ٴىـ	ـٴىـ	ـٴى	ɨ
ڭ	ڭـ	ـڭـ	ـڭ	ŋ					

Table 11 The Arabic alphabet for Kazakh

ٴۇرىمجى اۋدانى ساياپىل اۋىلىنىڭ شۋلاقتەرەك قىستاعى بوعدا-شىڭىنىڭ باتىس
باۋرايىندا ورنالاسقان مال شارۋاشىلىعىن نەگىزگى كاسىپ ەتەتىن قىستاق.

Translation:

Located west of Mt Bogeda, the village of Shulaketienielieke of the town of Sayapule in Wu-lu-mu-qi (Urumchi) County has a population who mainly live on livestock raising.

Figure 7 Sample sentence of Kazakh in Arabic script

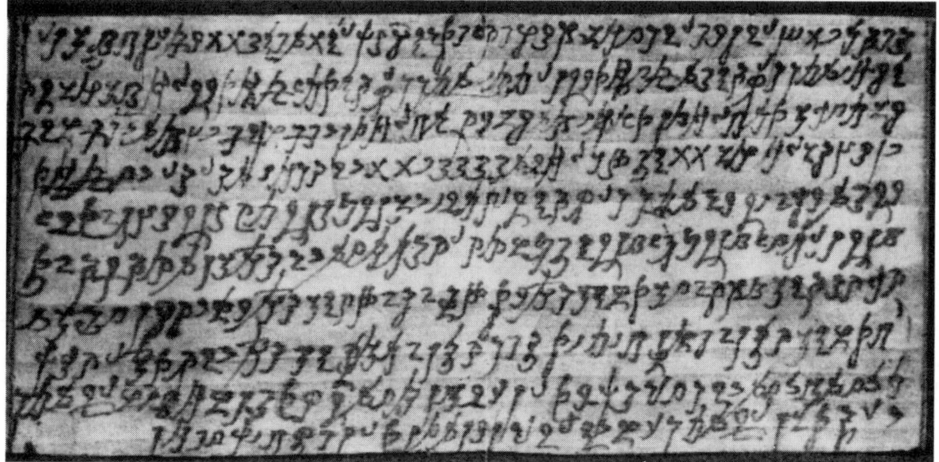

Figure 8 Kharoṣṭhī inscription on wood, third century CE *(National Museum, New Delhi)*

Aramaic	Kharosthī	Aramaic	Kharosthī
ʔ	a	l	la
b	ba	m	ma
g	ga	n	na
d	dha	s	sa
h	ha	p	pa
w	va	ṣ	ca
z	ja	q	kha
ḥ	śa	r	ra
y	ya	š	ṣa
k	ka	t	ta

Table 12 Kharoṣṭhī letters and their Aramaic models
Source: *adapted from Jensen 1969*

13). It has been hypothesized that this kind of V indication may have originated from the Semitic practice of optional V indication by means of MATRES LECTIONIS, but so far no epigraphic evidence confirming this hypothesis has been found.
See also BRĀHMĪ WRITING; INDIAN WRITING SYSTEMS.
Reading Jensen 1969.

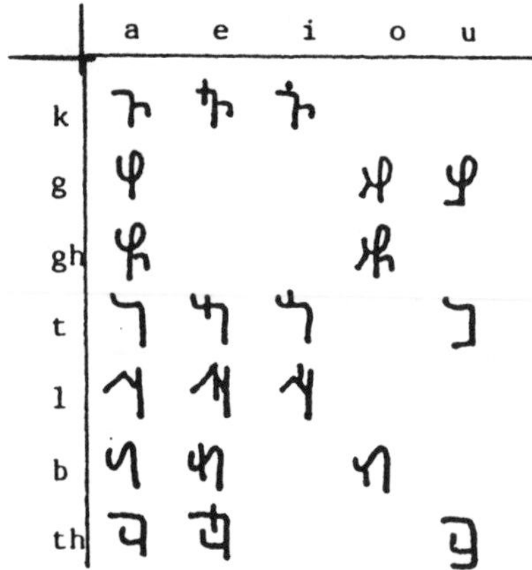

Table 13 Vowel indication in the Kharoṣṭhī script

Khmer writing Khmer, the national language of Cambodia, has a literary tradition that goes back to the seventh century CE. Its script is a syllabic alphabet derived from the BRĀHMĪ WRITING through the southern Indian Pallava script which is first attested in Old Khmer inscriptions dating from 611 CE. Over the centuries a distinct system evolved with some properties not found in other syllabic alphabets of the Indian type. The most conspicuous characteristic of the Khmer system is that it makes use of two series of C graphemes (table 14). Originally these corresponded to the series of graphemes for voiced and unvoiced phonemes in Indian scripts, but in the Khmer script they serve a different function. Those of the first series have an inherent /a/ and those of the second series an inherent /o/. This twin representation of Cs in two parallel series of equivalent letters has consequences for the representation of Vs. V indication follows

1st series + a	2nd series + o	value	1st series + a	2nd series + o	value
ក	គ	k	ប៉	ព	p
ខ	ឃ	kh	ផ	ភ	ph
ង៉	ង	ŋ	ម៉	ម	m
ច	ជ	c	យ៉	យ	y
ឆ	ឈ	ch	រ៉	រ	r
ញ៉	ញ	ñ	ឡ	ល	l
ដ	ឌ	d	វ៉	វ	w
ត	ទ	t	ស	ស៊	s
ថ	ធ	th	ហ	ហ៊	h
ឋ	ឍ	th	អ	អ៊	q
ណ	ន	n	ហ្គ	ហ្គ៊	g
ប	ប៊	b	ហ្វ	ហ្វ៊	f
			ហ្ស	ហ្ស៊	ž

Table 14 Khmer consonant graphemes: the last three items occur only in loan words

the general Indian pattern of diacritic satellites grouped around the basic C graph (table 15). However, the value of the V diacritic is determined by the series of the C graph to which it is added. Independent V graphemes are pronounced with initial glottal stop, transcribed as *q* in table 16. C clusters are written with subscript ligatures. In most cases the subscript graphs are smaller versions of the standard graphs, but some subscripts no longer bear any similarity with their full-sized counterparts (table 17).

	□	□ា	□ិ	□ី	□ឹ	□ឺ	□ុ	□ូ	□ួ	□ើ
First series	a	ā	e	ey	e	eɨ	o	ou	ue	ae
Second series	o	ie	ɨ	ii	ɨ	ɨɨ	u	uu	ue	ei

	□ឿ	□ៀ	□េ	□ែ	□ៃ	□ោ	□ៅ	□ំ	□ះ
First series	ɨe	ie	ei	ae	ay	ao	aw	om	ah
Second series	ɨe	ie	ee	ē	iy	oo	ɨw	um	eh

Table 15 Khmer vowel diacritics

Independent vowel graphemes

	First series	Second series
ឥ	qe	qɨ
ឦ	qey	
ឧ	qo	qu
ឪ	qew	
ឩ	qou	qū
ឯ	qae	
ឰ	qay	
ឱ	qao	
ឳ	qaw	

Consonant-vowel combinations

ឫ	rɨ
ឬ	rɨɨ
ឭ	lɨ
ឮ	lɨɨ

Table 16 Khmer vowel graphemes and special consonant-vowel combinations

Table 17 Khmer consonant graphs with corresponding subscript forms

Modern Khmer orthography is quite systematic but many spellings are etymological. In modern Khmer there are no words with final [-r], yet many words continue to be spelt with final រ. Some etymological spellings are marked with a special diacritic placed above a letter to indicate that it is not to be pronounced. Predictable phonetic distinctions are often ignored. For example, the grapheme ត /t/ is pronounced [d] when a nasal follows at the end of the same syllable.

Khmer is written horizontally from left to right without word spacing; spacing occurs at junctures roughly equivalent to pause groups in speech.

Reading Huffman 1970.

Kirghiz writing *See* KYRGHIZ WRITING

Kiswahili writing The most important language of East Africa, which enjoys official status in Tanzania and Kenya and is also widely spoken in Uganda, Rwanda, Burundi and Zaïre, Kiswahili has a literary tradition which extends back to the fourteenth century. This is attested by Arabic travellers of the time who visited the island of Kilwa where they met native poets who wrote Kiswahili poems and prose using the Arabic script. The oldest surviving manuscripts of poetry and religious works are dated from the early 1700s (figure 9). Around the turn of the nineteenth century the Arabic alphabet was gradually replaced by Roman letters which European colonialists and missionaries found more convenient. Following a decision reached at an international conference held in 1928 in Mombasa, standard Kiswahili is based on the Unguja dialect of Zanzibar which is generally accepted and used in Tanzania, but less so in Kenya where the dialects of Lamu and Mombasa had been used already in pre-colonial times for literary purposes.

In the early phase of writing Kiswahili with the Roman alphabet, some controversies arose about usage. One of the issues discussed was word division, because it was suggested by some that noun class prefixes and word stems should be written separately, while others argued that prefixes and concord morphemes should be written attached to the lexical morphemes. Some graphemic alternatives were also proposed. For instance, it was suggested that a simple <c> be used instead of the digraph <ch> for the palatal affricate [tʃ], and <ŋ> instead of <ng'> for the velar nasal. Eventually those spellings prevailed which had

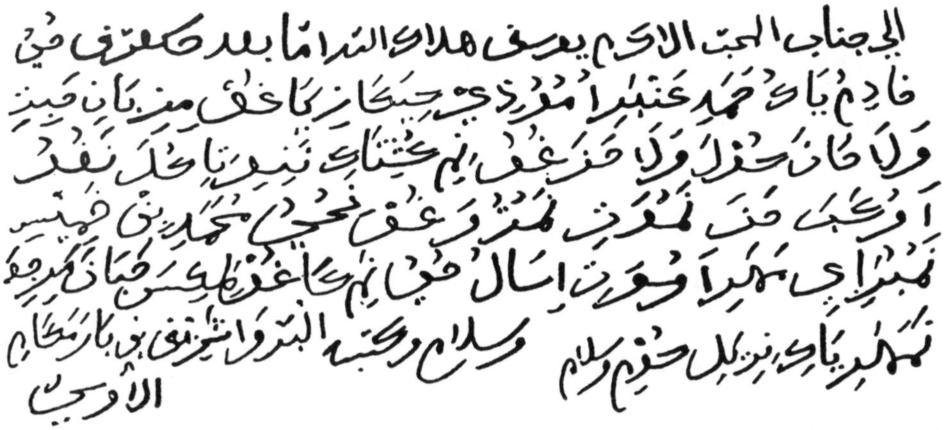

Transcription

Ila jenab ilmuhebb ilkram Jusuf. Hadak Allahu.
Ama baadu hukuarrifu huyu hadimu yako Hamadi Amabari umeozea kiyakazi kwangu Mizibani. Hapiti wala hana kula wala hana nguo. Nimekushitaki, na niwate kula na nguo; au kwamba hana. Na mtu wangu ni huyu Muhammadi bin Khamisi. Namburai mahari ao wate isaalo huyu. Nami kwangu nimekwisha, hapana maregeo. Na mahari yake ni reale kumi. Wasalaam. Wa katabahu ilbarua Sharifu bin bwana Makami ilAwi.

Translation

To his beloved and honourable Highness Joseph. God be your guide. And thus I report to you: this young servant Hamadi Ambari has wedded a girl here with me in Misbane. He does not come, and she has no food or drink. And now I plead with you that he may let me have food and clothes, otherwise she has nothing. And my man is Muhammed, son of Khamisi. And I don't want any of the dowry, or he should cease to do what he did. And I for my part am finished, there is no turning back. And the dowry is ten pounds. And greetings. And this letter was written by Sharifu, son of Makami, the Awi.

Figure 9 A nineteenth-century Kiswahili letter in Arabic script with Roman transcription
Source: *Büttner 1892, plate V*

first gained currency, i.e. <ch> and <ng'>. The standard orthography aims at a one-to-one correspondence between graphemes and phonemes, but some digraphs are necessary (table 18).
Reading Williamson 1947; Knappert 1979; Biersteker and Plane 1989.

<b>	[b']	<ch>	[tʃ]
<d>	[d']	<ng'>	[ŋ]
<g>	[g']	<sh>	[ʃ]
<h>	[h/x]	<dh>	[ð]
<j>	[ɟ']	<gh>	[ɣ]
<k>	[k]	<th>	[θ]
<l>	[r]	<nj>	[ndʒ]
<m>	[m̩]	<ny>	[nj]
<n>	[n]		
<p>	[p]		
<r>	[r]		
<s>	[s]		
<t>	[t]	<a>	[a]
<v>	[v]	<e>	[ɛ]
<w>	[w]	<i>	[i]
<y>	[j]	<o>	[ɔ]
<z>	[z]	<u>	[u]

Table 18 Kiswahili grapheme–phoneme correspondences

kokuji A Japanese term which literally means 'domestic character'. It refers to Chinese characters produced in Japan.
See also JAPANESE WRITING; KANJI.

Konkani writing Konkani belongs to the western group of Indo-Aryan languages and is spoken by some 2 million people centred in Goa and further to the south along the Karnataka coast. During the period of Portuguese colonial rule its status was elevated to that of a written language and it thus became the only Indian language for which a Roman orthography was devised and used. But although it was reduced to writing as long ago as the sixteenth century, it failed to develop a uniform standard. The reasons for this must be sought in the fact that Konkani is not used as a written language in all areas where it is spoken, and because it is surrounded by more prestigious literary languages, notably Marāṭhī and Kannada which many Konkani speakers prefer for purposes of written communication. Konkani is also written in the KANNADA SCRIPT.

Unlike its Portuguese model (and the common Roman transliteration systems for Indian languages), Konkani orthography avoids diacritics. Yet certain features of the spelling system, such as the grapheme <x> for the hushed sibilant /ʃ/, testify to the Portuguese heritage. Another characteristic is the indication of a final /-m/ by <mm>, a distinction which is necessary because final nasal Vs are expressed by the V letter plus <m>.
Reading Pereira 1973.

Korean writing

Historical development

The Koreans first learned the art of writing from China. From the first to the seventh centuries CE the Chinese written language was the official medium of written communication on the Korean peninsula. Once the Koreans started to use Chinese characters, called *hanja* in Korean, for writing their own language, they employed two adaptation strategies, one based on pronunciation, one on meaning. In the first, a *hanja* was used to represent a syllable irrespective of its meaning in Chinese. For example, Chinese 古 *kŭ* 'old' was used to write the Korean syllable *ko*. In the second, a *hanja* was used to represent a Korean word which corresponded in meaning to the Chinese word/morpheme written with it. For example, Chinese 水 *shŭi* 'water' was given the reading *mul*, the Korean word for 'water'.

The next step was to write *hanja* in Korean word order, a practice which led to the development of an extremely contrived written language called IDO. *Hanja* were used in both of the above functions side by side, that is semantically adapted characters for lexical stems and phonetically adapted characters for suffixes and all other grammatical morphemes. This made for difficult reading since the functional difference was not visible. One way of facilitating reading was to graphically distinguish the *hanja* used as phonograms. Accordingly, in the thirteenth century some of the grammatical morpheme characters were simplified and thus became graphically recognizable. These characters were first used as an auxiliary device for indicating readings in Classical Chinese texts. They were derived from standard Chinese characters by graphic simplification and came to be known as *kugyol* (figure 10). In spite of this simplification, writing Korean with Chinese characters remained a laborious exercise, resulting in a highly artificial written language which was far removed from any spoken variety of Korean and at the same time never really rivalled Classical Chinese in prestige.

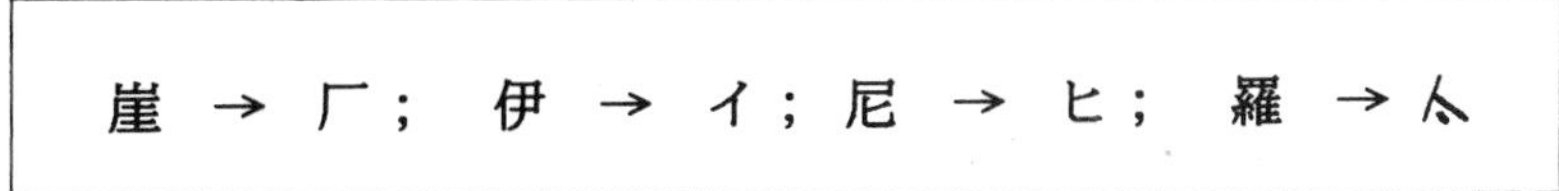

Figure 10 Korean kugyol, *simplified Chinese characters*

When large-scale printing with movable type was introduced in Korea early in the fifteenth century, the sense of dissatisfaction with the writing system became more acute and eventually led to the invention of what many consider the most scientific and elegant writing system in general use in any country, that known today as *han'gŭl* 'Korean letters'. *Han'gŭl* was developed in the early 1440s by a team of scholars under the leadership of King Sejong. It was promulgated in a royal rescript entitled *Hun min jong um* (訓民正音) 'The correct sounds for instructing the people', issued in 1446 out of 'pity with the common people' who were unable to express themselves properly in *ido*, and not without resistance on the part of the literati who were attached to the traditional system (figure 11). *Han'gŭl* is a simple phonetic script perfectly suitable for writing Korean (table 19).

訓民正音
國之語音異乎中國與文字
不相流通故愚民有所欲言
而終不得伸其情者多矣予
爲此憫然新制二十八字欲
使人人易習便於日用矣
ㄱ。牙音。如君字初發聲
並書。如虯字初發聲
ㅋ。牙音。如快字初發聲
ㆁ。牙音。如業字初發聲
ㄷ。舌音。如斗字初發聲
並書。如覃字初發聲
ㅌ。舌音。如呑字初發聲
ㄴ。舌音。如那字初發聲

Figure 11 Hun min jong um, *'the correct sounds for instructing the people', the royal rescript explaining the new Korean script*

Consonants	ㄱ	ㅋ	ㆁ	ㄷ	ㅌ	ㄴ	ㄹ	ㅂ ㅍ
	k'g	k	ŋ	t',d	t	n	r,l	p',b p
	ㅁ	ㅈ	ㅊ	ㅅ	ㅿ	ㆆ	ㅎ	ㅇ
	m	dʒ	tʃ	s, HS	z, ʒ	ʔ	h	
Vowels	ㆍ	ㅡ	ㅣ	ㅗ	ㅏ	ㅜ	ㅓ	ㅛ
	ɔ	ɯ	i	o	a	u	ə	jo
	ㅑ	ㅠ	ㅕ					
	ja	ju	jə					

Table 19 The original han'gŭl *letters*

Yet the educated classes looked on it with disdain and continued to use Chinese for scholarly and official writing. Although it came in time to be used for more popular literary purposes, *han'gŭl* did not supplant Classical Chinese until the twentieth century. It was only when Korea became independent in 1945 that *han'gŭl* was universally accepted as Korea's national script, after having been proscribed by the Japanese colonial authorities.

The han'gŭl system

The 한글 *han'gŭl* or *han-geul* is a phonemic notation which, like Chinese characters, treats the syllable as the unit of coding, but which is based on a phonological analysis which recognizes the segment and even the subsegmental distinctive

Simple vowel letters:

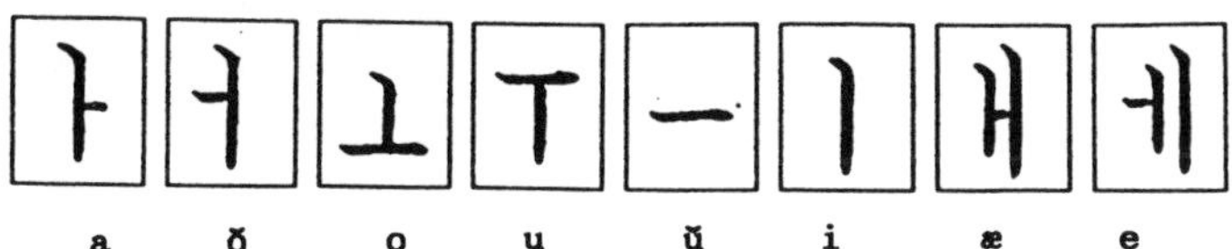

a ŏ o u ŭ i æ e

Diphthongs:

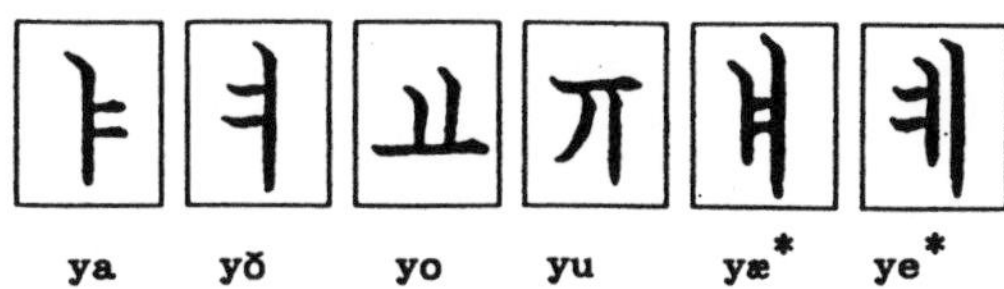

ya yŏ yo yu yæ* ye*

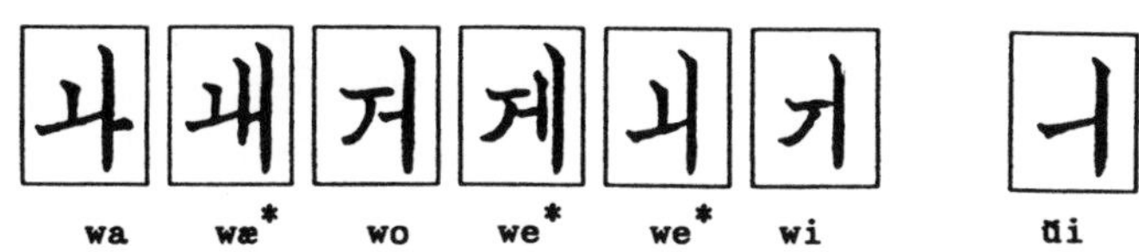

wa wæ* wo we* we* wi ŭi

Consonant letters:

Plain

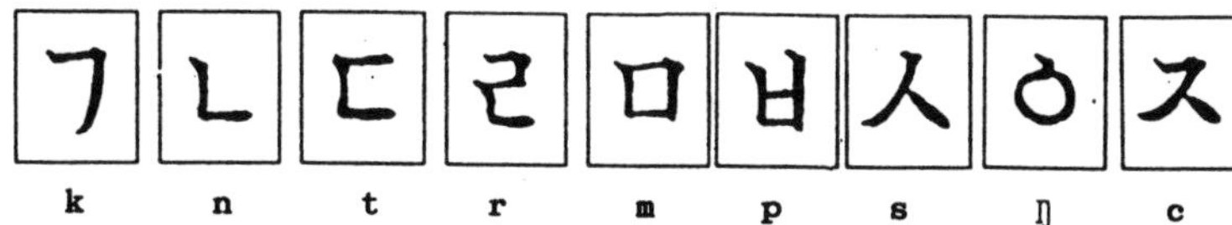

k n t r m p s ŋ c

Aspirated

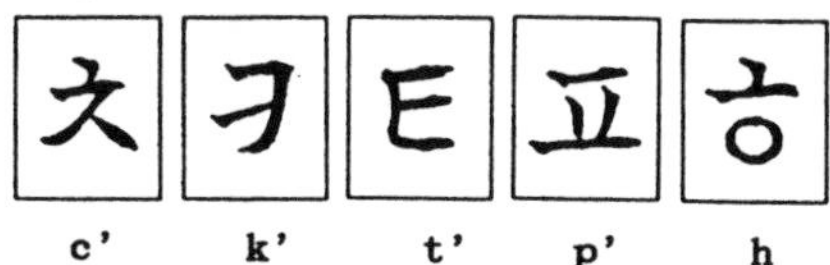

c' k' t' p' h

Glottalized

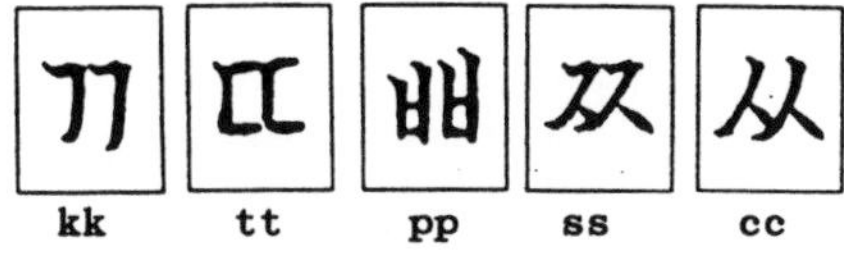

kk tt pp ss cc

*These distinctions are lost in speech.

Table 20 The basic han'gŭl *letters*

		ㅏ	ㅑ	ㅓ	ㅕ	ㅗ	ㅛ	ㅜ	ㅠ	ㅡ	ㅣ
		a	ya	eo	yeo	o	yo	u	yu	eu	i
ㄱ	g(k)	가	갸	거	겨	고	교	구	규	그	기
ㄴ	n	나	냐	너	녀	노	뇨	누	뉴	느	니
ㄷ	d	다	댜	더	뎌	도	됴	두	듀	드	디
ㄹ	r(l)	라	랴	러	려	로	료	루	류	르	리
ㅁ	m	마	먀	머	며	모	묘	무	뮤	므	미
ㅂ	b	바	뱌	버	벼	보	뵤	부	뷰	브	비
ㅅ	s	사	샤	서	셔	소	쇼	수	슈	스	시
ㅇ	※	아	야	어	여	오	요	우	유	으	이
ㅈ	j	자	쟈	저	져	조	죠	주	쥬	즈	지
ㅊ	ch	차	챠	처	쳐	초	쵸	추	츄	츠	치
ㅋ	k	카	캬	커	켜	코	쿄	쿠	큐	크	키
ㅌ	t	타	탸	터	텨	토	툐	투	튜	트	티
ㅍ	p	파	퍄	퍼	펴	포	표	푸	퓨	프	피
ㅎ	h	하	햐	허	혀	호	효	후	휴	흐	히

Table 21 The basic combinations of vowel and consonant graphemes in the Korean alphabet

사	샤	서	셔	소	쇼	수	슈	스	시
sa	sya	seo	syeo	so	syo	su	syu	seu	si

Table 22 Syllable blocks including the grapheme for /s/

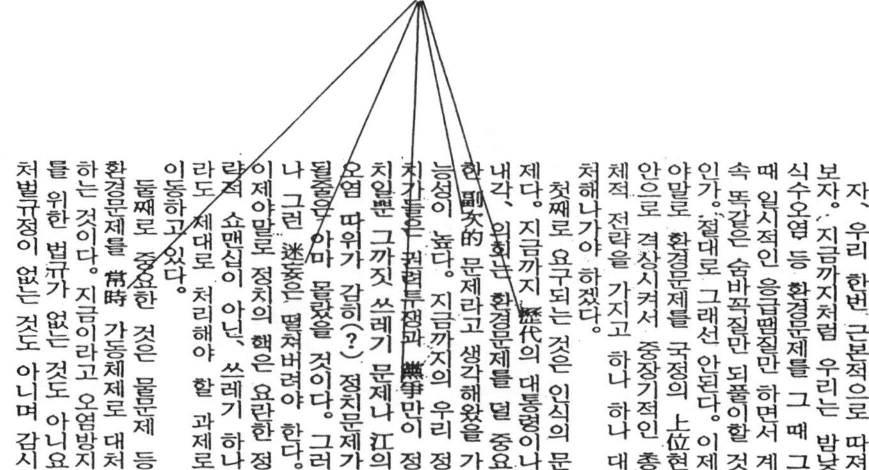

자、우리 한번 근본적으로 따져
보자。지금까지처럼 우리는 밤낮
식수오염 등 환경문제를 그 때 그
때 일시적인 응급땜질만 하면서 계
속 똑같은 숨바꼭질만 되풀이할 것
인가。절대로 그래선 안된다。이제
야말로 환경문제를 국정의 上位현
안으로 격상시켜서 중장기적인 총
체적 전략을 가지고 하나 하나 대
처해나가야 하겠다。
첫째로 요구되는 것은 인식의 문
제다。지금까지 歷代의 대통령이나
내각、의회는 환경문제를 덜 중요
한 副次的 문제라고 생각해왔을 가
능성이 높다。지금까지의 우리 정
치가들은 권력투쟁과 黨爭만이 정
치일뿐 그까짓 쓰레기 문제나 江의
오염 따위가 감히(?) 정치문제가
될줄은 아마 몰랐을 것이다。그러
나 그런 迷妄은 떨쳐버려야 한다。
이제야말로 정치의 핵은 요란한 정
략적 쇼맨십이 아닌、쓰레기 하나
라도 제대로 처리해야 할 과제로
이동하고 있다。
둘째로 중요한 것은 물문제 등
환경문제를 常時 가동체제로 대처
하는 것이다。지금이라고 오염방지
를 위한 법규가 없는 것도 아니요
처벌규정이 없는 것도 아니며 감시

Figure 12 Sample of contemporary Korean writing

feature. Instead of the basic signs being written in linear succession, as is usual in alphabetic scripts, they are stacked together to form blocks that represent syllables, each block being separated from the next by a space. These syllable blocks were designed to conform with the square frame of Chinese characters. Another extraordinary feature of *han'gŭl* is that its letters were designed to depict the places of articulation of the phonemes they represent. For example, the symbol ㄱ for /k/ pictures the tongue touching the palate.

The original system consisted of 28 basic graphemes; 24 of them are used today, ten Vs and 14 Cs (table 20). Simple Vs are indicated by vertical or horizontal straight lines with a short stroke (originally a dot) on one side or the other. For palatalized and other compound Vs another short stroke is added, the same principle of modifying the basic sign by a diacritic element being applied in all cases. C graphemes are angled lines, and their relationships are equally systematic. Aspirated Cs are indicated by a bar added to the corresponding unaspirated C form, and glottalized (tense) Cs are represented by reduplicating the simple C graph. V graphemes cannot be written alone. They are always combined with a preceding C grapheme, the grapheme ㅇ, in other contexts /ŋ/, serving as a zero marker when combined with a V grapheme to allow the expression of independent Vs (table 21). The spelling is largely phonemic. Predictable phonetic distinctions are ignored. That is, for example, what is transliterated as <k> in table 21 is phonetically [k] in initial position, but [g] in intervocalic position and unreleased [k] in final position.

Two basic principles for the formation of syllable blocks are as follows. V graphemes with their main stroke standing upright have the C grapheme at their left side, whereas V graphemes with their main stroke in horizontal position have the C grapheme on top (table 22). The arrangement of basic graphemes in syllable blocks makes it easy to combine *han'gŭl* with Chinese characters. Like Chinese characters the syllable blocks can be written with equal ease in vertical or horizontal lines.

In many Korean texts Chinese loan words are written with Chinese characters to be read in Sino-Korean (figure 12). The Democratic People's Republic of Korea has abolished the use of Chinese characters after the division of the country, while they continue to be used in South Korea. However, like their southern peers, North Koreans still learn some 3,000 Chinese characters at school.

See also ICON.

Reading Ledyard 1975; Lee 1989; Song 1970.

Kpelle syllabary Invented in the 1930s by Chief Gbili of Sanoyea, Liberia, the Kpelle syllabary consists of 88 graphemes written from left to right (table 23). Although the system is syllabic, it recognizes regular phonetic alterations by employing the same character for both members of mutational pairs. The script was apparently used by speakers of Kpelle in Liberia and Guinea during the late 1930s and early 1940s, but has never gained wide acceptance.

Reading Dalby 1967.

***kūfīc* script** [Arabic *kūfī*] An angular Arabic script initially associated with the copying of the Qur'ān. Named after the Mesopotamian city of Kufah, it is the

	i	a	u	e	ɛ	ɔ	o	-
p/b	[illegible]	[illegible]	[illegible]	[illegible]	[illegible]	[illegible]	[illegible]	
ɓ/m̀	[illegible]	[illegible]		[illegible]	[illegible]		[illegible]	
kp/gb	[illegible]	[illegible]	[illegible]	[illegible]	[illegible]	[illegible]	[illegible]	
f/v	[illegible]	[illegible]		[= fi/vi]	[illegible]	[illegible]	[illegible]	
t/d	[illegible] (also di [illegible])	[illegible]	[illegible]	[illegible]	[illegible]	[illegible] or [illegible] ([illegible])	[illegible]	
l/ǹ	[illegible]	[illegible]	[illegible]	[illegible]	[illegible]	[illegible]	[illegible]	
h(s)/j(z)	[illegible]	[illegible] or [illegible] ([illegible])	[illegible]	[illegible]	[illegible]	[illegible]	[illegible]	
y/ǹy	[illegible]	[illegible]		[illegible]	[illegible]			[illegible]
k/g	[illegible]	[illegible] (also ga [illegible])	[illegible]	[illegible]	[illegible]	[illegible]	[illegible]	
kw/gw	[illegible]			[illegible]	[illegible]			
ɣ (/ŋ̀)	[illegible]	[illegible]		[= ɣi]	[illegible]			
ɣ or w			[illegible] ([illegible] or [illegible])			[illegible]	[illegible]	
w (/ŋ̀w)	[illegible]	[illegible] / waŋ [illegible]	wuŋ [illegible]	[= wi]	[illegible]	wɔŋ [illegible]		
-		[= ɣa]		[illegible] or [illegible] ([illegible])				
NASAL SYLLABLES	**ĩ**	**ã**	**ũ**	**ẽ**	**ɛ̃**	**ɔ̃**		SYLLABIC NASAL
m	[illegible]	[illegible] or [illegible] ([illegible])	[illegible]			[illegible]		
n	[illegible]	[illegible]	[illegible]	[?] [illegible]				
ny		[illegible]		[?] [illegible]	[?] [illegible]	[illegible]		
ŋ		[illegible]						[illegible]

Table 23 The Kpelle syllabary
Source: *Dalby 1967*

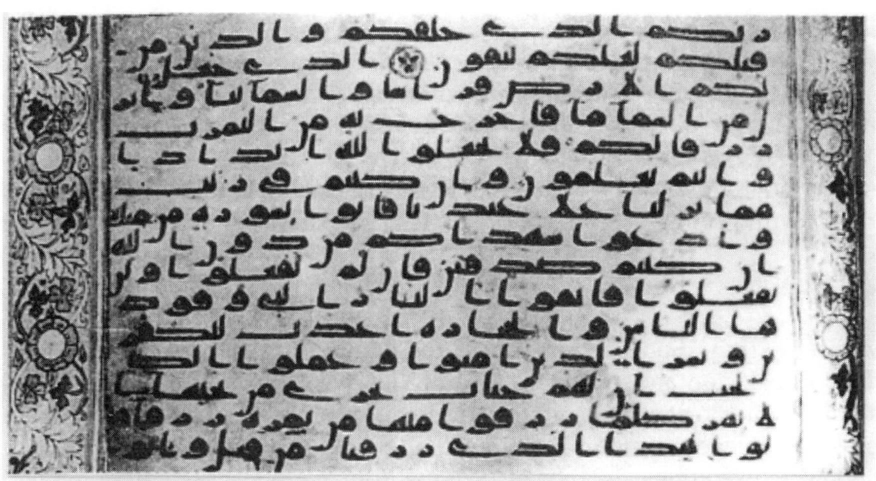

Figure 13 A page from the Qur'ān written in kūfīc script, seventh-century manuscript by Imam Ali (Raza Library, Rampur)

ا	ا		ﺎ	a
ب	ﺑ	ﺒ	ﺐ	b
پ	ﭘ	ﭙ	ﭗ	p
ن	ﻧ	ﻨ	ﻦ	n
ت	ﺗ	ﺘ	ﺖ	t
ج	ﺟ	ﺠ	ﺞ	ʤ
چ	ﭼ	ﭽ	ﭻ	tʃ
ح	ﺣ	ﺤ	ﺢ	x
ف	ﻓ	ﻔ	ﻒ	f
ق	ﻗ	ﻘ	ﻖ	q
ع	ﻋ	ﻌ	ﻊ	ʁ
ك .ک	ﮐ	ﮑ	ﻚ	k
گ	ﮔ	ﮕ	ﮓ	g
ڭ	ﯕ	ﯖ	ﯔ	ŋ
ل	ﻟ	ﻠ	ﻞ	l

م	ﻣ	ﻤ	ﻢ	m
و	و		ﻮ	o
ۉ	ۉ		ۉ	ø
ۇ	ۇ		ۇ	u
ۈ	ۈ		ۈ	y
ۋ	ۋ		ۋ	v
س	ﺳ	ﺴ	ﺲ	s
ش	ﺷ	ﺸ	ﺶ	ʃ
د	د		ﺪ	d
ر	ر		ﺮ	r
ز	ز		ﺰ	z
ە	ە		ﻪ	e
ى	ﯨ	ﯩ	ﻰ	ə
ئى	ﺋ	ﺌ	ﺌﻰ	i
ي	ﻳ	ﻴ	ﻲ	j

Table 24 The Kyrghiz alphabet

oldest Islamic script, appearing towards the end of the seventh century CE. It is characterized by heavy, bold lines suitable for monumental inscriptions (figure 13). As of the twelfth century the popularity of *kūfīc* began to decline.
See also ARABIC SCRIPTS; CALLIGRAPHY.

kugyol A set of simplified Chinese characters used as reading aids by Korean scribes for indicating pronunciations of Chinese characters in classical Chinese texts.
See also KOREAN WRITING.

Kyrghiz writing Spoken primarily in the Republic of Kyrgyzstan as well as in China, Uzbekistan and Afghanistan, Kyrghiz (also Kirghiz, Kirgiz) is a Turkic language which first achieved the status of a written language in the 1920s when it was recognized as one of the official languages of the USSR. Initially Arabic letters were used (table 24), but in 1926 the Roman alphabet was adopted which in turn was replaced by Cyrillic in 1940. In China, Kyrghiz continues to be written in the Arabic script (figure 14). A reformed spelling system was adopted there in 1983.

قىرعىز تىٔل - جازۋۇ قىزماتتىن ورعۇشتاپ وركوندوشۇن ەەرچىي، قىرعىزدىن ادابىئىي
تىٔلىن قالىپتاندىرۋۇ، جاڭى تەرمىندەردى شىتەپ چىعۇۇ سىياقتۇۇ ماسەلەلەر ۇچۇردا
قىرعىزدىن تىٔل - جازۋۇ قىزماتىنداعى نازار ووداروۇعا شاشىلىش كەرەك بولۇپ وتۇرعان
ماسەلەلەردەن بولۇپ تابىلات.

Translation:

With the booming development of research work on Kyrghiz, and with the standardization of the language and literature of the Kyrghiz nationality, the most urgent problem facing the current Kyrghiz language research is the creation of new words and terminology.

Figure 14 Sample sentence of Kyrghiz in Arabic script

L

L, l /el/ The twelfth letter of the English alphabet goes back to Semitic *lāmedh* through Greek *lambda* (Λ, λ). It arrived at its present form as a right angle facing right in Classical Latin. The small letter is a cursive variant of the capital.

Landa alphabet Bishop Diego de Landa was one of the first Spanish clergymen to go to Mexico. In the mid sixteenth century he spent several years in Yucatán where he came into contact with MAYA WRITING which he studied and professed to have deciphered. The 27 glyphs to which he assigned letter values came to be known as Landa's Maya 'alphabet' (table 1). Although Landa made an important contribution to the understanding of Maya writing in as much as he recognized that the glyphs could be read, he was misguided by his alphabetocentric assumptions. In the light of much later research it became clear that his Maya alphabet was not a phonetic transliteration as he suggested. Instead, the individual glyphs must be seen as syllabic rather than alphabetic graphemes. They apparently represent the responses Landa's Maya informants produced when asked how they wrote the letters of the Spanish alphabet as Landa pronounced them, thus corresponding to the Spanish alphabetic letter names rather than their actual sound values. In spite of this misunderstanding, the Landa alphabet was of great value for the eventual decipherment of Maya writing.
Reading Coe 1992; Knorosov 1955.

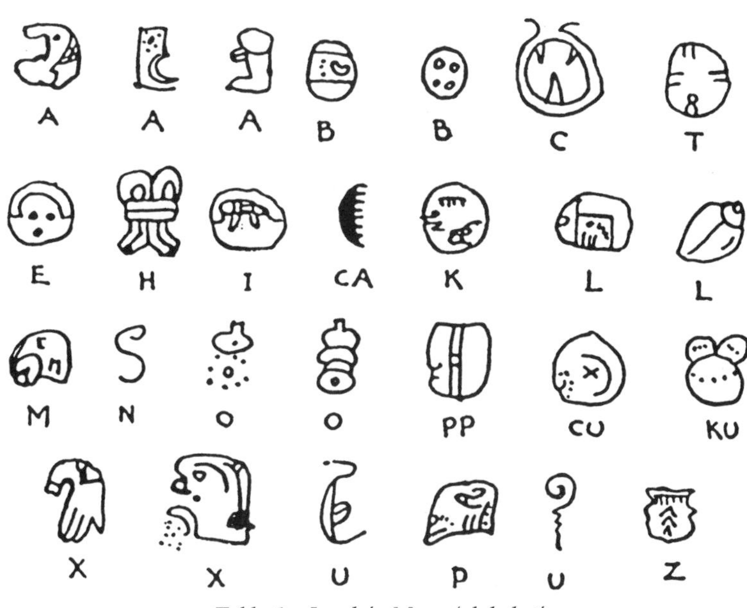

Table 1 Landa's Maya 'alphabet'

Laṇḍā script A member of the northern Indian group of scripts, the Laṇḍā script is derived from the tenth-century Śāradā (also Sharada) script. It was first used by Hindu merchants in Punjab and Sind, where it was called Baniyā̃, and is said to be the predecessor of the sixteenth-century Gurmukhī script. The earliest attested variety had only one independent V grapheme, that for *a*, which was used for all initial Vs (table 2). In 1868 the Laṇḍā script was adapted to serve as the medium of writing Sindhī. In this form it is equipped with a full set of V graphemes.
See also Indian writing systems.

Vowel letters

	Laṇḍā	Sindhī
a		
i		
u		
e		
o		
ā		

Consonant letters

	Laṇḍā	Sindhī		Laṇḍā	Sindhī		Laṇḍā	Sindhī		Laṇḍā	Sindhī
ka			ǰha			tha			ma		
kha			ñ			da			ya		
ga			ṭa			dha			ra		
gha			ṭha			na			la		
ṅa			ḍa			pa			va		
ča			ḍha			pha			śa		
čha			ṇa			ba			ṣa		
ǰa			ta			bha			ha		

Table 2 The Laṇḍā script in its old form and Sindhī adaptation

language dependency The reflection of structural peculiarities of individual languages in writing systems. All writing systems came into existence within the context of a particular language. On the most archaic stage the link with language was loose and imperfect, but as writing systems developed it became more precise and complete. As a result, writing systems bear the stamp of the language(s) for which they developed. Each writing system selects some aspects of language over others. For example, Semitic scripts emphasize Cs over Vs, a reflection of the importance of CONSONANT ROOTS in the grammar of Semitic languages. The language dependency of writing systems comes into evidence whenever a system is taken over for another language, a process which usually necessitates major adjustments. The adoption of the morphosyllabic Chinese system for Japanese gave rise to the development of a fully fledged syllabary (KANA), because Chinese characters, originally developed to express monosyllabic morphemes with no inflections, were ill-suited to represent the grammatical morphemes of Japanese, an agglutinative language. The adoption by the Greeks of a Semitic consonant script led to the development of more complete vowel indication, as vowels carry more lexical information in Greek than in Semitic languages. Language dependency is a property of all writing systems, including the alphabet. Although letters of the alphabet have been used for designing a language-neutral alphabet, IPA, this is not a writing system but a transcription system. The longer a writing system is used for a given language, the more pronounced its language dependency.

See also ETYMOLOGICAL SPELLING; ORTHOGRAPHY; WRITING SYSTEM.

Lao writing Derived from PĀLI WRITING and closely related to KHMER WRITING, the Lao script belongs to the northern branch of Brāhmī descendants. Its relation with the Thai script is uncertain. Mutual derivations have been claimed. As an independent system the Lao script emerges in the thirteenth century CE. The Old Lao script had a simple grapheme inventory of 22 letters of the common Indian C + *a* type with inherent V and four independent V letters (table 3). Since Lao belongs to the Tai subgroup of Sino-Tibetan languages, its sound system differs markedly from that of Indo-European Pāli. Hence, a number of Pāli letters

Vowel letters

a	i	u	e

Consonant letters

ka	kha	ṅa	ča	ta	da	na
pa	pha	ba	ma	ya	ra	la
va	śa	sa	ha			

Table 3 The Old Lao script

were not needed for Lao, especially those for retroflex Cs. Modern Lao writing was given its present form in a reform carried out in 1960. Many irregularities of the old system, such as silent letters in Pāli loan words, have been abolished, and the spelling system has been adjusted more closely to Laotian phonology (table 4).

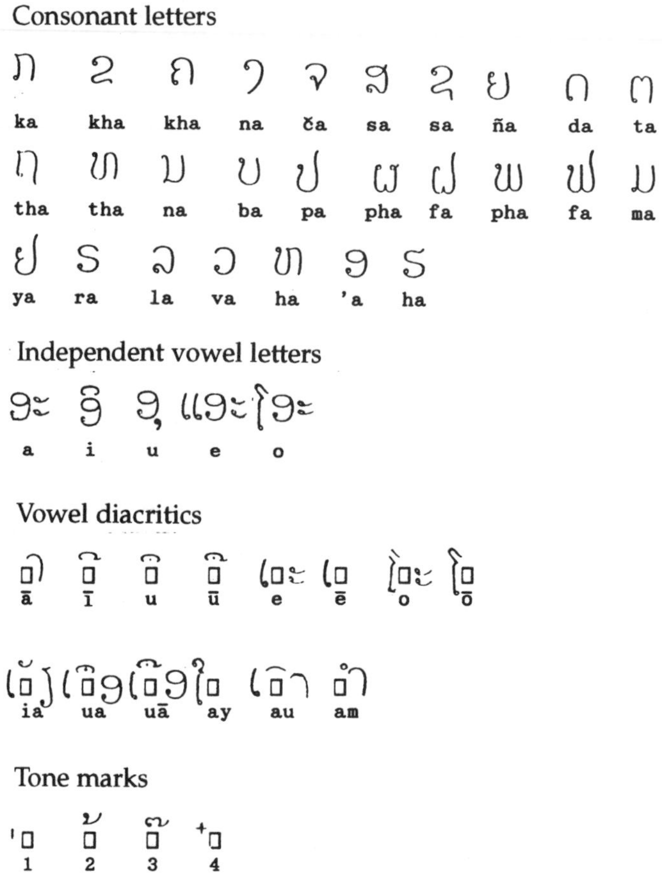

Consonant letters

ກ	ຂ	ຄ	ງ	ຈ	ສ	ຊ	ຍ	ດ	ຕ
ka	kha	kha	na	ča	sa	sa	ña	da	ta
ຖ	ທ	ນ	ບ	ປ	ຜ	ຝ	ພ	ຟ	ມ
tha	tha	na	ba	pa	pha	fa	pha	fa	ma
ຢ	ຣ	ລ	ວ	ຫ	ອ	ຮ			
ya	ra	la	va	ha	'a	ha			

Independent vowel letters

ອະ	ອິ	ອຸ	ແອະ	ໂອະ
a	i	u	e	o

Vowel diacritics

□າ	□ີ	□ຶ	□ື	ເ□ະ	ເ□	ໂ□ະ	ໂ□
ā	ī	u	ū	e	ē	o	ō

ເ□ັຽ	ເ□ຶອ	ເ□ືອ	ໄ□	ເ□ົາ	□ຳ
ia	ua	uā	ay	au	am

Tone marks

□່	□້	□໊	□໋
1	2	3	4

Table 4 The modern Lao script

Lao is a tone language. The writing system marks tones with four superscript diacritics placed over the C graphemes and on top of V diacritics, if any. C graphemes are divided into three classes, high, middle and low. In combination with the tone marks they determine the tone of a written syllable. The inherent V is phonetically realized as [ɔ] or [å]. Other Vs are indicated by diacritic satellites grouped around the C graph. These vary in form depending on whether the V occurs in medial or final position. Initial Vs are pronounced with a glottal stop and, accordingly, the C graph ອ for the glottal stop serves as the base graph for syllabic Vs. A special sign, ໆ is used for repetition.

Lapis Niger [Lat. 'black rock'] Dating from the sixth century BCE, the Lapis Niger bears the oldest known monumental Latin inscription. It was excavated in

1898 in the Forum Romanum. The inscription is written in Boustrophedon fashion with alternating lines running in opposite directions and some of the letters turned upside-down (figure 1). The script is an early form of Roman capital. Only a few words of the inscription can be understood: they say that 'he who damages this stone shall be doomed'. The word *recei*, dative of *rex* 'king', is also legible.

Figure 1 Ancient Latin inscription on the Lapis Niger, *sixth century* BCE
Source: *adapted from Steffens 1906*

Latin alphabet The alphabet of the Latin language which is attested in inscriptions as of the sixth century BCE. It descends from the Greek alphabet which spread from the Greek colonies in Sicily and southern Italy to other parts of the Italian peninsula, giving rise to a number of scripts which are usually referred to collectively as Old Italic scripts. One of them, the Etruscan alphabet, is the immediate forebear of the Latin alphabet. The adaptation to Latin took place during the seventh century BCE. The oldest known inscription dates from the early sixth century. It is written from right to left on a gold brooch, known as the Praeneste Fibula, and reads *MANIOS MED FHEFHAKED NVMASIOI* or, in Classical Latin, *Manios me fecit Numasio* 'Manius made me for Numasius' (figure 2).

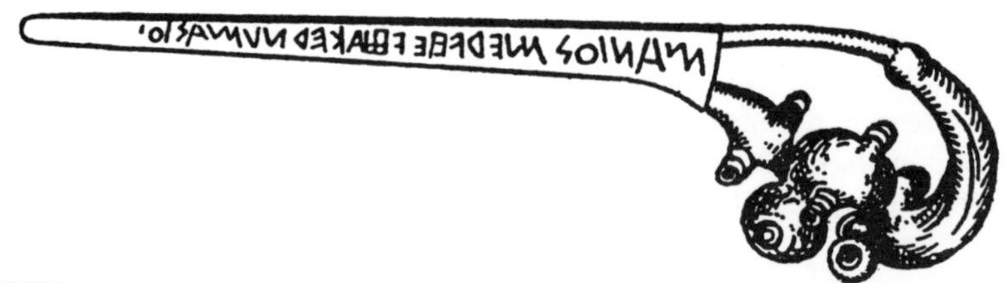

Figure 2 The earliest Latin inscription on the Praeneste Fibula *(Museo Preistorico Etnografico Luigi Pigorini, Rome)*

As in Etruscan, /f/ is written as *FH* in this inscription instead of later *F*. Other characteristics of the Latin alphabet which indicate its Etruscan origin (table 5) include the triple representation of /k/ by means of the three letters *K, O* and *C*. Eventually *K* fell out of use, and *O* came to be combined with *V*, pronounced [kw]. In Etruscan, no distinction was made between voiceless and voiced gutturals, *C* being used for both. In Latin, however, it was felt necessary to indicate this distinction in writing. Hence the letter *G* was created, probably in the third century BCE, by adding a stroke to *C*. The original Latin alphabet consisted of 21 letters.

Letters *Y* and *Z* were taken not from Etruscan but from Greek, when Greek loan words began to enter Latin. The French name of *Y*, *i-grec*, has its rationale in this specific adaptation. Three other letters of the Greek alphabet were never adopted, since Latin had no aspirated stops: *theta* Θ, *phi* Φ and *psi* Ψ. But they were taken over as numerals. As time went by, their forms were changed and they became identified with other letters, some of which were initials of Latin number words: Θ was halved and became *C* for *centum* 100; Φ was opened at the bottom and became *M* for *mille* 1,000; and Ψ first was straightened out to look like an upside-down T, ⊥, then subsequently lost the left half of its horizontal bar and became *L* for 50. (Letter *D* for 500 originates from the right half of the early sign for 1,000, ȸ.)

By the first century CE the Latin alphabet had 23 letters, making for a simple orthography which deviated from the one-letter/one-sound principle only in minor points. No distinction was made between long and short vowels, and both *V* and *I* had double values, the former standing for /v/ and /u/, the latter for /i/ and /j/. The graphic differentiation of both pairs took place much later. Gradually two variants of *V* developed which came to be written as *V* word initially and as *U* in the middle. By the tenth century, when the Latin alphabet was adopted for other languages, these variants were associated with different sound values: *V* with /v/ and *U* with /u/. Yet another sound, the voiced counterpart of /v/, came to be written as *VV* or *UU*, eventually resulting in the form *W*, called 'double *U*' in English, but 'double *V*' in French. The differentiation of *I* and *J* occurred even later, in the fifteenth century. As a separate letter, *J* took the form of the *I* as it was written in word-initial position. In the alphabetic sequence it was placed after *I*. Its Italian name, *I lungo* 'long I', reflects its derivation from *I*.

In the classical period of Rome the Latin alphabet was written in a variety of different styles. The *capitales quadratae*, or square capitals, are well known from

Etruscan	Latin	Roman
A A A	A Λ A A	A
	B B	B
Ɔ λ)	‹ C	C
	D	D
Ǝ Ǝ Ǝ	E II	E
ꟻ ꟻ	F I'	F
⊏ ± I	Z	Z
⊟ ⊟	H	H
O ⊗ ()		
I I	I	I
> K	K	K
⅃ ✓	L L	L
⋈ M M M	M M	M
N N N	N N	N
	O	O
1 Λ ⊓	Γ P	P
	Q	Q
D Ʊ ɑ q	R R	R
M ⋈ ≷ ≷	S S	S
T T	T	T
V V V	V	V
Φ ᗡ		
↓	X	X
8 (F		

Table 5 The Latin alphabet

many monumental inscriptions (figure 3). Using square, triangle and circle as its basic geometric forms, this script has served as a model of many modern typefaces. *See also* ROMAN ALPHABET.
Reading Diringer 1968.

Latinxua [Chinese 'Latinization'] An alphabetic transcription for Chinese based on Latin letters intended as an alternative orthography. Latinxua was devised in

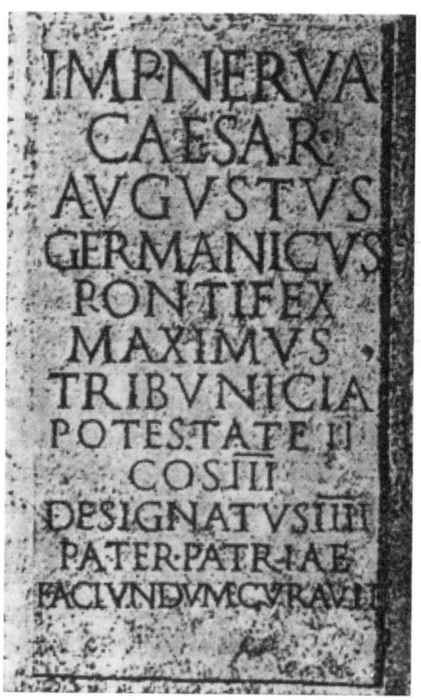

Figure 3 Latin inscription in capitales quadratae, *97* CE *(Vatican Museum, Rome)*

the Soviet Far East in 1931 and taken up in the communist-held north-western parts of China. It was replaced in the early 1950s by Pinyin as China's official alphabetic spelling system.
See also GWOYEU ROMATZYH; PINYIN.

Lepcha script A member of the Tibeto-Burman branch of Sino-Tibetan languages, Lepcha is mainly spoken in Sikkim and western Bengal. The Lepcha script, also known as 'Róng' (royal), is a syllabic alphabet which appears to have been derived from the DBU-MED form of the Tibetan script, although there is no agreement about its exact genealogy. Chinese influence is apparent in the vertical direction of old Lepcha manuscripts. The script was later turned 90 degrees counter-clockwise, but the direction of graphs on the line did not change (figure 4). The rotation occurred probably under Phyag-rdor-rnam-rgyal, at the beginning of the eighteenth century CE.

Lepcha scholars favour the theory that the Lepchas possessed their own script from ancient times. In support of this view they cite the peculiar mode of indicating final Cs not found in other INDIAN WRITING SYSTEMS. With respect to the basic C graphemes the script conforms to the common Indian pattern (table 6). C graphemes have an inherent V /å/, and other Vs are indicated by means of diacritic satellites grouped around the basic C graph. However, unlike other Indian writing systems, the Lepcha script also possesses signs for final Cs which are placed on top of the basic C + *a* graphemes much like V diacritics (table 7).

Figure 4 Hymn to the praise of Narok Rum, the Lepcha god of muse

Indication of independent Vs also differs from the usual Indian pattern, but is like Tibetan in that all independent V graphemes contain a common element.
Reading Chakraborty 1978.

Lepsius, Karl Richard (1810–1884) German Egyptologist and linguist who contributed to a better understanding of Egyptian writing by demonstrating that in addition to monoconsonantal signs it included many bi- and triconsonantal signs. Following a suggestion by the Church Missionary Society, London, Lepsius developed a uniform phonetic transcription system which was published in 1855 and 1863 in German and English, respectively. This system, with which Lepsius himself transcribed 120 languages, came to be known as the 'standard alphabet'. Much later Lepsius's pioneering work inspired the creation of the AFRICA ALPHABET.
Reading Lepsius 1863.

Vowel letters

Printed	Written	Value	Printed	Written	Value
		å			ů
		á			u
		a			e
		i			o
		í			ó

Consonant letters

Printed	Written	Value	Printed	Written	Value
		kå			må
		klå			mlå
		k			tså
		khå			thså
		gå			zå
		glå			yå
		ngå			y
		ng			rå
		chå		final	r
		čhå			r
		jå			lå
		nyå			l
		tå			hå
		t			hlå
		thå			vå
		då			så
		nå			sha
		n			wå
		på			
		plå			
		p			
		phå			
		få			
		flå			
		bå			
		blå			

Table 6 The Lepcha syllabic alphabet

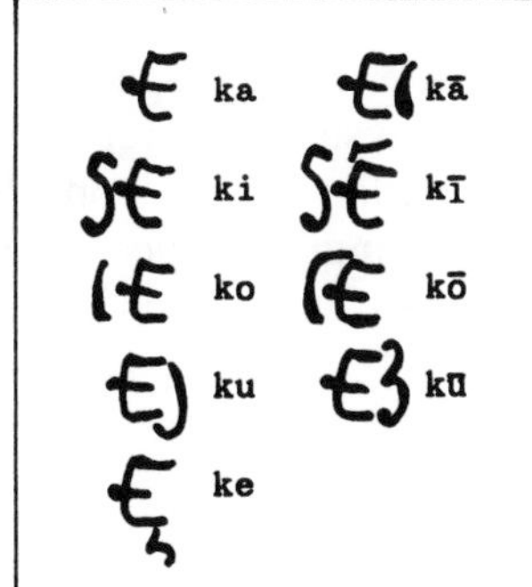

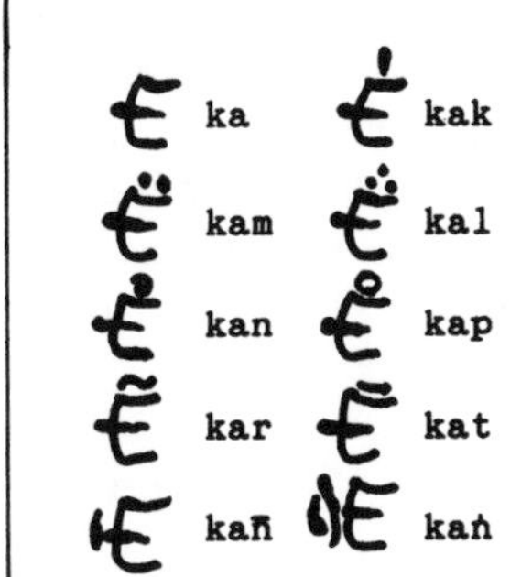

Table 7 Indication of vowels and final consonants in Lepcha

letter 1 One of a class of shapes which are recognized as instances of abstract graphic concepts which represent the basic units of an alphabetic writing system. Each of these units has a name, for example *ei, si, kei*. Thus the letter *em* is the class of all *M*s no matter how they are shaped; more precisely, it is the class of all conceivable letter shapes to which the name *em* applies (figure 5). We may write *em* in roman or italic, square capital, Caroline minuscule or any other type, or by hand. Although we associate prototypes with each letter name, it is difficult, if not impossible, to define these prototypes in terms of invariant graphical features such as permissible geometric elements, their syntactic relationships,

Figure 5 Various shapes of the letter em

curvature, thickness of lines, proportions, position on a base line, or minimal distinctions between similar letters such as *g* and *q*, *l* and *i*, or *f* and *t*. **2** A graphic symbol that represents one or more phonemes of a language. In this sense a letter is defined in terms of its function within a system that represents speech, its sound value. Since sound values of individual letters vary considerably across languages, such a definition is necessarily language specific. For example, a Dutch <g> differs from the same letter in Italian, German or English:

Dutch	<g>	[x], [ɣ̊]
Italian	<g>	[g], [dʒ]
German	<g>	[g], [k]
English	<g>	[g], [dʒ], [∅]

Assuming that <g> is the only letter so pronounced in Dutch, such a definition may be formulated thus: a Dutch <g> is any character or mark that speakers (and readers) of Dutch recognize as indicating [x] or [ɣ̊], where this recognition may be achieved by virtue of similarity to an assumed prototype or by virtue of contrast, that is, dissimilarity with all other elements of the same system. The same graphic elements which constitute the letters of individual language-specific writing systems are also used as scientific transcription symbols with invariant phonetic values, as in IPA. IPA symbols should not be confused with letters. **3** A letter shape that belongs to a particular style or typeface. In this sense the term 'letter' is used in statements such as 'This is a minuscule rather than an uncial letter', or 'The difference between capital and small letters developed only in the Middle Ages.' A letter in this sense is a geometrical shape constructed on the basis of certain formative principles common to all the letters of a given typeface (figure 6). **4** A piece of printing type used to produce a letter shape of which it bears a mirror image (figure 7).

See also FONT; GRAPHEME; TYPE; TYPOGRAPHY.

Reading Abercrombie 1949; Haas 1970.

letter names With the exception of *W* and *J*, which only came into existence in the Middle Ages, the letters of the alphabet have monosyllabic, meaningless names in modern European languages, such as English *ei*, *bi*, *si*. These names are an Etruscan and Latin heritage, for when the Etruscans adopted the Greek alphabet they did not take over the Greek letter names which still reveal their Semitic origin. The Semitic letter names have given rise to a great deal of research and speculation. In particular, it has been hypothesized that they might reveal the origin of Semitic writing. Several of the letter names could be identified as Semitic words. Thus *'āleph* means 'ox' in Semitic languages, *bēth* 'house', *mēm* 'water', *nūn* 'fish', *pě* 'mouth', *rēš* 'head' and *tāw* 'sign'. This observation led to the assumption that Semitic letters were originally pictographic signs of objects, their sound values being derived on the basis of the ACROPHONIC PRINCIPLE, that is, the initial sound of the word in question. However, the meanings of other letter names could not be ascertained, and some interpretations are dubious. For example, it was suggested that the letter *zayin* 'weapon' was earlier called *zayit* which means 'olive tree'. Further doubts about a pictographic origin of Semitic letters

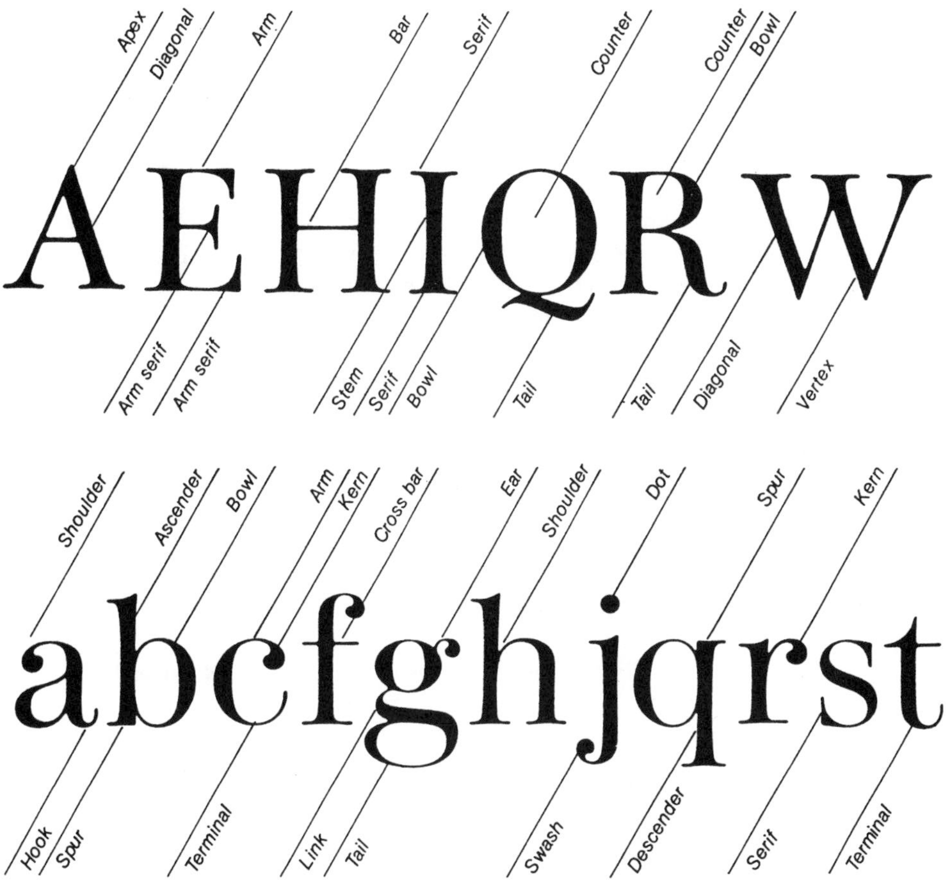

Apex Diagonal Arm Bar Serif Counter Counter Bowl

AEHIQRW

Arm serif Arm serif Stem Serif Bowl Tail Tail Diagonal Vertex

Shoulder Ascender Bowl Arm Kern Cross bar Ear Shoulder Dot Spur Kern

abcfghjqrst

Hook Spur Terminal Link Tail Swash Descender Serif Terminal

Figure 6 Parts of letters and their names

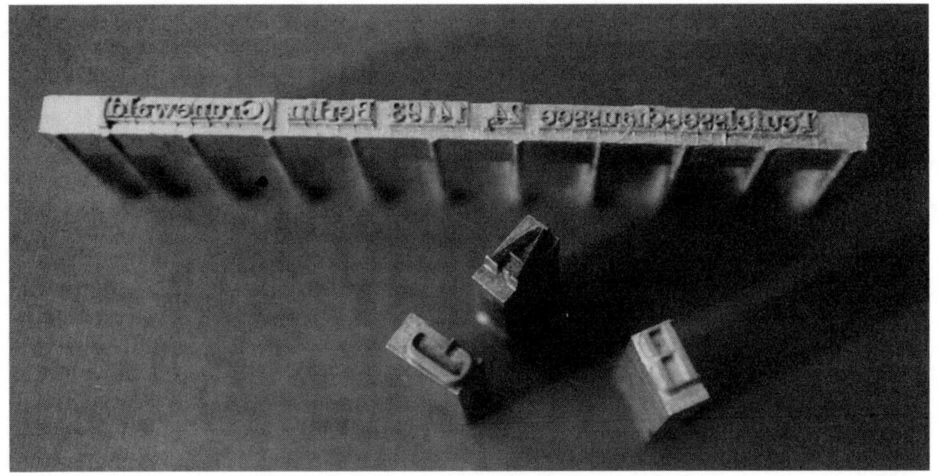

Figure 7 Letters cast in lead

arise from a comparison of some letter shapes. For instance, the pairs *hē/hēth* and *nūn/mēm* suggest that the latter were derived graphically from the former by adding a stroke to create a new sign for a different but similar sound. Further, although the interpretation of several letter names as Semitic words must be considered certain, it remains unclear what this implies for the origin of Semitic writing.

However, the letter names are an object of interest for another reason also. The Greek names are meaningless since they are derived from Semitic rather than Greek words (table 8). But a comparison of both and the reconstruction of the most ancient form of the Semitic names can shed light on the transmission process and thus help to answer the question of where the Greeks borrowed the alphabet, which was common to several Semitic languages. For example, the word *'āleph* 'ox' which became Greek *alpha* exists in Phoenician but not in Aramaic. This kind of philological evidence lends further support to the theory that Phoenician is the immediate source of the Greek alphabet, which is based primarily on the graphic similarity of the most ancient Greek letters with their Phoenician counterparts.

See also GREEK ALPHABET; LATIN ALPHABET; PHOENICIAN ALPHABET.
Reading Ullman 1927; Jensen 1969.

Meaning	Phoenician	Greek	Greek letter
ox	'ālaph	alpha	Α
house	bēth	beta	Β
	gīmel	gamma	Γ
door	dāleth	delta	Δ
	hē	epsilon	Ε
nail	wāw	vau (digamma)	Ϝ
weapon	zayin	zeta	Ζ
	hēth	eta	Η
	tēth	theta	Θ
hand	yōdh	iota	Ι
palm	kaph	kappa	Κ
	lāmedh	lambda	Λ
water	mēm	mu	Μ
fish	nūn	nu	Ν
mouth	pē	pi	Π
head	rēš	rho	Ρ
	sāmekh	sigma	Σ
sign	tāw	tau	Τ
eye	'ayin	omega	Ω

Table 8 Phoenician and Greek letter names and their Semitic meanings

letter recognition The process of identifying lines, curves and angles of visual stimulus items as letters. Considering the variety of letter shapes on the one hand, and the limited constitutive features of which they are composed on the other, letter recognition is a surprisingly complex task which competent readers carry out at great speed. The study of letter recognition can reveal much about the working of the human mind. How difficult a task it is became apparent when computer scientists started designing models of it which could function as the processing unit of reading machines able to handle a variety of fonts. Initially, such programs were thrown off course by every speck on a page and every broken letter. Also, it was extremely difficult to achieve a speed in machine scanning which came close to human performance.

In humans, letter recognition is a necessary although not a sufficient condition of reading. In the process of extracting meaning from a written text it interacts with other perceptual and cognitive mechanisms. An important indication of such interaction is the 'word-superiority effect': as parts of familiar words, letters are identified faster and easier than in non-words or, even more so, than in orthographically non-permissible letter sequences. The word-superiority effect plays a crucial role in reading research. In current scholarship it is taken as testifying to the dynamic nature of the reading process which involves different levels of processing – feature, letter, word – often proceeding concurrently.
See also Font; Letter **[1, 3]**.
Reading Massaro et al. 1980; Lee and Oldham 1990.

lettering In typography, the activity of putting Letters **[3]** on a surface by any technique suitable for the writing material, such as inscribing, painting, pasting and stamping.

ligature [Lat. *ligare* 'to bind'] A combination of two or more letters to form a single sign. Ligatures formerly used in English include Æ and Œ. The ampersand & developed from the abbreviation *etc.* Before the invention of movable type, ligatures were used extensively in printing. Since every page had to be cut in wood as a whole it was important to economize on space and effort, which could be achieved by condensing frequently cooccurring letters into a single sign. The earliest prints with movable letters still included many ligatures which, however, gradually disappeared as printers mastered the new technology which favours the reduction of the number of signs to be kept in stock (figure 8).

The return of the ligature

The return of the ligature

Figure 8 Design of modern ligatures by J. S. Scorsone

In Indian writing systems ligatures play an important role as the common means of representing C clusters. They are typically formed by conjoining parts of two or more C + *a* letters to form a distinct grapheme for a complex syllable.

These elements are conjoined horizontally or vertically. Since the composition of many ligatures is no longer self-evident, they have to be learned separately in addition to the basic letters (figure 9).

In alphabetic typography the term 'ligature' is also used for a line or bar connecting two letters.

See also GUTENBERG; INCUNABULA; INDIAN WRITING SYSTEMS; PRINTING.

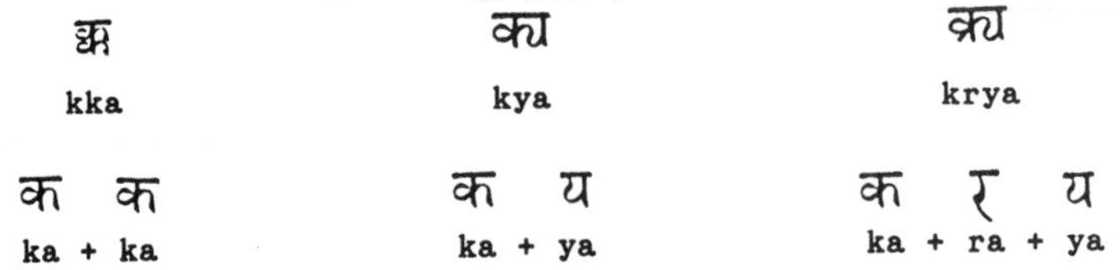

क्क	क्य	क्र्य
kka	**kya**	**krya**
क क	क य	क र य
ka + ka	**ka + ya**	**ka + ra + ya**

Figure 9 Some Devanāgarī ligatures

Limbu script A Tibeto-Burman language spoken in the border region of eastern Nepal and India, Limbu has a script which is related to the Lepcha script on which it appears to have been modelled. It is also called 'Kirant' script after the name of a group of related languages of the eastern Himalayas. It is a syllabic alphabet which shares with the LEPCHA SCRIPT and TIBETAN WRITING the characteristic of using a common element as the base of all independent V graphemes. C graphemes have an inherent V *a*, phonetically [å]. Subscripts are used to represent complex syllables (table 9).

Linear A One of three writing systems used in ancient Crete, as yet undeciphered. It is documented on clay tablets bearing short inscriptions mostly arranged in square fields with four to nine lines. The earliest Cretan script, also undeciphered, consists of pictorial signs, while the other two are linear in appearance. At the beginning of the twentieth century, clay tablets were excavated in large numbers at Knossos, at Hagia Triada, and at some other sites in Crete. Arthur EVANS, a pioneer of Minoan archaeology, called the earlier inscriptions from Hagia Triada 'Linear A' and the later ones from the deposits at Knossos 'Linear B'. Most Linear A tablets date from the eighteenth century BCE and later, but some finds, with what appears to be an earlier form of the script, pre-date these inscriptions by as much as 300 years (figure 10). The number of different signs – between 77 and 85 have been identified by different scholars – suggests a syllabic system. It has been hypothesized that Linear A was used to write a pre-Hellenic language. Other studies have tentatively linked Linear A with the Obɛri Ɔkaimɛ script of southern Nigeria (Hau 1967) and the script of the Old European Vinča culture (Haarmann 1990), but so far all interpretations remain speculative.

See also CRETAN WRITING; LINEAR B.

Reading Evans 1909; Hallagar 1980.

Linear B One of two linear scripts used in ancient Crete which were first discovered at the beginning of the twentieth century. While LINEAR A is still undeciphered, Linear B was demonstrated by Michael VENTRIS in 1952 to represent a Greek dialect used between 1400 and 1200 BCE. Hence, Linear B inscriptions represent the oldest documented form of Greek, now generally called 'Minoan

Vowel letters

Value	å	á	i	u	e	æ	o	ó	åh	a:

Consonant letters

Value	kå	khå	gå	nå	cå	chå	ǂå	ŋå
	tå	thå	då	dhå	på	phå	bå	bhå
	må	jå	rå	lå	vå	šå	så	hå

Subscripts

kå

yå kyå

rå krå

vå kvå

Table 9 The Limbu syllabic alphabet

Greek'. Linear B shares many of its signs with the older Linear A. It has been suggested, therefore, that it came into existence when Minoan scribes adapted Linear A to a new language, Greek. Most Linear B inscriptions have been found in the deposits of Knossos, but the script was also used on the Greek mainland. The texts are primarily of an administrative nature, such as lists of goods, statements of delivery or other commercial transactions (figure 11). The decipherment of Linear B was sensational because it produced evidence of a pre-alphabetic literate culture in Greece. Intellectually it was a great accomplishment, as it was achieved without a BILINGUIS and in the absence of collateral archaeological evidence that could have clarified the language of the inscriptions.

Linear B is a syllabic writing system consisting of 90 syllable signs of the form

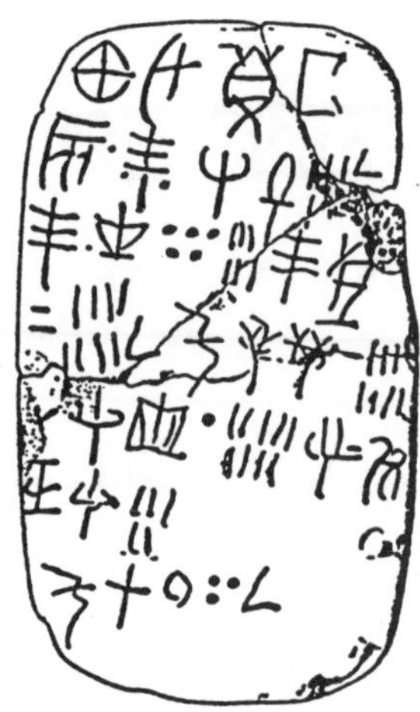

Figure 10 Linear A inscription on a clay tablet from Hagia Triada

CV or V and an indeterminate number of pictorial signs (table 10). It cannot represent C clusters, which makes it a rather deficient system for Greek. For instance, names such as *Knossos* and *Amnisos* had to be written as *ko-no-so* and *a-mi-ni-so*, respectively. Although most Linear B documents can be read, some features of the writing remain unclear. Not all syllable signs have been determined conclusively, and perhaps never will be. The imprecise representation of the language suggests that the system had been taken over from another language. The literary tradition of Linear B breaks off at about 1100 BCE.
See also DECIPHERMENT.
Reading Chadwick 1958; Hooker 1979; Heubeck 1982.

Lingala writing A Bantu language spoken on both sides of the Zaïre and one of the official languages of Zaïre, Lingala has served as a lingua franca since pre-colonial times. Its varieties were known by several different names including Ngala, Bangala and Mangala. When it was reduced to writing under Belgian colonial rule, missionaries created the name 'Lingala' as a designation for the emerging unified written standard variety. Lingala uses the Roman alphabet for its largely phonemic orthography.
Reading van Everbroek 1958.

linguistic awareness *See* LITERACY; PHONEME

lishu [Chinese 隷書 'clerical script'] A style of Chinese calligraphy, dating from the early Han dynasty (206 BCE to 25 CE), which developed from the small-seal script. An angular and formal style, it has been used ever since for inscriptions and serious writing (figure 12). It continues to be used for decorative purposes today.
See also CALLIGRAPHY; CHINESE SCRIPTS.

lists Many of the earliest palaeographic documents are inventories of objects and persons, stock itemizations of goods for trade, payments, rations, work

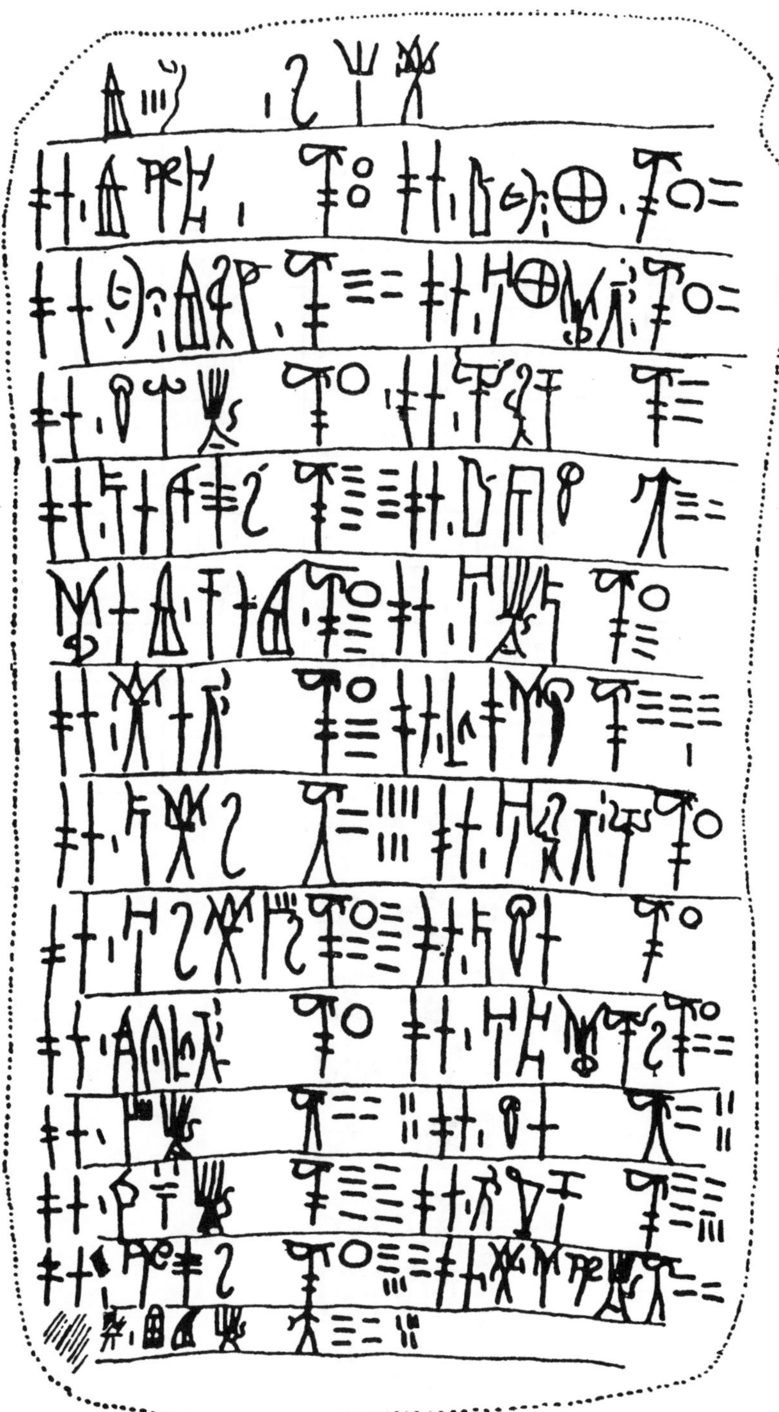

Figure 11 Specimen of Linear B: tablet 131 from the palace archive of Pylos, recording names of suppliers, goods and amounts

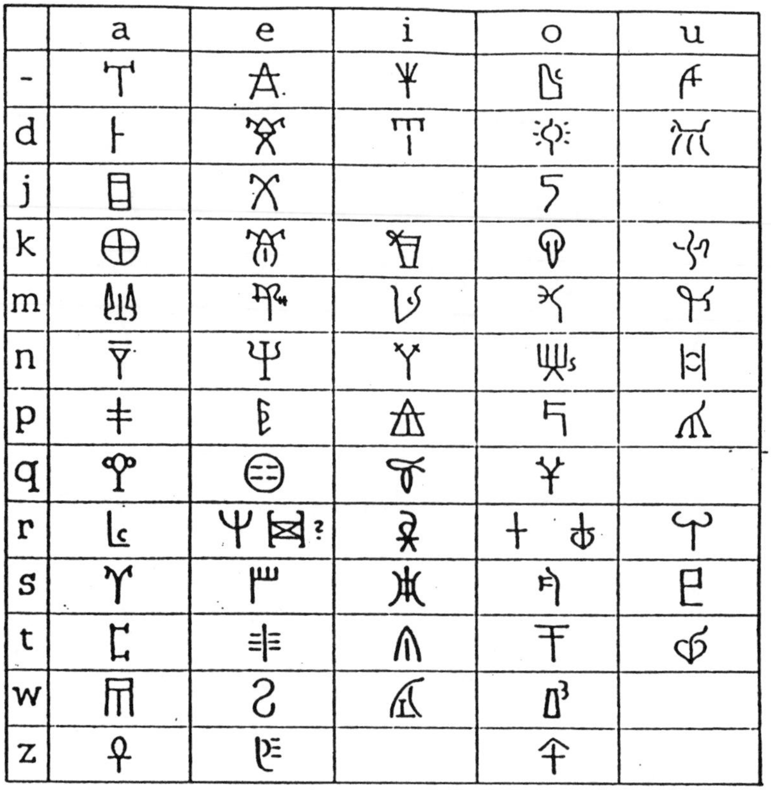

	a	e	i	o	u
-	𐀀	𐀁	𐀂	𐀃	𐀄
d	𐀅	𐀆	𐀇	𐀈	𐀉
j	𐀊	𐀋		𐀍	
k	𐀏	𐀐	𐀑	𐀒	𐀓
m	𐀔	𐀕	𐀖	𐀗	𐀘
n	𐀙	𐀚	𐀛	𐀜	𐀝
p	𐀞	𐀟	𐀠	𐀡	𐀢
q	𐀣	𐀤	𐀥	𐀦	
r	𐀨	𐀩 [illegible] ?	𐀪	𐀫 [illegible]	𐀬
s	𐀭	𐀮	𐀯	𐀰	𐀱
t	𐀲	𐀳	𐀴	𐀵	𐀶
w	𐀷	𐀸	𐀹	𐀺 [illegible]	
z	𐀼	𐀽		𐀿	

Table 10 The Linear B syllabary. Source: *Ekschmitt 1969*

漢武都大守阿陽李
翕字伯[illegible]動順經古

Figure 12 A specimen of the Chinese lishu, *clerical script, Ming dynasty (1368–1644)* requirements and so on. Rather than recording objects and events in connected prose, they were organized discontinuously in the forms of lists. The list is a form of communication which exploits the functional potential of writing to put unrelated items next to each other and to look at them item by item for purposes of keeping track of events or for comparison, in order to discover similarities and differences. Lists are a form of organizing knowledge; they are at the beginning of science (figure 13). So important were lists in the embryonic stages of literacy, especially in Mesopotamia, that the palaeographic study of ancient inscriptions gave rise to a branch of knowledge known as *Listenwissenschaft* or 'science of lists'. Lists embody the quintessence of decontextualized, discontinuous language use so immensely facilitated by writing. The most compelling example is the alphabet. Handed down through the generations for 3,000 years in a fixed though arbitrary sequence, it provides the ordering principle for all sorts of information storage and retrieval from dictionaries to library catalogues.

See also DICTIONARY.

Reading Goody 1977.

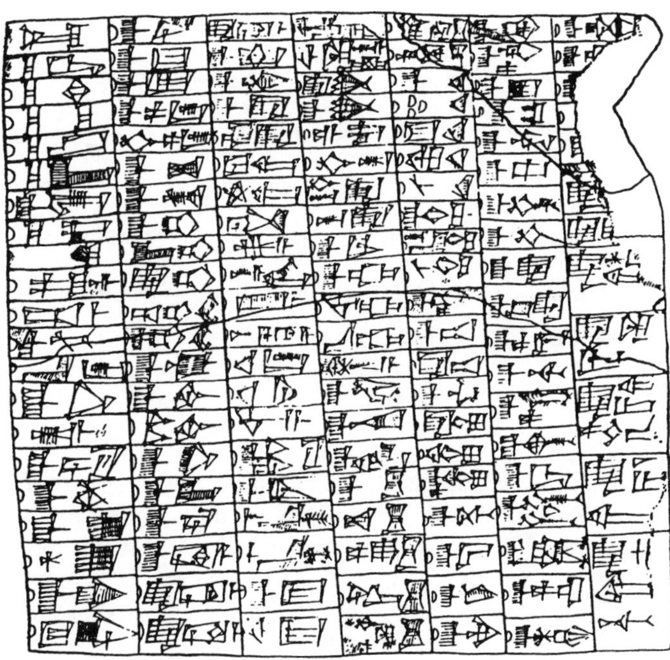

Figure 13 The Standard Professions List, one of the most ancient written documents of Babylonia, which was frequently copied: this copy dates from c.2500 BCE
Source: *Deimel 1923*

Lisu writing The Lisu are one of China's recognized minority nationalities. They live in the south-western part of the country in Yunnan province and on both sides of the border with Myanmar (Burma). Their language belongs to the Burmese-Lolo group of Sino-Tibetan languages and is known under a variety of names including Lishu, Lusu, Chung, Cheli and Yao Yen.

Two writing systems were created for Lisu, both based on the Latin alphabet.

The old Lisu writing was devised by Swedish-British missionary J. O. Fraser in 1912. The alphabet consists of 25 capital letters of the Latin alphabet, all except *Q*, plus 14 turned capital letters (table 11). Lisu is a tone language with no consonant clusters. Consonant letters denote a syllable C + *a*. Otherwise syllables are represented by combinations of consonant and vowel letters with tones indicated as diacritics at the lower right side of the letter: <.> for tone 1, <,> for tone 2, <..> for tone 3, <.,> for tone 4, <;> for tone 5, and <:> for tone 6. Tone marks are only written where necessary for disambiguation.

Vowel letters

I [i、ɿ]	E [e]	Ǝ [ø、y]	Ɐ [ɛ]	A [ɑ]
ɑ [ə]	U [u]	∩ [ɣ、ʅ]	O [o]	ꓶ [ɯ]

Consonant letters

B [b]	P [p]	ꓒ [ph]	D [d]	T [t]	ꓕ [th]
G [g]	K [k]	ꓘ [kh]	J [dʑ]	C [tɕ]	Ↄ [tɕh]
			[dʒ]	[tʃ]	[tʃh]
Z [dz]	F [ts]	Ⅎ [tsh]	M [m]	N [n]	L [l]
S [s]	R [ʒ]	ꓤ [z]	Λ [ŋ]	V [h]	H [x]
⅁ [ɦ]	W [uɑ]	X [ɕ]	Y [ʑ]	ɾ [f]	ꓭ [ɣɑ]
		[ʃ]			

Table 11 The Old Lisu alphabet

The new Lisu writing was devised in 1958 under the auspices of the Chinese government. It makes use of the Latin alphabet, both capital and small letters, with phonetic values which are close to those of the Chinese phonetic alphabet Pinyin (table 12). The six tones are indicated by letters that are added to CV syllables: <l> for tone 1, <q> for tone 2, <x> for tone 4, <r> for tone 5, and <t> for tone 6. The third tone is not indicated. Although scientifically sound and transparent, the new writing is not as popular as the old one which continues to be used in some measure today (figure 14). However, the use of Lisu for written communication is limited.
Reading Huang 1992; Kao 1992.

literacy Mastery of reading and writing skills. The term is used in a number of different senses by researchers in different fields. This diversity of meaning is obscured by the fact that they all have to do with linguistic communication in written form. The following three senses should be distinguished according to whether literacy is seen as an individual, a social, or a linguistic phenomenon.

Vowel letters

i[i、ɿ]	ei[e]	ai[ɛ]	a[a]	o[o]	u[u]
e[ɯ]	ia[ia、iɛ]	io[io]	ua[ua]	uai[uɛ]	ui[ui]
ao[ao]	iao[iao]	ou[ou]	uo[uo]		

Consonant letters

b[p]	p[ph]	bb[b]	m[m]	f[f]	v[v]
w[w]	d[t]	t[th]	dd[d]	n[n]	l[l]
g[k]	k[kh]	gg[g]	ng[ŋ]	h[x、h]	e[ɤ]
z[ts]	c[tsh]	zz[dz]	s[s]	ss[z]	j[tɕ]
q[tɕh]	jj[dʑ]	x[ɕ]	y[ʑ]	zh[tʃ]	ch[tʃh]
rr[dʒ]	sh[ʃ]	r[ʒ]			

Table 12 The New Lisu alphabet

Old Lisu

CO KUꓷ:KO.ꓛ T ꓞO Xꓵ: Cꓶ.ꓞꓯ: M NY-RO: KUꓷ:ꓞO Xꓵ ꓞO JI: MI- KUꓷ:CY Xꓵ: WU Tꓯ.KW:Xꓵ:W M- Tꓱ Tꓶ.M Cꓶ.Cꓵ. Jꓵ: W; W LE M LE: M: ꓞI.,- FAI.ꓕI: W TY.ZI;NY. M Mꓵ: KW NY- GO ꓕI: Mꓵ; KW NY CI.ꓛY: KW, Xꓵ, M YE SI.- CI.ꓛY ꓞO Xꓵ; Nꓯ. KW M Xꓵ: WU NY- CI.ꓛY: KW, M YE D LO=

New Lisu

Zhogot Goqchada coshit zheqcet ma nia, rot got coshit cojjit mi got ja shitvu dail guatshit wa ma deideq ma zheqzhiq rritwat wa'lei ma leir ma ci, zaiq titwa diaiq zzirniaq ma mut gua nia, ggo tit mut gua nia jilqait guat shit ma yei sil, jilqait coshit nail a gua ma shitvu nia, jilqait guat ma yei dda lo.

Translation

The nationality policy of the Communist Party of China not only allows all nationalities to participate in the national government, but also guarantees them autonomy and control over their own affairs.

Figure 14 Specimen of Old and New Lisu writing with translation

Individual aspects
Literacy conceived as the ability to read and write is investigated by psychologists and educationalists. The objects of research are individuals as they learn and utilize written language skills. The opposite of literacy in this sense is ILLITERACY. Rather than signifying an absolute contrast, both these terms refer to graded notions that may apply to individuals in varying degrees. Written language skills may be mastered only partially or, after having been learned, may degenerate for lack of use. Moreover, individuals are affected by literacy practices in their environment. An illiterate in a literate environment is more affected by medial and communicative properties of written language than an illiterate who is completely disconnected from literate communication practices. The notion of 'functional literacy' is intended to account for such differences and help conceive of literacy as diverse and graded rather than a uniform skill with a clearly defined threshold. What amounts to being functionally literate varies across historical periods and societies.

Individual mastery of written language involves both practical and theoretical problems. On the practical side, the learning and teaching of written language skills stand central. Relevant research questions in this connection include the following. How does literacy acquisition interact with cognitive development? How does literacy acquisition interact with language acquisition and language development? How do learning conditions differ for children and adults? How is literacy acquisition affected by different learning and teaching strategies, e.g. analytic, 'from word to letter', or synthetic, 'from letter to word'? How can impediments in literacy acquisition be explained and remedied? What is needed to avoid relapse into functional illiteracy after literacy campaigns which are prima facie successful, but eventually fail to produce sustained literacy?

On the theoretical side, questions have been raised about difficulties in grasping the underlying principles of writing systems and the relationship between speech and writing. This discussion led to the more specific question of how literacy influences linguistic awareness, that is, the ability to perceive and conceptualize units of language. In recent years ever more empirical evidence has been amassed that the linguistic analysis inherent in a writing system has a profound effect on how its users conceptualize language. It has been demonstrated that segmentation ability is greatly enhanced by, if not dependent on, written language skills. This insight has important consequences for the status of language as a reference system in models of mental operations. To what extent are such models influenced by the conception of language as suggested by written language? Arguably, the identification of thinking with manipulating discrete symbols is a by-product of literacy.

Social aspects
As a mode of communication, literacy is an attribute of socio-cultural systems studied by sociologists and cultural anthropologists. The opposite of literacy in this sense is orality. Sociologists have generally considered written language as an evolutionary advantage, since its possession increases the adaptive capacity of social systems by advancing differentiation and specialization. In current scholarship concerned with social aspects of literacy, there is an ongoing debate between

two schools of thought which may be called 'autonomist' and 'contextualist'. Autonomists conceive of written language skills as the key component of advanced or modern as opposed to 'primitive' or traditional societies, while contextualists deny that the dichotomy of literacy vs orality defines a meaningful demarcation between social systems, emphasizing that literacy practices vary greatly across cultures. The former tend to look at literacy as a technology which, of and by itself, brings about major changes in the way people interact with each other and with the physical and ideational world around them. By contrast, those in the contextualist camp stress the inextricable connection of literacy with cultural and power structures rather than conceptualizing it as an autonomous force in socio-cultural development. The autonomist position is exemplified by the work of Goody and Olson, while Graff and Street may be cited as representative contextualists. Some of the specific questions of the debate are as follows. What makes a society literate? How can societies be classified with respect to the functional distribution of literacy (e.g. magic, elite, restricted, function specific, sectoral, universal)? How is social organization different in oral and literate societies? To what extent can societal institutions be characterized in terms of their reliance on written discourse (religion, law, education, government)? How does literacy interact with other properties of social systems? Is literacy a consequence or a prerequisite of economic development?

For some time, especially when UNESCO sponsored many literacy campaigns in the 1960s and 1970s, much hope was placed on literacy as an agent of development, but there has been a growing recognition that in order for literacy to spread, a society must be ready for it, that is there must be a demand for literate people. The notion of literacy as a technology which, once introduced, works as an autonomous force in shaping social systems, is attractive for its simplicity. However, in recent years the focus of research has shifted from the question of how literacy affects societies to that of what societies do with literacy.

Linguistic aspects

As a linguistic phenomenon literacy pertains to the medium of expression, i.e. modulated air waves and penned or printed marks on a surface. Oral and literate modes of language production are investigated in terms of contrasts between the products of speech and writing, i.e. spoken and written language, respectively. With the exception of the Prague school, mainstream linguists in the twentieth century have paid little attention to the relationship between language, speech and writing, assuming for the most part that writing is just a secondary, if imperfect, representation of speech. This assumption has been called into question only during the last quarter of the twentieth century when many linguists began to realize that, despite the professed primacy of speech, the units of linguistic analysis – sentence, word, phoneme – are derivative of the units of WRITTEN LANGUAGE. As a consequence, the need was felt to reflect on the significance of writing for linguistic analysis in general and to more thoroughly investigate the specific properties of spoken and written language. The issues taken up in this connection can be divided into three sets of problems. Two of them correspond roughly to the common *langue/parole* distinction, and a third concerns properties of writing systems.

Parole issues have to do with characteristic differences in the organization of discourse in the oral and literate modes. These differences are sometimes described in terms of 'registers', where written language registers are characterized as more highly integrated, planned and context independent than spoken language registers. Typical features of literate discourse are said to be subordinative, hierarchical structures, while oral discourse is more additive and paratactic. Since it is evidently possible to use spoken language registers in writing and written language registers in speech, it has been suggested that the linguistic aspects of literacy and orality be conceived as a continuum. This notion has proved inadequate, however, because it suggests a single dimension of variation, while it has become obvious that oral and literal forms of discourse differ from one another in a multidimensional way. In order to come to grips with this diversity, linguistic research into the *parole* aspects of literacy focuses on how the physical conditions and the functional purposes of speech and writing are reflected in the respective products, i.e. spoken and written forms of language such as oral and literate narrative, or LITERATURE and oral poetry.

With respect to *langue*, literacy brings on the question of whether and how a language is affected by being used in writing. If writing affects *parole*, it stands to reason that *langue* too will be affected by it, because *langue* evolves with every speech and writing act. What then, if anything, does the written mode add to, or change in, the language system? Since language history depends on written records, causal effects of writing on the emergence of, for example, more complex syntactic structures are difficult to observe, although individual cases have been documented (e.g. Kalmár 1985). Linguists who conceive of writing as only the outer clothing of language have generally sidestepped this question, partly because their synchronic perspective leaves no room for external influences which may affect the language system over time, and partly because writing, being an artefact, interferes with the notion of 'natural' language as the proper object of linguistic analysis. Yet research into such areas as language standardization, language contact, the pluricentrality of languages, and the cleavage between spoken and written varieties usually captured under the notion of DIGLOSSIA, has made it clear that writing does affect language not only on the level of use, but also with respect to the underlying system. However, so far there is no conceptual framework for describing systemic differences (in grammar, lexicon and style) between languages used in both the oral and the literate modes and those confined to manifestation in speech alone.

Turning to the third set of linguistic problems concerning literacy, a number of hypotheses have been advanced about possible connections between systematic properties of writing systems and the social distribution of literacy. In particular, it has been suggested that universal literacy can be achieved only with alphabetic writing systems. Another hypothesis has linked the coming into existence of diglossia – a condition usually associated with restricted literacy – with phonetic as opposed to logographic writing systems. So far no indubitable evidence has been produced to confirm such hypotheses. The reasons for this must be sought on one hand in the fact that literacy levels are determined by a number of interacting factors, and on the other that too little is known about how writing systems work.

However, in recent years more linguists have taken an interest in the structural properties of writing systems which are now widely recognized to be linguistic subsystems which must be analysed accordingly. Each writing system can be described in terms of its systematic properties. On a structural level such a description can be independent of other linguistic subsystems, concentrating on the units of the system and the regularities underlying their combination. Once these regularities have been established, it must be determined in a subsequent step of the analysis how the writing system in question relates to other levels of the language system, i.e. the lexemic, morphemic and phonological levels. Only when such descriptions, as well as assessments of the relative complexity of writing systems based on them, are available on a wider scale for comparison will it be possible to pursue the question of how different writing systems affect the acquisition and spread of literacy.
See also BILITERACY; FUNCTIONS OF WRITING.
Reading (individual aspects) Levine 1980; Mann 1986; Scribner and Cole 1981; (social aspects) Goody 1977, 1986; Graff 1987; Olson 1994; Street 1984; 1993; Cook-Gumperz 1986; (linguistic aspects) Akinnaso 1982; Biber 1988, Coulmas 1989; Finnegan 1988; Harris 1980; Linell 1982; Tannen 1982.

literal meaning The usual meaning of a word or phrase as opposed to a metaphorical or figurative meaning. It has been argued that, as the term itself suggests, this distinction is a product of literacy or was at least accentuated by its advent. Writing, so the argument goes, not only represents speech but also turns its units into objects of contemplation which can be conceived as having a stable existence with fixed properties. It helps to conceptually distinguish between what a speaker means and what a word means. Writing makes it possible to isolate words, list them independent of any particular message intent, and provide them with a written definition of their meaning, their literal meaning. This literate mode of treating language is epitomized in the monolingual dictionary.
See also FUNCTIONS OF WRITING; LITERACY.
Reading Olson 1977; Harris 1980.

literature Writing makes literature permanent; in the strict sense of the word it makes literature possible. Etymologically 'oral literature' is a contradiction in terms, since 'literature' refers to letters (*litterae*) of the alphabet. While verbal art forms have been cultivated in the absence of writing, there is no question that the conditions for written and oral verbalization are essentially different and that, therefore, working with words for purposes of aesthetic expression is different in spoken and in written language. Writing locks words into a visual field, thus not only adding a dimension of artistic expression but also exposing it to inspection and criticism. While poetry is grounded in oral performance, other literary genres, such as novel or essay, are unthinkable without writing. Furthermore, a cultivated literary language affords its users a vocabulary many times larger than an oral language which lacks the support of a system of permanent recording independent of the individual speaker and even the collectivity of speakers. The question of what linguistic features distinguish literature from oral narrative and

poetry, both historically and synchronically, is the subject of a growing research literature.
See also FUNCTIONS OF WRITING; TEXT.
Reading Havelock 1979; Ong 1982; Baum 1987.

liù shū [Chinese 六書 'six writings'] The traditional classification of Chinese characters into six categories suggested by Xu Shen, the compiler of the *Shuowen jiezi* character dictionary (*c.*100 CE). The six categories are as follows:

1 pictographic characters
2 simple ideographic characters, e.g. a horizontal stroke with a dot on top for 'above'
3 compound ideographic characters whose meaning is a function of their parts, e.g. the character for 'honest' which is composed of the character for 'man' and that for 'word'
4 phonetic loan characters otherwise described as rebus
5 semantic-phonetic compound characters which consist of a RADICAL part which indicates meaning and a phonetic part which indicates sound
6 *chuan chu* or mutually interpretative signs.

The sixth category is not as clearly defined as the other five and is difficult to distinguish from the fifth. Most characters in the sixth category can be described as semantic extensions, i.e. characters which have been used to write a semantically related word and thus have acquired an additional pronunciation. As many as 90 per cent of all Chinese characters are thought to belong to the fifth category.
See also CHINESE WRITING SYSTEM.
Reading Karlgren 1923.

loan words In the history and development of writing, loan words have played an important role in shaping writing systems and conventions. The adoption of a writing for another language often led to an influx of loan words from the donor language into the recipient language which continued to be written as they were in the donor language. For example, many Sumerian words were incorporated into other languages which adopted cuneiform writing, such as Akkadian, Elamite and Hittite. They are known as Sumerograms because their written representation was not altered. Similarly, Chinese loans continued to be written with Chinese characters in Korean and Japanese even after phonetic writing systems had been developed for these languages, giving rise to hybrid systems. Similarly, in the process of adapting the Arabic alphabet to other languages no letters were ever dropped, because the Arabic script served as a channel for the introduction of Arabic loan words which again are usually spelled in the receiving languages as they are spelled in Arabic. Many orthographies thus mark loan words by applying conventions which deviate from the rest of the spelling system. This can also be observed in English. Usually the phoneme /f/ is written <f> but in words of Greek origin, such as *philistine, philosopher* and *phenotype,* /f/ is expressed by <ph>. Sometimes retaining the spelling of another language

for loan words leads to SPELLING PRONUNCIATION, because of the discrepancy between the conventions that guide spelling and pronunciation.
See also XENOGRAPHY.
Reading Coulmas 1989.

logogram [Gk λόγος 'word' + γράμμα 'letter'] (*also* logograph) A written sign which represents a word or morpheme. The term is often used interchangeably with 'ideogram' (IDEOGRAPHY), although the two should be carefully distinguished. Ideograms in the strict sense of the term are non-linguistic symbols which express concepts such as numbers. By contrast, logograms are signs which express units of a language. While the term suggests that only words, i.e. free morphemes, are represented, a somewhat wider interpretation to include bound morphemes is common. Logograms are the basic units of logographic writing systems which use the lexicon as the primary level of representation. Such systems are characterized by a large inventory of elementary signs numbering in the thousands, since the words (or morphemes) of a language are much more numerous than meaningless sounds such as syllables or phonemes. Archaic writing systems were to various degrees logographic, but in fully developed systems the logographic principle is generally supplemented in some measure by phonetic writing. The CHINESE WRITING SYSTEM is often cited as an example of logography, but it is better described as a morphosyllabic system. Logograms are also sometimes interspersed in basically phonetic writing, for example ©, ¥, $, %.
Reading Chao 1968; Coulmas 1989; DeFrancis 1989.

logograph *See* LOGOGRAM

Lolo writing *See* YI WRITING

Loma syllabary Devised in the 1930s by Wido Zobo of Boneketa, Liberia, the Loma script spread to some extent among the Loma in the following decades, but it was largely limited to personal correspondence and is no longer used. The system is a syllabary consisting of some 185 freely invented signs of the CV type (table 13). The direction of writing is from left to right.
Reading Dalby 1967.

Lycian alphabet An Indo-European language spoken in south-western Anatolia, Lycian is thought to be descended from Luwian, the language of HITTITE HIEROGLYPHIC. It is attested in inscriptions on tombstones as well as on coins dating from the eighth to the third centuries BCE. Some Greek-Lycian bilingual inscriptions have facilitated the decipherment, although they seem to be parallel only in sense rather than word for word. The script is derived from an early form of the western Greek alphabet, perhaps through contacts on the island of Ródhos, a western Greek colony. However, 12 of the 29 letters cannot be identified with Greek letters (table 14). The sound values of some remain uncertain. A connection with CYPRIOTE WRITING has been suggested to explain their origin, but so far there is no archaeological evidence to confirm this hypothesis.
Reading Neumann 1969.

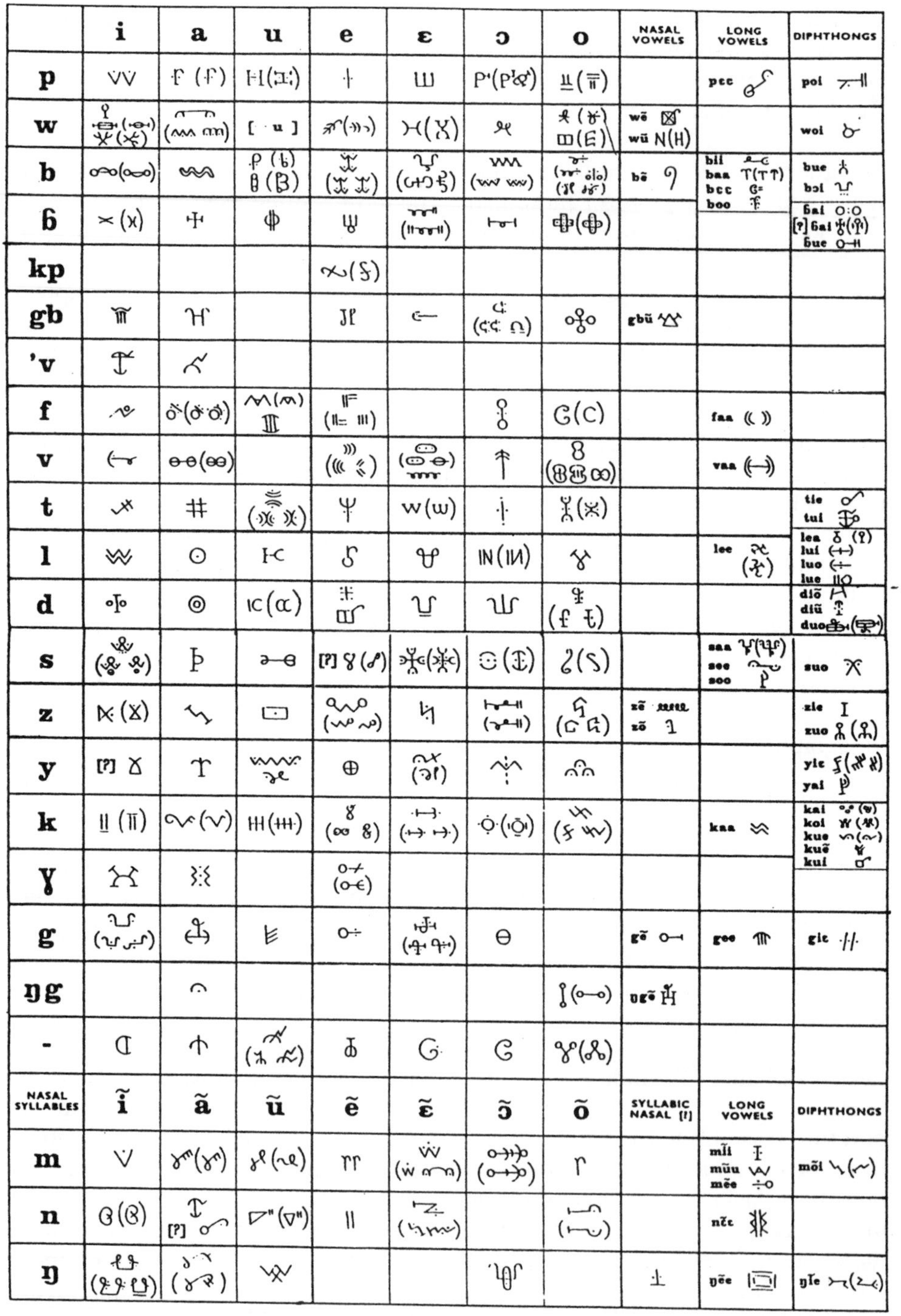

	i	a	u	e	ɛ	ɔ	o	NASAL VOWELS	LONG VOWELS	DIPHTHONGS
p									pɛɛ	poi
w			[u]					wẽ wũ		woi
b								bẽ	bii baa bɛɛ boo	bue bɔi
ɓ										ɓai [?] ɓai ɓue
kp										
gb								gbũ		
'v										
f									faa	
v									vaa	
t										tie tui
l									lee	lea lui luo lue
d										diõ diũ duo
s				[?]					saa see soo	suo
z								zẽ zõ		zie zuo
y	[?]									yie yai
k									kaa	kai koi kue kuẽ kui
ɣ										
g								gẽ	gee	gie
ŋg								ŋgẽ		
-										
NASAL SYLLABLES	**ĩ**	**ã**	**ũ**	**ẽ**	**ɛ̃**	**ɔ̃**	**õ**	SYLLABIC NASAL [ŋ]	LONG VOWELS	DIPHTHONGS
m									mĩi mũu mẽe	mõi
n		[?]							nɛ̃ɛ	
ŋ									ŋẽe	ŋĩe

Table 13 The Loma syllabary
Source: *Dalby 1967*

Greek		Lydian		Lycian	
A	*a*	A	*a*	P	*a*
				↑	*e*
B	*b*	8	*b*	B b	*b*
				ʌʌ	*β*
ʌ Γ	*g*			ΥΥV	*g*
Λ	*d*	⅄	*d*	Λ	*d*
Ε E	*e*	⋁	*e*	E	*i*
F	*v*	⅄	*v*	F	*w*
I	*z*	ǂ	*s*	I	*z*
⊙	*th*			X	*ϑ*
I	*i*	I	*i*	I	*j*
K	*k*	Ж K	*k*	K	*c*
				Ж	*q*
Λ L	*l*	1 1	*l*	Λ	*l*
M	*m*	M	*m*	M	*m*
N	*n*	N	*n*	N	*n*
				X	*m̃*
		Ξ	*τ (ñ?)*	Ξ	*ñ*
O	*o*	o	*o*	O	*u*
Γ	*p*			Γ	*p*
				◇	*x*
P	*r*	q	*r*	P	*r*
ξ ϟ	*s*	3 ξ	*ś*	ʃ ϟ	*s*
T	*t*	T	*t*	T	*t*
		Ϯ	*λ*	Ϯ	
				ΨΥΨΨ	*ĩ*
		Ψ	*ē*	ΨΨΨ	*ã*
		+	*p (h?)*	+ X	*ẽ*
Ψ Ψ	*kh*			ΨΥΥ	*h*
		a	*? (ə?)*		
		8	*f*		
		M	*ã*		
		ʔ	*v*		
ΥΥV	*u*	Y	*u*		
		↑	*? (q?)*		
		Ⴈ	*? (g?)*		

Table 14 The Lydian and Lycian alphabets and the western Greek alphabet from which they are derived

Lydian alphabet An Indo-European language of the Old Anatolian branch spoken at the western coast of Asia Minor before the spread of the Greek koine, Lydian is attested in inscriptions from Sardis, dating from the seventh to the third centuries BCE. Little is known about the language, although a Lydian–Aramaic bilinguis has helped to render some of the documents interpretable. The script is derived from an early form of the Greek alphabet. More than half of the 26 letters can be identified with Greek letters, but the remainder are of unknown origin, and the sound value of some is uncertain (table 14). The majority of the known inscriptions run from right to left.
Reading Heubeck 1969.

M

M, m /em/ The thirteenth letter of the English alphabet developed from Semitic *mēm* and Greek *mu* (M, μ).

macron [Gk μακρόν 'long'] A diacritic consisting of a horizontal bar <¯> placed over a letter. Its principal usage is to mark a V as long, as in Lat. *hērēditās* 'heritage'. IPA recommendation is as a transcription for a high-level tone. The Chinese PINYIN orthography has adopted this usage. In romanized transcriptions of Indo-Aryan languages it is also occasionally used as a C superscript to indicate palatal articulation, as in [r̄], [s̄] for palatalized [r], [s].

Madurese script A variety of the Kawi-derived JAVANESE WRITING.

maghribī script A calligraphic style of the Arabic script developed in twelfth-century Libya. The only cursive script developed from the *KŪFĪC* SCRIPT, its use was reserved for manuscripts. It is the most geographically limited of Muslim scripts, never extending beyond the Maghrib (Morocco, Algeria and Tunisia).

Maithilī script A variety of the Bengālī script used by Bihārī Brahmins in northern India. It is also known as Tiruṭe and belongs to the northern group of Indian syllabic alphabets.
See also BENGĀLĪ WRITING; INDIAN WRITING SYSTEMS.

majuscule [Lat. *mājuscula* (*littera*) 'larger letter'] Collective term for all alphabetic letters of the two-line system which are contained within a pair of parallel horizontal lines, all being of equal height; also called 'capital' or 'upper case letters' (figure 1). A contrast between majuscule and MINUSCULE did not originally exist. Both the Greek and Latin alphabets were initially written in majuscules only. The combined use of majuscules and minuscules which was introduced as part of the CAROLINGIAN REFORM is called 'dual alphabet'. The graphic perfection of Roman majuscules was achieved in imperial Rome in lapidary styles such as *capitalis quadrata* and *capitalis rustica* (figure 2).
Reading Morison 1949.

Figure 1 The two-line system: majuscules (Greek capital)

Makasarese script A syllabic alphabet of the Indian type which came into use in Sumatra in the seventeenth century. It is closely related to the BUGIS SCRIPT. Both are thought to derive from a common source which was a variant of the KAWI

IDALIAELVCOS'VBIM
FLORIBVS'ETDVLCIAD
IAMQ·IBATDICTOPAR

Idaliae lucos ubi m[ollis]
Floribus et dulci ad
Iamque ibat dicto parens

Figure 2 Specimen of majuscule writing in Latin: Virgil, fourth century CE

SCRIPT. There is a great deal of variation in both Bugis and Makasarese writing, but there are also some systematic differences reflecting differences in the sound systems of the two languages. For example, Buginese but not Makasarese has phonemic *shwa*. Consequently, Makasarese has no need for the V diacritic for *shwa*. Where it occurs in Makasarese texts, it indicates a final nasal. In addition to Makasarese and Buginese, the script has been used occasionally for some other languages such as Bimanese and Sumbawa of Sumbawa Island and Ende of the Lesser Sundas. It is no longer in use for any language.

A conspicuous feature of the script is the similarity of many of its graphemes, which makes it hard to read. Several pairs of characters, such as those for *na* and *ta*, *ma* and *da*, *pa* and *ga*, are distinguished by a single dot. Structurally, the system works like other Indian-derived scripts: the 19 basic C graphemes (table 1) have an inherent *a* and are modified with diacritic satellites for other V values.

The Makasarese had no written numerals of their own and hence used the common Arabic numerals. Figure 3 shows article 16 of the Bungaya treaty (1667) beginning with the numeral *'16'*. Where the end of the article is marked off, the next one begins with *'17'*.

Reading Matthes 1858; Noorduyn 1992.

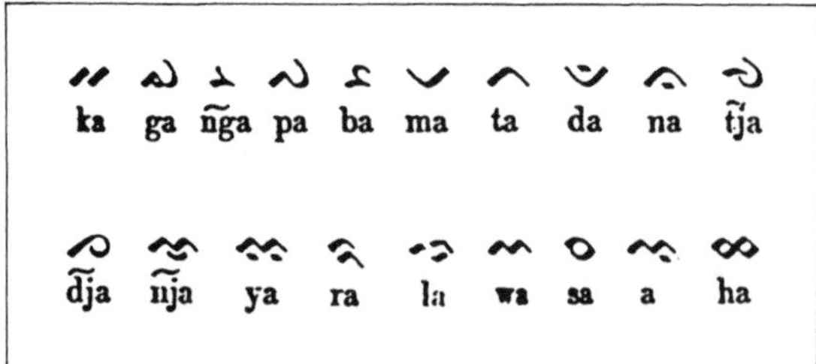

Table 1 The basic consonant letters of the Makasarese script

Malay writing The literary history of Malay begins with heavily Sanskritized inscriptions in the south Indian PALLAVA SCRIPT dating from the seventh century CE. In the Srivijaya Empire (seventh to fourteenth centuries) the Malay language was used in Devanāgarī script for official purposes. Malay inscriptions in Devanāgarī are found on Sumatra, Java and the Malay Peninsula. With the decline

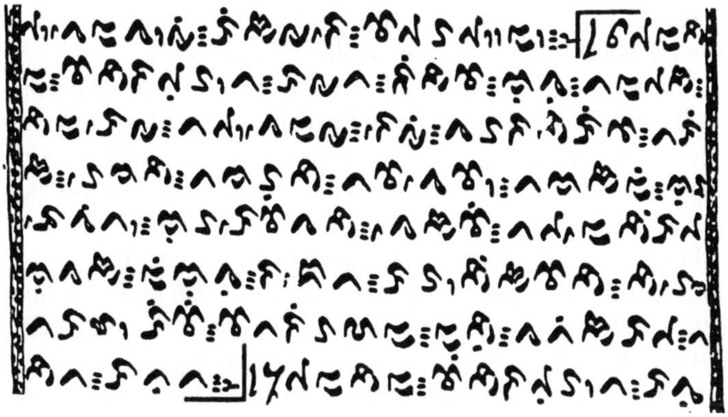

Transliteration

=16= paraka
ra/makasapulona/angana/sikama/butu/narapaya
karaenga/napoteranga/sengi/talasakaija/nai
ya/lebaka/nabaluka/namatemo/nabayari/bula
etino/bulaemataka/teyami/naparekiapa
butaya/ributu/sagena/alokiyamaka/kaleba
naadoimi/manasilawara/ruku/taniyaapa/na
kana/anuna

Transliteration

Article 16.

All people of Buton who were stolen by the King and are still alive must be returned by him, and those who died after being sold must be paid for in pure gold or silver, for he shall no longer make anything of the country of Buton until Doomsday, for after he agrees not even a blade of grass shall he call his own property.

Figure 3 Makasarese text of Bungaya treaty (1667), article 16 (transliteration and translation courtesy J. Noorduyn, Leiden)

from power of Srivijaya and the spread of Islam, Malay ceased to be written in Devanāgarī which was replaced by the Arabic script, called *Jawi* in Malay. Islamic Malay literature reached its peak in the manuscripts written during the fifteenth century at the courts of Riau and Johore, successors of the Sultanate of Malaka. In colonial times Malay was used by parts of the autochthonous populations of the Malay Peninsula and the East Indies, by Chinese traders and residents, as well as by Dutch administrators of the VOC (United East India Company) and British colonial officers, being written, as circumstances required,

in Javanese, Arabic or Latin script. The variety of the Malay lingua franca written in Latin script was called Pasar Maleis (Bazaar Malay) by colonial Dutchmen who, together with their British counterparts, did much to help the Latin alphabet gain ground, although two distinct conventions for using it developed under the influence of the Dutch and English spelling systems. From the beginning of the twentieth century, Bazaar Malay, which was considered too vulgar for official purposes, was replaced in government publications by an archaizing variety based on Riau-Johore Malay. The alphabetic script, however, was retained, and in 1972 a standardized and unified orthography was adopted for Bahasa Malaysia and Bahasa Indonesia, as the language is now called in Malaysia and Indonesia, respectively (table 2). The Arabic script has not been completely replaced by the Latin alphabet. In Malaysia it continues to be used for some publications in Malay. The 28 letters of the Arabic alphabet are supplemented by five additional ones: چ /č/, ڠ /ŋ/, ڤ /p/, ݢ /g/ and ڽ /ñ/.
See also INDONESIAN ALPHABET.
Reading Alisjahbana 1984; Lewis 1958.

Consonants	Digraphs	Vowels
<p> [p]	<ny> [ɲ]	<i> [i/I]
<b> [b]	<ng> [ŋ]	<e> [e/ɛ]
<t> [t]	<th> [θ]	<a> [a/ɜ]
<d> [d]	<dz> [ð]	<o> [o/ɔ]
<k> [k]	<sh> [ʃ]	<u> [u/v]
<k>* [ʔ]	<ch> [tʃ]	<ə> [ə]
<g> [g]	<ir> [I]	
<s> [s]	<or> [ɔ]	
<z> [z]	<ar> [a]	
<r> [r/ʁ]		
<l> [l]		
<m> [m]		
<n> [n]		
<h> [h/ħ]		
<j> [dʒ]		
<y> [j]		
<w> [w]		

*Final

Table 2 Grapheme–phoneme correspondence in Malay

Malayalam script A major member of the group of southern Indian scripts, the Malayalam system evolved in the eighth century CE out of the GRANTHA SCRIPT which in turn has its origin in the southern variety of Brāhmī. It is used primarily in Kerala for the Malayalam language, but also for some other languages such as neighbouring Konkani. Following the common Indian pattern, it is a syllabic alphabet consisting of independent V graphemes and C graphemes with inherent *a*, other Vs being expressed by diacritic satellites placed around the basic C graphs (table 3). Graphically, Malayalam is one of the more complex systems with contextually conditioned alternating letter shapes and many complex ligatures. For example, in pre-consonantal position the graph for *r*(*a*) is reduced to a superscript dot. Geminate Cs are written as ligatures, some horizontal, some vertical. The V muting *virāma* is a circle open at the top which is placed on the right shoulder of the C graph, but some Cs take a different mark. A circle placed to the right of a grapheme indicates nasalization, and two such circles placed above one another in the same position a glottal stop. Malayalam is written from left to right on horizontal lines.

Reading Meenakshisundaran 1966; Masica 1991.

a	അ	o	ഒ	ṭa	ട	bha	ഭ
ā	ആ	ō	ഓ	ṭha	ഠ	ma	മ
i	ഇ	au	ഔ	ḍa	ഡ	ya	യ
ī	ഈ	ka	ക	ḍha	ഢ	ra	ര
u	ഉ	kha	ഖ	ṇa	ണ	ra	ഴ
ū	ഊ	ga	ഗ	ta	ത	la	ല
ṛ	ഋ	gha	ഘ	tha	ഥ	la	ള
ṝ	ൠ	ña	ങ	da	ദ	va	വ
ḷ	ഌ	ča	ച	dha	ധ	śa	ശ
ḹ	ൡ	ča	ഛ	na	ന	ṣa	ഷ
e	എ	ǰa	ജ	pa	പ	sa	സ
ē	ഏ	ǰha	ഝ	pha	ഫ	ha	ഹ
ai	ഐ	ña	ഞ	ba	ബ	dʼa	ം

Vowel diacritics

□ാ	□ി	□ീ	□ു	□ൂ	□ൃ
ā	i	ī	u	ū	ru

െ□	േ□	ൈ□	െ□ാ	േ□ാ	െ□ൗ
e	ē	ai	o	ō	au

Table 3 The Malayalam syllabic alphabet

Maldivian script Not to be confused with the Old Maldivian script, a twelfth-century CE descendant of the Singhalese script known as DIVEHI HAKURA, the Maldivian script proper was created in the seventeenth century CE by an unknown inventor under the influence of the Arabic script. Like Arabic this script, which is called *Tana* or *Thaana*, is written from right to left. Arabic influence is apparent in the diacritic mode of V indication, although the Indian concept of C graphemes with inherent *a* is also in evidence. C graphemes are always written with V diacritics (table 4) or the V muting mark (a small circle placed above the C graph). The grapheme–phoneme correspondence of the system is quite efficient.

ka ކަ ki ކި ku ކު ke ކެ ko ކޮ

kā ކާ kī ކީ kū ކޫ kē ކޭ kō ކޯ

Table 4 Maldivian vowel diacritics for k-

Some of the letters of the alphabet are derived with certain modifications and simplifications from those of the *Divehi hakura*, but for the first nine letters, *h–w*, completely new forms were introduced (table 5). They resemble the Arabic numbers from *1* to *9* in the *nastaʿlīq* style. What motivated the adaptation of Arabic numerals as letters is not entirely clear. However, that the Arabic *9* was chosen as the letter for *w* is readily explained by the fact that *w* is the ninth letter of the Maldivian alphabet. This coincidence may have been the beginning of using Arabic numerals in this way.

Reading De Silva 1969.

ހ	ށ	ނ	ރ	ބ	ޅ	ކ	އ	ވ	މ	ފ	ދ
h	ś	n	r	b	ḷ	k	ɔ	w	m	f	d

ތ	ލ	ގ	ޏ	ސ	ޑ	ޒ	ޓ	ޔ	ޕ	ޖ	ޗ
t	l	g	ñ	s	ḍ	z	ṭ	y	p	j	c

١	٢	٣	٤	٥	٦	٧	٨	٩
1	2	3	4	5	6	7	8	9

*Table 5 The Maldivian alphabet (*Tana*) and the Arabic numbers from 1 to 9*

Maltese A Semitic language, Maltese is the only form of Arabic to be written in the Roman alphabet. The Christian population of the island of Malta has used Maltese Arabic in writing since the seventeenth century. Geographic proximity with Italy and cultural and political links with the European continent have led

to intensive language contact with European languages. In contradistinction to other forms of Arabic, Maltese is not in a Diglossia relationship with classical Arabic, but has evolved into an independent written language (figure 4). The Maltese alphabet makes use of an overdot and a crossbar as diacritics: <ħ> for a voiceless pharyngeal fricative; <għ> to lengthen the preceding V; <q> for the glottal stop; <ċ> for [č]; <ġ> for [ʒ]; <x> for [ʃ]; and <ż> for [z], contrasting with <z> for [ts].
Reading Aquilina 1959.

Il-Maltin jitkellmu lingwa antika ħafna li hi ta' nteress kbir għallingwisti.

Bażikament Semetika, maż-żmien assimilat għadd kbir ta' kliem rumanz, sakemm

illum hi tirrapreżanta l-għaqda ta' żewġ friegħi lingwistiċi.

Translation

The Maltese speak a very ancient language which is of great interest to linguists.

Though of Semitic stock, it has over the years assimilated a great number of

Romance words, and as a result represents a blending of two language families.

Figure 4 Maltese sample sentence

Manchu script An achievement of Nurhachi (1559–1626), uniter of the Jurchen tribes and founder of the Manchu state, the Manchu script was derived from the Uighur-Mongol script on his orders in 1599. In 1632 it was slightly modified. The Manchu script became an important medium of written communication in the wake of the Manchu conquest of China. As the language of the rulers of the Ch'ing empire (1636–1911), Manchu served as an administrative language and lingua franca for some 200 years. The early Ch'ing regime was bilingual, using both Chinese and Manchu. However, the Manchus eventually learned Chinese, many of them adopting it as their first language, thus indirectly acknowledging the superiority of Chinese culture. Nevertheless, they continued to translate Chinese documents into Manchu until the end of the dynasty and written Manchu was even used for a couple of decades thereafter. Today the language shift of the Manchus is all but complete, most members of China's Manchu nationality being monolingual speakers of Chinese (figure 5).

Like all scripts derived from Mongolian, e.g. Kalmyk writing, the Manchu script is written in vertical columns shifting from left to right. The graphemes have three different forms for initial, middle and final positions (table 6). As independent letters they are written with a rightward slanting base line or a left trailing curved descender. The graphemes for *dz, ts, tšh, dž, džh, ǵ, ḱh* and *s* were added to the Mongolian alphabet better to represent the many Chinese loan words.
Reading Möllendorff 1892.

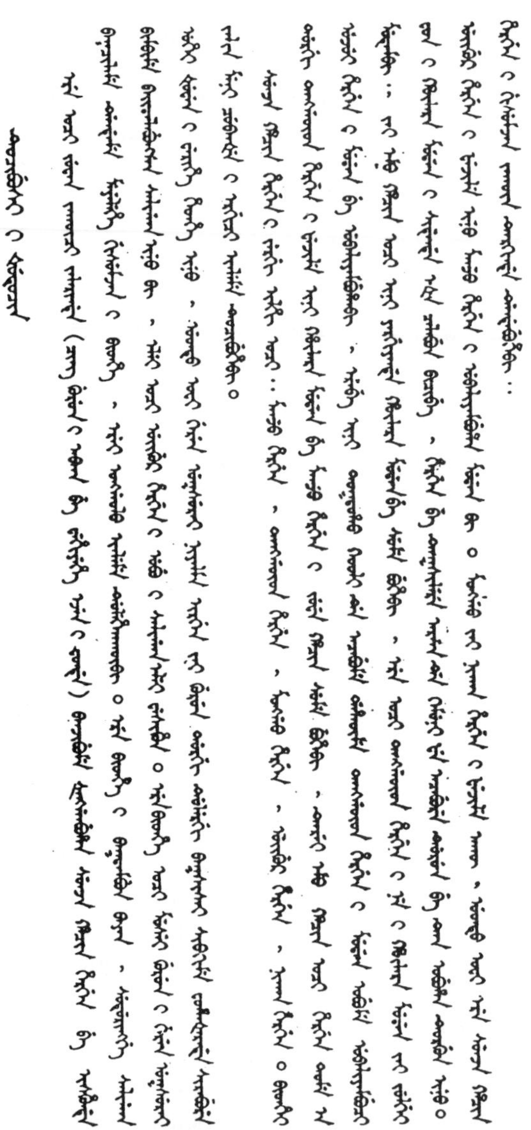

Figure 5 Preface and first page of quintolingual Manchu dictionary.

Mandean script A late Semitic script derived from the Aramaic. It was developed in the region of Basra at the Shatt al-Arab in the seventh century CE by the Mandeans, a Christian sect speaking a variety of Aramaic (table 7). The distinctive feature of the Mandean script is its developed mode of indicating Vs by means of MATRES LECTIONIS. The letters for ', *w*, *j* and ʒ are used to express both long and short Vs, rather than only long Vs as is usual in *plene* writing with *matres lectionis* in other Semitic scripts (table 8). In this sense, *matres lectionis* can be said to have evolved into V letters in the Mandean script.
Reading Nöldeke 1875.

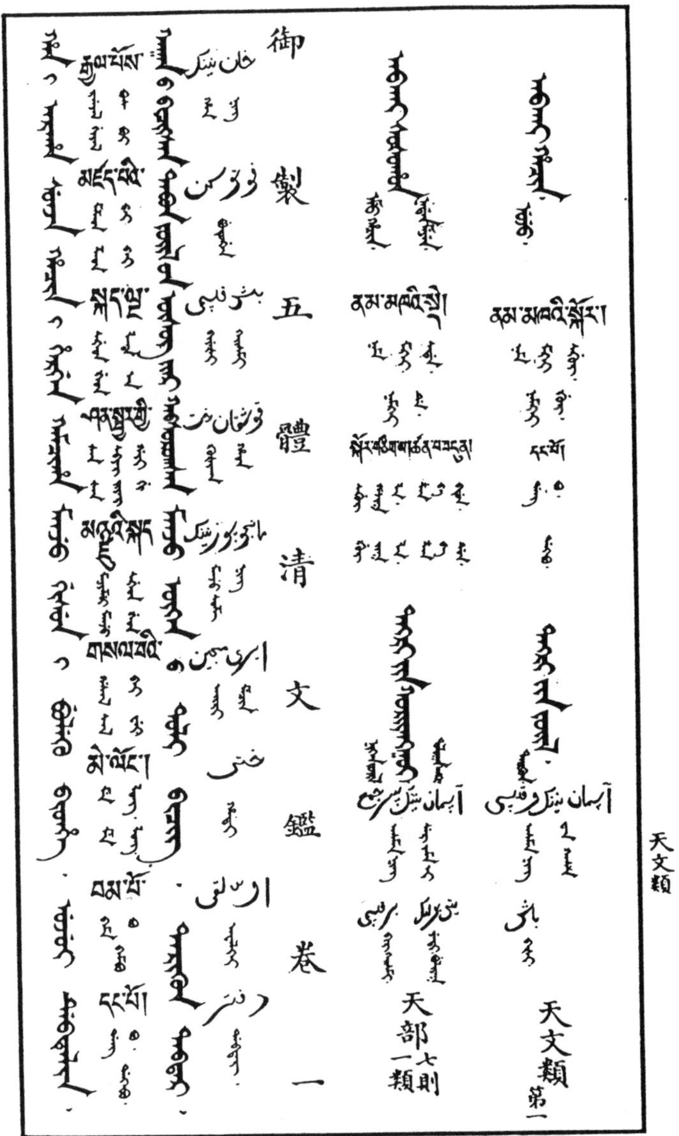

Figure 6 Languages from left to right: Manchu, Tibetan (written horizontally), Mongolian, Uighur (in Arabic script) and Chinese

Mangyan script A syllabic alphabet of the Indic type used by the Mangyans on the island of Mindoro, Philippines. Little is known about the origin of this script, because there are no epigraphic inscriptions on climate resistant surfaces like stone or metal, and the oldest document is from the nineteenth century. It is assumed that the Mangyan script is derived from the KAWI SCRIPT and was introduced to Mindoro by migrant Mangyans from Indonesia. Two varieties are distinguished, those of the Buhid Mangyans and the Hanunoo Mangyans. Table 9 presents the Hanunoo variety.

Independent	Initial	Medial	Final	Value	Independent	Initial	Medial	Final	Value
[illegible]	[illegible]	[illegible]	[illegible]	a	[illegible]	[illegible]	[illegible]		s
[illegible]	[illegible]	[illegible]	[illegible]	e	[illegible]	[illegible]	[illegible]	[illegible]	dz
[illegible]	[illegible]	[illegible]	[illegible]	i	[illegible]	[illegible]	[illegible]		ts
[illegible]	[illegible]	[illegible]	[illegible]	o	[illegible]	[illegible]	[illegible]	[illegible]	š
[illegible]	[illegible]	[illegible]	[illegible]	u	[illegible]	[illegible]			ž
[illegible]	[illegible]	[illegible]	[illegible]	ū	[illegible]	[illegible]	[illegible]	[illegible]	ṯ
[illegible]	[illegible]	[illegible]	[illegible]	ã	[illegible]	[illegible]	[illegible]		ḏ
[illegible]	[illegible]	[illegible]	[illegible]	n	[illegible]	[illegible]	[illegible]		t
[illegible]	[illegible]	[illegible]	[illegible]	k	[illegible]	[illegible]	[illegible]		d
[illegible]	[illegible]	[illegible]		g	[illegible]	[illegible]	[illegible]		tš
[illegible]	[illegible]	[illegible]		χ	[illegible]	[illegible]			tšh
[illegible]	[illegible]	[illegible]		ḱ	[illegible]	[illegible]	[illegible]		dž
[illegible]	[illegible]	[illegible]	[illegible]	ǵ	[illegible]	[illegible]			džh
[illegible]	[illegible]	[illegible]		χ́	[illegible]	[illegible]	[illegible]	[illegible]	l
[illegible]	[illegible]			ḱh	[illegible]	[illegible]	[illegible]	[illegible]	r
[illegible]	[illegible]			ǵh	[illegible]	[illegible]	[illegible]	[illegible]	m
	[illegible]			χ́h	[illegible]	[illegible]	[illegible]		y
[illegible]	[illegible]	[illegible]	[illegible]	b	[illegible]	[illegible]	[illegible]		v
[illegible]	[illegible]	[illegible]		p	[illegible]	[illegible]	[illegible]		f

Table 6 The Manchu alphabet

The V indication follows the general Indian pattern, although in a very simple form of just two diacritics, called *kulit* in Mangyan. The basic C graphemes have an inherent V *a*. For *i* and *e* a horizontal line is placed over the C graph, and a similar line is placed under the C graph for *u/o*. The script has no V muting sign, and hence only open syllables can be expressed. The script is therefore easy to write, but sometimes difficult to read. For example, both *magtepad* 'explicitly' and *matapang* 'harshly' are written *ma-ta-pa*, the disambiguation being left to contextual clues. Written as equidistant syllables without spacing between words, the direction of the script is different for writing and reading. Writing with a sharp pen or knife on bamboo is 'away from the body', that is, from bottom to top, while reading is from left to right, the result of turning the inscribed plate 90 degrees to the right (figure 6). Unlike other Philippine scripts which were abandoned during colonial times, the Mangyan script is reportedly still in use.

Reading Postma 1971; Miyamoto 1985.

Isolated form	Compound form	Value
ࡀ	ࡀ ࡀ	a/'
ࡁ	ࡁ ࡁ	b
ࡂ	ࡂ ࡂ	g
ࡃ	ࡃ	d
ࡄ	ࡄ	h, χ
ࡅ	ࡅ	w
ࡆ	ࡆ	z
ࡇ	ࡇ	ṯ
ࡉ	ࡉ	j
ࡊ	ࡊ	k
ࡋ	ࡋ	l
ࡌ	ࡌ	m
ࡍ	ࡍ	n
ࡎ ࡎ	ࡎ ࡎ	s
ࡏ ࡏ	ࡏ ࡏ	ʒ
ࡐ	ࡐ	f
ࡑ	ࡑ	ṣ
ࡒ	ࡒ	q
ࡓ	ࡓ	r
ࡔ ࡔ	ࡔ ࡔ	š
ࡕ	ࡕ	t

Table 7 The Mandean alphabet

Grapheme	Phoneme
'	a, ā
w	o,ō/u,ū
j	i,e
ʒ	ī,ē

Table 8 Mandean vowel indication

a	i	u
ba	bi	bu
ka	ki	ku
da	di	du
ga	gi	gu
ha	hi	hu
la	li	lu
ma	mi	mu
na	ni	nu
nga	ngi	ngu
pa	pi	pu
ra	ri	ru
sa	si	su
ta	ti	tu
wa	wi	wu
ya	yi	yu

Table 9 The Mangyan syllabic alphabet

Manichaean script Derived from a cursive form of the Aramaic script, the Manichaean alphabet came into existence in the third century CE as the script of the syncretistic Manichaean sect. It was used to record both Middle Persian and the east Turkic language of Central Asia where the Manichaeans settled after their expulsion from Persia. The 23-letter alphabet provides for complete V indication on the basis of regular Semitic *plene* writing, using the C letters with V values: ʾ(ʾ*āleph*) for /a/ and /ä/, *j* for /i/, *w* for /u/, and the digraph *wj* for /ö/ and /ü/ (table 10).
Reading Henning 1958; Jensen 1969.

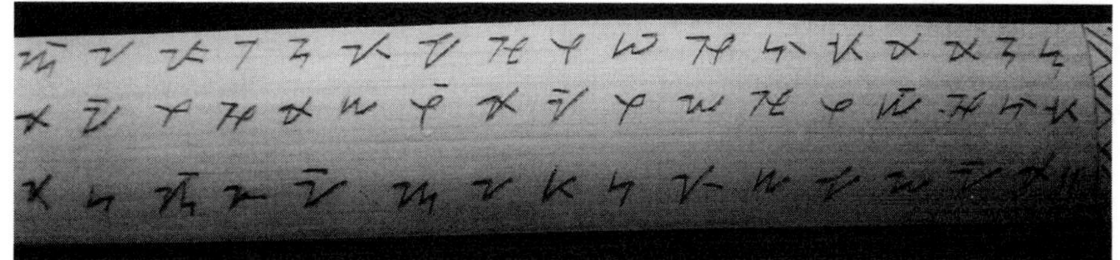

si ay- pod bay u- pa- dan no kang ti- na- gin- du- man may u- lang ma- di kang- nan may ta- kip ma- di kay- wan no kang ti- na- na- gin- du- man ga si- yon di sa ad- ngan ga pag- tang-da yon di-man

You, my friend, dearest of all, thinking of you makes me sad; rivers deep are in between, forests vast keep us apart. But thinking of you with love: as if you were here nearby, standing, sitting at my side.

Figure 6 Mangyan poem engraved in bamboo, with transliteration and translation
Source: *Postma 1972*

	ʼa		m
	b		n
	g		s
	d		e
	h		p
	w		f
	z		q
	ž		r
	ṭ		š
	j		t
	k		č
	l		

Table 10 The Manichaean alphabet
Source: *Jensen 1969*

Manipurī script Derived in the seventeenth century from the Bengālī script for writing the Meithei language of Manipur and Burma (modern Myanmar) (table 11). It is no longer in use, having been replaced by the Bengālī script.
See also INDIAN WRITING SYSTEMS.
Reading Jensen 1969.

Consonant letters

ka	kha	ga	gha	ṅa	ča	čha	ğa	ğha
ña	ṭa	ṭha	ḍa	ḍha	ṇa	ta	tha	da
dha	na	pa	pha	ba	bha	ma	ya	ra
la	va	śa	ṣa	sa	ha			

Vowel diacritics **Independent vowel letter**

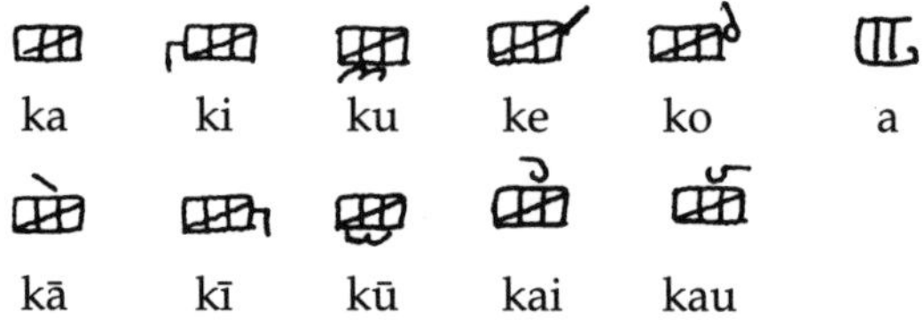

Table 11 The Manipurī syllabic alphabet

manuscript [Lat. (*libri*) *manu scripti* '(books) written by hand'] In occidental history this term refers to books produced by scribes prior to the introduction of printing, in the form of parchment or papyrus rolls and codices, that is, wax tablets held together with rings and, later, folded parchment sheets. It is chiefly in handwritten books that the history and literature of antiquity has come down to us (figure 7). In addition to inscriptions on other materials such as wood, stone and metal, manuscripts provide the most crucial material for the study of writing and the history of culture. The investigation of ancient and medieval manuscripts is the proper field of PALAEOGRAPHY. EPIGRAPHY, the study of inscriptions, diplomatics, the study of administrative and legal documents, and graphology, the study of (individual) handwriting, are related fields.
See also WRITING SURFACE; WRITING TOOLS.
Reading Febvre and Martin 1958; *Genesis*.

Sicut locutus est per os sco-
rum: qui a seculo sunt prophe-
tarum eius.
Salutem ex inimicis nris
et de manu omnium qui o-
derunt nos.
Ad faciendam miam cu
patribus nostris: et memora-
ri testamenti sui sancti.
Iusiurandum quod iu-
ravit ad abraham patrem
nrm daturum se nobis.
Ut sine timore de manu i-
nimicorum nrorum liberati
serviamus illi.

Figure 7 Page from a French manuscript book of hours, in Latin, mid fifteenth century

manyōgana Chinese characters used as phonograms to write the Japanese language. The name refers to the *Manyōshū*, an anthology of Japanese poems of the eighth century CE. Graphically *manyōgana* look like Chinese characters, but functionally they are different, representing syllables rather than morpheme-syllable units. They thus embody the initial stage of the Japanese *kana* syllabaries.
See also KANA.

Marāṭhī writing *See* MOḌISCRIPT

Maschtọtz *See* MESRỌP

mātrās The modifying vowel signs which are added as diacritic satellites to basic consonant graphemes in Indic scripts (table 12).
See also INDIAN WRITING SYSTEMS.

	Devanāgarī	Bengālī	Oṛiyā
kā	का	কা	କା
ki	कि	কি	କି
kī	की	কী	କୀ
ku	कु	কু	କୁ
kū	कू	কূ	କୂ
kr	कृ	কৃ	କୃ
kē	के	কে	କେ
kai	कै	কৈ	କୈ
kō	को	কো	କୋ
kau	कौ	কৌ	କୌ

Table 12 Mātrās *in three Indian scripts, exemplified with* ka

matres lectionis [Lat. *māter* 'mother' and *lēctio* 'reading', 'mothers of reading'] Reading aids in Semitic consonants scripts which have no graphemes for Vs. In certain texts it was found desirable to indicate Vs in order to ensure accurate pronunciation. To this end a convention developed of using certain C letters with vocalic values. These are called *matres lectionis*. The practice of using C letters as *matres lectionis* has been explained as a result of sound changes in Phoenician and other north-west Semitic languages. Certain final Vs were dropped. For example, the form /'abija/ 'of my father' was reduced to /'abij/. Before the reduction it was written as *'bj*. After the reduction its pronunciation merged with that of /'abī/ 'my father'. Now the *yōdh* <j> could conveniently be taken to represent the long final V of /'abī/. In this way a 'weak' C sign came to express a long V. By analogy, *wāw* <w> acquired a secondary function as a *mater lectionis* for /ū/ and subsequently also for /ō/ and /u/. *'Aššūr* 'Assyria', formerly written *'-š-r*,

was spelt *'s-w-r* with the *w* as a mater lectionis indicating that the V of the final syllable was /ū/. The C letters *hē* and *'āleph* were similarly employed for /ō/ and /ā/. This kind of writing is known as *plene* or 'full' writing as opposed to 'defective' writing, i.e. writing without Vs. *Plene* spelling is a precursor of full V indication in alphabetic writing, although it is not clear exactly how the Semitic *matres lectionis* influenced the formation of V letters in the GREEK ALPHABET. Initially only long Vs were expressed in *plene* writing, but in late Semitic scripts such as the MANDEAN SCRIPT *matres lectionis* were used for short Vs as well. In these systems they thus developed into fully fledged V letters.
See also BABYLONIAN POINTING; CONSONANT SCRIPT.
Reading Gelb 1963.

Maya writing The script of the Maya civilization of Central America (500 BCE to 1200 CE, with a classical period from 300 CE to 900 CE), Maya writing is a logosyllabic system combining logograms and syllable signs in a complex way with a great deal of POLYVALENCE. Because of its vivid graphical appearance the writing is often called 'hieroglyphic', in analogy to the EGYPTIAN SCRIPT. It is documented in many monuments such as stone stelae, lintels, altars and the like (figure 8), as well as on bark, wood, jade, ceramics and a few manuscripts, especially the Dresden, Paris and Madrid codices, so called after the cities where they came to be kept. Maya inscriptions have been found in southern Mexico, notably on the Yucatán peninsula, in Guatemala and in northern Belize, the oldest documents having been dated 200–100 BCE. The Maya script is the last of the independently created writing systems to be deciphered. Until recently, Maya civilization has been interpreted entirely from archaeological evidence, because Maya writing could not be read. Many Mayanists, epigraphers and other students of writing even doubted that the Maya glyphs were writing proper rather than a limited system of pictorial symbols.

The first report on Maya writing to reach the Old World was Bishop Diego de Landa's *Relación de las cosas de Yucatán* (*Account of the Affairs of Yucatán*), written in Spain around 1566. His assignment of alphabetic letters to 27 Maya glyphs which came to be known as the LANDA ALPHABET was based on the misconception that Maya writing was alphabetic. While this was a false premise, Landa pointed in the right direction in assuming that the Maya glyphs represented Maya speech sounds. Strangely, the obvious consequence of this assumption – to study Maya languages in order to be able to decipher the writing – was not seriously considered until the second half of the twentieth century (excepting a courageous but unsuccessful attempt by American linguist B. L. Whorf in the 1930s). The chief fault of early work on Maya was that no attempts were made to interpret the glyphs as a representation of language. Most of the scholars involved were trained as archaeologists and had no knowledge of any Maya language or linguistic methods which could be employed in establishing a link between language and writing.

It is now generally accepted that the writing evolved in the context of Cholan, the language of many of the monuments, and was later adopted by speakers of Yucatecan, the language of the codices. Both belong to the Cholan-Tzeltalan family of languages and are still spoken today, yielding valuable clues for the

Figure 8 Maya hieroglyphs on a lintel: blood offering among the Maya in Yaxchilan, Chiapas, southern Mexico, probably 781 CE (lintel 24, house G) (by permission of the British Museum)

interpretation of Maya texts. The main credit for advancing the cause of a linguistic approach to the decipherment of Maya belongs to Yuri Valentinovich Knorosov (1922–), a Russian ethnologist who in the early 1950s first proposed with specific examples that Maya writing was phonetic, representing Yucatec Mayan. His work met much resistance among his professional colleagues in the West, but he was eventually vindicated. During the 1970s and 1980s, as more linguists developed an active interest in Maya writing, the decipherment made dramatic progress, and now most Maya documents can be read with confidence. From the Mayas' sophisticated calendrical system which was understood long ago it has been clear that theirs was a highly history-conscious culture. The decipherment of their writing confirmed that they recorded just those things one would expect a literate civilization to register for posterity. Inscriptions could be shown to deal with birth, marriage, accession and death of rulers, royal deeds, concerns of warfare, and similar matters.

The writing system consists of multifunctional glyphs serving as both logograms and syllabic signs, the latter having acquired their phonetic values on the basis of the REBUS PRINCIPLE. Polyvalence is a prevalent feature of the writing, with both homophony (several graphemes for one reading) and polyphony (several readings for one grapheme) (figure 9). A total of about 800 glyphs have been identified, of which no more than 300 were in common use. Some 150 glyphs are known to have a syllabic function, enough to express everything in syllabic writing (table 13). However, as in other early writing systems, logograms were retained for reasons of aesthetics and prestige. A special group of more than 100 glyphs representing toponyms and/or names of tutelary divinities of cities are known as 'emblem glyphs' (figure 10). Although not all glyphs have been given

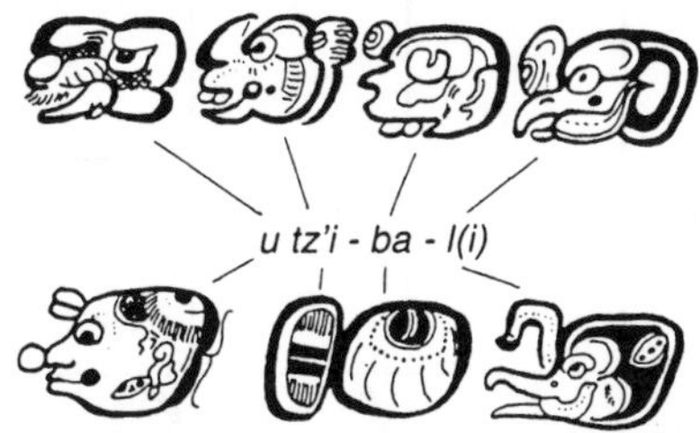

Figure 9 Polyvalence of Maya glyphs: two ways of writing u tz'ibal *'his writing'*

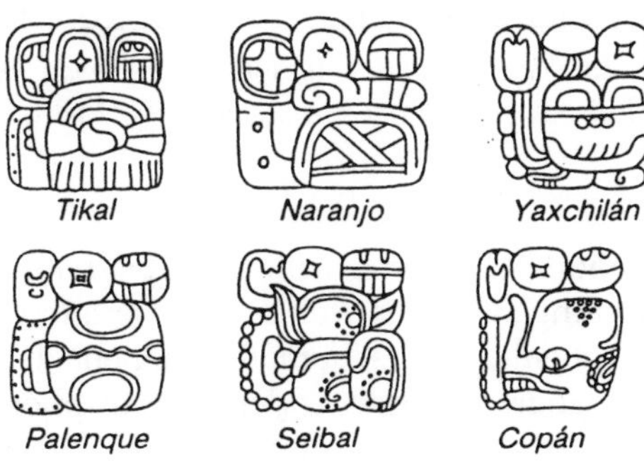

Figure 10 Maya glyphs of toponyms

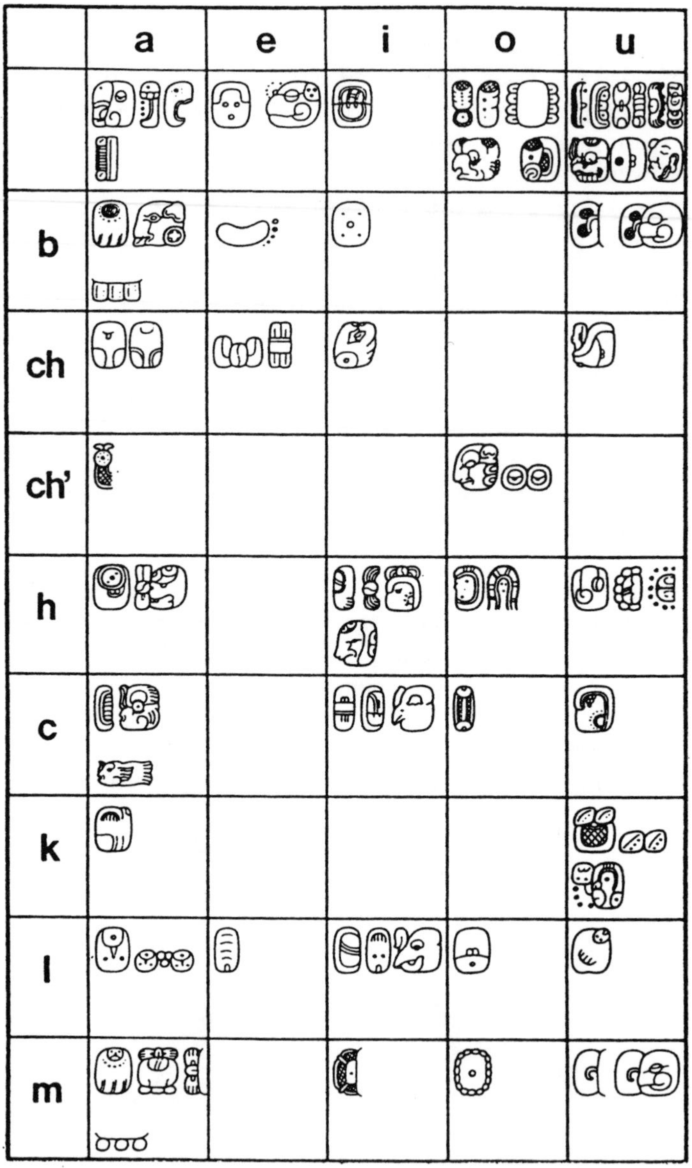

	a	e	i	o	u
b					
ch					
ch'					
h					
c					
k					
l					
m					

Table 13 The Maya syllabic chart with values given in Cholan, the language of the classical inscriptions (by permission of Michael Coe)

incontestable interpretations and some will, perhaps, remain obscure for ever, the core of the Maya writing system is well understood. In early inscriptions the glyphs have mostly morphemic values, but later phonetic determiners were used to disambiguate these logograms. Independent use of phonetic determiners as 'pure' phonetic signs is also attested. Language representation is not limited to the word level. Close correspondences have been established between Cholan

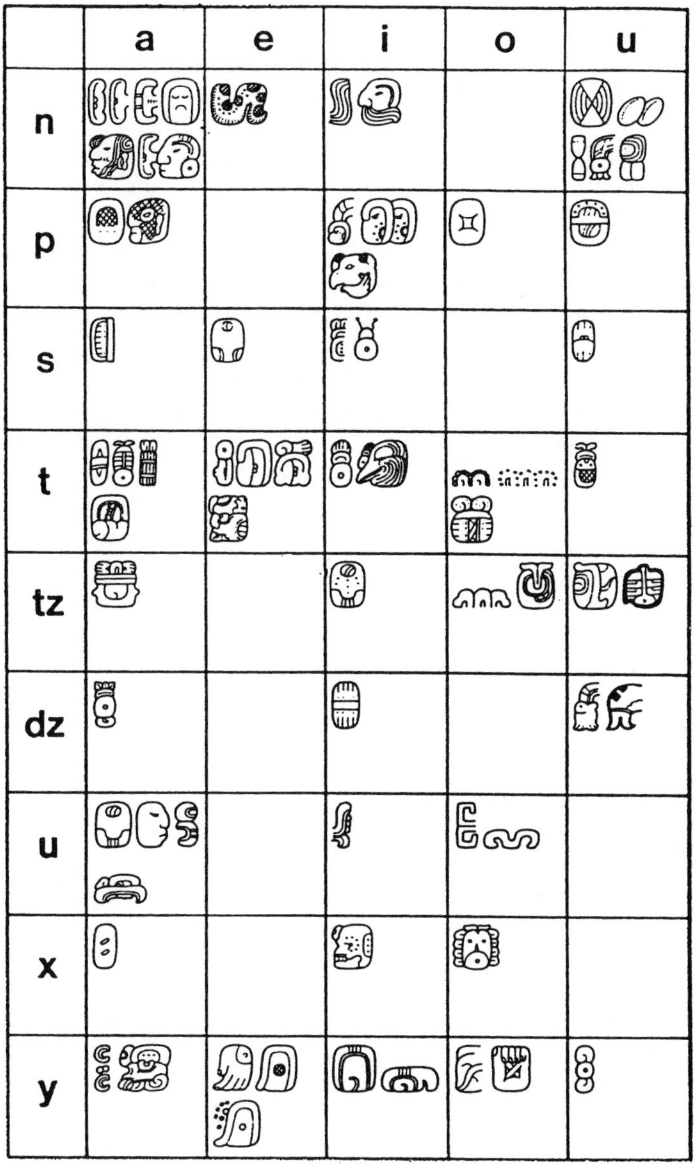

	a	e	i	o	u
n					
p					
s					
t					
tz					
dz					
u					
x					
y					

grammar and glyph grammar. The word order of Maya writing is typically VSO, that of Cholan.

Both vertical and horizontal inscriptions are known. Writing and pictorial representations are often closely linked, thematically and spatially. The characteristic arrangement of glyphs in longer texts is in two parallel vertical columns shifting from left to right.

See also Olmec writing.

Reading Bricker 1986; Coe 1992.

meaning, visual access to The principal function of all writing is to convey linguistic meaning, but writing systems vary greatly in how they encode meaning. In a purely phonetic transcription, access to meaning is mediated through sound representation, while a purely ideographic notation bypasses representation of sounds, encoding concepts instead. Actual writing systems belong to neither of these 'pure' categories, but are located somewhere along a continuum which ranges from sound-centred to meaning-centred. An example of the former is SERBO-CROATIAN WRITING with its closely phonemic alphabetic system, whereas the latter is exemplified by characters in CHINESE SCRIPTS which consist of mutually disambiguating components, one indicating sound and the other meaning. Other ancient systems such as Egyptian and Sumerian cuneiform, in order to help interpret phonetically written words, make use of semantic key signs called DETERMINATIVES. In contradistinction to Chinese, these are written separately rather than as components of logograms. The Semitic CONSONANT SCRIPTS, too, include a strong element of semantic coding, since there is a high degree of orthographic similarity between semantically related words. The written representation of words as C roots in unvocalized texts makes direct access to meaning feasible. Other sound-centred writing systems also afford direct visual access to meaning by a variety of graphic means, such as word separation, word class-specific capitalization of initials, e.g. proper names or nouns, and spelling differentiation of homophones like *right, rite, wright, write*. It is clear then that whether and how direct visual access to meaning is possible are not determined by the type of writing system in question, i.e. phonographic or logographic. Rather, writing systems of both types incorporate, to varying degrees, graphic representations of meaningful linguistic units which do not rely on phonetic coding.
See also LOGOGRAM; MORPHEMIC WRITING; ORTHOGRAPHY.
Reading Vachek 1973; Sampson 1985; Scheerer 1986.

memory Writing is both a physical and a mental memory aid. It enables the retention of records on a scale quite impossible when information is held in the memory alone. And it serves as an image of the memory perceived as a text or a list. In the study of writing the mnemonic function is the subject of discussion with respect to two major questions. First, what was the role of memory supportive devices, such as notches carved on sticks of wood (tallies), counter tokens of fired clay, or strings of knots, in the origin of writing? Second, how is the literate memory different from the oral, that is, what does the shift from memorizing things to writing them down imply for the organization of the human intellect?

The first question is investigated by epigraphers and archaeologists interested in tracing individual writing systems back to their earliest forms and precursors. In some cases, especially Sumerian, it is known that mnemonic devices employed for accounting and record keeping led to the development of writing. And in others where the origin remains obscure, it is evident that early writing served as an aid to, or substitute for, memory.

The second question is the concern mainly of historians and cultural anthropologists, but also of cognitive psychologists. Literacy brings about not merely an extension of memory, but a restructuring as well. The transition from orality to literacy brings with it a shift from committing to memory everything deemed worth knowing to recollecting where and how information can be retrieved. This shift from non-literate to literate ways of thinking is reflected in how the memory is conceived. Since antiquity models have been created of the human memory as imaginary places (*loci*) which are typically organized in literate terms. The items stored in the memory are thought of as written words 'imprinted in the mind' and arranged in some sort of alphabetic order (figure 11). The anonymous author of a Roman rhetoric textbook known as *Ad Herennium* (*c.*85 BCE) made the image explicit: 'The places [of the memory] are very much like wax tablets or papyrus, the images like the letters, the arrangement and disposition of the images like the script, and the delivery is like the reading.' How exactly the memory is organized is still largely a mystery, but it is clear that writing furnishes a powerful conceptual scaffold for structuring images of the memory store, as well as for consciously controlling it. Clichéd metaphors such as 'making a mental note of something' indicate how popular conceptions of memory have been shaped by writing.

See also FUNCTIONS OF WRITING; LITERACY; ORALITY; ORIGIN OF WRITING.

Reading (devices) Marshack 1972; Schmandt-Besserat 1978; (literate memory) Yates 1966; Ong 1982; Clanchy 1993.

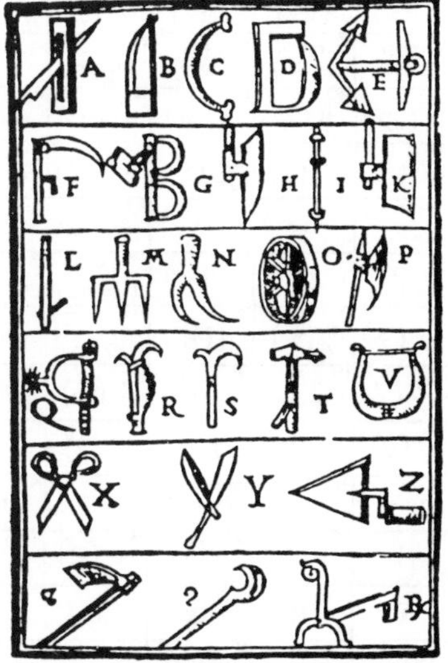

Figure 11 Visual alphabets as memory aids, from Johannes Romberch's Congestorium Artificiose Memorie, *Venice, 1533*

Mende syllabary Invented in 1921 by Kisimi Kamara, a native of Bari in Sierra Leone who was acquainted with the VAI WRITING of neighbouring Liberia. The script was used by individuals chiefly in personal correspondence, but it could not compete with Arabic literacy, of which the Mende had made limited use since the eighteenth century, and never gained wider currency beyond Kamara's chiefdom. Since about 1940 the roman AFRICA ALPHABET has been used for writing the Mende language which in effect led to the discontinuation of writing in Kamara's syllabary. The script consists of some 195 characters of the CV type including eight independent Vs (table 14). The first 42 characters make

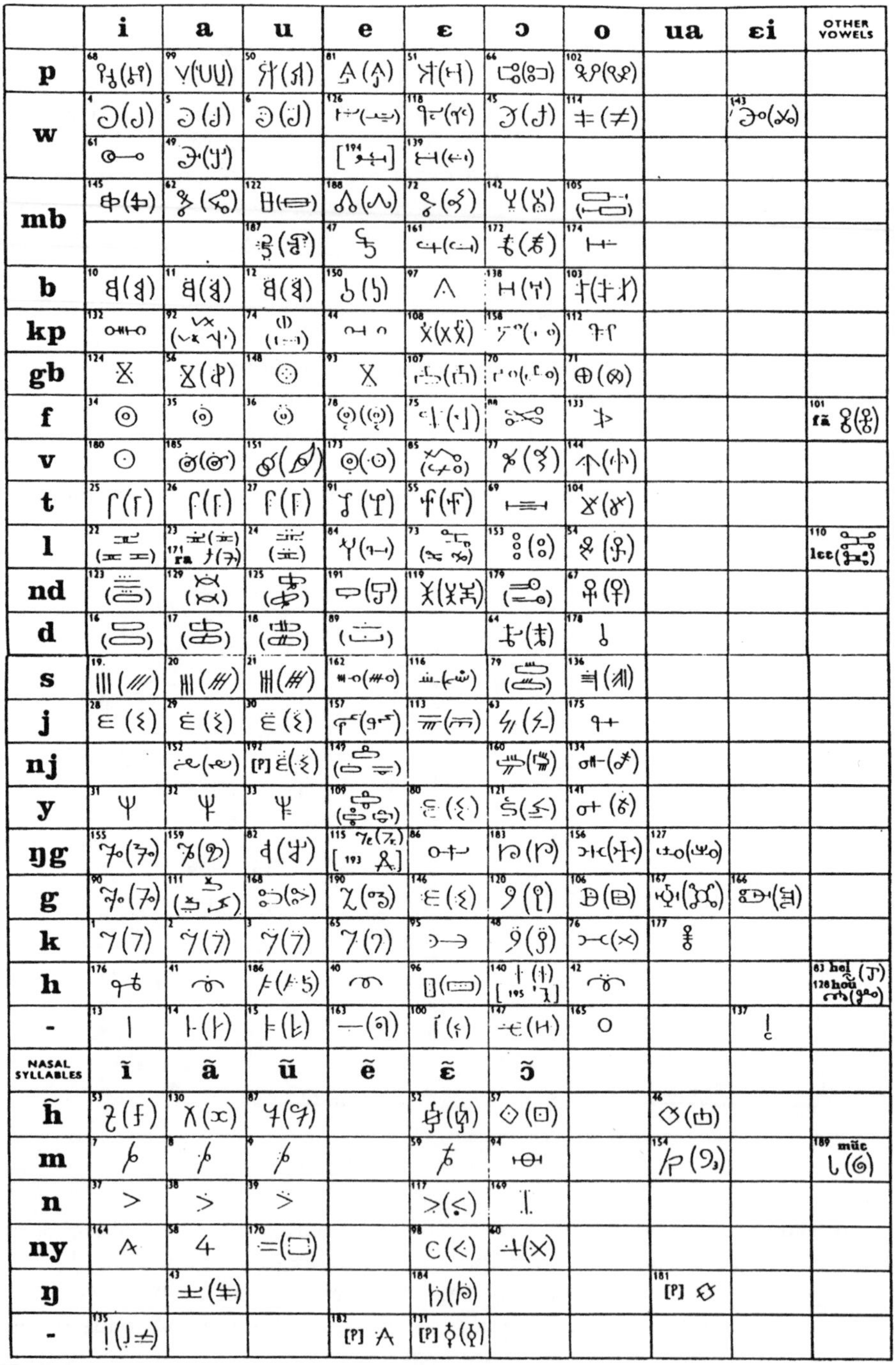

	i	a	u	e	ɛ	ɔ	o	ua	ɛi	OTHER VOWELS
p	68	99	50	81	51	66	102			
w	4	5	6	126	118	45	114		143	
	61	49		[194]	139					
mb	145	62	122	188	72	142	105			
			187	47	161	172	174			
b	10	11	12	150	97	138	103			
kp	132	92	74	44	108	158	112			
gb	124	56	148	93	107	70	71			
f	34	35	36	78	75	88	133			101 fã
v	180	185	151	173	85	77	144			
t	25	26	27	91	55	69	104			
l	22	23 171 ra	24	84	73	153	54			110 lɛɛ
nd	123	129	125	191	119	179	67			
d	16	17	18	89		64	178			
s	19	20	21	162	116	79	136			
j	28	29	30	157	113	63	175			
nj		152	192 [P]	149		160	134			
y	31	32	33	109	80	121	141			
ŋg	155	159	82	115 [193]	86	183	156	127		
g	90	111	168	190	146	120	106	167	166	
k	1	2	3	65	95	48	76	177		
h	176	41	186	40	96	140 [195]	42			83 hoi 128 hoũ
-	13	14	15	163	100	147	165		137	
NASAL SYLLABLES	ĩ	ã	ũ	ẽ	ɛ̃	ɔ̃				
h̃	53	130	87		52	57		46		
m	7	8	9		59	94		154		189 mũɛ
n	37	38	39		117	169				
ny	164	58	170		98	60				
ŋ		43			184			181 [P]		
-	135			182 [P]	131 [P]					

Table 14 *The Mende syllabary*
Source: *Dalby 1967*

use of diacritics to modify basic C signs for different Vs. Of the remaining characters many are also graphically related to each other through consonantal or vocalic diacritics in a less systematic fashion. The script is written horizontally from right to left.
Reading Dalby 1967.

Meroïtic writing A script derived in the second millennium from EGYPTIAN SCRIPTS for the Meroïtic language which was spoken in the Nile valley. It was used in northern Sudan until the fourth century CE when it was gradually superseded by Nubian. On the basis of inscriptions published in the nineteenth century by K. R. LEPSIUS, F. Ll. Griffith in 1911 published a successful decipherment of the script (table 15). Most inscriptions can hence be read, but the content of many remains obscure because the language, whose genetic affiliation is unknown, is little understood.
Reading Griffith 1911.

Hieroglyph	Cursive	Value	Hieroglyph	Cursive	Value
		ʾaleph or a			l
		e			ḫ (kh)
		o			ẖ (kh)
		i			s
		y			š (sh)
		w			k
		b			q
		p			t
		m			te
		n			to
		ñ			d
		r	⁝	:	stop to separate words

Table 15 The Meroïtic alphabet

Mesoamerican writing *See* AZTEC WRITING; MAYA WRITING; OLMEC WRITING; ZAPOTEC WRITING.

Mesrọp (*also* Maschtotz) (361–440 CE) An Armenian monk and clerk who created the alphabet of ARMENIAN WRITING and first translated the Bible into Armenian. He is also credited with creating the GEORGIAN ALPHABET.

Messapian script *See* OLD ITALIC SCRIPTS

Miao writing system The Chinese branch of the Hmong people who also settled in Vietnam, Laos and Thailand are called 'Miao'. Their language was first written in Chinese characters. In 1905, the British missionary Samuel Pollard in collaboration with Yang Yage and Li Sitifan devised a script for the north-eastern Miao dialect of Yunnan province (*Hwa Miao*) which became known as 'Pollard Miao writing'. This system consists of 32 capital letters for initial Cs, called *yunmu*, and 37 small letters for Vs, called *shengmu* (tables 16, 17). Arranged on horizontal lines from left to right, the letters are written as syllabic units in such a way that the C part of the syllable is the nucleus, while the V is written in smaller letters around it, placed according to tone. There are eight tones in all. The system can thus be described as semi-syllabic. Reminiscent of INDIAN WRITING SYSTEMS, its underlying linguistic analysis operates on the segmental level, but the unit of coding is the syllable (figure 12). The Pollard script was widely used among some Hmong groups, especially the Hwa Miao, although several competing Romanized systems also came into use. In 1957 the Chinese government introduced an alphabetic orthography for Miao which is largely based on PINYIN.
See also HMONG WRITING.
Reading Kao 1992; Huang 1992; Smalley et al. 1990.

Minoan writing A term which refers to pre-alphabetic literacy in Greece. The Minoan culture of Crete had three different writing systems, one pictorial which is called Cretan writing or Cretan hieroglyphic, and two of a linear nature known as LINEAR A and LINEAR B. Only Linear B has been deciphered.

minuscule [Lat. *minuscula* (*littera*) 'smaller letter'] Collective term for all alphabetic letters of the four-line system, where the body of the letter is contained between the base line and the *x* line (the height of an *x*), while ascenders of letters such as *h* and *b* and descenders of letters such as *p* and *y* extend, respectively, to an upper and lower line (figure 13). Minuscules were for the most part derived from the earlier MAJUSCULES, especially from the uncial style, a book hand. They first appeared in Roman manuscripts of the third century CE. Their popularity gradually increased, and in the mature form of the Caroline minuscule of the eighth century (figure 14) they became the major style of European writing.
See also TYPOGRAPHY.
Reading Bishop 1971.

Mkhedruli script *See* GEORGIAN ALPHABET

Moabite script An ancient north-west Semitic writing attested on a single document, the stele of King Meša of Moab, dating from the mid ninth century BCE

Y	ʔ	S	s
L	l, lɦ	3	z, zɦ
⅃	p, b, bɦ	Δ	tl̥, dl, dlɦ
T	t, d	Lo	l̥
+	ts, dz, dzɦ	6	ŋ, ŋɦ
Γ	f	I	ɣ, ɣɦ
ᒣ	h, x	J	ʂ
[	tʂ, dʐ, dʐɦ	R	ʐ, ʐɦ
]	k, g, gɦ	(⅃	mp, mb, mbɦ
ᒪ	ʈ, ɖ, ɖɦ	(+	nts, ndz, ndzɦ
J	q, ɢ, ɢɦ	([	ɳtʂ, ɳdʐ, ɳdʐɦ
(	n, nɦ	(]	ŋk, ŋg, ŋgɦ
)	m, mɦ	(T	nt, nd, ndɦ
U	w	(ᒪ	ɳʈ, ɳɖ, ɳɖɦ
V	v, vɦ	(J	ɴq, ɴɢ, ɴɢɦ
Λ	ʑ, ʑɦ	(Δ	ntl̥, ndl, ndlɦ

Table 16 Consonant letters of Pollard Miao writing

[illegible]	a	[illegible]	iu
[illegible]	ai	[illegible]	iai
[illegible]	ai, ei	[illegible]	iau
[illegible]	ʮ, ʯ	[illegible]	iɯ
[illegible]	ɿ, ʅ	[illegible]	iey
[illegible]	i	[illegible]	iə
[illegible]	u	[illegible]	iaɯ
[illegible]	rough breathing	[illegible]	in
[illegible]	ie	[illegible]	an
[illegible]	au	[illegible]	en
[illegible]	o	[illegible]	eŋ
[illegible]	y	[illegible]	ou
[illegible]	ɯ	[illegible]	ua
[illegible]	ey	[illegible]	uaŋ
[illegible]	ə	[illegible]	uei, uai
[illegible]	aɯ	[illegible]	un
[illegible]	ia	[illegible]	uo
[illegible]	ie	[illegible]	oŋ
[illegible]	io		

Table 17 Vowel letters of Pollard Miao writing

(figure 15). The Moabite language is closely related to neighbouring Phoenician, and the alphabet, too, bears a close resemblance to its Phoenician counterpart (table 18). A distinct feature of Moabite writing is the use of dots for marking word boundaries and dashes for sentences.

See also SEMITIC WRITING.

Reading Friedrich 1966.

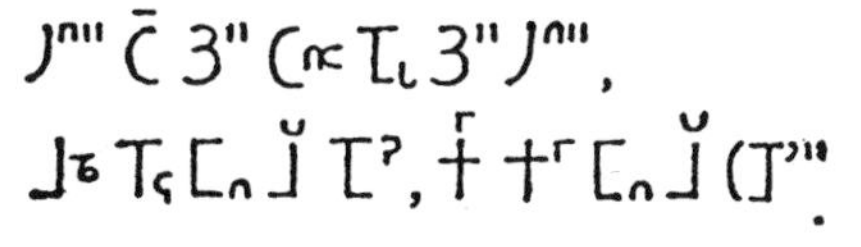

```
Once again we had a good year,
A myriad flowers bloomed, bearing plenty of fruit.
```

Figure 12 Sample sentence in Pollard Miao writing with translation

Figure 13 The four-line system: minuscules

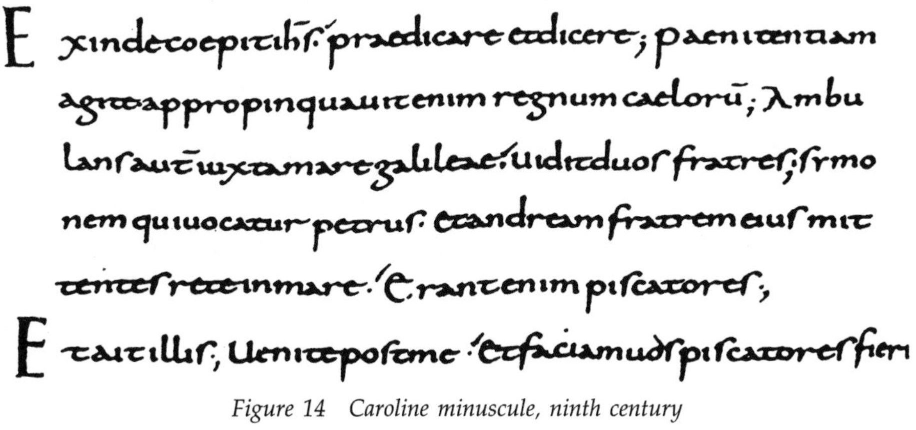

E xindecoepitihs. praedicare etdicere; paenitentiam
agiteappropinquauitenim regnum caelorū; Ambu
lans autē iuxtamare galileae. uiditduos fratres; simo
nem quiuocatur petrus. etandream fratrem eius mit
tentes reteinmare. Erantenim piscatores;
E tait illis, Uenite postme. etfaciamuos piscatores fieri

Figure 14 Caroline minuscule, ninth century

Figure 15 Moabite inscription on the stele of King Meša', ninth century BCE *(Musée du Louvre, Paris)*

A B C D E F Z H Th I K L M N S O P Ts Q R Sh T

Table 18 The Moabite alphabet (reversed, so as to read from left to right)

Moḍi script A cursive variety of DEVANĀGARĪ invented in the seventeenth century CE by a minister of Shivaji, formerly used for recording the Marāṭhī language. It shares with Devanāgarī the horizontal top line which joins the letters, but the vertical line which forms the skeleton component of Devanāgarī graphemes is less consistently developed (table 19).
See also INDIAN WRITING SYSTEMS.

Vowel letters

a i u e o ā

Consonant letters

ka kha ga gha ṅa ča čha ǧa ġa ña ṭa ṭha ḍa ḍha ṇa ta tha

da dha na pa pha ba bha ma ya ra la va śa ṣa sa ha

Table 19 The Moḍi syllabic alphabet

Mohen-jo-Daro script *See* INDUS SCRIPT

Mon script *See* PEGUAN SCRIPT

Mongolian writing The literary history of Mongolian begins in the twelfth century CE when the Mongols adopted the UIGHUR WRITING (table 20). It has subsequently been written in a variety of scripts reflecting the influence of political and religious developments. During the thirteenth and fourteenth centuries Mongolian was also written in Chinese characters and the 'PHAGS-PA SCRIPT, a Tibetan derivative especially designed for it. Mongolian documents in the Arabic script which had reached Central Asia in the wake of Islam are preserved from the thirteenth to the fifteenth centuries. In the twentieth century both a Roman and a Cyrillic orthography were developed for Mongolian (table 21). In Inner Mongolia (China), the Mongolian script continued to be used, but Mongolia, under Soviet pressure, introduced the Latin alphabet in 1931 which was replaced in 1937 by the Russian alphabet. In 1941 the government ordered the abolition of the Mongolian alphabet. It was only after the collapse of the Soviet Union and the communist regime that the Mongolian parliament adopted a bill in 1990 to restore the traditional Mongolian alphabet to official use (figures 16, 17).

When it was first adopted for Mongolian, the Uighur script had many shortcomings. With only 14 letters it was highly polyvalent. No more than three letters – *l*, *m* and *r* – were unambiguous in their sound values. To make reading yet more difficult, the classicized written variety differed considerably from the vernacular of the time, and the orthography was historical rather than phonemic. At the end of the sixteenth century when many Buddhist scriptures were translated

Initial	Medial	Final	Value
			a
			e
			i
			o u ụ
			ö ü ụ̈
			n
			ng (ŋ)
			q
			ġ γ
			b
			p
			s
			š
			t d
			l
			m
			č
			j
			y ị
			k g γ́
			r
			v
			h

Table 20 The Mongolian alphabet in Uighur letters

А	а	[a]	Р	р	[r]
Б	б	[b]	С	с	[s]
В	в	[w] [β]	Т	т	[t]
Г	г	[g, ɢ]	У	у	[o]
Д	д	[d]	Ү	ү	[ʉ, ɯ]
Е	е	[je, jθ]	Ф	ф	[f]
Ё	ё	[jɔ]	Х	х	[χ, x]
Ж	ж	[dʒ]	Ц	ц	[ts]
З	з	[dz]	Ч	ч	[tʃ]
И	и	[i]	Ш	ш	[ʃ]
	й	[j]	Щ	щ	[ʃtʃ]
К	к	[k]		ь	
Л	л	[l]		ы	[ɨ]
М	м	[m]		ъ	*
Н	н	[n] [ŋ]	Э	э	[e]
О	о	[ɔ]	Ю	ю	[jo, jʉ]
Ө	ө	[θ]	Я	я	[ja]
П	п	[p]			

*** only in Russian loanwords**

Table 21 The Mongolian alphabet in Cyrillic letters

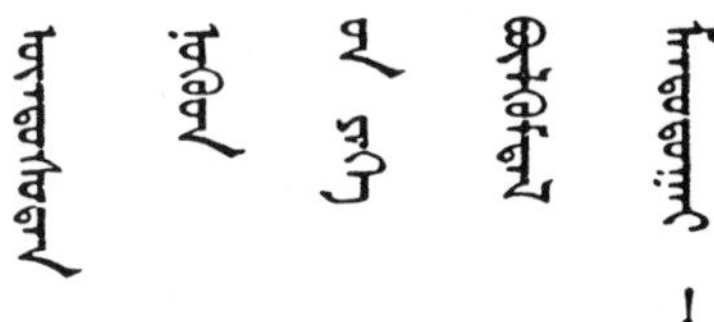

Long live the cooperation of all nationalities!

Figure 16 Mongolian sample sentence in traditional script

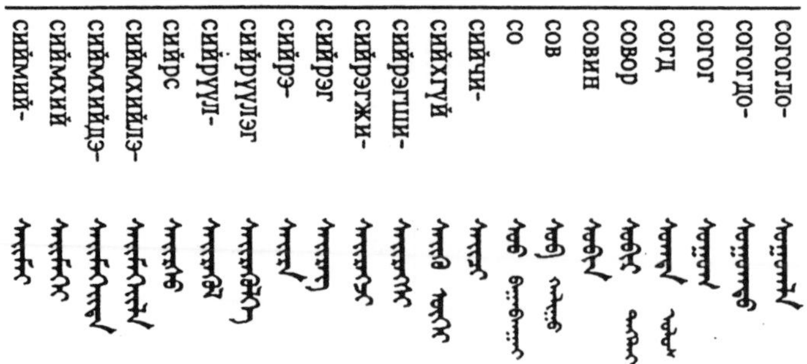

Figure 17   A page from a 1993 monolingual biscriptual Mongolian dictionary

and compiled, the Uighur script was reformed and freed of many inconsistencies of the older period. It has since been known as the Mongolian script. However, many intricacies remained, [o/u] and [ö/ü] were not distinguished at all and [k/g], [q/γ] and [t/d] only sometimes. Like the letters of the Syrian and Arabic scripts, Mongolian letters have three different forms for initial, medial and final position. The graphemes for [q] and [γ] are distinguished only by a diacritic which in older manuscripts often fails to be marked. The graphemes for [p], [v] and [h] occur in loan words only. The direction of Mongolian writing is from top to bottom in vertical columns shifting from left to right.
See also KALMYK WRITING.
Reading Doerfer 1964; Poppe 1974; Kao 1992.

monogenesis of writing The theory, once defended by influential scholars such as Ignace Gelb and Alfred Schmitt, that writing was invented only once, and that all writing systems, therefore, can be traced back to a common source. This theory refers to writing proper, that is, phonetic writing, and those who accept it credit the Sumerians with having made the decisive step from pictography to language-based writing. Once the advantages of this practice were recognized, it is thought to have spread through stimulus diffusion based on cultural contact to speakers of other languages who were in need of a visual recording system. Gelb discusses seven writing systems which could claim independent origin: Sumerian, proto-Elamite, Egyptian, Cretan, Hittite, Indus and Chinese. All except the last two are found in geographic proximity in the fertile crescent, the eastern Mediterranean and Mesopotamia. Many contacts between these cultures are well documented. There was also contact between Mesopotamia and the Indus valley civilization, as has been proven by archaeological evidence. That China does not fit into this scheme has often been remarked, but the greatest flaw of Gelb's argument is that he ignores Maya and other Mesoamerican writings which had evolved before the arrival of the Europeans. The monogenesis theory was born out of admiration for the overwhelming importance of writing in the history of the human species, and the conceptual difficulties involved in the conversion of language from the auditory into the visual medium. The writing systems developed by the Chinese and the Maya clearly refute the hypothesis that the transition from picture notation to sound writing was such an unlikely event that it could have been accomplished only once. Attractive as it appeared

for some time, the monogenesis theory must therefore be considered a dead end in the study of writing.
See also ORIGIN OF WRITING.
Reading Gelb 1963; Friedrich 1966.

Mormon alphabet A script created in the 1830s for English by Joseph Smith (1805–44), founder of the Mormon sect, who claimed that it was revealed to him in 1823 on golden plates by an angel. The characters are arbitrarily designed, although some of them resemble alphabetic letters (table 22). The script represents an attempt at designing a writing system for English which approximates a one-to-one mapping relation between sounds and symbols independent of traditional orthography.

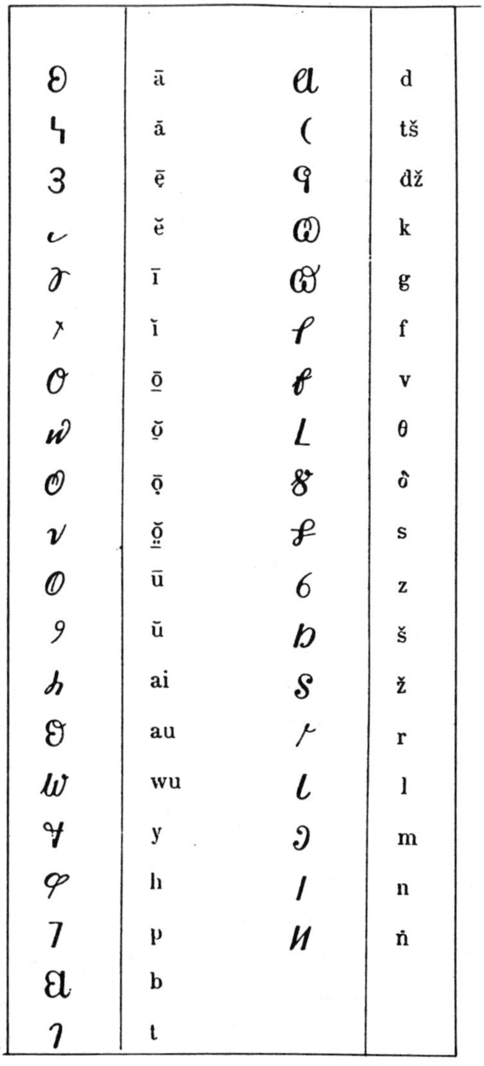

	ā		d
	ă		tš
	ę̄		dž
	ĕ		k
	ī		g
	ĭ		f
	ō̠		v
	ŏ̦		θ
	ọ̄		ð
	ọ̤̆		s
	ū		z
	ŭ		š
	ai		ž
	au		r
	wu		l
	y		m
	h		n
	p		ṅ
	b		
	t		

Table 22 The Mormon alphabet

morphemic writing A term sometimes used as a more accurate alternative to 'logographic writing'. A morpheme is defined as the smallest meaningful unit of language. Two kinds of morphemes are usually distinguished: free morphemes which can occur as words, and bound morphemes which can only occur in conjunction with free forms. In logographic writing systems the units of coding tend to be morphemes rather than words. The morpheme is also a relevant unit of many alphabetic writing systems, e.g. English, where GRAPHEME–PHONEME CORRESPONDENCES are often superseded by the principle of orthographic invariance of morphemes. This is obvious in inflections, e.g. *-ed* is pronounced differently in *wanted* and *wished*, and in derivations, e.g. differences in the pronunciation of vowels are not reflected in the spelling of such pairs as *divine–divinity, profane–profanity, know–knowledge*. In this sense morphemes can be said to have a graphic existence.
See also LOGOGRAM; ORTHOGRAPHY.
Reading Bolinger 1946; Chao 1968.

Morse code A system used in telegraphy to represent the letters of the alphabet as sequences of dots, spaces and dashes. These are produced by means of an electromagnetically activated stencil on a moving paper strip. Called after its inventor Samuel Morse (1791–1872), the Morse code was patented in Washington DC in 1837. Morse based his assignment of dots and dashes to the letters of the alphabet on frequency considerations, giving the simplest code to the most frequent letter (table 23). The letter *e* is thus represented by a single dot. As a

· —	a	— ·	n	· · · — —	3
· — — · —	å	— — —	o	· · · · —	4
· — · —	ä	— — — ·	ö	· · · · ·	5
— · · ·	b	· — — ·	p	— · · · ·	6
— · — ·	c	— — · —	q	— — · · ·	7
— — — —	ch	· — ·	r	— — — · ·	8
— · ·	d	· · ·	s	— — — — ·	9
·	e	—	t	— — — — —	0
· · — · ·	é	· · —	u	· · · · · ·	.
· · — ·	f	· · — —	ü	— · — · — ·	;
— — ·	g	· · · —	v	· — · — · —	,
· · · ·	h	· — —	w	— — — · · ·	:
· ·	i	— · · —	x	· · — — · ·	?
· — — —	j	— · — —	y	— — · · — —	!
— · —	k	— — · ·	z	— · · · · —	"
· — · ·	l	· — — — —	1	· — — — — ·	'
— —	m	· · — — —	2	— — — — — —	/

Table 23 The Morse code

Vowel letters

a	i	u

Consonant letters

ka	kha	ga	gha	ča	ǧa	ña	ṭa	ḍa	ḍha	ṇa	ta	tha

da	na	pa	pha	ba	bha	ma	ra	la	va	sa	ha

Table 24 The Multānī syllabic alphabet

measure of letter frequencies Morse used the quantities of type held for each letter in a printer's office. The Morse code is used universally, regardless of differing letter frequencies in other languages.

Moso writing *See* NAXI WRITING

movable type *See* PRINTING; TYPE

Multānī script A variety of the LAṆḌĀ script used for Siraiki, a language spoken in southern Punjab and northern Sind which is closely related to Punjabi (table 24).

Mycenean Greek syllabary *See* LINEAR B

N

N, n /en/ The fourteenth letter of the English alphabet derives from Semitic *nūn* through Greek *nu* (N, ν).

Nabataean script An offshoot of the Aramaic alphabet which developed in the first century CE on the Sinai peninsula and in north Arabia. It differs conspicuously from other Aramaic varieties by making extensive use of ligatures. Stone inscriptions in the Nabataean script are found from Petra, the capital of the Nabataean kingdom (*c.*150 BCE to 100 CE), to Damascus and Medina. The script is not attested in manuscripts, although its cursive character with letters frequently joined together indicates common use. The language of the inscriptions is Nabataean, a close cognate of Aramaic. Spread over a wide area, the script exhibits considerable variation with highly diverse letter shapes (table 1). Its significance for the history of writing lies in its being the immediate forebear of the Arabic script. Certain features of the Arabic character, such as the existence of separate final forms for certain letters, are already foreshadowed in Nabataean writing. Its transformation into the Arabic script took place in the fourth and fifth centuries CE.
See also ARABIC WRITTEN LANGUAGE.
Reading Driver 1976.

Nāgarī script [Sanskrit *nāgar* 'city', lit. 'city' or 'metropolitan' script] Derived from the old Brāhmī, Nāgarī is the most widely used script of India. It has official status for Hindi, Marāthī and Nepali, and is also used for literary varieties of Rajasthani, Dogri and Maithilī, as well as Pahari (Kumanni) when written.
See also DEVANĀGARĪ.

Nahuatl writing As the language of the Aztec empire, Nahuatl, a language of Uto-Aztecan stock, was written in pre-Columbian times in Aztec hieroglyphs. After the Spanish conquest, the traditional writing gave way to the Roman alphabet which became the medium of an extensive literature of a mainly historical and administrative nature. Nahuatl is now extinct, but several of its descendants survive in Mexico.
See also AZTEC WRITING.
Reading Prem and Riese 1983.

Nandināgarī A variety of the Brāhmī-derived Nāgarī script employed between the eighth and seventeenth centuries CE in south India. It differs in certain graphemic details, such as the use of the *anusvāra* (nasalization diacritic), from its northern counterpart DEVANĀGARĪ.
Reading Dani 1963.

Value	First century BCE	First century CE
ʾ		
b		
g		
d		
h		
w		
z		
ḥ		
ṭ		
j		
k		
l		
m		
n		
s		
ʿ		
p		
ṣ		
q		
r		
š		
t		

Table 1 The Nabataean alphabet

naskhī **script** Also known as 'Mecca-Medina script', this is one of the earliest Arabic book hands and is more cursive than the angular KŪFĪC SCRIPT which originated in Mesopotamia. It is thought to have been developed by Abū ʿAlī Muḥammad Ibn Muqlah (died 940), a famous calligrapher who introduced it at the court of Baghdad. Because of its elegance and legibility, the *naskhī* script as of the eleventh century gradually superseded *kūfīc* as the principal script for copying the Qur'ān (figure 1). For the same reason it has been widely used for languages other than Arabic, such as Persian, Turkish, Malay, Kiswahili, Hausa

Figure 1 An illustrated page from the Qur'ān, Samarkand school, later fifteenth century, in naskh'ī *script (National Museum, New Delhi)*

and Serbo-Croatian. From the *naskhī* script several other calligraphic styles developed, notably the *rīqā'*, *dīwānī* and *thuluth*.
See also ARABIC WRITTEN LANGUAGE; CALLIGRAPHY.
Reading Schimmel 1984.

***nasta'līq* script** A calligraphic style of the Arabic script developed around the end of the thirteenth century CE by Mīr 'Alī, a calligrapher from Tabriz. As the name indicates, it evolved as a combination of two other styles, *naskhī* and *ta'līq*. Like the latter, it is a smooth and elegant style used mainly for copying Persian literary works. From the fifteenth century it became the most widely used script of Persia, both in manuscripts and on architectural monuments (figure 2).
See also ARABIC WRITTEN LANGUAGE; CALLIGRAPHY.
Reading Schimmel 1984.

Figure 2 Specimen of nasta'līq *script from a sixteenth-century manuscript*

native American writing systems Unlike MAYA WRITING and other Mesoamerican scripts, none of the indigenous systems of North America pre-dates European contact. After European colonization had begun, various systems were devised for native American languages by indigenous inventors who had been exposed to European literacy, and by missionaries. Some of these systems gained wide currency among the speakers of the languages for which they were designed, notably the Cherokee syllabary. However, in the twentieth century their use has declined drastically if not discontinued altogether, because of the limited utility of native American languages for written communication and the necessity to become literate in English.
See also CHEROKEE SYLLABARY; CREE SYLLABARY; FOX SYLLABARY; YUPIC WRITING.
Reading Walker 1981; Krauss 1973.

Naxi writing A member of the Lolo branch of Burmese-Lolo languages, Naxi (also Nakhi, Naqxi, Nasi) is spoken in Yunnan province by one of China's recognized ethnic minorities, called *Moso* by the Chinese. Three different writing systems have evolved for Naxi, one pictographic, one syllabic and one alphabetic. The pictographic script, known as 'Tomba script', is the oldest, dating from the twelfth century CE. It is attested in numerous manuscripts and stone monuments (figure 3). Used primarily for Buddhist scriptures, it appears to be a limited system which functions as a memory aid in reciting texts that are already known. In excess of 90 per cent of its signs are pictographic, although some are occasionally employed as phonetic symbols in accordance with the REBUS PRINCIPLE. Rather than being a systematic feature of the underlying system, rebus writing is sporadic and appears late in the history of the script, perhaps under the influence of the syllabic system. The second, syllabic Naxi script is called *Geba* 'disciple', a designation which is interpreted as an indication that this script was created later than pictographic Tomba. Some Geba symbols were derived from

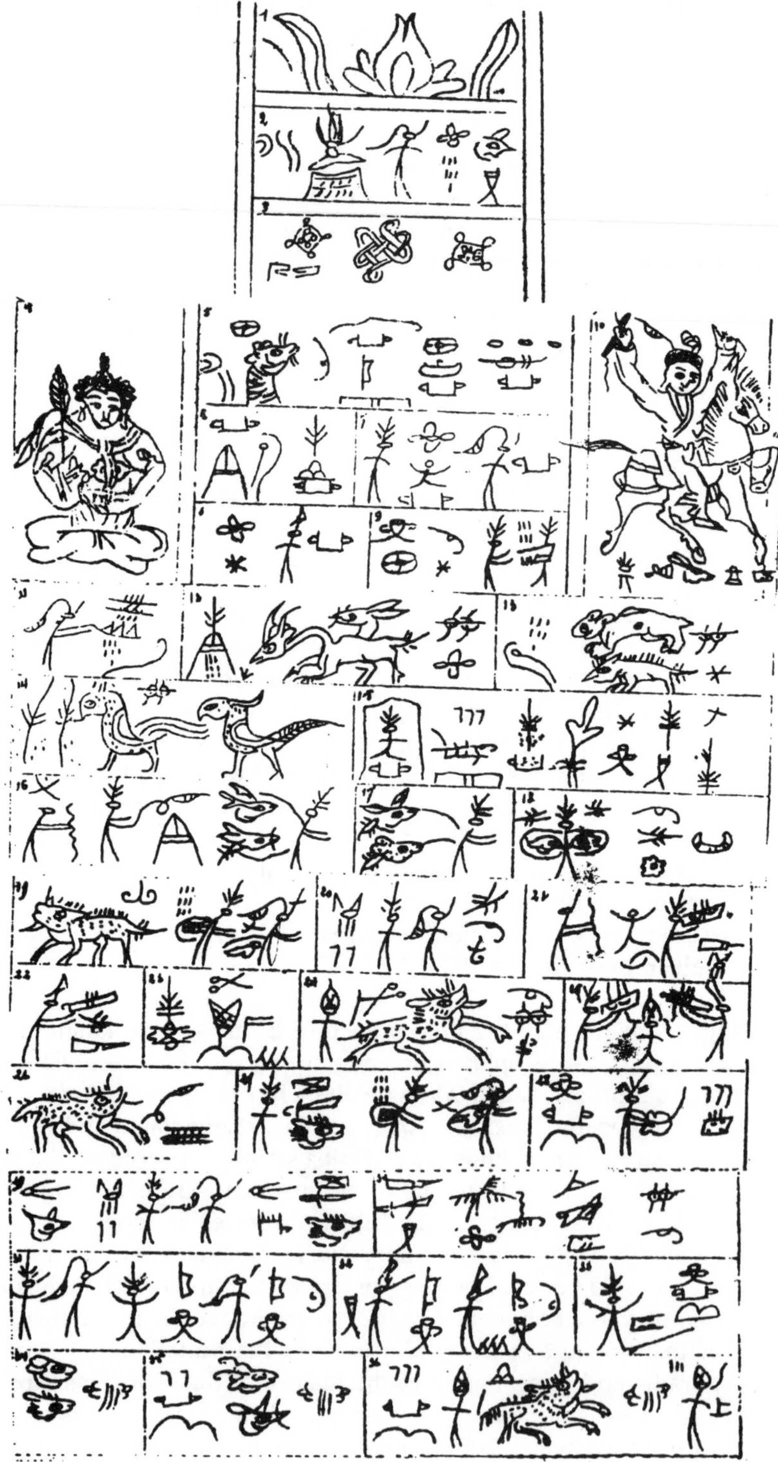

Figure 3 *A specimen of Naxi writing in the Tomba script*

Chinese characters, others from Tomba symbols, but in contradistinction to the pictorial nature of Tomba, it is linear in appearance (figure 4). This script is sparsely documented in only a few manuscripts and, accordingly, little understood. The third script for Naxi is the Roman alphabet, with which a phonemic orthography on the basis of PINYIN was devised in 1957 (figure 5).
Reading Kao 1992; DeFrancis 1989.

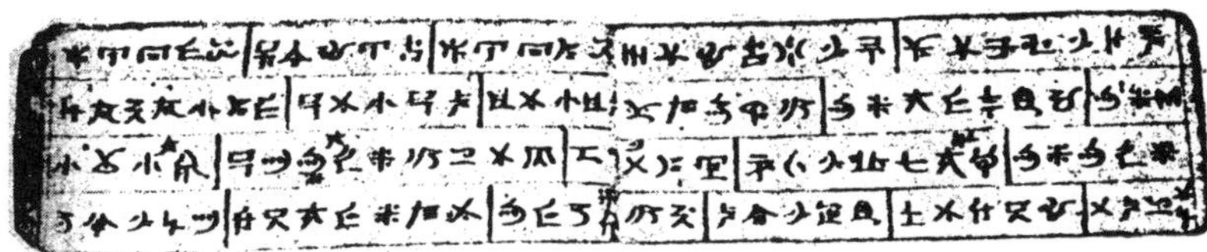

Figure 4 A specimen of Naxi writing in the Geba script

Naqxi tei'ee jju pil gguf, Naqxi balzhee tv ceeq sie. Naqxi tei'ee Naqxi bal, sseiweq leq gge ddee bbaq kail, bbaq leq bbaq ssi ddee ddoq nee, Naqxi xiyuq huahuaq seiq.

Translation

Since the Naxi people have their own script, they publish a Naxi newspaper. The Naxi script newspaper is as beautiful as a blooming flower. Seeing this beautiful flower, we know that the life of the Naxi people will be joyful.

Figure 5 A specimen of Naxi writing in the Roman script

Nestorian script *See* SYRIAC SCRIPTS

Norwegian writing Old Norwegian is attested in manuscripts dating from the mid-twelfth century CE, but as a written language Norwegian was replaced by Danish, which as of the sixteenth century became the standard language of church and State. Modern Norwegian represents a unique situation of two coexisting written standards recognized by the same speech community. As a written language Norwegian re-emerged in the nineteenth century after the Norwegians declared their independence from Denmark in 1814. Two written varieties were established as a result, now called *Bokmål* 'book language' (formerly *Riksmål* 'language of the kingdom') and *Nynorsk* 'New Norwegian' (formerly *Landsmål* 'language of the land'). Bokmål is based on standard Danish, whereas Nynorsk, which was codified by Norwegian nationalist Ivar Aasen (1813–96), reflects more conservative rural dialects. Both varieties enjoy official status and are taught at school, although Bokmål is favoured over Nynorsk at a rate of 4:1. Both varieties use the Roman alphabet based on Danish orthography. Independently occurring

<å> and <ø> distinguish both from Danish and Swedish, respectively. Written Nynorsk is readily distinguished from Bokmål by the orthographic words <ein>, <eit> and <dei>, the three gender forms of the indefinite article.
See also BOKMÅL.
Reading Jahr 1989.

notation [Lat. *notatio* 'designation', 'description'] Systems of graphic signs constituting a descriptive or meta-language, for example the notation of formal logic, calculus or chemical formulae. NUMERALS are notations to express numbers. Several notation systems have been developed to write down music (figures 6, 7). Linguistics makes use of various notations, such as the INTERNATIONAL PHONETIC ALPHABET or the VISIBLE SPEECH notation, both systems designed to represent speech. In a wider sense, writing systems too can be viewed as notations, since by representing languages they at the same time function as descriptions of languages which single out certain aspects rather than others.
See also TRANSCRIPTION; TRANSLITERATION.

Figure 6 Musical notation: autographed manuscript of Johann Sebastian Bach's 'Ricercar' of his Musical Offering, *composed 1747*

Nubian alphabet An offshoot of the COPTIC ALPHABET which is itself derived from the GREEK ALPHABET, the Nubian script (table 2) came into existence in the wake of the Christianization of the Nubians in the Nile valley of northern Sudan, where it was used from the eighth to the eleventh century.
Reading Damman 1980.

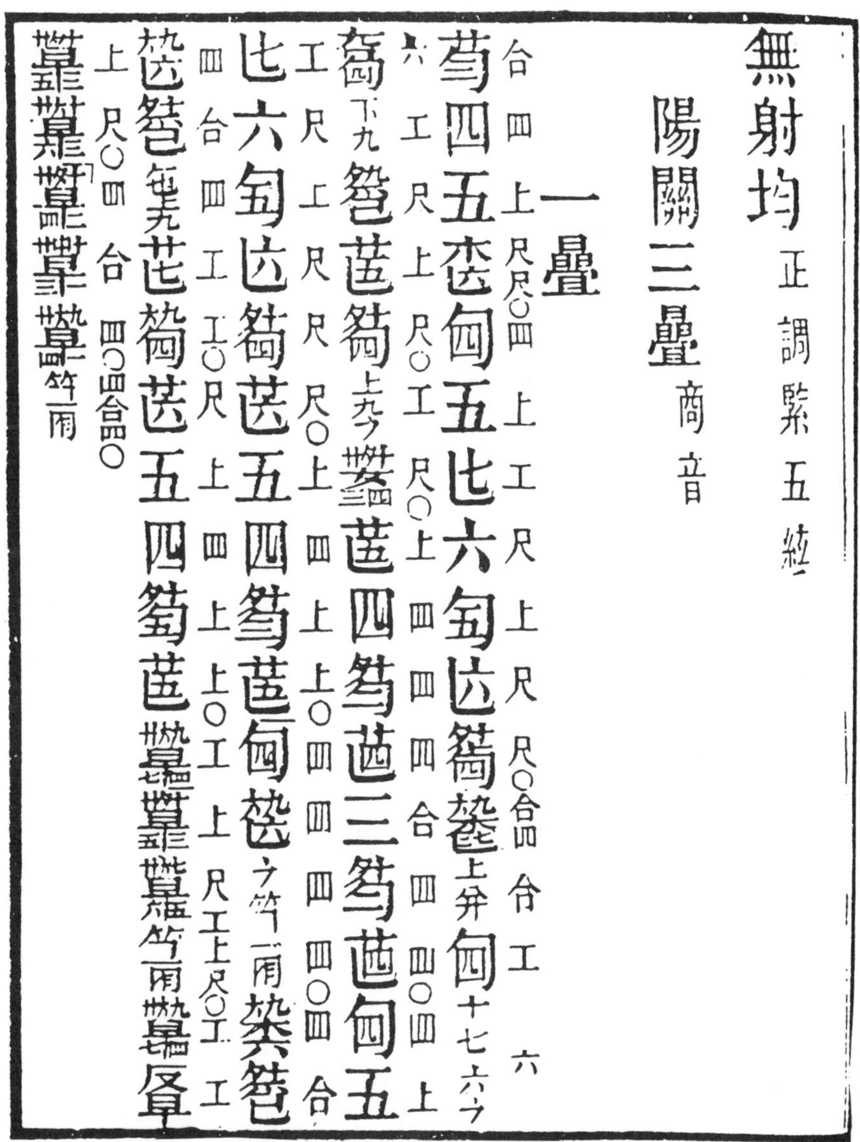

Figure 7 Chinese musical notation using a combination of standard Chinese characters and specially designed characters referring to stops (gupu) *and tones* (lülüpu)*. The notation begins in the fourth and fifth columns from right, the smaller characters indicating tones, the bigger ones stops*
Source: *Reinhard 1956*

numeral A figure or a group of figures expressing a number. Numerals played an important role in the development of writing. In at least one case, Sumerian cuneiform, there is compelling epigraphic evidence that writing grew out of a system of accounting. It has also been argued, on theoretical grounds, that numeracy must have preceded literacy. Since numbers are completely abstract entities, their symbolization – as distinguished from that of concrete sets of

Symbol	Translit-eration	Symbol	Translit-eration
ⲁ	*a*	ⲣ	*r*
ⲃ	*b*	ⲥ	*s*
ⲅ	*g*	ⲧ	*t*
ⲇ	*d*	ⲩ	*i*
ⲉ	*e*	ⲫ	(*ph*)
ⲍ	(*h*):*x*	ⲭ	(*ch*)
ⲏ	*i*	ⲯ	(*ps*)
ⲑ	(*th*)	ⲱ	*o*
ⲓ	*i*, *y*	ϣ	*š*
ⲕ	*k*	ϩ	*h*
ⲗ	*l*	8 (σ')	*ĝ*
ⲙ	*m*	ⳗ	*ñ*
ⲛ	*n*	ⳟ	*ṅ*
ⲟ	*o*	ⳙ ⳛ	*w*
ⲟⲩ	*u*, *u̱*		
ⲡ	*p*		

Table 2 The Nubian alphabet

objects – is a highly elaborate conceptual operation. The decisive abstraction is reflected by the step from a recording system which uses *x* signs of an object for *x* objects to a system which combines one sign of an object with one sign for *x*. Such a symbolization presupposes different underlying concepts for sets of objects and numbers.

Various systems of numerals have evolved. The decimal system, which is perhaps derived from the ten fingers of the human hands, is the most common today, although remnants of the vigesimal system (based on 20 as a unit) and the sexagesimal system (based on six and commonly used for measuring time) are still common. In early systems an iterative stroke notation is common: one stroke for *1*, two strokes for *2*, three strokes for *3* and so on. This pattern is iconic: the number of basic graphical elements corresponds to the number expressed. It is found on tally sticks, but can also be recognized in Sumerian, Egyptian, Chinese, Maya and Greek, among others (table 3). (The Maya system uses dots rather than strokes.) In order to reduce the inconvenience of iconic systems when dealing with large numbers, higher-level units evolved. Egyptian had elementary signs for *10* and *100* and used logograms for *1,000*, *10,000*, etc., a decimal system without zero, as it were. Semitic letters had numerical values, א for *1*, ב for *2*, ג for *3*, ד for *4*, ה for *5* etc., which is one reason why the order of the alphabet has been so remarkably stable since antiquity. The old Hindus used the initial Brāhmī letters of number words as numerals. In the fifth century BCE they invented something of the greatest importance for the development of science, particularly mathematics, namely the zero, which made possible a position notation of numbers in which the value of a symbol varies according to its place. The sequence

	Sumerian	Egyptian	Chinese	Maya
0				
1			一	
2			二	
3			三	
4			四	
5			五	
6			六	
7			七	
8			八	
9			九	
10			十	
100			百	
1,000			千	
10,000			万	
100,000			十万	
1,000,000			百万	

Table 3 Numerals of four independently created writing systems

12 is interpreted as the result of adding 1 times 10 to 2, whereas the sequence *102* is interpreted as the result of adding 1 times 100 to 2. The zero was also known to the Maya who, like the Indians, were capable of highly complicated calendrical and astronomical calculations. In their vigesimal system they used a dot for *1*, a bar for *5* and a shell for *0*. Numbers with higher values, such as the units of the Maya Long Count (calendar), are expressed with logograms.

It was only in the Middle Ages that, through Arab mediation, the revolutionary innovation of the Hindus reached Europe (table 4). The Greeks and Romans had to do their calculations with rather cumbersome number systems, which may be one reason why the Greeks excelled in geometry rather than arithmetic. Following the Semitic practice, the Greeks wrote numbers using letters of the alphabet with a prime <′> on the right shoulder. Later they used the letters Π for *5* (*pente*), Δ for *10* (*deka*), and H for *100* (*hekaton*). The Romans took some of their numerals from Etruscan and some directly from Greek, adjusting their forms so as to coincide with letters of the LATIN ALPHABET, *C* for *100* (*centum*) and *M* for *1,000* (*mille*). Structurally much like the Chinese system, Roman numerals made simple calculations a highly complicated matter. Both these systems are still used today, but mainly for decorative purposes. The old Mesopotamian system, also lacking a symbol for zero, is just as unwieldy, which makes the complicated computations carried out at the time by Sumerian (and later Babylonian) accountants, architects and astronomers that much more remarkable. The Sumerians had two systems, one sexagesimal and the other bisexagesimal, which were never used in combination, a fact which Sumerologists long failed to understand because both share basic signs for *1*, *10* and *60*. The sexagesimal system conceptualizes and symbolizes 600 as 10 × 60 and 3,600 as 6 × 600, whereas the bisexagesimal system has units for 120 = 2 × 60, 1,200 = 10 × 120 and 7,200 = 6 × 1,200.

Many writing systems have developed numerals, often using the first letters of the alphabetic sequence. However, today Arabic numerals are used everywhere

Decimal	Roman	Greek	Etruscan	Decimal	Arabic	Brāhmī
1	I	Ι	Ι	1	١	𑁧
2	II	ΙΙ	ΙΙ	2	٢	𑁨
3	III	ΙΙΙ	ΙΙΙ	3	٣	𑁩
4	VI	ΙΙΙΙ	ΙΙΙΙ	4	٤	𑁪
5	V	Π	Λ	5	٥	𑁫
6	VI	ΠΙ	ΛΙ	6	٦	𑁬
7	VII	ΠΙΙ	ΛΙΙ	7	٧	𑁭
8	VIII	ΠΙΙΙ	ΛΙΙΙ	8	٨	𑁮
9	IX	ΠΙΙΙΙ	ΛΙΙΙΙ	9	٩	𑁯
10	X	Δ	X	0	٠	𑁦
50	L	𐅄	↑			
100	C	Η	⊕			
500	D					
1,000	M	Χ	8			

Table 4 The coming of the zero

(tables 5, 6). In this form the position system invented by the Hindus has become one of the few truly universal notations.
See also ORIGIN OF WRITING.
Reading Destombes 1962; Ifrah 1989; Schmandt-Besserat 1977, 1978; Harris 1986; Hurford 1987; Schimmel 1992.

ا	1	ح	8	س	60	ت	400
ب	2	ط	9	ع	70	ث	500
ج	3	ى	10	ف	80	خ	600
د	4	ك	20	ص	90	ذ	700
ه	5	ل	30	ق	100	ض	800
و	6	م	40	ر	200	ظ	900
ز	7	ن	50	ش	300	غ	1000

Table 5 Numerical values of Arabic letters

1234567890

1234567890

Table 6 Arabic numerals in modern type

Numidian script *See* TIFINAGH

***nüshū* writing** A writing system developed in Jiangyong county, Hunan province, China. Its existence can be traced back to about the fifteenth century CE. A unique feature of this writing is its social distribution: it has always been used exclusively by women in personal correspondence and for recording folk tales for presentation at story-telling gatherings. Hence the name *nüshū* 'female writing'. Like Chinese characters, *nüshū* characters each represent a morpheme plus a syllable, but they are quite different in physical appearance (figure 8). The largest corpus of *nüshū* data available, collected by Xie Zhimin, contains some 1,700 different characters in 63,000 characters of running text.
Reading Xie 1991; Shi 1993.

Nüzhen script Also known as 'Jurchen', 'Ju-čen' and 'Niu-chih', the Nüzhen language is of Tungusic (Altaic) stock, and is now extinct. For a short period (1122–1234 CE) the Nüzhen, who called their dynasty the Chin (Golden), ruled over China. Excepting the Manchu, they are the only Tungus people who possessed a writing system of their own. It was derived in dynastic times from the

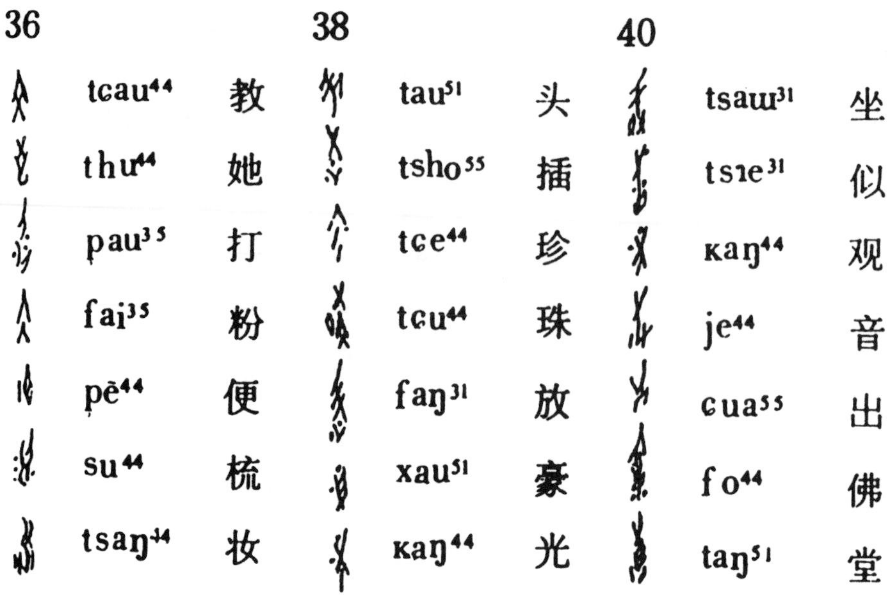

36		38		40	
tɕau^{44}	教	tau^{51}	头	tsaɯ^{31}	坐
thɯ^{44}	她	tsho^{55}	插	tsɿe^{31}	似
pau^{35}	打	tɕe^{44}	珍	ĸaŋ^{44}	观
fai^{35}	粉	tɕu^{44}	珠	je^{44}	音
pẽ^{44}	便	faŋ^{31}	放	ɕua^{55}	出
su^{44}	梳	xau^{51}	豪	fo^{44}	佛
tsaŋ^{44}	妆	ĸaŋ^{44}	光	taŋ^{51}	堂

Gloss

(36) 1. ask 2. her 3. apply 4. powder 5. and 6. comb 7. wear

(38) 1. head 2. put-on 3–4. pearl 5. beam 6. magnificent 7. shine

(40) 1. sit 2. like 3–4. Guanyin Bodhisattva 5. out of 6. Buddhist 7. shrine

Translation

They asked her to apply powder, comb her hair and ear jewlery.
On her head she was wearing pearls that were shining magnificently.
Sitting there she looked like the goddess Guanyin from a Buddhist shrine.

Figure 8 A specimen of nǚshū. *The* nǚshū *characters in the leftmost columns are provided with a phonetic transcription in the Jiangyong dialect (middle) and a transliteration in Chinese characters (right). The superscripts indicate relief tones*

Chinese script and used for the Nüzhen language until the mid seventeenth century when it was superseded by the MANCHU SCRIPT. However, the Nüzhen script never gained wide currency and extant text material is very limited (figure 9). Similar in its outer form to Chinese, with characters written in vertical columns shifting from right to left, the script is structurally very different. The system is basically syllabic with a prevailing pattern of one character per syllable, although some characters represent two or even three different syllables. In addition, some logograms are used for Chinese loan words.
Reading Grube 1896.

Nynorsk *See* NORWEGIAN WRITING.

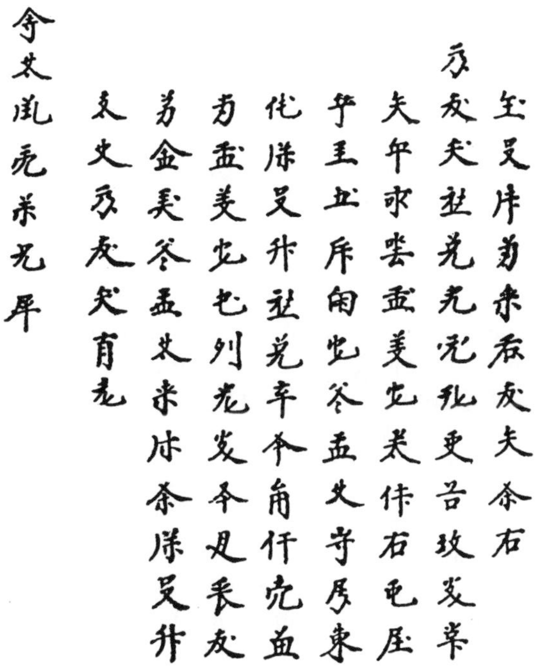

wúh-čè-tsò-wéi tū-tūh č'áh-lâh čè-čì-méi

čāo-lâh-mài 'á-hāh-`ái 'á-mîn mà-fâh piĉh-fûh-méh fûh-wān-tò čè-č'ē kīng náh méh-rh-kôh-ì t'ûh-t'i-méi 'óh-lîn-'óh hūh-sūn 'óh-léh-kîh čāh-ì wôh-šīh-pùh-lù .... -múh-lù (oder *šīh-rh*) *čū-léh 'óh-čè-hēi 'á-hāh-'ái t'éh-'óh tīh-wēn t'éh-t'éh-pùh-mâ méh-rh-kôh-ì hāh-č'ēng-yīn wàn-wān pán-tīh-hái čì-lâh-hīng póh -šēn wôh-šīh-pùh-lù tū-tūh t'ûng-či 'óh-čè-hēi wèi-léh-póh čāo-lâh-mài pāh-hāh-piĉh*

'á-č'ih-pùh-lù hàn-'ān-nì sāh-hī.

<u>Translation</u>

Petition by <u>Č'âh-lâh, Tū-tūh</u> from <u>Wúh-če-tsò-wéi</u> district

Since my ancestors did service at the frontier during their lifetime, they obtained the post which they held. Now it is my turn to offer products of the land as tribute, hoping for mercy and to be graciously awarded the post of <u>Tū-tūh-t'ûng-čī</u>.

Figure 9 Specimen of Nüzhen writing with transliteration and translation

O

O, o /əu/ The fifteenth letter of the English alphabet developed from Semitic *ʿayin*, a consonant sign which was revalued in Greek to become *omicron* (Ο, ο), the small *o*.
Reading Cohen 1982.

Ogham script [Celtic *ogham craobh*] An alphabetic script attested in some 500 stone inscriptions in southern Ireland, Wales and Scotland. The languages of these inscriptions dating from the fourth century CE are of Celtic stock, Old Irish and Pictish. A few digraphic inscriptions in Ogham (also Ogam) and Roman letters have been discovered. The script is not attested after 650 CE, by which time it had been replaced by the Roman alphabet. The outer form of the script is reminiscent of carved notches on tally sticks. It has been hypothesized, therefore, that the Ogham script evolved out of an accounting system which was transformed into an alphabet, the principle of alphabetic writing being known to the Celts through contact with the Romans. Formal similarities with runic scripts have also been pointed out. However, the exact origin of the Ogham script remains to be determined. Many of the inscriptions are very short; it is believed they consist mainly of proper names, which makes them difficult to read or interpret.

The Ogham alphabet consists of 20 letters, divided into four sets (paradigms) of five members, each marked by one to five strokes or dots above, below or intersecting a centre line (table 1). In many inscriptions the edge of the hewn stone serves as the centre line. Reading is usually from bottom to top, or from right to left. Figure 1 shows a sketch of a stone inscription from Kerry (*qerai* in the transliteration) in southern Ireland. Inscribed on two edges of the stone, it is to be read from bottom to top beginning at the left side. The reading is *coillabotas maqi corbi* | *maqi mocoi qerai* '[stone of] Coillab, son of Corb, son of the *qerai* tribe'.
Reading Macalister 1945; Gippert 1990; Ziegler 1992.

ᚁ	ᚂ	ᚃ	ᚄ	ᚅ	ᚆ	ᚇ	ᚈ	ᚉ	ᚊ
B	L	V	S	N	H*	D	T	C	Q
ᚋ	ᚌ	ᚍ	ᚎ	ᚏ	ᚐ	ᚑ	ᚒ	ᚓ	ᚔ
M	G	ŋ*	Z*	R	A	O	U	E	I

*** Uncertain sound values**

Table 1 The Ogham alphabet in its traditional order

Oirat script *See* KALMYK WRITING

okurigana In the JAPANESE WRITING system, syllabic *kana* signs added to a Chinese character (*kanji*) to represent inflectional or other endings. The principles for

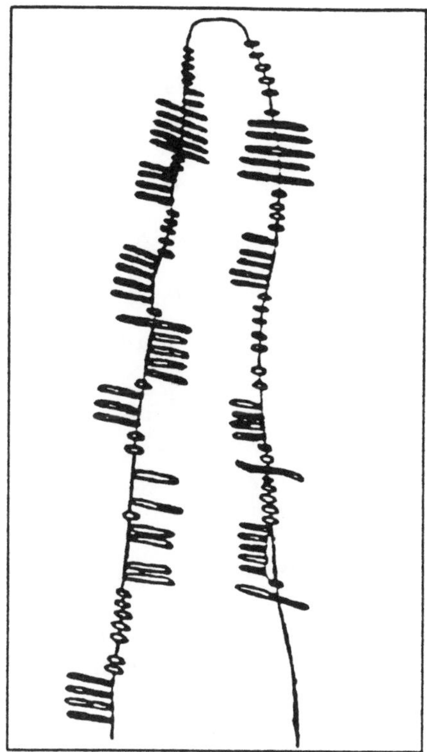

Figure 1 Sketch of Ogham stone inscription
Source: *Macalister 1945, no. 244*

using *okurigana* were laid down in government recommendations of 1959 and 1973, *Okurigana no tsukekata* 'Method of adding *okurigana*' (table 2). The general idea is that lexical stems are written with *kanji*, while *okurigana* are reserved for endings. However, usage of *okurigana* does not always reflect morphological analysis: other principles such as avoidance of homographs and disambiguation interfere.
See also KANA.

Old Bulgarian writing (*also* Old Church Slavonic) Old Bulgarian was the ecclesiastical language of orthodox Slavs throughout the Middle Ages. Never spoken as a mother tongue, it came into existence as a written language when in the ninth century CE the Slav apostles Konstantin (later known as Cyrillus) and Methodius translated religious texts from Greek into Slavonic, which to this end they first reduced to writing. For this purpose a new alphabet, the Glagolica, was created, usually attributed to Cyrillus. Another alphabet, the Kyrillica, was devised towards the end of the tenth century by his disciples who so called it in his honour.
See also CYRILLIC; GLAGOLITIC ALPHABET.
Reading Eckhardt 1989.

1959	1973	
異る	異なる	to differ
KOTONA-ru	KOTO-naru	
行なう	行う	to perform
OKO-nau	OKONA-u	
捕える	捕らえる	to catch
TORA-eru	TO-raeru	
表わす	表す	to express
ARA-wasu	ARAWA-su	

Table 2 Officially recommended okurigana *spellings of 1959 and 1973: transliteration of* kanji *in upper case, and of* okurigana *in lower case*

Old Church Slavonic *See* OLD BULGARIAN WRITING

Old European writing Excavations in south-east Europe have brought to light ceramics and other artefacts dating from between the seventh and the fourth millenniums BCE. They testify to an ancient sedentary neolithic civilization now commonly called Old European or Vinča culture, the latter after a major archaeological site near Belgrade. Many of the artefacts were found to be decorated with graphic symbols, some pictorial, others linear. Spanning a period of some 2,000 years from the sixth to the middle of the fourth millennium, when all traces of them disappear, these symbols have been interpreted by some scholars as what would be the most ancient writing not only in Europe but anywhere, predating the infant stage of writing in Mesopotamia by perhaps two millenniums. Most known sign sequences are very short, and all 'inscribed' objects were found at burial sites outside the settlements. It has been hypothesized that they are related to funeral rites. However, nothing is known about the language used by the Old Europeans, or whether their symbols represented language (figures 2, 3). Not surprisingly, there is no general agreement as to whether the Vinča signs constitute writing proper or should rather be regarded as a form of pre-writing. In the absence of longer texts which can reveal syntactic structures, this question may never be resolved.
Reading Masson 1984; Haarmann 1989.

Old Hungarian script Sometimes referred to as 'Hungarian runes' for its outer similarity with Germanic runes, the Old Hungarian script is documented in isolated inscriptions which have been dated variously to between the ninth and the twelfth centuries CE. The alphabetic script consists of 45 graphemes. Not all sound values could be established with certainty. The language written has been identified as a Turkish dialect, but the interpretation of most known documents is obscure. The similarity of most graphemes points towards a derivation of the Old Hungarian script from the TURKIC RUNES of Siberia, although a distant

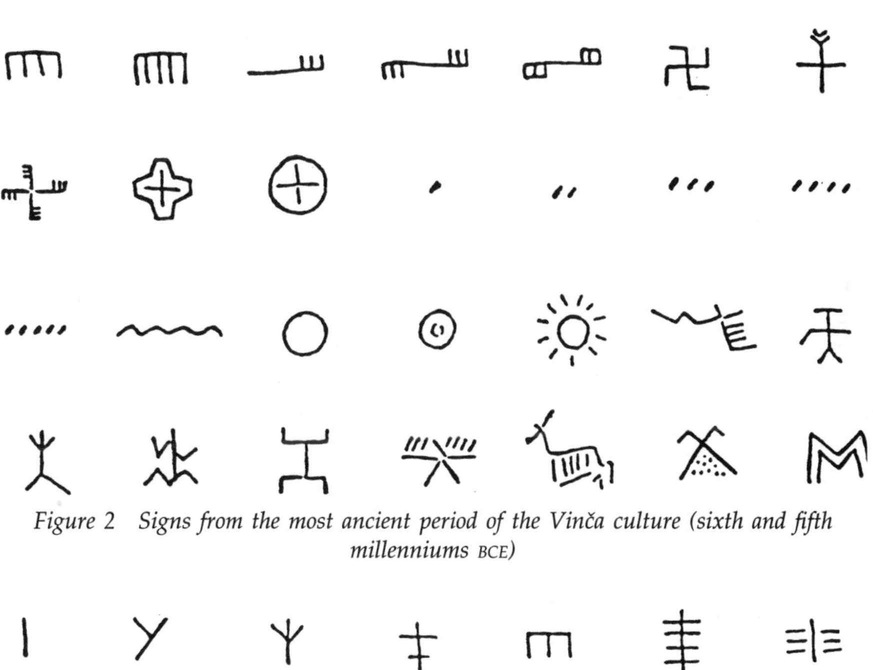

Figure 2 Signs from the most ancient period of the Vinča culture (sixth and fifth millenniums BCE)

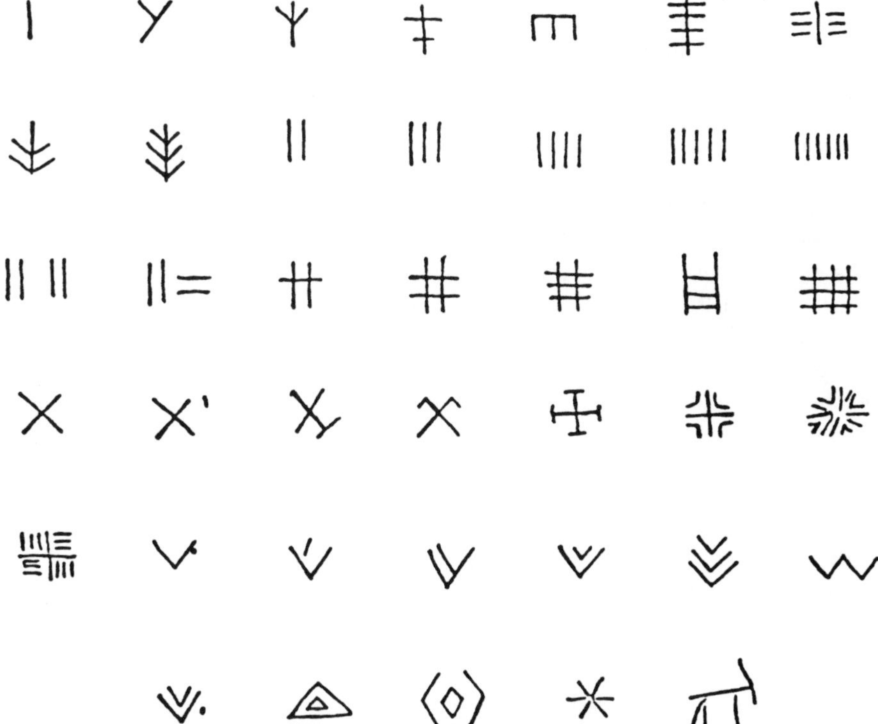

Figure 3 Signs of the Vinča culture used throughout

connection with the Greek alphabet and Glagolitic alphabet has also been suggested.
Reading Jensen 1969.

Old Italic scripts Alphabetic writing came to the Italian peninsula in the form of the west Greek alphabet used in the Greek colonies on Sicily and along the Tyrrhenian coast. From it several varieties arose which are generally referred to summarily as 'Old Italic scripts'. Most but not all of them were used for writing Italic languages. How exactly these varieties are related to each other is still a matter of some uncertainty, but in broad outline the genealogy is clear. The major Old Italic scripts are the Etruscan, Faliscan, Latin, Oscan, Umbrian and Messapic (table 3). Some other varieties of lesser importance include the Novilaran and the Siculic alphabets documented in isolated inscriptions.

The Etruscans, a non-Italic people which dominated large parts of Italy in the first half of the first millennium BCE, adopted a proto-Tyrrhenian variety of the west Greek alphabet, adjusting it to their phonemically quite different language. This happened not later than the sixth century BCE, perhaps earlier. From the Etruscan alphabet in turn derived the closely related Latin and Faliscan alphabets as well as the southern variety of the Oscans and the northern of the Umbrians. Etruscan-derived alphabets also emerged further to the north in Venetia and among speakers of other Italic varieties in alpine regions of northern Italy.

The alphabet of Faliscan, a close cognate of Latin, is attested in more than 100 inscriptions dating from *c.*400 to 250 BCE, excavated in Castellana. More than 300 Oscan inscriptions (400 BCE to 79 CE) have been excavated at various sites in southern Italy. Umbrian is known only from seven bronze tablets (*c.*350 to 50 BCE). The direction of most of these inscriptions is from right to left.

The alphabet of Messapic, a non-Italic language spoken in the fifth and fourth centuries BCE at the Adriatic coast, is attested in several inscriptions dating from the second and first centuries BCE. It is not thought to be derived from the Etruscan alphabet, since its earliest forms are still almost identical with the Greek alphabet, which suggests direct borrowing from Greece.

By far the most important of the Old Italic alphabets is the Latin, which supplanted all others once it had become the script of the Roman empire. As the script of Roman Christianity it was taken to every continent and has been adapted to more languages than any other script.
See also Etruscan alphabet; Latin alphabet.
Reading Vetter 1953; Jensen 1969.

Old Persian writing The latest and simplest of cuneiform scripts, Old Persian was the first to be deciphered. Old Persian cuneiform is documented on a number of monumental inscriptions as well as on clay and some small objects. The most important monument which is also generally considered the oldest Old Persian document is the trilingual (Elamite, Babylonian and Old Persian) inscription of Darius I (reign 522–486 BCE) on a cliff at Behistun, south-west Iran (520 BCE).

Many conflicting hypotheses have been advanced concerning the origin of the Old Persian cuneiform script. In the Behistun inscription Darius himself claims

Umbrian	Oscan	Faliscan	Messapic	Latin	modern value
𐌀	𐌀	𐌀	A A	A A A A	a
𐌁	𐌁		B	B B	b
	𐌂	𐌂 C	Γ	𐌂 C	g
	𐌃	𐌃	Δ	D	d
𐌄	𐌄	𐌄	E	E II	e
𐌅 𐌅	𐌅	𐌅	F 𐌅	F 𐌅	v, f
𐌆 𐌆	𐌆	𐌆 𐌆	𐌆 Z	Z	dz
⊗	𐌇	𐌇 H	H H	H	χ
⊙			⊙		θ
I	I	I	I	I	ι
𐌊	𐌊		K	K	k
𐌋	𐌋	𐌋 𐌋 𐌋	𐌋	𐌋 L	l
𐌌 𐌌 Λ	𐌌	𐌌	M	M M	m
𐌍 𐌍	𐌍	N	N	N N	n
		O	o	O	o
𐌐	𐌐	𐌐 𐌐	𐌐	𐌐 P	p
			Q		q
𐌓	𐌓	𐌓	R P	R R	r
𐌔 M	𐌔	S 𐌔	𐌔 Σ	𐌔 S	s
𐌕 𐌕	T	𐌕 𐌕	T	T	t
V	V	V		V	u
		𐌗	X	X	ks
8	8				f
𐌡					rs
𐌞	𐌝				ie

Table 3 *Old Italic scripts*

credit for its invention. While some scholars have dismissed this testimony, others have taken the possibility of a deliberate invention seriously, although Darius's scribes were the more probable inventors, since, in all likelihood, he was illiterate. The fact that Old Persian was not the language of the State chancellery of Achaemenid Persia, which was administered in imperial Aramaic, would seem to support the assumption that the Old Persian script is the result not of historical evolution but of conscious design. There is evidence to suggest that the Old

Persian version was the last to be inscribed on the rocks of Behistun, as a translation of the Elamite and Babylonian, although the original language of the inscription, that in which it was first dictated or drafted, is still a matter of controversy. In any event, Elamite and Babylonian were more widely used in writing than Old Persian in the Achaemenid empire. The scarcity of preserved inscriptions – 56 from Darius I, 20 from Xerxes, four from Artaxerxes I, three from Darius II, and even fewer from further successors – indicates that literacy in Old Persian cuneiform was very limited. Its use had already ceased under the successors of Xerxes. What, then, were the reasons for the creation of the Old Persian script? Considering the historical circumstances as well as other cases of script invention, the most convincing motivation is the desire to adorn the Persian language with the prestige of writing. On this theory, Darius wanted to see the spoken language of the Achaemenid elite side by side with the acknowledged literary idioms of antiquity and, therefore, ordered the creation of a script for Persian.

The structural properties of Old Persian cuneiform also point towards a planned system. Consisting of only 41 signs, it is at the threshold of alphabetic writing. These 41 signs comprise the 36 phonograms given in table 4, one word divider (an oblique wedge in the south-eastern direction) and five frequently used logograms. The 36 phonograms have both syllabic and phonemic interpretations, a design feature which probably reflects the inventors' familiarity with the Aramaic consonant script. Thus the Old Persian writing system is affiliated with the cuneiform tradition as regards the outer form of its graphemes, but the underlying structural principles derive from west Semitic letter writing. This convergence of

a, ā	ġ, ġa	b, ba	v, vi
i, ī	ġ, ġi	f, fa	r, ra
u, ū	t, ta	n, na	r, ru
k, ka	t, tu	n, nú	l, la
k, ku	d, da	m, ma	s, sa
g, ga	d, di	m, mí	z, za
g, gu	d, du	m, mǔ	š, ša
ḫ, ḫa	ϑ, ϑa	y, ya	ϑr, ϑra
č, ča	p, pa	v, va	h, ha

Table 4 Old Persian cuneiform

two utterly different traditions made for a system where the cuneiform graphemes could stand for syllables in one context and for individual Vs and Cs in another.
See also CUNEIFORM WRITING; DECIPHERMENT; GROTEFEND.
Reading Gershevitch 1979; Dandamaev and Lukonin 1989.

Olmec writing Originally the name of a historical people, the Huixtotin Olmecs living in Caoutchouc at the Gulf of Mexico prior to the arrival of the Spaniards, the term 'Olmec' has been used variously to refer both to the most ancient period of civilization in the New World which flourished in southern Mexico from the twelfth to the fifth centuries BCE, and to the period immediately preceding the 'golden age' of Mesoamerican culture, i.e. from about 150 BCE to 250 CE. The early Olmec culture had massive stone monuments and pyramids, and most scholars agree that the Maya calendar as well as Maya hieroglyphic writing have their origin in this period. The latter Olmec period is characterized by a distinctive literary tradition, called epi-Olmec because it seems to descend from that of the earlier Olmecs, although the scarcity of epigraphic material does not yet allow a reconstruction of the exact nature of the relationship between the two.

A better understanding of epi-Olmec writing became possible through the discovery in 1986 of a stele with a long inscription at La Mojarra, Veracruz, Mexico (figure 4). The script was found to be closely related to Mayan hieroglyphic writing, as had been suspected for some time. It is basically syllabic with individual graphemes representing CV syllables, and in addition makes use of logograms. Grammatical endings are mostly spelled by syllabograms. The language of the La Mojarra stele has been identified as pre-proto-Zoquean, which has been reconstructed based on a comparison of modern Mixe-Zoquean languages still spoken in southern Mexico. The decipherment of epi-Olmec writing must be considered as still in progress, since sound values and/or meanings of many glyphs remain to be determined. However, based on grammatical analysis and comparison with Mayan calendar glyphs, Justeson and Kaufman have made significant headway (table 5).
See also MAYA WRITING.
Reading Coe 1992; Justeson and Kaufman 1993.

onmun [Korean 'vulgar script'] The new writing system promulgated in 1446, now called *han'gŭl*.
See also KOREAN WRITING.

onomasiography [Gk ὄνομα 'name' + γράφειν 'to write'] A term rarely used as an alternative to IDEOGRAPHY.

opisthograph [Gk ὄπισθεν 'behind' + γραφος 'written'] A manuscript written on the back as well as on the front of the papyrus. The obverse of the papyrus with fibre in the vertical direction was more suitable for writing than the reverse, which was therefore often used for recording texts of secondary importance or for practising writing.
See also PAPYRUS; WRITING SURFACE.

Figure 4 Drawing of the La Mojarra stele (courtesy Justeson and Kaufman 1993: copyright 1993 by the AAAS)

oracle-bone script [Chinese 甲骨文字 *jiagu wenzi* (*chia-ku-wentsi*)] The oldest extant form of Chinese script dating from *c.*1300 to 1050 BCE, corresponding to the later part of the Shang dynasty. Oracle-bone inscriptions were found on tortoise shells and on ox and sheep scapulas. Systematic investigation began only in the twentieth century. In excess of 100,000 inscriptions have been unearthed, yielding more than 4,000 different characters, of which about one-third can be

A

	i	e	ʉ	a	u	o
p	179/180 pi			143 pa		122 po
t		56 te	102 tʉ			
tz						
k	170 ki		124 kʉ		37 ku	45 ko
ʔ	39 38 ʔi			49 ʔa		
s	101 si					
j	138 ji			85 ja		
m			46 mʉ	63 ma		
n		149 + 42 ne	43 nʉ	44 na		
w		25 we	20 wʉ			
y						

Table 5 Hypothetical epi-Olmec syllable grid (courtesy Justeson and Kaufman 1993: copyright 1993 by the AAAS)

identified with characters listed in the *Shuowen jiezi*, the earliest Chinese dictionary, or other lexicographic works. The 13-volume *Jiaguwen heji* (Beijing 1978–82) contains all oracle-bone inscriptions known up to the mid-1970s. Some of the inscriptions record the receipt of precious items, but most are divinationary texts. Questions were incised on bones and shells which were then exposed to intensive heat (figure 5). The resulting cracks in the surface, often following the path of holes drilled on the reverse, supplied the answer whose significance court diviners then interpreted. Many oracle-bone inscriptions can be read (figure 6). The characters of the inscriptions are quite linear in appearance, far removed from a purely naturalistic representation of objects. Judging by the extent to which these signs were conventionalized, it must be assumed that in China writing was present considerably earlier.

See also CHINESE SCRIPTS.

Reading Mickel 1986.

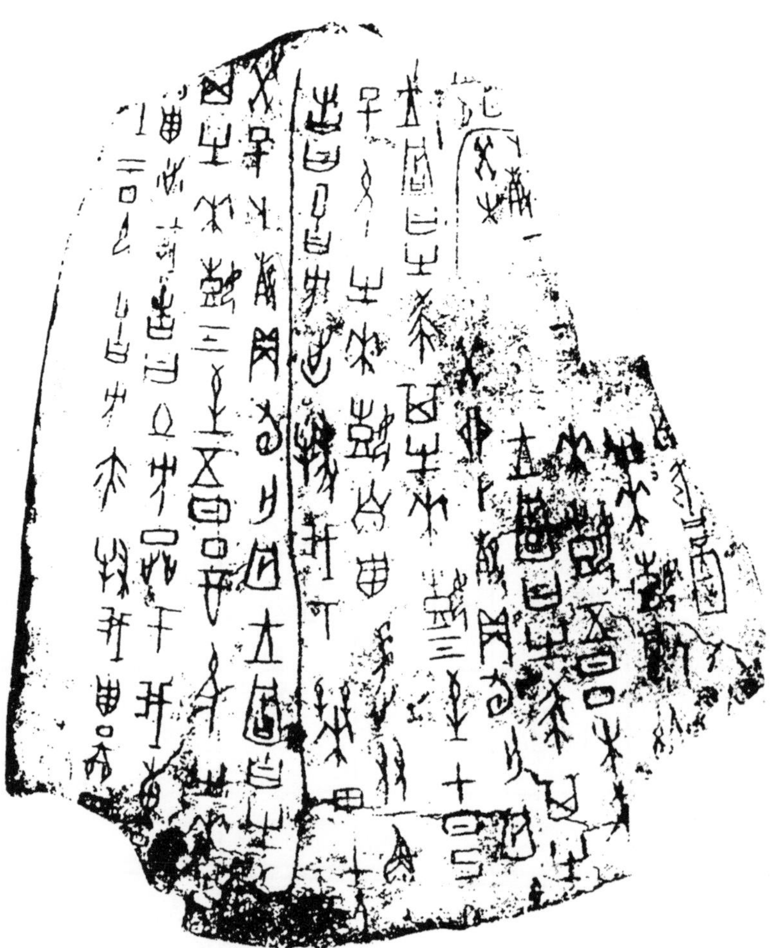

Figure 5 Chinese oracle-bone inscription on a scapula

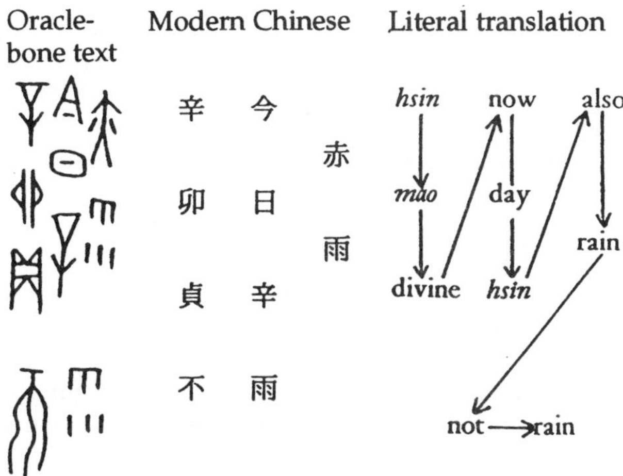

Figure 6 Oracle-bone inscription from Shang dynasty (fourteenth century BCE*) with modern Chinese transliteration and literal translation. Paraphrase of the text: [On this day]* hsin-mao*, it is divined whether on this* hsin *day it will rain or not rain'.*
Source: *adapted from Fairbank et al. 1973, p. 25*

orality A term coined as an opposite to 'literacy', which has come into vogue in the wake of the scientific investigation of how linguistic communication differs in speech and writing. Research has focused on two different phenomena: speech as opposed to writing in literate societies, and communication in non-literate societies. With respect to the first, 'orality' refers to the mode of linguistic production and the specific characteristics of oral language use as well as to the products thereof, for instance oral composition (narrative), spontaneous speech, and conversation. The focal question is how the oral mode used by co-present speakers determines structural features of oral texts. In traditional grammatical analysis written language has often been taken as the standard of which its oral manifestation deviated in various respects. Oral styles are characterized as more situation bound, personal, specific, concrete and redundant than their literate counterparts. Social registers, such as Basil Bernstein's 'restricted' and 'elaborated' codes, have also been likened to oral and literate styles, respectively.

In regard to the second phenomenon, 'orality' refers to the social organization of non-literate cultures. Genuine orality in this sense is a state of affairs where the alternative between the spoken and the written mode is unknown. Social systems with and without literacy have been found to differ in how they organize their economy, religion, law, education and cognition. Parry's (1971) study of Homer is a seminal work about the transition from orality to literacy. He was the first to demonstrate that the Classical Greek epics exhibit certain features characteristic of oral composition such as fixed formulas and frequently repeated useful phrases. Metre and rhyme were given a new interpretation as mnemonic rather than primarily aesthetic devices, enabling oral transmission of long texts. Involving several different disciplines such as cultural anthropology, rhetoric, linguistics, literary criticism and psychology, the comparative study of orality and literacy usually takes literacy as its point of departure in trying to determine whether and

how the functions assigned to literacy are served in non-literate societies, and how attitudes to language, knowledge, society and self reflect oral and literate modes of communication. In recent years, rather than literacy being conceived as a monocausal factor in social development, orality and literacy have been put into context with other aspects of sociocultural organization.
See also LITERACY.
Reading Parry 1971; Duggan 1975; Cook-Gumperz and Gumperz 1981; Goody 1986; Chafe 1986; Ong 1982; Olson and Torrance 1991.

Orchon script *See* TURKIC RUNES

origin of writing Where, when, how, and why writing originated are questions of foremost importance to students of various disciplines such as archaeology, history, palaeography and cultural anthropology, among others. On the empirical level the origin of writing is a problem of archaeological evidence. The task of historians of writing is to trace a given script to its earliest forms and precursors, hoping to understand how it came into existence. For several otherwise well-documented writing systems, the question of origin is yet to be resolved. For instance, the origin of the CHINESE WRITING SYSTEM is obscure since the earliest known characters of the ORACLE-BONE SCRIPT already largely conform to the structural principles underlying the mature system. Whether any connection can be established with the earlier emblematic signs found on pottery of the *Ta wen k'ou* culture (4800–2000 BCE) is yet to be determined. The EGYPTIAN WRITING SYSTEM also appears suddenly as a full-blown system with no trace of incipient stages which could shed light on its origin. Also unknown is the origin of the OLD EUROPEAN WRITING. At the present state of knowledge, a proper interpretation of its signs is primarily a problem of collecting and classifying archaeological data.

However, even where plenty of epigraphic and palaeographic material is available, the documents do not speak for themselves, but require systematic interpretation. In this sense the origin of writing is a theoretical problem. Its solution presupposes a theoretically founded definition of writing. In the absence of such a definition new finds cannot be assessed properly. At the same time, new discoveries may force revisions of theoretical positions. For example Gelb, whose 1963 book remains the theoretically most ambitious attempt to date at a general theory of the evolution of writing, committed himself to a pictorial origin of all writing. In the light of extensive research about non-pictorial clay tokens which Schmandt-Besserat (1977; 1978) and others were able to link with precursors of Sumerian cuneiform, he had to modify his position and recognize that graphical symbols making use of abstract shapes and colours can also lead to writing proper.

The historian of writing is faced with an array of visual signs, often called 'proto-writing', used for information storage and communication. They include decorations on objects such as pottery vessels, message sticks, clay pebbles, knotted cords, and seal impressions marking property, among others. The theoretical problem is then to identify non-arbitrary and coherent criteria which distinguish proto-writing from writing proper.

It is now widely accepted that a systematic relationship between the symbol inventory and linguistic units is what distinguishes writing from other visual recording devices. In the abstract this criterion is, however, more clear-cut than when applied to historical instances of early writing where graphical symbols were only loosely connected with language. Examining the motivations underlying the use of the visual signs out of which writing eventually arose is an additional source of insight into the origin of writing. This functional approach leads to the conclusion that writing came into existence to record and communicate information, not as the result of intentional efforts to visually represent language. Rather, that graphical symbols representing objects were given a linguistic interpretation was a secondary achievement. When a visual recording system first emerged in Sumer, it was intended to register economical and administrative transactions. Up to a certain level this function could be, and actually was, fulfilled without the intermediary of language. Symbols were arranged in a graphically determined format rather than according to linguistic-syntactic criteria, and they had no fixed linguistic values. Yet, since all fully fledged writing systems do represent language, the crucial question is how a systematic mapping relationship between graphical symbols and language was brought about.

Recent scholarship converges on the view that the graphic manipulation of numbers was decisive for this relationship to be established. The crucial step is seen in the development of abstract numerals, that is, the step from an iconic iterative number system where the counted objects corresponded in a one-to-one fashion with the numerals representing them (five symbols of a cow for five cows) to a non-iterative emblematic notation (one symbol of a cow followed by one symbol for 'five'). In the context of the latter notation the numeral becomes a symbol of an abstract number 'fiveness' as opposed to 'five cows', while the symbol of 'cow' can be interpreted as a symbol of the word *cow*. As this secondary interpretation becomes systematized and conceptually prevalent, writing proper begins. Thus, numeracy in combination with the linguistic interpretation of symbols of objects led mankind into literacy.

A close relationship between counting and embryonic writing has been observed in several archaic cultures. For example, a highly elaborate calendrical system was at the heart of early Maya writing. But in no case is the link between an accounting system as a controlling device of the economy and writing more thoroughly documented and corroborated by palaeographic data than in the ancient Near East, where early Sumerian writing could be incontestably linked to the counter tokens preceding it by several millenniums. Because of this connection, the study of early number systems has become a focal domain of inquiry about the transformation of proto-writing into writing proper.

See also MONOGENESIS OF WRITING.

Reading Nissen 1985; Harris 1986; Gaur 1992; Schmandt-Besserat 1992.

Oṛiyā script Like all other scripts developed on the Indian subcontinent, the Oṛiyā script is a syllabic alphabet. It is a member of the northern group of Brāhmī-derived scripts and an offshoot of the proto-Bengālī script. Its inner form bears close resemblance to the BENGĀLĪ WRITING, although the curvilinear appearance of its outer form is reminiscent of southern Indian scripts, a feature which has been attributed to the fact that it was initially mostly written on palm leaves with a pointed stylus. Hence the vertical bar characteristic of Nāgarī and Bengālī has been transformed into a semicircle which appears at the top of most letters. V indication conforms to the usual Indian pattern: a full set of graphemes for independent Vs is supplemented by diacritic satellites to be added to C graphemes whenever a V other than the inherent *a* is to be indicated (table 6). Syllables with final C are written by means of the V muting diacritic (*hasanta*), an oblique stroke placed at the right foot of the C grapheme. The *anusvāra* for nasalization is a small circle on the right shoulder of C graphemes. Oṛiyā is written on horizontal lines running from left to right.

See also INDIAN WRITING SYSTEMS.

Reading Matson 1971; Masica 1991.

Independent vowel letters

ଅ	a	ଋ	ṛ
ଆ	ā	ଏ	e
ଇ	i	ଐ	ai
ଈ	ī	ଓ	o
ଉ	u	ଔ	au
ଊ	ū		

Vowel diacritics

◌	-a	◌ୃ	-ṛ
◌ା	-ā	େ◌	-e
◌ି	-i	ୈ◌	-ai
◌ୀ	-ī	େ◌ା	-o
◌ୁ	-u	େ◌ୗ	-au
◌ୂ	-ū		

Consonant letters

କ	ka	ଖ	kha	ଗ	ga	ଘ	gha	ଙ	ŋa
ଚ	ca	ଛ	cha	ଜ	ja	ଝ	jha	ଞ	ña
ଟ	ṭa	ଠ	ṭha	ଡ	ḍa	ଢ	ḍha	ଣ	ṇa
ତ	ta	ଥ	tha	ଦ	da	ଧ	dha	ନ	na
ପ	pa	ଫ	pha	ବ	ba	ଭ	bha	ମ	ma
ଯ	ya	ର	ra	ଲ	la	ଵ	va		
ଶ	śa	ଷ	ṣa	ସ	sa	ହ	ha		

Table 6 The Oṛiyā syllabic alphabet

Orrmulum A paraphrase of the Gospels in Middle English dating from *c.*1200, so called after its author Orrm or Orrmin (figure 7). The *Orrmulum* occupies an important position in the history of English, because it is the only document before the modern period which contains suggestions for a spelling reform. Among other things, Orrm anticipated by several hundred years the modern convention of doubling Cs to indicate short Vs. He failed, however, to attract any followers.

Annd tatt he loke wel, þatt he an bocstaff write twizzess,
Ezzwhær þær itt uppo þiss boc iss writenn o þatt wise.
Loke he wel þatt hēt write swa, forr he ne mazz nohht elless
Onn Ennglissh wrītenn rihht te word; þatt wite he wel to soþe.

Translation

And that he look well, that he one letter write twice,
Always where it upon this book is written in that way.
Let him look well that he write it so, for he can not else
In English write the words right; let him know that well in truth.

Figure 7 Orrmulum, *from the introduction*

orthoepy [Gk ὀρθός 'straight, correct' + ἔπη 'word'] Correct pronunciation and that part of grammar that deals with correctness of diction. Although phonetic writing is thought to be a faithful representation of speech, orthoepy reflects a normative attitude towards language which is strongly influenced by its written form. Since the *ad litteras* movement of Charlemagne's pronunciation reform, the graphic representation of words has often been taken as a model of their correct pronunciation. At the time the idea was that, because vernacular Latin was widely felt to be too divergent and corrupted, each word should be articulated such that each letter could be 'heard' in a way that was thought to have been the pronunciation of those letters in classical times. Orthoepy also depends on writing in as much as pronunciation norms cannot be established easily without being given a written representation. Phonetic alphabets such as IPA were originally created with the stated purpose of ascertaining correct pronunciation.
See also Carolingian reform; Orthography; Spelling pronunciation.

orthography [Gk ὀρθός 'straight, correct' + γράφειν 'to write'] Correct spelling and that part of grammar that deals with the rules of correct spelling. An orthography is a normative selection of the possibilities of a script for writing a particular language in a uniform and standardized way. All orthographies are language specific. As the most visible and most consciously learned linguistic subsystems, orthographies are often codified by official decree. In alphabetically written languages, the aspects of writing most commonly codified by means of orthographic rules are grapheme–phoneme correspondence, word division, hyphenation, capitalization, and the spelling of loan words. Punctuation is sometimes also subsumed under orthography. Sound–letter correspondence is also a central component in orthographies of other writing systems, as for instance the representation of C clusters by means of conjunct letters in INDIAN WRITING SYSTEMS, or the composition of complex *han'gŭl* letters in Korean. Punctuation for V indication is a major concern of the orthographies of Semitic consonant scripts such as HEBREW WRITING and ARABIC SCRIPTS. In Chinese, the graphic composition of characters is a matter of orthographic regulation. The term 'orthography' thus covers both graphotactic and grapheme–phoneme correspondence rules.

Orthographies are based on historically evolved writing conventions and hence often involve different structural principles of linguistic representation. This makes it difficult to codify the spelling of a language by means of a set of rules alone. Orthographic codes, therefore, consist of two parts, a set of rules and a word list. For languages with a long literary tradition the latter usually takes the form of an orthographic dictionary. Since orthographies represent languages, they reflect meta-linguistic knowledge about the units of language, segmentation and derivation. Alphabetic orthographies vary with respect to phonological abstraction and the transparency of the relation between spelling and phonology. Orthographies such as the ENGLISH SPELLING and FRENCH SPELLING systems which preserve morphologic at the expense of phonetic information are called 'deep' orthographies. Identical or similar spellings denote the same morpheme, which implies that the same grapheme can represent different phonemes in different contexts (as in *heal* vs *health*). In 'shallow' orthographies, by contrast, grapheme–phoneme correspondence is less polyvalent and more transparent on a surface level. The orthography of SERBO-CROATIAN WRITING, which never varies with morphologic derivations, is often cited as an example of this type. The mapping relation on which it relies is simpler than that of deep orthographies, but this does not mean that shallow systems operate on the basis of the one-sound/one-symbol principle. Since the phonemes of most languages are more numerous than the letters of the alphabet, alphabetic orthographies typically include DIGRAPHS and TRIGRAPHS. Also, shallow orthographies should not be confused with narrow transcriptional representations. Like deep systems they are abstractions designed for practical use by speakers competent in the language. Exact phonetic transcription is too complicated and unnecessary for the purposes of practical orthographies.

See also GRAPHEMICS; HETEROGRAPH; IPA; ORTHOGRAPHY REFORM; SPELLING.

Reading *Orthography Studies* 1963; Vachek 1973; Catach 1978; Augst 1986; Luelsdorff 1987; Günther 1988; Frost 1992.

orthography reform A domain of language planning concerning deliberate changes in the writing conventions of a language without altering its script or writing system. According to this definition neither the changeover from a logographic to a phonographic writing system for Vietnamese, nor the replacement of the Arabic by the Roman alphabet for Turkish, count as orthography reforms. By contrast, the various regulation schemes of Dutch spelling adopted over the past 100 years are genuine orthography reforms. The changes that were effected pertained to grapheme–phoneme correspondences as well as individual word spellings, but did not affect the (Roman) script or the (phonographic) writing system.

The principles and criteria for effecting orthography reforms are of two kinds, psycholinguistic-technical and sociolinguistic. The former have to do with the utility of an orthography, while the latter involve the social conditions of implementing reforms. The need or desire for orthography reform usually arises as a result of real or perceived discrepancies between speech and writing and inconsistent or overly opaque grapheme–phoneme correspondences. Amending such deficits requires a thorough understanding of the principles underlying the orthography in question and a clearly defined standard of excellence to be met or approximated by the reformed system. Both of these criteria are of the psycholinguistic-technical kind. Their proper assessment is more complicated than is often assumed, and reforms carried out in disregard of either may be counterproductive.

The underlying principles of extant orthographies are highly abstract and hardly ever uniform. Unless an orthography is created from scratch there is no absolute measure for the ideal level of phonetic abstraction, because every reform has to take as its point of departure the existing conventions which, for the sake of continuity, cannot be abolished altogether. Also, apparently obvious reform measures such as increasing the simplicity (reducing the polyvalence of graphemes), regularity (eliminating irregular spellings) and economy (eliminating seemingly redundant graphemes, e.g. <x> in English) of the orthography in question can have unpredictable consequences. Likewise, the standard of excellence is not easily defined in a uniform and objective way. Advantages for the writer, e.g. greater simplicity of grapheme–phoneme correspondence, may not benefit the reader; and what is easiest to learn is not necessarily easiest to use. Historical experience with spelling reforms is still quite limited and hardly warrants any general statement about what kinds of effects are brought about by what kind of adjustment.

Furthermore, technical considerations are only one aspect of orthography reforms and, as many aborted attempts would suggest, not the critical one. Whether or not a reform can be implemented successfully depends more on social attitudes than on linguistic sophistication and utility. Like scripts, orthographies are often an object of sentimental attachment and viewed as a symbol of ethnic or national identity. Many reform proposals, however moderate and technically sound, have therefore met with public opposition, especially on the part of opinion leaders such as professional literati who value tradition and stability higher than whatever unknown advantages the new system may offer. It is also common that technical considerations are compromised in order to accommodate socially desirable features. Thus, although the contents of orthography reforms mainly concern technical aspects of the written form of a language, they highlight the fact that in addition to instrumental functions orthographies also fulfil symbolic functions.

See also Script reform; Spelling reform; Writing system.

Reading Fishman 1977; Berry 1958, 1977; (case studies) Garbe 1971; de Rooij and Verhoeven 1988; Rabin 1971; Thimonnier 1967.

Oscan script *See* Old Italic scripts

Figure 8 Potsherds with the names of Themistocles, Pericles, Aristides and Kimon scratched on them for ostracism (Agora Museum, Athens)

ostracon [Gk ὄστρακον 'earthen vessel, tile, potsherd'] In the city state of Athens ostracism was a method of temporary banishment effected by public vote, where the name of the person whom it was proposed to banish was written on pieces of broken pottery (figure 8). In addition to providing valuable epigraphic data, *ostraca* are an indication of the spread of literacy in ancient Athens and its role in Greek democracy. A person could be banished from Athens only if his name was written on *ostraca* by at least 6,000 citizens – clear evidence that the art of writing was not confined to a class of professional scribes.

outer form of writing systems A term used in the study of writing to refer to the graphic design features of writing systems as opposed to their inner form, which has to do with the underlying structural principles of how writing systems represent language.
See also INNER FORM OF WRITING SYSTEMS.

P, p /piː/ The sixteenth letter of the English alphabet is a descendant from Semitic *pē* through Greek *pi* (Π, π) and Latin, where it got its present form. The small letter is a variant of the capital.

Pahawh Hmong writing *See* HMONG WRITING

Pahlavi script The principal script of Middle Persian, spoken from the third century BCE to the ninth century CE, the Pahlavi script (also Pehlevi) is a derivative of the Aramaic consonant script. Since Persian is an Indo-European language, a consonant script with its inherently imperfect V indication is not very suitable. The Pahlavi script is attested in slightly different varieties on coins, in inscriptions and in manuscript literature from the Arsakidan (256 BCE to 226 CE) and Sassanidan (226 to 642 CE) periods. A great deal of the extant literature is religious in nature, concerning Zoroastrianism (Book Pahlavi). Religious texts of the Manichaeans of roughly the same time are written in the MANICHAEAN SCRIPT (Turfan Pahlavi).

The direction of the Pahlavi script is from right to left. Word division is marked by a dot. Consisting of only 20 letters, it is hard to read because of polyvalent V indication and graphic similarity of several letters, e.g. those for *u/w*, *n* and *r* (table 1). Another feature which adds to the complexity of Pahlavi writing is that

	',a		m
	i,y		n
	u,w		l,r
	h,x		s
	k		z
	g		c
	t		š
	d		č, ž
	f,p		ḥ
	b		r

Table 1 The Pahlavi (Middle Persian) alphabet

many words are written as *xenograms* or *heterograms*, spelt in regular Aramaic fashion but read in Middle Persian, a practice presumably inherited from Achaemenid scribes who interspersed Old Persian writing with many xenograms of other languages. In Pahlavi, lexical stems are often written as xenograms, whereas inflexional endings are added in Persian phonetic spelling. In Romanized transliteration these different uses of Pahlavi, letters are conventionally reflected by representing xenograms in upper case and phonetic spellings in lower case. The Pahlavi script shares most of its letters with the Avestan script which was derived from it, but the latter has more than twice the number of letters, allowing for a more accurate rendition of the Persian language. After the Islamic conquest Zoroastrians continued for centuries to write their scriptures in the Pahlavi script.
See also AVESTA ALPHABET; OLD PERSIAN WRITING; PERSIAN ALPHABET; XENOGRAPHY.
Reading Henning 1958; Mackenzie 1967; Nyberg 1964–74.

palaeography [Gk παλαῖο 'old' + γράφειν 'to write'] An auxiliary science of historiography concerned with the study of ancient forms of writing, especially manuscripts. The designation was first introduced in 1708 by Bernard de Montfaucon (1655–1741) in his seminal work *Palaeographia Graeca* which for the next two centuries set the standard for investigating Greek codices. A comprehensive systematization of palaeographic knowledge was accomplished by Ludwig Traube (1861–1907) who laid the foundations of the historical study of abbreviations and ligatures. Within the context of Western scholarship, palaeography has since become organized as a separate discipline, while palaeographic research about writing other than Greek and Latin is usually closely affiliated with the respective philologies. Looking at handwriting as a source of historical knowledge, palaeography examines letter forms, ligatures, punctuation marks and other features characteristic of individual hands which, when systematically compared, can be used for dating manuscripts, identifying their place and/or scriptorium of origin, and, in medieval times, the scribe of a given piece of writing.
See also EPIGRAPHY; MANUSCRIPT; PALIMPSEST.
Reading Brown 1990; Bischoff 1986; Ullman 1980.

Pāli writing Closely related to Sanskrit, Pāli is the language of Buddhist scriptures. It originated in Maghada, the land of Buddha's birth in the foothills of the Himalayas (modern Bihar), and was carried as a written language to south India, Ceylon, Pegu (modern Burma or Myanmar), Cambodia and Siam. The Pāli language was initially written in a variety of the Old Brāhmī script (BRĀHMĪ WRITING). When Buddhism spread to Burma early in the first millennium CE, the PEGUAN SCRIPT evolved which in turn gave rise to the BURMESE WRITING. Together with other Indian-derived South East Asian scripts of the Hindu kingdoms in Fu-nam and Champa (modern Vietnam) these have sometimes been referred to as the Pāli branch of Indian scripts. This designation is misleading, as it suggests a uniform development and a relationship with the Pāli language. However, Pāli has no script of its own: in each of the countries where it is used as a religious language it is written in the local script (table 2).
See also INDIAN WRITING SYSTEMS.
Reading Elizarenkova and Toporov 1976.

Vowel letters

अ	आ	इ	ई	उ	ऊ	ए	ओ
අ	ආ	ඉ	ඊ	උ	ඌ	එ	ඔ
a	ā	i	ī	u	ū	ē	ō

Consonant letters

क	ख	ग	घ	ङ
ක	ඛ	ග	ඝ	ඞ
ka	**kha**	ga	gha	ṅa
च	छ	ज	झ	ञ
ච	ඡ	ජ	ඣ	ඤ
ca.	cha	ja	jha	ña
ट	ठ	ड	ढ	ण
ට	ඨ	ඩ	ඪ	ණ
ṭa	ṭha	ḍa	ḍha	ṇa
त	थ	द	ध	न
ත	ථ	ද	ධ	න
ta	tha	da	dha	na
प	फ	ब	भ	म
ප	ඵ	බ	භ	ම
pa	pha	ba	bha	ma

य	र	ल	व	स	ह	ळ
ය	ර	ල	ව	ස	හ	ළ
ya	ra	la	**va** or wa	sa	ha	la

Table 2 The Pāli syllabic alphabet in Devanāgarī (above) and Sinhalese script (below)

palimpsest [Gk παλίμψηστος 'scraped again'] A manuscript from which the original writing has been scraped off in order to reuse the leaves for fresh writing. This procedure was applied in antiquity before the invention of paper as well as in medieval times when writing material was still expensive and hard to obtain. Often the text on a roll of vellum or parchment was erased only imperfectly. Thus slight traces of the first writing remained and showed through the second writing on the *codices rescripti*, as palimpsests were called in Latin, or they could once again become legible (figure 1). With chemical treatment and/or ultraviolet rays many ancient texts were recovered by palaeographers from palimpsest manuscripts.
See also MANUSCRIPT; PALAEOGRAPHY; WRITING SURFACE.

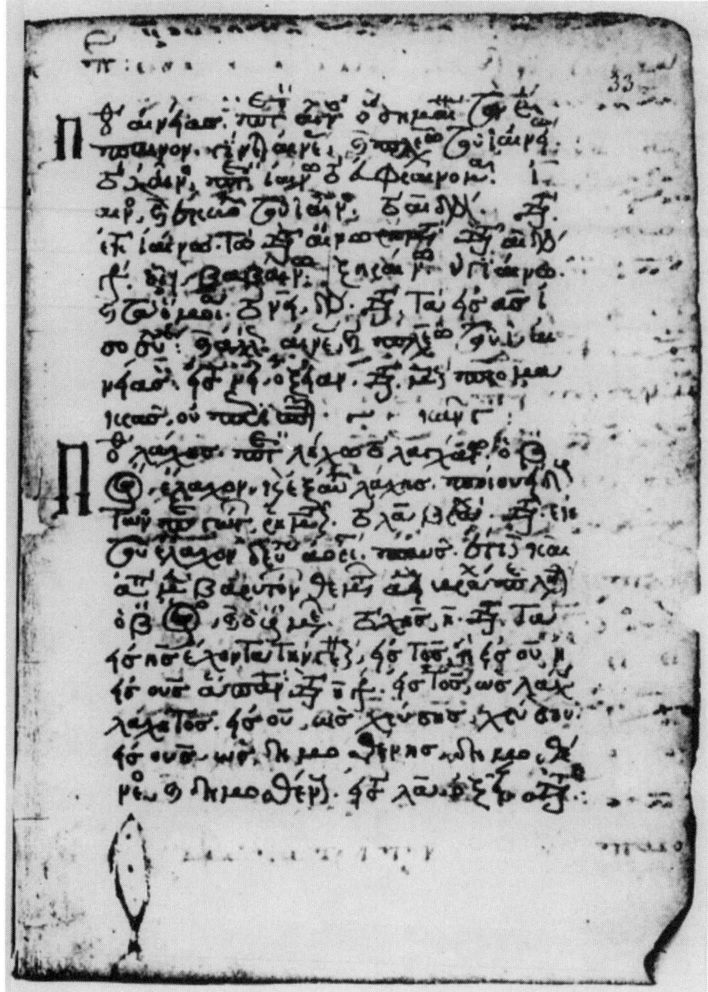

Figure 1 Page from a medieval parchment palimpsest. The upper writing is from a grammar textbook of the late thirteenth century CE *written in an Italo-Greek hand. The first writing underneath consists of several Greek texts, probably dating from the eleventh century (Herzog August Bibliothek Wolfenbüttel)*

palindrome [Gk παλίνδρομος 'running back'] A word or phrase reading the same backwards as forwards, such as *Laval* and *Madam, I'm Adam*, or French *Esope reste ici et se repose*. A wider definition includes phrases which can be read backwards yielding a different though meaningful expression, e.g. *Roma, Amor*. For entertainment and magic purposes palindromes of hundreds of letters have been constructed. A Latin palindrome of rather obscure meaning has been handed down since the first century CE, *SATOR AREPO TENET OPERA ROTAS* (lit. 'The sower Arepo holds the wheels through his work'), which can also be arranged as a magic square:

S A T O R
A R E P O
T E N E T
O P E R A
R O T A S

The palindrome depends on alphabetic writing. In other writing systems the conditions for reading an expression backwards the same as forwards are different, because the units of segmentation are different. In Japanese, KANA, for example, the loan word *tomato* is a palindrome, since the segmentation is syllabic: とまと *to-ma-to*. In music the palindrome is an important composition technique known as 'crab', for example, in Bach's *Musical Offering* and Schönberg's *Twelve Tone Music*.
See also WORD PLAY.

Pallava script A southern Indian script originating in the kingdom of Pallava (northern Mysore), the Pallava script is a variety of the GRANTHA SCRIPT. It is found on numerous inscriptions in south India and Sri Lanka dating from the fifth to the eighth centuries CE. This script has also been transplanted to the Indonesian archipelago where it became the parent script of the Old Kawi script as known from Old Javanese inscriptions from about the middle of the eighth century.
See also KAWI SCRIPT; INDIAN WRITING SYSTEMS.
Reading Bühler 1980; Casparis 1975.

Palmyran script A derivative of the ARAMAIC WRITING which was used in the desert town of Palmyra (modern Tadmor, Syria) from the beginning of the current era until the destruction of the Palmyran kingdom by Aurelian in 273 CE. It is attested in various monumental inscriptions found at the ruins of Palmyra, many of them bilingual in Greek and Palmyran. This facilitated its decipherment which was achieved in the mid-eighteenth century CE in Paris by Abbé Barthélemy shortly after its modern discovery (table 3).
Reading Barthélemy 1754; Naveh 1982.

paper According to the *Hou han shu* (*Annals of the Later Han Dynasty*, 25–220 CE) the Chinese invented paper in 105 CE. It became popular in China from the later part of the second century CE. From China paper spread to Korea and Japan in the seventh century, first the material and then the technology of producing it, based on vegetable fibres (figure 2). Through contacts in Samarkand, paper became known in the Arab world around the middle of the eighth century. It took another four centuries before Arab traders introduced the new writing material to Europe. It made its first appearance on the continent in Spain and Italy in the twelfth century and then spread to the north. Linen rags were used as the basis of the first quality paper produced in Europe. As it was cheap and good, paper was quickly accepted as a supplementary writing material, although for a long time PARCHMENT remained the preferred material for official documents. The increased availability of writing material made possible the production of more

Hebrew	Name	Transliteration
א	Aleph	'
ב	Beth	b
ג	Ghimel	g
ד	Daleth	d
ה	He	h
ו	Vau	w
ז	Zain	z
ח	Heth	h
ט	Teth	t
י	Jod	j
כ	Caph	k
ל	Lamed	l
מ	Mem	m
נ	Nun	n
ס	Samech	s
ע	Aïn	ʿ
פ	Pe	p
צ	Tzade	s
ק	Koph	q
ר	Resch	r
ש	Sin or Schin	š
ת	Thau	t

Table 3 Abbé Barthélemy's decipherment of the Palmyran alphabet (Roman transliteration added)

books and indirectly contributed to the search for new methods of reproducing manuscripts, which eventually Printing provided.

Once paper had reached the European continent, its value was quickly recognized. Paper making became an important and prestigious craft, and each manufactory used its own watermark to identify its product. Italy, where paper has been produced since 1276 (Fabriano), was the main supplier of the European market until paper mills opened in Germany (1389), England (1494) and Russia (1565).

Reading Blum 1932; Tsien 1962.

papyrus Made from the fibrous enclosure of the marrow of the papyrus plant, a kind of reed native to the Nile region, papyrus was the material the Egyptians used for manuscript writing in the Hieratic script and the Demotic script (figure 3). The marrow was cut into thin strips which were laid flat side by side in two layers, one at right angles to the other. The two layers were pressed on to each other, treated with a gum solution, and flattened until the surface was smooth enough to receive writing in ink with a brush. The resulting sheets were glued together and rolled up. The inside of the roll with fibres running in the horizontal direction was used for writing. It is called *recto* in Palaeography. The

Figure 2 Paper making in Han China, as reconstructed by Chinese archaeologists
Source: *reproduced from Wen Wu, 1977/1, 57*

verso or reverse with fibres running in the vertical direction was not inscribed in ancient Egypt but, as writing became more common, it was often used for lack of fresh material.

Papyrus was exported from Egypt throughout the Mediterranean world of antiquity and extensively used for writing by the Greeks and Romans. Being susceptible to damage from both dampness and dryness, it was by no means an ideal writing material, but for centuries it was unrivalled for its flexibility and light weight. Many important documents from Egypt, Greece and Rome have been preserved on papyrus rolls. The latest known papyrus manuscript is a

Figure 3 Papyrus harvest illustrated in an Egyptian inscription of the early fifteenth century BCE

papal bull of 1022 CE, a time when PARCHMENT had long replaced papyrus as the most common writing material in Europe.

The word *papyrus* is only attested in Greek and Latin but is probably of Egyptian origin, meaning 'that of the king'. Greek βύβλος of which Latin *liber* is derived came to mean 'book'.

See also MANUSCRIPT; WRITING SURFACE.

Reading Lewis 1974.

parchment Treated skins of animals used for writing. The parchment made from calfskin (vellum) was the best. Hides were used for writing in Egypt as early as 2000 BCE but, in the form of sheets that were prepared by splitting, tanning and bleaching, the material was not commonly used until the second century BCE. Although parchment was both heavier and more expensive, it replaced the fragile PAPYRUS to become the most widely used writing material in the ancient and medieval world. It was valued especially for its durability. Because of the high cost of producing parchment, the material was commonly recycled. Texts that were no longer needed were scraped off so that the surface could be inscribed once again. Manuscripts of this kind are known as PALIMPSESTS. The name *parchment* derives from the kingdom of Pergamum in Asia Minor whence it was exported into the Roman world. There it became known as *pergamena*.

See also WRITING SURFACE.

parenthesis A pair of rounded brackets, so called in British English, used as punctuation marks to introduce a word or phrase into a context upon which it has a bearing in a purely subordinate way. Syntactic constructions do not become incomplete when elements enclosed in parentheses (additional explanations, translations, references etc.) are deleted.

See also PUNCTUATION.

Pashto writing An Iranian language spoken by the Pathans of Afghanistan as well as north-western Pakistan, Pashto has been written in Arabic letters since the sixteenth century CE. In addition to the four letters added to the Arabic PERSIAN ALPHABET, the Pashto alphabet has another ten supplementary letters to accommodate Pashto sounds (table 4). The resultant alphabet of 42 letters allows for a near-phonemic orthography.

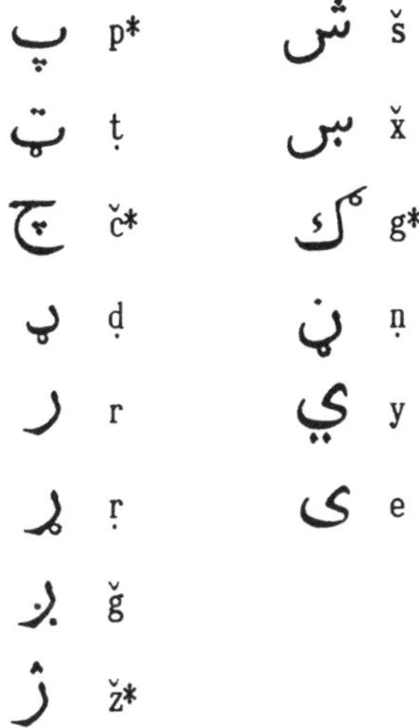

Table 4 Pashto letters added to the Arabic alphabet (also in Persian)*

pasigraphy [Gk πασ- 'all' + γράφειν 'to write'] A system of signs designed to express meaning visually without reference to speech. The underlying idea of attempts at constructing pasigraphic systems is universal communication unhindered by the specifics and limitations of individual languages.
Reading Freudenthal 1960.

Passepa script *See* 'PHAGS-PA SCRIPT.

Peguan script A northern Indian Brāhmī derivative which came to Burma (modern Myanmar) with the spread of Buddhism, the Peguan (also Pyu) script as of the eighth century served for writing the Mon language, also known as 'Peguan' or 'Talaing'. It is the parent script of the modern BURMESE WRITING (table 5).
See also INDIAN WRITING SYSTEMS.

Pehlevi script *See* PAHLAVI SCRIPT.

period A dot <.> on the line, called a *full stop* in British English, functioning as a punctuation mark of most alphabetic orthographies to indicate the end of a sentence in the declarative or imperative mood. It contrasts in this function with the question mark <?> and the exclamation mark <!> as final marks of sentences in other moods. The period is also used as an element of many abbreviations, such as *e.g., ed., Rev., etc.* Its use as a decimal point in writing figures is also common.
See also PUNCTUATION.

Persian alphabet After having been recorded in the OLD PERSIAN WRITING, AVESTA ALPHABET and PAHLAVI SCRIPT, the Persian language came to be written in Arabic letters in the wake of the Arabic conquest of Iran (642 CE). Four letters

Vowel letters

a i u e ā

Consonant letters

ka kha ga gha ṅa

ča/čha ǧa ǧha ña

ṭa ṭha ḍa/ḍha ṇa

ta tha/da/dha na

pa pha ba bha ma

ya ra la va

śa ṣa sa ha

Table 5 The Old Peguan syllabic alphabet

for sounds which do not occur in Arabic were added to the Arabic alphabet: پ /p/, چ /č/, ژ /ž/ and گ /g/. Naskhī is the script generally used in books and newspapers.

Largely unchanged since the ninth century CE, the Persian orthography is quite involved, because many graphemes are polyvalent (table 6). This is a result of the practice, common to all languages which have adopted the Arabic alphabet as the script of the holy Qur'ān, of retaining the spelling of Arabic loan words although their pronunciation may differ significantly from the Arabic model. Another difficulty is that short Vs are not written, giving rise to numerous homographs whose pronunciation and meaning must be determined from context. Modern standard Persian is the national language of Iran, where it is called 'Farsi'.
See also Arabic scripts; Arabic written language; Tajik writing.
Reading Dresden 1958.

Persian cuneiform *See* Old Persian writing

ا	aː a, ɪ, o	د	d	ط	tʻ	م	m
ب	b	ذ	z	ظ	z	ن	n
پ	pʻ	ر	r	ع	ʔ	و	v; uː, oːw
ت	tʻ	ز	z	غ	q	ه	h, -ɛ
ث	s	ژ	ʒ	ف	f	ی	j; iː, eːj
ج	dʒ	س	s	ق	q	ء	ʔ
چ	tʃ	ش	ʃ	ک	kʻ		
ح	h	ص	s	گ	g		
خ	x	ض	z	ل	l		

Table 6 The Persian alphabet: independent letter forms (for other letter forms see ARABIC SCRIPTS*)*

petroglyph [Gk πέτρα 'rock' + γλυφή 'carving'] Although the term seems to refer to any writing engraved in stone, it is usually reserved for prehistoric carved or painted (then known as petrogram) signs which are not writing proper but pictorial or linear representations of objects (figure 4).

Figure 4 Prehistoric petroglyphs from the north-west coast of the American continent: Petroglyph Park in Nanaimo, Vancouver Island

'Phags-pa script A syllabic alphabet derived from the TIBETAN WRITING, the 'Phags-pa script was created in 1269 CE at the order of Khubilai, Great Khan of the Mongols, by Matidhvaja Śrībhadra (1239–1280), a Tibetan sage better known by his honorary title 'Phags-pa Lama. The Chinese transliteration is *p'a-ssĕ-pa,* whence 'Passepa script'. Because of the square form of its letters, it is also known as 'square script' (*dörbelǰin üsüg* in Mongolian).

Khubilai's reasons for having a new script designed for Mongolian were two. One was that the Uighur script in which Mongolian was written at the time was ill-suited to express Mongolian phonology. The first requirement was thus that

Figure 5 'Phags-pa Mongolian inscription on a metal tablet serving as a passport for safe passage through the Mongol realm (Kansu Provincial Museum, China)

the new script should more accurately reflect the sounds of Mongolian. The second rationale was more ambitious. Khubilai ruled over a multilingual empire and had designs for the new script to serve as a unifying bond which could also be used to write other languages (figure 5). Referring to the alphabet devised by 'Phags-pa Lama initially as the Mongolian script, he therefore eventually designated it as the 'state script' (Chinese *kuo-tzŭ*). In 1275 the Han-lin Academy was charged with its supervision and cultivation. In addition to (an eastern dialect of) Mongolian the 'Phags-pa script was used for an educated vernacular variety of Chinese. Individual inscriptions in Tibetan, Sanskrit and Turkish have also been preserved. However, although the government actively promoted use of the 'Phags-pa script, for example by subjecting publication of Mongolian books in the Uighur script to court permission, Khubilai's script policy ended in failure, because his Chinese officials did not adopt it and neither did ordinary literate Chinese and Mongols. The latest known 'Phags-pa inscription dates from 1352, a fragment of birch bark discovered at the Volga.

'Phags-pa Lama's design followed the Tibetan pattern with independent V graphemes and C graphemes of the Indian type with inherent *a* (table 7). He also

	Tibetan	'Phags-pa		Tibetan	'Phags-pa
ka	ཀ	ꡀ	*tsa*	ཙ	ꡐ
kha	ཁ	ꡁ	*thsa*	ཚ	ꡑ
ga	ག	ꡂ	*dza*	ཛ	ꡒ
ṅa	ང	ꡃ	*wa*	ཝ	ꡓ
ča	ཅ	ꡄ	*ža*	ཞ	ꡔ
čha	ཆ	ꡅ	*za*	ཟ	ꡕ
ǧa	ཇ	ꡆ	*ˏa*	འ	ꡖ
ña	ཉ	ꡇ	*ya*	ཡ	ꡗ
ta	ཏ	ꡈ	*ra*	ར	ꡘ
tha	ཐ	ꡉ	*la*	ལ	ꡙ
da	ད	ꡊ	*ša*	ཤ	ꡚ
na	ན	ꡋ	*sa*	ས	ꡛ
pa	པ	ꡌ	*ha*	ཧ	ꡜ
pha	ཕ	ꡍ	*'a*	ཨ	ꡝ
ba	བ	ꡎ	*fa*		ꡤ
ma	མ	ꡏ			

'Phags-pa vowels

a	ꡝ	o	ꡡ
i	ꡞ	ō	
ī		au	
u	ꡟ	ē	ꡦ
ū		ai	

Table 7 The 'Phags-pa syllabic alphabet and its Tibetan model

Figure 6 Drawing of the Phaistos disk-obverse

borrowed certain principles of other Central Asian scripts. For example, the representation of /ö/ and /ü/ with the graphemes for *eo* and *eu*, respectively, is modelled on the Uighur Brāhmī script. Following Mongolian custom, the 'Phags-pa script is written in vertical columns which, unlike Chinese, are arranged from left to right.

See also MONGOLIAN WRITING.

Reading Pelliot 1925; Poppe 1974.

Phaistos disk A clay disk measuring 16 cm in diameter which was excavated in 1908 at the Minoan palace at Hagia Triada, Crete (figure 6). Both sides of the disk are imprinted with stamped signs arranged in a single spiral line circling around the centre. The entire 'text' consists of 214 signs which are grouped in sets of between two and six elements divided by vertical lines. Except for what is revealed by its physical appearance, very little is known about the disk. The number of different signs, 45, suggests a syllabic system, but since the Phaistos disk is the only document of its kind and since nothing is known about the language it presumably represents, this is no more than a conjecture (table 8).

Figure 6 Drawing of the Phaistos disk-reverse

Dating is also uncertain. On the basis of collateral archaeological evidence it is considered likely that the disk was made in the seventeenth century BCE. However, some scholars dispute both the disk's tentative date and its place of origin which may, they claim, not be Minoan. Even the direction of the inscription poses a problem. The only hypothesis that is not completely arbitrary has to do with the directionality of the faces in the pictorial signs. It has been argued that the text on the disk starts at the outside, because in other scripts that make use of pictorial signs the faces are facing towards the beginning of a line rather than away from the beginning. The rudimentary state of knowledge has invited interpretations that range from the fanciful to the bizarre. However, despite various claims to the contrary, the Phaistos disk remains undeciphered. The signs of the inscription bear no resemblance to CRETAN WRITING or other writings from adjacent areas of the eastern Mediterranean, and the method of imprinting them into the plastic clay with stamps that must have been especially cut for this purpose is likewise without any parallel. Thus, this peculiar document stands alone in the history of writing.
Reading Schwarz 1959; Duhoux 1977.

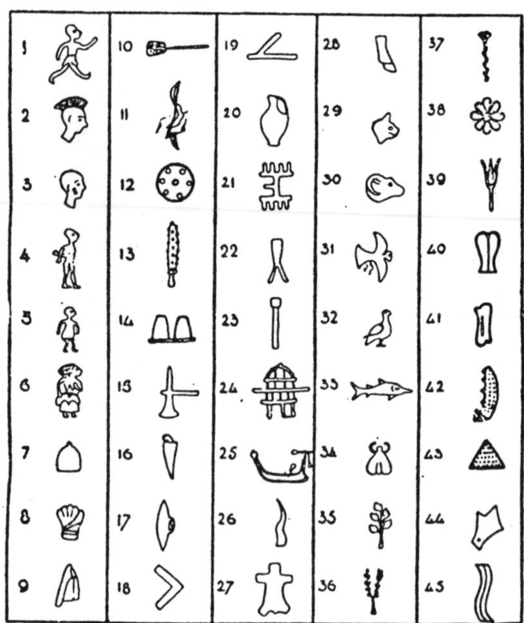

Table 8 The sign inventory of the Phaistos disk

Philippine scripts Prior to European contact in the sixteenth century, writing was known in the Philippines in the form of syllabic alphabets of the Indian type and probably of Indian descent. As in Central America, the Spanish *conquistadores* had little esteem for the native literary tradition and, in their efforts to Christianize the country, are thought to have burned or otherwise destroyed many manuscripts written on palm leaves and bamboo tubes. It is for this reason that palaeographic documentation is scanty. Except for the MANGYAN SCRIPT which is reportedly still occasionally used on the island of Mindoro, none of the ancient scripts have survived.

The origin and transmission of the Philippine scripts is not documented, but on the basis of comparative analysis of variant forms of the individual letters, there is wide agreement among students of Philippine palaeography that they are derived from the Old KAWI SCRIPT of Java which is itself of Indian extraction. A number of different forms are documented in extant manuscripts of different regional origin and language, but they are generally considered to be varieties of the same proto-alphabet, called *Baybayin* in Tagalog. It consists of 17 graphemes, three for independent Vs and 14 for Cs with inherent *a* (table 9). Indication of other Vs is by means of diacritics, following the Indian pattern. Judging from the alphabets that have been recorded by Spanish missionaries, there was no device for indicating syllable-final Cs (*virāma*).

The principal languages written in these scripts are Tagalog, Ilocano, Pampangan, Pangasinan and Binisaya (Visaya in table 10). Pardo de Tavera's table has been copied time and again, and many more or less accurate copies of copies are found throughout the literature on this subject. The names in the table are those of scholars who have published reports on Philippine scripts: Pedro

Table 9 Philippine syllabary from the island of Palawan (on the basis of data collected by José Rilla, made available by Antoon Postma)

Anciens Alphabets des Philippines

Langues	Equivalents	a	e, i	o, u	ka	ga	ñga	ta	da	na	pa	ba	ma	ya	la	wa	sa	ha
Tagale	N°. 1 Chirino																	
	„ 2 Sⁿ. Agustin																	
	„ 3 De Mas																	
	„ 4 De Mas																	
Ilocano	„ 5 De Mas																	
	„ 6 Jacquet																	
Visaya	. 7 Ezguerra																	
	. 8 Mentrida																	
Pangasinan	. 9 De Mas																	
Pampango	. 10 De Mas																	
(?)	. 11 Riedel																	
	„ 12 Riedel																	

Table 10 Ancient Philippine alphabets, compiled by Pardo de Tavera 1884

Chirino y Delgado, Gaspar de San Agustín, Sinibaldo de Mas, M. Eugene Jacquet, Domingo Ezguerra, Alonso Méntrida and J. G. F. Riedel. A collection of such accounts was compiled by Marcilla y Martín.

See also INDIAN WRITING SYSTEMS; MANGYAN SCRIPT; TAGALOG WRITING.

Reading Pardo de Tavera 1884; Marcilla y Martín 1895; Francisco 1977; Postma 1988.

Phoenician alphabet The most widely used variety of the west Semitic consonant alphabet, the Phoenician script is attested inscriptionally from the tenth to the first centuries BCE. The earliest known inscription is from the stone sarcophagus of Ahiram, king of Byblos (figure 7). It dates from about 1000 BCE. From the coastal strip of Palestine the script was taken to Phoenician colonies throughout the Mediterranean. Its latest variant from Carthage is the PUNIC SCRIPT. As the major medium of west Semitic writing the Phoenician script was eventually supplanted by the Aramaic script which also extended to the east, displacing cuneiform.

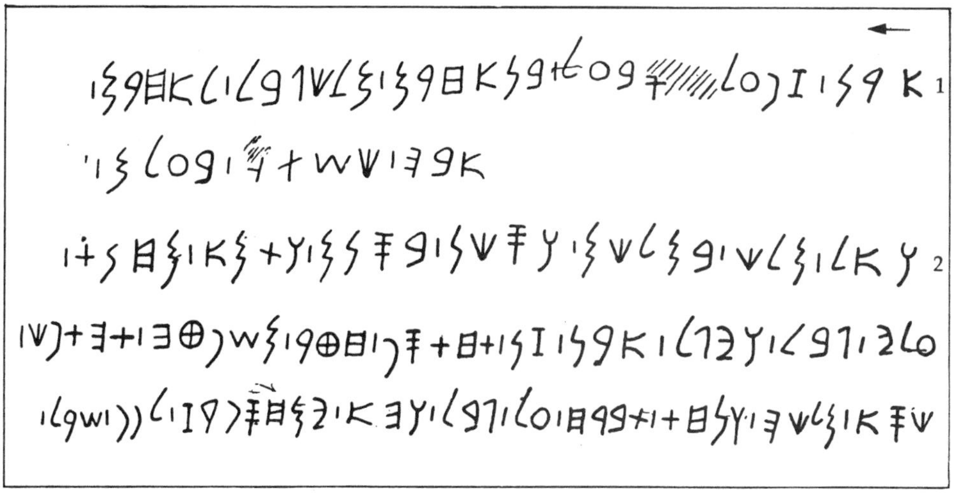

1 'rn z p' l[. . .]b' 1 bn 'ḥrm mlk Gbl l 'ḥrm 'bh k šth b ' lm

2 w–' l mlk b–mlkm w–skn b–snm w–tm' mḥnt ' lj Gbl w–jgl 'rn zn
tḥtsp htr mšpth thtpk ks'mlkh w–nḥt tbrḥ ' l Gbl w–h' jmḥ

1 Sarcophagus made by Ba' l, son of Ahiram, king of Gubla, for Ahiram, his father, when he laid him to rest in eternity

2 And when a king of the kings, a governor of the governor and the commander of the camp ascends to Gubla to uncover this coffin, shall the sceptre of his judiciary be removed, the thrône of his reign be toppled over, and shall peace flee from Gubla and he be eradicated

Figure 7 Phoenician inscription from the sarcophagus of King Ahiram, Byblos, eleventh century BCE

The Greeks used the term *phonikē* to refer to the eastern Mediterranean coast. It seems to correspond to the biblical (*Kenaʿ an*) and Akkadian (*Kinahhu*) names for Canaan. Both the Greek and the Semitic terms originally referred to a purple dye exported by Phoenician traders: hence the overlap in usage of 'Phoenician' and 'Canaan'. The Phoenician alphabet developed from the proto-Canaanite script which came into existence in the seventeenth or eighteenth century BCE and seems to have adopted the principle of representing only the consonants of their language from the Egyptians (table 11). The Phoenician letter names have been interpreted in accordance with the ACROPHONIC PRINCIPLE. Fourteen of them seem to represent the initial sounds of names of objects designated by their pictorial predecessors documented in various inscriptions in Palestinian and PROTO-SINAITIC SCRIPTS. For example, Semitic *dāleth* means 'door'. The triangular symbol which came to stand for *d* may have been a representation of a three-cornered tent door. By the eleventh century the 22 consonant letters of the Canaanite alphabet were purely linear symbols. Whatever pictographic form and logographic value they may have possessed at an earlier stage of development were lost. The direction of writing was stabilized from right to left. In early Phoenician inscriptions, word division was marked with vertical strokes or dots, but from the eighth century onwards words were written consecutively without division.

What exactly the lack of vowel letters in the Phoenician and other west Semitic scripts implies for the representation of language is still a matter of controversy. While Gelb (1963) hypothesized that each Canaanite/Phoenician letter stood for a C plus any contiguous V, Naveh (1982) insists that the letter values were strictly consonantal. In any event, the writing is focused on CONSONANT ROOTS which in Semitic languages carry the gist of lexical information. The use of the Phoenician script for a millennium, and its structural similarity to other Semitic alphabets including modern Hebrew and Arabic, underscore its general suitability for the Phoenician language.

The Phoenician alphabet gave rise not only to other Semitic scripts such as the Old Hebrew, Moabite and Samaritan, but also, and most importantly for the further development of writing, to the GREEK ALPHABET. That the Greeks traditionally call their own writing φοινικήια γράμματα 'Phoenician letters' is evidence of the fact that they adopted writing from the Phoenicians, as reported by Herodotus (v, 58):

> The Phoenicians with Cadmus brought arts and letters to the Greeks, since as I think the Greeks did not have them before but the Phoenicians were first to use them. With the passage of time they changed the form as well as the sound of letters . . . rightly calling the letters Phoenician after those who had introduced them into Greece.

See also SEMITIC WRITING.

Reading Dunand 1945; Friedrich 1951; Gelb 1963; Millard 1976, 1986; Naveh 1982.

Name	Symbol	Value
ʼāleph	𐤀	ʼ
bēth	𐤁	b
gīmel	𐤂	g
dāleth	𐤃	d
hē	𐤄	h
wāw	𐤅	w
zayin	𐤆	z
hēth	𐤇	ḥ
tēth	𐤈	t
yodh	𐤉	j
kaph	𐤊	k
lāmedh	𐤋	l
mēm	𐤌	m
nūn	𐤍	n
sāmekh	𐤎	s
ʻayin	𐤏	ʻ
pē	𐤐	p
sādhē	𐤑	s
qōph	𐤒	q
rēš	𐤓	r
šin	𐤔	š
tāw	𐤕	t

Table 11 The Phoenician alphabet

phoneme A group of similar speech sounds signified by an alphabetic letter. Although this definition is not universally accepted, it is the most relevant regarding the representation of linguistic units in writing. It may also be the best definition currently available. The relationship between phonemes and the letters of the Greek alphabet has been either ignored (by most linguists in this century) or considered a chicken-and-egg problem. Recent scholarship, however, has made it clear that 'phoneme' is an alphabet-induced concept. The complicated adaptation to their own language of the Phoenician CONSONANT SCRIPT, which was a rather imperfect but, for C root languages, a sufficient model of pronunciation, led the Greeks to recognize the resulting alphabet as an inventory of signs of segmental speech sounds. Ever since, the most common view of alphabetic writing has been that letters signify independently existing speech sounds, i.e. phonemes. However, the discrete nature of alphabetic notation makes the phonemes of a language appear a more clearly defined set than they actually are. That the alphabet is not, and never was, a transcription system is a relatively recent insight, and the idea that letters signify rather than create or pinpoint phonemes lingers on.

The term 'phoneme' was first coined in the late nineteenth century and has been used with a variety of different meanings. Many writing systems recognize the phoneme as a sense-discriminative speech sound in one way or another, e.g. Korean HAN'GŬL. Before the term 'phoneme' came into currency, other terms with similar meanings were used, notably LETTER which was especially common among eighteenth- and nineteenth-century grammarians. Whether or not the phoneme has an independent existence is a controversial question. On the psychological level there is evidence that phoneme identification, i.e. the segmentation of normal continuous speech, is facilitated by alphabetic literacy. This observation lends support to the notion that grammatical concepts, including that of the phoneme, are strongly dependent on the written form of language, if only because linguists are typically literate.
See also GRAMMAR; GRAPHEME; IPA; LITERACY.
Reading Abercrombie 1949; Krámsky 1974; Lüdtke 1969; Faber 1992.

phonemic orthography A spelling system which operates primarily on the level of phonemic representation, such as the Spanish, rather than recognizing higher-level units, such as the English orthography which operates on the morphophonemic level, or lower-level units, i.e. phonetic features, which are represented in the *han'gŭl* script of Korean.
See also ORTHOGRAPHY.

phonetic The sound-indicating part of a Chinese character, as opposed to the meaning-indicating part which is usually called a RADICAL. About nine out of ten Chinese characters contain a phonetic. Of these, many also occur as independent characters, such as 付 *fu* (table 12). The effectiveness of phonetics as indicators of the pronunciation of characters varies. Some are pronounced consistently the same when they occur independently and as elements of other characters; in other cases the tone of the characters of which they are a part varies; and in yet others there is correspondence only in some segmental phonemes, such that characters with the same phonetic would be pronounced variously as /pa/, /fa/

付	fù	to pay
府	fǔ	officialdom
附	fù	additional
符	fú	a seal
俯	fǔ	condescend
拊	fǔ	to beat

Table 12 The phonetic 付 fu *as a character and as part of other characters*

or /ba/. The total number of phonetics in the Chinese writing system is close to 900.
See also CHINESE WRITING SYSTEM.
Reading DeFrancis 1984b.

phonetic alphabet *See* INTERNATIONAL PHONETIC ALPHABET.

phonetic complement A phonetic sign added to a logogram which has more than one reading to indicate which is intended. Phonetic complements play an important role in AKKADIAN cuneiform because many logograms were polyvalent, having an Akkadian as well as a Sumerian reading. Thus for *šamu* 'sky' the Akkadians wrote *šamu-u*, where the final *u* is a phonetic complement which is not pronounced but only indicates Akkadian rather than Sumerian reading. Without it, the same logogram could also be read as *an*, the Sumerian word for 'sky'. In Egyptian, too, phonetic complements were used to reinforce intended readings. In English *-nd* and *-rd* can be regarded as phonetic complements when attached to 2 and 3, respectively, to indicate the readings *second* and *third*.

phonetic signs *See* PHONOGRAPHY.

phonetic transcription *See* INTERNATIONAL PHONETIC ALPHABET; TRANSCRIPTION.

phonetization The process in the development of writing by which pictorial or linear signs of objects are associated with stable sound values, typically word forms, and thus become elements of an incipient writing system (figure 8). There is wide agreement among students of the history of writing that phonetization is the decisive step from forerunners of writing to writing proper.
See also ORIGIN OF WRITING.
Reading Gelb 1963; DeFrancis 1989.

phonography Writing which expresses the sounds of speech as opposed to higher-level units, i.e. words and morphemes, is called 'phonographic'. This definition does not rule out that writing systems belonging to this category may express linguistic meaning in ways other than mediated through the representation

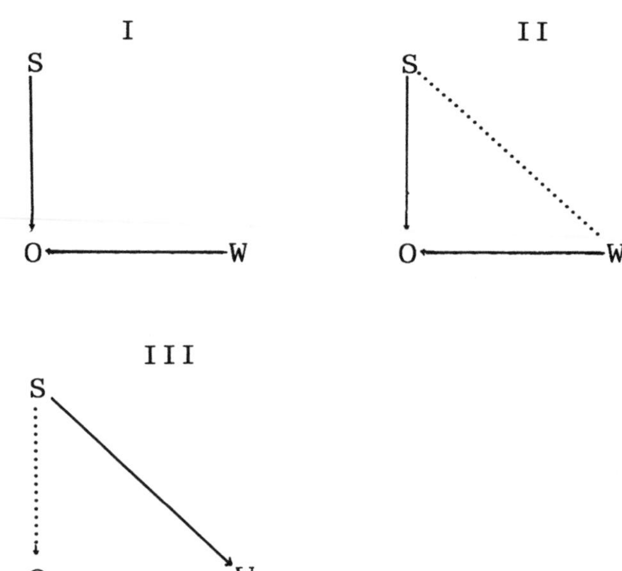

Figure 8 *Three steps of phonetization. (1) A visual sign S designates an object O which is also designated by a word W. No conventional relation exists between S and W. (II) In addition to the relations between S and O and between W and O, a relation is perceived between S and W, as yet unstable and secondary. (III) The relation between S and O is superseded by that between S and W. S thus becomes a sign which has a word as its primary referent*

of sound. It is focused on the minimal units of representation, i.e. the graphemes of the system, such as alphabetic letters, C + *a* letters of the Indian type, and Japanese *kana* signs which in isolation signify meaningless sounds. *See also* LOGOGRAM; WRITING SYSTEM.

Phrygian alphabet An early offshoot of the west Greek alphabet, the Phrygian script was used to write an Old Anatolian language of Indo-European extraction. Old Phrygian is attested inscriptionally in north and west Anatolia. The extant text corpus is limited to a few inscriptions dating from between the late eighth and the sixth centuries BCE. New Phrygian is better known from a large number of bilingual inscriptions, the parallel text being in Greek. These date from the second century CE. Except for some variant forms of the letters Z, Σ and Ψ, the alphabet is identical with its west Greek model.
Reading Young 1969; Brixhe and Lejeune 1984.

pictogram [Lat. *pīctus* 'drawn' + Gk γράφειν 'to write'] (*also* pictographic symbol) Visible sign expressing meaning without being conventionally associated with fixed linguistic form. The term is sometimes applied to writing systems such as the EGYPTIAN WRITING SYSTEM, HITTITE HIEROGLYPHIC and MAYA WRITING, as well as to SUMERIAN WRITING and the CHINESE WRITING SYSTEM in their earliest forms which are composed of symbols depicting objects or actions. Here the term refers to the outer form of the system alone, rather than to its mapping relation to language. Although the term 'picture writing' is sometimes used, in as much as writing is a visual representation of a specific language, no writing system is pictographic with respect to its inner form. Historically, sign systems which rely primarily on iconic relations (ICON) between pictures and objects, such as Amerindian PETROGLYPHS, are classified as pre-writing. Pictographic symbols of this sort can be interpreted but not read in the same sense as writing. While this upsets any attempt to create a universal visual writing system which is as potent in its expressive power as a natural language, it is exactly this limitation, i.e. the independence from language, wherein the utility of modern pictograms is grounded. They can be used conveniently to communicate information to a multilingual public or in environments where reliance on written messages is impractical (figure 9).

See also INNER FORM OF WRITING SYSTEMS; ORIGIN OF WRITING; OUTER FORM OF WRITING SYSTEMS.

Reading Ginneken 1939; Mallery 1893; Coulmas 1989, ch. 2; DeFrancis 1989, ch. 6.

Figure 9 Some modern pictograms for escalator, drinking fountain, cloakroom, shower, telephone, mail, currency exchange, first aid

pictographic symbol *See* PICTOGRAM

Pilipino alphabet Based on the educated variety of Tagalog as spoken in Manila and augmented with many loans from Spanish, English and other Philippine languages, Pilipino (also Filipino) is the official language of the Philippines. Prior to the Spanish colonization, Tagalog had been written in a syllabary of Indian descent which was, however, supplanted by the Roman alphabet. The modern Pilipino alphabet, called *abakada*, consists of 20 letters, including the digraph *NG* for /ŋ/, in the order *A, B, K, D, E, G, H, I, L, M, N, NG, O, P, R, S, T, U, W, Y*. Pilipino dictionaries are arranged in this order: the seven letters *C, F, J, Q, V, X*

and Z occur only in foreign proper names. The orthography is based on fairly simple grapheme–phoneme correspondences, although phonemic V length is not marked. There is no grapheme for the glottal stop, and /h/ is only written in syllable-initial position. Two abbreviated spellings for high-frequency morphemes are non-phonemic: the plural marker /maŋah/ and the case particle /naŋ/ are spelt *mga* and *ng*, respectively.
See also PHILIPPINE SCRIPTS; TAGALOG WRITING.
Reading Gonzalez and Bautista 1981.

Pinyin (*also hànyǔ pīnyīn*) Since 1958 the standard system of writing the Chinese language with Roman letters. The UN has adopted Pinyin as the official system of Romanization of Chinese names. Former *Peking, Nanking, Taipei* and *Sinkiang* are now generally spelled *Beijing, Nanjing, Taibei* and *Xinjiang*. Pinyin is a largely phonemic orthography which indicates the four tones of modern standard Chinese with accent marks on the tone-bearing Vs: flat <ā>, rising <á>, falling-rising <ǎ> and falling <à> (table 13).

Thanks to its systematicity and transparency, Pinyin was accepted rapidly and has largely replaced various other Romanization systems for Chinese which have been in use since the seventeenth century. However, the functions of the new Roman orthography are still very limited. Some recent dictionaries are arranged in alphabetical order, and it is used for annotating Chinese characters, especially for foreign readers (figure 10). It is also taught at the elementary school level, but although there are some periodicals published in Pinyin, it has not captured a place in everyday life as a medium of written communication.

When analysing the units of their language, the Chinese put the syllable central. The Pinyin alphabet is therefore explained for the Chinese in terms of the elements that combine to form a syllable, namely onsets and rhymes, as shown in table 14.
See also CHINESE WRITING REFORM.
Reading Chen 1996.

***plene* writing** [Lat. *plēnē* 'full'] **1** In Semitic philology, the use of the C letters *yōdh, wāw, hē* and *'āleph* as MATRES LECTIONIS to represent the long Vs /i:/, /u:/, /o:/ and /a:/, respectively. In older Semitic writings long Vs were generally left unindicated, but as of the ninth century BCE *plene* writing became more common. In late Semitic scripts such as the PUNIC SCRIPT and the MANDEAN SCRIPT the device of V indication reached a high degree of systematization. The *scriptio plena* contrasts with the *scriptio defectiva*, or writing without V indication. **2** In a wider sense the term *plene writing* is used to refer to redundant V indication. In Greek palaeography it is used to describe the practice in LINEAR B to represent C clusters and final Cs with a sequence of syllabic signs of the CV type. Thus κνοσος and τρι are spelt *ko-no-so-so* and *ti-ri*, respectively.
Reading Gelb 1963; Weinberg 1985.

pleremic writing Formed upon Gk πλήρης 'full', this term is used in the study of writing to designate writing systems consisting of elements which express both meaning and sound. It contrasts with CENEMIC WRITING, i.e. writing by means of signs which are void of meaning and express sound alone. Writing

CONSONANTS

Letter	IPA
b	b̥
p	pʻ
m	m
f	f
d	d̥
t	tʻ
n	n
l	l
g	g̊
k	kʻ
h	x
j	d̥ʑ
q	tɕʻ
x	ɕ
z	d̥z
c	tsʻ
s	s
zh	d̥ʐ
ch	tʂʻ
sh	ʂ
r	ʐ
ng	ŋ
y	j
w	w

VOWELS

Letter	IPA
a	a, (ɑ, ɛ)
o	ɔ, (o, ʊ)
e	ɵ, ʌ, ɛ
i, yi	i, (ɪ, ɹ, ɯ)
u, wu	u
ü, yu	y

DIPHTHONGS and TRIPHTHONGS

Letter	IPA
ai	aɪ
ao	ao
ou	ou
ei	ɛɪ
ia, ya	ĭa
iao, yao	ĭao
iou, iu, you	ĭou
ie, ye	ĭɛ
ua, wa	ŭa, wa
uai, wai	ŭaɪ, waɪ
uo, wo	ŭɔ, wɔ
uei, ui, wei	ŭeɪ, weɪ
üe, yue	yɛ
er	ɵɹ
-*i* (in *zhi, chi, shi, ri*)	ɹ
-*i* (in *zi, ci, si*)	ɯ

VOWELS + *n* or *ng*

Letter	IPA
an	an
ian, yan	ĭɛn
uan, wan	wan
üan, yuan	y̆ɛn
en	ɵn
uen, un, wen	wɵn
in, yin	ɪn
ün, yun	yn
ang	aŋ
iang, yang	ĭaŋ
uang, wang	wɑŋ
ong	ʊŋ
iong, yong	ĭʊŋ
eng	ʌŋ
ueng, weng	wʌŋ
ing, ying	ɪŋ

Table 13 The Pinyin alphabet of Chinese

systems such as the Egyptian, Sumerian and Chinese which operate partly on the lexical or morphemic levels of representation are pleremic.
See also Writing system.
Reading French 1976; Coulmas 1989.

point size In typography a point is the unit of type measurement in the generally recognized Didot system (so called after the Parisian typographer François

CAI LING
Yún dàndàn, fēng qīngqīng,
Xiǎoxiǎo niǎor qiàqià míng.
Shuǐ qīngqīng, gē shēngshēng,
Wǒ cǎi língr hú zhōngxīn.
Qīnglíng xiāng, hónglíng nèn,
Cǎi ya cǎi ya shǒu bù tíng.
Chuánr xiǎo, língr duō,
Língr sòng lǎoshī chángcháng xiān.

采　菱
云淡淡，风轻轻，
小小鸟儿恰恰鸣。
水清清，歌声声，
我采菱儿湖中心。
青菱香，红菱嫩，
采呀采呀手不停。
船儿小，菱儿多，
菱儿送老师尝尝鲜。

Translation

Picking water chestnuts

Thin clouds, a light breeze,
Little birds chirping in tune.
The water clear and clean, singing a song,
I pick water chestnuts at the central lake.
The green ones have a fragrance, the red ones are mellow.
Pluck, pluck, my hands don't halt.
Few boats, many water chestnuts,
I shall send some to my teacher to enjoy the fresh taste.

Figure 10 Chinese text in characters and Pinyin

Ambroise Didot, 1730–1804). Originally, the point was a measure used to subdivide the foot in an attempt to standardize printing. It still is a non-metric measure. One point equals 1/72 in or 0.3513 mm. In continental Europe, 2660 points equal 1 m, that is, one point is 0.3759 mm or 0.0148 in. The most common abbreviation is 'pt'; 'p' and 'P' are also used. Certain sizes of type have conventional names (table 15).
See also PRINTING; TYPE.

Polish writing A member of the west branch of Slavic languages, Polish is attested in writing since the mid-twelfth century CE, although Polish texts date only from the fourteenth century. The earliest written evidence is in medieval church documents written in Latin. A Polish literary language developed from the middle of the fifteenth century, as Latin gradually lost ground. An orthographic dissertation written about 1440 by Jacub Parkoszowic of the University of Cracow is among the first pieces of scholarly writing. Jan Kochanọwski's *Treny* of the sixteenth century is considered the first great literary work in Polish. The modern Polish standard language, re-established as Poland's national language

Onsets

b	p	m	f	d	t	n	l
ㄅ玻	ㄆ坡	ㄇ摸	ㄈ佛	ㄉ得	ㄊ特	ㄋ讷	ㄌ勒

g	k	h		j	q	x
ㄍ哥	ㄎ科	ㄏ喝		ㄐ基	ㄑ欺	ㄒ希

zh	ch	sh	r	z	c	s
ㄓ知	ㄔ蚩	ㄕ诗	ㄖ日	ㄗ资	ㄘ雌	ㄙ思

Rimes

	i ㄧ 衣	u ㄨ 乌	ü ㄩ 迂
a ㄚ 啊	ia ㄧㄚ 呀	ua ㄨㄚ 蛙	
o ㄛ 喔		uo ㄨㄛ 窝	
e ㄜ 鹅	ie ㄧㄝ 耶		üe ㄩㄝ 约
ai ㄞ 哀		uai ㄨㄞ 歪	
ei ㄟ 欸		uei ㄨㄟ 威	
ao ㄠ 熬	iao ㄧㄠ 腰		
ou ㄡ 欧	iou ㄧㄡ 忧		
an ㄢ 安	ian ㄧㄢ 烟	uan ㄨㄢ 弯	üan ㄩㄢ 冤
en ㄣ 恩	in ㄧㄣ 因	uen ㄨㄣ 温	ün ㄩㄣ 晕
ang ㄤ 昂	iang ㄧㄤ 央	uang ㄨㄤ 汪	
eng ㄥ 亨的韵母	ing ㄧㄥ 英	ueng ㄨㄥ 翁	
ong (ㄨㄥ)轰的韵母	iong ㄩㄥ 雍		

Table 14 The Pinyin alphabet with grapheme values given in the Chinese spelling alphabet

Points	Name
48	Canon
44	2-line double pica
36	2-line great primer
28	2-line English
24	2-line pica
22	Double pica
20	Paragon
18	Great primer
14	English
12	Pica
11	Small pica
10	Long primer
9	Bourgeois
8	Brevier
7	Minion
6	Nonpareil
5	Pearl
1-2	Diamond

Table 15 Names of sizes of type

<ą>	[õ]	<ć>	[ć]	<cz>	[tš]
<ę>	[ẽ]	<ł>	[w]	<dz>	[dž]
<ó>	[u]	<ń>	[n']	<sz>	[š]
		<ś>	[ś]	<rz>	[ž]
		<ź>	[ź]		
		<ż>	[ž]		

Table 16 Diacritics and digraphs of the Polish alphabet

after World War II, is based on the literary variety which is close to the dialect of the Poznań area. Throughout its literary history Polish has been written in the Roman alphabet. The acute accent mark, the slanted slash, the overdot and the Polish hook are used as diacritics to distinguish specific Polish sounds (table 16, figure 11).

Reading Brooks 1975.

Fryderyk Wielki i Krasicki
[frīderīk velki i krašitski

Razu jednego, gdy Krasicki w świetnym płaszczu biskupim
razu jednegɔ gdī krašitski fšvetnīm pwaštšu biskupim

przyszedł do króla na wielką ucztę, Fryderyk chciał go w
pžišet dɔ krula na velkɔ utšte frīderīk xtšaw gɔ w

obecności wielu gości niespodzianie zmieszać i rzekł:
ɔbetnɔštši velu gɔštši ɲespɔdʑaɲe zmešatć i žekw]

Translation

Frederick the Great and Krasicki

Once, when Krasicki attended the king's grand festivity in a magnificent episcopal coat, Frederick wanted to unexpectedly embarrass him in front of many guests and said:

Figure 11 Specimen of Polish grapheme–phoneme correspondence

Pollard Miao writing *See* MIAO WRITING SYSTEM

polyvalence The property of a written sign to have more than one phonetic value. Polyvalence is very common in the writing systems of the world, attesting to the fact that most writings are underdetermined with respect to speech. To both epigraphers and learners of a script it poses a major difficulty, especially where rules for the variation of phonetic values are hard to establish. Orthography reforms often strive to reduce the degree of polyvalence. However, the ubiquity of the phenomenon suggests that it is not so much of a problem for the typical user of a writing system, i.e. the literate native speaker of the language in question.

Polyvalence is frequently fairly systematic. In AKKADIAN cuneiform many signs have two readings, one Sumerian and one Akkadian, much like Japanese *kanji*, many of which have a Sino-Japanese and a Japanese reading. The PHONETICS of Chinese characters often designate several phonetically similar syllables. Polyvalence is also rampant in alphabetic orthographies. V graphemes are typically polyvalent, because most languages have more than the five Vs designated by the Greek alphabet, and only relatively few have augmented their sign inventories with extra letters or diacritics. Polyvalent C letters such as Portuguese <x> for [s, z, š, ks] are also common. Rather than being a fundamental defect, polyvalence is an inherent property of most writing systems which results from the primary function of writing to serve as a model of pronunciation rather than a transcription of speech.

Portuguese writing First attested in writing in the twelfth century CE in a northern variety, literary Portuguese developed from the thirteenth century onwards based on the south-central dialect of Lisbon/Coimbra. As a colonial language Portuguese spread to Africa (Angola, Mozambique), Asia (Goa, Ceylon,

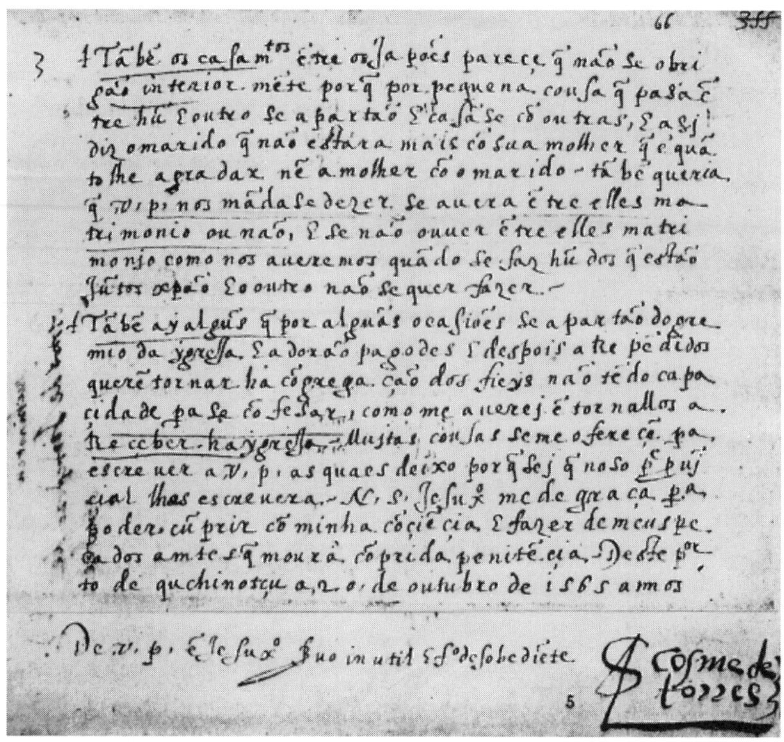

Figure 12 Manuscript by Padre Cosme de Torres, a Portuguese missionary, signed 20 October 1565 (Archive of the Society of Jesus, Rome)

Macao) and South America (Brazil) to become one of the numerically strongest languages of the world (figure 12).

Codification of Portuguese began in the sixteenth century with the publication in 1576 of Nunez do Lião's *Orthographia da Lingoa Portuguesa*. In 1779 the Academia das Ciências was founded in Lisbon and it has since played a significant role in regulating the orthography.

A Romance language, Portuguese has always been written in the Roman alphabet, although Arabs and Jews have also written it in their own alphabets. Twenty-three letters of the Roman alphabet are used, <k, w, y> occurring in foreign proper names only. Owing to the intricate phonology, the orthography is rather complicated. The nine V phonemes [u, ɔ, o, ɐ, a, ə, ɛ, e, i] are expressed by the five graphemes <u, o, a, e, i> and three accent marks, the acute, grave and circumflex, e.g. *avô* [ɐvo] 'grandfather' vs *avó* [ɐvɔ] 'grandmother'; *se* [sə] 'if', *sé* [sɛ] 'cathedral', *sê* 'be'. Nasalization is indicated by a superscript tilde on V graphemes or by the graphemes *-m* and *-n*, as in *ideação* 'ideation' and *sim* 'yes'. The *c cedilla* as in *fôrça* [forsɐ] 'force' is used as in French to indicate a fricative value for the letter <c> in contexts where otherwise a stop would be expected. Of the 18 C graphemes, one, <h>, is always silent, serving etymological spellings only, while most others have multiple values. For example, depending on context, <s> represents [s], [z], [š] or [ğ], and <x> can stand for [s], [z], [š] and [ks]. The digraphs <ch>, <nh>, <lh> and <rr> represent [š], [ɲ], [ʎ] and [ʀ], respectively.

The spelling prescriptions of the Portuguese academy were generally recognized in African and Asian overseas territories, but not always in Brazil, which in 1896 founded its own Academia Brasileira de Letras. The principal varieties of Portuguese today are those of Portugal and Brazil. The latter exhibits significant phonological and morphosyntactic differences from the former, and despite various attempts since the 1911 reform at unifying the orthography, the spelling conventions are still different. A spelling convention was signed by the Portuguese and Brazilian governments in 1943, and another in 1945. Following this scheme, 'silent' Cs were to be abolished where the letter was not pronounced in either country; accents were to be simplified; and the use of the apostrophe was to be reduced. Although this proposal was accepted by both countries, it was implemented only in Portugal, while Brazil adhered to the 1943 standard. The principal differences between Portuguese and Brazilian spelling have to do with the following:

Hyphenation In Portugal, but not in Brazil, the preposition *de* is attached to inflected forms of the verb *haver* 'to have to', as in *hão-de* 'they have to'.
Diaeresis In Brazil, but not in Portugal, <u> is used with <¨> when it occurs between <g, q> and <i, e> as in *agüentar* 'to tolerate'.
Accents In Brazil, but not in Portugal, the <e> in the ending *-eia* is marked with a grave accent, as in *idéia* 'idea', and the first of two final <oo> is marked with a circumflex, as in *vôo* 'flight'. These and some other differences correspond largely to differences in the position and pronunciation of tonic Vs.
Consonants in etymological spellings Brazil has abolished unpronounced etymologically motivated Cs, whereas Portugal continues to write such Cs in contexts after unstressed open /a, e, o/. Hence Portuguese *adoptar, baptismo, director* vs Brazilian *adotar, batismo, diretor*.
Reading Teyssier 1980; Castro et al. 1986.

printing The mechanical reproduction of written text. Since the invention of writing, the replacement of manuscript copying by printing has been the most dramatic change in the development of human communication.

Printing with wood blocks (xylography) was practised in China as early as the eighth century CE. Buddhist monks viewed the manual copying of the scriptures as a virtuous activity and initially resisted mechanical multiplication, but prayer sheets were printed in great numbers and distributed to monasteries throughout the country (figure 13). From China wood block printing spread to Central Asia, Korea and Japan. When Marco Polo visited the Mongol empire he was confronted with another print product, paper money, which well illustrates the multiple applications of this technology.

The Chinese were also the first to experiment with and successfully employ movable type. Since ancient times they had used ornate seals cut in relief and in reverse, and it was on the basis of these seals that they developed movable type made of wood and clay. This technology was known in China and Korea, where the first metal types were produced no later than the twelfth century (figure 14). Very early specimens of printing with movable type also survive from the Uighurs of Central Asia who could take advantage of the new technology more easily

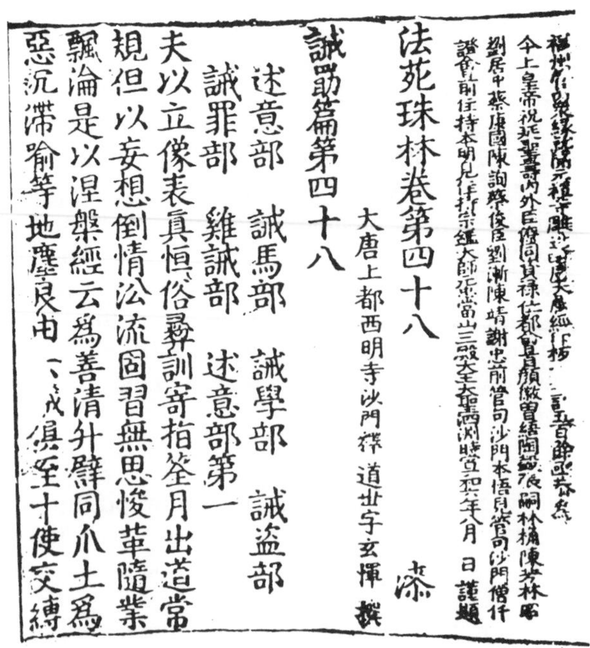

法苑珠林卷第四十八
大唐上都西明寺沙門釋道世字玄惲撰
誡勗篇第四十八
述意部　誡馬部　誡學部　誡盜部
誡罪部　雜誡部　述意部第一
夫以立像表真恒俗彝訓寄指筌月出道常
規但以妄想倒情泌流罔習無思悛革隨業
飄淪是以涅槃經云爲善清升辟同爪土爲
惡沉滯喻等地塵良由[illegible]俱至十使交縛

Figure 13 Page from a Buddhist book printed in 1124. The vertical lines proceed from right to left. The first large line is a chapter heading, followed by a smaller line giving the author's name and affiliation with a temple. The language is Chinese

Figure 14 Movable type: Korean letters dating from the twelfth century CE

than the Chinese, because being alphabetic in nature their writing system required no more than a few dozen types, while for Chinese characters several thousand were needed. This must be seen as a major reason why, for centuries after movable type had become available, wood block printing remained the preferred method of text reproduction in China (figure 15).

Answering the growing need for cheaper reproduction of texts in the wake of the introduction of PAPER to Europe, the invention of printing with movable type

Figure 15 A Chinese printing office of the eighteenth century CE

by GUTENBERG in Germany in the mid-fifteenth century was independent of the Chinese precedent. It was based on metal-processing technologies – engraving, casting and punching – which had been developed since antiquity for minting coins. Printing with movable type is now generally regarded as the key element of a communications revolution which marked the beginning of the modern age. Within 25 years of Gutenberg's printing of the 42-line Vulgate Bible in 1455, printing presses using the new technology were operating in more than 100 towns all across western Europe (figure 16).

While the Gutenberg Bible was in Latin, German texts also issued from the printing office in Mainz. With the mass production and circulation of catechisms, primers and pamphlets, literacy lost its elitist character, creating a public sphere

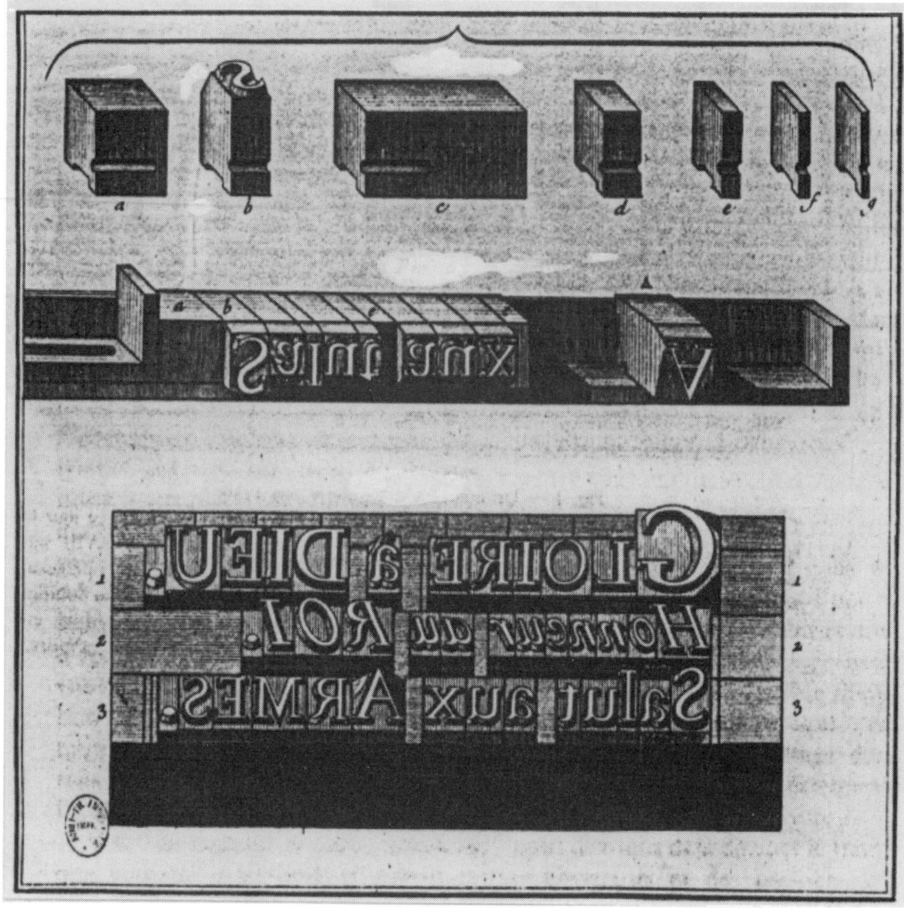

Figure 16 Movable type at a French printing office in the eighteenth century

of knowledge and debate vastly greater than intellectual life when individual copies of manuscripts and block prints were circulated among a select class of literati. The ability to satisfy the steadily growing demand for both religious and secular writing in vernacular languages greatly advanced movements towards officially accepted national languages. As an industry, printing favoured the spread of the vernaculars and the establishment of large territories throughout which a single language was written. In the century following Gutenberg, Luther's German translation of the Bible greatly influenced the development of modern High German. Likewise William CAXTON, who brought printing to England from the continent, is rightly regarded as an important agent in the shaping of modern English. Searching for the largest possible markets for their products, publishers throughout Europe supported adherence to uniform, cross-regional rules. They advanced the standardization of spelling and grammar, eliminating traces of local dialects. In other European countries similar processes of unification and consolidation took place. As a result, Latin was replaced as the major language of writing by the vernaculars which in turn came to monopolize the literary

domain at the expense of minor languages such as Provençal and Irish. The standardization not only of language but of many other aspects of social life is, perhaps, the most significant sociocultural effect of printing with movable type.
See also BOOK; INCUNABULA; LITERACY; MEMORY; TYPE.
Reading Carter 1955; Febvre and Martin 1958; Sohn 1959; Steinberg 1975; Gray 1979; Eisenstein 1979; Comentale 1984; Raabe 1990.

proper name A noun that refers to a single place, person, animal, god or object, such as *Knossos, Xerxes, Bucephalos, Thoth* or *Balmung*, as opposed to a common noun which refers to a class of objects, such as *palace, king, horse, deity* or *sword*. Because proper names are not necessarily meaningful words, they do not lend themselves easily to translation. This made proper names an important word class both in the history of writing and in its scientific investigation.

Many peoples have borrowed writing from their literate neighbours. While initially the writing was firmly linked with the (foreign) written language, the desire to write about their own people, places, gods or kings led the borrowers to modify the writing system in such a way that it could represent their own language. The changes that were brought about in the process transformed logographic systems in the direction of syllabographic or logo-syllabographic systems. The adaptation of Sumerian cuneiform to Akkadian and that of Chinese characters to Korean and Japanese are pertinent examples.

In the study of writing, proper names provided crucial clues for the decipherment of unknown scripts. Since their primary function is to identify a person or place, rather than to express a meaning, proper names are not usually translated but are represented phonetically. Many of the important decipherments took advantage of this fact. The international contracts of the ancient Near East were recorded in a great variety of languages and documents, and hence archaeological findings often supplied enough collateral information to look systematically for the occurrence of certain names. Herodotus's historical account of the Achaemenid kings and their names was crucial for the decipherment of the CUNEIFORM WRITING of Persia and Mesopotamia. The names of Ptolemy, Cleopatra and Alexander the Great were the opening wedge needed for deciphering the Egyptian HIEROGLYPHS. The identification of the name of the Canaanite goddess Ba'alat was the first step in the decipherment of the PROTO-SINAITIC SCRIPT. And solving the riddle of Linear B was greatly aided by the occurrence of the place names *Knossos* and *Pylos* in texts from Knossos and Pylos, respectively. To the decipherer, proper names are significant for two reasons: first because they are the most promising words to look for on the basis of historical evidence; and second because they are most likely to supply the data needed for establishing the first phonetic values of elements of the system.

The special status of proper names is reflected by the fact that in many writing systems they are graphically distinguished. In Egyptian hieroglyphic writing the names of dignitaries were enclosed in cartouches; the Maya had special name and title glyphs; in Javanese a set of special letters are reserved for proper names; and in many alphabetic orthographies proper names are capitalized.
See also DECIPHERMENT.
Reading Pope 1975; Coulmas 1989.

proto-Sinaitic script The writing of inscriptions discovered on the Sinai peninsula and in south Palestine dating from the early second millennium BCE. Also known as 'Sinai script', this writing was employed by turquoise miners in Sinai. Since these apparently belonged to a Semitic tribe, the discovery of this writing at the beginning of the twentieth century attracted a great deal of attention. The renowned Egyptologist A. H. Gardiner in 1916 first interpreted it as the earliest form of alphabetic writing. He was led to this conclusion and convinced several of his colleagues of its soundness by his identification of the name of the Canaanite goddess Ba'alat in the inscriptions (figure 17). Furthermore, Gardiner advanced the important hypothesis that the Sinai script was a stage of writing intermediate between Egyptian hieroglyphics and the Semitic alphabet. His assumption was that the letters of the Sinai script were derived from Egyptian hieroglyphs on the basis of the ACROPHONIC PRINCIPLE. If this connection could be substantiated, one of the most conspicuous gaps in the known history of writing could be closed, the origin of the Semitic consonant scripts.

Attractive though Gardiner's suggestion was, little progress has been made since his spectacular reading of the goddess's name. The epigraphic data are few,

Figure 17 Varieties of proto-Sinaitic inscription assumed to represent the name of the Canaanite goddess Ba'alat

and knowledge about the Semitic variety spoken in Canaan of the late Bronze Age is limited. So far there is no generally agreed decipherment of the proto-Sinaitic inscriptions. However, most scholars in the field are inclined to accept the alphabetic nature of the script. Whether it was really derived, wholly or in part, by acrophony from Egyptian hieroglyphs, and where exactly it stands in the history of the Semitic alphabet, being separated as it is by some 400 years from the oldest inscriptions in the PHOENICIAN ALPHABET, are questions for which satisfactory answers are yet to be found.
See also SEMITIC WRITING.
Reading Gardiner 1916; Sznycer 1972.

proto-writing Artificially produced graphical marks designed to record information without being systematically related to language. Property marks, mnemonic devices such as tally sticks, painted sea shells, knotted cords and pictorial signs are generally subsumed under 'proto-writing'. However, the notion is sometimes reserved to signs which were actual forerunners of a full writing system, such as the Middle Eastern counter tokens which are linked through their imprints in clay to the earliest form of what became the cuneiform script.
See also ORIGIN OF WRITING.

punctuation **1** The rules for graphically structuring written language by means of a set of conventional marks such as dots and horizontal, vertical or oblique strokes. The earliest beginnings of present punctuation in alphabetic writing are found in ancient Greek inscriptions. A vertical stroke <|> set off paragraphs; a double point <:> was occasionally used to close a sentence; and a dash <–> was used for separating the speeches of different characters. A more regular system was developed in the Greek schools of Alexandria in the third century BCE. Points were placed in different positions: the high point as a full stop; the point on the line marking a short pause; and a point in a middle position for a longer pause. Latin grammarians adopted and further developed the Greek system of punctuation by points, although usage was not consistent for a long time. Marks reflecting syntactic or functional distinctions such as the question mark appear as of the Carolingian period. Punctuation is generally the last part of orthographic systems to be standardized. There is hence a great deal of variation within and across languages. The basic punctuation signs used in English and other European languages are as follows: the full stop <.> to mark the end of a sentence; the colon <:> to introduce a new idea, a quotation or an enumeration; the semicolon <;> to separate two sentences which are closely connected in sense, or clauses in an enumeration; the comma <,> to separate clauses, appositions and other dependent parts of speech; brackets or parentheses <(...)> to enclose explanations or references; the dash <–> to mark, singly or in pairs, interjections; the exclamation mark <!> and the question mark <?> to indicate the emphatic and interrogative force of a sentence; and quotation marks <"..." '...'> to enclose direct speech or words not used in their proper sense. In English, variation in punctuation is more readily tolerated than in spelling. **2** A system of dots and dashes used in Semitic scripts to indicate V quality. In the history of Hebrew various systems of diacritical V marks evolved. The Babylonian system distinguishes six Vs, the

ִ	ֵ	ֶ	ַ	ָ	ֹ	ֻ	ְ
/i/	/e/	/ä/	/a/	/ɔ/	/o/	/u/	/ə/

Table 17 The basic signs of the Tiberian punctuation system

ט שֵׁשֶׁת
יָמִים תַּעֲבֹד וְעָשִׂיתָ כָּל־מְלַאכְתֶּךָ׃ י
וְיוֹם הַשְּׁבִיעִי שַׁבָּת ׀ לַיהוָה אֱלֹהֶיךָ לֹא־
תַעֲשֶׂה כָל־מְלָאכָה אַתָּה ׀ וּבִנְךָ וּבִתֶּךָ
עַבְדְּךָ וַאֲמָתְךָ וּבְהֶמְתֶּךָ וְגֵרְךָ אֲשֶׁר
בִּשְׁעָרֶיךָ׃

ששת ימים תעבד ועשית כל מלאכתך
ויום השביעי שבת ליהוה אלהיך
לא תעשה כל מלאכה
אתה ובנך ובתך עבדך ואמתך
ובהמתך
וגרך אשר בשעריך

šešät yā̈mi(y)m ta^{ca}vod wə^{c}aś(y)tā kol–məla(')ktäkā̈
wəyo(w)m hašəvi(y)^{c}i(y) šabbāt ləYHWH '^{ä}lohä(y) kā̈
lo(')–ta^{ca}śä(h) kol–məlā (')kā 'attā (h)
u(w)vinkā u(w)vittäkā̈ ^{c}avdəkā wa'^{a}mātəkā
u(w)vəhämtäkā
wəgerəkā '^{a}ṣ̌är biš^{ə} arä(y)ka

9 Six days shalt thou labor, and do all thy work.
10 But the seventh day is the sabbath of the Lord thy God: in it thou shalt not do any work, thou, nor thy son, nor thy daughter, thy manservant, nor thy maidservant, nor thy cattle, nor thy stranger that is within thy gates.

Figure 18 The fourth commandment of the Hebrew Bible with and without punctuation: translation from the King James version: Exodus 20. In the transliteration matres lectionis *are in brackets*

various Palestinian systems between five and seven. The Tiberian system – so called after the city of Tiberias in northern Israel – also distinguishes seven different V qualities (table 17). It became dominant around the ninth century CE, and the other systems were abandoned. Vs are not usually represented in writing, except in holy books, poetry and children's books, where the Tiberian system is employed for fully vowelized Hebrew (sometimes called 'pointed'). The V diacritics are mostly placed below the consonant letters, but in some cases in their middle or above them (figure 18).
See also **2** HEBREW WRITING.
Reading **1** Carly 1958; Wingo 1972; Parkes 1993.

Punic script The last variety of the Phoenician script used in the Phoenician colony of Carthage and other parts of north Africa from the ninth century BCE to the first century CE (figure 19). It is also inscriptionally attested in Spain, the Balearic Islands, southern France, Sicily and Malta. Early inscriptions rarely indicate Vs, but as of the mid-third century BCE PLENE WRITING is common and systematic. The Neo Punic script of the Roman period is extremely cursive and hard to read.
See also PHOENICIAN ALPHABET.
Reading Friedrich 1951.

Figure 19 Punic inscription from Carthage, third century BCE
Source: *Lidzbarski 1970*

Punjabi writing *See* GURMUKHĪ SCRIPT.

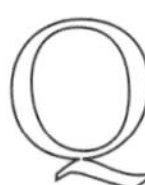

Q, q /kj:/ The seventeenth letter of the English alphabet can be traced back to Semitic *qōph*. In the oldest Greek inscriptions it is used to represent /k/ in front of back rounded Vs. After the introduction of the Attic alphabet it fell into disuse in east Greek alphabets where it was retained only as a number sign for 90. In the west Greek alphabet, however, it survived and thence was taken over into Latin where it was likewise used for /k/, for instance in archaic *pequnia* 'money'. In English, as in most Latin-derived alphabets, *q* is always followed by *u*, a practice already common in Latin. Hence <qu> can be considered a single grapheme: its sound value is /kw/ in English, Italian and German; it is /k/ in French, Spanish and Portuguese. In Albanian <q> alone has the value /kj/.
Reading Weidmüller 1977.

Quechua writing Although Quechua, or 'Runa Simi' as called by its speakers, was reportedly used as the principal lingua franca throughout the Inca empire, it was never written in pre-Hispanic times. During the sixteenth century it was first reduced to writing by Spanish missionaries who used it for proselytizing. Quechua is today widely spoken in Peru, Ecuador and Bolivia, although not much used in writing. No generally recognized standard variety exists. An official orthography was drafted in 1939 and adopted in 1946 for Ayacucho Quechua, the main Peruvian dialect. Spelling conventions are largely based on those of Spanish. Since 1975 it has been recognized in Peru as a national language together with Spanish.

The language has a three-V system /i/, /a/, /u/, represented by the three graphemes <i>, <a>, <u> and the diaeresis <¨> to indicate V length. However, in Peru /i/ is spelt <e> when pronounced [e], and /u/ is spelt <o> when pronounced [o], although these variations are predictable. The following digraphs are employed: <ch> for /č/, <ll> for /l^y/, and <rr> for /ř/. C graphemes have Spanish-like values. The tilde <˜> is used to mark palatal /n/. To give expression to a three-way contrast between surd, glottalized and aspirated stops and affricates, <p, t, k, q, ch> are used by themselves; with one accent mark to show glottalization; and with two accent marks to show aspiration.
Reading Parker 1969.

quipu [Quechua 'Knot'] (*K'ipu*) An information storage system consisting of groups of connected, knotted strings of various colours, used for record keeping by the accountants of Inca Peru. The Inca empire which flourished in the century prior to the arrival of Pizarro and other Spanish *conquistadores* in 1531 is exceptional in world history in that it developed a complex infrastructure in the absence of true writing. The *quipus* compensated for this deficiency to some extent. Kept by the *quipu-campayocs* or *quipu*-masters, they were used to register census statistics, taxation and other economic data (figure 1). That they also chronicled mythology and history has been suggested by Spanish and native sources, but if

Figure 1 Inca bureaucrat with quipu*: drawing by Felipe Gumán Poma de Ayala*

this was the case, the knowledge to interpret *quipus* storing this kind of information was lost after the Spanish conquest. It is more likely that with reference to non-numerical information *quipus* served the function of *aides-mémoire*, but could not be 'read' by anyone other than the *quipu*-master who had tied the knots.

In some parts of Peru and Bolivia a system of knotted strings called *chiumpu* is still used. Together with early Spanish accounts of *quipus* it has been instrumental in reconstructing the underlying numeral system of decimal place notation. The numbers from one to nine are represented by corresponding numbers of loops in a knot, the zero by the absence of a knot. Bigger numbers and sums are represented by different kinds of knots tied at specific intervals (figure 2). The colours of the strings distinguish different reference domains.

See also QUECHUA WRITING.

Reading Bankes 1977.

quoc-ngu The Roman alphabet of Vietnamese introduced in the seventeenth century by Christian missionaries. The term means 'national language'.

See also VIETNAMESE ALPHABET.

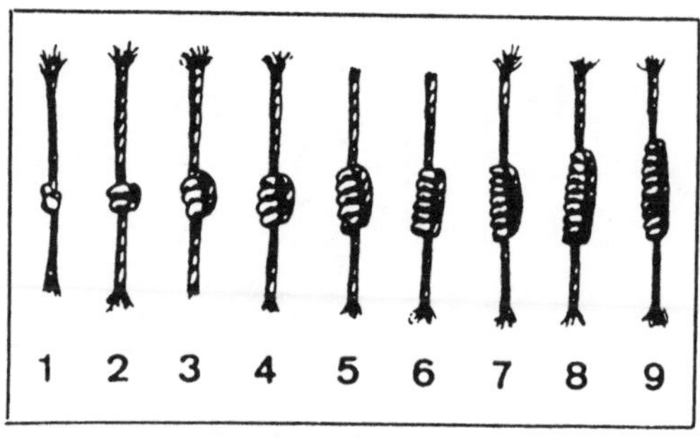

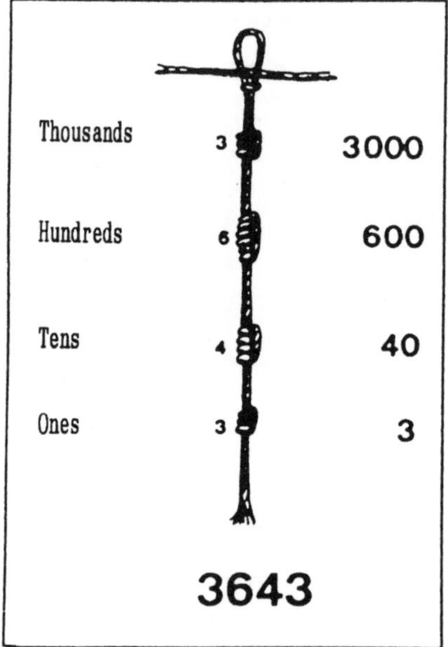

Figure 2 The numbers one to nine and 3643 in quipu *notation*
Source: *Ifrah 1989*

quotation marks A punctuation mark used in pairs to enclose reported speech or other expressions to be set off from the rest of the text. Such expressions can be: (1) titles of articles or songs (*He really hated 'The Sound of Music'.*); (2) real or imagined words of others (*'I bow to passion,' he said.*); (3) words that are mentioned rather than used (*The meaning of 'if' is 'provided that'.*); (4) expressions not intended in their literal meaning, as in irony (*The 'music' they are playing there sounds like a pneumatic drill.*). Where several of these functions occur in the same text, two sets of graphically distinct marks, such as single <'...'> and double quotes <"...">, are commonly used (*'I have no idea', he replied, 'what "graphetics" means.'*).

Conventions for single and double quotation marks and for combining them with other punctuation vary between British and American usage. The full stop and final comma are always placed before the end quotation mark in American usage, even where the quoted expression is a subordinate part of the sentence or clause. In cases of the latter kind, British usage has punctuation marks follow the end quotation mark. *She claimed it was called 'The Middle Passage'.* is British usage, whereas . . . *it was called "The Middle Passage."* Is American. Beginning and end quotation marks are usually distinguished in print <‘“...”’> but not in handwriting.
See also PUNCTUATION.

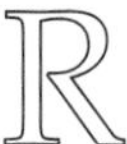

R

R, r /ɑ:/ The eighteenth letter of the English alphabet descended from Semitic *rēš* through Greek *rho* (Ρ, ρ). Its present form was arrived at in Latin, where a local Greek variant with a stroke at the right was added.

radical [Lat. *rādīx* 'root'] **1** The building blocks of Chinese characters. Every HÀNZÌ is either a radical or is composed of two to four radicals. Also called 'keys', 'classifiers' or 'determinatives', radicals are the meaning-indicating elements of Chinese characters as opposed to the PHONETICS. Characters which share the same radical designate semantically related morphemes, although this relation is sometimes less than self-evident. Radicals provide the basic principle for the organization of dictionaries, 540 in Xu Shen's etymological dictionary *Shuowen jiezi* of some 10,000 characters compiled about 120 CE (figure 1), and 214 since the *Kang xi* dictionary of 1716 CE which comprises more than 40,000 characters (tables 1, 2). **2** In Semitic philology, the lexical root Cs of a word. Radicals represent

說文解字弟十三上
漢太尉祭酒許慎記
銀青光祿大夫守右散騎常侍上柱國東海縣開國子食邑五百戶臣徐鉉等奉敕校定
二十三部 文七百 重一百二十四
凡八千三百九十八字
文三十六 新附

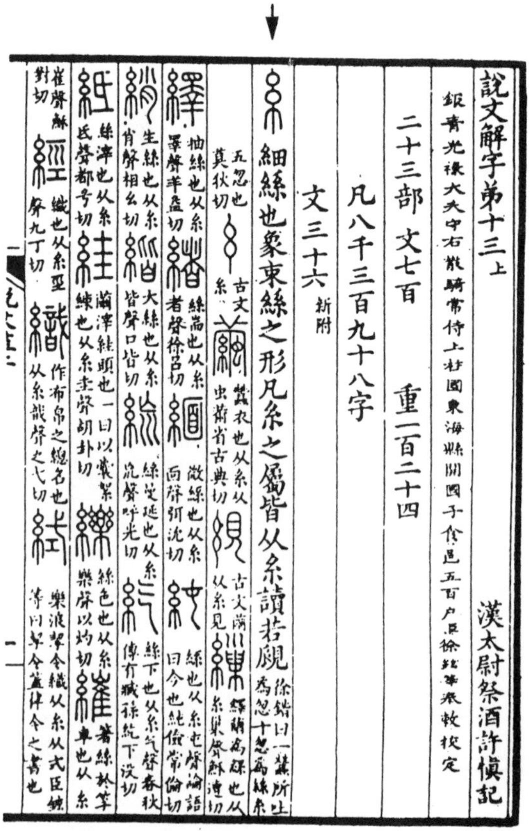

Figure 1 Page from the Shuowen jiezi *with the 'silk' radical, head of sixth column from right*

Strokes													
1	一 1	丨 2	丨 (2)	丶 3	丿 4	㇀ (4)	乛 (4)	乙 5	乚 (5)	乚 (5)	亅 6		
2	二 7	亠 8	人 9	亻 (9)	𠆢 (9)	儿 10	入 11	八 12	八 (12)	丷 (12)	冂 13	冂 (13)	
	冖 14	冫 15	几 16	凵 17	刀 18	刂 (18)	力 19	勹 20	匕 21	匚 22	匚 (22)	匸 23	十 24
	十 (24)	十 (24)	卜 25	⺊ (25)	卜 (25)	卩 26	厂 27	厶 28	又 29	辶 (162)	阝 (163)	阝 (170)	
3	口 30	囗 31	土 32	土 (32)	土 (32)	士 33	夂 34	夊 (34)	夊 35	夕 36	大 36	大 (37)	
	女 38	子 39	宀 40	寸 41	小 42	⺌ (42)	尢 43	尸 44	屮 45	山 46	川 47	巛 (47)	工 48
	己 49	巾 50	干 51	幺 52	广 53	廴 54	廾 55	弋 56	弓 57	彐 58	⺕ (58)	彡 59	彳 60
	忄 (61)	扌 (64)	氵 (85)	丬 (90)	犭 (94)	艹 (140)	辶 (162)	阝 (163)	阝 (170)				
4	心 61	⺗ (61)	忄 (61)	戈 62	戈 (62)	戶 63	戸 (63)	手 64	扌 (64)	支 65	攴 66	攵 (66)	
	文 67	斗 68	斤 69	方 70	无 71	旡 (71)	日 72	曰 73	月 74	木 75	欠 76	止 77	歹 78
	歺 (78)	殳 79	毋 80	母 (80)	比 81	毛 82	氏 83	气 84	水 85	氵 (85)	氺 (85)	火 86	灬 (86)
	爪 87	爫 (87)	父 88	爻 89	爿 90	丬 (90)	片 91	牙 92	牛 93	牜 (93)	犬 94	王 (96)	⺪ (103)
	礻 (113)	内 (114)	耂 (125)	月 (130)	艹 (140)								
5	旡 (71)	母 (80)	比 (81)	氺 (85)	牙 (92)	玄 95	玉 96	王 (96)	瓜 97	瓦 98	甘 99	生 100	
	用 101	田 102	疋 103	⺪ (103)	疒 104	癶 105	白 106	皮 107	皿 108	目 109	矛 110	矢 111	石 112
	示 113	礻 (113)	禸 114	禾 115	穴 116	立 117	罒 (122)	艮 (138)	衤 (145)				
6	竹 118	⺮ (118)	米 119	糸 120	缶 121	网 122	罒 (122)	羊 123	⺶ (123)	羽 124	老 125	耂 (125)	
	而 126	耒 127	耒 (127)	耳 128	耳 (128)	聿 129	⺻ (129)	肉 130	月 (130)	臣 131	自 132	至 133	臼 134
	舌 135	舛 136	舟 137	舟 (137)	艮 138	艮 (138)	色 139	艸 140	艹 (140)	虍 141	虫 142	血 143	行 144
	衣 145	衤 (145)	西 146	覀 (146)	豕 (152)	⻊ (157)							
7	臣 (131)	舛 (136)	見 147	角 148	言 149	谷 150	豆 151	豕 152	豸 153	貝 154	赤 155	走 156	
	足 157	身 158	車 159	辛 160	辰 161	辰 (161)	辵 162	辶 (162)	邑 163	阝 (163)	酉 164	釆 165	里 166
	麦 (199)												
8	金 167	長 168	門 169	阜 170	阝 (170)	隶 171	隹 172	雨 173	青 174	非 175	食 (184)	斉 (210)	
9	面 176	革 177	韋 178	韭 179	音 180	頁 181	風 182	飛 183	食 184	飠 (184)	首 185	香 186	
10	韋 (178)	馬 187	骨 188	高 189	髟 190	鬥 191	鬯 192	鬲 193	鬼 194	鬼 (194)	竜 (212)		
11	魚 195	鳥 196	鹵 197	鹿 198	麥 199	麻 200	麻 (200)	黄 (201)	黒 (203)	亀 (213)			
12	黃 201	黄 (201)	黍 202	黑 203	黒 (203)	黹 204	歯 (211)						
13	黽 205	鼎 206	鼓 207	鼠 208									
14	鼻 209	齊 210	斉 (210)										
15-17	齒 211	歯 (211)	龍 212	竜 (212)	龜 213	亀 (213)	龠 214						

Table 1 The 214 historical radicals, ordered for number of strokes: bracketed items are variant forms

Radical	Character	Meaning
女	妊	pregnant
	妹	younger sister
	姉	elder sister
	姫	princess
	娘	daughter
	姓	surname
	娼	prostitute
	媛	beauty
	婦	woman
	妻	wife

Table 2 Radical 38 'woman' and examples of characters in which it occurs

basic meanings. Most Semitic lexemes have three radicals, from which different words can be derived by varying the V positions. Dictionaries of Semitic languages are traditionally arranged for C roots.
See also CHINESE WRITING SYSTEM; CONSONANT ROOTS; DICTIONARY.

Raschi script A variant of the Hebrew square script in which Raschi wrote a commentary of the Talmud (figure 2). *Raschi* is an acronym of Rabbi Schelomo ben Isaak (1040–1105 CE), a Jewish scholar from Troyes, Champagne. More cursive than the square script, the Raschi came to be used widely in Jewish writing in medieval Italy and Germany (table 3).
See also HEBREW WRITING.

reading **1** The process of deriving meaning from written text. Reading is a highly complex activity involving the interplay of visual-perceptual, linguistic and conceptual systems. Historically, reading was associated with reciting, i.e. reading aloud, but in modern times reading is generally thought of as a silent, solitary activity. **2** An interpretation or meaning of an inscription or text. **3** The sound value of a Chinese character in Chinese, Korean, Japanese or Vietnamese writing. In the Japanese writing system most Chinese characters have two or more different readings.
See also **1** LITERACY; READING PROCESS. **3** JAPANESE WRITING.
Reading **1** Saenger 1982.

reading disability Disturbance in reading ability in children (developmental) or in adults (acquired). It can be due to or associated with a number of different

Figure 2 Title page of a handwritten Raschi commentary, twelfth century CE

א	'a	ל	l
ב	b, v	מ	m
ג	g, γ	נ	n
ד	d, ð	ס	s
ה	h	ע	ʕ
ו	w	פ	*p, f
ז	z̤	צ	s̱
ח	χ	ק	q
ט	t̲	ר	r
י	y	ש	š
כ	k, χ́	ת	t, θ

Table 3 Raschi, the Italian Jewish script

factors including slow development of verbal skills; difficulty with the perception of auditory or visual stimuli; difficulty with audiovisual integration; difficulty in forming memory images of orthographic words; difficulty in grasping the orthographic principles of the language in question. Four main types of reading disability are commonly distinguished:

Deep dyslexia A disturbance in phonological recoding of the orthographic word as evidenced by semantic substitutions. Instead of the stimulus word a semantically

similar but orthographically and phonologically different word is sometimes produced.
Phonological dyslexia Characterized by the inability to read pseudo-words, which points to an abnormality in establishing and/or processing grapheme–phoneme correspondences. This syndrome is not accompanied by semantic substitutions.
Word form dyslexia, word blindness A dysfunction of the word recognition process. Rather than recognizing an orthographic word as a whole, the reader spells it out 'letter by letter' and thus derives the word form. Reading performance is markedly slowed down.
Surface dyslexia Consists of grapheme–phoneme conversion errors. In typical misreadings graphemes of closely related phonemes are confused, as in *just* for *guest* or *bargain* for *barge*.

Reading disabilities often cooccur with agraphia.
See also DYSLEXIA; READING PROCESS.
Reading Patterson 1981.

reading process Based on an abundance of experimental psycholinguistic research, various models of the reading process have been proposed. They all try to identify the perceptual and cognitive stages and activities leading from visual input to understanding the content of the written message. At least the following modules are distinguished: (1) eye fixation; (2) iconic representation; (3) character identification; (4) recognition of character sequences as orthographic words; (5) associating orthographic words with meanings; (6) application of syntactic and semantic rules to combine words into meaningful phrases; and (7) in oral reading, the application of phonological rules to map orthographic words on to phonological words which are then given a phonetic form by the vocal system.

Much research has focused on the question of whether, and if so under what circumstances, the phonological system can be passed by in silent reading. Numerous experiments have been carried out in order to determine whether readers can access the mental lexicon without going through the process known as phonic recoding, that is, associating letter sequences with phonological representations which are then mapped on to morphemes. Comparative studies of reading in different writing systems, such as Chinese (logosyllabic), Japanese *kana* (syllabic) and Hebrew (consonant) as well as deep (e.g. English) and surface (e.g. Serbo-Croatian) alphabetic systems, have shown that the nature of the writing system has a marked effect on the reading process. Although proficient readers do not generally rely on phonic recoding, it is more likely to occur in systems involving very little graphic encoding of semantic information, especially surface alphabetic systems. However, it could be demonstrated that even in strongly meaning-oriented systems such as Chinese, silent reading may be accompanied by phonic recoding. Subliminal phonetic activity, moreover, varies with frequency of words, highly frequent words being more likely to be processed without phonic recoding; with proficiency level, proficient readers depending less on phonic recoding; and with individual reading strategies.
See also LITERACY; READING DISABILITY.
Reading Henderson 1984; Gough 1972; Günther 1988; Morais 1987; Oakhill and Garnham 1988; *Reading Research Quarterly*.

reading readiness The developmental stage at which the child is able to respond to reading instruction. Since the 1920s various tests have been developed to assess the reading readiness in a standardized way. Readiness tests are widely used, but the value of such tests has been called into question in early reading research. While reading readiness testing assumes that readiness can be predicted on the basis of testing knowledge and skills of a general nature, early reading research emphasizes the need to disconnect the teaching of reading from other skills, especially from teaching new language or concepts.
Reading Smith 1971; Pumfrey 1985.

reading span The number of characters/words which can be perceived and processed by the reader in a single fixation period, that is, the period between eye movements in the reading process.

rebus principle Representing a word by means of the logogram of another which is phonetically similar or homophonous, for instance using the sign ¤ for 'son'. The rebus principle played an important role in the development of writing as the cardinal strategy for increasing the expressive power of logographic systems. In the beginning, word writing relied heavily on pictographic signs representing concrete objects. Words which cannot be represented easily by means of a picture, such as proper names and function words, were difficult to write. The rebus provided the means to overcome this limitation. It is found in all ancient writing systems. Examples in early SUMERIAN WRITING include the sign *ti* 'arrow' for *ti(l)* 'life', *íb* 'hip' for *íb* 'wrath', and *gi* 'reed' for *gi* 'to reimburse' (figure 3). In the EGYPTIAN WRITING SYSTEM *wr* 'swallow' was used for *wr* 'big'. The CHINESE WRITING SYSTEM has a whole class of characters known as 'phonetic loans', of which *ləg* 'grain' for *ləg* 'to come' is an early example. Maya writing, too, is essentially based on the rebus principle, although this has been recognized only recently. A glyph consisting of a pair of fish fins illustrates the transformation from pictographic ICON to PHONOGRAPHY accomplished by the application of the rebus principle. It was first used as the sign of Maya *xoc* 'fish' and then also for *xoc* 'to count'.

The rebus, then, is a re-employed sign which strengthens the phonetic aspect of a writing system by exploiting phonetic similarities. While initially rebus signs

Figure 3 Sumerian rebus sign of Jemdet Nasr period. The sign in the upper left corner of the tablet is a pictograph of gi *'reed', here used for the homophonous word* gi *'reimburse'*
Source: *Vaiman 1974, p. 18*

were typically transfers from one word to another, the principle was subsequently also applied to syllables. Thus, the Egyptian word *msdr* 'ear' was written by combining the hieroglyphs *ms* 'fan' and *dr* 'basket'. Where signs are employed in such a way, a complete shift has taken place from logogram to phonogram (figure 4).
See also PHONETIZATION; WRITING SYSTEM.

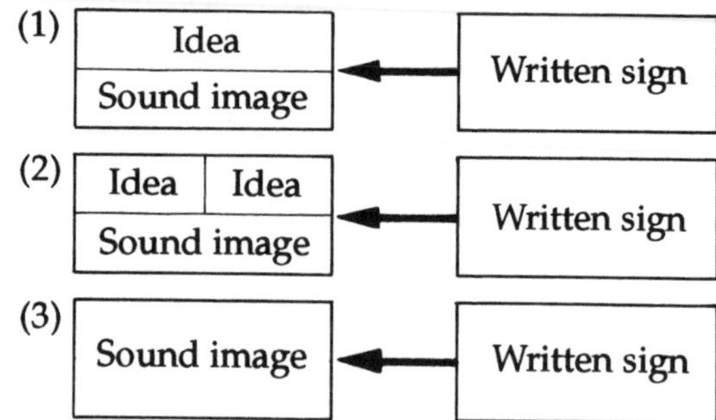

Figure 4 The transition from (1) logography resting on a unique relation between word form, word meaning and written sign, via (2) rebus writing based on homophony, to (3) phonography

recoding *See* READING.

Redjang script (*also* Redžan script) Derived from the Javanese KAWI SCRIPT during the fifteenth century, the Redjang is native to south-east Sumatra. Compared with Kawi, it is much reduced in graphic complexity and number of graphemes. A syllabic alphabet of the Indian type, it consists of just 16 C + *a* letters (table 4). The texts in which the script is attested are known as *Ka-ga-nga* texts (figure 5). The language of these is a literary form of Old Malay.
See also INDIAN WRITING SYSTEMS.
Reading Jaspan 1964.

ka		na	
ga		ma	
ṅa		ya	
ča		ra	
ža		la	
ńa		wa	
ta		sa	
da		ha	

Table 4 The Redjang syllabic alphabet

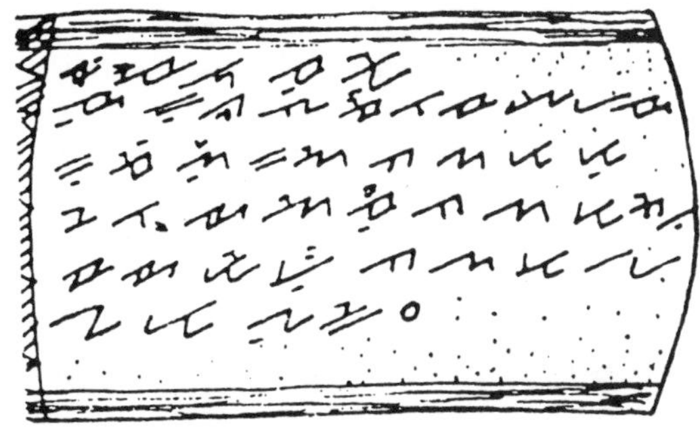

Figure 5 Redjang inscription
Source: *Jaspan 1964*

reduction to writing Providing an unwritten language with a means of writing. Rather than referring to historically evolved writings, this term is limited to modern, deliberately created systems which take an alphabet with close grapheme–phoneme correspondence as the standard of excellence. Reduction to writing is a necessary prerequisite of subjecting a language to grammatical analysis. In this sense it is the same as making a phonemic analysis of a language. Conversely, every writing system is based on an implicit or explicit analysis of the relevant units of its language. Such an analysis is a 'reduction', because every graphic representation of a language – for purposes of both written communication and phonological analysis – is inevitably selective in the features of speech it depicts and makes the language system appear more stable and clear-cut than it actually is.
See also ALPHABET MAKING; ORTHOGRAPHY.
Reading Pike 1947; Berry 1958, 1977; Gudschinsky 1970.

Redžan script *See* REDJANG SCRIPT.

religion and writing The history of writing, its development and dissemination, is profoundly and diversely interconnected with religion. Many literate cultures credit DEITIES OF WRITING with the creation of written signs, thus underscoring the significance of this invention. While early writing in Mesopotamia and elsewhere was primarily used as a means of controlling economic life, this function was carried out by priests who were at the same time accountants. The Sumerian precedent of an economy centred on, and administered in writing by, the temple set a precedent repeated in many variations throughout history. The etymology of the English word *clerk* still reflects the same connection. The clerk or cleric in the original sense was a man consecrated to the service of God. Since during the second half of the first millennium CE outside the Roman heartland most of those versed in Latin, the written language of the time, were churchmen, the term *clericus* came to mean 'knowledgeable about letters'. In many early civilizations literacy was limited to clerics, who often carefully guarded their knowledge as a secret or magic power. And although cult and ritual developed orally, all major world religions produced sacred texts. God's word is often revealed in the form of holy books, which a prophet is appointed by Providence to interpret. For Jews, Christians and Muslims *the* book thus became the locus of authority guiding individual and social conduct. Similarly, Mahayana Buddhists consider a great number of sūtras sacred. Many other religions and sects have their 'scriptures' or particular variants of sacred texts.

Another important aspect of religion and writing relates to scripts. The spread of the most important scripts the world over has generally followed that of religions. Although the term 'hieroglyph' in the sense of 'holy letter' is misleading, the EGYPTIAN SCRIPT was intimately linked with cult. HEBREW WRITING is the script of Judaism and Jewish languages. When Hebrew ceased to be a spoken language, the Jewish Masoretes devised a system of PUNCTUATION to make sure that the phonological form of the language could be preserved. The ROMAN ALPHABET is the script of Roman Christianity, while CYRILLIC is the script of the Orthodox Church. This distinction still divides the Slavic world: west Slavic languages belonging to the Roman Catholic domain use the Roman alphabet, while the languages of the Orthodox east Slavs are all written in Cyrillic. In the south the split is along religious lines: Catholic Croats use Roman, Orthodox Serbs use Cyrillic. The Copts distinguished themselves from other Egyptians by using their own Greek-derived alphabet. The Syriac, Ethiopian, Armenian and Mandean Christians likewise all had their own scripts. The ARABIC ALPHABET is, of course, the script of Islam, and for many still the only script in which the Muslims' holy book, the Qur'ān, should be copied and read. Examples from other religious spheres can be added. The sphere of Chinese characters is, by and large, co-extensive with the sphere of Confucianism. The Zoroastrians in Persia (PAHLAVI SCRIPT), the Lamaists in Tibet (TIBETAN WRITING), the Sikhs in the Punjab (GURMUKHĪ SCRIPT) all created scripts as vehicles of their religious texts.

Further, modern script creations were often inspired by, or presented as the result of, divine revelation. The MORMON ALPHABET, BAMUM WRITING and HMONG WRITING are pertinent examples from North America, Africa and East Asia, respectively. SEQUOYAH'S syllabary for the Cherokee language also belongs to this group of scripts.

Typography, too, became a means of expressing religious distinctions. Almost all of the books printed in the fifteenth century were of a religious nature, and when the Reformation jolted the European continent, the schism was made visible: Roman was Catholic, *Fraktur* Protestant.

The positive association of a religion with a script also had its negative implications: other scripts were condemned as savage and heathen, if not devilish. Thus the literature and the literary traditions of the Mayas and other Mesoamerican cultures were eradicated by the Spanish *conquistadores* in the name of God. Conversely, Christian missionaries have provided numerous languages with a writing system for the first time, invariably using the Roman alphabet. As a result, the reading materials available in a large number of languages are limited to Christian religious texts.

In sum, clergymen have always understood the power of the written word and the symbolic significance of a distinct script that goes with a doctrine, giving it a visually recognizable appearance.

Reading Diringer 1968; Goody 1986.

Riksmål *See* BOKMÅL

rīqāʿ script One of the six SITTA styles of the Arabic script developed by Abū ʿAlī Muḥammad Ibn Muqlah (*d.*939 CE) and further perfected by Yaqut al-Mustaʿsimi (*d.*1298) and his disciples of the calligraphy school of medieval Baghdad. Ahmad as-Suhrawardi is credited with the perfection of the *rīqāʿ* which came to be used mainly for correspondence and was the preferred style of Ottoman Turks (table 5).

See also ARABIC SCRIPTS; CALLIGRAPHY.

Reading Schimmel 1984.

Final	Medial	Initial	Independent	Value
ـا			ا	a
ـب	ـبـ	بـ	ب	b, p
ـپ	ـپـ	پـ	پ	p
ـت	ـتـ	تـ	ت	t
ـح ح	ـحـ	حـ	ح	hʿ
ـخ خ	ـخـ	خـ	خ	χ
ـد			د	d, t
ـر ر			ر ر	r
ـس س	ـسـ	سـ	س س	s
ـش ش	ـشـ	شـ	ش ش	š
ـص	ـصـ	صـ	ص	ṣ
ـض	ـضـ	ضـ	ض	ẓ
ـط	ـطـ	طـ	ط	t, th
ـع	ـعـ	عـ	ع	ʒ
ـف	ـفـ	فـ	ف	f
ـق	ـقـ	قـ	ق	q, kh
ـك ك	ـكـ	كـ	ك	k'
ـل ل	ـلـ	لـ	ل	l
ـم	ـمـ	مـ	م	m
ـن	ـنـ	نـ	ن	n
ـو			و	w
ـه ـة	ـهـ	هـ	ه	h, t
ـلا			لا	la
ـى ـي	ـيـ	يـ	ى	y, i

Table 5 The Arabic alphabet for Turkish, rīqāʿ *style*

rōmaji [Japanese ***rōma*** 'Roman' + *ji* 'letter'] Systems of transliterating Japanese with Roman letters. The reference system is the *kana* syllabary, although the pronunciation of the syllables represented by the *kana* system is also taken into account in the various Romanization schemes. The Roman alphabet was introduced to Japan in the sixteenth century by Portuguese missionaries who were the first to write Japanese texts with alphabetic letters. They used the alphabet largely along the lines of Portuguese spelling conventions. A Dutch-based system followed. In the nineteenth century various other systems came into existence. That which became, and still is, most widely used is known as the HEPBURN SYSTEM (table 6). The *Nipponsiki* system was developed by Tanakadate Akitsu, founding member of one of the most active Romanization societies which promoted an alphabetic orthography as a replacement for rather than a supplement to the JAPANESE WRITING system. Although in 1937 this scheme was officially authorized by the Japanese government, it was never very popular. In 1954, a 'government notification' (*kunrei*) was issued recommending a modified version of this scheme, which became known as the *kunrei* system (*kunreisiki*).
See also KANA; ROMANIZATION; TRANSLITERATION.
Reading Reischauer 1940; Saeki and Yamada 1977.

Roman alphabet The adaptation to the Latin language in the seventh century BCE of the ETRUSCAN ALPHABET, which was itself a descendant of a west Greek script. Until the first century BCE it consisted of the following 21 letters: *A, B, C, D, E, F, G, H, I, K, L, M, N, O, P, Q, R, S, T, V, X.* (figure 6). Subsequently, *Y* and *Z* were added, initially to write Greek proper names and loan words. Their appearance at the end of the conventional sequence still bears witness to the fact that they were not originally taken over from the Etruscan alphabet where, as in Greek, Z was the seventh letter. The differentiation of *V* and *U* as well as *I* and *J* and the addition of the ligature *VV* as a separate letter *W* were later developments.

The resultant 26 letters form what in modern times is referred to as the 'Roman' or 'roman' alphabet. The spelling with a small initial *r* is indicative of the general significance of the script which is no longer exclusively associated with Roman culture, but serves as the basis of the writing systems of more languages than any other script. It also forms the nucleus of the INTERNATIONAL PHONETIC ALPHABET and many varieties thereof which are universally used in dictionaries and foreign language textbooks. The Roman alphabet is, therefore, also the most commonly used script for providing unwritten languages with a written form, although the sound values of Roman letters vary widely across orthographic systems. The term ROMANIZATION has hence become all but tantamount to providing a language with an alphabetic script.

The vast majority of all library catalogues are arranged in the order of the Roman alphabet, and electronic media of text processing and information storage have further enhanced its importance. The Roman alphabet has been the principal medium of the technologization of the word. Even where other scripts are implemented for word processing, keyboards are more often than not laid out in Roman. The International Organization for Standardization (ISO) uses Roman as its reference system, and data banks around the globe are accessed through the

phonetisch	Hepburn	Kunreisiki	Nipponsiki
ɑ i ɯ ɛ ɔ	*a i u e o*		
kɑ ki kɯ kɛ kɔ	*ka ki ku ke ko*		
sɑ ʃi sɯ sɛ sɔ	*sa shi su se so*	*si*	*si*
ta tʃi tsɯ tɛ tɔ	*ta chi tsu te to*	*ti tu*	*ti tu*
nɑ ni nɯ nɛ nɔ	*na ni nu ne no*		
ha çi Φɯ hɛ hɔ	*ha hi fu he ho*	*hu*	*hu*
mɑ mi mɯ mɛ mɔ	*ma mi mu me mo*		
ĭɑ ĭɯ ĭɔ	*ya yu yo*		
ɾɑ ɾi ɾɯ ɾɛ ɾɔ	*ra ri ru re ro*		
ŭɑ ɔ	*wa (w)o*		
n(ŋ)	*n*		
gɑ gi gɯ gɛ gɔ	*ga gi gu ge go*		
zɑ ʒi zɯ zɛ zɔ	*za ji zu ze zo*	*zi*	*zi*
dɑ ʒi zɯ dɛ dɔ	*da ji zu de do*	*zi*	*di du*
bɑ bi bɯ bɛ bɔ	*ba bi bu be bo*		
pɑ pi pɯ pɛ pɔ	*pa pi pu pe po*		
kĭɑ kĭɯ kĭɔ	*kya kyu kyo*		
ʃɑ ʃɯ ʃɔ	*sha shu sho*	*sya syu syo*	*sya syu syo*
tʃɑ tʃɯ tʃɔ	*cha chu cho*	*tya tyu tyo*	*tya tyu tyo*
nĭɑ nĭɯ nĭɔ	*nya nyu nyo*		
çĭɑ çĭɯ çĭɔ	*hya hyu hyo*		
mĭɑ mĭɯ mĭɔ	*mya myu myo*		
ɾĭɑ ɾĭɯ ɾĭɔ	*rya ryu ryo*		
gĭɑ gĭɯ gĭɔ	*gya gyu gyo*		
ʒɑ ʒɯ ʒɔ	*ja ju jo*	*zya zyu zyo*	*zya zyu zyo*
ʒɑ ʒɯ ʒɔ	*ja ju jo*	*zya zyu zyo*	*dya dyu dyo*
bĭɑ bĭɯ bĭɔ	*bya byu byo*		
pĭɑ pĭɯ pĭɔ	*pya pyu pyo*		

Table 6 Rōmaji: *three Romanization systems for Japanese. In the* Kunreisiki *and* Nipponsiki *columns only deviations from the Hepburn system are listed*

Roman code which at the same time serves as the ordering system. The only universal stabilized transliteration of proper names world-wide is in Roman. The Universal Postal Union (UPU) periodically issues in Roman script lists of post offices in all five continents. All of these factors and the necessity for a common code for global communication within one language, i.e. English, and across languages have made the Roman alphabet the world's predominant script.

See also Latin alphabet; Roman type.

Reading Schiaparelli 1921; Morison 1949; Cardona 1986.

Figure 6 Roman capital, first century CE

Roman notation The style of recording dates in the colophons or on the title pages of early printed books using Roman numerals, e.g.

M iiiiC iiiiXX Viij
1,000 + 4 × 100 + 4 × 20 + 8 = 1,488

roman type In typography, ordinary vertical type as distinct from Black letter and Italic, so called because the letters were derived from manuscript forms used in Rome. The first roman types were those of Adolf Rusch, Strasbourg, 1467. In France, the Netherlands, Switzerland and Spain roman types were introduced during the last two decades of the fifteenth century. The first English book set in roman type was the *Oratio in pace nuperrime composita* of Richard Pace (1518) (figure 7).

Romani alphabet A language of Indo-Aryan extraction, Romani (also Romany) is the tongue of the Romanes or Gypsies. Its many dialects have never been used much in writing, although texts of Gypsy folklore, poetry and religious content have been collected and published in both Roman and Cyrillic. Romani was recognized as a literary language during the early years of the USSR, and its

mander ayde au peuple de Rome, &
iamaiz ne faire refus de ſe ſoubmettre
a lauctorite & empire des ſequa:
noys. ¶ Dauantage Diuiciacus me cer
tifia que entre tous les heduez / il eſtoit
ſeul, lequel iamais on nauoit ſceu in:
duyre a faire ſerment ou bailler ſes en:
fans en ouſtage. Et que pour ceſte
cauſe il eſtoit parti de ſa cite, & ſan
eſtoit alle a Rome pour demander
ayde au Senat, pource que luy ſeul ne:

Figure 7 Roman type, 1520

various dialects have appeared in print in several other countries, notably in eastern and northern Europe. Script and spelling conventions were usually based on those of the national or majority language of the environment.

Since the nineteenth century many attempts have been made to create a standard

Pal–i ćàarta e UTh–enqiri ta e obiekti ve e Unisarde Themenqe Organizaciaqere, te spelel anglal o pućhipe e ṁanuśikane progresaqo general thaj te vàzdel o status, e hakaja ta o laćhipee Rromenqoro, sar jekh sel indiaqe originaθar, and–e savore thema, kaj amaro khetanipe ivel, asave ćhandesee te aźutil eemergència thaj dikăripe jekhe hakajutne socialone sistemaqo e lumiaqeresqo, bazisardo opr–o barabaripe thaj phralipe.

Translation

In accordance with the UN Charter and the aims of the United Nations Organization, to advance the cause of human progress in general and to uplift the status, rights and welfare of Romanis, as a people of Indian origin, in all countries in which our communities exist, in such ways as may assist the emergence and maintenance of a just social world order based on equality and brotherhood.

Figure 8 Specimen of Romani writing
Source: *Statutes of the Romani Union, section 5*

alphabet for the Romani language. So far they have all been frustrated by three factors: (1) extreme dialect variation; (2) lack of a tradition of writing; (3) dispersal of the speech community throughout the world. The last problem implies that there is no government or other official body that can select a variety as the basis of a written norm and impose a standard alphabet on the entire speech community. Yet, since the first World Romani Congress in 1971 the International Romani Union, an umbrella organization of Romanes bodies in some 25 countries, has worked towards establishing a common written language, and at a meeting in Warsaw in 1990 the Commission for the Standardization of the Romani Language formally adopted the 'Romani alphabet'.

The Romani alphabet is based on the Latin script with some modifications. It consists of the following 31 graphemes, five Vs and 26 Cs: <a, b, c, ć, ćh, d, e, f, g, h, x, i, j, k, kh, l, m, n, o, p, ph, r, s, ś, t, th, u, v, z, ź, ʒ>. For some dialects an additional digraph, <rr>, is recognized to express the opposition of simple and retroflex /r/. Further, there are three 'post-positional' graphemes to indicate sandhis, i.e. characteristic phonological changes at morpheme boundaries. They are <θ> = [d], <ç> = [c] and <q> = [g]. The grave accent is used to mark stress where it is not final.

The adoption of this alphabet by the Romani Union is a significant step in the direction of a common standard language (figure 8). How and to what extent it will contribute to the codification of Romani will depend on its acceptance and use in publications, especially dictionaries.

Reading Kenrick 1981; Rromani Unia 1990; Hancock 1993.

Romanian writing The earliest Romanian (also Rumanian) texts date from the sixteenth century. Under the influence of the Eastern Church and its liturgical language, Old Church Slavonic (OLD BULGARIAN WRITING), Romanian was first written in Cyrillic letters. Around the end of the eighteenth century a Latinist movement emerged whose promoters sought to deepen relations with other Romance language countries, especially France. As a consequence Cyrillic was abandoned in 1860 in favour of the Roman alphabet. Moldavian, the Romanian dialect of the Moldavian principality which became a Soviet republic, was written in an adjusted form of the Cyrillic alphabet for Russian until 1989. Modern written Romanian is based on the Daco-Romanian dialect of Bucharest which derives from the Latin vernacular of the Roman colony of Dacia (second century BCE to third century CE) (figure 9).

The modern Romanian alphabet has 27 letters: seven Vs, <a, ă, e, i, î, o, u>, and 20 Cs, <b, c, d, f, g, h, j, k, l, m, n, p, r, s, ş, t, ţ, v, x, z>. Phonetic values of the diacritically distinguished letters are as follows: <ă> = [ə], <î> = [ω], <ş> = [š] and <ţ> = [ts]. The letter <e> is pronounced [je] in initial and post-vocalic position. The letter <h> is used, much as in Italian, after <g> and <c> to indicate that these are pronounced as velar stops, e.g. *chema* 'to call'. Since the present spelling system has been codified only in the nineteenth century, it is largely phonemic with straightforward grapheme–phoneme correspondences. In contradistinction to other Romance languages, accent marks are not used for word accent, but mainly to distinguish homographs, such as *cópii* 'copies' vs *copíi* 'children'.

Reading Lombard 1974.

Locuitorii României

Românii sînt de religie creştină ortodixă. Unii din ei sînt uniţi cu biserica romano–catolică a Romei. În fruntea bisericii ortodoxe române stă un patriarh, cu sediul în Bucureşti. Acesta are subt ascultarea sa mai mulţi mitropoliţi şi episcopi. În România mai trăiesc afară de români şi alte naţionalităţi; în primul rînd maghiari sau unguri, apoi germani, slavi, greci, armeni, evrei şi alţii.

Translation

Romania's inhabitants

The Romanians are of Christian Orthodox religion. Some of them belong to the Roman Catholic Church. At the head of the Romanian Orthodox Church is a patriarch who resides in Bucharest. He directs many metropolitans and bishops. In addition to Romanians, other nationalities live in Romania; in the first place there are Magyars and Hungarians, and then there are Germans, Slavs, Greeks, Armenians, Jews and others.

Figure 9 Specimen of Romanian writing

Romanization Providing a language which is written with a non-alphabetic script with an alphabetic writing using the Roman script. A system of Romanization is either a TRANSLITERATION or a TRANSCRIPTION. In a wider sense the term includes conversion conventions of non-Roman into Roman alphabets, such as Greek and Cyrillic. A comparison of systems of Romanization for the same language is instructive, demonstrating the multiple ways in which the ROMAN ALPHABET can be used to represent a language. For example, numerous schemes have been developed for Chinese which differ significantly from each other. The major modern systems, none of which can be said to be based on the orthography of another language, as many earlier systems were, all represent Chinese tones differently: GWOYEU ROMATZYH gives different internal spellings to all Vs in all four tones; WADE-GILES ROMANIZATION uses superscript ciphers; PINYIN, the official Romanization of Chinese, represents tones with accent marks. Similar differences in grapheme–phoneme correspondence can be observed in the various systems of Japanese RŌMAJI. The main criteria for designing and evaluating systems of Romanization resemble those of ALPHABET MAKING: (1) systematic transparency of grapheme–phoneme correspondence; (2) ease of learning; and (3) ease of reading and writing (both manually and mechanically/electronically).

Róng script *See* LEPCHA SCRIPT.

Rongo-rongo script *See* EASTER ISLAND SCRIPT.

Rosetta Stone A large black stone inscribed in two languages, Egyptian and Greek, but in three scripts, the Egyptian version of the text being redacted in both HIEROGLYPHS and DEMOTIC SCRIPT. The stone, which was discovered in 1799 in a small village in the Nile delta called Rosetta by Europeans, held the key for the decipherment of Egyptian hieroglyphic writing. The inscription is a copy of a decree of the Egyptian clergy dating from 196 BCE. The partly damaged stone monument weighs 762 kg and measures 114 cm in height, 72 cm in width and 11 cm in thickness. It is kept in the British Museum.
See also DECIPHERMENT; BILINGUIS (for illustration).
Reading Andrews 1981.

rotunda A script developed in the fifteenth century in Italy, also known as 'round Gothic'. Characterized by rounded forms, it retains many features of the Carolingian script (figure 10).

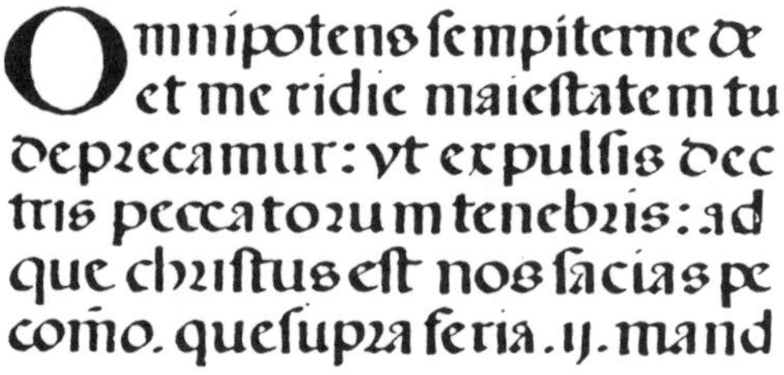

Omnipotens sempiterne de
et me ridie maiestatem tu
deprecamur: ut expulsis dec
tris peccatorum tenebris: ad
que christus est nos facias pe
como. quesupra feria .ij. mand

Figure 10 Rotunda

rune A letter from an old Germanic alphabetic writing. Runes are inscriptionally attested on stone monuments, coins and various other portable objects scattered across Europe from the Balkan and the Alps to Germany, the British Isles and Scandinavia where the great majority of all of the some 5,000 known inscriptions have been found. The runic alphabet is called *fuþark* (*futhark*) for the first six letters of the traditional sequence of 24. It is divided into three sets of eight runes, which are known by the Icelandic term *ættir*. In some inscriptions, such as the Rök stone (figure 11), the position of a rune in its *ættir* is used as a code for writing it. Etymologically, the word *rune* means 'mystery' and 'secret' in old Germanic languages, a name which is indicative of the important part runes played in Germanic ritual and magic, referred to in Plutarch's *Marius*, Caesar's *De bello gallico* and Tacitus's *Germania*. The fact that runic writing never developed into a cursive script and is attested mainly in epigraphic inscriptions is explained by its primary usage which was symbolic rather than utilitarian. Runes were incised in wood, metal and stone and are therefore characterized by straight lines and angular forms (table 7).

The earliest runic inscriptions date from about the beginning of the current era.

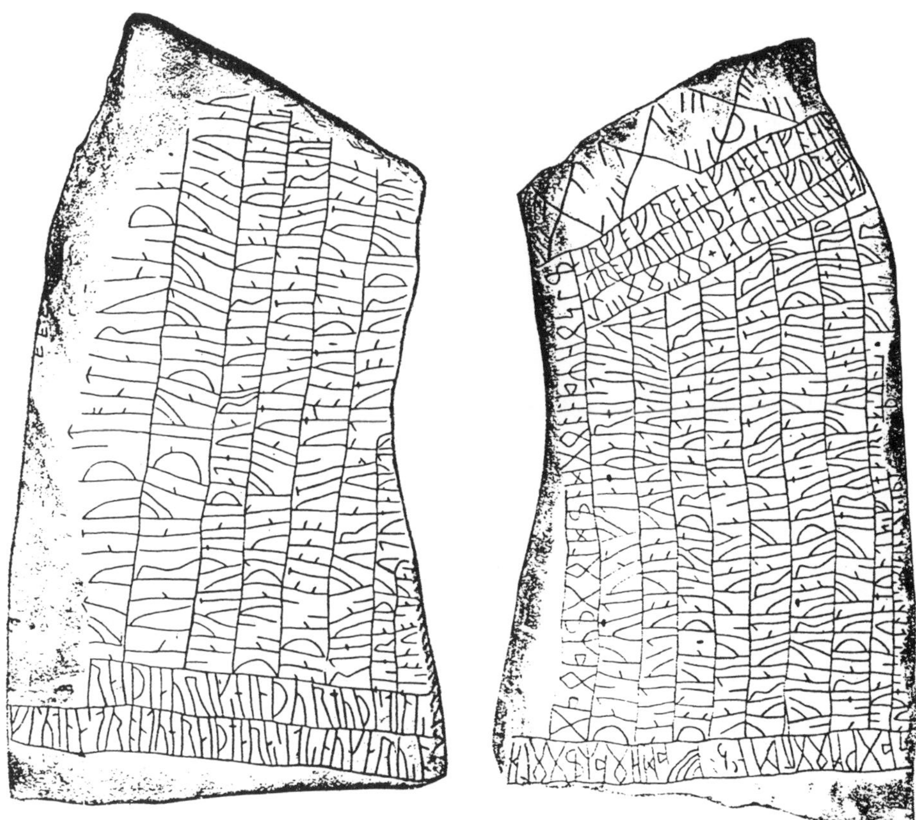

Figure 11 The Rök stone, front (left) and back, inscribed with runes of the Swedish-Norwegian futhark, *mid-ninth century* CE

Initially the direction of writing is variable, but later it is from left to right. Word divisions are not usually recognized, although one or several dots are used in some inscriptions to distinguish words or larger linguistic units. Another feature of runic writing which is attested only occasionally is the use of ligatures. These are contractions of two runic letters into one sign.

Judging from the preserved documents, runic writing was used most during the period from the fourth to the seventh centuries. After that it gradually gave way to the Latin alphabet. Use of the 33-letter Anglo-Saxon runic alphabet ceased around the ninth century. In Denmark the latest monuments are from the twelfth century, and in Sweden runes continued to be inscribed on monuments for another couple of centuries (table 8). Isolated ornamental uses and inscriptions on charms in a reduced script of 16 runic letters occur as late as the seventeenth century.

The origin of runic writing remains enigmatic. However, recent scholarship concurs on the following points:

1 The *futhark* is an individual creation rather than the result of historical evolution.
2 Runic writing first appeared in south Europe and was carried from there by Germanic tribes to the north.

Early runes		Later runes			
Common Germanic	Value	Danish (9th – 11th C. CE)	Nordic	Value	Name
ᚠ	*f*	ᚠ	ᚠ	*f*	*fē*
ᚢ ᚢ	*u*	ᚢ	ᚢ ᚢ	*u, o, w*	*ūr*
ᚦ ᚦ	*þ*	ᚦ	ᚦ	*þ, ð*	*þurs*
ᚨ	*a*	ᚬ	ᚭ	*ą, å*	*ą̄ss*
ᚱ ᚱ	*r*	ᚱ	ᚱ	*r*	*reið*
ᚲ ᚲ ᚲ	*k*	ᚴ	ᚴ	*k, g, ng*	*kaun*
ᚷ	*g, γ*				
ᚹ ᚹ	*w*				
ᚺ ᚻ	*h*	ᚼ	ᚽ	*h*	*hagall*
ᚾ	*n*	ᚾ	ᚿ	*n*	*nauð*
ᛁ	*i*	ᛁ	ᛁ	*i, e*	*īss*
ᛃ ᛃ ᛃ ᛃ	*j*	ᛅ	ᛆ ᛅ ᛆ	*a*	*ār*
ᛇ	*é*				
ᛈ ᛈ ᛈ	*p*				
ᛉ ᛉ ᛉ	*-z, -R*				
ᛊ ᛊ	*s*	ᛋ ᛋ	ᛌ	*s*	*sōl*
ᛏ	*t*	ᛏ	ᛐ	*t, d, nd*	*tȳr*
ᛒ ᛒ	*b*	ᛒ ᛒ	ᛓ ᛓ	*p, b, mb*	*bjarkan*
ᛖ ᛖ	*e*				
ᛗ	*m*	ᛘ ᛘ	ᛙ ᛘ	*m*	*maðr*
ᛚ	*l*	ᛚ	ᛚ ᛚ	*l*	*lǫgr*
ᛜ ᛜ ᛜ ᛜ	*ŋ (ng)*				
ᛞ ᛞ	*d, ð*				
ᛟ ᛟ	*o*				
		ᛦ		*R*	*ȳr*

Table 7 Early and later runic signs

Table 8 *Runic numerals from the fourteenth century*

3 Of the three southern European scripts that have been proposed as the paradigm on which the *futhark* was modelled, i.e. Greek, Latin and Etruscan, a northern Italic variety of the last is the most probable.
4 The creator(s) of the *futhark* was (were) also familiar with the Latin alphabet, as evidenced by the Latin–runic parallels: *F* ᚠ, *R* ᚱ, *H* ᚺ, *S* ᛋ, *C* ᚲ (*k*).

The letter names of the *futhark* follow the ACROPHONIC PRINCIPLE: that is, the initial sound of the name is the sound value of the rune. Most of the names are meaningful words. How the order of the letters and their names became fixed is unknown.
Reading Odenstedt 1990; Krause 1970; Elliott 1971.

Russian writing Russian emerges as a distinct member of the eastern branch of Slavic languages around the middle of the fourteenth century CE with the earliest written documents belonging predominantly to the religious domain. Russian coexisted in a DIGLOSSIA relationship with Old Church Slavonic which, as the language of the Christianization of the Slavs, remained the principal liturgical and cultural language until the end of the seventeenth century (OLD BULGARIAN WRITING).

Russian, like the other east Slavic languages as well as Bulgarian, Macedonian and Serbian in south Slavic, is written in the CYRILLIC alphabet, the script of the Orthodox Church. As a result of the reform initiated by Peter the Great (1708–10), the Cyrillic letters were adapted so as to bear greater formal resemblance to the Latin alphabet, since known as the 'civil script' (*grashdanskaja asbuka*). Two new letters, ё [jɔ] and Й [j], were added later. Another orthography reform designed to simplify Russian spelling was enacted in 1917 and 1918 when the letters i [i], ѣ [jɛ], and A [f] were abolished by government decree (table 9, figure 12).

Russian	Transliteration	Russian	Transliteration	Russian	Transliteration
а	a	к	k	х	x
б	b	л	l	ц	c
в	v	м	m	ч	č
г	g	н	n	ш	š
д	d	о	o	щ	šč
е	je/e	п	p	ъ	″
ё	jo	р	r	ы	y
ж	ž	с	s	ь	′
з	z	т	t	э	è
и	i	у	u	ю	ju
й	j	ф	f	я	ja

Table 9 *The Russian alphabet*

Всё затихло в Москве. Редко, редко где слышится визг колес по зимней улице. В окнах огней уже нет, и фонари потухли. От церквей разносятся звуки колоколов и, колыхаясь над спящим городом, поминают об утре. На улицах пусто. Редко где промесит узкими полозьями песок с снегом ночной извозчик и, перебравшись на другой угол, заснет, дожидаясь седока.

Transliteration

Vsjo zatixlo v Moskve. Redko, redko gde slyšitsja vizg koljes po zimnej ulice. V oknax ognej uže njet, i fonari potuxli. Ot cerkvej raznosjatsja zvuki kolokolov i, kolyxajas nad spjaščim gorodom, pominajut ob utre. Na ulicax pusto. Redko gde promesit uzkimi polozjami pesok s snegom nočnoj izvoščik i, perebravšis na drugoj ugol, zasnjet, dožidajas sedoka.

Translation

All is quiet in Moscow. Once in a while screeching wheels are heard on the frozen road. No windows are lit, and the streetlamps have gone out. The chime from the church reverberates across the sleeping town, heralding the approaching daybreak. The streets are empty. Here and there a sleigh, its slender runners mixing the street sand with snow, glides to the next street corner where, expecting a customer, the coachman soon falls asleep. (From Leo N. Tolstoj, *Kazaki*)

Figure 12 Specimen of Russian writing: Leo N. Tolstoj, Kazaki

Grapheme–phoneme correspondence is characterized by some measure of polyvalence, because the alphabetic principle of one-to-one mapping relations is often compromised for the sake of preserving grapheme–morpheme identity. The letters ъ and ѣ are the so-called 'hard' and 'soft' signs respectively. The former has no sound value, while the latter indicates that an ambivalent C is palatalized.

Reading Stilman 1941; Issatschenko 1980–3.

S, s /es/ The nineteenth letter of the English alphabet developed from Semitic *šin* through Greek *sigma* (Σ, ς), which was similar in form to its Phoenician model but turned 90 degrees to the right. It acquired its present form in Latin.

Sabaic writing The principal member of the southern branch of south Arabian consonant scripts. Sabaic (also Sabaean) is epigraphically attested in numerous inscriptions of the ancient cultures of south-west Arabia going back to the middle of the first millennium BCE. The script is linear and predominantly angular and symmetric in appearance (table 1). The direction on most monuments is typically from right to left, but some of the most ancient inscriptions are BOUSTROPHEDON. The origin of this script and its relationship with north Semitic scripts are obscure, but like those of north Semitic the 29 letters of the Sabaic script represent Cs only. The script has no means of V indication. A conspicuous feature of the script is the four graphemes for different *s* sounds. Their phonetic characteristics have been tentatively described as follows: (1) a voiceless palato-alveolar central fricative; (2) a voiceless alveolar lateral fricative; (3) a voiceless alveolar central fricative; and (4) an emphatic velar fricative. (As is common among Arabists, the underdot is used in table 1 to represent emphatic Cs.) In Arabia, the Sabaic script fell into disuse in the sixth century CE.

During the final centuries of the first millennium BCE, colonists from south-west

glottal	𐩱 ʾ	𐩠 h	𐩲 ʿ	𐩢 ḥ
palatal	𐩭 ḫ	𐩶 ġ	𐩤 q	
	𐩫 k	𐩴 g		
dental	𐩩 t	𐩵 d	𐩻 ṯ	𐩹 ḏ
alveolar	𐩪 s¹	𐩦 s²	𐩯 s³	𐩸 z
emphatic	𐩷 ṭ	𐩳 ḍ	𐩮 ṣ	𐩼 ẓ
labial	𐩰 f	𐩨 b		
liquid/nasal	𐩡 l	𐩧 r	𐩣 m	𐩬 n
semi-vowel	𐩥 w	𐩺 y		

Table 1 The south Arabian alphabet for Sabaic, monumental style

Arabia began to settle in Abyssinia. Their language, known as *Ge'ez* (South Arabic 'emigrant'), which became the language of the Ethiopic Church, was initially written in the familiar Sabaic script. This was subsequently modified to yield the right-running Classical Ethiopic script of which, in turn, the modern Amharic script is derived.
See also SEMITIC WRITING; SOUTH ARABIAN SCRIPT.
Reading Avanzini 1977/1980; Beeston 1984.

Samaritan script A north Semitic alphabet of 22 C letters which was derived in the fifth century BCE from the Old Hebrew script by the Samaritans – a Mesopotamian tribe which had moved to Palestine around the beginning of the first millennium BCE and assimilated to Jewish culture and religion. While the Old Hebrew script was superseded by the Hebrew square script, an Aramaic offshoot, the Samaritan script continued to be used as the script of the Samaritan sect (figure 1). In the city of Nablus a few members of the sect still carry on the tradition of this script.
See also SEMITIC WRITING.
Reading Jensen 1969; Lidzbarski 1907.

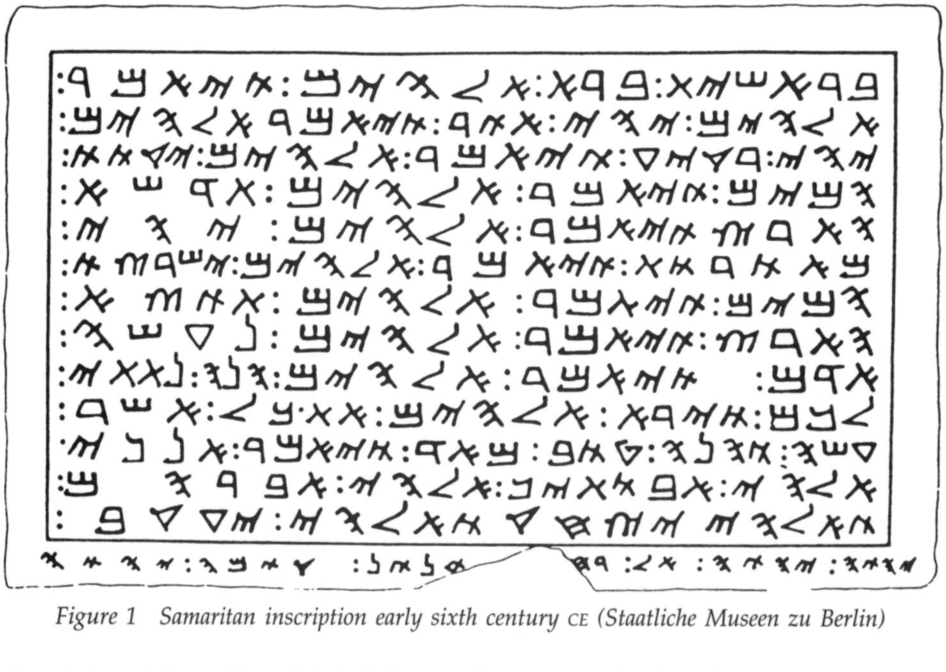

Figure 1 Samaritan inscription early sixth century CE (Staatliche Museen zu Berlin)

Sanskrit writing The classical literary language of India, Sanskrit (from *saṃskṛta* 'elaborated') is the language described in the grammar of Pāṇini (*c.*sixth century BCE). It has been India's pre-eminent language of learning for two and a half millenniums and continues to be studied widely. The oldest form of Sanskrit, Vedic, the language of the Hindu scriptures, is distinguished from epic and Buddhist Sanskrit. During its long history Sanskrit has been written in various scripts in and outside India. Early inscriptions are in BRĀHMĪ WRITING. As of the fourth century CE it was followed by one of its derivatives, the GUPTA SCRIPT, which in turn gave way to the NĀGARĪ SCRIPT. BENGṚĀLĪ WRITING and the OṚĪYĀ SCRIPT have also been used, as have the local scripts of Dravidian languages in south India, especially TAMIL WRITING. Sanskrit has furthermore been written in Old Kawi, Tibetan and Chinese characters, a fact which is of great importance for the history of printing. In the eighth century CE, 'one million' Buddhist charms (*dhāraṇī*) were printed in Japan for distribution to the temples and monasteries of the land. The texts were taken from the *Raśmi vimaviśuddha prabhā nāma dhāraṇī* and printed in Chinese characters used as phonograms on strips of paper. In Japanese they are commonly referred to as *Hyakumantō-dhāraṇī* or 'mantras of the million stupas' (figure 2). Some of them are kept at the temple Hōryūji in Nara. With the possible exception of a *dhāraṇī* of a stupa at the temple Pulgugk-sa in Korea, these charms are the oldest known printed texts.

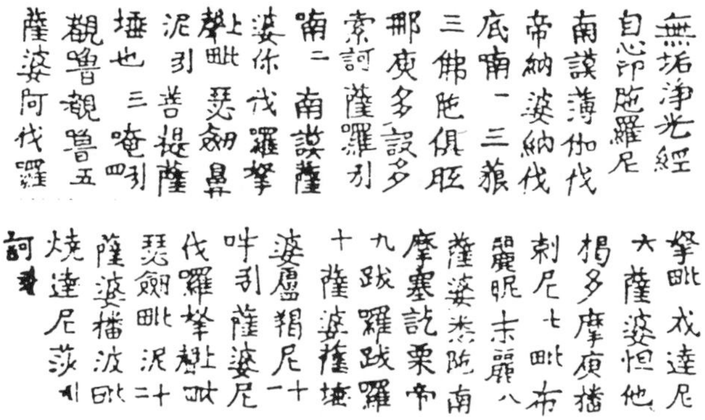

Figure 2 A Buddhist charm from the 'mantras of the million stupas' in Sanskrit, printed in Chinese characters: the original appears on a long strip of paper that was rolled up

However, the script in which the bulk of the massive Sanskrit literature is written is DEVANĀGARĪ. Its 48 letters – 13 Vs and 35 Cs with inherent *a* – are thought to faithfully reflect the sounds of the classical Sanskrit language (table 2). Both the ordering of letters for organs and places of articulation, and the writing conventions developed for Sanskrit, reflect a high degree of linguistic insight. Word boundaries are not marked, unless they coincide with breath pauses.

	Hard (tenues)	Hard aspirates	Soft (mediæ)	Soft aspirates	(Soft) nasals	(Soft) semi-vowels	Hard spirants	Soft Vowels Short	Soft Vowels Long	Soft Diphthongs
Gutturals	क k	ख k-h	ग g	घ g-h	ङ ṅ	ह h	: ḥ	अ a	आ ā	ए e ऐ ai
Palatals	च c	छ c-h	ज j	झ j-h	ञ ñ	य y	श ś	इ i	ई ī	
Cerebrals	ट ṭ	ठ ṭ-h	ड ḍ	ढ ḍ-h	ण ṇ	र r	ष ṣ	ऋ ṛ	ॠ ṝ	
Dentals	त t	थ t-h	द d	ध d-h	न n	ल l	स s	ऌ ḷ		
Labials	प p	फ p-h	ब b	भ b-h	म m	व v	: ḥ	उ u	ऊ ū	ओ o औ au

Table 2 The Devanāgarī syllabic alphabet for Sanskrit, ordered for organs and places of articulation

Sentences, on the other hand, are always marked by a perpendicular stroke. Devanāgarī is written from left to right (figure 3).
See also Indian writing systems.
Reading Macdonell 1927; Filliozat 1963; Lambert 1953.

नासदासीन्नो सदासीत् तदानीं नासीद्रजो नो व्योमा परो यत् ।
किमावरीवः कुह कस्य शर्मन्नम्भः किमासीद्गहनं गभीरम् १
न मृत्युरासीदमृतं न तर्हि न रात्र्या अह्न आसीत् प्रकेतः ।

Transliteration
1. nāsad āsīn nosad āsīt tadānīṃ; nāsīd rajo viomā paro yat.
kim āvarīvaḥ? kuha? kasya sarmann? ambhaḥ kim āsīd gahanaṃ gabhīram?

Translation
1. Then, there was not the existent, nor the non-existant; space was not, nor the heavens beyond. What was latent? Where? By whom sheltered? Was water there, unfathomable, deep?

Figure 3 Specimen of Sanskrit writing in Devanagārī: Rig-Veda, *book X, hymn 129*

Santhali writing An Austro-Asiatic language of the Munda group, Santhali is spoken in four north-eastern states of India, each with its own distinct script. These are Orissa, West Bengal, Bihar and Assam. Following a common practice in India of writing minority languages in the script of the regional language of the state in which they are spoken, Santhali, which has no long literary tradition of its own, has been written in the Oṛiyā, Bengālī, Devanāgarī and Roman scripts. Opposition on the part of the Santhalis to the use of four different scripts for writing their language led to the development of a Santhali script, known as *Ol chiki*, which combines elements of the Bengālī, Devanāgarī and Roman scripts.
See also Indian writing systems.
Reading Mahapatra 1979.

Śāradā script An Indian syllabic alphabet derived between the eighth and tenth centuries CE (table 3) from a western variety of the Gupta script. The oldest known Śāradā (also Sharada) inscriptions from Kīragrāma are dated 804 CE (figure 4). This script is also attested on coins of the Varma dynasty of Kashmir. In some restricted domains it continued to be used for writing Kashmiri texts until the twentieth century. It is furthermore the parent of the Gurmukhī script, that associated with the Punjabi language and Sikh religious writing.
See also Indian writing systems.
Reading Bühler 1980; Dani 1963.

Saussure, Ferdinand de (1857–1913) Eminent Swiss linguist and Indo-Europeanist who laid the foundations of structuralist linguistics. He taught that in the study of language a strict distinction should be made between a diachronic

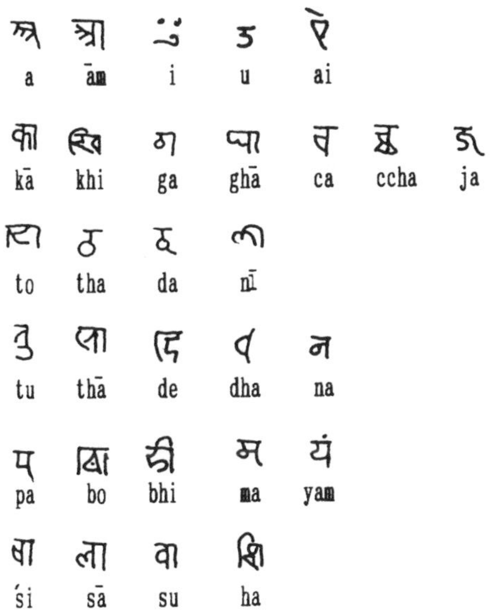

a	ām	i	u	ai		
kā	khi	ga	ghā	ca	ccha	ja
to	tha	da	nī			
tu	thā	de	dha	na		
pa	bo	bhi	ma	yam		
śi	sā	su	ha			

Table 3 The Sāradā syllabic alphabet
Source: *adapted from Bühler 1980, plate V*

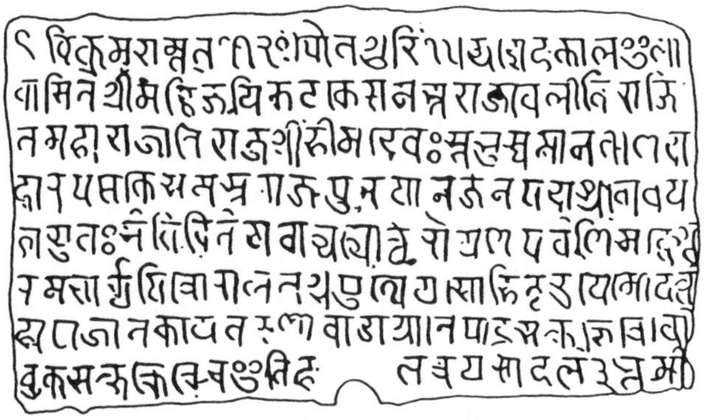

Figure 4 A Sāradā inscription, eighth century CE

and a synchronic approach, the latter constituting the heart of structural analysis. To this end, linguists should focus their attention on spoken language, because 'the linguistic object is not both the written and the spoken forms of words; the spoken forms alone constitute the object'. Saussure's exclusion of writing from the proper domain of linguistic inquiry has been very influential, leading many linguists to disregard writing and the relations between written signs and speech signs.
See also SCRIPTISM.
Reading Saussure 1916.

schwa A Roman lower case *e* rotated 180 degrees, <ə>. This symbol is commonly used in phonetic transcriptions to represent a mid-central unrounded unstressed V. The name *schwa* or *shva* derives from Hebrew *šewa*, the diacritic subscript <.> introduced by the medieval Masoretes to represent the absence of a V or a neutral V in Hebrew writing.

script **1** In the study of writing, the graphic form of a writing system. In non-technical contexts the term is often used interchangeably with 'writing system' or 'alphabet', from which it should be distinguished, however. A writing system needs a script for its physical representation, but both are conceptually independent of each other. The same writing system may be written in a variety of scripts. For example, the Roman, Cyrillic, Greek, Russian and runic scripts are different graphic instantiations of the same writing system, the alphabet. Similarly, syllabic alphabets of the C plus inherent *a* type are instantiated by the various Indian scripts. Scripts, in turn, come in different varieties in both handwriting and print, for example the many typefaces that have evolved for the Roman script. **2** In typography, typefaces designed to imitate the appearance of handwriting.

script reform A deliberate and often officially sanctioned change in a speech community's script, to be distinguished from orthography reform which affects spelling conventions but not the script. Script reform usually consists of two steps: script choice and orthography formation. Only in some cases does a script reform not entail the selection of a script, but consist of the reduction or elimination of a system or part of a system. A case in point is North Korea's decision to use *han'gŭl* exclusively and to abolish Chinese characters which formerly had been used in combination with it. This is a rather unique example, but script reforms involving the shift from one system to another have been carried out many times.

It is quite common that in the course of history languages have been written in different scripts. For example, Indonesian (Malay) was successively written in three different scripts, Nāgarī, Arabic and finally Roman. Vietnamese shifted from Chinese characters to an alphabetic script based on Roman. Turkish, Somali, Kiswahili and Hausa all shifted from Arabic to Roman. In India a large number of languages have been written in different scripts, and for some of them the discussion about a linguistically suitable and culturally acceptable script continues. In the 1920s and 1930s many languages of the Soviet Union underwent changes in the scripts from Arabic to Latin and then Cyrillic. After the demise of the USSR, several of these reforms were reversed. For instance, in 1992 Tajikistan adopted the Perso-Arabic alphabet of neighbouring Iran, while Azerbaijan opted for Roman.

As such examples show, script reforms often have political overtones and symbolize changes in ideological orientation. In antiquity, the Copts, who were Christians, dissociated themselves from the Egyptian tradition by writing their language in a Greek-based alphabet. Kubilai Khan's promotion of the 'Phags-pa instead of the Uighur script for Mongolian was a bold attempt to establish a common script for his empire. One of the best-documented cases is Turkey's shift from Arabic to Roman in the 1920s which was part of Kemal Atatürk's Westernization policy.

Sometimes script reforms have been implemented only partially in the sense

that parts of the speech community continued to use the old system. For example, when in 1860 Romanian writing changed from Cyrillic to Roman, the Moldavian dialect of this language continued to be written in Cyrillic letters. The resulting situation of two scripts for one language is known as Digraphia or Digraphic literacy.
See also Orthography reform; Religion and writing; Spelling reform.
Reading Gallagher 1971; Henze 1977; Fishman 1977; Daswani 1975.

scriptism The tendency of linguists to base their analyses on writing-induced concepts such as Phoneme, Word, Literal meaning and 'sentence', while at the same time subscribing to the principle of the primacy of speech for linguistic inquiry. Since most fundamental concepts of linguistics are derived from writing, linguists cannot quite do what they profess to do, that is, analyse spoken language without being influenced by writing. From its inception, grammar has been the science of letters, and in some ways it still is.
See also Functions of writing; Literacy.
Reading Harris 1980; Linell 1982.

scriptorium In medieval Europe, the room in a monastery in which copyists (*clerici* or clerks) wrote manuscripts from an exemplar. As of the mid-ninth century virtually every monastery and abbey had its own scriptorium. The scriptorium was the centre of European manuscript culture and the main agency of text reproduction before printing. It was a place of highly regarded and specialized work, usually shared by several copyists. Although most scribes were members of the monastery, secular specialists were sometimes brought in to carry out certain duties, such as illumination. The scriptorium was under the direction of an *armarius* who was charged with supervising the work and dispensing Parchment, ink, pens, knives and other implements necessary for the scribes' work. It was also his responsibility to administer the strict rules that governed conduct in the scriptorium. Silence was imperative so as to ensure maximum concentration and thus avoid copying errors. During working hours standardized gestures were used for communication. Work in the scriptoria was limited to daylight hours, artificial light being forbidden in order to guard against the risk of fire. Manuscripts produced by copyists of the scriptoria are called 'scribal copies' as distinct from those written or dictated by the author.
Reading Banks 1989.

scriptura continua Writing without word separation. This term usually refers to Greek and Latin epigraphic monuments and manuscripts which were written in this manner, although in the earliest Greek inscriptions word boundaries were marked by interpuncts (figure 5). There is general agreement among reading

(testaturque deos iterum se ad proelia cogi bis iam
Italos hostis haec altera foedera)

Figure 5 Scriptura continua: *two lines from a manuscript of Virgil in rustic capitals* specialists that word separation facilitates reading. Why then was this simplification of the reading process ever given up, to be reintroduced only in the early Middle Ages?

Two main factors were responsible for this development. First, while word separation was essential in the Semitic consonant scripts, the addition of V letters to the north Semitic alphabet that the Greeks adapted to their language made it possible to dispense with word separation in writing. The text could still be interpreted, although the reader had to take over what formerly was the writer's task, to divide the written string of letters into words. Second, in antiquity, reading was typically aloud and not associated with the swift consultation of books. Rather than speed, scrutiny was valued. Many texts were recited over and over again. Since the message of a text was recovered through oralization, reading was still a practice which was closely associated with rhetoric. It was only when reading material became more plentiful and the solitary practice of SILENT READING more common that spaces were reintroduced in writing as a code to separate words.

The first to break away from the *scriptura continua* tradition were Irish and Anglo-Saxon scribes in the early Middle Ages, perhaps because they had more difficulties with Latin, a language foreign to them, than their colleagues in Romance language areas.

See also WORD BOUNDARY.

Reading Saenger 1991; Ullman 1980.

scriptura quadrata The Hebrew square script which came into existence after the decline of the Persian empire as an offshoot of the Aramaic script. The earliest inscriptions date from the middle of the third century BCE. The *scriptura quadrata*, or 'Hebrew square', replaced the Old Hebrew (Canaanite) script as the script of the Jewish scriptures and thus became the Jewish script as such. Its name refers to the equidimensional frames of the letters. Initially, only Cs were expressed in square Hebrew but, when biblical Hebrew was superseded as a spoken language by Aramaic, systems of vocalization by means of MATRES LECTIONIS and PUNCTUATION evolved. In the early Middle Ages the masoretes systematized V diacritics. Well-proportioned and regular in appearance, the Hebrew square script proved to be remarkably consistent over the centuries (figure 6). Three slightly different styles evolved: (1) the formal book hand, which is still used almost unchanged; (2) the rabbinical hand mostly used for commentaries of the scriptures, e.g. the Italian RASCHI SCRIPT; (3) cursive hands for everyday usage.

See also HEBREW WRITING; SEMITIC WRITING.

Reading Birnbaum 1971.

seal A device impressed on a piece of plastic material as a mark of ownership or evidence of authenticity. Seals made of stone, clay, metal and other hard materials have been used in various forms throughout history. In neolithic Mesopotamia the practice of impressing seals with geometric, human and animal forms on clay may well have been a decisive step in the development of writing.

Figure 6 Scriptura quadrata: *a Jewish wedding contract written at Maddelena, Italy, 23 August 1839 (From the collections of the Hebraic Section, African and Middle Eastern Division, Library of Congress.)*

Both stamp seals and cylinder seals which were rolled across the wet clay to render a continuous impression had great vogue not only in Assyria and Babylonia but also beyond these limits in a wide area from Anatolia to India (figure 7). Cylinder seals continued to be used for signatures when writing was fully developed. Pierced longitudinally, they were carried by their owners on a string around the neck. Since they are made of very durable material, many cylinder seals bearing elaborately incised scenes and inscriptions have been excavated throughout the

Figure 7 A Babylonian cylinder seal from Ur, third dynasty, c.2050 BCE: *two deities introduce Hashamer, governor of the city of lshkun-Sin, to King Ur-Nammu (British Museum)*

ancient Near East. A much larger number have been preserved in the form of their impressions on clay tablets. Documents were commonly signed in this way, with several seals belonging to the scribe and the parties involved in whatever transaction was recorded.
See also TOKEN.
Reading Nissen 1977; Collon 1990.

Sejong (*also* Solch'ong) The fourth monarch of the Korean Yi dynasty (1392–1910) who reigned from 1418 to 1450. An enlightened ruler, King Sejong was known for his devotion to scholarship. He took an active interest in the spread of learning beyond the narrow confines of the educated classes, and to this end initiated two major innovations in Korean literacy. One was the development of movable type to facilitate the reproduction of Chinese books and reduce the cost of printing. The other was the creation of a Korean alphabet, later to be called HAN'GŬL. Against the prevailing sentiment among the literati elite, he advocated the idea of writing the vernacular language. It is generally thought that he actively partook in designing the new script which was suitable to faithfully represent all sounds of the Korean language. Simple, elegant and more systematically structured than any other writing system, it was announced in 1443, but not officially promulgated until 1446. The official document, entitled 'The correct sounds for instructing the people', was prefaced by King Sejong himself, advocating literacy for everyone for daily use. This document was rediscovered in this century.
See also KOREAN WRITING.
Reading Ledyard 1975; Kim 1954.

semasiography [Gk σῆμα 'sign' + γράφειν 'to write'] Broadly, writing systems consisting of graphemes which denote meaningful elements of speech, such as Chinese characters and Egyptian hieroglyphs. More specifically, writing systems which express ideas without being related to language. That semasiographic systems in the narrower sense exist is disputed by many students of writing, but

some define the notion of writing so broadly that it includes semasiography. The latter view is defended in Sampson (1985) and criticized in DeFrancis (1989).
See also ORIGIN OF WRITING; WRITING SYSTEM.

semicolon [Lat. *sēmi* 'half' + 'colon'.] Consisting of a dot placed on top of a comma <;>, this punctuation mark came into existence in medieval times. First written as a comma placed next to a full stop on the line <.,>, it has always been used to separate grammatically independent clauses which could be marked with a full stop between them, but which are closely related in sense. Modern usage also includes the separation of potentially ambiguous items in a series: for example, *Among those present were Adam Black, president; Bertrand White, vice-president; Rosetta Stone, provost; and Victoria Clay, dean*. Sometimes the semicolon is used instead of the conjunction *and*, and in combination with conjunctive adverbs such as *therefore, however, hence*: for example, *A mere comma is not enough; therefore a semicolon is used*.
See also COLON; COMMA; PUNCTUATION.
Reading Carey 1958; Parkes 1993.

Semitic writing The grouping of Semitic writing systems and scripts is usually based on the geographic distribution of the languages they represent: the eastern group, sometimes referred to as north-eastern, in Mesopotamia; the northern or north-western group in Syria and Palestine; and the southern group in Arabia and Ethiopia (figure 8). The writing of the languages of the eastern group – AKKADIAN, BABYLONIAN and ASSYRIAN being its most important members – is the heart of the cuneiform tradition with its very involved writing system consisting of LOGOGRAMS, SYLLABOGRAMS and DETERMINATIVES. The writing of the languages of the northern group – Moabite, Canaanite, Phoenician, Aramaic, Hebrew, Palmyran, Samaritan, Syriac, Nabataean and Arabic – is typologically different from, and genetically unrelated to, cuneiform. There is one point of contact between the two traditions, however. This is the script of the city of Ugarit (*c*.1400–1200 BCE) which consists of cuneiform signs, but is structurally a north Semitic alphabet. The south Semitic group has two branches, the north Arabian scripts of Safaitic and Thamudic and the south Arabian SABAIC WRITING, which is also attested inscriptionally in Qatabanic, Himyaritic and Hadhramautic. Both the north and south Arabian scripts pre-date by several centuries the Arabic script which eventually replaced them.

Although some questions about the origin of north Semitic writing and its relation with the south Semitic group remain to be answered, the major lines of development are well understood. The earliest north Semitic alphabet emerged in the period between 1700 and 1500 BCE. A connection with the PROTO-SINAITIC SCRIPT has been suggested, but not conclusively proven. North Semitic divided into three main branches: Phoenician, Canaanite and Aramaic. The 22-letter alphabet of the Phoenicians is clearly discernible in the eleventh century BCE and continued to be used with few alterations for at least 700 years until the third century BCE. Phoenician traders and colonists took it to many places throughout the Mediterranean. Its greatest significance, however, is that it became the parent script of the Greek alphabet. The Canaanite branch included several local varieties

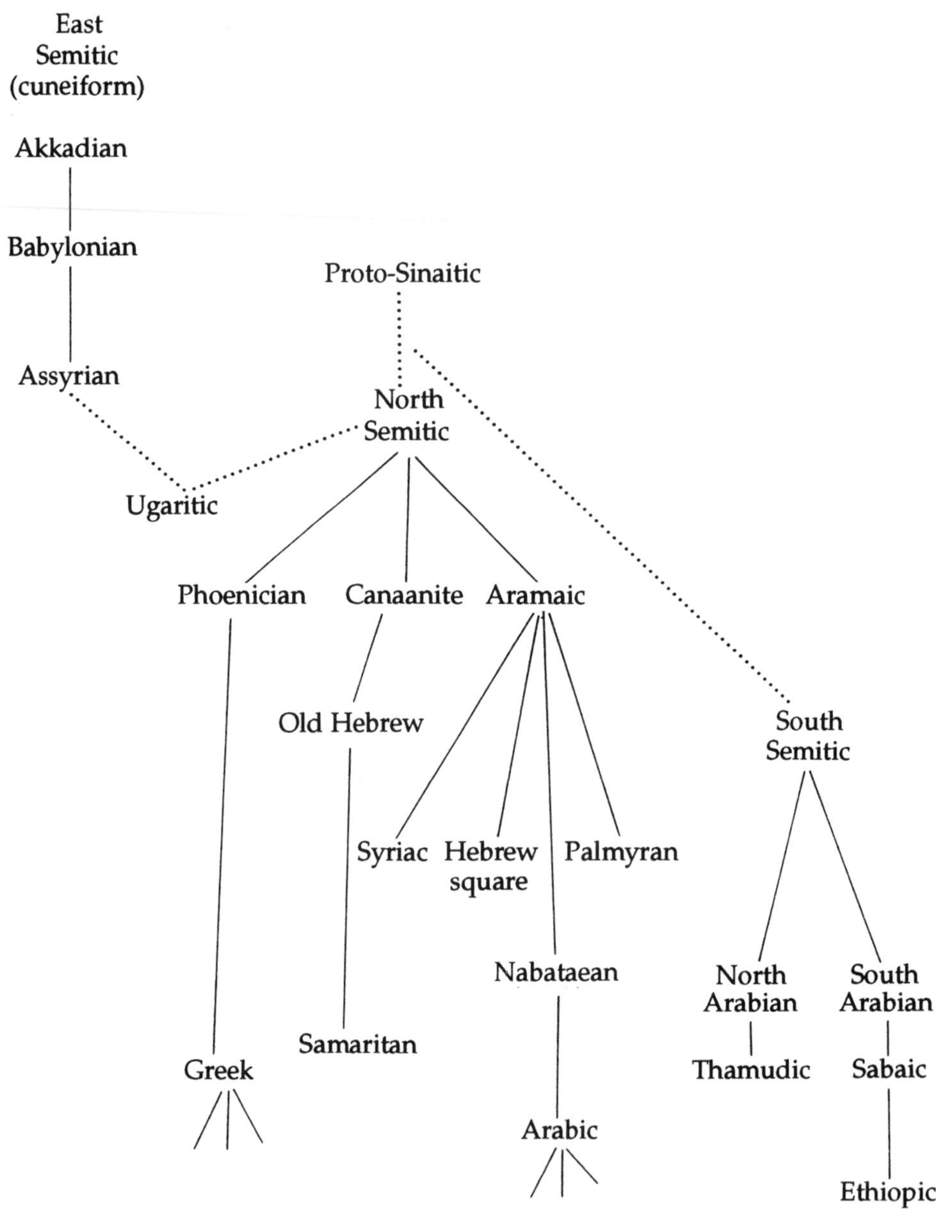

Figure 8 Semitic writing, the major junctures: dotted lines indicate assumed connections which are not well documented

west of Syria, among them the Old Hebrew script and the Samaritan script. Of these, the former was replaced by an offshoot of the Aramaic script, Hebrew square. Other varieties, too, became extinct in antiquity; only Samaritan continued to be used until modern times. The third main derivative of north Semitic is the Aramaic script of which dozens of alphabetic writings east of Syria were derived. The earliest Aramaic inscriptions date from the ninth century BCE. By the end of the eighth century its use had spread through wide parts of the Assyrian empire, where eventually Aramaic in its own script became the official administrative language (imperial Aramaic). The written form of the major lingua franca of the time, the Aramaic alphabet spread throughout the ancient Near East from Mesopotamia to Egypt. Through its offshoots it further contributed to the history of writing. They include the Hebrew, Syriac, Palmyran, Mandean and Manichaean scripts as well as the NABATAEAN SCRIPT: the last gave rise to the ARABIC ALPHABET which, except for the Latin alphabet, is the most widely used script today. The Aramaic script was also adapted to non-Semitic languages, as exemplified by Persian (PAHLAVI SCRIPT, SOGDIAN WRITING and UIGHUR WRITING). Whether it was also the source of the Indian Brāhmī is not known, but is likely in view of the fact that Aramaic was used right up to the borders of India.

South Semitic writing is much younger than the north Semitic systems, dating from the middle of the first millennium BCE. By default of a clearly identifiable link with any member of the three main branches of the north Semitic group, a derivation from proto-Sinaitic or from the north Semitic proto-alphabet has been suggested, but there is no conclusive evidence that south Semitic descended directly from either of these. The scripts of the north Semitic languages are the beginning of sound writing proper with no meaning-bearing signs. With the writing of the languages of the southern group they share the general structural principle underlying all of the scripts of both groups, with the exception of ETHIOPIAN WRITING in the southern group: each grapheme represents a C, and Vs are not indicated. The Ethiopic script alone, which is a derivative of the Sabaic, is a syllabary rather than a consonant alphabet. Conspicuous though it is, the absence of Vs in Semitic writing has yet to be explained in a universally accepted manner. One view is that the vowellessness of the ancient Semitic scripts exhibits Egyptian influence mediated through proto-Sinaitic writing. It is thought that, once the principle of sound writing was understood, the Semites deliberately did not mark the Vs, because the Cs are so obviously more important, forming as they do the roots of Semitic words. Another theory, advocated by Schmitt (1938) and Gelb (1963), assumes that Semitic writing was originally syllabic and that the syllable signs were gradually reduced to pure C letters. However, the fact that the most ancient north Semitic epigraphic documents appear to be purely consonantal remains to be accounted for.

See also CONSONANT ROOTS; CONSONANT SCRIPT; WRITING SYSTEM.

Reading Driver 1976; Diringer 1968; Jensen 1969; Gaur 1992; Naveh 1982; Gelb 1963; Lidzbarski 1907.

sentence writing A term occasionally used for certain forerunners of writing such as pictorial representations of proverbs, where the whole picture can be said to have a linguistic referent which, however, can only be determined by those who know the proverb in question. Representations of this kind, which were found for example among the Ewe of West Africa, do not constitute writing proper.

Reading Friedrich 1966; Gelb 1963.

Sequoyah (1760–1843) A monolingual, illiterate Cherokee, also known as George Guess, who between 1810 and 1820 invented the Cherokee syllabary

which was adopted widely by members of the Cherokee tribe after it had been introduced to some of its leaders in 1821. Since Sequoyah's invention called into question the exclusivity of English as a necessary precondition of literacy and hence civilized life, it was not universally welcomed by white Americans who took an interest in Indian affairs. The Cherokee, however, adopted the syllabary so enthusiastically that within a few years the tribe started a newspaper printed in Sequoyah's script. The syllabary was well adapted to the phonology of the Cherokee language and easy to learn, and its invention secured Sequoyah a place in Cherokee history and in the history of writing.
See also CHEROKEE SYLLABARY.
Reading Foreman 1938.

Serbo-Croatian writing A member of the southern branch of Slavonic languages, Serbo-Croatian exists in two main varieties, the eastern, Serbian variety centred on Belgrade, and the western, Croatian variety centred on Zagreb. The literary tradition of both varieties goes back to the twelfth century. Since the Middle Ages the speech community has been divided by divergent religious affiliations, Serbia being largely Orthodox, Croatia Catholic. This distinction was given expression in writing by using the Cyrillic and Roman alphabets, respectively. In the nineteenth century various attempts were made at establishing a literary standard, and in 1850 an accord was reached, recognizing the Štokavian dialect as the basis of the unified written language. This continued to be written in the two scripts, for which a one-to-one transliteration was established (figure 9). The Serbian Cyrillic alphabet was based on that first presented in Vuk Stefanović Karadžić's 1818 dictionary. It deleted several letters of the Old Slavonic alphabet and introduced new ones for compound letters. The similarity of Serbian Cyrillic with Russian was thus noticeably reduced, which was widely criticized at the time. However, the new orthography was much more regular, being based on a simple principle: 'Write as you speak and read as it is written.' In order to secure unambiguous transliteration the three digraphs <dž, lj, nj> were adopted in the Croatian Roman alphabet where they are treated as separate letters for lexicographic purposes. The order of the two alphabets is slightly different. The Cyrillic order is: А, Б, В, Г, Д, Ђ, Е, Ж, З, И, Ј, К, Л, Љ, М, Н, Њ, О, П, Р, С, Т, Ћ, У, Ф, Х, Ц, Ч, Џ, Ш. The Roman order is given in table 4.

The Serbo-Croatian orthography is called 'shallow' or a 'surface orthography' because it operates on the level of surface phonology. It was designed to represent the phonology of the language in an unequivocal manner, each letter denoting only one phoneme, and each phoneme being represented by only one letter. Too little time has passed since the orthography standardization of the nineteenth century for major sound changes to occur; therefore the system has hardly deviated from the one-to-one principle. In order to preserve simple grapheme–phoneme correspondence, the orthographic form of a root morpheme is sometimes altered, rather than leaving contextually predictable variations in pronunciation graphically unexpressed. For example, *snah-a* and *snas-i* are the nominative and dative singular forms of the same word 'daughter-in-law'.
See also DIGRAPHIA.
Reading Partridge 1972; Turvey et al. 1984.

Gradovi Jugoslavije

1. Najveći grad Jugoslavije je Beograd, koji je glavni grad Srbije, a istodobno i glavni grad Jugoslavije.

2. Beograd ima otprilike jedan milijun stanovnika.

3. Nalazeći se na brijegu, gdje se sastaju Dunav i Sava, Beograd je danas, kao i u prošlosti, važna spona između Zapada i Istoka.

4. Povijest kaže da su Kelti u četvrtom stoljeću prije Krista na tom mjestu sazidali grad (Singidunum).

Градови Југославије

1. Највећи град Југославије је Београд, који је главни град Србије, а истовремено и главни град Југославије.

2. Београд има отприлике један милион становника.

3. Налазећи се на брегу, где се састају Дунав и Сава, Београд је данас, као и у прошлости, важна спона између Запада и Истока.

4. Историја каже да су Келти у четвртом веку пре Христа на том месту сазидали град (Сингидунум).

Translation

Yugoslav cities

1 Yugoslavia's biggest city is Belgrade, the capital of Serbia which is at the same time the capital of Yugoslavia.

2 Belgrade has approximately one million inhabitants.

3 Situated at the river bank where the Sava flows into the Danube, Belgrade is today, as it was in the past, an important junction between East and West.

4 According to historical records, the Celts founded a city (Singidunum) here in the fourth century BC.

Figure 9 Specimen of Serbo-Croatian in Roman and Cyrillic letters

serif (*also* **ceriph**) One of the fine lines projecting from a letter stem, especially at the top and bottom of capitals (figure 10). The absence of these lines characterizes typefaces known as 'sanserif'. Modern examples of sanserif fonts include Futura, Gill, Helvetica and Noble.

Serṭō script *See* SYRIAC SCRIPTS.

Shavian *See* BERNARD SHAW ALPHABET.

Shikastah script A calligraphic style of the Arabic script developed in Iran in the sixteenth century. The word *shikastah* means 'broken', a reference to the deviation upwards and downwards from horizontal lines characteristic of this script. It had little currency beyond the borders of Iran.
See also ARABIC SCRIPTS; CALLIGRAPHY.
Reading Schimmel 1984.

Latin		Cyrillic	
A	a	А	а
B	b	Б	б
C	c	Ц	ц
Č	č	Ч	ч
Ć	ć	Ћ	ћ
D	d	Д	д
Dž	dž	Џ	џ
Đ	đ	Ђ	ђ
E	e	Е	е
F	f	Ф	ф
G	g	Г	г
H	h	Х	х
I	i	И	и
J	j	Ј	ј
K	k	К	к
L	l	Л	л
Lj	lj	Љ	љ
M	m	М	м
N	n	Н	н
Nj	nj	Њ	њ
O	o	О	о
P	p	П	п
R	r	Р	р
S	s	С	с
Š	š	Ш	ш
T	t	Т	т
U	u	У	у
V	v	В	в
Z	z	Э	э
Ž	ž	Ж	ж

Table 4 The alphabets of Serbo-Croatian

shorthand A method of writing derived from the spelling system and script of a particular language. Also known as 'stenography' (narrow writing) and 'tachygraphy' (quick writing), shorthand contrasts with 'longhand', that is, the standard way of writing that language. The speed of oral speech production is about five times that of competent handwriting. Shorthand systems are designed to reduce this difference. In order to approximate the speed of speech, shorthand systems enhance the economy of effort involved in jotting down texts by hand. This is done in two ways: by reducing the graphic redundancy of written characters, and by reducing the redundancy of the orthographic code. The various shorthand systems that have evolved all rely on these two strategies to save time. The basic signs of most shorthand systems are derived from longhand letters or simple geometrical forms. In addition, abbreviations, ligatures and word signs are used. The orthographic code only serves as a reference system of what is largely sound writing. All SILENT LETTERS are ignored, and complex orthographic rules are simplified.

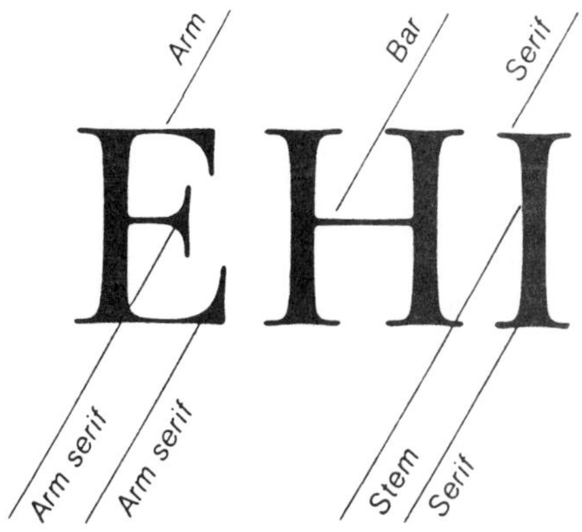

WRITING WITH SERIFS
WRITING SANS SERIF

Figure 10 Serifs

The history of shorthand writing goes back to antiquity. The most ancient known example is an inscription on the Acropolis in Athens dating from the fourth century BCE. In Rome, Cicero's secretary Tiro invented or improved a system which allowed him to record his master's speeches. Recording political oration and court proceedings were the earliest, and have proved to be the most durable, functions of shorthand.

In modern times, shorthand was introduced in England by John Willis (1602). The most widely used systems are Isaac Pitman's (1813–1897) 'English phonography' in Britain, and John R. Gregg's (1867–1948) in the USA (table 5). French shorthand was developed in the eighteenth century by Felix Conen de Prépéan. A stenographic institute was founded in 1872 in Paris by Albert Delauney and Emil Duployé. In Germany, Franz Xaver Gabelsberger (1789–1849) created a system that operates on the level of morphemic structure. Shorthand systems have also been evolved outside the sphere of alphabetic writing, for instance in China, Japan and India (table 6).
See also TIRONIAN NOTES.
Reading Butler 1951; Glatte 1959.

sign **1** In the study of writing systems, a basic unit of visual communication. The term is often used interchangeably with 'character', 'glyph', 'letter' or 'grapheme', although the meaning of all of these is more specific than that of 'sign'. **2** In semiotics, any mark which by virtue of convention, iconicity, causality or contiguity indicates something other than itself. In linguistics the concept of the sign gained prominence through the work of Ferdinand de SAUSSURE, who emphasized the importance of the arbitrary relationship between the sign vehicle (the signifier) and its meaning (the signified).
See also ICON.
Reading Eco 1973; Saussure 1916.

CONSONANTS

Written forward:

K G R L N M T D TH or

Written downward:

P B F V CH J S or SH

H NG NK

VOWELS

ă	ĭ	ŏ	ŭ
ä	ĕ	aw	ŏŏ
ā	ē	ō	o͞o

DIPHTHONGS

	Composed of			Composed of
ū	ē-o͞o as in *unit*		*oi*	aw-ē as in *oil*
ow	ä-o͞o as in *owl*		*ī*	ä-ē as in *isle*

BLENDED CONSONANTS

The consonants are so arranged that two strokes joining with an obtuse or blunt angle may assume the form of a large curve, thus:

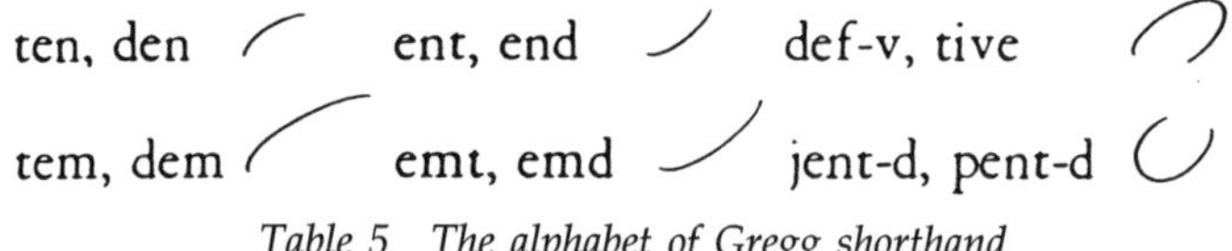

Table 5 The alphabet of Gregg shorthand

signary The total number of elementary signs in a writing system. Writing systems vary on a large scale in the size of their signaries, ranging between several thousands and fewer than two dozen signs. These differences correlate with structural differences, since the number of necessary signs is determined by the linguistic level on which the writing system operates. Logographic systems require a larger signary than syllabaries, which in turn need more signs to function than alphabetic systems. The history of writing has, therefore, been described as a continuous improvement in economizing effort by reducing the number of signs to be memorized. Probably the most economical writing system is the CREE SYLLABARY invented in 1840 by James Edwards, which makes do with a signary of just 13 basic signs used in four different orientations. At the other end of the scale, in excess of 40,000 characters are listed in the most comprehen-

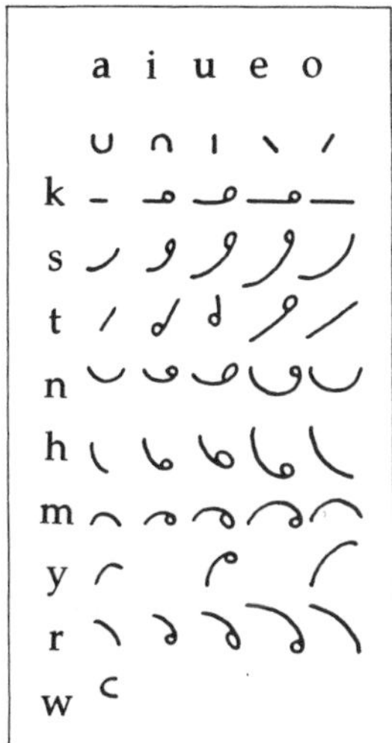

Table 6 The Waseda shorthand system for Japanese, 1931

sive Chinese dictionaries, of which 2,000 to 3,000 are needed for contemporary literature.
See also GRAPHEME; WRITING SYSTEM.

signature 1 The name of a person written with his or her own hand to authenticate a document such as a letter or a will (figure 11). **2** In printing, letters of the alphabet or numbers printed at the left margin of the first page of each section of a book. When letters are used, *J*, *V* and *W* are traditionally omitted, because in the Latin alphabet of the INCUNABULA *I* and *U* included *J* and *V*, respectively, and there was no *W*.

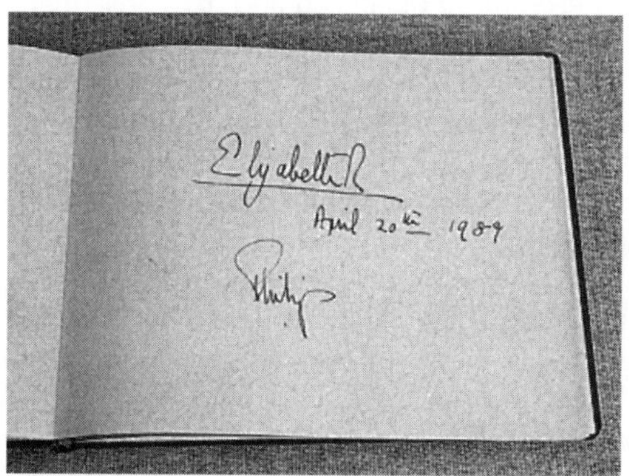

Figure 11 Signature of Elizabeth II and Prince Philip

silent letter An ill-defined term referring to any letter which in the spelling of certain words does not represent a sound. Two kinds of silent letters can be distinguished. One is a letter which is part of the grapheme inventory of a language and occurs in some of its orthographic words, but is never pronounced,

irrespective of context. For example, modern French and Italian have no phoneme /h/, but words such as *habitude* [abityd] and *hanno* [an'no] retain the <h> as etymological spellings. The other kind of silent letter has a zero pronunciation as one of its sound values. For example, in English the digraph <gh> is silent in *though*, but corresponds to [f] in *tough*. Similarly, in *signal* <g> has a sound value, but in *sign* it is 'silent'. Its presence in the latter word is etymologically motivated, indicating as it does a morphological relationship with the former. As a result of sound changes not reflected in writing, the spelling systems of phonographically written languages with a long literary tradition often contain silent letters of either kind. Since ENGLISH SPELLING has remained relatively unchanged for several centuries, it has many silent letters, such as <e> in final position (*knife, code*) and in the past *-ed* ending (*drowned*), or <p> and <b> in preconsonantal position of words of Greek and Latin origin such as *psycho* and *debt*, respectively. Other examples include <t>, <h>, <c> and <g> in *listen, honour, indict* and *gnome*, respectively. However, that a letter does not correspond to a sound in the sequence of graphemes of the orthographic word does not always mean that it fulfils no sound-indicating function. For example, if the 'silent' *e* of *knife* were deleted, the word would have to be pronounced [nif] rather than [naif], according to the rules of English orthography. Its function is thus to determine the quality of the preceding V. As this example shows, the underlying system of most alphabetic orthographies cannot be properly analysed on the basis of ascertaining the sound values of individual letters linearly. Rather, GRAPHEME–PHONEME CORRESPONDENCES have to be determined by taking morpho-phonological processes and word forms into account. Silent letters often fulfil disambiguating functions, as in French *héros* 'hero' vs *éros* 'Eros'.
See also ORTHOGRAPHY.

silent reading As a result of the developmental process of PHONETIZATION, writing became a representation of speech and, by consequence, reading became an activity of retrieving meaning from written characters through vocalization. Because of this conceptual link between writing and speech, reading in antiquity was reading aloud. The written message could only be decoded by reconstructing the speech form it represented. Within the tradition of alphabetic literacy, the dissociation of voice and content in silent reading is a medieval achievement. As literacy spread, reading was transformed from a social into a solitary activity, and it became evident that text understanding could be achieved without going through speech as an intermediary state of decoding. This speeded up the reading process considerably, as it could now proceed unconstrained by the physical conditions of the speech apparatus. For a long time, though, inner phonetic recoding was nevertheless taken for granted. The breakthrough to speed reading only came after, as a by-product of PRINTING, word forms became so fixed that the possibility of direct lexical access from the graphic code was recognized and exploited. It is of some interest in this connection that silent reading habits vary with the properties of writing systems. That silent reading was common in China earlier than in Europe has been explained by properties of the CHINESE WRITING SYSTEM. Chinese characters, which each encode a morpheme plus syllable and are hence more meaning oriented than alphabetic writing, afford better condi-

tions for direct lexical access. Also, proficient readers of Chinese achieve a higher reading speed than readers of alphabetically written languages.
See also Reading; Scriptura continua.
Reading Saenger 1982; Taylor and Taylor 1983.

Sinai script *See* Proto-Sinaitic script

Sindhī writing An Indo-Aryan language of the north-western group spoken in the province of Sind, Pakistan, as well as by a large group of Sindhī Hindus in India, Sindhī has been written in various scripts since the eighteenth century CE, if not earlier. Under the influence of first Arabic and subsequently Persian, the Perso–Arabic script has always been prevalent among Muslims. In the nineteenth century, the Laṇḍa script was adapted to Sindhī (called 'Sindhī script' by Jensen 1969). At the same time, the British rulers recognized an augmented version of the Perso-Arabic script as the official script for Sindhī (1853). Additional letters were introduced for the retroflex series /ṭ, ṭh, ḍ, ḍh, ṇ, ṛ/; the aspirates /ph, bh, th, čh, ǰh, gh/; the implosives /ɓ, ʄ, ɗ̣, ɠ, g/; and the nasals /ñ, ŋ/ (table 7). For almost a century thereafter the bulk of Sindhī publications were in Perso-Arabic script. However, after the partition of India, the Indian government declared a change of script, first in 1950 making Devanāgarī the official script of Sindhī in India, and a year later allowing both the Devanāgarī and Perso-Arabic scripts for Sindhī (figure 12). In Pakistan the language continued to be written in the Perso-Arabic script.
Reading Daswani 1979.

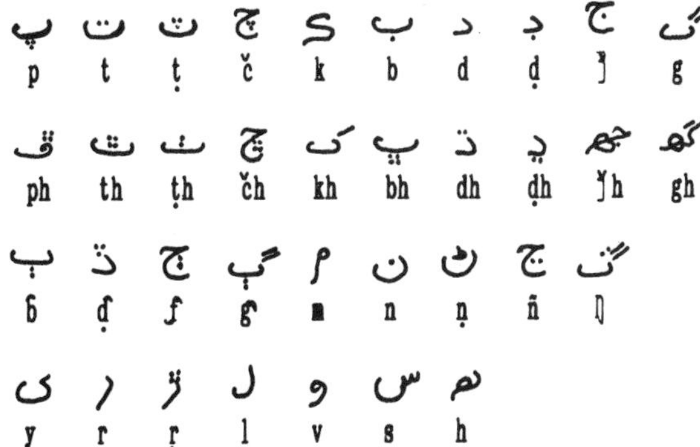

Table 7 The Sindhī alphabet in Perso-Arabic script, independent letter forms

Sinhalese script Indo-Aryan speech was carried to Sri Lanka probably in the fifth century bce by settlers from the Indian west coast. It was written in styles of writing associated with the activities of India's Buddhists. Absorbing influences from the southern and northern Brāhmī derivatives of the Kadamba and Pallava-Grantha scripts, respectively, the Sinhalese script emerged in the seventh to eighth centuries CE and has been used ever since. The syllabic alphabet conforms to the regular Indian pattern, consisting of 34 graphemes of Cs with inherent *a* and 16 graphemes for Vs (including /ṛ/ and /ṝ/) and diphthongs (table 8). The orthography of modern Sinhalese has some etymological elements. The

صبوح آيو

نئين سورج نئون پرڪاش ڦهلايو،
صبوح آيو!

सुबह आयो

नए सूरज नओं प्रकाश फहिलायो,
सुबह आयो !

Translation

Morning

The new sun has spread new light,
The morning has arrived.

Figure 12 *Title and first two lines of a Sindhī poem in Perso-Arabic and Devanāgarī scripts (courtesy C. J. Daswani)*

graphemic distinctions between /l/ and /ḷ/ and /n/ and /ṇ/ no longer represent distinct pronunciations. A peculiar feature of Sinhalese spelling conventions is the superscript *virāma* for V muting which, in contradistinction to other Indian scripts where this device is usually limited to word-final position, is added to C graphemes to indicate both C clusters and final Cs. With some additional letters the Sinhalese alphabet, then known as the *miśra hōḍiya* or 'mixed alphabet', is also used for Pāli and Sanskrit. On account of the rounded forms of its letters, the Sinhalese script is similar in appearance to the south Indian scripts of Dravidian languages. In the thirteenth century, Sinhalese literature reached its classical form which became the standard of literary Sinhalese (figure 13). As a result of continuing divergence of the spoken varieties from the highly Sanskritized written variety, modern Sinhalese exists in a situation of diglossia.
See also INDIAN WRITING SYSTEMS; PĀLI WRITING.
Reading Dani 1963; Masica 1991.

sitta The six major cursive styles of Arabic calligraphy as developed by Abū 'Alī Muḥammad Ibn Muqlah (*d.*939 CE) and his disciples. These styles were further

Vowel letters					
අ	a	ඍ	ṛ	ඓ	ai
ආ	ā	ඍ		ඔ	o
ඉ	i	ඎ	ṝ	ඕ	ō
ඊ	ī	ඎ		ඖ	au
උ	u	එ	e	ඇ	æ
ඌ	ū	ඒ	ē	ඈ	ǣ

Consonant letters					
ක	ka	ඩ	ḍa	ම	ma
ඛ	kha	ඪ	ḍha	ය	ya
ග	ga	ණ	ṇa	ර	ra
ඝ	gha	ත	ta	ල	la
ඞ	ṅa	ථ	tha	ව	va
ච	ca	ද	da	ශ	sa
ඡ	cha	ධ	dha	ෂ	ṣa
ජ	ja	න	na	ස	sa
ඣ	jha	ප	pa	හ	ha
ඤ	ña	ඵ	pha	ළ	ḷa
ට	ṭa	බ	ba		
ඨ	ṭha	භ	bha		

Table 8 The Sinhalese syllabic alphabet

perfected by Yaqut al-Musta'simi (*d.*1298) at the court of Baghdad and assigned to different kinds of writing: *rīḥānī* for Qur'ān copies; *thuluth* for instruction and practice; *rīqā'* for correspondence; *naskhī* for commentaries of the Qur'ān; *tauqī'* for official documents; and *muḥaqqaq* for poetry.
See also ARABIC SCRIPTS; CALLIGRAPHY.

slips of the pen Writing errors involving omission, conversion, intrusion, repetition or other rearrangements in sequences of discrete elements such as letters, orthographic words and punctuation marks. Lapses of this kind, where it can be shown with reasonable certainty that they are not due to the writer's ignorance of the correct form, are considered valuable data for investigating the psycholinguistic process of writing performance, that is, the cognitive, linguistic and neuro-motor processes that are carried out when a written message is conceptualized, verbalized and written down. Distributional and other characteristics can help to clarify the psychological status of graphic units of writing.
See also HANDWRITING.
Reading Hotopf 1980; Ellis 1984a.

Sogdian writing A derivative of the ARAMAIC WRITING developed in Sogdiana (Samarkand) and used by Persian colonists in Chinese Turkestan to record their Middle Iranian language. The oldest known documents are the 'Ancient Letters', tentatively dated 312–313 CE, which were discovered in 1920 by Sir Aurel Stein in a watchtower of the Chinese wall west of Tun-huang. They are written on the most ancient paper with writing on it that has come down to us. Most extant

මල් රැසකින් බොහෝ මල් දම් ගොතන්නේ
යම් සේ ද, එසේ ම, උපන් මිනිසා විසින් බොහෝ කුසල්
කටයුතු ය.

සාමාන්‍ය මල් සුවඳක් හෝ සඳුන්, තුවරලා
ඉද්ද වැනි මල්වල සුවඳක් හෝ උඩු සුළඟට නො යයි.
එහෙත් සත්පුරුෂයන්ගේ (සිල්) සුවඳ උඩු සුළඟට ද යයි.
සත්පුරුෂයා සියලු දිශාවල ම සිල් සුවඳ පතුරුවයි.

සඳුන්, තුවරලා, මහනෙල්, දෑසමන් යන සියලු
මල් ජාතීන්ගේ සුවඳට වඩා සිල් සුවඳ උසස් ය.

Transliteration

Mal resakin bohō mal dam gothan nē yam sē da, esēma, upan minisā visin bōho kusal katayuthuya.
Sāmānya mal suwadak hō sadun thuwaralā idda vani malwala suwadak hō udu sulagata no yai.
Eheth sathpurushayanange (sil) suwada udu sulagata da yai.
Sath purushayā siyalu dishawala ma sil suwada pathuruwai.
Sadun thurawalā, mahanel, dāsaman yana siyalu mal jathinge suwadata wada sil suwada usasya.

Translation

As many kinds of garlands can be made from a heap of flowers, so many good works should be achieved by a mortal when once he is born.
The scent of flowers does not travel against the wind, not that of sandalwood, of tagara, or jasmine. But the fragrance of good people travels even against the wind. A good man pervades every quarter.
Sandalwook, tagara, a lotus flower, jasmine among these kinds of perfumes the perfume of virtue is unsurpassed.

Figure 13 Sinhalese verse from Dhammapada, *Buddhist scriptures*

manuscripts were preserved in Turfan, an important oasis town on the Silk Road. Three different styles of the Sogdian script are attested. In the script of the Ancient Letters, the graphemes are clearly distinct and mostly written separately. A slightly different book hand, often called 'sūtra script', developed around 500 CE for Buddhist scriptures. Finally, in the course of the seventh century the Sogdian cursive script with letters connected by a base line was invented. It has sometimes been attributed to Ahriman the devil, because several of its letters are so similar as to be all but indistinguishable. It is therefore extremely hard to read, posing sometimes insurmountable difficulties for decipherment. Both the sūtra and cursive scripts were taken over in the eighth century by Buddhist Uighurs, which is why the Sogdian and Uighur scripts are often discussed together. In some palaeographic works the sūtra script is identified as the Sogdian script proper, whereas cursive Sogdian is called 'Uighur'.

The Sogdian script is a C alphabet which, like other Aramaic offshoots, is written from right to left. A 90 degree rotation of the script, resulting in vertical columns progressing from left to right, has often been attributed to the Uighurs or Mongols, who adopted the Uighur script. However, from the orientation of annotations to early Sogdian documents in Chinese script it must be inferred that this change in the direction of the script was brought about by the Sogdians themselves (figure 14).

The alphabet consists of 17 C letters most of which have variant forms for initial, medial and final position (table 9). In addition, a number of diacritics were developed which, however, were used rather inconsistently. A subscript double hook distinguishes an *l* from an *r*; an underdot turns a *z* into a *ž*. V indication

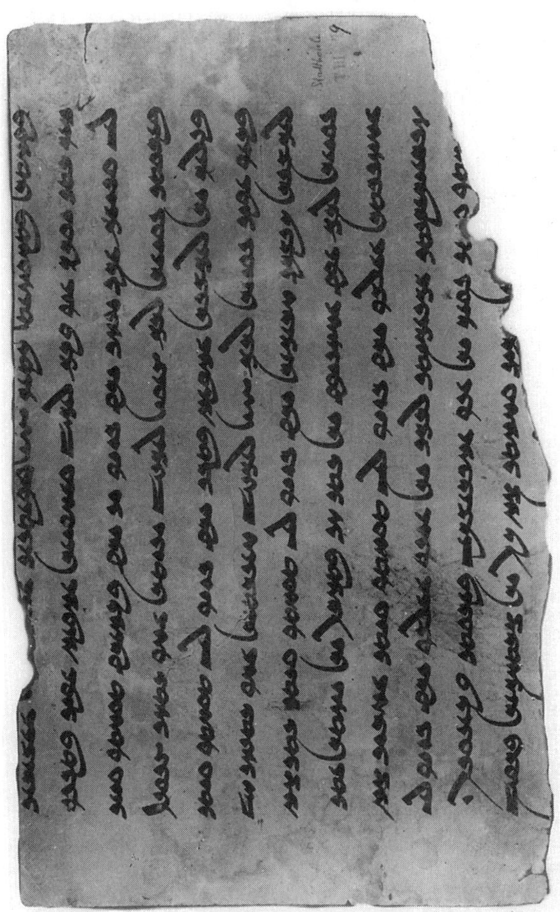

Figure 14 A page of a Sogdian manuscript in vertical cursive script, eighth to ninth centuries CE *(Museum für Indische Kunst, Berlin, no. III, 105) (by permission Staatliche Museen Berlin)*

Final	Medial	Initial	Value
			a, ε
			γ, χ, q
			g, k
			i, j, ī, e, ē
			r
			l
			t
			δ, θ
			č, ǰ
			s
			š
			z, ž
			n
			b, p
			v, β
			w, u, ū, o, ō
			m
			h (final)

Table 9 The Sogdian alphabet

by and large follows the practice, common in imperial Aramaic, of using the C graphemes *y* and *w*, initially for the long Vs and *ī* and *ū* and later for other Vs as well. The writing of Sogdian documents is highly involved, many words being represented in historical or pseudo-historical spelling, without Vs, in inverted spelling, or as Aramaic xenograms.

See also MANICHAEAN SCRIPT; PAHLAVI SCRIPT.

Reading Gershevitch 1954; Henning 1958; Sims-Williams 1975, 1981.

Somali alphabet A modern creation patterned on the Arabic alphabet and augmented by five V graphemes for /i, u, o, a, e/ following the Italian model

(table 10). As the scripts of Islam and the colonial administration, respectively, the Arabic and Latin alphabets were current in Somalia when the question of the choice of a writing system for Somali arose early in the twentieth century. The alphabet was designed by Cismaan Kenadiid, brother of the Sultan of Obbia, in 1922. Although some letter forms are reminiscent of Roman letters, they seem to be freely invented. The script was used for some 50 years, but was very limited in its dissemination. In 1972 the Somali government promulgated an official Somali orthography using the Roman alphabet with no additional letters. Sounds peculiar to the Somali language are represented by a number of digraphs, <kh, sh, dh, aa, ee>, and by letters which are assigned new values, <q> for the glottal stop, and <c> and <x> for voiced and unvoiced pharyngeal fricatives.
Reading *L'Afrique et la lettre* 1986.

𐒀	𐒁	𐒂	𐒃	𐒄	𐒅	𐒆	𐒇	𐒈	𐒉	𐒊	𐒋	𐒌	
ʾ	b	t	ǵ	ḥ	ḫ	d	r	s	š	ḍ	g	ʿ	
𐒍	𐒎	𐒏	𐒐	𐒑	𐒒	𐒓	𐒔	𐒕	𐒘	𐒚	𐒙	𐒖	𐒗
f	q	k	l	m	n	w	h	y	i	u	o	a	e

Table 10 The Somali alphabet

south Arabian script Prior to the spread of Arabic language and writing throughout Arabia, a number of south-west Semitic languages were spoken and written on the Arabian peninsula of which Sabaic, Qatabanic, Himyaritic, and Hadhramautic are the most important ones. These languages are epigraphically attested in inscriptions dating from between the sixth century BCE and the sixth century CE (figure 15). An alphabet of 22 to 29 C letters, the south Arabian script is a member of the south Semitic group of scripts. It is written from right to left like other Semitic scripts. Angular in form and very regular, the varieties of this

Figure 15 Himyaritic inscription in south Arabian script

script have been remarkably stable over the centuries in pre-Islamic times. Recently a cursive variety of the script has been discovered (table 11).

See also SABAIC WRITING; SEMITIC WRITING.

Reading Ryckmans 1986; Ryckmans et al. 1994.

Table 11 The south Arabian script: above, monumental style; below, cursive style
Source: *Ryckmans 1986*

Spanish writing The history of written Spanish is taken to begin in the tenth century with the Hispano-Latin glosses of the monastery San Millán in Burgos dated 977 CE. Recognizable literature based on the speech of Castile emerges in the twelfth century. In the thirteenth century Castilian, which so far had been used mainly for lyric and epic verse, became a medium of scholarly writing as well. After the political union with Aragon and Catalonia in 1479, literary Castilian was extended to these provinces, leading to dialect levelling in most of southern Spain. Castilian hence became the principal language of Spain, 'Spanish' (figure 16). Serious concern with grammar began in the fifteenth century, and when the Real Academia de la Lengua was founded in 1714, Spanish was given a codified standard. Following the Spanish example, other academies were later established in Latin American countries, most of them in the 1880s with a second wave of foundations in the 1920s. Thanks to their cooperation with the Real Academia, the written language has been quite homogeneous throughout the extensive language area. Although there is some divergence in pronunciation and lexical innovation, standard grammar and spelling are largely uniform.

Spanish has always been written in the Latin alphabet, although the Moors and Jews have also used the Arabic and Hebrew (Raschi) scripts, respectively. (Judezmo, or Judaeo-Spanish, which was originally based on a south Spanish variety, is still used in writing in the *Aki Yerushalayim*, a newspaper which caters to the small community of Judezmo speakers in Israel.)

The Spanish alphabet includes the digraphs <ch> = /tš/, <ll> = /ʎ/, <qu> = /k/ and <rr> = /r/, as well as the grapheme <ñ> for palatal /n/. *Ch, ll* and *ñ* used to be alphabetized separately after *c, l* and *n*, respectively. In view of the requirements of data banks and other alphabetically ordered reference systems this practice was abolished in 1994. The Spanish orthography is a surface system with relatively close grapheme–phoneme correspondences. Some predictable phonetic variations are ignored in writing. For example, <c> represents /k/ and /θ/ before back and front Cs, respectively. In initial position <b> stands for /b/, but in intervocalic position for /β/. <g> is pronounced /g/ before /i/, /e/ and /x/ in all other environments. The ACUTE ACCENT is used on Vs to mark stress. A peculiar feature of Spanish writing is the introduction of questions and

Quixote de la Mancha. 171

prouecho,di en oluidalla. Y ſi algo ſe me acuerda, es aquello del ſobajada, digo del ſoberana ſeñora, y lo vltimo, vueſtro haſta la muerte, el cauallero de la triſte Figura. Y enmedio deſtas dos coſas, le puſe mas de trezientas almas, y vidas, y ojos mios.

Cap. XXXI. De los ſabroſos razonamientos que paſſaron entre don Quixote, y Sancho Pança ſu eſcudero: con otros ſuceſſos.

TODO eſſo no me deſcontenta, proſigue adelante, dixo don Quixote. Llegaſte, y que hazia aquella reyna de la hermoſura? a buen ſeguro, que la hallaſte enſartando perlas, o bordando alguna empreſa, con oro de cañutillo, para eſte ſu cautiuo cauallero. No la hallè, reſpondio Sancho, ſino ahechando dos anegas de trigo, en vn corral de ſu caſa. Pues haz cuenta, dixo don Quixote, que los granos de aquel trigo, eran granos de perlas, tocados de ſus manos. Y ſi miraſte amigo, el trigo era candeal, o trechel? No era ſino rubion, reſpondio Sancho. Pues yo te aſſeguro, dixo don Quixote, que ahechado por ſus manos hizo pan candeal, ſin duda alguna: pero paſſa adelante. Quando le diſte mi carta beſola? Puſoſela ſobre la cabeça? hizo alguna ceremonia, digna de tal carta? o que hizo? Quando yo ſe la yua a dar, reſpódio Sancho, ella eſtaua en la fuga del meneo, de vna buena parte de trigo, que tenia en la criua. Y dixome, poned amigo eſſa carta ſobre aquel coſtal, q̃ no la puedo leer haſta que acabe de acriuar todo lo que aqui

Y 4 eſtá.

Figure 16 Specimen of Spanish writing: a page from Miguel de Cervantes's Don Quixote, *1st edn, Madrid, 1605*

exclamations with inverted question and exclamation marks: *¿Crees que irá?* 'Do you think he will go?', *¡Que lástima!* 'What a pity!'

Reading Real Academia Española 1973; Menéndez Pidal 1987.

spelling The conventions which determine how the graphemes of a writing system are used to write a language. The term is sometimes used interchangeably with, or encompassing that of, ORTHOGRAPHY, but there is a difference. In the strict sense, an orthography is a *standardized* spelling system, where the standard has been codified, explicitly in official guidelines, or implicitly through to a tradition developed over the centuries and perhaps laid down in a generally accepted reference work such as a dictionary.

Within the context of the written vernaculars of medieval Europe, spelling long remained subject to the whims of individual writers, as no orthographies existed. This was due to two factors. There was great variety in the language forms that different authors wrote, and there was great variety in the ways they

employed the alphabet to represent these. The advent of printing did much to change this. Although there was little in terms of *a priori* principles for establishing rules, printers had a material interest in eliminating peculiar spellings and promoting uniformity. To a large extent the standardization of spelling went hand in hand with the standardization of language and the consolidation of a written norm, which was in turn reinforced by the spread of LITERACY. Compulsory schooling made correct spelling an elementary and central part of education, which exercises a strong influence on laypeople's conception of language. Since spelling is typically taught and learned with little or no understanding of the principles underlying the spelling system or the relationship between spoken and written language, it is commonly assumed that correct spelling reflects the standard language, as if the standard language had an independent existence. Arguably, however, the standardized spelling system is what best defines the standard language, for example standard English. Once a standard has been established, it has a strong tendency to perpetuate itself. When in doubt about the correct spelling of a word, authors and editors, rather than risk appearing uneducated, consult dictionaries which invariably are based on the usage of the most highly regarded authors. Speller programs in word-processing software further reinforce existing spelling conventions. All this puts a brake on any spontaneous spelling innovation. In its standardized form as an orthography, spelling has thus become one of the most conservative institutions of modern society.
See also SILENT LETTER; SPELLING REFORM.
Reading Haas 1970; Stubbs 1980.

spelling pronunciation The pronunciation of a word based on the regular grapheme–phoneme correspondences characteristic of the language to which it belongs. The term refers to words which have undergone a change in pronunciation because they were more commonly seen than heard, or because the written form is considered correct. English examples include many words of Latin or Greek origin. As late as the eighteenth century, words such as *hospital, habit, heretic, hotel, herb* were pronounced with an initial V. Having entered the English language from French at a time when the <h> was already mute, the spelling with <h> was historical to begin with, but by analogy with words such as *hog, hand, head* the pronunciation with initial /h/ became standard, although some speakers still use initial V on some of these words. Similarly, the <th> in words such as *anthem, author, theatre* was formerly pronounced [t] as in *Thomas* rather than [θ] as in *thought, thin* etc.; and the <t> in *often* and *soften* was not pronounced at all, but is now by some speakers. Spelling pronunciation testifies to the influence of writing on the speech community's linguistic awareness and its importance for the formation of a linguistic standard.
See also SPELLING.

spelling reform A deliberate change in the grapheme–phoneme correspondences of a language. The rationale of spelling reforms is to make spelling more regular and transparent and thus easier to learn. The fact that they have to be accepted by readers and writers who have mastered the existing system has frustrated many reform proposals. For the generation that has to implement the reform it implies more inconvenience than relief. Consequently, reform projects are often protracted by endless discussion and eventually lead to nothing.

ENGLISH SPELLING has never been fundamentally reformed, although it could undoubtedly be much simpler and more linguistically appropriate. Numerous proposals for a better spelling have, therefore, been advanced during the past three centuries by individuals as well as several learned societies, notably the (British) Simplified Spelling Society and the (American) Simplified Spelling Board. The only noticeable modification of English spelling was achieved in the wake of the American Revolution as an act of linguistic nationalism: Noah WEBSTER'S rules for American spelling. However, Webster's simplifications were superficial, leaving many of the underlying structural problems of the spelling system untouched. These problems reflect the fact that the system is based on a number of different, sometimes conflicting, principles. Grapheme–phoneme correspondences are obscured by such principles as morpheme invariance, ETYMOLOGICAL SPELLING, homograph avoidance, loan word identification and deviant PROPER NAME spelling. If all of these principles were to be abolished in favour of a strictly phonemic system, English writing would be all but unrecognizable.

The basic task is to reduce the rampant polyvalence in grapheme–phoneme relations. As it is, English spelling represents the 40 phonemes of the language in more than 1,000 different ways. Two kinds of reform proposal designed to remedy this situation can be distinguished: those aiming at simplification by deleting irregularities and systematizing the existing conventions without altering

Mont Follick

'Ei tuisted flash ov pein shot akros dhu peinter's feis. Hie poazt for ei moment, and ei waild fieling ov piti keim ouver him ¿After oal, huot rait had hie tuu prai intuu dhu laif ov Dorian Grei? ¡If hie had dun ei taidh ov huot uos ruumert abaut him, hau mutsh hie must have sufert!

ITA

'a twisted flash ov pæn shot across the pæntər's fæs. hee pausd for a mœment and a wield feeliŋ ov pity cæm œvər him. aftər aul, whot riet had hee too prie into the lief ov dorian græ? if hee had dun a tieth ov whot wos roomərd about him, hou much hee must hav suffərd!

Bernard Shaw Alphabet

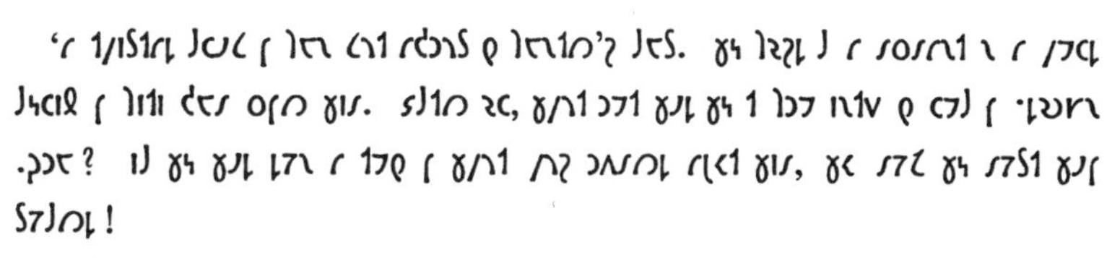

[illegible]

Figure 17 *Three alternative spellings for English: Mont Follick, ITA, Bernard Shaw alphabet* the sign inventory; and those improving grapheme–phoneme correspondences by adding new signs and diacritics. Serious recent reform schemes of the first kind include Mont Follick's 1946 proposal *Reform English Spelling*, the Simplified Spelling Society's *Nue Spelling* (1948), and *Regularized English* proposed by Axel Wijk (1959), among others. Benjamin FRANKLIN's 1768 reformed alphabet is an early example of the second kind, followed by many others. The two decades after World War II saw a renewed interest in the problem of spelling simplification, with specific proposals such as James Pitman's INITIAL TEACHING ALPHABET (ITA), the BERNARD SHAW ALPHABET, and John Malone's UNIFON. The latter two go beyond mere spelling reforms, involving as they do, respectively, a significant extension of the existing signary and an entirely new script and writing system.

Virtually all reform proposals would simplify and in this sense improve the spelling system of English (figure 17). That, nevertheless, no proposal has ever come close to being accepted shows that more is involved in spelling reform than functional criteria of simplicity and systematic coherence. Opponents of spelling reforms invariably emphasize three reasons for rejecting change: (1) the historical depth of the literary traditions which may be jeopardized by drastic or successive moderate changes; (2) the value of the written form of the language as a symbol of national identity; and (3) the cost of implementation. As time passes without any changes in the spelling system, the significance of these reasons increases, making it ever less likely that a reform will be carried out.

See also ORRMULUM; ORTHOGRAPHY REFORM; SCRIPT REFORM.

Reading Fishman 1977; Stubbs 1980; Haas 1969; Venezky 1970; Vallins 1973.

standard alphabet *See* AFRICA ALPHABET; LEPSIUS

stenography [Gk στενός 'narrow' + γράφειν 'to write'] *See* SHORTHAND

stichometry A method of measuring the contents of manuscripts in antiquity. In poetry, the unit of measuring the extent of an author's work or a scribe's labour was the verse, but for prose works a different unit had to be found. This unit was a standard line of 15 or 16 syllables, or 34 to 38 letters. It was called στίχος, whence 'stichometry'.

stroke The basic graphic unit of Chinese characters. Each character consists of a definite number of strokes which are written in a fixed order. For example, a square is made up of three strokes: (1) the perpendicular stroke on the left, (2) the horizontal top which bends without a break into the right side, and (3) the bottom stroke. Both number and order of strokes must be learned, because the number of a character's constituent strokes determines its position in a dictionary, and because, in the absence of a fixed order of strokes, handwriting would be impossible to read.

See also CHARACTER; (illustration) CHINESE WRITING SYSTEM; RADICAL.

subscript A small letter, number or symbol placed below the main line at the right foot of a full character, as X_1 (or, less commonly, at the left). In computer languages subscripts are usually represented in parentheses written on the main line, as X(1).

Sumerian writing Of unknown extraction, Sumerian is considered to be the first language ever written. Having its origin in impressions on TOKENS and SEALS, Sumerian writing was always on clay. It evolved gradually in the fourth millennium BCE from pictorial representations of objects which were recorded for mnemonic and bookkeeping purposes. While clearly serving the function of record keeping, the most ancient Sumerian inscriptions cannot be 'read' in the usual sense of the word, since no firm relationship between sign and language had been established. Pictorial images are not the only source of the Sumerian writing system. Among the earliest signs were numerals, such as the round and semi-spherical impressions on the clay tablet shown in figure 18 which dates from about 3300 BCE. While pictorial signs came to be associated with words, the graphic signs were increasingly stylized in form (table 12). Curved lines were straightened and broken down into parts. From about 3000 BCE each of these parts was impressed into the wet clay by means of a triangularly shaped stylus, leaving a wedge-shaped mark. Cuneiform writing had thus come into existence. Like ancient Chinese, Sumerian words were largely monosyllabic with many homonyms. It is thought that extensive homonymy made early Sumerian scribes recognize the possibility of rebus writing which led to PHONETIZATION. From about the middle of the third millennium, Sumerian texts consist of logograms and phonetic signs (C, CV, VC and CVC syllabograms) for grammatical morphemes. DETERMINATIVES were introduced to specify the intended reading of homographs. The mature system comprised a large number of logograms which was gradually reduced as it became adapted to Akkadian and other languages and phonography gained prominence. Sumerian was displaced by Akkadian, and early in the second millennium ceased to be a spoken language, but it survived

Figure 18 Archaic Sumerian clay tablet of the Uruk III stratum detailing the allotment of malt to a number of people and with stock accounts of barley on the reverse (photograph courtesy Margret Nissen)

3100	3000	2500	2000	assumed reading	meaning
				ninda	bread
				sag	head
				gu	ration
				suhur	dried fish
					1
					10

Table 12 Graphical development of some early Sumerian signs (years BCE)

as a medium of the cult and other literary functions for more than 1,000 years. Having become a classical language, it also enriched other languages such as Elamite and Old Persian, which borrowed the writing system and with it many Sumerian words.
See also AKKADIAN; CUNEIFORM WRITING.
Reading Civil 1973; Nissen 1985; Falkenstein 1964.

Sumerogram A Sumerian loan word in other languages which have adopted the cuneiform writing system, e.g. Elamite, used in its original Sumerian spelling.
See also XENOGRAM.

Sundanese writing A syllabic alphabet of the Indian type consisting of C letters (*akṣara*) with inherent V *a*, the script of Old Sundanese inscriptions is derived from the Old KAWI SCRIPT. It is palaeographically first attested in inscriptions of western Java dating from the fourteenth century CE. Most of the inscriptions were discovered in Batutulis, a former capital of Sunda, and in Kĕbantĕnan, a site east of Jakarta. The date, place and circumstances of the origin of the Old Sundanese script are not well understood. It is evidently related to, but differs in many ways from, the JAVANESE WRITING by which it was superseded. Its most conspicuous feature is that the V muting *patèn* (*virāma*) has developed into a separate *akṣara* which follows the C whose inherent *a* it cancels. Until the nineteenth century Sundanese was written in the Javanese alphabet, called *tjarakan*. In the wake of Islamization the Arabic alphabet with some supplementary letters, called *pégon* with a Javanese loan word, has also been used to write Sundanese; and early in the nineteenth century the Dutch colonial government began to use the Roman alphabet on the basis of Dutch spelling conventions (*akṣara Walanda*). Guidelines of an orthography were laid down in J. H. Oosting's *Soedasch-Nederduitsch Woordenbook* of 1879.

superscript A small letter, number or symbol placed on the right shoulder of a full character, as X^1 (or, less commonly, at the left).

Swahili writing *See* KISWAHILI WRITING.

Swedish writing The history of Swedish is commonly divided between Old Swedish (thirteenth to early sixteenth centuries CE) and modern Swedish. Runic inscriptions dating from the ninth to the thirteenth centuries CE represent the common eastern Scandinavian speech which branched out to form the Scandinavian languages. The emergence of modern literary Swedish written in the Roman alphabet is commonly dated in the 1520s when the union with Denmark was dissolved and the Lutheran Church gained general recognition at the expense of Catholicism. In addition to the 26 letters of the common Roman alphabet, Swedish makes use of three distinctive graphemes: <å> for [o,ɔ:], <ä> for [ɛ] and <ö> for [ø]. While spoken Swedish is characterized by significant dialect variation in Sweden and across the border in Finland, the written language is highly standardized. The word list periodically published by the Swedish Academy (*Svenska Akademiens ordlista*) is generally accepted as reflecting the norm for spelling.
Reading *Svenska Akademiens* 1986.

syllabary The signary of a writing system where speech is represented by means of graphemes each of which has a SYLLABLE as its value. The unit of a syllabary, i.e. each of its graphemes, is a syllabogram. Syllabograms may be of the following types: V, CV, VC, CVC or CVCV. Structurally more complex syllables are not usually coded as units.
See also SYLLABIC ALPHABET.

syllabic alphabet A writing system which treats the syllable as the unit of representation, while at the same time recognizing the segment as the unit of analysis. All Indian scripts that can be traced back to the old BRĀHMĪ WRITING, including Indo-Chinese and Indonesian derivatives, conform to this pattern. The only other historically evolved syllabic alphabet is that of ETHIOPIAN WRITING. Syllabic alphabets consist of two kinds of graphemes, Vs and Cs with an inherent neutral V, typically transliterated *a*. V graphemes come in two different forms: independent forms for word-initial (syllabic) Vs, and conjunct forms to be combined with C + *a* letters. When combined with a C + *a* letter, the conjunct V

supersedes the inherent V. In addition, there are some auxiliary devices, such as the V muting *virāma* and the *visarga* to indicate nasalization.
See also INDIAN WRITING SYSTEMS; WRITING SYSTEM.

syllabic writing *See* SYLLABOGRAPHY

syllable [Gk συλλαβή 'fetters'] The intuitively elementary, but scientifically ill-defined, smallest suprasegmental sound unit of speech. Phonologically the syllable is analysed as consisting of a V 'nucleus' and initial and final C 'margins', which are optional. A syllable with no final C margin is an 'open syllable', as opposed to a 'closed syllable' with a final C. Another structural division commonly recognized is that between initial 'onset' and following 'rhyme' or 'coda'. Syllables can be long or short. A short syllable is a 'mora', i.e. a minimal unit of metrical time. Syllabic writing systems analyse the sound continuum of speech into syllables. They differ in what they recognize as syllables. For example, length may or may not be distinguished. Hence, the syllable as represented in writing is a language specific unit.

syllabogram [Gk συλλαβή 'fetters' + γράμμα 'letter'] A written sign that denotes a speech syllable, forming the basic unit of a syllabary or syllabic writing system.
See also SYLLABARY.

syllabography (*also* syllabic writing) A system that treats the speech syllable as the unit of representation. Historically syllabic writing evolved from word writing by application of the REBUS PRINCIPLE.

Three main types of syllabic system can be distinguished. The first type is exemplified by cuneiform writing, a mixed system of logograms and phonograms. The phonograms are syllabic signs each of which represents a syllable holistically, that is, the graphic structure of the signs is in no way related to the phonetic structure of the syllables they stand for. Japanese KANA and the West African VAI WRITING are other systems of this type.

In syllabic systems of the second type the graphic structure of the individual syllabogram does relate to the phonetic structure of the represented syllable in such a way that a recognizable graphic component of the sign represents a part of a syllable, and that this component represents the same part in all syllables of which it is a part. The basic unit of such systems is a C with inherent *a*, the 'neutral V' which is superseded when other graphic elements are added to indicate other Vs. Systems of this kind are called SYLLABIC ALPHABETS or 'alpha-syllabic'. The Brāhmī-derived INDIAN WRITING SYSTEMS as well as the ETHIOPIAN WRITING belong to this type.

In systems of the third type the C element of the syllable is central, as it is in the second, but the V element is unspecified. That is, the basic sign is of the form C + *x*, where *x* can be any V. Both the phonographic use of Egyptian HIEROGLYPHS and the oldest forms of north Semitic writing have been described as belonging to this type, although the validity of this characterization is a matter of dispute. Many scholars prefer to categorize these systems as C alphabets.

In a strict sense only systems of the first type constitute syllabography. Here the unit of the underlying analysis of the sound continuum and the unit of written representation are the same, the syllable of speech. The other two types are characterized by a systematic difference between unit of analysis and unit of representation. The graphemes of Indian scripts represent syllables, but they consist of a central C component to which diacritics are added for V indication. The graphemes of Egyptian (monoconsonantal) phonograms and early north Semitic letters represent C-initial syllables, but the V must be specified by the reader.

No syllabic writing system is complete in the sense that each syllable of the language in question has its own sign. Complex syllables are often represented synthetically by two or more syllabograms. For example, in Akkadian cuneiform CVC syllables were typically broken up into two parts and represented as CV-VC, where the two Vs indicate the same segment, as in *šar* written as *ša-ar*, *lum* written as *lu-um*, or *gir* as *gi-ir* (figure 19). Similar strategies are found in CYPRIOTE WRITING, LINEAR B and MAYA WRITING. Japanese has a very simple syllable structure with no C clusters or final Cs. The *kana* syllabaries, therefore, come close to being a complete system, but the number of Japanese syllables is still about twice that of basic *kana* signs. A complete system of syllabic writing for phonologically more complex languages such as Russian would require many hundreds of elementary signs.

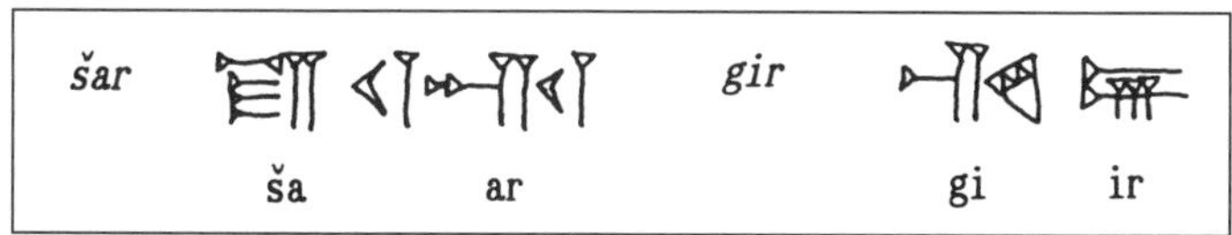

Figure 19 Complex syllable writing of the CV-VC pattern in Akkadian

synharmony A principle in syllabic writing where the last V in a pair of CV phonetic signs repeats the first, although it is unpronounced. Synharmonic V representation is found in several writing systems, as diverse as Cretan LINEAR B and MAYA WRITING.
See also SYLLABOGRAPHY.

Syriac scripts An offshoot of east Aramaic, the Syriac language is first epigraphically attested in inscriptions of the second century CE using the 22-letter alphabet of ARAMAIC WRITING. As Syriac became the medium of the extensive religious literature of the Syrian Christians, consisting of both original writings and translations from Greek, a distinctive form of the alphabet evolved. This script of the cultural centre of Edessa (fifth century) is known as *Esṭrangelā* (Gk στρογγύλη 'rounded'). It was mostly written without Vs (table 13). The schism in 489 CE between the east Syrian followers of Nestorius in Persia and the west Syrian followers of Jacob of Edessa led to a division. The east Syrians in the Persian empire used the conservative Nestorian script, preserving the traditional pronunciation of the language by means of V pointing on the Hebrew model. Like SOGDIAN WRITING, another Aramaic offshoot, the Nestorian script spread to Central Asia and was written vertically, as attested in bilingual Syriac-Chinese inscriptions of the eighth century. When written horizontally, Syriac scripts run in the

Syriac (old)	Syriac (common)	Value	Syriac (old)	Syriac (common)	Value
ܐ	ܐ	*ʼ*	ܠ	ܠ	*l*
ܒ	ܒ	*b*	ܡ	ܡ ܡ	*m*
ܓ	ܓ	*g*	ܢ ܢ	ܢ ܢ	*h*
ܕ	ܕ	*d*	ܣ	ܣ	*ṣ*
ܗ	ܗ	*h*	ܥ	ܥ	*ʻ*
ܘ	ܘ	*v*	ܦ	ܦ	*p*
ܙ	ܙ	*z*	ܨ	ܨ	*ẓ*
ܚ	ܚ	*ḥ*	ܩ	ܩ	*ḳ*
ܛ	ܛ	*ṭ*	ܪ	ܪ	*ṛ*
ܝ	ܝ	*y*	ܫ	ܫ	*sh*
ܟ ܟ	ܟ ܟ	*k*	ܬ	ܬ	*t*

Table 13 The Syriac alphabet in Esṭrangelā (old) and Nestorian scripts

Nestorian		Sertō	
ـܺ	ī	ܺ	i
ـܷ	ē	ܶ	e
ـܸ	e	ܳ	ā, o
ـܳ	ā	ܰ	a
ـܲ	a	ܽ	u
ܘܿ—	ō, o		
ܘܼ—	ū, u		

Table 14 Syriac vowel indication in Nestorian and Sertō

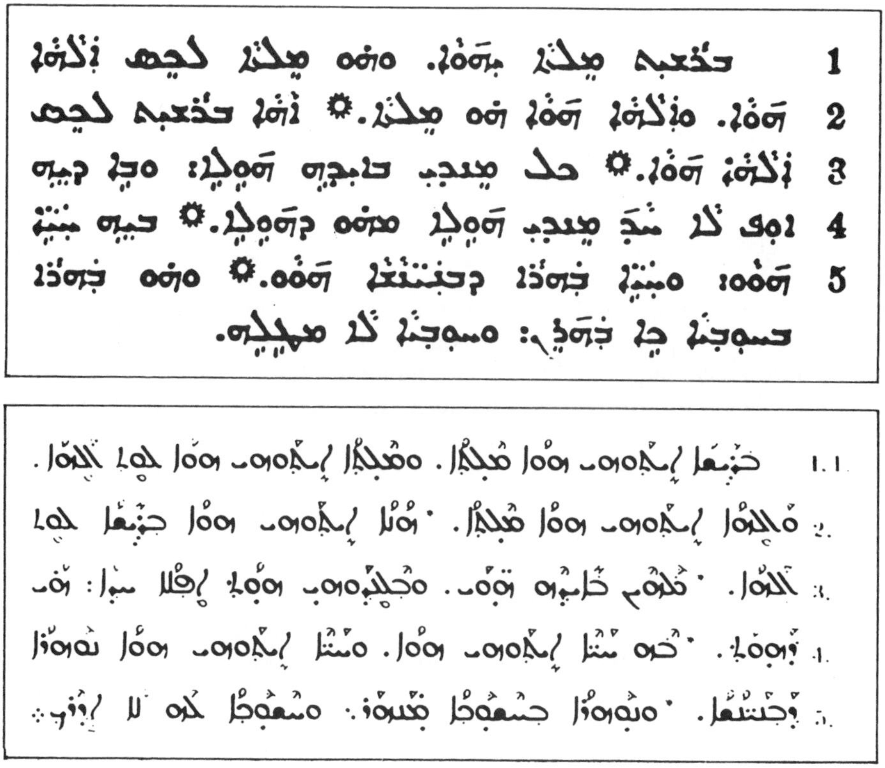

1 ܒܪܫܝܬ ܡܠܬܐ ܗܘܐ. ܘܗܘ ܡܠܬܐ ܠܘܬ ܐܠܗܐ
2 ܗܘܐ. ܘܐܠܗܐ ܗܘܐ ܗܘ ܡܠܬܐ.܀ ܗܢܐ ܗܘܐ ܒܪܫܝܬ ܠܘܬ
3 ܐܠܗܐ ܗܘܐ.܀ ܟܠ ܒܐܝܕܗ ܐܬܒܪܝ ܗܘܐ: ܘܕܠܐ ܗܘ
4 ܐܦ ܠܐ ܚܕܐ ܐܬܒܪܝ ܗܘܬ ܡܕܡ ܕܗܘܐ.܀ ܒܗ ܚܝܐ
5 ܗܘܘ: ܘܚܝܐ ܢܘܗܪܐ ܕܒܢܝܢܫܐ ܗܘܘ.܀ ܘܗܘ ܢܘܗܪܐ
ܒܚܫܘܟܐ ܗܘ ܢܗܝܪ: ܘܚܫܘܟܐ ܠܐ ܐܕܪܟܗ.

1.1 ܒܪܫܝܬ ܐܝܬܘܗܝ ܗܘܐ ܡܠܬܐ. ܘܡܠܬܐ ܐܝܬܘܗܝ ܗܘܐ ܠܘܬ ܐܠܗܐ.
2. ܘܐܠܗܐ ܐܝܬܘܗܝ ܗܘܐ ܡܠܬܐ. ܗܢܐ ܐܝܬܘܗܝ ܗܘܐ ܒܪܫܝܬ ܠܘܬ
3. ܐܠܗܐ. ܟܠ ܒܐܝܕܗ ܗܘܐ. ܘܒܠܥܕܘܗܝ ܐܦܠܐ ܚܕܐ: ܗܘܬ ܡܕܡ
4. ܕܗܘܐ. ܒܗ ܚܝܐ ܐܝܬܘܗܝ ܗܘܐ. ܘܚܝܐ ܐܝܬܘܗܝ ܗܘܐ ܢܘܗܪܐ
5. ܕܒܢܝܢܫܐ. ܘܗܘ ܢܘܗܪܐ ܒܚܫܘܟܐ ܡܢܗܪ. ܘܚܫܘܟܐ ܠܐ ܐܕܪܟܗ܀

Translation

1 In the beginning God created the heaven and the earth.
2 And the earth was without form, and void; and darkness was upon the face of the deep. And the spirit of God moved upon the face of the waters.
3 And God said, Let there be light: and there was light.
4 And God saw the light, that it was good: and God divided the light from the darkness.
5 And God called the light Day, and the darkness he called Night. And the evening and the morning were the first day.

Figure 20 Specimen of Syriac writing from the Bible: Genesis 1:1–5

usual Semitic direction from right to left. The Jacobite script in the west, which is also known as *Serṭō* 'linear' script, was used to write a variety of Syriac closer to the vernacular. In the eighth century it developed a peculiar mode of V indication by inserting reversed Greek letters as diacritics, an innovation attributed to Theophilius of Edessa (table 14). As a spoken language Syriac was superseded in the fourteenth century by Arabic, but as a liturgical language it is still used by Christian communities in Syria, Lebanon and Iraq (figure 20).
See also CONSONANT SCRIPT; SEMITIC WRITING.
Reading Naveh 1982; Ungnad 1913.

T

T, t /ti:/ The twentieth letter of the English alphabet developed from Semitic *tāw*, which already had a cross-like form. The form of Greek *tau* (T, τ) was only slightly changed in Latin.

tachygraphy [Gk ταχύς 'swift' + γρὰφειν 'to write'] The art of quick writing. In Palaeography this refers to cursive, conjoined as distinguished from angular, separately written characters; to the Egyptian hieratic; and to the Greek and Latin writing of the Middle Ages with its characteristic abbreviations. The term is also applied to Shorthand. The Greeks appear to have had a shorthand system at a very early time; fragmentary inscriptions date back as far as the fourth century BCE.
Reading Boge 1973.

Tagalog writing A west Austronesian language which since 1939 has been the national language of the Philippines, Tagalog has a literary history that goes back to pre-colonial times. When in 1521 Magellan arrived in the Philippines, the local population used a number of closely related syllabic alphabets which had reached the islands in the wake of the spread of Indian culture and through the Indonesian Old Kawi script. Very little is known about the exact derivation of these scripts, but it is clear that they are of Indian extraction. The Tagalog syllabary is one of them. It consists of 17 basic graphs, three for initial Vs and 14 of the common Indian C plus inherent V type (table 1). Indication of Vs in other than initial positions is simple: an overdot on the C graphs causes the inherent *a* to be phonetically interpreted as /i/ or /e/, and an underdot changes it into /o/ or /u/.

Within about a century of the beginning of Spanish colonial rule in 1571, the Roman alphabet was generally used for writing Tagalog, and the old syllabic alphabet had fallen out of use along with most other ancient Philippine scripts (figure 1). Known as *abakada* for the names of the first four letters, the Roman alphabet for Tagalog consists of 20 letters in the following sequence: *a, b, k, d, e,*

Vowel letters

a	e, i	o, u

Consonant letters

ba	ka	da	ga	ha	la	ma
na	ŋa	pa	sa	ta	wa	ya

Table 1 The Tagalog syllabic alphabet

Ang gabay na ito ay nagsasaad ng mga paliwanag at mga bagay na kinakailangan sa iba' t–ibang uri ng pagpatala. Sagutin ang alin mang katanungan na naaayon sa inyong katayuan at hanapin ang pahina na tutugon sa bawat pamamaraan.

Translation

This guide provides a step-by-step explanation of what materials are needed for different types of registration. Check the situation which best applies to you and turn to the page which corresponds to each procedure.

Figure 1 Sample of modern Tagalog

g, h, i, l, m, n, ng, o, p, r, s, t, u, w, y. The digraph <ng> represents the phonemic velar nasal /ŋ/. The glottal stop has phonemic value in Tagalog, but is not represented in the alphabet. In word-final position it is indicated by an apostrophe <'>. The following digraphs are used to represent diphthongs: *ya, ye, yo, wa, we, wi, wo*. These occur mostly in loan words, since the typical syllable structure of Tagalog is (C)V(C) with no C clusters or diphthongs. The letters *c, f, j, q, v, x* and *z*, although not part of the *abakada*, are used in proper names and certain borrowings from Spanish and English. Older loans which are completely integrated are, however, generally spelt in accordance with Tagalog orthography, e.g. *tsip* < English *chief; taksi* < English *taxi; prito* < Spanish *frito; trabaho* < Spanish *trabajo*.
See also PHILIPPINE SCRIPTS.
Reading Marre 1901; Ramos 1986.

Tajik writing [Cyrillic таджики] An Iranian language closely related to modern Persian, Tajik (also Tadzhik) is spoken in Tajikistan, Iran, Uzbekistan and Afghanistan. The written language differs little from Persian, although under Soviet rule the Arabic alphabet was replaced, first by the Roman (1928–9) and then by the Cyrillic (1939–40). In addition to the Russian alphabet, the following six letters are used: Ғ, Ӣ, Қ, Ӯ, Ҳ, Ҷ. In Afghanistan the Arabic alphabet continues to be used.

Ṭākrī script A syllabic alphabet which is a variety of the north Indian ŚĀRADĀ SCRIPT, used widely until the early decades of the twentieth century in several states of the western Himalayas (table 2). It has given way to the Devanāgarī script.
See also INDIAN WRITING SYSTEMS.
Reading Masica 1991.

tally A primitive means of record keeping, the tally is a carved stick or rod of wood. Traverse notches are cut into the usually square stick to represent an amount of debt or payment received. The tally is split lengthwise across the notches, and the parties to the transaction each keep one half, with identical records which cannot be altered one-sidedly. Notched sticks of various sorts were used in many parts of the world. It has been suggested that the practice of

Independent vowel letters

𑚀 a	𑚆 e
𑚁 ā	𑚇 ai
𑚂 i	𑚈 o
𑚃 ī	𑚉 au
𑚄 u	
𑚅 ū	

Consonant letters

𑚊 ka	𑚋 kha	𑚌 ga	𑚍 gha	
𑚏 ca	𑚐 cha	𑚑 ja	𑚒 jha	
𑚔 ṭa	𑚕 ṭha	𑚖 ḍa	𑚗 ḍha	𑚘 ṇa
𑚙 ta	𑚚 tha	𑚛 da	𑚜 dha	𑚝 na
𑚞 pa	𑚟 pha	𑚠 ba	𑚡 bha	𑚢 ma
𑚣 ya	𑚤 ra	𑚥 la	𑚦 va	
𑚧 śa	𑚨 ṣa	𑚩 sa	𑚪 ha	

Table 2 The Ṭākrī syllabic alphabet

carving notches into wood or bone for mnemonic purposes was a step in the development of writing. In medieval Europe, however, tallies were used alongside and often in combination with writing (figure 2).
See also PROTO-WRITING.

Tamil writing A Dravidian language spoken in the southern Indian state of Tamil Nadu and in Sri Lanka, as well as in Malaysia and Singapore, Tamil is written with its own syllabic alphabet consisting of independent V graphs and C graphs with inherent *a*. It was derived from a north Indian script with south Indian influences of the GRANTHA SCRIPT and the PALLAVA SCRIPT. Tamil is first inscriptionally attested in documents dating from the early eighth century CE.

The Tamil script distinguishes itself from other Indian syllabic alphabets through the small number of basic signs, which is a reflection of phonological peculiarities. There is no distinction between voiced and voiceless Cs, and no series of aspirated Cs. Originally only 21 letters were used. In its present form, the Tamil syllabic alphabet consits of 30 letters. The list in table 3 contains six derived letters for *ū*, *ō*, *ai*, *ṇ*, *ẓ* and *n*. In addition, six Grantha letters are used for Sanskrit and other foreign words, and the *aaytam* which indicates fricates following a stop (table 4). V indication follows the general Indian pattern. Initial Vs have their

Figure 2 Tallies used in Surrey and Sussex, as receipts for payments into the treasury in the financial year 1293–4. Ginny Stroud-Lewis

own symbols, and Vs following a C are written by grouping diacritic satellites around the C graphs (table 5). The rules for using the V muting overdot (*hasanta*) with which the C graphs are given in table 3 differ somewhat from those of the VIRĀMA in other Indian scripts. Most conspicuously it is more freely used in non-final position than the *virāma*. The representation of C clusters is, therefore, easier in Tamil than in other Indian scripts.

Like several other Indian languages, Tamil exists in a situation of DIGLOSSIA. Literary Tamil, until recently the only variety used in writing, has changed little since the thirteenth century. It hence differs markedly from modern spoken Tamil.

Vowel letters

அ	ஆ	இ	ஈ	உ	ஊ
a	ā	i	ī	u	ū
எ	ஏ	ஐ	ஒ	ஓ	ஔ
e	ē	ai	o	ō	au

Consonant letters

க்	ங்	ச்	ஞ்	ட்	ண்
k	ng	c	ñ	ṭ	ṇ
த்	ந்	ப்	ம்	ய்	ர்
t	n	p	m	y	r
ல்	வ்	ழ்	ள்	ற்	ன்
l	v	ẓ	ḷ	ṛ	ṉ

Table 3 The Tamil syllabic alphabet

ஸ	ஜ	ஷ	ஹ	க்ஷ	ஸ்ரீ
sa	ja	sha	ha	ksha	shri
ஃ					
Aaytam					

Table 4 Grantha letters in Tamil

த்	த	தா	தி	தீ	து	தூ
t	ta	tā	ti	tī	tu	tū
	தெ	தே	தை	தொ	தோ	தௌ
	te	tē	tai	to	tō	tau

Table 5 Vowel indication in Tamil

In recent decades writers have experimented with writing varieties of modern Tamil (figure 3), and a modern standard seems to be emerging.
See also INDIAN WRITING SYSTEMS.
Reading Rao 1966; Schiffman and Arokianathan 1986.

Tangut writing *See* HSI-HSIA WRITING

Tatar writing [Cyrillic Татары] A Turkic language spoken in and around Kazan, Russia, as well as in Siberia and parts of Central Asia, Tatar (also Tartar) was

தமிழும் தனித்தமிழும்!

தமிழ் ஒரு மொழி. தனித் தமிழ் ஒரு முயற்சி. தனித் தமிழே தமிழ் மொழியல்ல. இந்தத் தெளிவு எனக்கிருப்பதால் தனித்தமிழ் மீது எனக்கு வெறுப்பில்லை. இந்தத் தெளிவு இல்லாததினால் தனித்தமிழ்ப் பிரியார்கள் தம்மை அறியாமலேயே தமிழை வெறுத்து வருகிறார்கள்.

tamiṟum taṉittamiṟum!

tamiṟ oru moṟi . taṉit tamiṟ oru muyaṟci . taṉit tamiṟe: tamiṟ moṟiyalla . intat teḷivu eṉakkiruppata:l taṉittamiṟ mi:tu eṉakku veṟuppillai . intat teḷivu illa:tatiṉa:l taṉittamiṟp piriya:rkaḷ tammai aṟiya:male:ye: tamiṟai veṟuttu varukiṟa:rkaḷ

Tamil and the Pure Tamil Movement

Tamil is a language. The Pure Tamil Movement is an endeavor. The *tanit tamiṟ* Movement all by itself is not the Tamil language. Just because I have this understanding does not mean that I hate the Pure Tamil Movement. Lacking this insight, the *tanit tamiṟ* separatists are themselves bringing Tamil into disrepute.

Figure 3 Specimen of modern Tamil writing with transliteration and translation: from Jeyakanthan, 'Munnooṭṭam', 1972, p. 189 (courtesy Harold Schiffman)

reduced to writing in the mid-nineteenth century using the Arabic alphabet. Two script reforms with changes to Latin (1927) and then to Cyrillic (1939) were carried out under Soviet rule. In addition to the Russian alphabet, the following six letters are used: ж, Н, һ, θ, Ү, ə.

Telugu writing A member of the Dravidian family, Telugu is the official language of the State of Andhra Pradesh, south India. Palaeographically, Telugu is first attested in inscriptions dating from the sixth to the eighth centuries CE. The oldest extant poetic work is considerably later, the *Mahābhārata* of the eleventh century. As with other literary languages of India, Telugu evolved in a situation of DIGLOSSIA as of that time. Until the twentieth century the written language of poetry and prose literature remained archaic. Based on the central coastal dialect of Godavari, modern standard Telugu emerged as a written language only during the latter half of the twentieth century. It is now used in newspapers, fiction and other writing.

The Telugu writing system is a syllabic alphabet belonging to the southern branch of Brāhmī-derived scripts. It is closely related to the KANNADA SCRIPT. During the early period of written Telugu (seventh to thirteenth centuries) the Telugu-Kannada script is considered a single system derived from the KADAMBA SCRIPT with minor local variations. As of the thirteenth century, the differences become more pronounced, but it was only with the introduction of printing early in the nineteenth century that the separation was completed. In Kannada the upper part of the letters bears some resemblance to the characteristic top line of northern scripts, but in Telugu it has been transformed into a hook. Still, it is easy for a person familiar with one of the scripts to read the other.

Telugu has 16 graphemes for initial, i.e. independent, Vs. Of these, 14 are paired for short and long Vs, the graphemes of the latter being derived from those of the former by minor graphical modifications (table 6). The 35 C graphemes are of the common Indian type with inherent *a*. The inherent V is neutralized by addition of diacritics for other Vs in post-consonantal position. Ligatures for C clusters are formed by subscribing succeeding Cs stripped of their top hook to preceding Cs. The V muting sign (*virāma*) is a superscript loop. Aspiration can be indicated by two small circles, one above the other, placed next to the C letter on the line (*visarga*); and nasalization is expressed by a bigger circle placed on the line like a letter. The direction of Telugu writing is from left to right, like all Indian scripts.

See also INDIAN WRITING SYSTEMS.

Reading Rao 1966; Šastri 1985.

text [Lat. *textus*, past participle of *texĕre* 'to weave', whence 'texture, web'] Any piece of connected language that is written or printed; more specifically, that part of a piece of writing which constitutes the original matter as distinct from additional notes or comments, as in scriptures. In philology, theology and literary studies, 'text' is understood as written language, but in linguistics the term has been extended to include self-contained pieces of spoken and signed language. The linguistic investigation of texts examines structural constraints above the sentence level which determine how sentences and lower-level linguistic units combine to form a coherent whole. In the sense in which it is used by discourse and conversation analysts, a text is a transcript of spontaneous speech including para-linguistic (pauses, stress) and non-linguistic (laughing, gestures) information. Usage of the term in literacy research is closer to the original meaning. Language as text is written and as such autonomous, that is, not dependent for its interpretation on the presence of the author or the situation in which it has been produced. This is contrasted with language as discourse which consists of situation-bound utterances. The principal concern here is with the structural,

Vowel letters

అ	ఆ	ఇ	ఈ	ఉ	ఊ	ఋ	ౠ
a	ā	i	ī	u	ū	ṛ	ṝ

ఌ	ౡ	ఎ	ఏ	ఐ	ఒ	ఓ	ఔ
ḷ	ḹ	e	ē	ai	o	ō	au

Consonant letters

క	ఖ	గ	ఘ	ఙ	చ	ఛ	జ	ఝ	ఞ
ka	kha	ga	gha	ña	ča	čha	ǧa	ǧha	ńa

ట	ఠ	డ	ఢ	ణ	త	థ	ద	ధ	న
ṭa	ṭha	ḍa	ḍha	ṇa	ta	tha	da	dha	na

ప	ఫ	బ	భ	మ	య	వ	ర	ల	ళ
pa	pha	ba	bha	ma	ya	va	ra	la	ḹa

స	శ	ష	హ	ఱ
sa	š́a	ša	ha	ṫa

Vowel diacritics

కా	కి	కీ	కు	కూ	కృ	కౄ
kā	ki	kī	ku	kū	kṛ	kṝ

కె	కే	కై	కొ	కో	కౌ
ke	kē	kai	ko	kō	kau

Table 6 The Telugu syllabic alphabet

functional and cognitive differences between autonomous text and situated utterance which result from the physical properties of the visual and the oral medium.

See also LITERACY; LITERATURE.

Reading Olson 1977; Danlos 1987; Stein 1992.

Thai writing A syllabic alphabet, the Thai writing system appears to be derived from the Khmer script which is itself an offshoot of the southern branch of Indian writing systems which spread to Indo-China in the wake of Buddhism. Traditionally, King Ramkhamhaeng (1275–1317) is credited with having early in his reign designed a writing for the Siamese language which developed into the Thai script. The oldest known inscription dates from 1283.

The writing system

Structured on the basis of the general Indian pattern, the Thai writing system consists of C plus inherent V letters (table 7). V indication is by diacritic satellites (table 8). A number of peculiarities set Thai writing apart from other Brāhmī-derived scripts. The 44 basic letters are all Cs with inherent V. Although no V muting device is used, the inherent V is sometimes not pronounced when two C letters are juxtaposed without additional V diacritic. C clusters are thus expressed without conjunct C letters. Further, there are no letters for initial, i.e. independent

ก	k	ฎ	ḍ	บ	b	ย	y
ข	kh	ฏ	ṭ	ป	p	ร	r
ฃ	k̈h	ฐ	ṭh	ผ	ph	ล	l
ค	k′	ฑ	ṭ′	ฝ	f	ว	w
ฅ	k̈′	ฒ	ṭ̂′	พ	p′	ศ	ś
ฆ	k̂′	ณ	ṇ	ฟ	f′	ษ	ṣ
ง	ng	ด	d	ภ	p̂′	ส	s
จ	c	ต	t	ม	m	ห	h
ฉ	ch	ถ	th			ฬ	ḷ
ช	c′	ท	t′			อ	ʼ
ซ	s′	ธ	t̂′			ฮ	h′
ฌ	ĉ′	น	n				
ญ	ñ						

Table 7 The Thai syllabic alphabet

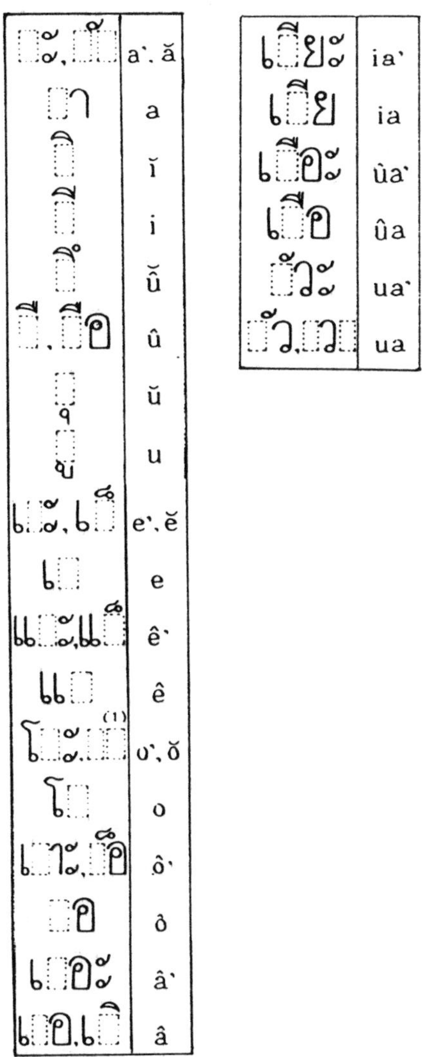

Table 8 Thai vowel diacritics

Vs. The inherent V is /ɔ/; other Vs are expressed by diacritics. For initial Vs the letter for the glottal stop is used as a base for the appropriate diacritic. The diacritics are for 18 Vs and six diphthongs. The vocalism of Thai is complicated by five tones (table 9). Four tone marks are used for low, falling, high and rising tones, while the flat middle tone is left unmarked. Finally, there are four letters for liquids and four diacritics for diphthongs and a nasal only used in Pāli loan words (table 10). Two special characters are used to indicate repetition and abbreviation.

Three factors account for the complexity of the Thai writing system. One is that there is no homology between the sequential order of segments in speech and writing. A phonetically simple CV syllable may be represented in writing with the V diacritic in any position relative to the base C, preceding or following it,

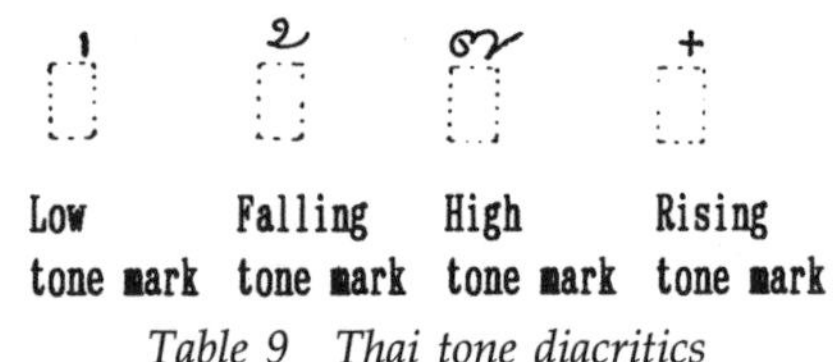

Table 9 Thai tone diacritics

ฤ	ṛŭ,ṛi	◌ำ	ăm
ฤๅ	ṛû	ใ◌	ai
ฦ	ḷŭ	ไ◌	ăi
ฦๅ	ḷû	เ◌า	au

Table 10 Thai syllabic letters used in Pāli loan words

above or below it, or on both sides. The linearity of speech is hence represented in writing not on the level of segments but only on that of syllables. However, a facilitating aspect is that each of the V diacritics always appears in the same position in relation to all Cs to which it can be attached.

Tone indication is another complication of the system, unknown in other Indian scripts. The four tone marks are added as secondary diacritics in an outer orbit to the base C with its inner orbit of V diacritics. The tone marks have variable values depending on the kind of C to which they are attached. Cs are subdivided into three classes: low, middle and high. This division is partly motivated by phonological distinctions, the letters of unaspirated Cs being grouped as middle, while those of aspirated Cs are either high or low. Thus the graph for /k/ is middle class, that for /kh/ high class. A low tone marker indicates a low tone when attached to a high- or middle-class C, but a falling tone when attached to a low-class C. A falling tone mark usually indicates a falling tone, except on low-class Cs where it indicates a high tone.

A third difficulty lies in the many idiosyncrasies, irregular spellings and polyvalent grapheme–phoneme correspondences. Historical spellings have preserved graphemes used only irregularly in some words. Some phonemes have multiple representations, and some are spelt differently in final and initial position in the syllable. Adding to these features, which make Thai writing relatively hard to read, is the practice of running syllable blocks together without spaces or other marks to indicate word boundaries. Thai is written on horizontal lines from left to right.

The script

Since its creation the script has undergone some modifications (table 11). The earliest form of King Ramkhamhaeng, which came to be known as 'Sukhothai script' after Sukhothai, the capital of Thailand at the time, was curvilinear in appearance. It was succeeded in 1357 during the reign of King Li Thai by the slightly different 'King Li Thai script'. The 'King Na Rai script' which followed

	b	p	p^h			f		w	m	d		t	
Sukhothai	[illegible]	[illegible]	[illegible]	[illegible]	[illegible]	[illegible]	[illegible]	[illegible]	[illegible]	[illegible]	[illegible]	[illegible]	[illegible]
King Li Thai	[illegible]	[illegible]	[illegible]	[illegible]	[illegible]	[illegible]	[illegible]	[illegible]	[illegible]	[illegible]	[illegible]	[illegible]	[illegible]
King Na Rai	[illegible]	[illegible]	[illegible]	[illegible]	[illegible]	[illegible]	[illegible]	[illegible]	[illegible]	[illegible]	[illegible]	[illegible]	
Modern Thai	บ	ป	พ	ภ	ผ	ฟ	ฝ	ว	ม	ด	ฎ	ต	ฏ

Table 11 Formal development of Thai letters

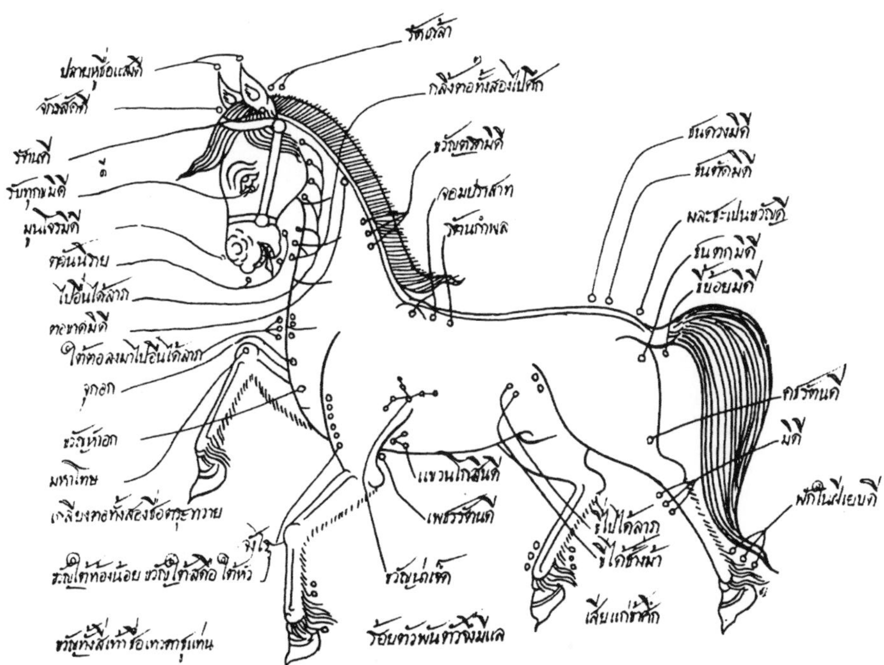

Figure 4 Illustration from a nineteenth-century Thai manual describing horses, with notes explaining body parts in Thai script

in 1680 was more angular with many pointed letter forms. A compressed variety of this script is the present Thai script (figure 4).
See also BRĀHMĪ WRITING; INDIAN WRITING SYSTEMS; KHMER WRITING.
Reading Danwiwat 1987; Haas 1956.

Thamudic script A member of the northern branch of SOUTH ARABIAN SCRIPTS used in pre-Islamic times in the northern part of the Arabian peninsula and Sinai. It is attested in several inscriptions which have been tentatively dated between the second century BCE and the third century CE. Consisting of 28 C letters, the

Thamudic script has no means of V indication (table 12). The direction of writing is usually from right to left, although the script has also been written from left to right and, in isolated cases, vertically from top to bottom.
See also SABAIC WRITING; SEMITIC WRITING.
Reading Jensen 1969.

Table 12 The Thamudic alphabet

Thoth The Egyptian ibis-headed god revered as the patron of letters. Sometimes represented as a baboon, he was the lord of writing, the master of PAPYRUS, and the god of the moon, keeping the score of time.
See also DEITIES OF WRITING.

***thuluth* script** A rounded calligraphic style of the Arabic script which came into existence in the late eighth century CE. One of the six major scripts of Islamic calligraphy (the SITTA), it is characterized by great plasticity which allows letters to be bent, stretched or compressed for decorative purposes. Its principal use is as a decorative script for architecture and small objects, but it also occurs in manuscripts (figure 5). It was popular among the Ottoman Turks who called it *sülüs* or *rīḥānī* after Rīḥān, a calligrapher credited with its design.
See also ARABIC SCRIPTS; CALLIGRAPHY.
Reading Schimmel 1984.

Figure 5 Specimen of thuluth *script, from a fourteenth-century Egyptian epitaph*

Tiberian pointing A system of diacritics used in HEBREW WRITING for vocalization. So called after the city of Tiberias in northern Israel, a centre of biblical studies since the eighth century CE, it is the system used for printing the Bible. The basic seven signs with their names and the sound values they indicate are as follows: <ָ> *qāmes* for *ā*, <ַ> *pathaḥ* for *ă*, <ֵ> *ṣēṛē* for *ē*, <ֶ> *sēgōl* for *ĕ*, <ִ> *ḥīreq* for *ī*, <ֹ> *hōlem* for *ō* and <ֻ> *šūreq* for *ŭ*. The *šewa* or *schwa*, <ְ>, for ə was added later. How each diacritic is attached to a C graph is shown with the letter *dāleth* (*d*) as follows:

דָ דֲ דֵ דֶ דִ דֹ דֻ דְ
dā dă dē dĕ dī dō dū də

See also Babylonian pointing.

Tibetan writing The literary history of Tibetan goes back to the eighth century CE. Tradition credits Thon-mi Sambhoṭa, a noble Tibetan scholar and minister of King Srong-btsan-sgam-po, with devising the Tibetan writing system on the model of a north Indian script. Although there is no documentary evidence to support this attribution, it is clear that the Tibetan system is patterned on the Brāhmī writing, the Gupta variety probably being its immediate forebear (figure 6). The oldest epigraphic monument is the stone pillar of Zhol, Lhasa, which has been dated 764 CE.

Figure 6 Tibetan talisman, the 'horse of good fortune'

The adaptation to Tibetan of the Gupta alphabet made significant changes necessary because, unlike the languages for which Brāhmī and its offshoots evolved, Tibetan is not an Indo-European language. The structural principle underlying the Tibetan script is that of Indian writing systems. The unit of representation is the syllable, but the unit of analysis is the segment.

The alphabet consists of 30 letters (table 13). In its basic form each letter represents a C plus an inherent V *a*. As with the Indian scripts, the inherent V is neutralized by attaching diacritic V satellites to the C letter. However, in contrast to the Indic systems, Tibetan has only one independent V letter, for *a*. By extending the principle of diacritical V indication, this letter is also used as the base to which diacritics for *i*, *u*, *e*, *o* are attached to indicate their syllabic occurrence

ཀ་ *ka*	ཁ་ *kha*	ག་ *ga*	ང་ *ṅa*
ཅ་ *tša*	ཆ་ *tšha*	ཇ་ *dža*	ཉ་ *ña*
ཏ་ *ta*	ཐ་ *tha*	ད་ *da*	ན་ *na*
པ་ *pa*	ཕ་ *pha*	བ་ *ba*	མ་ *ma*
ཙ་ *tsa*	ཚ་ *tsha*	ཛ་ *dza*	ཝ་ *wa*
ཞ་ *ža*	ཟ་ *za*	འ་ *'a*	ཡ་ *ja*
ར་ *ra*	ལ་ *la*	ཤ་ *ša*	ས་ *sa*
	ཧ *ha*	ཨ *a*	

Table 13 The Tibetan syllabic alphabet

ཨི *i*	ཨུ *u*	ཨེ *e*	ཨོ *o*

Table 14 Tibetan-derived independent vowel letters

ཊ	ཋ	ཌ	ཎ	ཥ
ṭa	*ṭha*	*ḍa*	*ṇa*	*sha*

Table 15 Tibetan inverted letters for loan words

(table 14). V length was not originally distinguished, but in order to represent long Vs in loan words from Sanskrit and other languages, the letter for *ha* (*achung*) is added to the C sign as a subscript. In addition, the letters of the dental series *ta, tha, da, na* and *ša* have been inverted to form letters for cerebral Cs which likewise occur in loan words (table 15). Ligatures are formed by writing the preceding Cs *ra, la* and *sa* above, and the succeeding Cs *ya, ra, la, wa* and *ha* below, the base C. A written syllable can thus be of considerable complexity, consisting of the base C with inherent V plus additional Cs and an additional V. There is no V muting sign. Instead, a dot, called *tseg*, placed on the right shoulder of a C letter indicates syllable closure. If no *tseg* is placed between two or more C letters, the group is to be read as a C cluster. If a syllable ends in a voiced laryngeal fricative, the *achung* འ is added to the syllable group.

Syllables are written from left to right one next to another with no word division. Never having been reformed since the standardization of the orthography during the reign of King Ralpacan (815–36), the spelling conventions of Tibetan are conservative with rather involved grapheme–phoneme correspondences which make for difficult reading. Many etymological spellings represent sounds no longer pronounced. For example, the word *gye* is spelt བརྒྱད which is transliterated as *ba-rgya-da*. Further, the script fails to mark a systematically important phonological distinction. Tibetan is a tone language, but there are no graphic means to indicate tone.

The outer appearance of the script is regular and elegant with an Indian-type top line which, however, does not link groups of syllables. In classical Tibetan, one and two perpendicular strokes, <|> and <||>, mark off clauses and sentences, respectively. In modern Tibetan, <,> and <.> are used. In addition to the printed style several cursive varieties have evolved, among them the *dbu-med* or 'headless' script.

Tibetan exists in a situation of DIGLOSSIA. Until recently, writing was largely restricted to classical Tibetan. A standard of modern literary Tibetan has emerged in the twentieth century. The Tibetan script is also used to write Ladakhi and Sikkimese.
Reading Miller 1956.

Tifinagh The writing used by the Tuareg for writing Tamasheq, one of the Berber languages of North Africa. The Tuareg live in a large section of the Sahara Desert and the Sahel. Their writing, the Tifinagh, is derived from the Old Numidian script which was created on the model of Semitic scripts in the sixth century BCE, perhaps as an offshoot of the PUNIC SCRIPT. The letters, which are known as *asekkil*, designate Cs only. Vs are mostly left unindicated (table 16). Modern attempts at using a modified form of the Tifinagh for writing the Berber languages of Morocco and Algeria have not met with success (figure 7).
Reading Aghali Zakara and Drouin 1978.

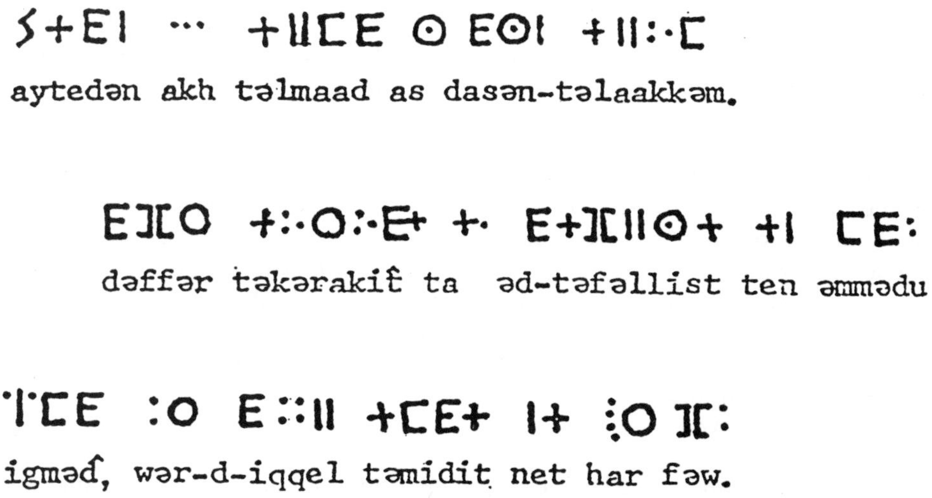

aytedən akh təlmaad as dasən-təlaakkəm.

dəffər təkərakit̂ ta əd-təfəllist ten əmmədu

igməd̂, wər-d-iqqel təmidit̲ net har fəw.

Figure 7 A short text in Tifinagh script with transliteration
Source: *Office of Literacy and Adult Education, Niger, 1970s*

Symbol	Transliteration	Arabic equivalent	Symbol	Transliteration	Arabic equivalent
◫	b	ب	ǁ	l	ل
ↄ	š	ش	⊐	m	م
V	d	ذ	ǀ	n	ن
∃	ḍ	ض (ظ)	ǂ	ɲ	—
)(	f	ف	:	w	و
x	g	ڮ	ⵔ	r	ر
·ǀ·	ġ	—	⋮	ɣ	غ
⁝	h	ه	⊙	s	س
ʒ	y	ي	+	t	ت
ⵊ	ž	ج	∃	ṭ	ط
·:	k	ك	I	z	ز
⋯	ḳ	ق	⋕	ẓ	ض
∷	x	خ	·	[vowel]	—

Table 16 The Tifinagh alphabet for Tamasheq

tilde The diacritic <˜> usually placed over V letters of the ROMAN ALPHABET to indicate nasal quality. In some languages it is also used to mark palatalization and then placed over C letters, as in Spanish *español*. In phonetic transcription the tilde indicates nasalization only, whereas in written words it often indicates both stress and nasalization, e.g. in Portuguese *capitão*.
See also DIACRITIC.

Tironian notes [Lat. *notae Tirōniānae*] A shorthand system in use in ancient Rome. Tiro, Cicero's freedman and secretary, is thought to have devised or at least improved the system, which hence came to be known as Tironian notes (table 17). Those who mastered it were called *notarii*. The system was later extended to include a great number of abbreviations of syllables, words, groups of words and, after the spread of Christianity, biblical names. Some 13,000 such abbreviations are known. Isidor of Seville's seventh-century work on the notes comprised 20 volumes.
Reading Boge 1973.

tjarakan The name of the Javanese alphabet, also *carakan* or *hanacaraca*, after the first letters of the traditional sequence.
See also JAVANESE WRITING.

Alphabet

a
b
c
d
e
f
g
h
i
k
l
m

n
o
p
q
r
s
t
u
χ
ph
ts

Prefixes

al
ac
an
ab
oc
de
di
ex
prae
pro

ap
ad
con
circa
in
inter
ob
per
re
sub

Suffixes

a
ae
am
amini
amur
amus
are
ari
aris
arum
as
at

ans
ant
antes
anticis
antur
anus
atis
atur
e
el
em
emur

Table 17 Variant letter forms of the Tironian notes

Tocharian writing An Indo-European language of which palaeographic remains were discovered only in the early years of the twentieth century, Tocharian is inscriptionally attested in fragmentary manuscripts dating from the sixth to the eighth centuries CE. These palaeographic materials were excavated along the northern Silk Road in Chinese Turkestan (modern Xinjiang Uygur Autonomous Region). They exhibit two distinct dialects: the eastern, Turfanian dialect and the western, Kuchean dialect. Both are written in an adjusted form of the old Brāhmī script that spread to Central Asia in the wake of Buddhism. The extant Tocharian literature is largely religious in nature, most texts being translations of Buddhist writings from Sanskrit; only a few secular texts are known (figure 8).

Figure 8 A specimen of Tocharian writing

The writing system consists of 45 graphemes, 11 Vs and 34 C plus inherent *a* letters (table 18). The letters of the long Vs /ā/, /ī/ and /ū/ are derived from their short counterparts. Vs in non-initial position are indicated by means of diacritic satellites grouped around the C letters. Like other Brāhmī-derived scripts, the direction of Tocharian writing is from left to right.
See also BRĀHMĪ WRITING; INDIAN WRITING SYSTEMS.
Reading Krause 1971.

token Geometrically shaped bits of fire-hardened clay which were used in Mesopotamia as early as 8000 BCE as a primitive accounting system for computation and record keeping. More than 10,000 of these objects have been found in some 100 archaeological sites (figure 9). Recent research by Denise Schmandt-Besserat and others has lent support to the notion that these clay tokens or 'count stones' were the precursors of the earliest Sumerian writing.

Initially, the sign relation between clay token and referent was simple: one token for one object, differently shaped tokens being used for different objects. In order to systematize the inventory of objects represented by the tokens, these

Consonant letters

ka	ḍa	ma
kha	ḍha	ya
ga	ṇa	ra
gha	ta	la
ṅa	tha	va
ča	da	śa
cha	dha	ṣa
ja	na	sa
jha	ṉä	ha
ña	pa	
ṭa	pha	
ṭha	ba	
	bha	

Independent vowel letters

a	e
ā	o
i	ai
ī	au
u	ṛ
ū	

Syllable final diacritics

-ṃ
-ḥ
-ḫ
-ẖ

Vowel indication

tha thā thi thī thu thū

the tho thaj thau tho

Table 18 The Tocharian syllabic alphabet

were kept in clay containers called *bullae*, which were also used as bills of lading to accompany shipments of goods. The recipient would open the container to verify that the correct quantity had arrived. At a later stage of development, a simpler method of verification was discovered, making it unnecessary to destroy the *bullae*. By impressing the tokens on the wet shell before it was sealed, it was possible to indicate on the outside what was contained inside and thus check the record without breaking the container.

The next step was that the impressions on the outside of the containers assumed

Figure 9 Clay tokens from Susa, fourth millennium BCE *(Musée du Louvre, Paris)*

the function of the primary signs, the tokens. In turn the latter became less and less important until finally they could be dispensed with, as a direct relation developed between the impressions and the objects (figure 10).

Two aspects of Schmandt-Besserat's work on the tokens are of major importance for the history of writing. One is the discovery that some of the earliest Sumerian pictographs correspond closely to token impressions (table 19). At least

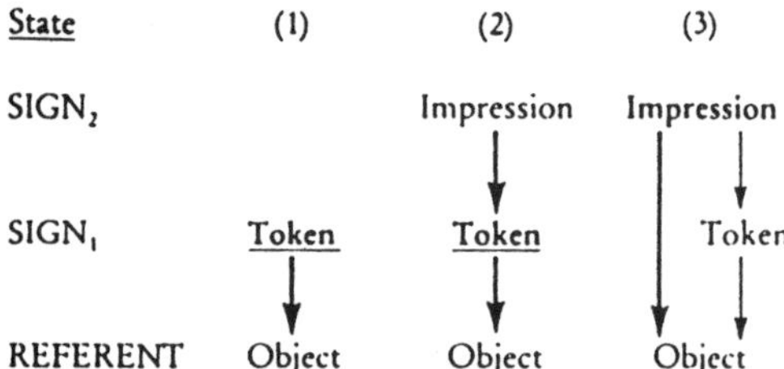

Figure 10 The relation between a token and an object is superseded by the relation between the impression of the token and the object

Token	Pictograph	Translation	Token	Pictograph	Translation
		Bread			Sheep
		Oil			Ewe
		Beer			Wool, fleece
		Sheep's milk			Metal

Table 19 Correspondences between tokens and early Sumerian pictographs
Source: *Schmandt-Besserat 1992*

30 Sumerian signs can be shown to have a clay token equivalent. Although this is a small number in comparison with the almost 2,000 Sumerian signs, they clearly play an important part in the first attempts to produce written records, if only because they marked the transition from three-dimensional objects to two-dimensional signs on a surface. Of equal importance is the fact that some of the earliest tokens represent numbers rather than concrete objects. Their use as number signs is evidence of the crucial link between reckoning and the origin of writing.
See also ORIGIN OF WRITING.
Reading Schmandt-Besserat 1992.

Tomba script *See* NAXI WRITING

tone Distinctive pitch at the syllable level. In tone languages, tone is a sense-discriminative feature which distinguishes lexical meanings. Tones are usually classified in terms of pitch range as high, low, middle etc., and of direction as rising, falling or rising-falling contour tones. Although a great many, if not the majority, of the world's languages are tone languages, only a few writing systems have developed devices for the representation of tones. The Chinese writing system, operating as it does on the syllabo-morphemic level, has no means to indicate tone, but it recognizes tone distinctions in that different characters are used for words which are phonetically identical except for tone. The various ROMANIZATION systems of Chinese indicate the four tones of Mandarin by various means such as accent marks (Pinyin) or additional letters (Gwoyeu Romatzyh). The same differences between level, rising, falling-rising and falling tones that Pinyin expresses as *fēn*, *fén*, *fěn* and *fèn* are given as *fen*, *fern*, *feen* and *fenn* in Gwoyeu Romatzyh. An example of a tone language which uses a phonographic system of writing without tone indication is TIBETAN WRITING; one with full tone indication is THAI WRITING.
Reading Voorhoeve 1962.

transcription The visual representation of verbal utterances by means of special phonetic symbols derived from alphabetic letters, such as the INTERNATIONAL PHONETIC ALPHABET. A distinction is made between a *broad phonemic* transcription, usually enclosed between slashes /. . . /, which ignores non-distinctive phonetic differences, and a *narrow phonetic* transcription, usually enclosed between square brackets [. . .], which indicates such differences as, for instance, aspirated vs non-aspirated bilabial stops – [pʰ] as opposed to [p] – even where such a contrast is contextually predictable, as in English. Another distinction is that between transcriptions of the citation forms of individual words, for example in pronunciation dictionaries, and transcriptions of actual speech, as from a recording.

Transcription is a by-product of alphabetic writing which suggests that it is possible in principle to represent units of speech as definite numbers of independent sounds, to each of which corresponds an alphabetic letter or supplementary symbol. Since, however, a word in connected speech is a continuous series of infinitely numerous sounds which, moreover, often blend with those of neighbouring words through processes of assimilation and elision, every transcription that makes use of discrete symbols is essentially an abstraction. However narrow, it can be no more than a theoretically informed approximation. Yet in this approximation lies a fundamental difference which distinguishes transcription from conventional, i.e. orthographic, writing. Both transcription and orthographic writing are based on theories about how to segment and analyse speech, but the purposes of the respective analyses are different. Transcription aims at fixing the phonemic or phonetic features of an individual utterance, mapping some aspects of a unique physical event. Orthographic writing, by contrast, is intended to abstract from individual differences. Orthographic words are highly abstract models which ignore many variations and allow for a great range of pronunciations. There is hence inevitably a structural divergence between orthographic text and transcribed speech.

See also ALPHABET; ORTHOGRAPHY; PHONEME.

Reading Haas 1970; Edwards and Lampert 1992.

transliteration A one-to-one conversion of the graphemes of one writing system into those of another writing system; not to be confused with TRANSCRIPTION. The general problem is that writing systems do not exist in the abstract, but are used in language-specific orthographies consisting of rules which determine how the sounds of a language are written and how the letters are pronounced. In an early study of the question of how to use the Roman alphabet to write languages usually written in other scripts, Sir William Jones (1807, p. 269) identified the principal difficulty:

> Our *English* alphabet and orthography are disgracefully and almost ridiculously imperfect; and it would be impossible to express either *Indian*, *Persian*, or *Arabian* words in *Roman* characters, as we are absurdly taught to pronounce them; but a mixture of new characters would be inconvenient, and by the help of the diacritical marks used by the *French* . . . we may apply our present alphabet so happily to the notation of all *Asiatick* languages, as to equal the *Dévanágarì* itself in precision and clearness.

Since the purpose of transliteration is, presumably, to enable those not familiar with the writing system of a language to nevertheless read words or even texts of that language, it is tempting for the benefit of such persons to use the transliteration system in a way they are familiar with. However, this would imply, for example in the case Jones was concerned with, the imposition of the spelling conventions of English on Sanskrit, Persian or Arabic when representing these languages with Roman letters. To avoid such oddities, transliteration conventions are defined explicitly, taking the signary of the language to be transliterated as a starting point and assigning to each of its elements a grapheme of the transliteration system which is then used consistently. The spelling conventions will then be those of the original writing system.

Transliteration conventions for writing systems of the same type, e.g. the Greek and Latin alphabets, pose no conceptual difficulties (table 20). Transliteration conventions for structurally different writing systems are more problematic. For example, the various Romanization systems for Chinese, Japanese and Korean include elements of transcription in that the question underlying their construction, 'How shall this character be represented alphabetically?', is sometimes

I[1]	II[2]	III[3]	IV[4]
α	a	a	a
β	b	b	b
γ	g	g	g
γγ	ng	gg	gg
γκ	nk	gk	gk
γξ	nx	gx	gx
γχ	nch	gh	gch
δ	d	d	d
ε	e	e	e
ζ	z	z	z
η	e	ē	ē
θ	th	th	th
ι	i	i	i
κ	k	k	k
λ	l	l	l
μ	m	m	m
ν	n	n	n
ξ	x	x	x

I[1]	II[2]	III[3]	IV[4]
ο	o	o	o
π	p	p	p
ρ	r	r	r
σ, ς	s	s	s
τ	t	t	t
υ[5]	y	u	y
φ	ph	f	ph
χ	ch	h	ch
ψ	ps	ps	ps
ω	o	ō	ō
’[6]			
‘[7]	h	‘	h
´[8]		´	´
`[8]		`	`
-[8]		-	-
., ι[9]		j	.
-[8]		¨	¨

[1]Greek letters (minuscules) and diacritics; [2]transcription; [3]ISO transliteration; [4]Classicists' transliteration; [5]αυ, ευ are au, eu in II and IV. ηυ is eu in II and ēu in IV; [6]Not transliterated or transcribed. [7]In front of geminate Vs; [8]Not transcribed. [9]Subscript iota is not in II, is, postposed j in III, and is underdot in IV.

Table 20 Roman transliteration and transcription of Classical Greek. Column heads: (I) Greek letters (minuscules) and diacritics (II) transcription (III) ISO transliteration (IV) classicists' transliteration

superseded by another, 'How shall this unit of speech be represented alphabetically?' Thus, transliteration has not always been clearly distinguished from transcription.

However, for the scientific study of epigraphic and palaeographic texts, for lexicographic purposes, and for cataloguing of reference systems, it is important that this distinction is not ignored. A great variety of transliteration systems have been designed for such objectives, and in many fields competing systems are in use. For example, biblicists and linguists use different systems for transliterating Hebrew texts in Roman letters. The most widely used systems today are those

developed by the International Organization for Standardization (ISO) and the Library of Congress.
See also SCRIPT REFORM.
Reading Wellish 1975; ISO 1955; Jones 1807; Chasseboeuf Volney 1818.

trigrams A notation system of the *I Ching*, the Book of Changes, of the sixth century BCE. In China's intellectual history the idea that things resonate with one another has a long tradition. It is this idea which finds expression in the *I Ching's* trigrams which are supposed to mirror all the processes of nature. The symbols are formed as sets of lines, perhaps originally representing long and short sticks used in divination. The possible combinations of the lines yield eight trigrams (sets consisting of three lines) and 64 hexagrams (six-lined sets). These symbols, which are known as *kua*, are arranged in a fixed order in the book. Each *kua* has a name and is associated with a number of concepts, as shown in table 21. Taken together, all *kua* provide a repository of concepts which are the basis of a cosmology which links human relations with nature (figure 11).

trigraph A sequence of three letters representing a single phoneme. Examples are German <sch> for /š/ as in *Schiff* 'ship', and French <eau> for /o:/ as in *oiseau* 'bird'.
See also GRAPHEME–PHONEME CORRESPONDENCE.

tuğra An imperial monogram written in special calligraphic style, used by Ottoman sultans (figure 12). *Tuğras* were designed by celebrated calligraphers, since the Ottomans held calligraphy to be the noblest of the arts.
See also CALLIGRAPHY; SIGNATURE.

Turkic runes Also known as 'Siberian' or 'Yenisey' runes, the Turkic runes appear to be the earliest form of writing any variety of Turkish. The relationship of this writing with the Nordic, Germanic or Anglo-Saxon runes is unclear, if there is one at all. The name is motivated in a certain formal resemblance of the letters which, like the runes proper, are linear and angular in appearance. The place and time of origin of this script, which is documented in stone inscriptions found in Orchon and other parts of Siberia, are still obscure. Two slightly different varieties of the script can be distinguished, that of the Orchon inscriptions (early eighth century CE) and that of the Yenisey inscriptions (late eighth century) (table 22). Genealogically, the script is an offshoot of the SOGDIAN WRITING to which some 20 extra signs were added for Old Turkish sounds. Inscriptions are mostly from right to left, but under Chinese influence the script has also been written vertically with the letters turned 90 degrees. Epigraphic material is very limited. Manuscript fragments discovered in eastern Turkestan suggest that Turkic runes were also used as a book hand, although not for long. By the ninth century the Turkic people of south Siberia and Central Asia used the UIGHUR WRITING.
Reading Doblhofer 1957.

Turkish writing From the conversion of the Turks to Islam until the 1920s, Ottoman Turkish was written in the rather unsuitable Perso-Arabic script. In particular, the indication of Vs was never satisfactory, but certain consonantal

Trigram Name	Kinship	Animal	Natural entity	Element	Compass point
乾	father	dragon	heaven	metal	S
坤	mother	mare	earth	earth	N
雲	eldest son	horse	thunder	wood	NE
坎	second son	pig	moon	water	W
艮	youngest son	dog	mountain	wood	NW
巽	eldest daughter	hen	wind	wood	SW
離	second daughter	pheasant	lightning	fire	E
兌	youngest daughter	sheep	sea	water	SE

Table 21 Trigrams each relating to the Chinese character of its name, a kinship relation, an animal, a natural entity, an element and a compass point

distinctions such as that between voiced and voiceless velar stops, /g/ and /k/, were also left unmarked. Apart from all political and cultural considerations, it was not difficult, therefore, to argue that a reform of Turkish writing was desirable.

Under President Kemal Atatürk (1881–1938) a script reform was enacted as part of his government's secularization and Westernization programme. A slightly modified form of the Roman alphabet was adopted as the obligatory alphabet of

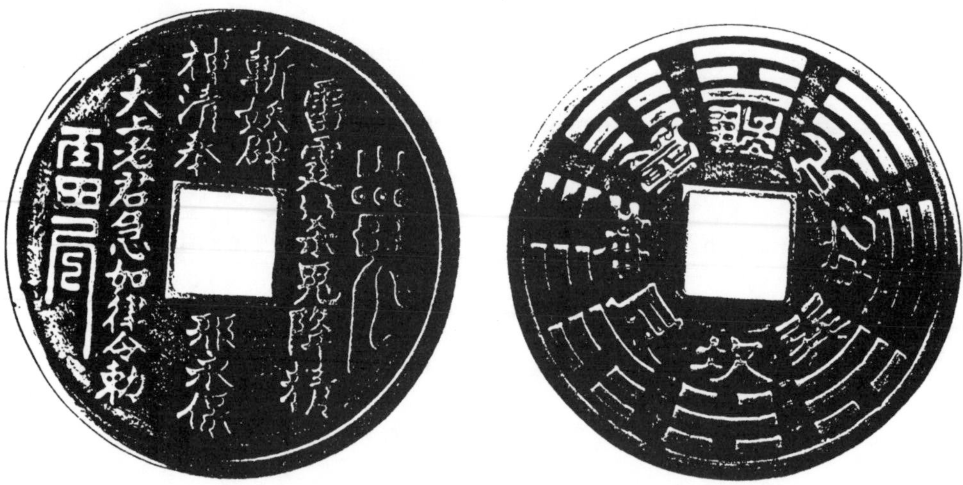

Figure 11 A coin with the eight trigrams on one side and a charm to guard against evil spirits on the other

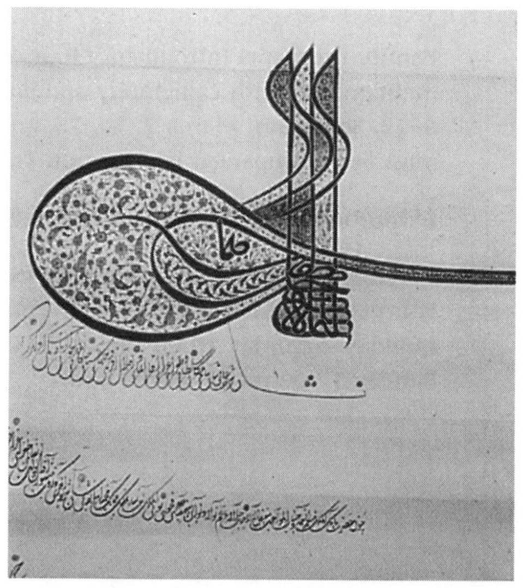

Figure 12 Illuminated tŭgra *of Süleyman the Magnificent decorated with flowers, dated 1552 (Topkapi Palace Museum, Istanbul)*

Turkish in 1928–9. As regards its implementation and acceptance by the population, the script reform was a success. The adjustment of the alphabet could arguably have been better.

The Turkish alphabet includes one non-Roman letter, the undotted <ı>, in addition to <i>, which retains the dot when capitalized <İ>. It also uses the following diacritics: <ö, ü, ç, ş, ğ>. Grapheme–phoneme correspondence is consistent and simple, although some sound values are somewhat unexpected: <c> = [dʒ]; <ç> = [tš]; <ş> = [š]; <j> = [ʒ]. The letter [ğ], *yamuşak* or 'soft g', is polyvalent: it lengthens a preceding V to give [γ] after back Vs, i.e. <a, ı, o, u>,

Orchon	Yenisei	
		A
		e
		I
		U
		Ü
		j̣
		j̣
		ḅ
		ḅ
		č
		č
		ḍ
		ḍ
		g̣
		g̣
		ḷ
		ḷ
		m
		ṇ
		ṇ
		ŋ
		ǰ
		n͜č
		n͜d
		p
		ḳ
		ḳ
		ḳ
		ḳ
		ḳ
		ṛ
		ṛ
		ṣ
		ṣ
		š
		š
		ṭ
		ṭ
		z
		l͜d

Table 22 The Orchon and Yenisei varieties of the Turkic runes with Roman transliteration

and [j] after front Vs, i.e. <e, i, ö, ü>. In non-final position <'> represents the glottal stop, mainly in words of Arabic origin. The circumflex, too, is found primarily in Arabic and Persian loan words where it marks a long V and palatalization of preceding *l, k, g*. The letters <q, w, x> are absent. The sequence of the Turkish alphabet is: *a, b, c, ç, d, e, f, g, ğ, h, ı, i, j, k, l, m, n, o, ö, p, r, s, ş, t, u, ü, v, y, z.*

A broad phonetic representation is the principal level with regard to which orthographic conventions are defined. Some variations which are contextually determined by processes such as V harmony and syllable-final devoicing are represented in spelling, while other predictable variations are not. The orthography fails to indicate the unpredictable distribution of V length, except in the Arabic loan words where <^> is used.

See also SCRIPT REFORM.

Reading Heyd 1954; Underhill 1976.

type A rectangular, prism-shaped piece of metal adapted for use in letterpress printing (figure 13). The term 'type' also refers to the assemblage of characters used for printing. The face of the type is the mirror-image letter which holds the ink to be impressed on the paper. Wooden types were used in China and Central Asia several centuries before the advent of printing with movable type in Europe. Early metal types are known from twelfth-century Korea. In Europe, printing with movable type made its appearance in the mid-fifteenth century, an invention which is closely associated with Johannes GUTENBERG (figure 14). The unit of measurement of type is a point.

See also FONT; LETTER; POINT SIZE; PRINTING.

Reading Updike 1937.

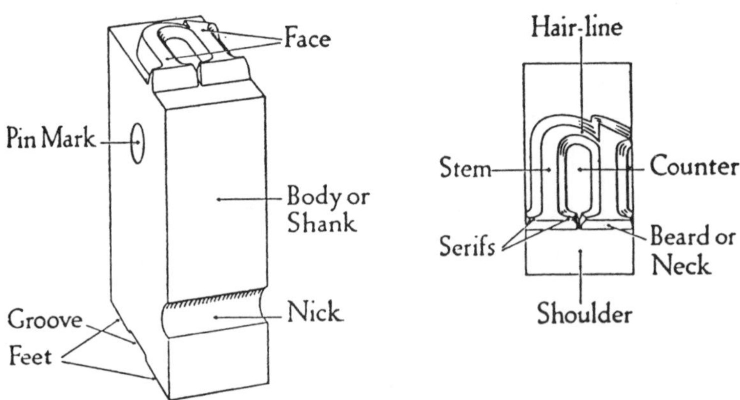

Figure 13 (left) Diagram of type and (right) plan of its face

typography **1** The craft of printing, involving composition, imposition and presswork. Early typographers did not immediately realize the potential of the new medium to change reading habits, but gradually the aesthetic demands of manuscript culture were augmented by those of greater visual economy. Thus words came to be arranged on the surface in ways not only pleasing to the eye, but also facilitating reading. Ever since, typography has been concerned with

zu hecuia Die dez keiſʒs võ cõſtãtinopel
was Alſo iſt ym begegent gar ein groſ
ſer has Vñ iſt dẽ turckẽ vil folkes nidd̃
gelegẽ Almechtig got du wolleſt diner
criſtẽheit plegẽ Vñ gnedeclich gebẽ crafft
fridd̃ vñ einikeit Vñ das ſie ſich mit ir
groſſen macht bereide Den vbeln turken
vñ ſin folck zuũtribẽ Vñ dz ſie ir keinen
lebendig laſſẽ blybẽ · wedd̃ in turky gre
cie aſye noch europa Dez helff vns die kõ
nigin maria Die do iſt ein muť d̃ heilgẽ
criſtẽheit Der ein ſwert pres mitlidens ir
hertz uſneit Do ir ſon in dotlichem vnge
mach Dirwont hãgẽ an dẽ crutz ſprach
Jch befelen dich dem iungern min Alſo
laſz dir die criſtenheit befolen ſin Vnd
bidde gnedeclich vor ſie in aller not Das
xiiij nuwe am himmel ſtat Vff dinſtag
noch nicolai des milden herren Vor mit
tage ſo ſehs ſtunde her zu heren
Eyn gut ſelig nuwe Jar

Figure 14 A page from Gutenberg's Türkenkalender *for 1455, printed in 1454, the oldest German print with movable type. The stripe through the bottom line is red in the original, for emphasis*

improving the quality of printed books by making them both more beautiful and easier to read. These efforts have engendered theories of letter deign which are concerned with sizes, proportions, letter forms (fonts), ligatures, layout and other graphic properties which affect the appearance of print (figure 15). As typographers designed new fonts, more options for the visual presentation of printed works became available. National preferences for type forms evolved – black letter and *Fraktur* in Germany, roman in France – and as these forms were associated with particular writing traditions they became symbolically charged, adding to written language an aesthetic dimension peculiar to the medium of print (figure 16). **2** A mode of writing contrasting with chirography, or handwriting. Typography is a specific representation of language with its own rules and regularities which can be studied and compared with the specifics of other modes of language representation. Typographic language differs in characteristic ways both from chirographic language and from speech.

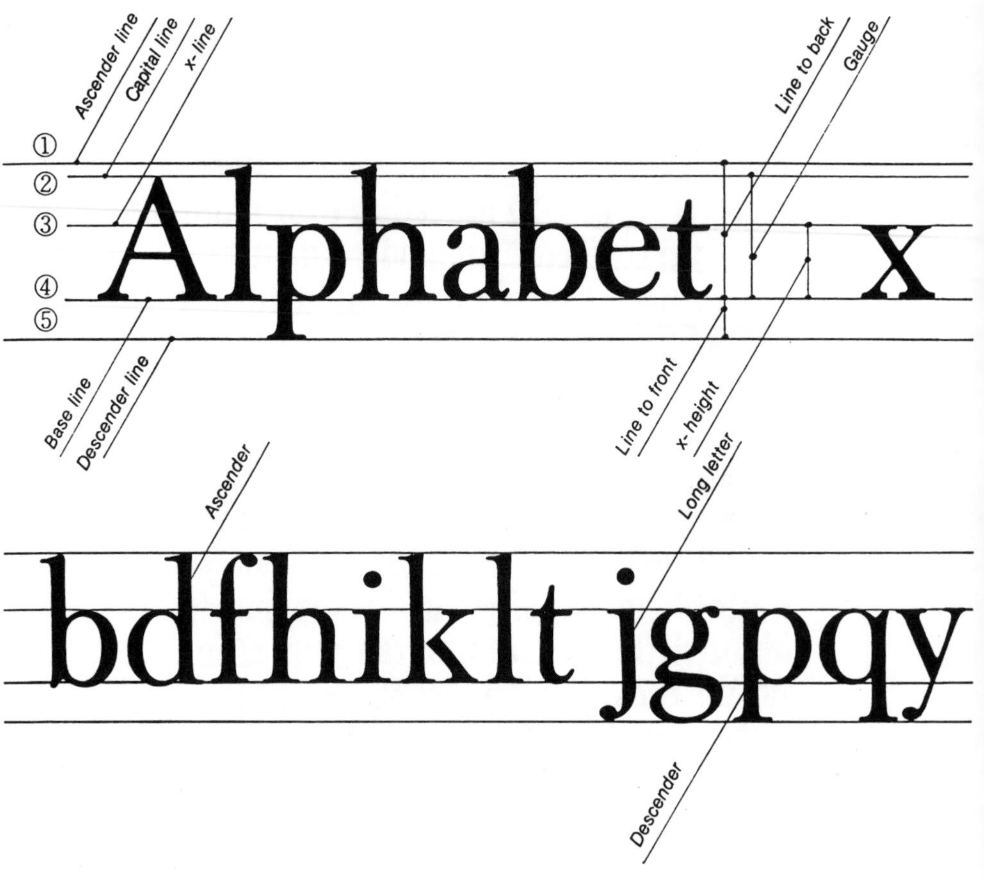

Figure 15 Roman type: how the letters are put on the line

FORCE

SÉRIEUX

MONUMENTALITÉ

MODERNISME

SIMPLICITÉ

Préciosité

FANTAISIE

ÉLÉGANCE

Archaisme

Figure 16 Typographic symbolism

LE TIERS LIVRE. FEVIL.XLIIII.

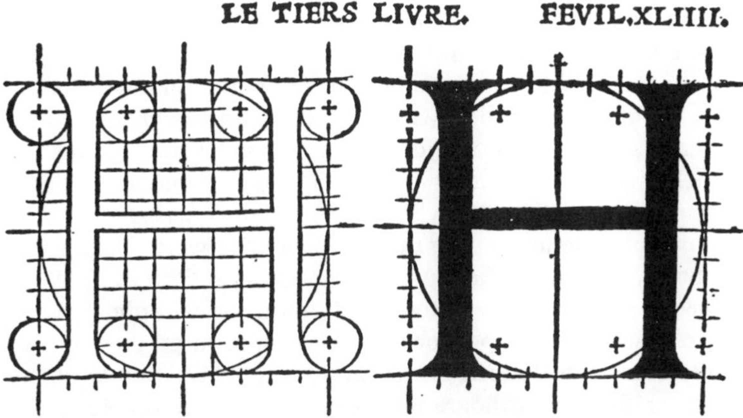

LA figure cy pres deſignee & faicte de le I. auec huit cẽtres, eſt de dix corps en Quarre. Ceſt a dire, auſſi large que haulte. Les Grammairiens, & meſmement ſelon Priſcian en ſon Premier liure ou il traicte De literarum poteſtate, diſent quelle neſt pas lettre, mais la note & enſeigne pour monſtrer quant quelque vocale, ou lune de ſes quatre conſones, C.P.R.T. doibt eſtre pronũcee graſſe & a plaine voix venant du profond de leſtomac. Iceluy Priſcian dit. H. autem aſpirationis eſt nota, & nihil aliud habet literæ, niſi figuram, & quod in vſu ſcribit inter alias lr̃as. Ceſt a dire. H. eſt la note de laſpiratiõ, & na aultre choſe deficace de lettre, ſi non la figure, & auſſi que par vſage elle eſt eſcripte. Priſciã.

H. a ſi peu de vertus auec les vocales, q̃ ſi on len oſte, le ſens ne ſera point diminue. mais ouy bien dauec leſſuſdictes quatre conſones. C.P.R.T. Exemple des vocales. Erennius. Oratius. Exemple deſdictes cõſones. Cremes pour Chremes. Et a ceſte cauſe comme dit Priſcian au ſuſdict lieu allegue, les Grecs ont faict ces ſuſdictes conſones aſpirees. Car pour Th, ilz ont faict Θ. pour Ph. Φ. pour Ch. X. Le Rho na point eſte mue de ſa figure, mais il prẽt ſus luy vne demye croix en lettres maiuſcules, ou vng point corbe en lettre courãt qui denote la dicte aſpiration. cõme on peult cleremẽt veoir es impreſſions du feu bon imprimeur Alde, que Dieu abſoille. Θ.Φ.Χ.Ρ. Alde.

AVlus Gellius au. III. Chapiſtre du Segõd liure de ſes nuyts Attiques dit, que H. a eſte miſe des Anciens & inſeree es dictions pour leur bailler vng ſon plus ferme & vigoreux quant il dit. H. litera, ſiue illam ſpiritũ magis quam literam dici oportet, inſerebant eam veteres noſtri pleriſq; vocibus verborũ firmandis roborãdiſq;, vt ſonus earum eſſet viridior vegetiorq;. Atq; id videntur feciſſe ſtudio & exemplo linguæ Atticæ. Satis notum eſt Attiquos ιχθυν ηρον. Multa itidẽ alia citra morẽ gentiũ Græciæ cæterarũ inſpirãtis primæ literæ dixiſſe ſic, lachrymas, ſic ſpechulũ, ſic ahenũ, ſic vehemẽs, ſic ichoare, ſic helluari, ſic hallucinari, ſic honera, ſic honuſtũ dixerũt. In his verbis oĩbus literæ ſeu ſpũs iſti⁹ nulla ratio viſa eſt, niſi vt firmitas & vigor vocis quaſi quibuſdã neruis additis intẽderet. Ceſt a dire. La lr̃e H. ou ſil conuiẽt myeulx la dire leſperit vocal, eſtoit ſouuãt iſeree des Anciẽs Latins en beaucop de dictiõs pour les firmer & roborer, afin q̃ leur ſon fuſt pl⁹ vertueux & vigoureux. Iceulx Anciẽs le faiſoiẽt a limitatiõ des Atheniẽs, au lãgage deſq̃lz ιχθυν ηρον. & beaucop de ſẽblables dictions eſtoiẽt aſpirees hors la coſtume des aultres Nations de Grece. Aiſi furẽt aſpirez Lachrymæ, ſpechulũ, ahenũ, vehemẽs, ichoare, hallucinari honera, & honuſt⁹. En ces vocables ſuſeſcripts laſpiratiõ na eſte veue raiſonna Aulus Gellius.

I.ij.

Figure 17 A page from Geofroy Tory's Champfleury, *Paris, 1529*

Since the sixteenth century, which is sometimes called typography's golden age, typography has exercised a major influence on written language and, however indirectly, also on speech. Most noticeably, it has greatly promoted standardization. That texts could be multiplied with little effort in exactly the same form fostered the idea that there was or should be one correct form. Early typographers were much aware of the fact that their craft gave language a potentially more stable form, transcending the whims of individual writers. They felt entitled to play an active role in shaping the language they were dealing with and in some cases had a profound effect on its orthography. For example, Geofroy Tory (born *c.*1480 in Bourges), one of the most famous typographers, who wrote *Champfleury*, a treatise on the proportions of letters, introduced the accent marks, apostrophe and cedilla into French orthography (figure 17). Similarly, some of the peculiarities of English orthography are directly attributable to William CAXTON's early typographic work. Thus, rather than being limited to a merely subservient role, typography exercised an active influence on the development of LITERACY and literary culture in Europe.

See also FONT; INCUNABULA; MAJUSCULE; MINUSCULE; PRINTING; TYPE.

Reading Sutton and Bartram 1968; Eisenstein 1979; Ong 1977.

typology of writing systems Writing systems have been typologically classified on the basis of various criteria reflecting theoretical differences in the analysis of how writing systems work and what they represent. The first problem is that of demarcating writing from its precursors and other visual notations. There is wide agreement in recent scholarship that the critical feature which distinguishes writing proper from other visual signs such as PETROGLYPHS, QUIPUS, TALLIES and isolated PICTOGRAMS is a stable conventional relationship between written sign and language. This is generally understood to mean systematically specifiable units of language, although in at least one typology a general relationship between pictograms and narrative content is recognized as writing: Hill (1967) classifies Amerindian pictograms as 'discourse writing'. Assuming that such a vague relationship between signs and language does not qualify as writing, the task of a typology based on grapho-linguistic relations is to determine the linguistic unit most relevant for a given writing system.

There is considerable diversity in this regard between the different typologies that have been proposed. For example, Gelb (1963) classifies Phoenician, Hebrew, Arabic, Linear B, *kana* and Cherokee as syllabic, whereas in DeFrancis's (1989) typology Linear B, *kana* and Cherokee are identified as cases of pure syllabic systems as distinct from pure consonantal systems such as Phoenician, Hebrew and Arabic. Chinese, too, is variously classified as logographic morphemic (Sampson 1985), morphemic (Hill 1967) and morphosyllabic (DeFrancis 1989). The typological position of the EGYPTIAN WRITING SYSTEM is a matter of dispute: Gelb designates it as word syllabic, Hill as morphemic and DeFrancis as morphoconsonantal.

Two important insights follow from such discrepancies. One is that, if at all meaningful, typologies are necessarily theoretically informed and selective, focusing on particular properties of writing systems rather than on others.

That writing systems are classified differently by different researchers, therefore, reflects different theoretical goals and definitions.

At the same time, it is also evident that the phenomena under consideration allow for different kinds of classification. This is so because, no matter on what criteria a typology is based, writing systems rarely embody a specific type in its pure form. Historically grown systems that they are, they tend to make use of different principles in representing language. Most writing systems are mixed, either in the sense that they use signs of different kinds (e.g. morphographic *kanji* and syllabographic *kana* in Japanese), or in the sense that the structural level of language on which the elementary signs of a system are defined is not the only one on which they operate. The latter is true of most alphabetic systems: not only phonemic distinctions but also morphophonemic, morphemic or lexical distinctions are commonly indicated. In INDIAN WRITING SYSTEMS the unit of coding is the syllable, but the unit of the underlying analysis is the segment. This is why in this dictionary these systems are classified as SYLLABIC ALPHABETS.

Thus, a typology based on minimal units of representation – morphemes, syllables, phonemes – must be augmented by stating how these units are used. A first distinction can be drawn between PLEREMIC WRITING and CENEMIC WRITING. Pleremic signs denote both linguistic meaning and form, while cenemic signs are devoid of meaning and denote only linguistic form. Fully developed pleremic systems invariably use cenemic signs also. Cenemic systems include syllabaries and alphabets. Both of these major pleremic and cenemic categories can be further subclassified, yielding the seven types listed below together with examples. For pleremic systems the way in which logograms are supplemented provides a suitable criterion. Different types of cenemic systems can be distinguished on the basis of the mode of V indication.

Pleremic
Logograms + phonograms Hittite hieroglyphic, with some 400 elementary signs, of which 50 are used as phonograms.
Logograms + phonograms + determinatives Sumerian-Akkadian cuneiform, with some 2,000 elementary signs, a number which was gradually reduced to 200 used at any one time and place.
Morphosyllabic signs Chinese, with some 50,000 elementary signs, of which 3,000 to 8,000 are used at any one time.

Cenemic
Syllabary Japanese *kana*, with 46 elementary signs each denoting a (C)V unit.
Consonant alphabet Phoenician, with 22 elementary signs for Cs only.
Syllabic alphabet Devanāgarī (for Sanskrit), with 48 elementary signs, 13 for Vs and 35 for Cs with inherent *a*, plus V diacritics.
Alphabet Latin, with 26 elementary signs, five for Vs and 21 for Cs.

See also ALPHABET; LOGOGRAM; ORTHOGRAPHY; PHONOGRAPHY; SCRIPT; SYLLABOGRAPHY.

Reading Cohen 1958; Voegelin and Voegelin 1961; Gelb 1963; Hill 1967; Pulgram 1976; Sampson 1985; Coulmas 1989; DeFrancis 1989.

U

U, u /ju:/ The twenty-first letter of the English alphabet derives from Semitic *wāw* through Greek *upsilon* (Υ, υ). Etruscan had its own letter for the same sound, a more pointed *V*, which came to be used in Latin interchangeably with *U*. A clear differentiation of the two only developed in medieval Latin.

Ugaritic alphabet Often called 'the oldest alphabet of the world', the Ugaritic script is a C alphabet consisting of 30 letters, each written as one or several wedges of the cuneiform type. A Semitic language closely related to Phoenician, Ugaritic is so called after the city state where it was spoken in northern Syria at the Mediterranean coast, close to present-day Ras eš-Šamra. A centre of overland and maritime trade, Ugarit flourished in the fourteenth and thirteenth centuries BCE. It was destroyed by invaders from the sea in 1200 BCE. As attested in numerous documents which have been excavated since 1928, the residents of Ugarit included other Semites, Egyptians, Minoans, Hurrians and Hittites, in addition to the local population. Various languages and writing systems were commonly used in this ancient port town, a fertile ground for designing a script to write the local language. This happened no later than in fourteenth century BCE.

Archaeological evidence suggests that, rather than being the result of a long development, the Ugaritic alphabet was created suddenly. In 1949 a student tablet was discovered at Ugarit which lists the signs in the order of the PHOENICIAN ALPHABET (figure 1). From this it must be concluded that the Phoenician alphabet or some Canaanite variety existed at the time and was known in Ugarit. However, the Ugaritic script differs from all other west Semitic scripts: it consists of cuneiform signs. Thus Ugaritic combines the outer form of the east Semitic, Akkadian-Babylonian tradition of writing with the inner form of the west Semitic, Canaanite-Phoenician tradition of C alphabets.

The Ugaritic alphabet has 30 signs, eight and seven more than Phoenician and Hebrew, respectively (table 1). This reflects a richer inventory of Cs, as is found in other Semitic languages, for example Arabic. Moreover, while the west Semitic alphabets consist of C letters only, Ugaritic has three signs for *'āleph* with vocalic values /a/, /i/ and /u/. Thus *ugrt*, the name of the city, is written 𐎜𐎙𐎗𐎚. The extra *'āleph* signs for /i/ and /u/, as well as the infrequently occurring letter for the second *s* which has proved hard to phonetically specify exactly, are thought to have been added to the original 27-letter alphabet. At a later stage some phonological distinctions were neutralized, and as a result the alphabet was simplified. Letter 21 dropped out, and letters 10 and 11 as well as 27 and 30 were fused into one.

The forms of Ugaritic letters seem to be freely invented. Derivational relationships for individual letters with other cuneiform scripts have not been established. During the period it was used, the script was stable, undergoing no substantial changes. The direction of writing, mostly on clay tablets, is typically

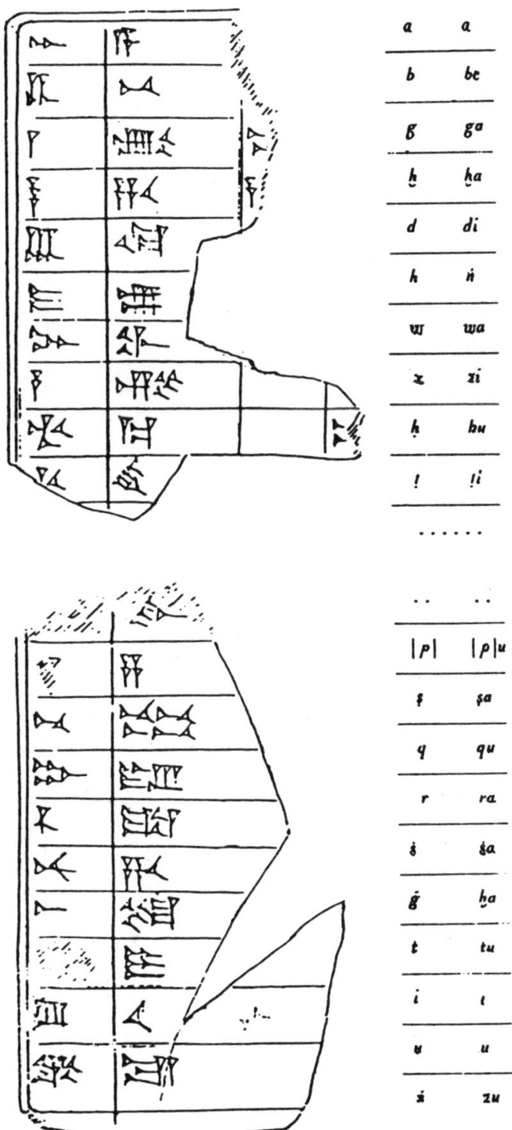

Figure 1 (left) A school tablet of the Ugaritic alphabet with (right) Akkadian key and transliteration
Source: *adapted from Virolleaud 1957*

from left to right, reflecting Akkadian usage. Only a few documents are written in Canaanite fashion from right to left. Words are often divided by a perpendicular stroke. Otherwise there is no punctuation.

The DECIPHERMENT of the Ugaritic script was accomplished within a couple of years of its discovery by Charles Virolleaud, Hans Bauer and Édouard Dhorme. Despite some remaining uncertainties about the exact sound values of individual

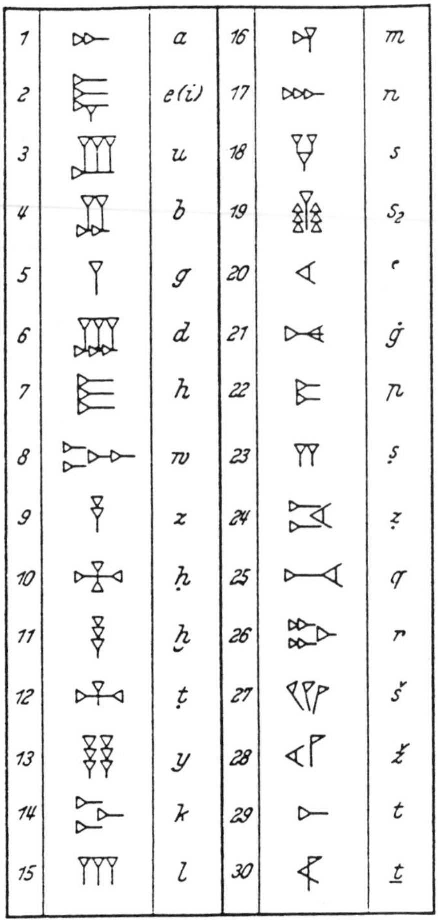

1		a	16		m
2		e(i)	17		n
3		u	18		s
4		b	19		s_2
5		g	20		ʿ
6		d	21		ġ
7		h	22		p
8		w	23		ṣ
9		z	24		ẓ
10		ḥ	25		q
11		ḫ	26		r
12		ṭ	27		š
13		y	28		ž
14		k	29		t
15		l	30		ṯ

Table 1 The sign inventory of the Ugaritic script

letters, for instance 14, 19 and 30, their work has made accessible an important part of ancient Semitic literature.

See also CUNEIFORM WRITING; SEMITIC WRITING.

Reading Virolleaud 1957; Segert 1984; Millard 1986.

Uighur writing The name 'Uighur' refers to a group of Turkic languages of Central Asia. Modern Uighur belongs to the east Turkic branch and is mainly spoken in the Xinjiang Uygur Autonomous Region, China, and in Kazakhstan. It was only in 1921 that at a conference in Tashkent the people of west Turkestan decided to call their language 'Uighur' (*Ujğur tili*). The name was subsequently adopted in Xinjiang, China. Modern Uighur is related to but not directly derived from Old Uighur, which belongs to the north Turkic branch and served as a major administrative language in Chinese Turkestan. The Old Uighur (also Uyghur) or Uighur Turkish script derives from the cursive Sogdian script, itself an offshoot of the 22-letter Aramaic alphabet which Persian colonists brought to Chinese Turkestan. It evolved gradually in the eighth century CE as a result of the attempt to write Turkish with the Sogdian alphabet. Because of differences between the sound systems of the two languages, certain adjustments were necessary. The Sogdian letters for *d, ṭ,* ʿ and *q* were omitted, while a letter for *l* was added. In Sogdian *l* was represented by the Aramaic letter for *r*, while *lāmedh* was used for *đ*. This practice was apparently continued in Uighur, although doubts remain about the exact sound value of this letter. In any event, a new letter was created for *l* by adding a diacritic mark to that of *r*, hence called 'hooked *rēš*' (*rēš* being the Semitic name of the letter). Spelling conventions in Sogdian and Uighur differ in a number of points, largely reflecting phonological differences. As in other Turkic languages, voiced and voiceless stops are distinct in Uighur, but since the Sogdian alphabet had no letters for *b* and *g*, those for *k* and *t* were made to serve a double function in Uighur. Further, the velar nasal /ŋ/ is represented in Uighur by the digraph *nk*, a combination which represents /ṁk/ in Sogdian. Like Sogdian, Uighur is written both horizontally, from right to left, and vertically, from top to bottom. In addition to the many manuscripts, printed books in Old Uighur have been preserved in considerable numbers (table 2, figure 2). Block prints of Old Uighur translations of Buddhist sūtras dating from the tenth century CE were found in Turfan, and as early as the fourteenth century the Uighurs made use of the Chinese invention of movable TYPE. Because they used an alphabet, the advantages of this technique could be better exploited in their writing than in Chinese.

As of the thirteenth century the Uighur script was adapted to the Mongolian language and thus became one of the most widely used scripts of medieval Asia. Modern Uighur was deliberately developed as a literary language written with the Arabic alphabet only in the twentieth century. In 1925 the Arabic alphabet was reformed in Soviet Turkestan, only to be replaced by the Latin in 1930, and eventually by the Cyrillic in 1947 (table 3). The Uighurs in Xinjiang adopted the Arabic alphabet after the foundation of the People's Republic of China in 1949. Attempts to introduce a Romanized orthography were made in the 1970s, but abandoned in the 1980s. Uighurs in China now use the Arabic alphabet.
See also MONGOLIAN WRITING; SOGDIAN WRITING; SYRIAC SCRIPTS.
Reading Sims-Williams 1981; Zieme 1991; Jarring 1981; Kao 1992.

Ukrainian alphabet A Slavonic language of the eastern branch, Ukrainian has developed a literary standard as of the early decades of the nineteenth century. Using the Cyrillic script, the Ukrainian alphabet is based on the Russian with the three additional letters є, I and Ї, but without Ë, ъ, ы and э (table 4).
See also CYRILLIC.
Reading Stechishin 1977.

Umbrian script *See* OLD ITALIC SCRIPTS; WORD BOUNDARY

umlaut [German *um* 'about' + *Laut* 'sound'] **1** A sound change which derives one V from another, as in *come* [kʌm] → *came* [keɪm]. **2** The diacritic <¨> to mark such a derivation in writing, for example in German orthography.
See also DIAERESIS.

Transliteration	10th C.	10th C.	1072	13th – 14th C.
1 ʾ				
2 β				
3 γ				
4 w				
5 z				
6 x				
7 y				
8 k				
9 d(δ)				
10 m				
11 n				
12 s				
13 p				
14 č				
15 r				
16 š				
17 t				
18 l				
19 ž				
20 -m				
21 q̋				

Table 2 Various forms of the Old Uighur alphabet from texts dating between the fourteenth and the tenth centuries BCE
Source: *adapted from Zieme 1991*

Figure 2 Fragment of a page of a Manichaean book in Uighur cursive script, eighth to ninth centuries CE *(Museum für Indische Kunst, Berlin)*

Roman	Arabic	Cyrillic	Value	Roman	Arabic	Cyrillic	Value
a	ئا ~ ا	а	a	v		в	v
b	ب	б	b	w	ۋ	в	v, w
c	(تس)	ц	ts‘, ts	x	ش	ш	ʃ
d	د	д	d	y	ي	й	j
e	ئې ~ ې	е	e	z	ز	з	z
f	ف	ф	f	ƣ	غ	ғ	ʁ
g	گ	г	g	ⱨ	ھ	h	h
h	خ	х	χ	ⱪ	ق	қ	q
i	ئى ~ ى	и	i	ə	ئە ~ ە	ә	ɛ
j	ج	ж	dʒ	ɵ	ئۆ ~ ۆ	ө	ø
k	ك	к	k	ü	ئۈ ~ ۈ	у	y
l	ل	л	l	ⱬ	ژ	ж	ʒ
m	م	м	m	ng	ڭ	ң	ŋ
n	ن	н	n	zh	(جژ)		tʂ
o	ئو ~ و	о	o	ch	چ		tʂ‘
p	پ	п	p	sh	ش		ʂ
q	چ	ч	tʃ			щ	ʃ′tʃ′
r	ر	р	r			ы	ɨ
s	س	с	s			ё	jo
t	ت	т	t			ю	ju
u	ئۇ ~ ۇ	у	u			я	ja

Table 3 The modern Uighur alphabets

uncial [Lat. *litterae unciales* 'inch-long letters'] The origin of the term is not quite clear, although it seems to refer to the measure *unciālis* 'of one-twelfth'. It is a MAJUSCULE form of writing used as a book hand for Christian manuscripts from the fourth to the sixth centuries, after which it was superseded by the half-uncial. Uncials developed from cursive styles in the fourth century CE. It is distinguished from Roman capital by large rounded forms of certain letters, especially *A, D, E, H* and *M* (figure 3). The shapes of uncial letters are thought to have been influenced by Byzantine art. Greek uncials are characteristic of many medieval manuscripts (figure 4).
See also ROMAN ALPHABET.
Reading Bischoff 1986.

underdot A diacritic <.> placed under a letter. Of its diverse uses the most important are as follows:

Ukranian		Transliteration	Ukranian		Transliteration
А	а	a	О	о	o
Б	б	b	П	п	p
В	в	v	Р	р	r
Г	г	h	С	с	s
Ґ	ґ	g	Т	т	t
Д	д	d	У	у	u
Е	е	e	Ф	ф	f
Є	є	je	Х	х	x
Ж	ж	ž	Ц	ц	c
З	з	z	Ч	ч	č
И	и	y	Ш	ш	š
І	і	i	Щ	щ	šč
Ї	ї	ji	Ю	ю	ju
Й	й	j	Я	я	ja
К	к	k	Ь	ь	'
Л	л	l		'	''
М	м	m			
Н	н	n			

Table 4 The Ukrainian alphabet

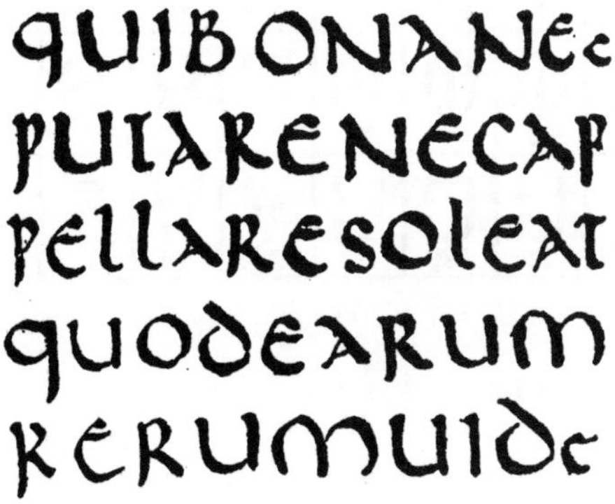

```
qui bona nec
putare nec ap
pellare soleat
quod earum
rerum vide[atur]
```

Figure 3 Specimen of Latin uncial majuscules: Cicero, De republica, *fourth century* CE

Figure 4 Greek uncials

1 In the transliteration of Indic scripts, of both Indo-Aryan and Dravidian languages, it indicates retroflex articulation of the letter so marked.
2 In Semitic philology, it denotes velarization or pharyngealization of 'emphatic' Cs.
3 IPA usage is to indicate higher V quality.

Unifon A phonemic transcription system devised in 1959 by John Malone from Chicago as a transitory alphabet intended to facilitate the learning of English spelling in first- and second-language classrooms. The 40-letter Unifon alphabet makes use of 18 new letters and eliminates two old ones, <q> and <x> (table 5). The idea is to use it as a pronunciation key in English dictionaries, thus bridging the gap between speech and spelling. Simple though it is, Unifon has not attracted many followers, and, like other script reform proposals, its chances of challenging the established standard spelling conventions are slim.
See also BERNARD SHAW ALPHABET; ENGLISH SPELLING; SCRIPT REFORM; SPELLING REFORM.

AT	ATE	ALL	BOW	CHAIR	DIP	HEN	HE	HER	FAST
GOAT	HAT	BIT	BITE	JAW	KISS	LOW	MUSIC	NO	KING
LOT	OLD	LOOK	OUT	BOY	PIPE	RUN	CELL SAY	SURE	TABLE
THERE	THIRST	UP	DUE	YOU	VEST	WIG	AZURE	YES	ZEBRA

Table 5 Unifon, a transitory alphabet for English

universal alphabet *See* VISIBLE SPEECH.

universal writing Since antiquity philosophers have been intrigued by the idea of developing a universal notation unrestricted by the arbitrary limitations of individual languages. Such a universal writing should be able to be read in any language. A measure of success was achieved only in mathematical notation and to some extent in logic, although the idea of a PASIGRAPHY was more ambitious. Through his interest in logic Leibniz was motivated to propose a project for a *characteristica universalis* by which he meant an alphabet of human thought. For some time he was led, erroneously, to believe that the Chinese writing system could serve as the basis of a universal writing. Other scholars who pursued the idea realized that no language-dependent writing system could serve as a starting

point. Early in the nineteenth century Juan Egaña in his *Ocios filosoficos y poéticos en la quinta de las delicias* remarked that Chinese CHARACTERS, Peruvian QUIPUS and Egyptian HIEROGLYPHS were all unsuitable as a model. Instead he proposed a system based on 20 thought categories. Frege's *Begriffsschrift* (1879) can also be understood as an outgrowth of the desire to visually represent conceptual relations by exploiting the two-dimensional character of the printed page (with antecedent and consequent of a conditional written on separate lines). However, the notion of a universal notation cannot strictly speaking be subsumed under writing proper, because by definition writing is representation of language, which inevitably means that, in one way or another, all writing systems refer to linguistic form – which is what universal writing is intended to avoid.
See also TYPOLOGY OF WRITING SYSTEMS.
Reading Patzig 1969.

universals of writing Design features shared by all writing systems due to physical conditions of the visual medium or structural conditions of their construction. Universals of writing can be understood as defining criteria of what writing is. Research into universals of writing is still in its infancy, but the following four features have been proposed as candidates of universals:

Language representation Writing systems operate on different levels and emphasize different units of language, but like speech they all serve the function of giving language a material form. Writing represents language rather than ideas. One of the major tasks of the study of writing is hence to determine how a given writing system represents a given language. Since all writing systems have come into existence in the context of a given language, they are biased in selectively reflecting some structural features rather than others.
Discreteness Every writing system is an abstraction incorporating a linguistic analysis. This analysis necessarily breaks up the continuum of speech into discrete visible segments. These segments may have internal graphical structures which correspond to nothing in the linguistic units they represent. Because analysis and transcoding from the auditory into the visual medium require segmentation, writing is always selective and incomplete with respect to speech.
Finite signary Every writing system consists of a finite set of basic symbols which are combined with each other in linear sequence according to fixed conventions. A finite set of symbols cannot represent an infinite variety of speech forms. Rather than mapping a specific pronunciation, writing is a model of speech which can be realized in a broad range of different ways.
Permanence In contradistinction to the ephemeral nature of oral language, the visual materialization of language is relatively permanent. In writing, language is given a fixed form. On the level of linguistic structure this implies that, as time goes by, GRAPHEME–PHONEME CORRESPONDENCES tend to get more complicated as speech evolves, while writing preserves established forms much longer. On the social level the permanence of writing translates into resistance to change, in extreme cases leading to a diglossic split between spoken and written language.

See also DIGLOSSIA; PHONETIZATION; TYPOLOGY OF WRITING SYSTEMS.
Reading DeFrancis 1989; Coulmas 1989.

upper case The compositor's type case in which capital letters, reference marks and accent marks are kept. Also, the capital letters on a typewriter or word-processor keyboard.

Urartian writing Closely related to Hurrian, Urartian was spoken north of Assyria in the Lake Van area between 1500 and 500 BCE. It was written in Assyrian cuneiform with minor adjustments. A distinguishing feature is that in Assyrian crossing wedges are superimposed one over the other, while in Urartian horizontal wedges are usually written separately when crossed by vertical ones. The oldest inscriptions date from the ninth century BCE, when bilingual Urartian scribes first adapted the cuneiform script to their own language. Decipherment was facilitated by a couple of bilingual Assyrian–Urartian inscriptions. The direction of Urartian writing, like that of Assyrian, is from left to right. The script comprises SYLLABOGRAMS, DETERMINATIVES and LOGOGRAMS. Under the influence of Assyrian writing, the Urartian scribes also used many SUMEROGRAMS. *See also* CUNEIFORM WRITING.
Reading Diakonoff and Starostin 1986.

Urdu writing The national language of Pakistan and the major language of Indian Muslims, Urdu is an offshoot of Dakani (also Delhavi), a seventeenth-century literary language of north India which is also the forebear of Hindi. Increasing Persianization since the early eighteenth century, the writing of Dakani literature in Perso-Arabic script, and the conscious attempt to eradicate Braj Bhasha or indigenous Hindi elements from the language, all contributed to the emergence of Urdu as a separate language. In the nineteenth century the replacement of Persian by Urdu as an official language of British India further consolidated the status of Urdu. Linguistic commonalities with Hindi are still very strong, but the sociosymbolic differences are highlighted by the two different scripts, DEVANĀGARĪ for HINDI WRITING and a modified form of Perso-Arabic for Urdu. The latter is moreover associated with Muslim religion, strongly adding to divergent communal attitudes.

The adaptation of the Perso-Arabic alphabet to Urdu made some modifications necessary. It consists of 35 letters, plus a number of supplementary signs (table 6). In addition to the four Persian letters which were added to the 28-letter Arabic alphabet – those for *p, c, ž* and *g* – three extra letters were created for Urdu, i.e. those for t^h, d^h and *ṛ*. Since diacritics are a systematic component of the Arabic alphabet, this was possible without upsetting the graphic equilibrium of the script. Several letters share a basic form, e.g. those for *b, p, t* and t^h as well as those for *j, c, h* and *x*. The four respective members of these two sets are distinguished from each other by dots written above, below or inside the basic form. Most letters have variant shapes for independent, initial, medial and final position.

The Cs of the language are all represented in writing, some redundantly by two different letters. This is a result of the neutralization of certain phonological differences between Urdu and Arabic loan words which, as in other languages using the Arabic script, are written as they are in Arabic. Thus ط /t/, ث /s/, ض /z/ and ح /h/ occur in Arabic or Persian loan words, whereas ت /t/, س /s/, ز /z/ and ه /h/ are their counterparts for native words.

ا	ā	خ	x	ش	š	ک	k
ب	b	د	d	ص	s	گ	g
پ	p	ده	d^h	ض	z	ل	l
ت	t	ذ	z	ط	t	م	m
ٿ	t^h	ر	r	ظ	z	ن	n
ث	s	ڙ	ṛ	ع	ʻ	و	v, ū
ج	j	ز	z	غ	ɣ	ہ	h
چ	c	ژ	ž	ف	f	ی	y, ē
ح	h	س	s	ق	q		

Table 6 The Urdu alphabet in naskhī *script: independent letter forms*

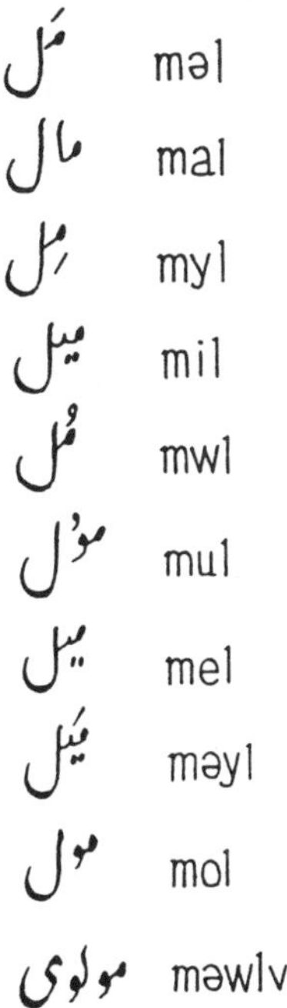

- məl
- mal
- myl
- mil
- mwl
- mul
- mel
- məyl
- mol
- məwlvi

Table 7 Urdu vowel diacritics, illustrated for the syllable m + V + l

Long Vs are generally indicated by assigning C graphemes secondary values: *alif,* the first letter, for /ā/, *v* for /ō/ and /ū/, and *y* for /ī/, /ē/, /ai/ (table 7). A variant form of the letter /y/, ے, is used to distinguish final /ē, ai/ from final /ī/. These are not distinguished, however, word internally. Short Vs are usually not written at all, although the signary includes diacritics for these as well: *zabar,* a stroke placed above a C letter for /a/; *zeer,* a stroke placed below a C letter for /i/; and *peeš*, a hook placed above a C letter for /u/. Yet another diacritic, *jazm*, a semicircle placed above a C letter, indicates the absence of a V following the C so marked. Similarly, nasalization is indicated by a diacritic. Two oblique strokes placed above a final *alif* denote /ã/ or /an/.

Following Arabic and Persian practice, the direction of Urdu writing is from right to left, but Urdu numerals are written from left to right. Commonly used punctuation marks are as follows: a dash is used for a full stop; an inverted comma for a comma; an inverted question mark for a question mark; and a semicolon turned 180 degrees for a semicolon. Special ornamental symbols are used in poetry (figure 5).

Reading Bright and Khan 1976; Mobbs 1981.

رات یُوں دِل میں تری کھوئی ہُوئی یاد آئی
جیسے وِیرانے میں چُپکے سے بہار آجائے
جیسے صحراؤں میں ہَولے سے چلے بادِ نسیم
جیسے بیمار کو بے وجہ قرار آجائے

Transliteration

Ash'ār
Rāt yūṅ dil meṅ tĕrī kho'ī hū'ī yād ā'ī
Jaise vīrāne meṅ chupke-se bahār ā-jā'e,
Jaise ṣaḥrāon meṅ haule-se chale bād-e-nasīm,
Jaise bīmār ko be-vajh qarār ā-jā'e.

Translation

Last Night
Last night your faded memory filled my heart
Like spring's calm advent in the wilderness,
Like the soft desert footfalls of the breeze,
Like peace somehow coming to a sick man.

Figure 5 Specimen of Urdu writing: poem by Faiz Ahmad Faiz, 1911–84 (courtesy Tariq Rahman)

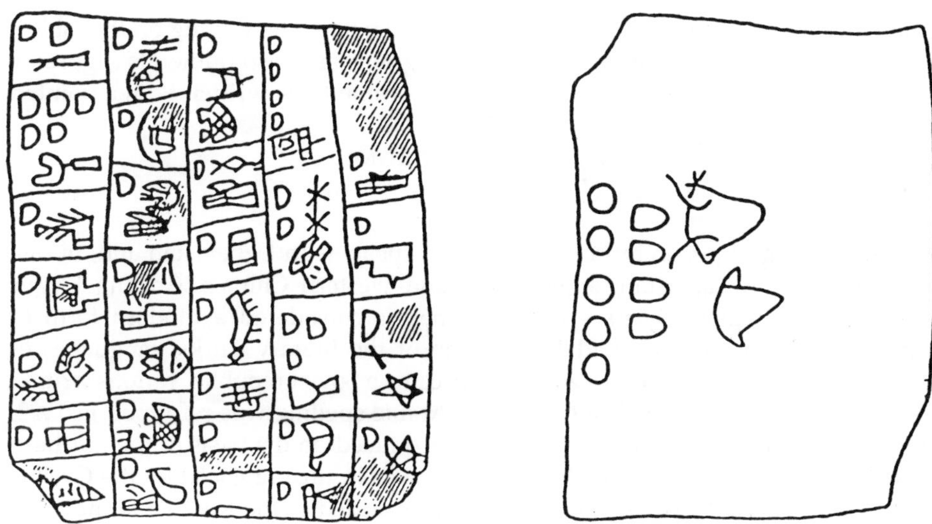

Figure 6 Archaic Uruk tablet

Uruk Archaeological site in southern Mesopotamia on the bank of the Euphrates, present-day Iraq. Because of a number of archaic inscribed clay tablets discovered at the site of Uruk level IV, the name is associated with the earliest

Cyrillic	Value	Arabic	Cyrillic	Value	Arabic
А а	a	ئه ه	Т т	t	ت
Б б	b	ب	У у	u	ئۇ
В в	w	ۋ	Ф ф	f	ف
Г г	g	گ	Х х	x	خ
Д д	d	د	Ц ц	ts	—
Е е	e	—	Ч ч	č	چ
Ё ё	yɔ	—	Ш ш	š	ش
Ж ж	ž	ژ	ъ	ʔ	ئ
З з	z	ج	ʼ	ʔ	ء
И и	i	ئـ	ь	—	—
Й й	y	ي ى	Э э	e	ئـ ـ
К к	k	ک ك	Ю ю	yu	—
Л л	l	ل	Я я	ya	—
М м	m	م	Ў ў	o	ئو
Н н	n	ن	Қ қ	q	ق
О о	ɔ	(ه) ئا/ئو	Ғ ғ	ɣ	غ
П п	p	پ	Ҳ ҳ	h	ح/ه
Р р	r	ر	НГ нг	ŋ	ڭ ݣ
С с	s	س			

Table 8 Uzbek alphabets

known writing, conventionally dated *c*.3200–2800 BCE. The writing on the tablets of Uruk IV shows more or less stylized pictograms and also numerals (figure 6). When the pictograms of the Uruk inscriptions came to be written with a pointed stylus, the cuneiform script evolved.
See also CUNEIFORM WRITING; SUMERIAN WRITING.
Reading Falkenstein 1936; Nissen 1986.

Uzbek writing Spoken by some 17 million speakers in Uzbekistan and, in distinct dialects, in Tajikistan, Afghanistan and western China's Xinjiang Uygur Autonomous Region. By its speakers Uzbek is considered a modern form of Chagatay which they call Old Uzbek, one of the literary Turkic languages of medieval Central Asia. When Uzbekistan became a Soviet republic, various writing reforms were carried out. The traditional Arabic spelling was reformed in 1923, and in 1929 a new written standard was introduced on the basis of the northern Uzbek dialect using the Latin alphabet. This was in turn replaced by the Cyrillic in 1939–40. The last five letters of table 8 were added to the Russian alphabet of which щ and ы are not used in Uzbek. In Afghanistan, Uzbek continued to be written in Arabic letters.
Reading Raun 1969.

V, v /vi:/ The twenty-second letter of the English alphabet can be traced back to Semitic *wāw*, a C letter which as Greek *upsilon* (Υ, υ) was given the vocalic value /u/. The Etruscans adapted this letter, changing its form slightly by reducing the length of its lower stem. They used it indiscriminately for /u/ and /w/, the same sound value it had in early and Classical Latin. Its use for a fricative dates from the Middle Ages. After the Norman conquest of England, it was used to distinguish the /w/ sound of English from the French /v/.

Va writing The language of one of China's ethnic minorities living in Yunnan province, Va was first reduced to writing in 1924 by Chen Dingxin, a Va man, and John Weiley, a British missionary. The writing system uses Roman letters. A reformed system was devised in 1949 because the original one failed to differentiate tense and lax Vs, aspirated and unaspirated voiced Cs, as well as syllable-final glottal stop and [h]. However, the old system has not been driven out by the new. Usage is split along religious lines: Christians favour the old spelling (figure 1), whereas secular writing is largely in the new system.
Reading Huang 1992.

Kui-ing e pa ot pehang meung raoma keh ceukau Mai Kwe kra yung kra yi heu-e.

Translation

Our Father in heaven, we pray your name will always be kept holy.

Figure 1 Specimen of Old Va writing

Vai writing A syllabary invented in the 1820s by Dualu Bukele (also Duwalu Bukɛlɛ) of Jondu, Liberia, who was inspired by a dream. Together with five colleagues he subsequently perfected the system which was then learned by many Vai who used it to write letters, diaries, travelogues and partial translations of the Qur'ān. The Vai system of writing became known to European travellers and scholars in the mid-nineteenth century and was introduced into the curriculum of mission schools, although its spread among the Vai was mostly through informal instruction outside the school setting. By the end of the nineteenth century European traders reported that 'most of the Vai can read their own characters'.

The Vai syllabary consists of up to 220 graphemes of which seven are independent Vs. The remainder represent syllables consisting of an initial C or a cluster of up to three Cs and a V. The graphemes are usually arranged as in table

1 with the seven Vs appearing in a horizontal line at the beginning. Underlined Roman letters in the table indicate implosive pronunciation of Cs and tense pronunciation of Vs. A tilde stands for nasalized sounds, the graphemes for which were added to the original syllabary by modifying existing graphemes with diacritics. Punctuation marks are shown in table 2.

The visual form of the graphemes testifies to the influence of traditional West African pictograms as well as symbols associated with Islamic charms and magical practices. Since they were first designed, some of the graphemes have undergone formal changes (table 3). A set of type for the Vai script was apparently

Table 1 The Vai syllabary

comma	∧
full stop	*
exclamation mark	**
question mark	[illegible]

Table 2 Vai punctuation marks

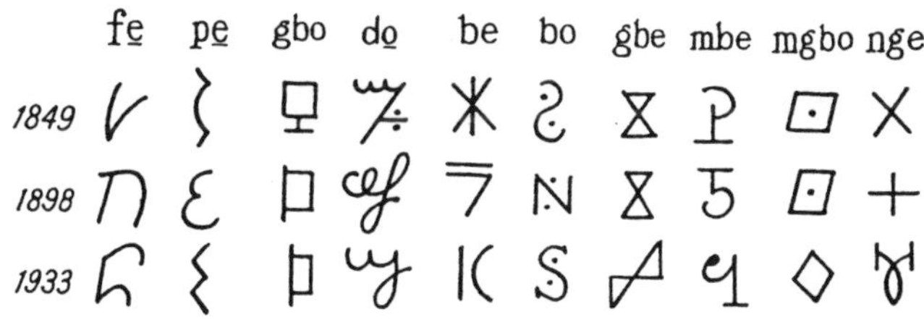

Table 3 Changes of Vai graphemes from 1849 to 1933

prepared in Germany in the 1920s by Professor Klingenheben of the University of Hamburg, but there is no evidence to show that it was used for printing. The standardization of the script with regard to both its inner and outer forms was achieved by the Standardization Committee at the University of Liberia in 1962. Literacy in the Vai script has attracted scholarly attention as it coexists with Arabic and Roman alphabetic literacy in Arabic and English, respectively.
See also AFRICAN WRITING SYSTEMS; INNER FORM OF WRITING SYSTEMS; OUTER FORM OF WRITING SYSTEMS.
Reading Klingenheben 1933; African Studies Program 1962; Dalby 1967; Scribner and Cole 1981.

vanishing vowel sign The diacritic mark placed above a C letter in the Arabic script and some Indian scripts to indicate that no V follows.
See also SCHWA; VIRĀMA; VOWEL INDICATION.

variation in writing The variability of spoken language is often contrasted with the stability of written language. In speech, linguistic expression is ephemeral and inherently variable. No two utterances of the same word or sentence can ever be the same, whereas writing gives language permanence and uniformity. However, although writing is the principal means of language standardization, it does not by itself eliminate variation. All early writing is characterized by extensive variation, a clear indication that no writing system is structured in such a way that it precludes alternative ways of representing speech.

In ancient inscriptions variable written forms of the same word often pose vexing problems for decipherment, because the decipherer has no way of knowing where variation is distinctive, indicating different meanings, and where it falls within a range of alternative forms representing the same linguistic unit. For example, in Egyptian the spatial arrangement of hieroglyphs used to spell a

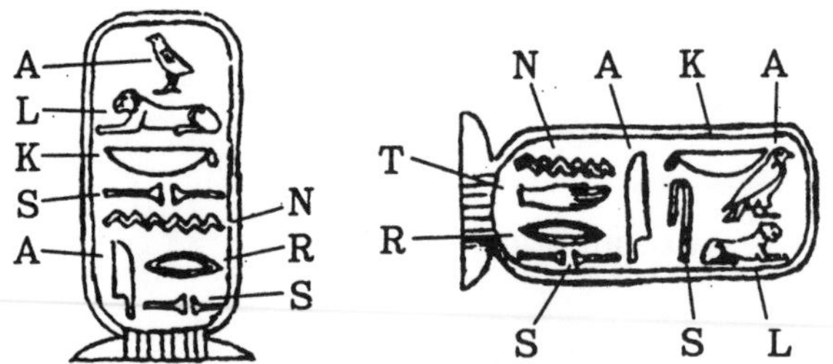

Figure 2 Variation in Egyptian hieroglyphic writing: two versions of the name of Alexander the Great

proper name allows for considerable variation within a CARTOUCHE (figure 2). In writing systems that are built on different structural principles making use, for example, of both logograms and phonograms, variation occurs in representing words by means of graphemes of each of these kinds or by using them in combination. This practice was a major obstacle to recognizing the phonetic nature of Maya writing (figure 3).

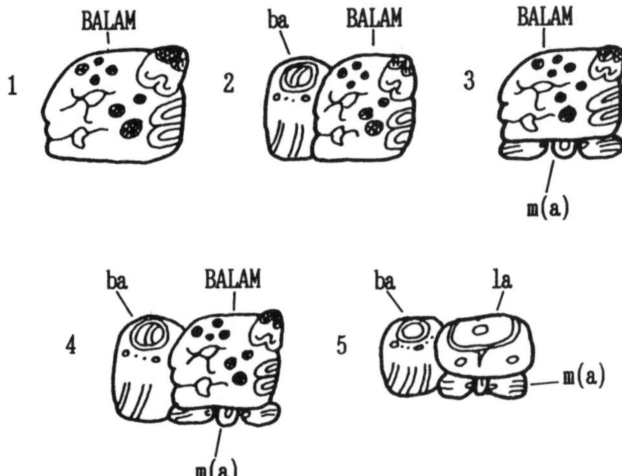

Figure 3 Variation in Maya writing. Five ways of spelling balam *'jaguar': (1) as a logogram: (2), (3), (4) as a logogram plus phonetic complement(s) (in lower case); (5) syllabically*

In alphabetic writing, regional differences in pronunciation contributed to variation because the alphabet was generally thought to work more or less as a TRANSCRIPTION system. Although the systematic reproduction of manuscripts in medieval SCRIPTORIA paved the way for greater uniformity, the notion of orthographic conventions, which often deviate from direct phonetic representation, only took root with the advent of printing. Early printed texts still exhibit considerable heterogeneity. As the following examples from William CAXTON'S *The Book of the Knight of the Tower* (1971, p. 31) illustrate, it was not uncommon for words to be spelt differently even within the same text:

There was a *damoyselle* that had a pye in a cage.
This *damoysell* was after moche scorned.

And it happed that the lord of the *hows* . . .
And in the *hous* therefore was grete sorowe.

But . . . yf ony man cam in to that *hows* that was *balled* or pylled . . .
The pye . . . so often remembryd it to suche as cam thynder so *ballyd* or pylled.

Proper names of people and places, often the first words written in a language, appear in many different forms in early documents, reflecting differences both in pronunciation and in the sound values assigned to the letters of the alphabet.

Writers did not attach much importance to uniformity and consistency in spelling, as long as what they put down in writing could be understood. As illustrated by the example of the fable 'The wolf and the lamb', of which three quite different versions were produced within a few decades, it was printers and editors who did most for reducing variation in spelling (figure 4). But it took several centuries of spreading literacy and compulsory education for the idea to develop that there is but one (correct) form of representing language in writing.

Vom Wolff vnd lemlin

Eiñ wolff vnd lemblin kamen beide on gefer an einen bach zu trincken, Der wolff tranck oben am bach, das lemblin aber fern vnden, Da der wolff des lemblins gewar ward,, ſprach er zu yhm, Warumb trubſtu mir das waſſer, das ich nicht trincken kan? Das lemblin antwortet, Wie kan ich dirs waſſer trüben, ſo du ober mir trinckeſt? Du mochteſt mirs wol trüben. Der wolff ſprach Wie? fluchſtu mir noch dazŭ,

Vom wolff vnd lemlin

Ein wolff vnd lemlin kamen on geferd, beide an einen bach zu trincken, Der wolff tranck oben am bach, Das lemlin aber, fern vñden Da der wolff des lemlins gewar ward, lieff er zu yhm, vnd ſprach, Warumb truͤbeſtu mir das waſſer das ich nicht trincken kan, Das lemlin antwortet wie kan ich dirs waſſer truben, trinckeſtu doch ober mir, vnd mochteſt es mir wol truben Der wolff ſprach, Wie? flucheſtŭ mir noch dazû?

Vom Wolff vnd Lemlin

EJn Wolff vnd Lemlin kamen on gefehr beide an einen Bach zu trincken. Der Wolff tranck oben am Bach, das Lemlin aber fern vnten. Da der Wolff des Lemlins gewar war, lieff er zu jm, und ſprach, Warumb truͤbeſtu mir das Waſſer, das ich nicht trincken kan? Das Lemlin antwortet, Wie kan ich dirs Waſſer truͤben, trinckeſtu doch vber mir und moͤchteſt es mir wol truͤben? Der Wolff ſprach, Wie? Fluchſtu mir noch dazu?

Figure 4 Variation in writing: three versions of the fable 'The wolf and the lamb' in German, the first two from 1530, the last from 1557

Canonical spelling conventions with a uniform standard recognized by the entire speech community are a modern notion which developed together with other aspects of the rationalization of society. The monolingual dictionary, a Renaissance invention, became the principal reference work for establishing a standard spelling and effectively curbing variation.
See also DICTIONARY; ORTHOGRAPHY; WRITTEN LANGUAGE.
Reading Biber 1988; Haas 1982.

Vaṭṭeḻuttu script A syllabic alphabet belonging to the group of south Indian Brāhmī derivatives, this script is closely related to the TAMIL WRITING, although it is more cursive in appearance. The Vaṭṭeḻuttu is palaeographically attested in a number of inscriptions in Tamil Nadu and Kerala dating from the sixth to the fourteenth centuries CE. It has been characterized as the 'round hand' because its letters are written with a single curvilinear stroke (table 4). As in all Indian scripts, the direction of writing is from left to right. With Tamil inscriptions of the eleventh and later centuries, Vaṭṭeḻuttu inscriptions share the usual omission of the *virāma* V muting device.
See also INDIAN WRITING SYSTEMS.
Reading Bühler 1980.

Vowel letters	a	i	u	e	ā			
Consonant letters	ka	ṅa	ča	ña	ṭa	ṇa	ta	na
	pa	ma	ya	ra	la	va	ṛa	ḷa

Table 4 The Vaṭṭeḻuttu syllabic alphabet

vellum [Lat. *vellus* 'sheepskin'] A writing surface made from treated animal skins. The term originally referred to the skin of the newborn calf only, but was extended to include that of a lamb or a kid. Prepared for writing by scratching, stretching and polishing with alum, these skins are collectively called parchment.
See also WRITING SURFACE.

Ventris, Michael An architect by training, Ventris (1922–56) developed an interest in Minoan culture when, still at school, he listened to a lecture by Sir Arthur EVANS. He became famous for his decipherment of the Cretan LINEAR B script which he accomplished in 1953 with the help of John Chadwick, a classicist. After the publication in 1951 of tablets which were discovered at Pylos in south-western Greece but written in one of the Minoan scripts known from

Knossos, Crete, Ventris explored the hypothesis that the language of these tablets was Greek. His famous article 'Evidence for Greek dialect in the Mycenaean archives' which he coauthored with Chadwick appeared in the *Journal of Hellenic Studies* for 1953.
See also DECIPHERMENT.
Reading Chadwick 1967.

versals [Lat. *verto* 'to turn, to change'] Ornamented capital letters used in Latin manuscripts. Versals were not used to compose entire texts, but rather served as chapter openings and headlines to draw the reader's attention to the beginning of a new chapter, verse or section of a text, often written marginally or partly in the text. Since there were no corresponding small letters, they would be used in combination with uncial, half-uncial or Caroline minuscule letters. In early manuscripts ornamentation was simple, being mostly elongated serifs or contrasting colour. As of the fourteenth century they became more elaborate, developing into illuminated initials.
Reading Bischoff 1986; Callery 1993.

Vietnamese alphabet Contemporary Vietnamese is written with an alphabetic writing system using Roman letters. First attempts at designing an alphabetic orthography for Vietnamese were made by Portuguese, French and Italian missionaries in the seventeenth century. The earliest alphabetically written dictionary of the language was published in 1651 under the auspices of the Vatican in Rome, the trilingual Vietnamese–Portuguese–Latin *Dictionarium Annamiticum – Lusitanum et Latinum* by Alexandre de Rhodes. At the time, Vietnamese was usually written in a Chinese-derived script known as CHỮ'NÔM or 'southern [i.e. Vietnamese] script, a highly intricate system which, however, was a significant symbol of Vietnamese identity. The inroads of alphabetic writing in Vietnamese literacy were therefore slow, and it was not until 1910 that the Roman alphabet was recognized as the official Vietnamese script.

The orthography is based on the conventions developed by Alexandre de Rhodes. The Vietnamese alphabet consists of 37 letters (table 5), including complex graphemes such as digraphs and graphemes composed of a basic Roman letter and an additional mark, for instance the barred *D* <Đ> and the *A* with a breve sign <Ă> for [ă], a V which is further back than [a] = <a>. The letters *F, J, W,* and *Z* are not used, except in foreign proper names. In addition to the 37 letters, six superscript and subscript diacritics are used to differentiate phonemic tones. All Vietnamese syllables have the structure C_1 (C_2) VC_3, where C_2 is always the semivowel /w/. Tone diacritics are attached to V letters as indicated in table 6.
Reading Trúóng 1970.

```
A, Ă, Â, B, C, Ch, D, Đ, E, Ê, G, Gi, H,
I, K, Kh, L, M, N, Ng, Nh, O, Ô, Ơ, P,
Ph, Qu, R, S, T, Th, Tr, U, Ư, V, X, Y
```

Table 5 The Vietnamese alphabet

a	ê
à	ề
á	ế
ả	ể
ã	ễ
ạ	ệ

Table 6 Vietnamese vowel letters with diacritics

virāma A diacritic letter of the Sanskrit syllabic alphabet indicating the absence of a V. In the DEVANĀGARĪ script the *virāma* has the form of an oblique stroke added as a subscript to the C letter which is to be stripped of its inherent V; thus त *ta,* but अत् *at.* Most Indian scripts have a *virāma,* but there is considerable variation in usage.
See also SANSKRIT WRITING; SYLLABIC ALPHABET.

visarga A diacritic letter of the Sanskrit (DEVANĀGARĪ) syllabic alphabet having the form of a colon placed behind other letters to indicate hard breathing. It is usually pronounced as [h] followed by a short repetition of the preceding V.
See also SANSKRIT WRITING.

visible speech A graphic notation system developed in 1867 by Alexander Melville Bell and applied by his son, Graham Bell, to teaching the deaf, 'Visible speech' is one of several physiologically oriented alphabets devised in the nineteenth century (figure 5). Its purpose was to enable the deaf to learn English, although the notation was intended as a 'universal alphabet' by means of which all speech sounds made by the human voice could be expressed. Following William Thornton, Isaac Pitman and other advocates of the oral method, Melville Bell regarded the non-phonetic nature of English spelling as a major obstacle to the acquisition of speech by the deaf. He thought that a proper remedy could be found in a strictly phonetic transcription system making use of basic letters whose sound values are defined in terms of places of articulation.
See also TRANSCRIPTION.
Reading Bell 1900.

vowel indication In the history of writing, Vs occupy a different position from Cs. The introduction of V letters into the Semitic writing that the Greeks adopted from the Phoenicians is often considered the origin of alphabetic writing proper. Some phonetic writing systems do not represent Vs, but no such system fails to represent Cs. The mode of V indication has, therefore, been used as a criterion for classifying writing systems. Four major modes of V indication can be distinguished:

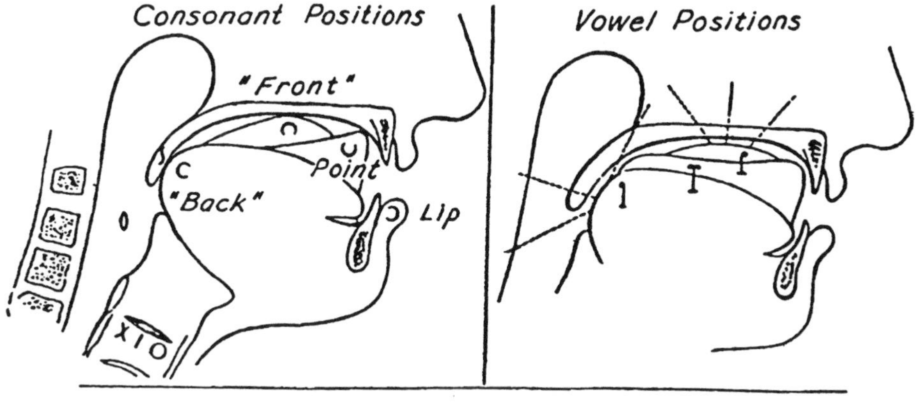

THE UNIVERSAL ALPHABET.

Columns 1, 2, 3, 4, *Consonants.* Column 5, *Glides.* Columns 6, 7, 8, *Vowels.* Columns 9, 0, *Throat Sounds and Modifiers.*

Lines a to f, Voiceless Consonants, Lingual Glides, Lingual Vowels. *Lines g to m, Vocalized Consonants, Labialised Glides, Labialised Vowels.*

*** The Marginal Numbers and Letters may be used, instead of the Visible Speech Letters, to express the mechanism of sounds in common type. The following examples show the English, Scotch, and Irish pronunciations of the words 'Visible Speech :'—**

English 4i 8d 2h 8d 4l 3i ob 2b 4e 8a ob 3e 3b

Scotch 4i 8a 2h 7b 4l 3i ob 2b 4e 8a 3e 3b

Irish 4i 8d 2h 8a 4l 3i ob 2b 4e 5f 8a ob 3e 3b

Figure 5 Alexander Melville Bell's 'visible speech' alphabet

No V indication Semitic writings such as ancient and contemporary HEBREW WRITING represent C roots only, leaving the correct vocalization to be inferred from context by the reader.

Auxiliary V indication Basic graphemes represent Cs but can be modified or used to represent Vs. Two subtypes, both of which evolved within the context of Semitic literacy, are MATRES LECTIONIS and PUNCTUATION. In systems of the former type, C letters – especially those for /', j, w/ – are used in certain contexts

to represent Vs. Systems of the latter type attach diacritics to C letters to mark the V that follows.
Inherent V indication In Indian SYLLABIC ALPHABETS and in the AMHARIC WRITING, C graphemes contain an inherent neutral V, usually *a*. Other Vs in post-consonantal position are indicated by adding to the C grapheme a diacritic which cannot occur independently to represent a V. Many of the Indian systems also have independent V graphemes.
Independent V indication Carrying the *matres lectionis* type one step further, the Greeks created the prototype of a writing system based on this mode of V indication. Ever since they revalued Semitic C letters as Vs, such as א for /a/, Vs were represented separately in all subsequent descendants of the Semitic alphabet. However, very few alphabets have enough graphemes for all Vs of the language in question. V letters often represent several different phonemes and are modified by diacritics such as accent marks and diaeresis. This poverty of V graphemes testifies to the Semitic origin of the alphabet.

See also TYPOLOGY OF WRITING SYSTEMS.
Reading Voegelin and Voegelin 1961; Driver 1976; Coulmas 1989.

vowel muting The C letters of Indian SYLLABIC ALPHABETS have an inherent V, usually *a*. In order to write C clusters or final Cs, this inherent V must be muted. Two devices are used to write syllable-final Cs. One is the combination of C letters to form conjuncts of two or more Cs, of which all but the last are understood to lose their inherent V. The other is a diacritic sign, called VIRĀMA in Sanskrit, indicating zero V.
See also AKSARA; VANISHING VOWEL SIGN.

W, w /ˈdʌblju/ The twenty-third letter of the English alphabet was created in the Middle Ages as a ligature to distinguish *UU* from *UV*. The fact that until medieval times *U* and *V* were not distinguished is reflected in the different names given to the letter *W*, 'double *U*' in English and 'double *V*' in French.

Wade-Giles Romanization Prior to the official adoption of PINYIN by the UN and other international agencies in the 1980s, Wade-Giles (WG) was the most widely used Romanization system of Chinese in Western scholarship. Although it is quite systematic in its make-up, representation of Chinese sounds is often rather indirect, using neither a strictly phonetic notation nor the spelling conventions of English. For example, the retroflex *r* which Pinyin simply gives as <r> is written <j> in WG on the grounds that French <j> represents a sound that comes close to the Chinese *r*. Thus WG *jen*² corresponds to Pinyin *rén*. WG indicates tones by means of superscript numerals.
See also ROMANIZATION.
Reading Newnham 1987.

wax tablets Wooden writing tablets coated with black wax used from the very earliest times of literacy in Greece and Rome. Known as δέλτος, δέλτίον in Greek and *tabulae* in Latin, such tablets were single or of several pieces. A set of tablets held together by rings formed a *caudex* or *codex*. Wax tablets were usually made of common wood, but sometimes a more precious material such as ivory was used.
See also WRITING SURFACE.

Webster, Noah (1758–1843) An American nationalist, Webster followed in the footsteps of European Romanticists who promoted the idea that an independent nation should have a language of its own. He devoted much of his life to providing the newly independent American republic with a language recognizably different from that of the former colonial motherland. In his writings he often referred to 'federal English' and the 'American language'. Deliberately deviating from the standard set in Samuel Johnson's dictionary, which he denounced as both conservative and vulgar, Webster codified a number of American spellings in his *American Spelling Book*. First published in 1783, it became a huge commercial success. Total sales of the 'blue-backed speller', as it was known at the time, are estimated to have reached more than 100 million copies (figure 1). Superficial as they were, Webster's proposals for a reformed spelling are to date the only ones that have been accepted in large parts of the English-speaking world. The reformed spellings he proposed in his *Compendious Dictionary of the English Language* of 1806, e.g. *bred* for *bread, bilt* for *built, giv* for *give, laf* for *laugh,* were far-reaching and often eccentric. However, those codified in his *American Dictionary*

OF PRONUNCIATION. 35

com-mon	dol-lar	of-fer	ker-nel
con-duct	fod-der	of-fice	mer-cy*
con-cord	fol-ly	pot-ter	per-fect*
con-greſs	fop-piſh	rob-ber	per-ſon
con-queſt	hor-rid	ſot-tiſh	ſer-mon
con-ſul	joc-ky	2	ſer-pent
con-vert	jol-ly	cler-gy	ſer-vant
doc-tor	mot-to	er-rand	ver-min
droſſ-y	on-ſet	her-mit	

* Not Marcy, Parfect, &c.

TABLE V.

Eaſy Words of Two Syllables, *accented on the* Second.

N. B. In general when a vowel, in an unaccented ſyllable, ſtands alone, or ends a ſyllable*, it has its firſt ſound, as in *pro-ject*; yet as we do not dwell upon the vowel, it is ſhort and weak. When the vowel, in ſuch ſyllables, is joined to a conſonant, it has its ſecond ſound; as, *ad-dreſs*.

A-baſe	com-pute	de-pute	en-tice
a-bide	com-plete	de-rive	en-tire
a-dore	confine	diſ-like	e-vade
a-like	con-jure	diſ-place	for-ſworn
al-lude	con-ſume	diſ-robe	fore-ſeen
a-lone	cre-ate	diſ-taſte	im-brue
a-maze	de-cide	di-vine	im-pale
aſ-pire	de-clare	e-lope	in-cite
a-tone	de-duce	en-dure	in-flame
at-tire	de-fy	en-force	in-trude
be-fore	de-fine	en-gage	in-ſure
be-have	de-grade	en-rage	in-vite
be-hold	de-range	en-rol	miſ-name
com-ply	de-note	en-ſue	miſ-place

* *But if a vowel unaccented ends the word, it has its ſecond ſound, as in ci-ty.*

Figure 1 A page from Noah Webster's American Spelling Book

of the English Language which was first published in 1828 are less extensive and less erratic.

See also AMERICAN SPELLING; SPELLING REFORM.

Reading Warfel 1936; Baron 1982.

wényán The Chinese term for 'classical literary Chinese', the Chinese written language which was the norm for literary and official writing for some 2,000 years prior to the May 4th Movement of 1919 which promoted the unification of written and spoken Chinese. Its grammar is by and large based on Classical

Chinese from the Han dynasties (206 BCE to 220 CE) when the written language is thought to have been relatively close to the spoken language. Since *wényán* came to be regarded as an unalterable standard, the spoken and written language continued to diverge, leading to a diglossic relationship between the two.
See also CHINESE WRITTEN LANGUAGE; DIGLOSSIA.
Reading Hsu 1979.

Winnebago syllabary An adaptation of the Fox SYLLABARY for writing Winnebago, a native American language of the Siouan family spoken in Wisconsin and Nebraska.
Reading Walker 1981.

Wolof alphabet A member of the west Atlantic subgroup of the Niger–Congo family, Wolof is the most widely spoken language of Senegal, with smaller groups of speakers in Gambia, Mali, Mauritania and Guinea. Although important as a trade language in West Africa since the early period of European contact, Wolof has no significant literary tradition. It has been written occasionally in Arabic and Roman letters, but systematic instruction in Romanized Wolof was begun only in the 1960s. At the same time Asane Faye, the first president of the African Language Teachers' Movement in Senegal, devised the Wolof alphabet. Much like Arabic letters, its 25 graphemes have two forms for initial and non-initial positions (table 1). The influence of Arabic is also apparent in the direction of

Consonant letters									Vowel letters	
	Initial	Non-init.		Initial	Non-init.		Initial	Non-init.	Provisional identification	
[ā] (1)	[illegible]	[illegible]	w (8)	[illegible]	[illegible]	y (40)	[illegible]	[illegible]	a	[illegible]
c (2)	[illegible]	[illegible]	l (9)	[illegible]	[illegible]	t (50)	[illegible]	[illegible]	ɛ	[illegible]
m (3)	[illegible]	[illegible]	g (10)	[illegible]	[illegible]	r (60)	[illegible]	[illegible]	e	[illegible]
k (4)	[illegible]	[illegible]	ŋg	[illegible]	[illegible]	ɲ (70)	[illegible]	[illegible]	ö	[illegible]
b (5)	[illegible]	[illegible]	ŋ	[illegible]	[illegible]	ʃ (80)	[illegible]	[illegible]	i	[illegible]
mb	[illegible]	[illegible]	d (20)	[illegible]	[illegible]	n (90)	[illegible]	[illegible]	ɔ	[illegible]
j (6)	[illegible]	[illegible]	nd	[illegible]	[illegible]	p (100)	[illegible]	[illegible]	o	[illegible]
nj	[illegible]	[illegible]	x (30)	[illegible]	[illegible]	Diacritics: long vowel (postscript)	—		u	[illegible]
s (7)	[illegible]	[illegible]	h	[illegible]	[illegible]	zero vowel (postscript)	c		ə	[illegible]
						double consonant (superscript)	^		ii	[illegible]

Numerals	1	2	3	4	5	6	7	8	9	10
	[illegible]	[illegible]	[illegible]	[illegible]	[illegible]	[illegible]	[illegible]	[illegible]	[illegible]	[illegible]

Table 1 The Wolof alphabet

writing from right to left and in the mode of V indication. A teaching manual of the Wolof alphabet was published in Dakar in 1966.
Reading Dalby 1969; *L'Afrique et la lettre* 1986.

word Pre-theoretical notions of the word as a linguistic unit are strongly influenced by the graphic representation of words in writing. These notions are, therefore, dependent on particular literary and lexicographic traditions, reflecting the fact that every writing system is based on and manifests a linguistic analysis. In this sense a word is a linguistic unit consisting of a group of graphemes which is separated from other such groups by a space. As this definition shows, the written word is an artefact which does not necessarily correspond to a distinct unit of speech.

Non-literate cultures, not being prompted by the visual appearance of linguistic units, have a different concept of the word than literate cultures. The same can be said of pre-literate children who tend to identify any meaningful utterance irrespective of length as a word and fail to recognize function words as words.

That literacy has a bearing on the notion of the word is also evidenced by the vague and polysemous nature of the meta-linguistic terms of early Western literacy, such as Greek λόγος, λέξις, ῥῆμα and Latin *dictio, verbum,* which are usually translated as 'word'. Theoretical attempts at clarifying the concept have not been very successful. Most linguists prefer not to use the term 'word', or make a distinction between orthographic, phonetic and semantic words which are not necessarily congruous. Although such a distinction helps to avoid some conceptual confusion, it does little to solve the problems of how spoken and written words relate to each other, and whether words have an existence as linguistic units independent of their realization in speech and writing. Lexicographers have never been much concerned about these theoretical issues since their data are invariably the words of written language. The result of their work, dictionaries, reinforces the general and rather circular notion of what words are: graphically separable units of language, that is, those units one finds in a dictionary.
See also DICTIONARY; GRAMMAR; WORD REPRESENTATION; WRITTEN LANGUAGE.
Reading Kràmsky 1969; Blanche-Benveniste 1993.

word blindness *See* AGRAPHIA

word boundary Three different ways of treating word boundaries are found in the writing systems of the world: no marking, indirect marking and overt marking.

Systems of no marking are exemplified by Chinese which separates morphemes but not words. In alphabetic writing the SCRIPTURA CONTINUA of ancient Greek and Latin inscriptions ignores word boundaries, putting letters next to each other with equal spaces within and between words.

Indirect marking of word boundaries occurs in writing systems that encode grammatical or semantic information which coincides with word boundaries. For example, Egyptian DETERMINATIVES can be thought of as serving the secondary function of marking word boundaries, although not all words include a determinative.

Many writing systems indicate word boundaries with special markers. For instance, Old Persian had a slanted stroke in the south-eastern direction, and Ugaritic used a perpendicular stroke as a word separator. Hebrew, Aramaic, Syriac and Arabic were always written with word boundaries marked by spaces between words, although these divisions were not always consistent. The Ethiopic script used two dots, one above the other. In Latin and other Old Italic inscriptions, words were also usually separated by dots (figure 2), a practice which was given up when the *scriptura continua* came into vogue. It was only in medieval times that German and Anglo-Saxon scribes, who used Latin as a foreign language, reintroduced word boundary marking to facilitate understanding. However, instead of the earlier single or double dots they used spacing, which became the standard form of word separation in alphabetic writing. In alphabetic calligraphy the width of an o is often taken to determine the space between words. Before orthographies were standardized in the wake of Printing and Typography, indication of word boundaries was quite inconsistent. In particular, function words such as prepositions and conjunctions were often joined to the words they followed.

See also Word; Word representation.

Reading Beck 1963; Schenkel 1976; Saenger 1982.

Figure 2 Word boundaries marked by a colon in an Umbrian inscription of the third century BCE

word play Playing with words is a universal pastime found in all cultures throughout history. While the playful manipulation of words often involves homophony, rhyme, alliteration and other phonetic properties, many word plays depend on the medium of writing. The Rebus principle – representing a word by a picture or a combination of pictures with a similar name – was an important step in the development of some writing systems such as cuneiform, Egyptian hieroglyphic and Chinese. Playful applications are known from the early periods of all of these literacies. When paper became a household item, word play also became a pastime in alphabetic cultures. Transcribing foreign proper names by means of meaningful Chinese Characters is popular throughout the sphere of Chinese writing. Other Chinese word plays include writing sequences of similar-sounding characters which, when pronounced, are meaningless, but reveal some

sense to the eye. Alphabetic writing induced word plays involving the arrangement of letters in a special sequence so as to form PALINDROMES, also called sotadices, and word squares or acrostics. The crossword puzzle, first devised in 1913, is likewise an essentially alphabetic entertainment, as is the popular parlour game 'Scrabble'. In languages that use consonant alphabets, such as Hebrew, these games often play with the multivalence of C roots (figure 3). In other word plays the letters of a word may be scrambled or combined in a way involving deliberate segmentation errors (*a jar, ajar; an apron, a napron*). That some words are 'other words backwards' – *evil, part* – is true and detectable in writing only. Cryptograms have often been produced for purposes of entertainment, although the encoding of messages to shield them from uninvited readers has become a matter of devising highly sophisticated computer programs. New word plays making use of the same basic techniques – rebus, anagram, palindrome, encoding, circumscribing, substituting differently spelt homophones – are continuously invented, giving expression as they do to the various functions of writing beyond the domains of practical application in visual communication.
Reading Shipley 1960; Manchester 1976.

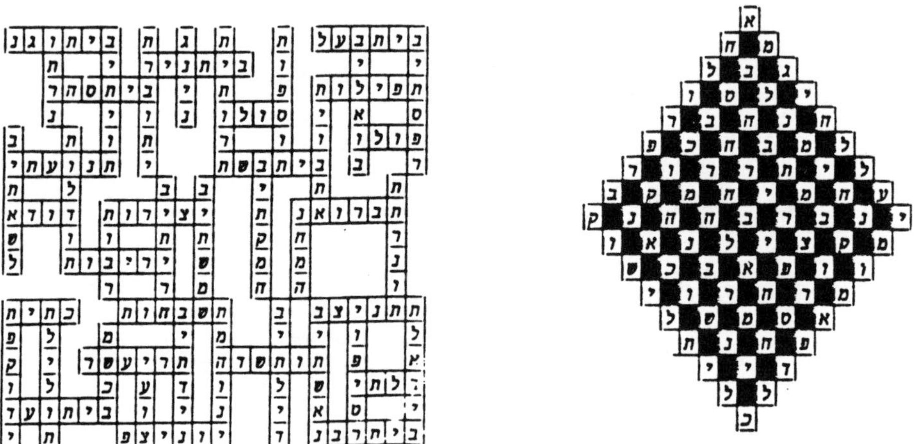

Figure 3 Hebrew crossword puzzles

word processing A writing technology which enables the writer to produce texts by means of a computer using a software program designed to automatically carry out tasks formerly handled by writer, typist, editor and typographic designer. The input is through an alphabetic keyboard not unlike that of a typewriter, but word processing differs from typewriting in significant ways. Multiple character sets can be accessed through the same keyboard, allowing authors to integrate not only a great variety of symbols into their texts, but also material in other languages and scripts, including those which run in different directions. Before a text is printed out it appears on a computer screen and can thus be inspected and edited. While producing a typewritten manuscript makes it necessary to coordinate in advance the contents and physical appearance, word processing allows the author to separate both. Layout features that determine the printed document's appearance can be decided after the text input has been completed, and changed without retyping.

Some of the functions which are part of standard word-processing programs are the following. Documents are formatted in a uniform way; among the features that can be determined by the program are fonts, number of characters per line, number of lines per page, justification of margins, width of margins, footnotes and endnotes, page numbers and their position, running heads, columns, spacing between paragraphs, and numbering of sections, paragraphs, lines, tables and figures. Editor functions include the ability to copy, move and delete parts of a document and to compose documents by combining already existing text blocks of other documents. The writer can work at two or more documents simultaneously, incorporating quotations from one into the other. The writer also has immediate access on the screen to a thesaurus and an orthographic dictionary. The spelling of words or entire documents can be checked. Words can be marked for indexing and indices compiled. Bibliographies and other lists can be arranged in alphabetical order.

These and several other functions of word-processing programs assist authors in various ways. They incorporate not only formatting features, but also many features of general writing style for which authors would formerly rely on their own judgement or consult a reference book such as the *Chicago Manual of Style.* Word-processing equipment has spread rapidly among writing professions during the 1980s and 1990s. Like other writing technologies, word processing is therefore likely to have an influence, however subtle, on how written words are handled in societies where it is widely used. However, so far there has been little systematic research about the effects of this technology on the writing process or the texts that are produced using it.

See also LITERACY; PRINTING; WRITING TOOLS.

Reading Schanze 1987; Sharples 1992.

word recognition The process of identifying groups of graphemes or phonemes as words in writing and speech, respectively. As this process is an essential prerequisite of reading comprehension and speech understanding, word recognition strategies have been the object of much psycholinguistic and reading research. A focal question has been whether and to what extent phonetic recoding takes place in graphic word recognition. There is general agreement that word recognition in reading usually involves some subliminal phonetic activity, although allowances must be made for individual variation as well as variation across structurally different writing systems.

Reading Ives et al. 1979; Günther 1988; Kolinsky et al. 1991.

word representation Because of their contextual distribution, words are intuitively obvious units of speech. Yet there is great variation and arbitrariness in the ways words are represented in writing. Three main factors are responsible for this. One is that the morphosyntactic status of words varies greatly across typologically different languages. In inflecting languages such as Greek many words are clearly recognizable as such by virtue of their inflected forms. Isolating languages such as Chinese are characterized by a high degree of morphemic independence which allows almost all morphemes to function as separate words or as parts of compounds. And in polysynthetic languages such as Yupik the morphemes are so closely interconnected that what appears as one unit, i.e. a 'word', is expressed in an inflecting language by a sentence consisting of several words.

The second factor is that the segmentation and grammatical analysis that necessarily precede reducing a language to writing are of a preliminary, rough-and-ready kind. In-depth grammatical analysis has traditionally been based on written data and thus tends to reinforce pre-theoretically motivated units.

The third factor is that breath pauses in speech do not consistently cooccur with word boundaries. Word separation in speech thus interferes with faithful mapping of speech. This is obvious where phonetic groups reach across word boundaries as in the so-called *liaison* of French. For instance, French *les amis* 'the friends' is the orthographic representation of what is phonetically [le za·mi:]. In many Indian scripts, for example DEVANĀGARĪ, this phenomenon is represented at the expense of marking word boundaries which are indicated only where they cooccur with breath pauses.

For this reason, writing is not neutral but rather exhibits analytic patterns in the representation of external word structure. Modern alphabetic orthographies mark external word structure, but ignore internal word structure, except in some cases such as *re-elect* where a hyphen may be inserted to prevent unintended pronunciations, i.e. [ri:lɛkt].

See also GRAMMAR; WORD; WORD BOUNDARY.

Reading Günther 1988; Filliozat 1990.

word separation *See* WORD BOUNDARY

word writing *See* LOGOGRAM

world orthography A system proposed by the International Phonetic Association. The graphemes and their sound values are largely identical with those of the INTERNATIONAL PHONETIC ALPHABET (IPA), except that <j> and <y> have the consonantal values they have in English (table 2). World orthography is an attempt to standardize the handwritten forms of graphemes not contained in the 26-letter Roman alphabet. It has been adopted for the practical writing of some African languages which have been reduced to writing recently, such as Dinka in Sudan and Igbo, Efik, Twi and Ewe in West Africa.

See also AFRICA ALPHABET; UNIVERSAL WRITING.

Reading International Institute of African Languages and Cultures 1930.

writ A written command in the name of a ruler addressed to an official or other subordinate. An important means of establishing a centralized government, writs were closely connected with the expansion of the common law in medieval times. Many writs were used repeatedly in the same form and hence assumed a conventionalized, formulaic pattern.

See also FUNCTIONS OF WRITING.

Reading Clanchy 1993.

[1] r to be written ɹ (not ɾ) in languages containing r and ɽ.
[2] The latter in languages not requiring ɑ.

Table 2 The 'world orthography' proposed by the International Phonetic Association

writer's cramp A painful spasm of the muscles of fingers, hand and forearm of psychogenic origin which makes HANDWRITING and typing difficult or impossible.

writing At least four different meanings are associated with this term in non-technical usage:

1 a system of recording language by means of visible or tactile marks which relate in a systematic way to units of speech, for example alphabetic vs logographic writing

2 the activity of recording language by means of such a system
3 a script style, e.g. cursive writing vs block letter writing
4 a professional occupation.

See also FUNCTIONS OF WRITING; HANDWRITING; LITERACY; SCRIPT; WRITING SYSTEM.

writing community A term coined in analogy with 'speech community', occasionally used in the sociology of language. As the most tangible subsystem of language, writing is often associated with ethnocentric, national and religious attachment. For example, AMERICAN SPELLING is a symbol of linguistic and cultural independence, as is the Swiss convention of using <ss> instead of German <ß>. In economic terms, a writing community is a market for print products whose extension is defined by the range of an orthographic norm. In a wider sense, as scripts take on an emotional symbolic significance, they define cultural and religious spheres and thus communities. For this reason, in the history of writing, once a system or style had become accepted by a community it tended to last for centuries. Where a language is first reduced to writing or a writing system is reformed, the social aspects of writing as a pivot of community identification are particularly obvious.
See also FUNCTIONS OF WRITING; ORTHOGRAPHY REFORM; RELIGION AND WRITING.
Reading Fishman 1977; Stubbs 1980.

writing, development of From its precursors – pictures and mnemonic devices such as counter tokens, tally sticks, knot strings – to the diversity of full-blown systems around the world, writing has undergone complex developments. There is wide agreement that PHONETIZATION and writing according to the REBUS PRINCIPLE are important steps in the history of writing, and that the transfer of writing systems to languages other than that for which they originally evolved often brought about significant developments involving changes from PLEREMIC WRITING to CENEMIC WRITING. Beyond these general factors, which have had an undeniable influence on the development of writing, the histories of writing systems are so diverse and subject to so many different determinants that it is risky to posit a single history of writing, although theoretical attempts in this direction have been made.

Some historians of writing have tried to account for the genesis of the various writing systems by identifying common causes and principles underlying changes which are documented and others which can be inferred. Such attempts, while necessary for advancing the formulation of a general theory of writing, have sometimes yielded over-simplistic results. The evolution of writing is accordingly portrayed from a teleological viewpoint which posits a necessary order of development from pictography, through ideography, logography, logosyllabic and syllabic writing, to alphabetic writing. I. J. GELB in particular has put heavy stress on the inevitability and irreversibility of these stages. They are grounded in what has been called 'the principle of economy', i.e. the supposedly natural tendency to reduce the size of the signary of a writing system: the smaller the unit of representation (word → syllable → phoneme), the fewer the elementary signs. However, elegant as it is, such a theory cannot account for a number of important phenomena in the history of writing, of which only two shall be mentioned here. One has to do with the place of the syllabic alphabets of India in such an order of development, and the other with developments in alphabetic writing.

If it is true, as is commonly assumed, that the Old Brāhmī script is derived from the ARAMAIC WRITING, this represents a case of 'developmental regression', because Aramaic is a C alphabet of just 22 letters, whereas Brāhmī is a syllabic alphabet with a much larger signary. Apparently, the principle of writing individual speech sounds was given up for representing syllables instead.

The alphabet as adapted from the Phoenician model by the Greeks with separate letters for Cs and Vs cannot be viewed, as it often is, as essentially the end of the development of writing. Very different systems operating on different levels of linguistic structure have evolved which cannot be described satisfactorily if the alphabet is viewed as a notation where each sign represents a speech sound. In alphabetic systems such as ENGLISH SPELLING and FRENCH SPELLING, word and morpheme, i.e. pleremic units, are at least as important units of representation as smaller cenemic units. Again, this would appear to be a retrogression, because writing has become more complicated rather than simpler, as the representation of sounds has been partially superseded by the representation of words. Thus the history of alphabetic writing shows clearly that many developments contradict the principle of economy.

A teleological theory of the development of writing systems which assumes a necessary sequence of developmental stages is bound to run into difficulties for two principal reasons. One is that there are no language-neutral writing systems. All writing systems, including the alphabet, reflect features of the languages in whose context they first evolved. In this sense their development cannot be studied properly unless the structural properties of how they represent particular languages are taken into account. The other reason is the asynchrony of changes in a language and in the writing system it uses. In the long run this is bound to affect the basic structural relationships underlying the writing system. For these two reasons the development of writing is not a steady progression aiming in a quasi-natural manner at optimal efficiency, but rather a meandering path where hard-gained advantages are sometimes lost along the way.

See also MONOGENESIS OF WRITING; ORIGIN OF WRITING.

Reading Gelb 1963; Harris 1986; DeFrancis 1989; Coulmas 1989; Gaur 1992; Daniels 1990.

***writing*, etymology of** Words for *writing* in various languages testify in their etymology to the mechanics of the writing process. The Greek verb γράφειν 'to write' originally meant 'to carve, to engrave, to scratch', a meaning similar to that of Latin *scribere*, whence English *scribe, inscribe*, German *schreiben*, French *écrire* etc. In Semitic languages, relations between the words for 'write' and 'cut' or 'excavate' are apparent by common roots. The root *shf* in south Semitic languages, for instance, meant both 'to write' and 'to hollow'. The Chinese term *shu* originally meant 'to paint', pointing to the typical implement of Chinese writing, the brush. Similarly, in ancient Egyptian the same word was used for 'writing' and 'drawing'. The English word *write* (Old English *wrítan*) derives from an Old German root meaning 'to cut, to score', designating the process of outlining a shape on a surface.

writing surface There is virtually no limit to the materials that have been used for writing from its earliest precursors to the present. Bone, sea shells, rock, pebbles, clay and wood were among the earliest writing surfaces. Initially they were used more or less as they were found. At a more advanced stage various materials were especially prepared to receive writing: clay tablets in Mesopotamia and in the Aegean; wooden stripes and silk in China; palm leaves and bamboo tubes in South and South East Asia; animal skins in various parts of the Mediterranean and the ancient Middle East; and bark in Central America. Monumental inscriptions in stone are known from almost every literary culture, and metal – copper, silver, gold, lead, tin, iron – as a writing surface in the form of coins, thin sheets and various implements such as vessels, swords and mirrors has also been used widely. The next step was to produce materials particularly suited to receive writing: dressed stone, potsherds and leather were routinely used in Palestine, Syria and adjacent areas of Semitic writing as well as in Greece; wax tablets – wooden tablets coated with a thin layer of black wax – were common in Greece and Rome; and PAPYRUS was the typical surface of other than monumental writing in Egypt. From there it was exported to Palestine, the Phoenician colonies around the Mediterranean, as well as the Roman empire. Since, however, papyrus tends to rot or disintegrate in most climatic conditions, a more durable substitute was sought. In Christian Rome, PARCHMENT – treated animal skins – drove out papyrus as the preferred writing surface, which it remained for centuries until it was in turn replaced by PAPER. This Chinese invention was introduced to Europe in the eleventh century and, because of its cheapness and ease of processing, has been the unchallenged medium of written communication ever since the invention of the printing press. As the twentieth century draws to a close, the importance of paper is still undiminished, although electromagnetic media are rapidly taking over many of its functions for recording, storing and transmitting information.

In addition to the preferred surfaces of practical writing, writing has been executed for decorative purposes on every conceivable surface. Stamped, painted, scratched, engraved, incised, chiselled, impressed, burned, knitted, woven, planted or sprayed, writing is found on landmarks and gravestones; on tapestry, cloth and any other fabric; in flowerbeds and in the bark of live trees; as a tattoo on the human skin; in mosaics and tessellated floors; and in the icing on birthday cakes. Everything that belongs to someone is prone to bear an inscription, and decorative objects such as jewellery have been produced in the form of letters. Seaweed flakes in the form of Chinese characters, alphabet noodles and chocolate letters are for physical consumption; and messages written in the sky by an aircraft with its vapour trail are for the accidental observer.

Among the many surfaces that have been employed to bear writing a few stand out because they influenced the graphic development of the writing systems for which they were first used. Most notably, clay has been the formative medium of CUNEIFORM WRITING. The form of cuneiform signs as patterns of wedge-shaped marks is an immediate result of impressing a pointed stylus on soft clay (figure 4). Likewise, the angularity of Chinese characters bears witness to the fact that the sheep scapulas and tortoise shells incised with a pointed implement were at the beginning of writing in China. The rounded forms of south Indian scripts and their derivatives in Burma, Indonesia and the Philippines have been explained by reference to the typical writing surface: palm leaves were less likely to break when curvilinear forms were cut into them rather than straight lines and sharp angles. Writing surfaces, therefore, are more than superficial aspects of the history of writing. Traditionally, EPIGRAPHY is the study of

Figure 4 Clay, the most durable of writing surfaces. A letter in Old Babylonian written almost three and a half thousand years ago by the Prince of Alashija to Pharaoh Amenophis III of Egypt (by permission of Staatliche Museen Berlin)

inscriptions carved or incised on hard materials, whereas PALAEOGRAPHY tends to concentrate on manuscript writing on papyrus and parchment.
See also WRITING TOOLS.
Reading Gaur 1992; Healey 1990.

writing system A set of visible or tactile signs used to represent units of language in a systematic way, with the purpose of recording messages which can be retrieved by everyone who knows the language in question and the rules by virtue of which its units are encoded in the writing system. The term 'writing system' is sometimes confused with, or used interchangeably with, others from which it should be distinguished, at least in theoretical contexts. Of these, ALPHABET, ORTHOGRAPHY, SCRIPT, SPELLING and WRITING are treated in separate entries of this encyclopedia.

As a technical term, 'writing system' is used in two different senses. One refers to the basic types of graphic systems designed to represent language, i.e. logographic and logosyllabic systems as well as syllabic alphabets, consonant alphabets and full alphabets. A major distinction is between PLEREMIC WRITING systems (the first two of these types), which consist of signs that represent sound–meaning units, and CENEMIC WRITING systems (the remaining three types), which consist of signs that are devoid of meaning, representing speech sounds only. For instance, Chinese is said to have a morphosyllabic writing system which is pleremic, whereas the scripts of India are instances of a cenemic writing system of a particular kind, a syllabic alphabet. Writing systems in this sense are not bound to individual languages, although they typically reflect some of the features of the language in whose context they evolved. For example, word-syllabic systems came into existence to represent languages characterized by a large proportion of monosyllabic lexemes, i.e. Sumerian, Chinese and Maya; and C alphabets emerged for Semitic languages where C roots bear lexical information.

In the other sense a writing system is what is also referred to as spelling, i.e. a system of rules underlying the use of the GRAPHEMES of a language. For instance, the English writing system is described as highly involved because its rules operate on different levels of grammatical structure. It is understood in this usage that English writing is alphabetic, but what is meant by 'system' here has to do with how alphabetic letters are combined to represent the phonemes, morphemes and words of English. In this sense a writing system is language specific, being a subsystem of the grammar of a language.
See also ORIGIN OF WRITING; TYPOLOGY OF WRITING SYSTEMS.
Reading Gelb 1980; DeFrancis 1989; Coulmas 1989; Sampson 1985.

writing tools Hand-held devices for marking a surface with visual signs representing language. The earliest writing implements included reeds and rushes used in ancient Egypt; styluses cut from reed with a triangular tip to be impressed on clay in Mesopotamia; and brushes made of camel's or rat's hair in China. Like rushes, reeds and brushes the hollow reed was a writing tool for delivering a coloured liquid to a surface. First introduced in the sixth century CE, the quill pen worked basically on the same principle of storing a small column of liquid which was released when pressure was applied to the tip. Yet it was an improvement, since it allowed delivery of the ink in a more controlled fashion. Made of the large wing feathers of large birds, the quill was the chief writing tool in Europe for over 1,000 years (figure 5). It was gradually driven out by the split steel-point pen which was first introduced in England in the eighteenth century. Metal was used much earlier to make pens; a bronze pen came to light in the excavation of Pompeii. However, it was only the steel pen that became a common writing tool. In the early nineteenth century a replenishable ink reservoir was attached to the steel pen to produce the fountain pen. This was a further improvement, since it removed the inconvenience of frequently dipping the pen to replenish the ink while writing.

Cancellaresca Circonflessa.

C. Perche partecipi siate dello scriuere, che nell'età mia giouenile solamente da Iddio imparai col mezo
del dilettarmi houui in publico dimostrato breue et facile il modo, cò che presto saperete le mie lre
formare, se ui piaceranno. Ma prima temperarete la penna, che sia d'oca domestica dura tonda et
traluc.nte; la qual fregata tanto cò panno nero di lana ch'egli non resti imbiancato da lei ridurre-
te cò simigliante coltello
in questa forma canale et lauatele la medol-
la col riuoglierle per dentro la propria coda cosi
li farete il primo taglio al diritto del suo canale cosi
dipoi li farete due tagli uguali cominciati nel mezo del primo cosi
et fra il principio e fine delli detti due tagli assottigliarete in modo che formiate una punta cosi

Figure 5 How to make a quill pen

The end of the eighteenth century saw the invention by Nicholas Jacques Conté, a French chemist, of the lead pencil. Graphite, the material responsible for the black marks that lead pencils produce, was used for marking purposes much earlier. The Aztecs are known to have used graphite before their first contact with Europeans. In England a graphite mine was discovered near Borrowdale, Cumberland, in the sixteenth century, and chunks of graphite called 'marking stones' were used for writing. Conté succeeded in blending graphite powder with clay and other substances to produce pencil lead.

The next significant change in handwriting equipment came with the introduction of the ballpoint pen in the 1940s. Although a first patent for a pen using a rotating ball to deliver ink was issued in 1888 to John H. Loud, an American, the technology was not developed for mass production until 60 years later. The most recent innovation, the felt-tip pen, which because of its soft tip allows for very rapid and fluid writing, was first introduced in Japan.

Many other implements have been invented to satisfy the writing needs peculiar to various occupations, such as the blackboard chalk and whiteboard marker; pens for writing on special surfaces such as glass, polished metal, polymeric films and cloth; and pens for special environments, e.g. under water. In addition, a great variety of wax crayons and synthetic soft-tip pens are also used.
See also CALLIGRAPHY; MANUSCRIPT.
Reading Smith 1966; Kao 1979.

written language While WRITING is often defined as the visual representation of speech, where the principal difference is seen as concerning the medium of physical realization, the term 'written language' is in opposition to 'spoken language', emphasizing as it does the structural differences between the two. The assumption of a close relationship between written and spoken language, traditionally implicit in Western scholarship, is responsible for the relative neglect of these differences in modern linguistics. However, although there is considerable variation in degree across languages, it is safe to say that there are structural differences between the spoken and written forms of all languages that have been used in writing for any length of time. This is so because written language and spoken language are functionally distinct.

The most conspicuous case is that of speech communities in which a language that is unrelated to the spoken vernacular is used for written communication: for instance, SUMERIAN WRITING continued to be used and cultivated by the Akkadians for centuries after it had ceased to be spoken natively. Other examples include classical languages such as Latin, Arabic and Chinese, or colonial languages such as English, French, Portuguese and Dutch in non-native environments. In other cases spoken and written language are related, but the relationship is so remote that the speakers do not recognize the two as forms of the same language, for instance, Haitian Creole and French. In speech communities with a relatively long literary tradition and high literacy, spoken and written language are usually so closely related that they are perceived as stylistic variants of the same system. Yet, even in these cases significant differences exist between the two. Vagueness, ambiguity, repetition and other forms of redundancy are features which are characteristic of spoken language, but disfavoured in written language.

Systematic research into the specific consequences that follow from these general differences began, in the 1970s, as a by-product of the study of spoken language. Empirical analyses of speech on the basis of real-life recordings by sociolinguists and discourse analysts revealed forms of linguistic expression quite different from the isolated, well-formed sentences which usually constitute the object of grammar modelling. It was promising, therefore, to take a closer look at the structural specifics of both oral and written forms of language.

While many aspects of the structure of language are independent of its mode of physical expression, and while spoken and written language do not correspond to categorical differences, a number of significant pragmatic, lexical and grammatical contrasts were uncovered. Pragmatic differences result from the fact that writer and reader are not usually collocated. Typically, written language is context independent. Therefore, deictic expressions – pronouns, adverbs, nouns and verbs denoting 'me, you, here, now', movements, directions etc. – cannot be anchored in a shared field of reference. Syntactic differences involve the complexity and length of sentences. Written language is characterized by greater length and more complex embedding, whereas paratactic constructions are preferred in spoken language. Further, the great amount of syntactically incomplete sentences observed in spoken language has raised the question of whether the concept of a sentence itself is not an artefact induced by the conventions of writing, and should hence be reserved to the study of written language. Lexical differences between spoken and written language are also conspicuous: vernacular and slang expressions have a higher currency in the former, while learned words are more common in the latter. In order properly to appreciate these and many other features, it should be noted that their presence or absence is a matter of proclivity rather than absolute distinction, and that spoken language can be made to resemble written language and vice versa.

The study of differences between written and spoken language is of theoretical interest not just because it may explain a particular kind of variation in linguistic expression, but because it may reveal to what extent the theoretical foundations of linguistics are grounded in written rather than in spoken language.
See also DIGLOSSIA; GRAMMAR; WRITTEN NORM.
Reading Akinnaso 1982; Biber 1986; Devitt 1989; Halliday 1990; Horowitz and Samuels 1987.

written norm A term introduced by Josef Vachek and also used by other members of the Prague school of linguistics. It is intended to highlight the fact that a language system for which two modes of physical realization, speech and writing, coexist develops two different norms which cannot be simply reduced to one another. The longer a language is used in both speech and writing, the more its written norm develops properties which cannot be explained as derived from the spoken norm. As a language forms a literary tradition, its further evolution is characterized by a complex interaction between its spoken and written norms.
See also GRAMMAR; LITERACY; WRITTEN LANGUAGE.
Reading Vachek 1973; Baum 1987.

X, x /ɛks/ The twenty-fourth letter of the English alphabet descended from Semitic *tāw*, where it had a /t/-like value. The Greeks revalued it to represent a velar fricative or the C cluster /ks/, making it the only letter of the alphabet to represent a combination of sounds which can be denoted by other individual letters, <k> and <s>. The Latin *X* with this value occurs in final position only, e.g. *rex, lex*. In English <x> represents three different sounds – [ks] as in *excellent*, [gz] as in *exist*, [z] as in *xenography* – as well as the syllable [ɛks] as in *Xmas* and *Xing*, with alternative pronunciations [kris] and [kros].

xenography [Gk ξένος 'guest, stranger' + γράφειν 'to write'] The practice of adopting the original spelling of a LOAN WORD while pronouncing it in one's own language. Examples are found in various writing systems. Many Sumerian words were given an Akkadian pronunciation when the Akkadians adopted the Sumerian script for writing their own language. As SUMEROGRAMS these words were subsequently incorporated into other literary languages of the ancient Near East. Middle Persian texts in the PAHLAVI SCRIPT contain (imperial) Aramaic words in Aramaic spelling which were pronounced in Middle Persian. Xenograms are also known from the sphere of Chinese writing. In Japan a great many Chinese characters were given a Japanese pronunciation in addition to the Chinese one. In English certain abbreviations of Latin origin are habitually or occasionally treated as xenograms, e.g. the pronunciation 'pound' for *lb* instead of 'libra'; 'and so on' instead of 'et cetera' for *etc*. Other terms that have been used for this phenomenon are 'allogram' and 'heterogram'.

xiaozhuan [Chinese 小篆] (*hsiao-chuan*) The Chinese small-seal script, also called lesser or standard seal script, is a calligraphic style traditionally attributed to Li Ssu (*d*.208 BCE), the statesman who carried out the first government standardization of the forms of Chinese characters. A further development of DAZHUAN or large-Seal script, *xiaozhuan* was hence widely adopted by the scribes of the Ch'in dynasty (221–206 BCE) (figure 1). It was with this script style that the arrangement of characters from top to bottom in vertical columns became fixed and uniformity of Chinese writing was achieved.
See also CALLIGRAPHY; CHINESE SCRIPTS; CHINESE WRITING SYSTEM.
Reading Liang 1959; Tsien 1962.

xingshu [Chinese 行書] (*hsing-shu*) The running script of Chinese which came into use from about the fourth century CE. *Xingshu* is a cursive style which leaves the calligrapher more freedom and potential for personal expression than the formal standard script, KAISHU, from which it developed. It is still one of the generally recognized and practised calligraphic styles (figure 2).
See also CALLIGRAPHY; CHINESE SCRIPTS.
Reading Fu 1977.

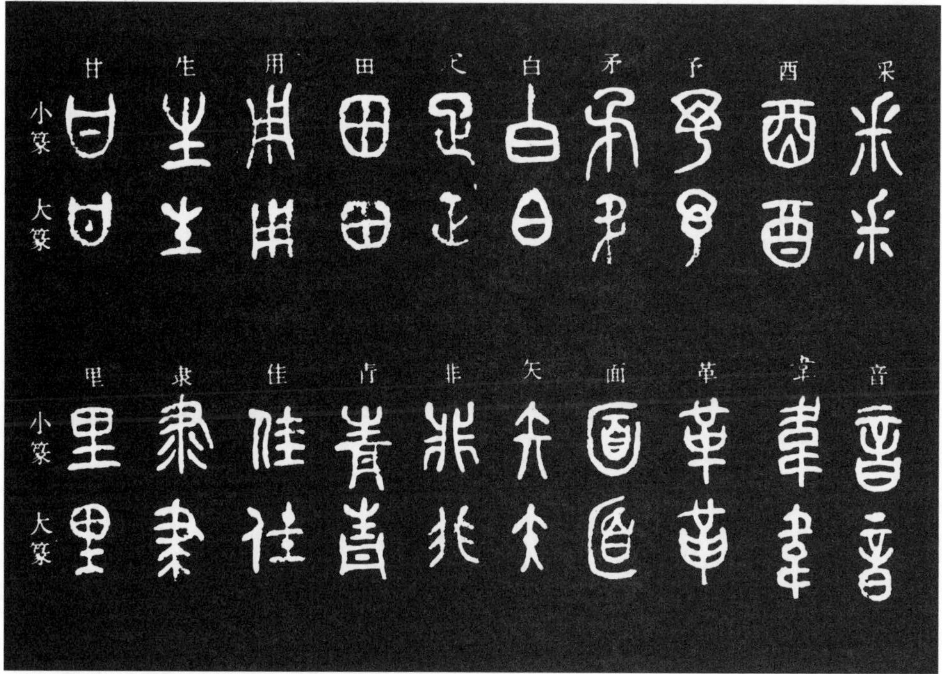

Figure 1 *Chinese seal scripts: (above)* xiaozhuan *'small seal' and (below)* dazhuan *'large seal', with modern printed characters on top*

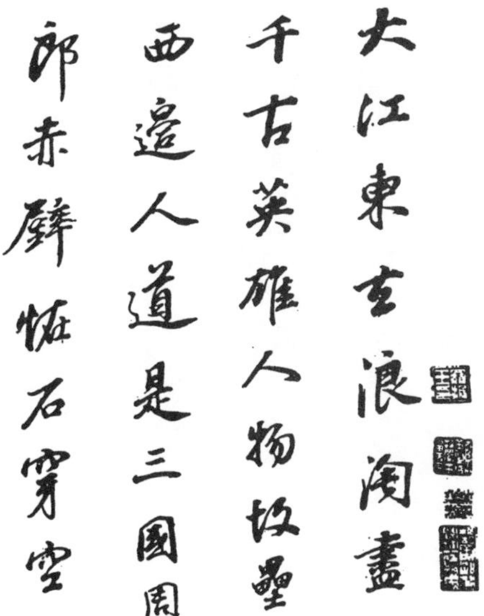

Figure 2 *A specimen of the Chinese* xingshu *'running script' (Ming dynasty, 1368–1644)*

Figure 3 Xylography: Japanese wood block print by Kunisada, a page from a book printed 1860

Xīxīà writing *See* HSI-HSIA WRITING

Xu Shen (Hsü Shu) A Chinese scholar-official who around 100 CE compiled the first comprehensive character dictionary, the *Shuowen jiezi*, containing 9,353 characters. It is the most important source of the early history of Chinese writing. *See also* CHINESE WRITING SYSTEM; DICTIONARY; RADICAL.
Reading DeFrancis 1984b.

xylography [Gk ξύλον 'wood' + γράφειν 'to write'] Wood engraving and wood block printing as distinguished from type. Xylography was used in China for printing books as of the sixth century CE. There and in neighbouring countries that were under the influence of Chinese literacy it became an art combining pictorial designs with calligraphic text which is still cultivated today (figure 3). In Europe it was not until the twelfth century CE that this technique was applied to the production of books. This delay was due to the poor level of chemical knowledge which did not enable the production of proper inks or a suitable printing surface, i.e. PAPER.
See also PRINTING.
Reading Drège 1984.

Y, y /waɪ/ The twenty-fifth letter of the English alphabet has the same origin as *V*: it derives from the Semitic C letter *yōdh* through Greek *upsilon* (Υ, υ) which had the sound value [u] or [y]. The *Y* form was used in Latin to transcribe Greek *upsilon*. In Etruscan and Roman capital and uncial inscriptions the form of the letter without a lower stem still resembles that found in early Greek manuscripts. The lower stem was added to avoid confusion with *V*. In medieval manuscripts it was drawn out slanting to the left, and as of the sixth century a superscript dot or triangular mark was added. The names of the letter in several languages, for instance French *i-grec* and Spanish *i griega*, testify to the origin of *Y* as a 'Greek *i*'. The origin of its English name, *wy* [waɪ], is unknown.

Yale Romanization A system developed at the Chinese Department of Yale University shortly after the US became entangled in the Pacific War. Designed as a learning aid rather than a linguistic transcription system, it is largely phonetic rather than analytic on the morphological level. Morphemic compounds are written together as words, much as they are in PINYIN. Yale stresses distinctions that speak to the eye. Tones are indicated by accent marks. The letters *w* and *y* are used extensively to indicate V quality in order to avoid diacritics, e.g. *ywànyi* for *pinyin yùanyi* and *lwun* for *pinyin lün*.
See also ROMANIZATION.
Reading Newnham 1987.

Yi writing Also known by the Chinese name 'Lolo', which they consider pejorative, the Yi are a minority nationality of China living in Yunnan province and the Yi autonomous prefecture in Sichuan. Yi is a member of the Loloish branch of Tibeto-Burmese languages.

The literary tradition of Yi can be traced back to stone inscriptions dating from the sixteenth century CE, but the origin of Yi writing is unknown, although the inner form of the system points to Chinese influence. Yi is a syllabic system where each grapheme stands for a distinct syllable. Although the syllable structure of Yi is simple, allowing for no C clusters, the total number of tone syllables is between 700 and 800, depending on the variety of Yi. For centuries the script was used for religious and secretive writing, with new and idiosyncratic signs being introduced continuously by individual writers, leading to a total of more than ten times that number. Attempts at reducing the number of current signs and standardizing the script were first undertaken under the auspices of the government of the People's Republic of China. The 'Yi writing standard scheme' was officially adopted in 1975 and introduced into the school system in 1978. It consists of 819 graphemes, 756 for Yi syllables and 63 for syllables occurring in Chinese and other loan words (table 1). The principle underlying the standard scheme is that each tone syllable is represented by one grapheme, and that each grapheme stands for one tone syllable. Tone is thus treated as a feature on a par

		b	p	bb	nb	hm	m	f	v	d	t	dd	nd	hn	n	hl	l	g	k	gg	mg	hx	ng	h	w	z	c	zz	nz	s	ss	zh	ch	rr	nr	sh	r	j	p	jj	nj	ny	x	y	[illegible]
i	[illegible]	[illegible]	[illegible]	[illegible]	[illegible]	[illegible]	[illegible]	[illegible]	[illegible]	[illegible]	[illegible]	[illegible]	[illegible]	[illegible]	[illegible]	[illegible]	[illegible]	[illegible]	[illegible]	[illegible]		[illegible]		[illegible]		[illegible]	[illegible]	[illegible]	[illegible]	[illegible]	[illegible]							[illegible]	[illegible]	[illegible]	[illegible]	[illegible]	[illegible]	[illegible]	t p
ie	[illegible]	[illegible]	[illegible]	[illegible]	[illegible]	[illegible]	[illegible]		[illegible]	[illegible]	[illegible]	[illegible]	[illegible]	[illegible]	[illegible]	[illegible]	[illegible]	[illegible]	[illegible]	[illegible]	[illegible]	[illegible]	[illegible]	[illegible]		[illegible]	[illegible]	[illegible]	[illegible]	[illegible]	[illegible]							[illegible]	[illegible]	[illegible]	[illegible]	[illegible]	[illegible]	[illegible]	t p
a	[illegible]	[illegible]	[illegible]	[illegible]	[illegible]	[illegible]	[illegible]	[illegible]	[illegible]	[illegible]	[illegible]	[illegible]	[illegible]	[illegible]	[illegible]	[illegible]	[illegible]	[illegible]	[illegible]	[illegible]	[illegible]	[illegible]	[illegible]	[illegible]	[illegible]	[illegible]	[illegible]	[illegible]	[illegible]	[illegible]	[illegible]	[illegible]	[illegible]	[illegible]	[illegible]	[illegible]	[illegible]								t p
uo	[illegible]	[illegible]	[illegible]	[illegible]		[illegible]	[illegible]			[illegible]	[illegible]	[illegible]		[illegible]	[illegible]	[illegible]	[illegible]	[illegible]	[illegible]	[illegible]	[illegible]	[illegible]	[illegible]	[illegible]	[illegible]	[illegible]	[illegible]		[illegible]	[illegible]		[illegible]	[illegible]	[illegible]		[illegible]	[illegible]	[illegible]	[illegible]	[illegible]	[illegible]	[illegible]	[illegible]	[illegible]	t p
o	[illegible]	[illegible]	[illegible]	[illegible]	[illegible]	[illegible]	[illegible]	[illegible]	[illegible]	[illegible]	[illegible]	[illegible]	[illegible]	[illegible]	[illegible]	[illegible]	[illegible]	[illegible]	[illegible]	[illegible]	[illegible]	[illegible]	[illegible]	[illegible]	[illegible]	[illegible]	[illegible]	[illegible]	[illegible]	[illegible]	[illegible]	[illegible]	[illegible]	[illegible]	[illegible]	[illegible]	[illegible]	[illegible]	[illegible]	[illegible]	[illegible]	[illegible]	[illegible]	[illegible]	t p
e	[illegible]	[illegible]		[illegible]			[illegible]		[illegible]	[illegible]	[illegible]	[illegible]	[illegible]	[illegible]	[illegible]	[illegible]	[illegible]	[illegible]	[illegible]	[illegible]	[illegible]	[illegible]	[illegible]	[illegible]	[illegible]	[illegible]	[illegible]	[illegible]	[illegible]	[illegible]	[illegible]	[illegible]	[illegible]	[illegible]	[illegible]	[illegible]	[illegible]								t p
u		[illegible]	[illegible]	[illegible]	[illegible]	[illegible]	[illegible]	[illegible]	[illegible]	[illegible]	[illegible]	[illegible]	[illegible]	[illegible]	[illegible]	[illegible]	[illegible]	[illegible]	[illegible]	[illegible]	[illegible]					[illegible]	[illegible]	[illegible]	[illegible]	[illegible]	[illegible]	[illegible]	[illegible]	[illegible]	[illegible]	[illegible]	[illegible]	[illegible]	[illegible]	[illegible]	[illegible]	[illegible]		[illegible]	t p
ur		[illegible]	[illegible]	[illegible]	[illegible]	[illegible]	[illegible]	[illegible]	[illegible]	[illegible]	[illegible]	[illegible]	[illegible]		[illegible]	[illegible]	[illegible]	[illegible]	[illegible]	[illegible]	[illegible]					[illegible]	[illegible]	[illegible]	[illegible]	[illegible]		[illegible]	[illegible]	[illegible]	[illegible]	[illegible]	[illegible]	[illegible]	[illegible]	[illegible]	[illegible]			[illegible]	
y		[illegible]	[illegible]	[illegible]	[illegible]	[illegible]	[illegible]	[illegible]	[illegible]							[illegible]	[illegible]									[illegible]	[illegible]	[illegible]	[illegible]	[illegible]	[illegible]	[illegible]	[illegible]	[illegible]	[illegible]	[illegible]	[illegible]	[illegible]	[illegible]	[illegible]	[illegible]		[illegible]	[illegible]	t p
yr		[illegible]	[illegible]		[illegible]	[illegible]			[illegible]							[illegible]	[illegible]									[illegible]	[illegible]	[illegible]	[illegible]	[illegible]	[illegible]	[illegible]	[illegible]	[illegible]	[illegible]	[illegible]	[illegible]	[illegible]	[illegible]		[illegible]		[illegible]	[illegible]	

Table 1 *The Yi syllabary: a list of 756 syllabic signs selected and standardized in 1975 from thousands of symbols used for centuries by the Yi or Lolo nationality in south-west China*

with other phonological features differentiating syllables, rather than being indicated by means of diacritics added to graphemes for toneless syllables. Since the graphemes have no meaning but are purely phonetic, the Yi system of writing is the largest existing syllabary and probably the largest syllabic system that has ever been standardized.

In the twentieth century, an alphabetic writing system using Roman letters was devised for Yi with the help of an Australian-British missionary known only by his Chinese name Zhang Erchang. This system, which is generally referred to as 'black Yi writing', is used by Yi Christians, but has not supplanted the traditional syllabic script.

Reading Kao 1992; DeFrancis 1989; Huang 1992.

Yiddish writing Also known as 'Judaeo-German', Yiddish is the only Germanic language not written in the Roman alphabet. The earliest extant records are glosses in biblical commentaries dating from the twelfth century, but the oldest known manuscript, a medical treatise, is only from 1396. Modern literary Yiddish is based on eastern dialects (figure 1). It is written in the Hebrew alphabet, with several standardized diacritics (table 2). A standard for the spelling system was promulgated in 1936.

The modern orthography is largely phonemic with relatively simple grapheme–phoneme correspondences, although words of Hebrew-Aramaic origin retain the traditional historical-etymological spelling which often deviates considerably from one-to-one phonographic mapping. Since the letters of the Hebrew alphabet stand for Cs only, V indication is by means of diacritics, largely following the Hebrew pattern (TIBERIAN POINTING). PLENE WRITING is also common, i.e. certain C letters are used to represent Vs and diphthongs. Already attested in the fourteenth century, *plene* writing has become increasingly standardized in the course of time: א for /a/ and /o/, ע for /ɛ/, יי for /ej/, and ו plus י for /oj/. Initial א before י, ו and diphthongs is silent. When V points are used, Cs with no following Vs are marked with a subscript colon (SCHWA) which indicates the absence of a V. Like Hebrew, Yiddish is written from right to left.

See also HEBREW WRITING.

Reading Committee for the Unified Yiddish Spelling 1994; Wexler 1981.

yogh The name of the letter ȝ used in Old English manuscripts for <g>. It came to represent three diferent sounds, [j], [g] and [ʤ]. In Middle English it was used for the fricative [x], as in *loch*. Subsequently it was replaced by <gh>.

Yoruba writing A member of the Kwa branch of Niger-Congo languages spoken in south-west Nigeria and in Benin and Togo, Yoruba has been written in Roman letters since the beginning of the nineteenth century, when European missionaries first used it in writing. The alphabet of modern standard Yoruba, which enjoys official status in Nigeria, consists of 25 letters, seven Vs and 18 Cs (table 3). Letters <ẹ> and <ọ> are counted as separate graphemes denoting open [ɛ] and [ɔ] as distinct from [e] and [o], respectively. Letter <ṣ> designates a palato-alveolar fricative [š]. The digraph <gb>, likewise a separate grapheme, stands for a co-articulated bilabial velar. In addition, the acute and grave accent marks are

אַלפֿסנדר שפּיגלבלאַט / פּתח־תּקוה

אויפֿן וועג צו אַ סך־הכּל

די מאָדערנע ייִדישע ליטעראַטור האָט אַ וויליונגישן צאַפּל געטאָן איבער די מיזרחדיקע, היימישע לענדערײַען, און זיך שטילערהייט, מיט אַ פֿאַרשײַט חנדל, אַראָפּגעלאָזט אויף די רײַכע מירמלנע טרעפּ פֿון דער אייראָפּעיִשער קולטור־בעל־הבתּישקייט.

עשׂרה בטלנים — די אמתע מבֿינים אויף אַזאַ מין באַשעפֿעניש — זענען געווען עדות פֿונעם דאָזיקן מעמד און זיי האָבן טאַקע מלא־התפּעלות זיך אָנגערופֿן איינער צום צווייטן:

— פֿאַר וואָר, די גאָלדענע פּאַווע?

— אַוודאי, די גאָלדענע פּאַווע!

Transliteration

Afn veg tsu a sakh-haki
Di moderne yidishe literatur hot a voylyungishn tsapl geton iber di mizrekhdike, heymishe lenderayen, un zikh shtilerheyt, mit a farshayt kheyndl, aropgelozt af di raykhe mirmlme trep fun der eyropeyisher kultur-balebatishkeyt.
Asore batlonem – di emese meyvinem af aza min bashefenesh zikh ungerufn eyner tsum tsveytn:
Far vor, di goldene pave?
Avade, di goldene pave!

Translation

En route to a summing-up
Modern Yiddish literature wriggled mischievously across the folksy eastern landscape, and quietly, with a saucy smile, it descended on the rich marble steps of the European cultural establishment.

The ten Ne'er-Do-Wells – who were the only real connoisseurs of such matters – were witness to these circumstances and they actually called out to one another, gleefully:

'Is this, indeed, the golden peacock?'
'Definitely, the golden peacock!'

Figure 1 Specimen of Yiddish writing: Aleksander Shpiglblat, Goldene keyt, *1990, 130, p. 195 (transliteration, Library of Congress system; translation courtesy Joshua A. Fishman)*

		Final			Final
א	Aleph		ל	Lamed	
ב	Beth		מ	Mem	ם
ג	Gimel		נ	Nun	ן
ד	Daleth		ס	Samek	
ה	He		ע	Ayin	
ו	Waw		פ	Pe	ף
ז	Zayin		צ	Tsadeh	ץ
ח	Heth		ק	Qoph	
ט	Teth		ר	Resh	
י	Yodh		ש	Shin	
כ	Kaph	ך	ת	Taw	

Table 2 The Yiddish alphabet

a	f	j	o	ṣ
b	g	k	ọ	t
d	gb	l	p	u
e	h	m	r	w
ẹ	i	n	s	y

Table 3 The Yoruba alphabet

used to indicate rising and falling register tone. The Roman letters *c, q, v, x, y* are not used, except in foreign proper names.

Yue writing Yue is the Chinese language spoken in Guangdong (Canton) and Guangxi in south China and usually referred to as Cantonese in Western literature. It is written in the CHINESE SCRIPT with a number of additional characters and variant characters not found in standard Chinese writing (table 4). However, the Yue-made characters conform to the construction principles of Chinese CHARACTERS.

Yue	啲	di^{1}	possessive	嚟	lai^{5}	to come
Chinese	的	dē		来	lái	

Table 4 Specimen of Yue characters that differ from Chinese: superscript numbers indicate tone

Yupik writing A syllabic writing system for central Yupic, an Eskimoan language of Alaska, invented around 1900 by Uyakoq (1860–1924), a native speaker of that language who had been exposed to English writing through his literate son, but was not himself literate. The script has attracted considerable interest

	Vowel letters						
	1	a	[illegible]		4	i	[illegible]
	2	i	[illegible]		5	ai, i, y	[illegible]
	3	u	[illegible]				
	Consonant letters						
			a	i	u	schliessend	„vorlesen.“
Labials	6	p	[illegible]	[illegible]	[illegible]	[illegible]	[illegible]
	7	v	[illegible]	[illegible]	[illegible]	[illegible]	[illegible]
	8	m	[illegible]	[illegible]	[illegible]	[illegible]	[illegible]
Dentals	9	t	[illegible]	[illegible]	[illegible]	[illegible]	[illegible]
	10	s, ts	[illegible]	[illegible]	[illegible]	[illegible]	[illegible]
	11	n	[illegible]	[illegible]	[illegible]	[illegible]	[illegible]
Velars	12	k	[illegible]	[illegible]	[illegible]	[illegible]	[illegible]
	13	g	[illegible]	[illegible]	[illegible]	[illegible]	[illegible]
	14	ng [ŋ]	[illegible]	[illegible]	[illegible]	[illegible]	[illegible]
Uvulars	15	q	[illegible]	[illegible]	[illegible]	[illegible]	[illegible]
	16	r	[illegible]	[illegible]	[illegible]	[illegible]	[illegible]
	17						[illegible]
	18	y	[illegible]	[illegible]	[illegible]		
	19	l	[illegible]	[illegible]	[illegible]	[illegible]	[illegible]
	Special features						
	20	ar	[illegible]		25	u(i)t	[illegible]
	21	ag	[illegible]		26	kut	[illegible]
	22	ig	[illegible]		27	qoq	[illegible]
	23	mik	[illegible]		28	tlo	[illegible]
	24	lit	[illegible]		29	uga	[illegible]

Table 5 The Yupik syllabary: latest developmental stage of the script
Source: *adapted from Schmitt 1951, figure 13*

among scholars of writing because it quickly evolved from a logographic system, based on traditional pictograms, to a syllabic system. Uyakoq apparently learned to write some English words which, however, he used holistically via XENOGRAPHY for Yupik words which could be combined with graphemes denoting Yupik inflectional endings. The Yupik language is now mostly written in the Roman alphabet which has been used in various forms since the early nineteenth century. A systematic orthography was worked out in the 1960s at the University of Alaska (table 5).

Reading Schmitt 1951; Jacobsen 1995.

Z

Z, z [zɛd] The twenty-sixth letter of the English alphabet derives from Semitic *zayin* through Greek *zeta* (Z, ζ). It appears in Latin only after the conquest of Greece by the Romans in the first century BCE. Letter ζ occupied the seventh position in the Greek alphabet, but since it was not used in early Latin inscriptions, it was added as the final letter to the Latin alphabet to transcribe Greek words with an initial /z/ sound like *Zeus*. The two forms of the small letter, one between the lines <z> and one with a descender below the base line <ʒ>, were already known in early medieval times.

Zaiwa writing One of China's recognized minority languages, Zaiwa is a variety of the Jingpo language. A writing system based on the modified Roman alphabet for Lisu was created in 1912.
See also LISU WRITING.

Zapotec writing A member of the Otomanguean group of Mesoamerican languages, Zapotec is thought to be the language associated with the earliest form of writing in Mesoamerica. The Zapotec culture occupied a prominent position in the Monte Albán region, Oaxaca, south Mexico, between 500 BCE and 700 CE. Sculptures and ceramics of the so-called *dazante* style exhibit a formalized calendar and genealogical registers, which are the oldest written documents known from Mesoamerica. The Zapotec word for 'book' or 'document', *quichi tija colaça,* means 'paper of old lineage people'. So far the glyphs of Zapotec inscriptions are poorly understood, although parallels with the Maya calendar, which is likely to derive from the Zapotec prototype, allow for the interpretation of numeral glyphs as well as glyphs of years and days (figure 1). Interpretations of longer inscriptions

Figure 1 Zapotec glyphs of days with numbers
Source: *Caso 1965*

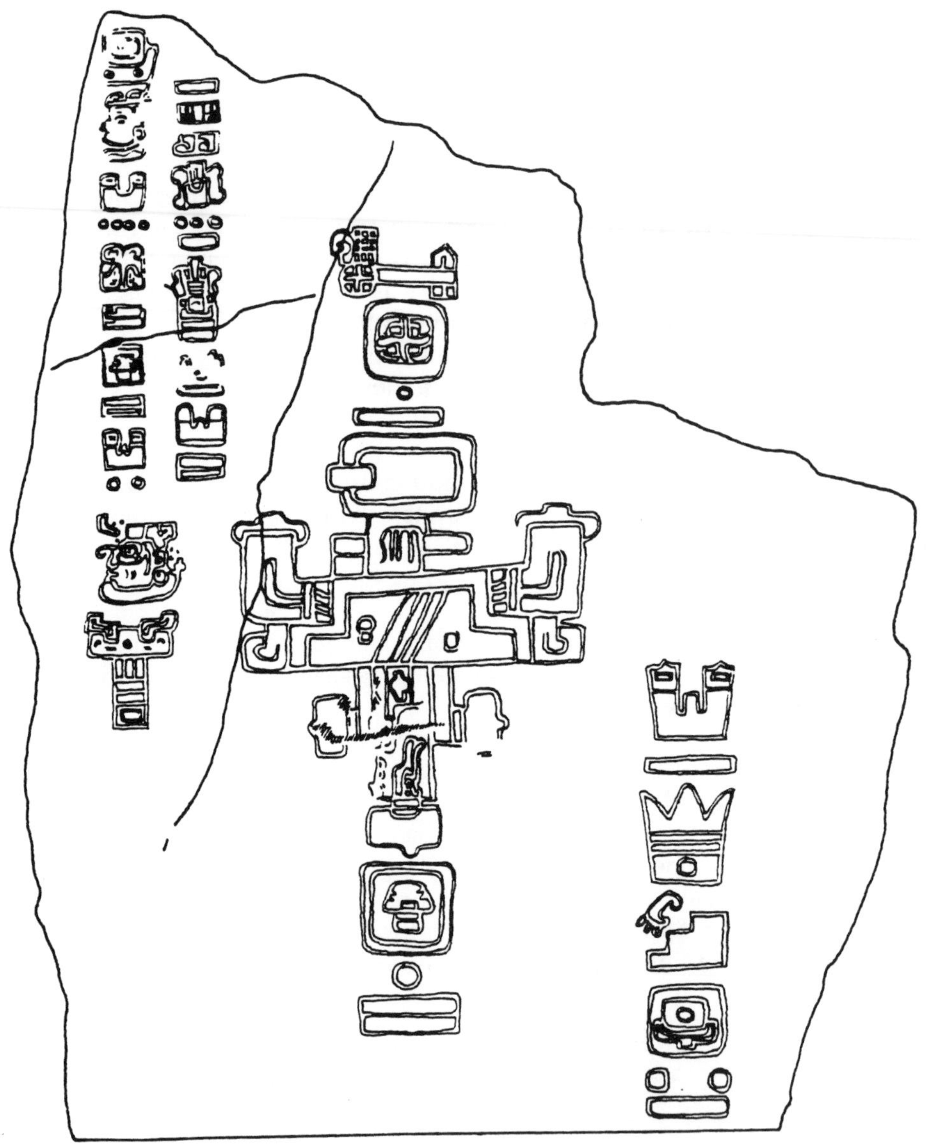

Figure 2 Zapotec inscription Lápida 14, Mound J, Monte Albán
Source: *Caso 1965*

have also been attempted, but a great deal of uncertainty remains (figure 2). However, much progress has been made in analysing Maya writing and Olmec writing, and because Zapotec survives as a spoken language there is hope that eventually it will be discovered how the glyphs relate to linguistic units.

Modern Zapotec is written in the Roman alphabet with nine additional letters: <c̲, ə, j̲, l̲, n̲, ñ, š, x̲, ž>. The digraphs <cw, gw> stand for labialized /k°, g°,/, respectively.

Reading Caso 1965; Benson 1971; Marcus 1980; Whittaker 1980.

	Consonant letters												Vowel letters							
MPS	ㄅ	ㄆ	ㄇ	ㄈ	ㄪ	ㄉ	ㄊ	ㄋ	ㄌ	ㄍ	ㄎ	ㄫ	ㄚ	ㄛ	ㄜ	ㄝ	ㄧ	ㄨ	ㄩ	ㄦ
CPA	b	p	m	f	w	d	t	n	l	g	k	ng	a	o	e	ê	i	u	ü	er
IPA	p	pʻ	m	f	v	t	tʻ	n	l	k	kʻ	ŋ	ʌ	o	ɤ	ɛ	i	u	y	ər
MPS	ㄏ	ㄐ	ㄑ	ㄬ	ㄒ	ㄓ	ㄔ	ㄕ	ㄖ	ㄗ	ㄘ	ㄙ	ㄞ	ㄟ	ㄠ	ㄡ	ㄢ	ㄣ	ㄤ	ㄥ
CPA	h	j	q	n	x	zh	ch	sh	ri	z	c	s	ai	ei	ao	ou	an	en	ang	eng
IPA	x	tɕ	tɕʻ	ȵ	ɕ	tʂ	tʂʻ	ʂ	ʐ	ts	tsʻ	s	ai	ei	au	ou	an	ən	aŋ	əŋ

Table 1 Zhùyīn zìmǔ *or Mandarin phonetic symbols (MPS) with sound values indicated in the Chinese phonetic alphabet (CPA) and the international phonetic alphabet (IPA)*

zhuanshu (*chuan-shu*) The Chinese seal script.
See also DAZHUAN; XIAOZHUAN.

zhùyīn zìmǔ (Mandarin phonetic symbols, MPS) A system of 40 phonetic signs, 24 for C onsets and 16 for V nuclei, which are typographically derived from Chinese characters, for representing the Mandarin pronunciation of Chinese syllables as the national standard (table 1). The system was adopted under government auspices in 1913. Initially called *zhùyīn zīmǔ* 'phonetic alphabet', it was renamed *zhùyīn fúhào* 'phonetic symbols' in 1930 in order to avoid the impression that an alphabetic system of writing was in use in China. Since the official adoption of PINYIN the system is no longer used in China, but in Taiwan it still serves as the basis of early school instruction and is occasionally used for character annotation.
Reading DeFrancis 1984b.

BIBLIOGRAPHY

Aalto, Pentii. 1964. 'Schrift-Oriatisch.' *Handbuch der Orientalistik* I/4, 185–99. Leiden, Cologne: Brill.

Abercrombie, David. 1949. 'What is a "Letter"?' *Lingua* 2, 54–62.

African Studies Program. 1962. *The Standard Vai Script.* Monrovia: University of Liberia.

Aghali Zakara, M. and Drouin, J. 1978. 'Recherches sur le tifinagh.' *Comtes rendus du Group linguistique d'études chamito-sémitique* 18/23, 245–9, 279–84.

Agrawala, V. S. 1966. 'The Devanagari Script.' In: *Indian Systems of Writing.* Delhi: Publications Division, 12–16.

Akinnaso, F. Niyi. 1982. 'On the Difference between Spoken and Written Language.' *Language and Speech* 25/2, 97–125.

Albright, R. W. 1958. *The International Phonetic Alphabet: Its Background and Development.* Bloomington: Indiana University Press.

Albrow, K. H. 1972. *The English Writing System: Notes towards a Description.* London: Longmans.

Alisjahbana, S. Takdir. 1984. 'The Concept of Language Standardization and its Application to the Indonesian Language.' In: F. Coulmas (ed.) *Linguistic Minorities and Literacy.* Berlin, New York: Mouton, 77–98.

Allchin, Bridget and Allchin, Raymond. 1982. *The Rise of Civilization in India and Pakistan.* London: Cambridge University Press.

Alleton, Viviane. 1970. *L'Écriture chinoise.* Paris: Presses universitaires de France.

Andrews, Carol. 1981. *The Rosetta Stone.* London: British Museum Publications.

Ansell, Michael. 1979. 'Handwriting Classification in Forensic Science.' *Visible Language* XIII, 239–51.

Aquilina, J. 1959. *The Structure of Maltese.* Valetta: Royal University of Malta.

Aronson, Howard I. 1982. *Georgian: A Reading Grammar.* Columbus, Ohio: Slavica.

Augst Gerhard (ed.). 1986. *New Trends in Graphemics and Orthography.* Berlin, New York: DeGruyter.

Avanzini, Alessandra. 1977/1980. *Glossaire des inscriptions de l'Arabie du Sud 1950–1973*, vols I, II. Florence: Instituto di Linguistica e di lingue orientali, Universita di Firenze.

Baines, J. 1983. 'Literacy and Ancient Egyptian Society.' *Man* NS 18, 572–99.

Bankes, George. 1977. *Peru before Pizzarro.* Oxford: Phaidon.

Banks, Doris H. 1989. *Medieval Manuscript Bookmaking: A Bibliographic Guide.* Metuchen, NJ: Scarecrow Press.

Baron, Dennis E. 1982. *Grammar and Good Taste: Reforming the American Language.* New Haven and London: Yale University Press.

Barr, James. 1976. 'Reading a Script without Vowels.' In: W. Haas (ed.) *Writing without Letters.* Manchester: Manchester University Press, 71–100.

Barthel, T. S. 1969. 'Entzifferung früher Schriftsysteme in Alt-Amerika und Polynesien.' In: *Frühe Schriftzeugnisse der Menschheit.* Göttingen: Vandenhoek und Ruprecht, 151–76.

Barthélemy, J. J. 1754. *Reflexions sur l'alphabet et sur la langue dont on se servoit autrefois à Palmyre.* Paris: Académie des Inscriptions.

Barton, Paul Alfred. 1991. *Afrikuandika: The African Hieroglyphic Writing System.* New York: Vantage Press.

Battestini, Simon P. X. 1994. *Ecriture, texte et Afrique: Pour une théorie de l'écriture et du texte.* Washington, DC: Georgetown University, MS.

Baugh, Albert C. 1951. *A History of the English Language.* London: Routledge and Kegan Paul.

Baum, Richard. 1987. *Hochsprache, Literatursprache, Schriftsprache.* Darmstadt: Wissenschaftliche Buchgesellschaft.

Bauer, Hans and Leander, Pontus. 1922. *Historische Grammatik der hebräischen Sprache des Alten Testaments.* Halle: Niemeyer, reprinted Hildesheim: Olms, 1965.

Beck, H. 1963. 'Problems of Word Division and Capitalization.' In: William A. Smalley et al. *Orthography Studies: Articles on New Writing Systems.* London: United Bible Societies, 156–60.

Beckett, Brian. 1988. *Introduction to Cryptology.* Oxford: Blackwell.

Beeston, Alfred F. L. 1970. *The Arabic Language today.* London: Hutchinson.

—— 1984. *Sabaic Grammar.* Journal of Semitic Studies monograph no. 6. Manchester: University of Manchester Press.

Bell, Alexander Graham. 1900. 'Historical Notes Concerning the Teaching of Speech to the Deaf.' *Volta Review* 2, 113–15; 489–510.

Bender, Marvin L., Bowen, J. Donald, Cooper, Robert L. and Ferguson, Charles A. (eds). 1976. *Language in Ethiopia.* London, New York: Oxford University Press.

Bennett, Jo Anne and Berry, John W. 1991. 'Cree Literacy in the Syllabic Script.' In: D. R. Olson and N. Torrance (eds). *Literacy and Orality.* Cambridge: Cambridge University Press, 90–104.

Benson, Elizabeth P. (ed.). 1971. *Mesoamerican Writing Systems.* Washington, DC: Dumbarton Oaks Research Library Collection.

Berdan, Frances F. and Rieff Anwalt, Patricia. 1992. *The Codex Mendoza.* 4 vols. Berkeley, Los Angeles, Oxford: University of California Press.

Berry, Jack, 1958. 'The Making of Alphabets.' In: *Proceedings of the Eighth International Congress of Linguists.* Oslo: Oslo University Press, 752–64.

—— 1977. ' "The Making of Alphabets" Revisited.' In: J. A. Fishman (ed.) *Advances in the Creation and Revision of Writing Systems.* The Hague, Paris: Mouton, 3–16.

Biber, Douglas. 1986. 'Spoken and Written Textual Dimensions in English: Resolving the Contradictory Findings.' *Language* 62/2, 384–414.

Biber, Douglas. 1988. *Variation across Speech and Writing.* Cambridge: Cambridge University Press.

Bibliothèque nationale. 1990. *Mémoires d'Egypte: Homage de l'Europe à Champollion.* Strasbourg: Nuée bleue.

Biersteker, A. and Plane, M. 1989. 'Swahili Manuscripts and the Study of Swahili Literature.' *Research in African Literature* (Austin) 20/3, 449–72.

Birnbaum, Solomon Asher. 1971. *The Hebrew Scripts.* Leiden: Brill.

Bischoff, Bernhard. 1986. *Paläographie des römischen Altertums und des abendländischen Mittelalters.* Berlin: Erich Schmidt Verlag.

Bishop, T. A. M. 1971. *English Caroline Minuscule.* Oxford: Clarendon Press.

Blanche-Benveniste, Claire. 1993. 'Les Unités: langue écrite, langue orale.' In: C. Pontecorvo and C. Blanche-Benveniste (eds) *Proceedings of the Workshop on Orality versus Literacy: Concepts, Methods and Data.* Strasbourg: European Science Foundation, 139–93.

Bleek, D. F. 1926. 'Note on Bushman Orthography.' *Bantu Studies* 2, 71–4.

Bloomfield, Leonard. 1933. *Language.* New York: Holt, Rinehart and Winston.

Blum, A. 1932. *Les Origines du papier, de l'imprimerie et de la gravure.* Paris: Editions du Trianon (Engl. trans. *On the Origin of Paper.* New York: R. R. Bowker, 1934).

Boge, Herbert. 1973. *Griechische Tachygraphie und Tironische Noten: Ein Handbuch der mittelalterlichen und antiken Schnellschrift.* Berlin: Akademie-Velag.

Bolinger, Dwight. 1946. 'Visible Morphemes.' *Language* 22, 333–50.

Bonfante, G. and Bonfante, L. 1983. *The Etruscan Language: An Introduction.* Manchester: Manchester University Press.

Borger, Rykle. 1981. *Assyrisch-babylonische Zeichenliste.* Neukirchen-Vluyn: Neukirchener Verlag.

Bottéro, J. 1982. 'Écriture et civilisation en Mésopotamie.' In: B. André-Leiknam and C. Ziegler (eds) *Naissance de l'écriture: Cuneiformes et hiéroglyphes.* Paris: Ministère de la Culture.

Bowdre, Paul H., Jr. 1982. 'Eye Dialect as a Problem in Graphics.' *Visible Language* XVI/2, 177–82.

Bradley Holmes, R. and B. Sharp Smith. 1976. *Beginning Cherokee.* Norman, OK: University of Oklahoma Press.

Bricker, Victoria A. 1986. *A Grammar of Mayan Hieroglyphs.* New Orleans: Tulane University Middle American Research Institute Publications 56.

Bright, William and Khan, Saeed A. 1976. *The Urdu Writing System.* Ithaca, New York: Spoken Language Services, Inc.

Brincken, Anna Dorothea von der. 1972. 'Tabula alphabetica: von den Anfängen alphabetischer Registerarbeiten zu Geschichtswerken.' In: Max-Planck-Institut für Geschichte (ed.) *Festschrift für Hermann Heimpel.* Göttingen: Vandenhoeck and Ruprecht.

Britto, Francis. 1986. *Diglossia: A Study of the Theory with Application to Tamil.* Washington, DC: Georgetown University Press.

Brixhe, C. and Lejeune, M. 1984. *Corpus des inscriptions paléo-phrygiennes.* 2 vols. Paris: Institut français d'études anatoliennes.

Brooks, Maria Zagórska. 1975. *Polish Reference Grammar.* The Hague: Mouton.

Brown, M. P. 1990. *A Guide to Western Historical Scripts from Antiquity to 1600.* London: British Library.

Brunner, Helmut. 1973a. 'Hieratisch.' In: *Ägyptische Schrift und Sprache: Handbuch der Orientalistik.* Erste Abteilung. Leiden, Cologne: E. J. Brill, 40–7.

—— 1973b. 'Demotisch.' in: *Ägyptische Schrift und Sprache: Handbuch der Orientalistik.* Erste Abteilung. Leiden, Cologne: E. J. Brill, 48–51.

Bühler, Georg. 1980. *Indian Palaeography.* New Delhi: Oriental Reprint. (German original published in 1896.)

Bullough, D. A. 1991. *Carolingian Renewal: Sources and Heritage.* Manchester: Manchester University Press.

Bundgard, J. A. 1965. 'Why Did the Art of Writing Spread to the West? Reflections on the Alphabet of Marsiliana.' *Annalecta Romana Instituti Danici* 3, 11–72.

Butler, Edward H. 1951. *The Story of British Shorthand.* London: Pitman.

Büttner, C. G. 1892. *Suaheli-Schriftstücke in Arabischer Schrift.* Stuttgart, Berlin: W. Spemann.

Callery, Emma. 1993. *The Complete Calligrapher: A Comprehensive Guide from Basic Techniques to Inspirational Alphabets.* London: New Burlington Books.

Cardona, Giorgio R. 1986. *Storia universale della scrittura.* Milano: Mondadori.

Carey, G. V. 1958. *Mind the Stop: A Brief Guide to Punctuation.* London: Cambridge University Press.

Carter, Thomas F. 1955. *The Invention of Printing in China and its Spread Westward.* New York: Columbia University Press.

Caso, Alfonso. 1965. 'Zapotec Writing and Calendar.' In: Robert Wauchope, and Gordon Willey (eds) *Handbook of Middle American Indians.* vol. 3, part 2. Austin, TX: University of Texas Press, 931–47.

Casparis, J. G. de. 1975. 'Indonesian Palaeography: A History of Writing in Indonesia from the Beginnings to c. AD 1500.' *Handbuch der Orientalistik* III/4.1. Leiden, Cologne: Brill.

Castro, I., Duarte, I. and Leiria, I. (eds). 1986. *A demanda da ortografia Portuguesa: Comentário do acordo ortográfico de 1986 e subsídios para a compreensão da questão que se lhe seguiu.* Lisbon: Sá da Costa.

Catach, Nina. 1978. *L'Orthographe.* Paris: Presses universitaires de France (Collection Que sais-je).

Chadwick, John. 1958. *The Decipherment of Linear B.* Cambridge: Cambridge University Press, 2nd edn 1967.

Chafe, Wallace. 1986. 'Writing in the Perspective of Speaking.' In: Charles R. Cooper and Sidney Greenbaum (eds) *Studying Writing: Linguistic Approaches.* Beverly Hills, London, New Delhi: Sage, 12–39.

Chakraborty, Ashit. 1978. *Read Lepcha: An Introduction to the Lepcha or Róng Script and Self-Instructor for Reading the Language.* New Delhi: Chaya Chakraborty.

Champollion, Jean-François. 1833. *Lettres écrites d'Egypte et de Nubië en 1828 et 1829.* Geneva: Slatkine Reprints, 1973.

Chao, Yuen Ren. 1968. *Language and Symbolic Systems.* Cambridge, MA.: Harvard University Press.

Chasseboeuf Volney, C. F. Compte de. 1818. *L'Alphabet européen applique aux langues asiatiques.* Paris: Didot.

Chatterji, Suniti Kumar. 1966. 'Brahmi – The Mother of Indian Scripts.' In: *Indian Systems of Writing.* Delhi: Publications Division, 7–11.

Chen, Ping. 1996. 'Towards a Phonographic Writing System of Chinese: A Case Study in Writing Reform.' *International Journal of the Sociology of Language.*

Chiera, Edward. 1938. *They Wrote on Clay.* Chicago, London: The University of Chicago Press.

Chomsky, Noam and Halle, Morris. 1968. *The Sound Pattern of English.* New York: Harper and Row.

Civil, Miguel. 1973. 'The Sumerian Writing System: Some Problems.' *Orientalia* 42: 21–34.

Clanchy, M. T. 1993. *From Memory to Written Record,* 2nd edn. Oxford: Blackwell.

Clédat, L. 1930. *Précis d'Orthographe française.* Paris: Hatier.

Clemens, Samuel. 1967. 'Simplified Spelling.' In: B. DeVoto (ed.) *Letters from the Earth.* New York: Fawcett World Library, 131–3.

Coe, Michael. 1992. *Breaking the Maya Code.* London: Thames and Hudson.

Cohen, George Leonard. 1982. 'The Origin of the Letter Omicron.' *Kadmos* 21, 122–4.

Cohen, Marcel. 1958. *La Grande Invention de l'écriture et son évolution.* 3 vols. Paris: Klincksieck.

Cohen Stuart, Abraham B. 1875. *Kawi Oorkonden in Facsimile, met inleiding en transcriptie.* 2 vols. Leiden: E. J. Brill.

Collon, Dominique. 1990. *Near Eastern Seals.* London: British Museum Publications.

Comentale, Cristophe. 1984. 'Les Techniques de l'imprimerie à caractères mobiles (XIe–XVIIIe siècles).' *Revue Française d'Histoire du Livre* 42, 41–55.

Committee for the Unified Yiddish Spelling. 1994. *Takones fun yidishn oysleyg,* naye uflage. *Rules of Yiddish Spelling,* new edition. New York: League for Yiddish and YIVO Institute for Jewish Research.

Cook-Gumperz, Jenny (ed.). 1986. *The Social Construction of Literacy.* Cambridge: Cambridge University Press.

Cook-Gumperz, Jenny and Gumperz, John J. 1981. 'From Oral to Written Culture: The Transition to Literacy.' In: M. Farr Whiteman (ed.) *Writing: The Nature, Development, and Teaching of Written Communication,* vol. 1. Hillsdale, NJ: Lawrence Erlbaum, 89–109.

Cooper-Clark, James. 1938. *The Codex Mendoza.* 3 vols. London: Taylor and Francis.

Coulmas, Florian. 1983. 'Writing and Literacy in China.' In: F. Coulmas and K. Ehlich (eds) *Writing in Focus.* Berlin, New York, Amsterdam: Mouton, 239–53.

—— 1984. 'Arbitrariness and Double Articulation in Writing.' In: L. Henderson (ed.) *Orthographies and Reading.* London: Lawrence Erlbaum, 57–66.

—— 1989. *The Writing Systems of the World.* Oxford: Blackwell.

—— 1991. 'The Future of Chinese Characters.' In: R. L. Cooper and B. Spolsky (eds) *The Influence of Language on Culture and Thought.* Berlin, New York: Mouton, 227–43.

—— 1992. *Language and Economy.* Oxford: Blackwell.

Dalby, David. 1967. 'A Survey of the Indigenous Scripts of Liberia and Sierra Leone: Vai, Mende, Loma, Kpelle and Bassa.' *African Language Studies* 8: 1–51.

—— 1968. 'The Indigenous Scripts of West Africa and Surinam: Their Inspiration and Design.' *African Language Studies* 9: 156–97.

—— 1969. 'Further Indigenous Scripts of West Africa: Manding, Wolof, Fula Writing and Yoruba "Holy" Writing.' *African Language Studies* 10, 161–81.

Dale, Ian R. H. 1980. 'Digraphia.' *International Journal of the Sociology of Language* 26, 5–13.

Daly, L. W. and Daly B. A. 1964. 'Some Techniques in Medieval Latin Lexicography.' *Speculum* 39, 231–9.

Damman, E. 1980. 'Nilnubisches Schrifttum.' *Africana Marburgensia* 13, 3ff.

Dandamaev, Muhammad A. and Lukonin, Vladimir G. 1989. *The Culture and Social Institutions of Ancient Iran.* Cambridge, New York: Cambridge University Press.

Dani, Ahmad Hasan. 1963. *Indian Palaeography.* Oxford: Clarendon Press.

Daniels, Peter T. 1990. 'Fundamentals of Grammatology.' *Journal of the American Oriental Society* 110, 727–31.

—— 1992. 'The Syllabic Origin of Writing and the Segmental Origin of the Alphabet.' In: P. Downing, S. D. Lima and M. Noonan (eds) *The Linguistics of Literacy.* Amsterdam, Philadelphia: John Benjamins, 83–110.

Danlos, Laurence. 1987. *The Linguistic Basis of Text Generation.* Cambridge: Cambridge University Press.

Danwiwat, Nanthana. 1987. *The Thai Writing System.* Hamburg: Buske (Forum Phoneticum 39).

Daswani, C. J. 1975. 'The Question of One Script for Indian Languages: Devanagari or Roman.' *Indian Linguistics* 36/3, 182–5.

—— 1976. 'A Common National Script for Indian Languages – Augmented Devanagari.' *Journal of the School of Languages,* Winter 1975–6, 36–42.

—— 1979. 'Movement for the Recognition of Sindhi and for the Choice of a Script for Sindhi.' In: E. Annamalai (ed.) *Language Movements in India.* Manasagangotri, Mysore: Central Institute of Indian Languages, 60–9.

DeFrancis, John. 1984a. 'Digraphia.' *Word* 35/1, 59–66.

—— 1984b. *The Chinese Language: Fact and Fantasy.* Honolulu: University of Hawaii Press.

—— 1989. *Visible Speech: The Diverse Oneness of Writing Systems.* Honolulu: University of Hawaii Press.

Deimel, A. 1923. 'Schultexte aus Fara.' *Wissenschaftliche Veröffentlichungen der Deutschen Orientalischen Gesellschaft* 43.

de Rooij, Jaap and Verhoeven, Gerard. 1988. 'Orthography Reform and Language Planning for Dutch.' *International Journal of the Sociology of Language* 73, 65–84.

Derrida, Jacques. 1967. *De la grammatologie.* Paris: Les Éditions de Minuit.

Derwing, Bruce L. 1992. 'Orthographic Aspects of Linguistic Competence.' In: P. Downing, S. D. Lima and M. Noonan (eds) *The Linguistics of Literacy.* Amsterdam, Philadelphia: Benjamins, 193–210.

De Silva, M. W. S. 1969. 'The Phonological Efficiency of the Maldivian Writing System.' *Anthropological Linguistics* 11/7, 199–209.

De Silva, M. W. S. 1976. *Diglossia and Literacy.* Manasagangotri, Mysore: Central Institute of Indian Languages.

Destombes, Marcel. 1962. 'Un Astrolabe carolingien et l'origine de nos chiffres arabes.' *Archives Internationales d'Histoire des Sciences* 58/9, 3–23.

Devitt, A. J. 1989. *Standardizing Written English.* London: Cambridge University Press.

Devos, J. P. and Seligman, H. 1967. *L'Art de dechiffrer.* Louvain: Publications Universitaires de Louvain.

Dhorme, E. 1948. 'Déchiffrement des inscriptions pseudo-hiéroglyphiques de Byblos.' *Syria* XXV, 1–35.

Diakonoff, Igor M. and Starostin, S. A. 1986. *Hurro-Urartian as an Eastern Caucasian Language.* Munich: Kitzinger.

Dimock, Edward C. 1976. *Introduction to Bengali.* Columbia, MO: South Asia Books.

Diringer, David. 1943. 'The Origin of the Alphabet.' *Antiquity* 17: 77–90.
—— 1968. *The Alphabet: A Key to the History of Mankind.* London, New York: Hutchinson.
—— 1977. *A History of the Alphabet.* Old Woking: Unwin.
Doblhofer, Ernst. 1957. *Zeichen und Wunder: Entzifferung verschollener Schriften und Sprachen.* Vienna: Paul Neff Verlag.
Doerfer, Gerhard. 1964. 'Die mongolische Schriftsprache.' *Handbuch der Orientalistik* I/5, 81–95. Leiden, Cologne: Brill.
Dournon, J.-Y. 1974. *Dictionaire d'orthographe et des difficultés du français.* Paris: Hachette.
Dow, Sterling. 1954. 'Minoan Writing.' *American Journal of Archaeology* LVIII, 77–129.
Drège, Jean-Pierre. 1984. 'La Livre manuscript et les débuts de la xylographie.' *Revue Française d'Histoire du Livre* 42, 19–38.
Dresden, Mark. J. 1958. *Reader in Modern Persian.* New York: American Council of Learned Societies.
Driver, G. R. 1976. *Semitic Writing: From Pictograph to Alphabet,* rev. edn. London: Oxford University Press.
Druet, Roger and Grégoire, Herman. 1976. *La Civilisation de l'ecriture.* Paris: Fayard et Dessain et Tolra.
Duden. 1991. *Die deutsche Rechtschreibung,* 20th edn. Mannheim: Bibliographisches Institut.
Duden. 1994. *Informationen zur neuen deutschen Rechtschreibung.* Nach den Beschlüssen der Wiener Orthographiekonferenz vom 22. bis 24. 11. 1994 für Deutschland, Österreich und die Schweiz. Mannheim: Dudenverlag.
Duggan, Joseph J. (ed.). 1975. *Oral Literature.* Edinburgh and London: Scottish Academic Press.
Duhoux, Yves. 1977. *Le Disque de Phaistos: Archéologie, épigraphie, édition critique, index.* Louvain: Editions Peeters.
Dumont, C. F. H. 1923. *Het Javaansche Letterschrift.* Leiden: Gebroeders van der Hoek.
Dunand, Maurice. 1945. *Byblia grammata: Documents et recherches sur le developpement de l'écriture en Phenicie.* Beirut: Series Liban, Direction des antiquites, études et documents d'archéologie.
Eckhardt, Thorvi. 1989. *Azbuka: Versuch einer Einführung in das Studium der slavischen Paläographie.* Vienna, Cologne: Böhlau.
Eco, Umberto. 1973. *Il Segno.* Milano: Istituto Editoriale Internazionale.
Edwards, Jana A. and Lampert, Martin D. (eds). 1992. *Talking Data: Transcription and Coding Methods for Discourse Research.* Hillsdale, NJ: Erlbaum.
Edzard, Dietz O. 1980. 'Keilschrift.' In: D. O. Edzard (ed.) *Reallexikon der Assyrologie und vorderasiatischen Archäologie,* vol. 5, 7/8. Berlin: deGruyter, 544–68.
Ehlich, Konrad, Coulmas, Florian and Graefen, Gabriele. 1995. *Bibliography on Writing and its Use.* Berlin, New York: Mouton de Gruyter.
Eisenberg, Peter. 1985. 'Graphemtheorie und phonologisches Prinzip: Vom Sinn eines autonomen Graphembegriffs.' In: G. Augst (ed.) *Graphematik und Orthographie.* Frankfurt: Lang, 122–8.
—— 1993. 'Linguistische Fundierung orthographischer Regeln.' In: J. Baurmann,

H. Günther and U. Knoop (eds) *Homo scribens: Perspektiven der Schriftlichkeitsforschung.* Tübingen: Niemeyer, 67–93.

Eisenman, R. and Robinson, J. 1991. *A Facsimile Edition of the Dead Sea Scrolls.* 2 vols. Washington, DC: Biblical Archaeology Society.

Eisenstein, Elizabeth L. 1979. *The Printing Press as an Agent of Change: Communications and Cultural Transformations in Early-Modern Europe.* Cambridge: Cambridge University Press.

Ekschmitt, Werner. 1969. *Die Kontroverse um Linear B.* Munich: Beck.

Elizarenkova, T. V. and Toporov, V. N. 1976. *The Pali Language.* Moscow: Nauka.

Elliott, Ralph W. V. 1971. *Runes: An Introduction,* 2nd edn. Manchester: Manchester University Press.

Ellis, Andrew W. 1984a. 'Slips of the Pen.' *Visible Language* XIII, 265–84.

—— 1984b, *Reading, Writing, and Dyslexia: A Cognitive Analysis.* London and Hillsdale, NJ: Erlbaum.

Ettinghausen, Richard. 1974. 'Arabic Epigraphy: Communication or Symbolic Affirmation.' In: D. K. Kouymijian (ed.) *Near Eastern Numismatics, Iconography, Epigraphy and History.* Beirut: American University of Beirut.

Evans, Arthur J. 1909. *Scripta Minoa.* Oxford: Clarendon.

—— 1921. *The Palace of Minos.* London: Macmillan.

Ewing, James. 1801. 'The Columbian Language.' *New-England Palladium* 18/27 (2 October).

Faber, Alice. 1992. 'Phonemic Segmentation as Epiphenomenon: Evidence from the History of Alphabetic Writing.' In: P. Downing, S. D. Lima and M. Noonan (eds) *The Linguistics of Literacy.* Amsterdam, Philadelphia: John Benjamins, 111–34.

Fairbank, Alfred. 1970. *The Story of Handwriting.* London: Faber and Faber.

Fairbank, John K., Reischauer, Edwin O. and Craig, Albert M. 1973. *East Asia: Tradition and Transformation.* Boston and Tokyo: Houghton Mifflin and Charles E. Tuttle.

Falkenstein, Adam. 1936. *Archaische Texte aus Uruk.* Leipzig: O. Harrassowitz.

—— 1964. *Das Sumerische.* Leiden: Brill.

Febvre, Lucien and Martin, Henri-Jean. 1958. *L'Apparition du livre.* Paris: Editions Albin Michel (Engl. trans. *The Coming of the Book.* London: Verso Editions, 1984).

Feldbusch, Elisabeth. 1985. *Geschriebene Sprache: Untersuchungen zu ihrer Herausbildung und Grundlegung ihrer Theorie.* Berlin: deGruyter.

Ferguson, Charles A. 1978. 'Patterns of Literacy in Multilingual Situations.' In: J. E. Alatis (ed.) *Georgetown University Roundtable on Languages and Linguistics.* Washington, DC: Georgetown University Press.

Filliozat, J. 1963. 'Les Écritures indiennes: Le Monde indien et son système graphique.' In: Marcel Cohen (ed.) *L'Écriture et la psychologie des peuples.* Centre International de synthèse, XXIIe semaine de synthèse, Paris: Colin.

Filliozat, Pierre-Sylvain. 1990. 'La Notion de mot chez les grammairiens indiens.' *Modèles linguistiques* XII/1, 10–20.

Finnegan, R. 1988. *Literacy and Orality: Studies in the Technology of Communication.* Oxford: Blackwell.

Fischer, Wolfdietrich (ed.). 1982. *Grundrisse der arabischen Philologie,* vol. 1, *Sprachwissenshaft.* Wiesbaden: Reichert.

Fishman, Joshua A. (ed.) 1977. *Advances in the Creation and Revision of Writing Systems.* The Hague, Paris: Mouton.

Fleckstein, Josef. 1953. *Die Bildungsreform Karls des Großen als Verwirklichung der norma rectitudinis.* Freiburg/Br.: Albert.

Foreman, Grant. 1938. *Sequoya.* Norman, OK: University of Oklahoma Press.

Francisco, Juan R. 1977. 'Two Views on the Origin of the Philippine Script: The Sanskrit Factor.' *Filipino Heritage* 3, 598–601.

French, M. A. 1976. 'Observations on the Chinese Script and the Classification of Writing Systems.' In: W. Haas (ed.) *Writing without Letters.* Manchester: Manchester University Press.

Freudenthal, H. 1960. *Lincos: Design of a Language for Cosmic Intercourse.* Amsterdam: North Holland.

Friedrich, Johannes. 1951. *Phönizisch-punische Grammatik.* Rome: Analecta Orientalia 32.

—— 1954. *Entzifferung verschollener Schriften und Sprachen.* Berlin: Springer.

—— 1960. *Hethitisches Keilschrift-Lesebuch.* Heidelberg: Carl Winter.

—— 1966. *Geschichte der Schrift.* Heidelberg: Carl Winter.

Frost, Ram. 1992. 'Orthography and Phonology: The Psychological Reality of Orthographic Depth.' In: P. Downing, S. D. Lima and M. Noonan (eds) *The Linguistics of Literacy.* Amsterdam, Philadelphia: John Benjamins, 255–74.

Fu Shen, C. Y., 1977. *Traces of the Brush: Studies in Chinese Calligraphy.* New Haven: Yale University Press.

Fu Shen, C. Y., Lowry, Glenn D. and Yonemura, Ann. 1986. *From Concept to Context: Approaches to Asian and Islamic Calligraphy.* Washington, DC: Freer Gallery of Art.

Gallagher, Charles F. 1971. 'Language Reform and Social Modernization in Turkey.' In: J. Rubin and B. H. Jernudd (eds) *Can Language be Planned?* Honolulu: University of Hawaii Press, 159–78.

Garbe, Burkhard (ed.). 1971. *Die deutsche Rechtschreibung und ihre Reform 1722–1974.* Tübingen: Niemeyer.

Gardiner, A. H. 1916. 'The Egyptian Origin of the Semitic Alphabet.' *Journal of Egyptian Archaeology* 3: 1–16.

Gaur, Albertine. 1992. *A History of Writing.* Cross River: Abbeville Press.

—— 1994. *A History of Calligraphy.* Cross River/Abbeville Press.

Gelb, I. J. 1963. *A Study of Writing*, 2nd edn. Chicago, London: The University of Chicago Press.

—— 1965. 'The Ancient Mesopotamian Ration System.' *Journal of Near Eastern Studies* 24, 230–43.

—— 1974. 'Records, Writing, and Decipherment.' *Visible Language* 8/4, 293–318.

—— 1980. 'Principles of Writing Systems within the Frame of Visual Communication.' In: Kolers, Paul A. et al. (eds) *Processing of Visible Language*, vol. 2. New York: Plenum Press, 7–24.

Genesis. Manuscrits, Recherche, Invention. Revue internationale de critique génétique. Paris: CNRS.

Gérard, Albert. 1984. *Essais d'histoire littéraire africaine.* Paris: Agence de Coopération Culturelle et Technique.

Gerschel, L. 1960. 'Comment comptaient les anciens Romains?' In: *Hommages à Léon Herrmann*. Bussels: Latomus, 386–97.

Gershevitch, Ilya. 1954. *A Grammar of Manichean Sogdian*. Oxford: Blackwell.

—— 1979. 'The Alloglottography of Old Persian.' *Transactions of the Philological Society*, 114–90.

Gill, Harjeet Singh and Gleason, Henry A. 1963. *A Reference Grammar of Punjabi*. Hartford, CT: Hartford Seminary Foundation.

Ginneken, J. van. 1939. 'Die Bilderschrift-Sprachen.' *Travaux du Cercle Linguistique de Prague* 8.

Gippert, Jost. 1990. 'Präliminarien zu einer Neuausgabe der Ogaminschriften.' In: A. Bammesberger and A. Wollmann (eds) *Britain 400–600: Language and History*. Heidelberg: C. Winter, 291–304.

Glatte, Hans. 1959. *Shorthand Systems of the World*. New York: Philosophical Library.

Gomez-Moreno, Manuel. 1962. *La escritura bastulo-turdetana (Primitiva hispanica)*. Madrid: Revista de Archivos, Bibliotecas y Museos.

Gonzalez, Andrew and Bautista, M. Lourdes S. (eds). 1981. *Aspects of Language Planning and Development in the Philippines*. Manila: Linguistic Society of the Philippines.

Goody, Jack. 1977. *The Domestication of the Savage Mind*. Cambridge: Cambridge University Press.

—— 1986. *The Logic of Writing and the Organization of Society*. London, New York: Cambridge University Press.

Goody, Jack and Watt, Ian. 1968. 'The Consequences of Literacy.' In: J. Goody (ed.) *Literacy in Traditional Societies*. Cambridge: Cambridge University Press, 27–68.

Gopal, Lallanji. 1977. 'Early Greek Writers on Writing in India.' In: L. Gopal (ed.) *In Commemoration of D. D. Kosambi*. Varanasi: Banaras Hindu University, 41–54.

Gordon, Cyrus H. 1970. 'The Accidental Invention of the Phonemic Alphabet.' *Journal of Near Eastern Studies* 29, 193–7.

Gough, Philip B. 1972. 'One Second of Reading.' In: J. F. Kavanagh and I. G. Mattingly (eds) *Language by Ear and by Eye: The Relationship between Speech and Reading*. Cambridge, MA: MIT Press, 331–58.

Graff, Harvey J. 1987. *The Labyrinths of Literacy*. Basingstoke: Falmer Press.

Gramkrelidze, T. V. 1961. 'The Akkado-Hittite Syllabary and the Problem of the Origin of the Hittite Script.' *Archiv Orientální* 29, 406–18.

Gray, Basil. (ed.). 1979. *The Art of the Book of Central Asia*. Paris: UNESCO.

Green, M. W. 1981. 'The Construction and Implementation of the Cuneiform Writing System.' *Visible Language* 15/4, 345–72.

Gregersen, E. A. 1977a. *Language in Africa: An Introductory Survey* (Library of Anthropology, vol. 3). New York, Paris, London: Gordon and Breach.

—— 1977b. 'Success and Failure in the Modernization of Hausa Spelling.' In: J. A. Fishman (ed.) *Advances in the Creation and Revision of Writing Systems*. The Hague: Mouton, 421–40.

Grevisse, Maurice. 1980. *Le Bon Usage*, 11th edn. Paris: Duculot.

Griffith, F. L. 1911. 'Karanòg: The Meroitic Inscriptions of Shablul and Karanòg.' In: *Eckley B. Coxe Jr. Expedition to Nubia,* vol. 6. Philadelphia: University of Philadelphia Museum.

Grube, W. 1896. *Die Schrift der Ju-čen.* Leipzig: O. Harrassowitz.

Gudschinsky, Sarah C. 1970. 'More on Formulating Efficient Orthographies.' *The Bible Translator* 21, 21–5.

Guion, Jean. 1974. *L'Institution orthographe.* Paris: Éditions du Centurion.

Gundersen, Dag. 1977. 'Successes and Failures in the Reformation of Norwegian Orthography.' In: J. A. Fishman (ed.) *Advances in the Creation and Revision of Writing Systems.* The Hague: Mouton, 247–65.

Günther, Hartmut. 1988. *Schriftliche Sprache: Strukturen geschriebener Wöter und ihre Verarbeitung beim Lesen.* Tübingen: Max Niemeyer.

Gupta, S. P. and Ramachandran, K. S. (eds). 1979. *The Origin of Brahmi Script.* Delhi: DK Publications.

Haarmann, Harald. 1989. 'Writing from Old Europe to Ancient Crete – A Case for Cultural Continuity.' *The Journal of Indo-European Studies* 17, 251–75.

—— 1990. *Universalgeschichte der Schrift.* Frankfurt/New York: Campus.

Haas, Mary R. 1956. *The Thai System of Writing.* Washington, DC: American Council of Learned Societies.

Haas, William. 1969. *Alphabets for English.* Manchester: Manchester University Press.

—— 1970. *Phono-graphic Translation.* Manchester: Manchester University Press.

—— (ed.). 1982. *Standard Languages: Spoken and Written.* Manchester: Manchester University Press.

—— 1983. 'Determining the Level of a Script.' In: F. Coulmas and K. Ehlich (eds) *Writing in Focus.* Berlin, Amsterdam, New York: Mouton, 15–29.

Hakulinen, Lauri. 1961. *The Structure and Development of the Finnish Language.* Bloomington: Indiana University Publications.

Hallagar, Erik. 1980. 'A New Linear A Inscription from Khania.' *Kadmos* 19, 9–11.

Halliday, M. A. K. 1990. *Spoken and Written Language.* Oxford: Oxford University Press.

Hancock, Ian. 1993. 'The Emergence of a Union Dialect of North American Vlax Romani, and its Implications for an International Standard.' *International Journal of the Sociology of Language* 99, 91–104.

Hargreaves, Gloria. 1992. *How They Write: Secrets of the Famous Revealed by Leading Graphologists.* London: Peter Owen.

Harris, Roy. 1980. *The Language Makers.* Ithaca. NY: Cornell University Press.

—— 1986. *The Origin of Writing.* London: Duckworth.

Harris, Zellig. 1954. 'Distributional Structure.' *Word* 10, 146–62.

Hartleben, Hermine. 1906. *Champollion: sein Leben und sein Werk.* 2 vols. Berlin: Weidmann.

Hau, Kathleen. 1967. 'The Ancient Writing of Southern Nigeria.' *Bulletin de l'Institut Français d'Afrique Noir. Série B* 1–2: 150–78.

Haugen, Einar. 1961. 'Language Planning in Modern Norway.' *Scandinavian Studies,* 33, 68–81.

Havelock, Eric A. 1979. 'The Ancient Art of Oral Poetry.' *Philosophy and Rhetoric* 19, 187–202.

—— 1982. *The Literate Revolution in Greece and its Cultural Consequences.* Princeton, NJ: Princeton University Press.

Hawkins, J. David. 1979. 'The Origin and Dissemination of Writing in Western Asia.' In: P. R. S. Moorey (ed.) *Origins of Civilization.* Oxford: Oxford University Press.

—— 1986. 'Writing in Anatolia: Imported and Indigenous Systems.' *World Archaeology* 17/3, 363–76.

Healey, John F. 1990. *The Early Alphabet.* London: British Museum Press.

Helck, W. (ed.). 1973. *Ägyptologie. Handbuch der Orientalistik* I. Leiden, Cologne: Brill.

Hellinga, L. 1982. *Caxton in Focus: Beginning of Printing in England.* London: British Library.

Henderson, Leslie (ed.). 1984. *Orthographies and Reading.* London: Erlbaum.

—— 1986. 'On the Use of the Term "Grapheme".' *Language and Cognitive Processes* 1, 135–48.

Henning, W. B. 1958. 'Mitteliranisch.' *Handbuch der Orientalistik* I/4.1, 20–130. Leiden, Cologne: Brill.

Henze, Paul B. 1977. 'Politics and Alphabets in Inner Asia.' In: J. A. Fishman (ed.) *Advances in the Creation and Revision of Writing Systems.* The Hague: Mouton, 371–420.

Herbert, Robert K. 1990. 'The Sociohistory of Clicks in Southern Bantu.' *Anthropological Linguistics* 32/3–4, 295–311.

Hertz, Herbert. 1970. *La Graphologie.* Paris: Presses universitaires de France.

Heubeck, Alfred. 1969. 'Lydisch.' *Handbuch der Orientalistik* I/2, 397–427. Leiden, Cologne: Brill.

—— 1982. 'L'origine della lineare B.' *Studi Micenei ed Egeo-anatolici* (Rome) 23, 202f.

Heyd, Uriel. 1954. 'Language Reform in Modern Turkey.' *Oriental Notes and Studies* 5 (Jerusalem).

Hilgers-Hesse, Irene. 1967. 'Schriftsysteme in Indonesien: Makassaren und Buginesen.' *Studium Generale* 20, 548–58.

Hill, Archibald A. 1967. 'The Typology of Writing Systems.' In: William M. Austin (ed.) *Papers in Linguistics in Honor of Léon Dostert.* The Hague: Mouton, 92–9.

Hodgson, Richard and Sarkonak, Ralph (eds). 1987. 'Bi-Graphic Differences: Languages in Con(tact)(flict).' *Visible Language* XXII.

Hooker, J. T. 1979. *The Origin of the Linear B Script.* Salamanca: Ediciones Universidad de Salamanca.

Horowitz, Rosalind and Samuels, S. Jay (eds). 1987. *Comprehending Oral and Written Language.* New York/London: Harcout Brace Jovanovich.

Hotopf, Norman. 1980. 'Slips of the Pen.' In: U. Frith (ed.) *Cognitive Processes in Spelling.* New York: Academic Press, 287–307.

Hsu, Raymond S. W. 1979. 'What is Standard Chinese?' In: R. Lord (ed.) *Hong Kong Language Papers.* Hong Kong: Hong Kong University Press, 115–41.

Hu, Y.-H., Qiou, Y. G. and Zhong, G.-Q. 1990. 'Crossed Aphasia in Chinese.' *Brain and Language* 39, 347–56.

Huang Xing. 1992. 'On Writing Systems for China's Minorities Created by Foreign Missionaries.' *International Journal of the Sociology of Language* 97, 75–85.

Huffman, Franklin E. 1970. *Cambodian System of Writing and Beginning Reader.* New Haven, London: Yale University Press.

Hudson, Alan (ed.). 1991. 'Studies in Diglossia.' *Southwest Journal of Linguistics* 10/1.

Hurford, I. R. 1987. *Language and Number: The Emergence of a Cognitive System.* Oxford: Blackwell.

Ibrahim, Muhammad H. 1989. 'Communicating in Arabic: Problems and Prospects.' In: F. Coulmas (ed.) *Language Adaptation.* Cambridge, New York: Cambridge University Press, 39–59.

Ifrah, G. 1989. *Universalgeschichte der Zahlen.* Frankfurt, New York: Campus.

Illich, Ivan and Sanders, Barry. 1988. *A B C: The Alphabetization of the Popular Mind.* San Francisco: North Point Press.

International Institute of African Languages and Cultures. 1930. *The Practical Orthography of African Languages.* London: Oxford University Press.

ISO 1955. *International System for the Transliteration of Cyrillic Characters.* International Organization for Standardization, Geneva: ISO Recommendation R9.

Issatschenko, Alexander V. 1980–3. *Geschichte der russischen Sprache.* 2 vols. Heidelberg: Winter.

Isserlin, Benedikt S. J. 1983. 'The Antiquity of the Greek Alphabet.' *Kadmos* 22, 151–63.

Ives, J. P., Bursuk, L. Z. and Ives, S. A. 1979. *Word Identification Techniques.* Chicago: Rand McNally.

Jacobsen, Steven A. 1995. *A Practical Grammar of the Central Alaskan Yup'ik Eskimo Language.* Fairbanks Alaska: Native Language Center.

Jahr, Ernst H. 1989. 'Limits of Language Planning? Norwegian Language Planning Revisited.' *International Journal of the Sociology of Language* 80, 33–9.

Jarring, G. 1981. 'The New Romanized Alphabet for Uighur and Kazakh and some Observations on the Uighur Dialect of Kashghar.' *Central Asiatic Journal* 25, 230–45.

Jaspan, M. A. 1964. *Redjang Ka-ga-nga Texts.* Canberra: Australian National University.

Jaspert, W. P., Berry, W. T. and Johnson, A. F. 1970. *The Encyclopedia of Type Faces.* London: Blandford.

Jeffery, L. H. 1982. 'Greek Alphabetic Writing.' In: J. Boardman et al. (eds) *The Cambridge Ancient History,* vol. 3, part I. London: Cambridge University Press, 819–33.

Jensen, Hans. 1925. *Geschichte der Schrift.* Hannover: Orientbuchhandlung H. Lataire.

Jensen, Hans. 1969. *Die Schrift in Vergangenheit und Gegenwart,* 3rd edn. Berlin: VEB Deutscher Verlag der Wissenschaften (*Sign, Symbol and Script.* New York: Putnam, 1969).

Jones, William. 1807. 'A Dissertation on the Orthography of Asiatick Words in Roman Letters.' *The Works of William Jones,* vol. 3. London: Robinson, 253–318.

Justeson, John S. and Kaufman, Terrence. 1993. 'A Decipherment of Epi-Olmec Hieroglyphic Writing.' *Science* 259 (March 1993), 1703–11.

Kabashima Tadao. 1979. *Nihon no moji: Hyōki taikei-o kangaeru* (*Japanese Letters: Considerations about the Writing System*). Tokyo: Iwanami.

Kalmár, I. 1985. 'Are there Really no Primitive Languages?' In: D. R. Olson, N. Torrance and A. Hildyard (eds) *Literacy, Language and Learning: The Nature and Consequence of Reading and Writing.* Cambridge: Cambridge University Press, 148–66.

Kao, H. S. R. 1979. 'Handwriting Ergonomics.' *Visible Language* XIII/3, 331–9.

—— G. P. van Galen, and R. Hoosain (eds). 1986. *Graphonomics: Contemporary Research in Handwriting.* Amsterdam: North Holland.

Kao Shi-fen (ed.). 1992. *Zhongguo shaoshuminzu wenzi* (The Writings of China's Minorities). Beijing: Zhongguo zangxue chubanshe.

Karlgren, Bernhard. 1923. *Analytic Dictionary of Chinese and Sino-Japanese.* Paris: Geuthner.

Kelly, J. 1981. 'The 1847 Alphabet: An Episode of Phonotypy.' In: R. E. Asher and E. Henderson (eds). *Toward a History of Phonetics.* Edinburgh: Edinburgh University Press, 248–64.

Kenrick, Donald. 1981. 'The Development of a Standard Alphabet for Romani.' *The Bible Translator* 32/2, 215–19.

Kim Won-Young. 1954. *Early Movable Type in Korea,* series A, vol. 1. Seoul: National Museum of Korea.

Klingenheben, A. 1933. 'The Vai Script.' *Africa* VI, 158–71.

Knappert, Jan. 1979. *Four Centuries of Swahili Verse: A Literary History and Anthology.* London: Heinemann.

Knorosov, Yuri V. 1955. *Diego de Landa: Soobshchenie o delakh v Yukatani, 1566* (*Diego de Landa: Report on Work in Yukatán, 1566*). Moscow: Akademia Nauk SSSR.

Knuth, Donald E. 1982. 'The Concept of a Meta-Font.' *Visible Language* XVI, 3–27.

Kohrt, Manfred. 1986. 'The Term "Grapheme" in the History and Theory of Linguistics.' In: G. Augst (ed.) *New Trends in Graphemics and Orthography.* Berlin, New York: DeGruyter, 80–96.

—— 1987. *Theoretische Aspekte der deutschen Orthographie.* Tübingen: Niemeyer.

Kolinsky, Régine, Morais, José and Segui, Juan (eds). 1991. *La Reconnaissance des mots dans les différentes modalités sensorielles: Etudes de psycholinguistique cognitive.* Paris: Presses universitaires de France.

Komai, Akira and Rohlich, Thomas H. 1988. *An Introduction to Japanese Kanbun.* Nagoya: The University of Nagoya Press.

Komatsu Shigemi. 1968. *Kana: Sono seiritsu to hensen (Kana: Its Formation and Development).* Tokyo: Iwanami.

Krámsky, Jirì. 1969. *The Word as a Linguistic Unit.* The Hague/Paris: Mouton, Janua Linguarum Series Minor no. 75.

—— 1974. *The Phoneme.* Munich: Wilhelm Fink.

Krause, Wolfgang. 1970. *Runen.* Berlin: Walter de Gruyter.

—— 1971. *Tocharisch: Handbuch der Orientalistik* I/IV. Leiden/ Cologne: E. J. Brill.

Ku-kung fa-shu. 21 vols. 1962–8. Taipei: Kuo-li ku-kung powu-yuan.

Kyle, J. G. and Woll, B. 1985. *Sign Language: The Study of Deaf People and their Language.* Cambridge, New York: Cambridge University Press.

Labat, R. and Malbran-Labat, F. 1988. *Manuel d'épigraphie akkadienne,* 6th edn. Paris: Geuthner.

Lacouture, Jean. 1988. *Champollion: Une Vie de lumieres.* Paris: B. Grasset.

Ladefoged, Peter and Traill, Anthony. 1984. 'Linguistic Phonetic Description of Clicks.' *Language* 60, 1–20.

L'Afrique et la lettre (Africa and the Written Word). 1986. Exposition Catalogue, published by Centre Culturel Français, Lagos and Fête de la Lettre, Paris.

Lambert, Hester M. 1953. *Introduction to the Devanagari Script*. London: Oxford University Press.

Laroche, E. 1960. *Les Hiéroglyphes hittites: I L'Écriture*. Paris: Editions du Centre national de la recherche scientifique.

Ledderose, Lothar. 1979. *Mi Fu and the Chinese Tradition of Calligraphy*. Princeton, NJ: Princeton University Press.

Ledyard, Gari Keith. 1975. *The Korean Language Reform of 1446: The Origin, Background, and Early History of the Korean Alphabet*. Ann Arbor, MI: University Microfilms.

Lee, Hansol H. 1989. *Korean Grammar*. New York: Oxford University Press.

Lee, M. and Oldham, W. 1990. 'Font Recognition by a Neural Network.' *International Journal of Man-Machine Studies* 33, 41–61.

Leon, N. H. 1981. *Character Index of Modern Chinese*. London: Curzon Press.

Lepschy, Anna Laura and Lepschy, Giulio C. 1988. *The Italian Language Today*, 2nd edn. London: Huchinson.

Lepsius, Karl Richard. 1863. *Standard Alphabet for Reducing Unwritten Languages and Foreign Graphic Systems to a Uniform Orthography in European Letters*, ed. J. Alan Kemp. Amsterdam Studies in the Theory and History of Science 5. Amsterdam: John Benjamins, 1981.

Leslau, Wolf. 1987. *Comparative Dictionary of Ge'ez (Classic Ethiopic)*. Wiesbaden: Harrassowitz.

Levine, Kenneth. 1980. *Becoming Literate*. London: Social Science Research Council.

Lewis, M. B. 1958. *A Handbook of Malay Script*. London: Macmillan.

Lewis, Nephtali. 1974. *Papyrus in Classical Antiquity*. Oxford: Clarendon Press.

Liang Donghan. 1959. *Hanzide jieguo mai qi liu bian* (*Form and Development of Chinese Characters*). Shanghai: Wenzi gaige chubanshe.

Lidzbarski, M. 1907. *Kanaanäische Inschriften*. Gießen: A. Töpelmann.

Linell, Per. 1982. *The Written Language Bias in Linguistics*. Linköping: University of Linköping Department of Communication Studies.

Literacy Mission. Journal published by the Directorate of Adult Education, Government of India, New Delhi.

Lombard, Alf. 1974. *La Langue roumaine: une présentation*. Paris: Klincksieck.

Lou Chengzhao. 1992. 'Transliterating Non-Chinese Proper Nouns into Chinese: A Comparative Study of Usage in Mainland China, Taiwan, and Hong Kong.' *International Journal of the Sociology of Language* 97, 121–33.

Lucas, Elizabeth. 1984. *Calligraphy: The Art of Beautiful Writing*. Cambridge, MA: PH Press.

Lüdtke, H. 1969. 'Die Alphabetschrift und das Problem der Lautsegmentierung.' *Phonetica* 20, 147–76.

Luelsdorff, Philip A. (ed.). 1987. *Orthography and Phonology*. Amsterdam: Benjamins.

Macalister, R. A. S. 1945. *Corpus Inscriptionum Insularum Celticarum*. Dublin: Stationery Office, Irish Manuscript Commission.

MacCarthy, P. A. D. 1969. 'The Bernard Shaw Alphabet.' In: W. Haas (ed.) *Alphabets for English.* Manchester: Manchester University Press, 105–17.
Macdonell, Arthur A. 1927. *A Sanskrit Grammar for Students.* Oxford: Clarendon Press.
Mackenzie, D. N. 1967. 'Notes on the Transcription of Pahlavi.' *Bulletin of the School of Oriental and African Studies* XXX, 17–29.
Mahapatra, B. P. 1979. 'Santali Language Movement in the Context of Many Dominant Languages.' In: E. Annamalai (ed.) *Language Movement in India.* Manasagangotri, Mysore: Central Institute of Indian Languages, 107–17.
Mahmoud, Youssef. 1979. *The Arabic Writing System and the Sociolinguistics of Orthography Reform.* PhD dissertation. Georgetown University Press.
Mallery, Garric. 1893. 'Picture Writing of the American Indians.' *Tenth Annual Report of the Bureau of Ethnology.* Washington, DC: Smithsonian Institution.
Manchester, Richard B. 1976. *Mammoth Book of Word Games.* New York: Hart Publishing.
Mann, V. A. 1986. 'Phonological Awareness: The Role of Reading Experience.' *Cognition* 24, 65–92.
Marcilla y Martin, Cipriano. 1895. *Estudios de los Antiguos Alfabetos Filipinos.* Malabon: Asilio de Herfanos.
Marcus, Joyce. 1980. 'Zapotec Writing.' *Scientific American* 242/2, 46–60.
Marre, Aristide. 1901. 'Grammaire Tagalog, composée sur un nouveau plan.' *Bijdragen tot de taal-, land- en volkenkunde van Nederlandsch-Indië* 53, 547–92.
Marshack, A. 1972. *The Roots of Civilization: The Cognitive Beginnings of Man's First Art, Symbol and Notation.* New York: McGraw-Hill.
Martin, M. 1962. 'Revision and Reclassification of the Proto-Byblian Signs.' *Orientalia,* NS 31, 250–71; 339–63.
Martinet, André. 1965. *La Linguistique synchronique: études et recherches.* Paris: Presses universitaires de France.
Masica, Colin P. 1991. *The Indo-Aryan Languages.* Cambridge, New York: Cambridge University Press.
Massaro, Dominic W., Taylor, G. A., Venezky, R. L., Jastrzembski, J. E. and Lucas, P. A. 1980. *Letter and Word Perception.* Amsterdam: North-Holland.
Masson, E. 1984. 'L'Écriture dans les civilisations danubiennes néolithiques.' *Kadmos* 23, 89–123.
Masson, Olivier. 1961. *Les Inscriptions chypriotes syllabiques: Recueil critique et commenté.* Paris: E. de Boccard.
Matson, Dan M. 1971. *Introduction to Oriya and the Oriya Writing System.* East Lansing: Michigan State University Asian Studies Center.
Matthes, B. F. 1858. *Makassaarsche Spraakkunst.* Amsterdam: Frederik Muller.
McCarter, P. Kyle Jr. 1975. *The Antiquity of the Greek Alphabet and the Early Phoenician Scripts.* Missoula: Scholars Press (for Harvard Semitic Museum).
McGregor, Ronald S. 1977. *Outline of Hindi Grammar,* 2nd edn. Delhi: Oxford University Press.
McLean, J. 1890. *James Evans: Inventor of the Syllabic System of the Cree Language.* Toronto: William Briggs.
McLuhan, Marshall. 1962. *The Gutenberg Galaxy.* Toronto: University of Toronto Press.

Meenakshisundaran, T. P. 1966. 'The Scripts of South India (Tamil, Malayalam, Grantha, etc.).' In: *Indian Systems of Writing.* Delhi: Publications Division, 23–8.

Meltzer, E. S. 1980. 'Remarks on Ancient Egyptian Writing with Emphasis on its Mnemonic Aspects.' In: P. Kolers, M. E. Wrolstad and H. Bouma (eds) *Processing of Visible Language,* vol. 2. New York: Plenum Press, 43–66.

Menéndez Pidal, Ramon. 1987. *Manual de gramática histórica española.* Madrid: Espasa-Calpe.

Mickel, Stanley Lewis. 1986. 'Literary Aspects of Shang Bone Inscriptions.' In: William H. Niehauser, Jr (ed.) *The Indiana Companion to Traditional Chinese Literature.* Bloomington, In: Indiana University Press, 255–7.

Millard, A. R. 1976. 'The Canaanite Linear Alphabet and its Passage to the Greeks.' *Kadmos* 15, 130–44.

—— 1986. 'The Infancy of the Alphabet.' *World Archaeology* 17/3, 390–8.

Miller, Roy A. 1956. *The Tibetan System of Writing.* Washington, DC: American Council of Learned Societies.

Mills, Lawrence Hayworth. 1913. *A Dictionary of the Gâthic Language of the Zend Avesta,* reprinted 1977 from the 1913 Leipzig edn. New York: AMS Press.

Milroy, James and Milroy, Leslie. 1985. *Authority in Language: Investigating Language Prescription and Standardization.* London: Routledge and Kegan Paul.

Miyamoto Masaru. 1985. 'Firipin no manyan moji' ('The Mangyan Script of the Philippines'). *Gekkan Minpaku* (Monthly of the National Museum of Ethnology, Osaka) 6, 12–13.

Mobbs, Michael C. 1981. 'Two Languages or One? The Significance of the Language Names "Hindi" and "Urdu".' *Journal of Multilingual and Multicultural Development* 2, 203–11.

Möllendorff, P. G. von. 1892. *A Manchu Grammar, with Analysed Text.* Shanghai: American Presbyterian Mission Press.

Monod, T. 1958. 'Un nouvel alphabet ouest-africain: le bété (Côte d'Ivoire)'. *Bulletin de l'Institut Français d'Afrique Noir* XX/1–2, 432–553.

Morais, J. 1987. 'Phonetic Awareness and Reading Acquisition.' *Psychological Research* 49, 147–52.

Morenz, S. 1973. 'Das Koptische.' *Handbuch der Orientalistik* I, 90–104. Leiden, Cologne: Brill.

Morison, Stanley. 1949. *Notes on the Development of Latin Script from Early to Modern Times.* Cambridge: Cambridge University Press.

Morris, Charles W. 1938. *Foundations of the Theory of Signs.* Chicago: The University of Chicago Press.

Morton, J. and Sasanuma, Sumiko. 1984. 'Lexical Access in Japanese.' In: L. Henderson (ed.) *Orthographies and Reading.* London: Erlbaum, 25–42.

Mulugeta Seyoum. 1988. 'The Emergence of the National Language in Ethiopia: A Historical Perspective.' In: F. Coulmas (ed.) *With Forked Toungues: What are National Languages Good for?* Ann Arbor: Karoma, 101–45.

Murdoch, John. 1982. 'Cree Literacy in Formal Education.' In: W. Cowan (ed.) *Papers of the Thirteenth Algonquian Conference.* Ottawa: Carleton University, 23–8.

Nakata Yūjirō. 1973. *The Art of Japanese Calligraphy,* trans. Alan Woodhull. New York, Tokyo: Wetherhill/Heibonsha.

Naveh, Joseph. 1982. *Early History of the Alphabet: An Introduction to West Semitic Epigraphy and Palaeography.* Leiden: E. J. Brill.
Nelson, A. N. 1962. *The Modern Reader's Japanese–English Character Dictionary.* Rutland, VT, Tokyo: Tuttle.
Neumann, Günter. 1969. 'Lykisch.' *Handbuch der Orientalistik* I/2, 358–96. Leiden, Cologne: Brill.
Newnham, Richard. 1987. *About Chinese.* Harmondsworth: Penguin Books.
Nguyên Đình Hoà. 1959. 'Chữ'Nôm: The Demotic System of Writing in Vietnam.' *Journal of the American Oriental Society* 79/4. 270–4.
Nishida Tatsuo. 1982. *Ajia no mikaidoku moji* (*Undeciphered Scripts of Asia*). Tokyo: Taishūkan.
Nissen, Hans J. 1977. 'Aspects of the Development of Early Cylinder Seals.' *Bibliotheca Mesopotamica* 6, 15–23.
—— 1985. 'The Emergence of Writing in the Ancient Near East.' *Interdisciplinary Science Reviews* 10/4, 349–61.
—— 1986. 'The Archaic Texts from Uruk.' *World Archaeology* 17, 317–34.
Nissen, Hans J., Damerow, Peter and Englund, Peter. 1990. *Zur Schrift und Techniken der Wirtschaftsverwaltung im alten Vorderen Orient: Informationsspeicherung und -verarbeitung vor 5000 Jahren.* Bad Salzdetfurth: Franz Becker.
Nöldeke, Thomas. 1875. *Mandäische Grammatik.* Halle: Niemeyer.
Noorduyn, J. 1992. *Variation in the Bugis and Makasarese Scripts.* Leiden: Royal Institute of Linguistics and Anthropology: International Workshop on Indonesian Studies no. 7.
Nyberg, H. S. 1964–74. *A Manual of Pahlavi.* Wiesbaden: Harrassowitz.
Nyikos, Julius. 1988. 'A Linguistic Perspective of Illiteracy.' In: Sheila Empleton (ed.) *The Fourteenth LACUS Forum 1987.* Lake Bluff, IL: Linguistic Association of Canada and the United States, 146–63.
Oakhill, J. and Garnham, A. 1988. *Becoming a Skilled Reader.* Oxford: Blackwell.
O'Connor, M. 1991. 'Early Witnesses of Alphabetic Order.' In: P. Swiggers (ed.) *L'Écriture (Writing).* Leuven: Peeters, La Pensée linguistique no. 5.
Odenstedt, Bengt. 1990. *On the Origin and Early History of the Runic Script: Typology and Graphic Variation in the Older Futhark.* Uppsala: Gustav Adolfs Akademien.
Ohala, Manjari 1983. *Aspects of Hindi Phonology.* Delhi: Motilal Banarsidass.
Olson, David R. 1977. 'From Utterance to Text: The Bias of Language in Speech and Writing.' *Harvard Educational Review* 47/3, 257–81.
Olson, David R. 1994. *The World on Paper.* London: Cambridge University Press.
Olson, David R. and Torrance, Nancy (eds). 1991. *Literacy and Orality.* New York: Cambridge University Press.
Ong, Walter J. 1977. *Interfaces of the Word: Studies in the Evolution of Consciousness and Culture.* Ithaca and London: Cornell University Press.
—— 1982. *Orality and Literacy: The Technologizing of the Word.* London, New York: Methuen.
Orthography Studies. Articles on New Writing Systems by William A. Smalley and others. 1963. Helps for Translators vol. VI. London: United Bible Societies.
Pardo de Tavera, T. H. 1884. *Contribucion para el Estudio de los Antiquos Alfabetos Filipinos.* Losana: Jaunin Hermanos (French trans. *Annales de l'extrême orient et de l'afrique,* 1884, 1885, 204–10; 232–9).

Parker, Gary J. 1969. *Ayacucho Quechua Grammar and Dictionary.* The Hague: Mouton.

Parkes, M. B. 1993. *Pause and Effect: An Introduction to the History of Punctuation in the West.* Berkeley, CA: University of California Press.

Parpola, Asko. 1993. *Deciphering the Indus Script.* Cambridge: Cambridge University Press.

Parry, Milman. 1971. *The Making of Homeric Verse: The Collected Papers of Milman Parry,* ed. Adam Parry. Oxford: Clarendon Press.

Partridge, Monica. 1972. *Serbo-Croat Practical Grammar and Reader.* Belgrade: Izdavački Zavod Jugoslavia.

Pattanayak, D. P. 1979. 'The Problem and Planning of Scripts.' In: G. Sambasiva Rao (ed.) *Literacy Methodology.* Manasagangotri: Central Institute of Indian Languages, 43–59.

Patterson, K. 1981. 'Neuropsychological Approaches to the Study of Reading.' *British Journal of Psychology* 72, 151–74.

Patzig, Georg. 1969, 'Leibniz, Frege und die sogenannte lingua characteristica universalis.' *Studia Leibnitiana Supplementa III,* 103–12.

Pearlman, Moshe. 1980. *Digging up the Bible: The Stories behind the Great Archaeological Discoveries in the Holy Land.* London: Weidenfeld and Nicholson.

Pelliot, Paul. 1925. 'Les Systèmes d'écriture en usage chez les anciens Mongols.' *Asia Major* OS 2/2, 284–9.

Pereira, Jose. 1973. *Literary Konkani: A Brief History.* Dharwar: Konkani Sahitya Prakashan.

Peyraube, Alain. 1991. 'Some Diachronic Aspects of Diglossia/Triglossia in Chinese.' *Southwest Journal of Linguistics* 10/1 (Studies in Diglossia), 105–24.

Pichl, W. J. 1966. 'L'Écriture bassa au Libéria.' *Bulletin de l'Institut Français d'Afrique Noire* XXVIII, B, 1/2, 481–4.

Piehl, W. 1940. 'Die Hsi-hsia-Schrift.' *Asien-Berichte* II, 25ff.

Pigeaud, Theodore G. Th. 1975. *Javanese and Balinese Manuscripts and some Codices Written in Related Idioms Spoken in Java and Bali.* Wiesbaden: Franz Steiner Verlag.

Pike, Kenneth L. 1947. *Phonemics: A Technique for Reducing Languages to Writing.* Ann Arbor: University of Michigan Press.

Pitman, James and St John, J. 1969. *Alphabets and Reading.* London: Pitman.

Pope, Maurice. 1975. *The Story of Decipherment: From Egyptian Hieroglyphic to Linear B.* London: Thames and Hudson.

Poppe, Nicholas. 1974. *Grammar of Written Mongolian.* Wiesbaden: Harrassowitz.

Postma, Antoon. 1971. 'Contemporary Mangyan Scripts.' *Philippine Journal of Linguistics* 2, 1–11.

—— 1972. *Treasure of a Minority: the Ambahan.* Manila: Arnoldus Press.

—— 1988. *Annotated Mangyan Bibliography 1570–1988.* Mansalay (Oriental Mindoro): Mangyan Assistance and Research Center.

Powell, Marvin A. 1981. 'Three Problems in the History of Cuneiform Writing: Origins, Direction of Script, Literacy.' *Visible Language* 15/4, 419–40.

Prem, Hanns J. and Riese, Berthold. 1983. 'Autochthonous American Writing Systems: The Aztec and Maya examples.' In: F. Coulmas and K. Ehlich (eds) *Writing in Focus.* Berlin, New York, Amsterdam: Mouton, 167–86.

Pulgram, Ernst. 1976. 'The Typologies of Writing Systems.' In: W. Haas (ed.) *Writing without Letters.* Manchester: Manchester University Press, 1–27.

Pulte, William. 1976. 'Writing System and Underlying Representation: The Case of the Cherokee Syllabary.' In: F. Ingemann (ed.) *1975 Mid-America Linguistics Conference Papers.* Lawrence, KS: University of Kansas, 388–93.

Pumfrey, P. D. 1985. *Reading: Tests and Assessment Techniques,* 2nd edn. London: Hodder and Stoughton.

Raabe, Paul (ed.). 1990. *Gutenberg: 550 Jahre Buchdruck in Europa.* Wolfenbüttel: Herzog-August-Bibliothek (exhibition catalogue).

Rabin, Chaim. 1971. 'Spelling Reform – Israel 1968.' In: Joan Rubin and Björn H. Jernudd (eds) *Can Language Be Planned?* Honolulu: University of Hawaii Press, 95–121.

Ramos, Teredsita. 1986. *Introduction to Tagalog.* Honolulu: University of Hawaii Press.

Rao, K. V. 1966. 'The Scripts of South India (Telugu-Kannada and Nandināgarī).' In: *Indian Systems of Writing.* Delhi: Publications Division, 28–33.

Raun, A. 1969. *Basic Course in Uzbek.* Bloomington, In.: Bloomington University (USA vol. 59).

Ray, John D. 1986. 'The Emergence of Writing in Egypt.' *World Archaeology* 17/3, 307–16.

Reading Research Quarterly. Newark, Delaware: The International Reading Association.

Real Academia Española. 1973. *Esbozo de una nueva gramática de la lengua española.* Madrid: Espasa-Calpe.

Reichelt, H. 1909. *Awestisches Elementarbuch.* Heidelberg: Universitätsverlag.

Reiner, Erica. 1966. *A Linguistic Analysis of Akkadian.* London, Paris, The Hague: Mouton.

—— 1973. 'How we Read Cuneiform Texts.' *Journal of Cuneiform Studies* 25, 3–58.

Reinhard, Kurt. 1956. *Chinesische Musik.* Kassel: Röth-Verlag.

Reischauer, Edwin O. 1940. 'Rōmaji or Rōmazi', *Journal of the American Oriental Society* 60/1, 82–9.

Renz, Johannes and Röllig, Wolfgang. 1995–. *Handbuch der Althebräischen Epigraphik.* 3 vols. Darmstadt: Wissenschaftliche Buchgesellschaft.

Rohsenow, J. S. 1986. 'The Second Chinese Character Simplification Scheme.' *International Journal of the Sociology of Language* 59, 73–85.

Roop, D. Haigh. 1972. *An Introduction to the Burmese Writing System.* New Haven: Yale University Press.

Rosenthal, Franz. 1948. 'Penmanship.' *Ars Islamica* 13–14, 1–31.

Rossini, Stéphane. 1989. *Hiéroglyphes: Lire et Ecrire,* 3rd edn. Lavaur: Editions Trismégiste.

Rromani Unia. 1990. *Statutes of the Romani Union.* Warsaw: Prima Białystok.

Ryckmans, J. 1986. 'Une Écriture minuscule sud-arab ancienne récemment découverte.' In: H. L. J. Vanstiphout, K. Jongling, F. Leemhuis and G. J. Reinink (eds) *Scripta Signa Vocis.* Groningen: Egbert Forsten.

Saeki Kōsuke and Yamada Hisao. 1977. *The Romanization of Japanese Writing: Hepburn vs. Kunrei system controversies.* Tokyo: Nippon Romazi-sya (distributed by ISO as TC46).

Saenger, Paul. 1982. 'Silent Reading; Its Impact on Late Medieval Script and Society.' *Viator* 13, 367–414.

—— 1991. 'The Separation of Words and the Physiology of Reading.' In: David R. Olson and Nancy Torrance (eds) *Literacy and Orality*. Cambridge: Cambridge University Press, 198–214.

Sampson, Geoffrey. 1985. *Writing Systems.* London: Hutchinson.

Šastri, Korada Mahadeva. 1985. *Descriptive Grammar and Handbook of Modern Telugu.* Stuttgart: F. Steiner.

Sato Habein, Yaeko. 1984. *The History of the Japanese Written Language.* Tokyo: Tokyo University Press.

Saussure, Ferdinand de. 1916. *Cours de linguistique générale* (Engl. trans. *Course in General Linguistics.* New York: Philosophical Library, 1959).

Scancarelli, Janine. 1992. 'Aspiration and Cherokee Orthographies.' In: P. Downing, S. D. Lima and M. Noonan (eds) *The Linguistics of Literacy.* Amsterdam, Philadelphia: John Benjamins, 135–52.

Scatton, Ernest A. 1984. *Reference Grammar of Modern Bulgarian.* Columbus, Oh: Slavica.

Schanze, H. 1987. 'Writing, Literacy and Word-Processing: Changes in the Concept of Literature in the Framework of New Media.' *Literary and Linguistic Computing* 2/1, 24–9.

Scheerer, Eckart. 1986. 'Orthography and Lexical Access.' In: Gerhard Augst (ed.) *New Trends in Graphemics and Orthography.* Berlin, New York: De Gruyter, 262–86.

Schenkel, Wolfgang. 1976. 'The Structure of Hieroglyphic Script.' *Royal Anthropological Institute News* 15, 4–7.

Schenker, Alexander M. and Stankiewicz, Edward (eds). 1980. *The Slavic Literary Languages: Formation and Development.* New Haven: Yale Concilium on International and Area Studies.

Schiaparelli, Luigi. 1921. *La scrittura latina nell'età romana.* Como: C. Nani.

Schiffman, Harold and Arokianathan, S. 1986. 'Diglossic Variation in Tamil Film and Fiction.' In: Bh. Krishnamurti (ed.) *South Asian Languages: Structure, Convergence and Diglossia.* Delhi: Motilal Banarsidass, 371–81.

Schimmel, Annemarie. 1984. *Calligraphy and Islamic Culture.* New York, London: New York University Press.

—— 1992. *The Mystery of Numbers.* New York: Oxford University Press.

Schlott, Adelheid. 1989. *Schrift und Schreiber im Alten Ägypten.* Munich: C. H. Beck.

Schmandt-Besserat, Denise. 1977. 'An Archaic Recording System and the Origin of Writing.' *Syro-Mesopotamian Studies* 1, 31–70.

—— 1978. 'The Earliest Precursor of Writing.' *Scientific American* 238/6, 50–9.

—— 1992. *Before Writing.* 2 vols. Austin: University of Texas Press.

Schmitt, Alfred. 1938. *Die Erfindung der Schrift.* Erlanger Universitätsreden 22. Erlangen: Deichert.

—— 1951. *Die Alaskaschrift und ihre schriftgeschichtliche Bedeutung.* Marburg: Simons.

—— 1963. *Die Bamum-Schrift.* 3 vols. Wiesbaden: Harrassowitz.

Scholes, Robert J. and Willis, Brenda J. 1991. 'Linguists, Literacy, and the Intensionality of Marshall McLuhan's Western Man.' In: D. R. Olson and N.

Torrance (eds) *Literacy and Orality*. Cambridge, New York: Cambridge University Press, 215–35.

Schott, Siegfried. 1973. 'Das Schriftsystem und seine Durchbildung.' *Handbuch der Orientalistik* I, 22–31. Leiden, Cologne: Brill.

Schulz, Herbert C. 1939. *The Gothic Script of the Middle Ages*. San Francisco: D. Magee.

Schwarz, Benjamin. 1959. 'The Phaistos Disk.' *Journal of Near Eastern Studies* XVII, 105–12; 227f.

Schwarz, P. 1915. 'Die Anordnung des arabischen Alphabets.' *Zeitschrift der deutschen morgenländischen Gesellschaft* 69, 59–67.

Scribner, Sylvia and Cole, Michael. 1981. *The Psychology of Literacy*. Cambridge, MA: Harvard University Press.

Seeley, Christopher. 1991. *A History of Writing in Japan*. Leiden: Brill.

Segert, Stanislav. 1975. *Altaramäische Grammatik mit Bibliographie, Chrestomatie und Glossar*. Leipzig: VEB Verlag Enzyklopädie.

Segert, Stanislav. 1984. *A Basic Grammar of the Ugaritic Language*. Berkeley, CA: University of California Press.

Seybolt, Peter J. and Gregory Kuei-ke Chiang. 1979. *Language Reform in China: Documents and Commentary*. White Plains, NY: M. E. Sharpe.

Sharples, Mike (ed.). 1992. *Computers and Writing: Issues and Implementations*. Dordrecht: Kluwer.

Shi Dingxu. 1993. 'Review of *Jiāngyǒng nüshū zhī mí* (*The Enigma of Jiangyong Female Writing*), by Xie Zhimin.' *Language* 69/1, 174–8.

Shipley, J. T. 1960. *Word Play*. New York: Hawthorn Books.

Sims-Williams, Nicholas. 1975. 'Notes on Sogdian Palaeography.' *Bulletin of the School of Oriental and African Studies*, University of London, XXXVIII/1, 132–9.

—— 1981. 'The Sogdian Sound-System and the Origin of the Uyghur Script.' *Journal Asiatique* 269, 347–60.

Sirat, C. 1987. 'La Morphologie humaine et la direction des écritures.' *Comptes Rendus; Académie des Inscriptions et Belles Lettres*. Paris: Boccard.

Skousen, R. 1982. 'English Spelling and Phonemic Representation.' *Visible Language* 16, 28–38.

Smalley, William A., Chia Koua Vang and Gnia Yee Yang. 1990. *Mother of Writing: The Origin and Development of a Hmong Messianic Script*. Chicago, London: The University of Chicago Press.

Smith, Frank. 1971. *Understanding Reading*. New York: Holt, Rinehart and Winston.

Smith, K. U. 1966. 'Human Factors in Penmanship and the Design of Writing Instruments: A Special Report to The National Science Foundation.' Madison, WI: University of Wisconsin, Behavioral Cybernetics Laboratory.

Smith, P. T. 1980. 'Linguistic Information in Spelling'. In: U. Frith (ed.) *Cognitive Processes in Spelling*. London: Academic Press, 33–49.

Soden, Wolfram von and Röllig, Wolfgang. 1967. *Das akkadische Syllabar*, 2nd rev. edn. Rome: Pontificium Institutum Biblicum (Analecta orientalia 42).

Sohn Pow-Key. 1959. 'Early Korean Printing.' *Journal of the American Oriental Society* 79/2, 96–103.

Song, Chong-man. 1970. *A New Explication of Sino-Korean Characters (sinhae hanja)*. Seoul: Namhyang Munhwa.

Speiser, Ephraim A. 1941. *Introduction to Hurrian*. Annual of the American School of Oriental Research. New Haven: American Oriental Society.

Stechishin, J. W. 1977. *Ukrainian Grammar*. Winnipeg: Ukrainian Canadian Committee.

Steffens, Franz. 1906. *Lateinische Paläographie*. Freiburg: Universitätsbuchhandlung.

Stein, Dieter (ed.). 1992. *Cooperating with Written Texts: The Pragmatics and Comprehension of Written Texts*. Berlin, New York: Mouton de Gruyter.

Steinberg, S. H. 1975. *Five Hundred Years of Printing*, 3rd edn. Harmondsworth: Penguin.

Stilman, Leon. 1941. *Russian Alphabet and Phonetics*. Columbia Slavic Studies. New York: Columbia University Press.

Street, Brian. 1984. *Literacy in Theory and Practice*. Cambridge, London: Cambridge University Press.

—— (ed.). 1993. *Cross-Cultural Approaches to Literacy*. Cambridge: Cambridge University Press.

Stubbs, Michael. 1980. *Language and Literacy: The Sociolinguistics of Reading and Writing*. London: Routledge and Kegan Paul.

Stutterheim, W. F. 1930. *Outheden van Bali*. 2 vols. Singaradja, Bali: Kirtya Liefrinck van der Tuuk.

Sutton, James and Bartram, Alan. 1968. *An Atlas of Type Forms*. London: Lund Humphries.

Svenska Akademiens ordlista (*Word-list of the Swedish Academy*) 1986. Stockholm: Norstedts Förlag.

Szerdahelyi, I. 1984. 'Entwicklung des Zeichensystems einer internationalen Sprache: Esperanto.' In: I. Fodor and C. Hagége (eds) *Language Reform: History and Future*, vol. 3. Hamburg: Buske, 277–308.

Sznycer, M. 1972. 'Protosinaïtiques (inscriptions).' *Supplément au dictionaire de la Bible*. Paris: Letouzey et Ané, 8, cols 1384–95.

Tannen, Deborah. 1982. 'The Oral/Literate Continuum in Discourse.' In: D. Tannen (ed.) *Spoken and Written Language: Exploring Orality and Literacy*. Norwood, NJ: Ablex, 1–16.

Taylor, Insup and Taylor, Martin M. 1983. *The Psychology of Reading*. New York: Academic Press.

Terrien de Lacouperie, Albert E. 1894. *Beginnings of Writing in Central and Eastern Asia, or Notes on 450 Embryo-Writings and Scripts*. London: D. Nutt.

Teyssier, Paul. 1980. *Histoire de la langue portugaise*. Paris: Presses universitaires de France (Portuguese version: *História da língua portuguesa*. Lisbon: Sá da Costa, 1982).

Thimonnier, René. 1967. *Le Système graphique du français (projet de réforme)*. Paris: Plon.

Thompson, Edward M. 1906. *Handbook of Greek and Latin Palaeography*. London: Kegan Paul, Trench, Trübner.

Thomson, Robert W. 1975. *An Introduction to Classical Armenian*. Delmar, NY: Caravan.

Trúóng Văn Chinh. 1970. *Structure de la langue viêtnamienne*. Paris: Geuthner.

Tsien Tsuen-Hsuin. 1962. *Written on Bamboo and Silk: The Beginnings of Chinese Books and Inscriptions*. Chicago and London: University of Chicago Press.

Tucker, A. N. 1971. 'Orthographic Systems and Conventions in Sub-Saharan Africa.' In: Th.A. Sebeok (ed.) *Current Trends in Linguistics*, vol. 7. The Hague, Paris: Mouton, 618–53.

Turvey, M. T., Feldman, L. B., Lukatela, G. 1984. 'The Serbo-Croatian Orthography Constrains the Reader to a Phonologically Analytic Strategy.' In: L. Henderson (ed.) *Orthographies and Reading*. London: Erlbaum, 81–9.

Ulatowska, Hanna K., Baker, Temple and Freedman Stern, Renee. 1979. 'Disruption of Written Language in Aphasia.' In: Haiganoosh Whitaker and Harry A. Whitaker (eds) *Studies in Neurolinguistics*, vol. 4. New York: Academic Press, 241–68.

Ullman, B. L. 1927. 'The Etruscan Origin of the Roman Alphabet and the Names of the Letters.' *Classical Philology* XXII, 372–7.

—— 1980. *Ancient Writing and its Influence*, 2nd edn. Toronto: Toronto University Press.

Underhill, Robert. 1976. *Turkish Grammar*. Cambridge, MA: MIT Press.

Unger, J. M. 1984. 'Japanese Orthography in the Computer Age.' *Visible Language* 18/3.

Ungnad, Arthur. 1913. *Syrische Grammatik*. Munich: C. H. Beck.

Updike, Daniel B. 1937. *Printing Types: Their History, Forms, and Use*. Cambridge, MA: Harvard University Press.

Vachek, Josef. 1973. *Written Language: General Problems and Problems of English*. The Hague: Mouton.

Vaillant, Pierre. 1972. *Champollion et le dechiffrement des hieroglyphes*. Grenoble: La Bibliothèque.

Vaiman, A. A. 1974. 'Über die protosumerische Schrift.' *Acta Antiqua Academiae Scientiarum Hungaricae* 22, 15–27.

Vallat, F. 1986. 'The Most Ancient Scripts from Iran: the Current Situation.' *World Archaeology* 17/3, 335–47.

Vallins, G. H. 1973. *Spelling*, 2nd edn (1st edn 1965). London: André Deutsch.

van der Molen, W. 1993. *Javaans schrift*. Leiden: Vakgroep Talen er Culturen van Zuidoost-Asië en Oceanië (Semaian 8).

van Everbroek, Nestor. 1958. *Grammaire et Exercises Lingala*. Antwerp, Léopoldville.

Van Sommers, Peter. 1989. 'Where Writing Starts: The Analysis of Action Applied to the Historical Development of Writing.' Paper presented at the Fourth International Graphonomics Society Conference, Trondheim.

Vellutino, Frank R. 1979. *Dyslexia: Theory and Research*. Cambridge, MA: MIT Press.

Venezky, Richard L. 1970. *The Structure of English Orthography*. The Hague: Mouton.

Ventris, Michael and Chadwick, John. 1953. 'Evidence for Greek Dialect in the Mycenaean Archives.' *The Journal of Hellenic Studies* LXXIII, 84–103.

Verma, Thakur Prasad. 1971. *The Palaeography of Brahmi Script in North India, from c.236 BC to c.200 AD*. Varanasi: Siddharth Prakashan.

Vernus, P. 1977. 'L'Écriture de l'Egypte ancienne.' *L'espace et la lettre. Cahiers Jussier* 3, 60–77.

Vetter, Emil. 1953. *Handbuch der italischen Dialekte*. Heidelberg: Winter.

Vikør, L. S. 1989. 'The Position of Standardized vs Dialectal Speech in Norway.' *International Journal of the Sociology of Language* 80, 41–59.

Virolleaud, C. 1957. *Textes en cunéiformes alphabetiques*. Vol. II of Claude Frédéric A. Schaeffer (ed.) *Le Palais Royal d'Ugarit*. Paris: Imprimerie nationale.

Voegelin, C. F. and Voegelin, F. M. 1961. 'Typological Classification of Systems with Included, Excluded and Self-Sufficient Alphabets.' *Anthropological Linguistics* 3, 2: 54–94.

Voorhoeve, J. 1962. 'Some Problems in Writing Tone.' *The Bible Translator* 13/1, 34–8.

Wagner, Daniel (ed.). 1987. *The Future of Literacy*. Oxford: Pergamon Press.

Walker, C. B. F. 1987. *Reading the Past*. Berkeley, CA: University of California Press.

Walker, Willard. 1981. 'Native American Writing Systems.' In: C. A. Ferguson and S. Brice Heath (eds) *Language in the USA*. Cambridge: Cambridge University Press, 145–74.

Warfel, Harry R. 1936. *Noah Webster, Schoolmaster of America*. New York: Macmillan (reprint Octagon Books, 1966).

Weidmüller, Wilhelm. 1977. 'Der Buchstabe "q": Herkunft und Entwicklung.' In: *Mélanges de l'Université Saint-Joseph* (Beyruth) 48, 77–93.

Weinberg, Werner. 1985. *The History of Hebrew Plene Spelling*. Cincinnati: Hebrew Union College Press.

Wellish, H. H. 1975. *Transcription and Transliteration: An Annotated Bibliography on Conversion of Scripts*. Silver Springs, MD: Institute of Modern Languages.

Westermann, Diedrich. 1930. *Practical Orthography of African Languages, Memorandum 1*, 2nd edn. London: International Institute of African Languages and Cultures.

Wexler, Paul. 1981. 'Ashkenazic German (1760–1895).' *International Journal of the Sociology of Language* 30, 119–30.

Whittaker, Gordon. 1980. *The Hieroglyphics of Monte Albán*. Yale, PhD dissertation.

Wilcox, William B. 1972. *The Papers of Benjamin Franklin*. New Haven, CT: Yale University Press.

Wilhelm, Gernot. 1982. *Grundzüge der Geschichte und Kultur der Hurriter*. Darmstadt: Wissenschaftliche Buchgesellschaft.

Williamson, J. 1947. 'The Use of Arabic Script in Swahili.' *African Studies*, Supplement 6,4.

Wing, Alan M. (ed.) 1979. *Behavioural Studies of the Handwriting Skill*. Special issue *Visible Language* XIII/3.

Wingo, E. O. 1972. *Latin Punctuation in the Classical Age*. The Hague: Mouton.

Winter, Werner. 1983. 'Tradition and Innovation in Alphabet Making.' In: F. Coulmas and K. Ehlich (eds) *Writing in Focus*. Berlin, Amsterdam, New York: Mouton, 227–38.

Winterowd, W. Ross. 1989. *The Culture and Poltics of Literacy*. New York: Oxford University Press.

Woordenlijst. 1954. *Woordenlijst van de Nederlandse Taal – samengesteld in opdracht van de Nederlandse en de Belgische regering*. The Hague: Staatsuitgeverij.

Wright, Roger (ed.). 1991. *Latin and the Romance Languages in the Early Middle Ages*. London, New York: Routledge.

Xie Zhimin. 1991. *Jiāngyǒng nǚshū zhī mí* (*The Enigma of Jiangyong Female Writing*). Henan, China: Henan People's Press.

Yadin, Yigael. 1984. 'The Latest Dead Sea Scroll.' *Biblical Archaeology Review* X, 5.
Yates, Frances A. 1966. *The Art of Memory*. Chicago: The University of Chicago Press.
Yi Ki-moon. 1975. 'Language and Writing Systems in Traditional Korea.' In: Peter H. Lee (ed.) *The Traditional Culture and Society of Korea: Art and Literature*. Honolulu: University of Hawaii, 15–32.
Yin Huan-xian. 1979. *Fǎnquiè shìyào* (*Explanation of fanqiè*). Shandong: Shandong renmin chubanshe.
Yoshino Masaharu. 1988. *Kanji no fukken* (*The Rehabilitation of Chinese Characters*). Tokyo: Nichū shuppan.
Young, R. S. 1969. 'Old Phrygian Inscriptions from Gordion: Toward a History of the Phrygian Alphabet.' *Hesperia* 38, 252–96.
Zapf, Hermann. 1960. *About Alphabets*. Cambridge, MA: MIT Press.
Zgusta, Ladislav (ed.). 1992. *History, Languages, and Lexicographers*. Tübingen: Max Niemeyer.
Ziegler, Sabine. 1992. *Die Sprache der altirischen Ogham-Inschriften*. Göttingen: Vandenhoek and Ruprecht.
Zieme, Peter. 1991. *Die Stabreimtexte der Uiguren von Turfan und Dunhuang: Studien zur alttürkischen Dichtung*. Budapest: Akadémiai Kiadó.
Zima, Petr. 1969. 'Language, Script and Vernacular Literature in West Africa.' *African Language Review* 8: 212–24.